The law of the sea

Melland Schill Studies in International Law
Series editor Professor Dominic McGoldrick

The Melland Schill name has a long-established reputation for high standards of scholarship. Each volume in the series addresses major public international law issues and current developments. Many of the Melland Schill volumes have become standard works of reference. Interdisciplinary and accessible, the contributions are vital reading for students, scholars and practitioners of public international law, international organisations, international relations, international politics, international economics and international development.

The law of the sea

third edition

R. R. Churchill and A. V. Lowe

Juris Publishing

Manchester University Press

First edition published 1983 by Manchester University Press
Reprinted with addenda 1985
Revised edition printed 1988

This edition published 1999 by
Manchester University Press
Oxford Road, Manchester M13 9NR, UK
http://www.man.ac.uk/mup

British Library Cataloguing-in-Publication Data
A catalogue record for this book is available from the British Library

ISBN   0 7190 4381 6   *hardback*
          0 7190 4382 4   *paperback*

First published in the USA and Canada by Juris Publishing, Inc.
Executive Park, One Odell Plaza, Yonkers, NY 10701

Library of Congress Cataloging-in-Publication Data applied for

ISBN   1 57823 029 2   *hardback*
          1 57823 030 6   *paperback*

This edition first published 1999

11 10 09 08 07 06   10 9 8 7 6 5

Typeset in 10/12pt Times
by Graphicraft Limited, Hong Kong
Printed in Great Britain
by Biddles Ltd, King's Lynn, Norfolk

Contents

Contents

Contents

Contents

List of tables

List of figures

List of figures

Series editor's foreword

The third edition of this classic text will be warmly welcomed by the international legal community. *The law of the sea* is of systemic importance to the discipline of public international law. It teaches us much about the historical, social, economic and political forces that play upon the formation and interpretation of legal rules. It evidences the tensions in devising rules of order and conduct for the communal resources of a functioning international society. It has also displayed some legal ingenuity in devising an accommodation that should allow universal participation in the Law of the Sea Convention. All of these elements and many more are expertly analysed in this text.

Dominic McGoldrick
International and European Law Unit
University of Liverpool

Preface

The aim of the third edition of this book remains broadly the same as that of the first two editions, namely to provide an introduction to the law of the sea, surveying not only the 1982 United Nations Convention on the Law of the Sea but also the customary and conventional law which supplements it. In covering such a large body of law in a relatively short space, our discussion of a number of topics has had to be more concise than we would have wished. To economise on space we have been sparing with footnotes. We give references to the sources of conventions and cases mostly in the tables of cases and conventions at the front of this book and not in the text itself. As a guide and, we hope, a stimulus to further reading and research, a select list of books and articles appears at the end of each chapter.

Since the previous edition of this book was published in 1988, much has happened in the law of the sea. Most notably, the 1982 Convention has entered into force and is now widely ratified. In addition a number of important multilateral treaties have been concluded (including the two Agreements of 1994 and 1995 relating to the implementation of the Convention), there have been several judgments by international courts and tribunals, and there has been a vast amount of bilateral treaty-making, national legislation and other forms of State practice. This new edition has been completely revised and extensively rewritten, although the basic structure of the book remains unchanged. Except where otherwise indicated in the text, we have endeavoured to state the law as at 31 August 1998.

In preparing this book we have received much help. We would like to thank our publishers for their patience as deadlines came and went; Dominic McGoldrick for reading the entire manuscript and making many helpful comments; Rob Cryer for research assistance; Chris Bleby for help with the tables; Lisa Comley for scanning the previous edition of this book which greatly facilitated production of this edition; and Thomas Churchill and Helen Wright for word processing. More generally we would like to thank all those, too numerous to mention individually, who over the years have discussed law of the sea issues with us, thereby helping to develop and broaden our knowledge and understanding of the subject.

Robin Churchill and Vaughan Lowe
Cardiff and Cambridge

Abbreviations

ACOPS	Advisory Committee on Pollution of the Sea, London
AD	*Annual Digest of Public International Law Cases*
AFDI	*Annuaire Français de Droit International*
AJIL	*American Journal of International Law*
ALR	*Australian Law Reports*
art.	article
BYIL	*British Yearbook of International Law*
Cm. and Cmnd.	*Command Paper* (of the United Kingdom)
CSC	(Geneva) Convention on the Continental Shelf, 1958
CTS	*Consolidated Treaty Series*
DLR	*Dominion Law Reports*
DUSPIL	*Digest of United States Practice in International Law*
EC	European Community
ECOSOC	Economic and Social Council of the United Nations
EEC	European Economic Community
EEZ	Exclusive Economic Zone
EFZ	exclusive fishing zone
ER	*English Reports*
FAO	(United Nations) Food and Agricultural Organisation
FOCP	Foreign Office Confidential Print
GA	(United Nations) General Assembly
GATT	General Agreement on Tariffs and Trade
GESAMP	Group of Experts on the Scientific Aspects of Marine Environmental Protection
HELCOM	Baltic Marine Environment Protection Committee
HSC	(Geneva) Convention on the High Seas, 1958
IA	Implementation Agreement
IAEA	International Atomic Energy Agency
ICAO	International Civil Aviation Organisation
ICES	International Council for the Exploration of the Sea
ICJ	International Court of Justice
ICJ Rep.	*ICJ Reports*
ICLQ	*International and Comparative Law Quarterly*
IJECL	*International Journal of Estuarine and Coastal Law*
IJIL	*Indian Journal of International Law*

IJMCL	*International Journal of Marine and Coastal Law*
ILC	(United Nations) International Law Commission
ILC Yearbook	*Yearbook of the International Law Commission*
ILM	*International Legal Materials*
ILO	(United Nations) International Labour Organisation
ILR	*International Law Reports*
IMCO	(United Nations) Intergovernmental Maritime Consultative Organisation
IMO	(United Nations) International Maritime Organisation
INMARSAT	(Convention on the) International Maritime Satellite Organisation
IOC	(United Nations) Intergovernmental Oceanographic Commission
IOMAC	(Organisation for) Indian Ocean Marine Affairs Co-operation
ISA	International Sea Bed Authority
ITLOS	International Tribunal for the Law of the Sea
JDI	*Journal du Droit International*
Jessup	P. C. Jessup, *The Law of Territorial Waters and Maritime Jurisdiction*, New York, 1927
JMLC	*Journal of Maritime Law and Commerce*
Limits in the Seas	*Limits in the Seas*, published by the Geographer, United States Department of State
LNTS	*League of Nations Treaty Series*
LOSB	(United Nations) *Law of the Sea Bulletin*
LOSC	(United Nations) Law of the Sea Convention, 1982
LQR	*Law Quarterly Review*
MARPOL	International Convention for the Prevention of Pollution from Ships, 1973
Moore, *Digest*	J. B. Moore, *A Digest of International Law*, 8 vols, 1906
Moore, *Int. Arb.*	J. B. Moore, *History and Digest of the International Arbitrations to which the United States has been a Party,* 5 vols, 1898
NAFO	Northwest Atlantic Fisheries Organisation
ND	*New Directions in the Law of the Sea*, ed. R. R. Churchill *et al.*, Dobbs Ferry, NY, Oceana, vols I–IX, 1973–81
NYIL	*Netherlands Yearbook of International Law*
O'Connell	D. P. O'Connell, *The International Law of the Sea*, 2 vols (Oxford, Clarendon), 1982, 1984
ODAS	Ocean data acquisition systems
ODIL	*Ocean Development and International Law*
OECD	Organisation for Economic Co-operation and Development
OGLTR	*Oil and Gas Law and Taxation Review*
OJEC	*Official Journal of the European Communities*
Oppenheim I	Sir Robert Jennings and Sir Arthur Watts (eds), *Oppenheim's International Law*, 9th edn, Vol. I, *Peace* (Harlow, Longman), 1992
Oppenheim II	H. Lauterpacht (ed.), *Oppenheim's International Law*, Vol. II, *Disputes, War and Neutrality*, 7th edn (London, Longman), 1952
PCIJ	Permanent Court of International Justice
P.D.	Law Reports, Probate and Divorce
PREPCOM	Preparatory Commission for the International Sea Bed Authority and for the International Tribunal for the Law of the Sea

Abbreviations

Recueil des Cours	*Recueil des cours de l'Académie de droit international* (The Hague)
Res.	Resolution
RGDIP	*Revue générale de droit international public*
RIAA	(United Nations) *Reports of International Arbitral Awards*
S.I.	Statutory Instrument (of the United Kingdom)
Smith	R. W. Smith, *Exclusive Economic Zone Claims: An Analysis and Primary Documents* (Dordrecht, Nijhoff), 1986
SOLAS	Safety of Life at Sea (Conventions)
SOPAC	South Pacific Applied Geoscience Commission
STCW	(International Convention on) Standards of Training, Certification and Watchkeeping for Seafarers
TIAS	*Treaties and other International Acts Series*
TSC	(Geneva) Convention on the Territorial Sea and the Contiguous Zone, 1958
UKMIL	*United Kingdom Materials in International Law* (section in the *British Yearbook of International Law*)
UKTS	*United Kingdom Treaty Series*
UN	United Nations
UNCED	United Nations Conference on Environment and Development, 1992
UNCITRAL	United Nations Commission on International Trade Law
UNCLOS I	First United Nations Conference on the Law of the Sea, 1958
UNCLOS II	Second United Nations Conference on the Law of the Sea, 1960
UNCLOS III	Third United Nations Conference on the Law of the Sea, 1973–82
UNCTAD	United Nations Conference on Trade and Development
UNEP	United Nations Environment Programme
UNESCO	United Nations Educational, Scientific and Cultural Organisation
UN Leg. Ser.	*United Nations Legislative Series* (see p. 26 below)
UNTS	*United Nations Treaty Series*
US	*United States Reports*
USC	United States Code
UST	*United States Treaties and other International Agreements*
VJIL	*Virginia Journal of International Law*
Whiteman	M. M. Whiteman, *Digest of International Law*, 15 vols (Washington DC, US Government Printing Office), 1963
WMO	World Meteorological Organisation
WTO	World Trade Organisation
ZAOVR	*Zeitschrift für Ausländisches Öffentliches Recht und Völkerrecht*

Table of cases and incidents

Table of conventions

The various conventions referred to in this book are listed in chronological order. Protocols are listed following their parent convention and not in the year of their adoption. In each case information is given as to the place and date of signature; the date of entry into force; the number of ratifications (in the case of multilateral conventions); and references to the source of the convention. As regards ratifications, in the case of conventions for which the UN Secretary General is the depositary (indicated *) the information is correct as at 12 November 1998. In the case of conventions for which the IMO is the depositary (#) it is correct as at 1 October 1998. With other conventions the number of ratifications (where known) is accurate as at the date shown.

1494 Treaty of Tordesillas, 1494 204

1661 Denmark–Sweden. Convention, Naslebacke, 26 October 1661. 6 *CTS* 495 182

1774 Russia–Turkey. Treaty of Perpetual Peace and Amity, Kucuk Kainardji, 10 July 1774. In force 13 January 1775. 45 *CTS* 349 115

1815 Act of the Congress of Vienna, Vienna, 9 June 1815. 2 BFSP 3 64

1857 Treaty for the Redemption of Sound Dues, Copenhagen, 14 March 1857. In force 31 March 1857. Fifteen ratifications. 116 *CTS* 357; *ND IV*, p. 320 114

1868 Convention for Rhine Navigation, Mannheim, 17 October 1868, as amended. In force 17 April 1869. Six ratifications. 1967 *UKTS* 66 443

1881 Argentina–Chile. Boundary Treaty, Buenos Aires, 23 July 1881. In force 22 October 1881. 159 *CTS* 45 114

1884 Convention for the Protection of Submarine Cables, Paris, 14 March 1884. In force 1 March 1888. Forty ratifications. 163 *CTS* 391 209, 218

1888 Convention respecting the Free Navigation of the Suez Canal, Constantinople, 29 October 1888. In force 22 December 1888. Nine ratifications. 171 *CTS* 241 65

1890 General Act of the Brussels Conference relating to the African Slave Trade, Brussels, 2 July 1890. In force 2 July 1891. Eighteen ratifications. 173 *CTS* 293 212

1903 Panama–USA. Convention for the Construction of a Ship Canal, Washington, 18 November 1903. In force 26 February 1904. 194 *CTS* 263 65

Table of conventions

1925 Convention for the Suppression of the Contraband Traffic in Alcoholic Liquors, Helsinki, 19 August 1925. In force 24 December 1925. Eleven ratifications. 42 *LNTS* 75 134

1926 International Convention for the Unification of Certain Rules concerning the Immunity of State-owned Ships, Brussels, 10 April 1926. In force 8 January 1937. Twenty-nine ratifications (as of January 1997). 176 *LNTS* 199 98

Slavery Convention, Geneva, 25 September 1926. In force 9 March 1927. Seventy-nine ratifications. 60 *LNTS* 253 212

1927 Great Britain–Johore. Agreement concerning the Johore Strait, 19 October 1927. No information on date of entry into force. Schedule to the Straits Settlement and Johore Territorial Waters (Agreement) Act, 1928 182

1928 Treaty providing for the Renunciation of War as an Instrument of National Policy, Paris, 27 August 1928. In force 25 July 1929. Sixty-three ratifications. 94 *LNTS* 57 422

1930 International Treaty for the Limitation and Reduction of Naval Armament, London, 22 April 1930. In force 27 October 1930. Nine ratifications. 112 *LNTS* 65. *Procès-verbal* relating to the Rules of Submarine Warfare, London, 6 November 1936. In force 6 November 1936. Forty-four ratifications. 173 *LNTS* 353 429, 430

Hague Convention on Certain Questions relating to the Conflict of Nationality Laws, The Hague, 12 April 1930. In force 1 July 1937. Nineteen ratifications. 179 *LNTS* 89 257

1932 Denmark–Sweden. Declaration concerning the Boundaries of the Sound, Stockholm, 30 January 1932. In force 30 January 1932. 127 *LNTS* 62 182

1936 Convention regarding the Regime of the Straits, Montreux, 20 July 1936. In force 9 November 1936. Eleven ratifications. 173 *LNTS* 213; *ND II*, p. 535 106, 110, 115, 263

1937 Nyon Arrangement, Nyon, 14 September 1937. In force 14 September 1937. Nine ratifications. 181 *LNTS* 135 430

1940 Finland–USSR. Agreement concerning the Aaland Islands, 11 October 1940. In force 11 October 1940. 67 *UNTS* 139 114

1942 Great Britain–Venezuela. Treaty relating to the Submarine Areas of the Gulf of Paria, Caracas, 26 February 1942. In force 22 September 1942. 205 *LNTS* 121 143, 184

1944 Convention on International Civil Aviation, Chicago, 7 December 1944. In force 4 April 1947. 185 ratifications. 15 *UNTS* 295 173, 443

International Air Services Transit Agreement, Chicago, 7 December 1944. In force 30 January 1945. 114 ratifications. 84 *UNTS* 389 443

International Air Transport Agreement, Chicago, 7 December 1944. In force 8 February 1945. Twelve ratifications (as of 21 October 1997). 171 *UNTS* 387 443

1945 Charter of the United Nations, San Francisco, 26 June 1945. In force 24 October 1945. 185 ratifications.* 1946 *UKTS* 67 107, 217, 422, 424, 449, 454, 459

Statute of the International Court of Justice, San Francisco, 26 June 1945. In force 24 October 1945. 187 ratifications.* 1946 *UKTS* 67 451–3

1946 International Convention for the Regulation of Whaling, Washington, 2 December 1946. In force 10 November 1948. Forty-one ratifications (as of February 1998). 161 *UNTS* 72, *ND I*, p. 418 317

1947 General Agreement on Tariffs and Trade, Geneva, 30 October 1947. In force 1 January 1948. 126 ratifications.* 55 *UNTS* 187 64, 113, 250, 441–2

1948 Convention on the Intergovernmental Maritime Consultative Organisation, Geneva, 6 March 1948. In force 17 March 1958. 156 ratifications.* 289 *UNTS* 3; *ND IV*, p. 519 23, 259

Convention concerning the Regime of Navigation on the Danube, Belgrade, 18 August 1948. In force 11 May 1949. Seven ratifications. 33 *UNTS* 181 65, 443

1949 ILO Convention No. 92 concerning Crew Accommodation on Board Ship, Geneva, 18 June 1949. In force 29 January 1953. Forty-two ratifications. 160 *UNTS* 223 270

Convention on Road Traffic, Geneva, 19 September 1949. In force 26 March 1952. Ninety ratifications.* 125 *UNTS* 3 443

Agreement for the Establishment of the General Fisheries Council for the Mediterranean, Rome, 24 September 1949. In force 20 February 1952. Twenty-three ratifications. 126 *UNTS* 237 297

Amendments, July 1976. In force December 1976. 297

Amendments, 13–16 October 1997. In force 6 November 1997. 297

Convention for the Establishment of the Inter-American Tropical Tuna Commission, Washington, 31 May 1949. In force 3 March 1950. Eleven ratifications. 80 *UNTS* 3 311

1952 International Convention for the High Seas Fisheries of the North Pacific Ocean, Tokyo, 9 May 1952. In force 12 June 1953. Three ratifications. Terminated 1993. 205 *UNTS* 65; *ND I*, p. 383. Protocol to the Convention, Tokyo, 25 April 1978. In force 20 February 1979. Three ratifications. *TIAS* 9242 297

International Convention relating to the Arrest of Seagoing Ships, Brussels, 10 May 1952. In force 24 February 1956. Sixty-nine ratifications (as of January 1998). 439 *UNTS* 193 64, 98

International Convention for the Unification of Certain Rules relating to Penal Jurisdiction in Matters of Collision or Other Incidents of Navigation, Brussels, 10 May 1952. In force 20 November 1955. Sixty-six ratifications (as of August 1997). 439 *UNTS* 233 98, 208

International Convention on Certain Rules concerning Civil Jurisdiction in Matters of Collision, Brussels, 10 May 1952. In force 14 September 1955. Sixty-four ratifications (as of August 1997). 439 *UNTS* 217 98, 208

1953 Convention for the Preservation of the Halibut Fishery of the Northern Pacific Ocean and Bering Sea, Ottawa, 2 March 1953. In force 28 October 1953. 22 *UNTS* 77 295

Protocol, Washington, 29 March, 1979. In force 15 October 1990. *TIAS* 9855 295

Table of conventions

1954 International Convention for the Prevention of Pollution of the Sea by Oil, London, 12 May 1954. In force 26 July 1958. Sixty-five ratifications. 327 *UNTS* 3; *ND II*, p. 557 339

Amendments to the Convention, adopted at London, 11 April 1962. In force 18 May and 28 June 1967. 600 *UNTS* 332; *ND II*, p. 567 54

Amendments to the Convention, adopted at London, 21 October 1969. In force 20 January 1978. 1140 *UNTS* 340; *ND II*, p. 580 54

1956 Supplementary Convention on the Abolition of Slavery, the Slave Trade and Institutions and Practices similar to Slavery, Geneva, 7 September 1956. In force 30 April 1957. 117 ratifications. 266 *UNTS* 3 212

1957 Treaty establishing the European Community, Rome, 25 March 1957. In force 1 January 1958. Fifteen ratifications. 1973 *UKTS* 1 63

International Convention relating to the Limitation of the Liability of Owners of Sea-Going Ships, Brussels, 10 October 1957. In force 31 May 1968. Thirty-five ratifications (as of January 1997). 1968 *UKTS* 52 277, 363

Interim Convention on North Pacific Fur Seals, Washington, 9 February 1957. In force 14 October 1957. Terminated 1985. Four ratifications. 314 *UNTS* 105 320

1958 Poland–USSR. Protocol concerning the Delimitation of Polish and Soviet Territorial Waters in the Gulf of Gdansk in the Baltic Sea, Warsaw, 18 March 1958. In force 29 July 1958. 340 *UNTS* 94 182

Convention on the Territorial Sea and the Contiguous Zone, Geneva, 29 April 1958. In force 10 September 1964. Fifty-one ratifications* (for further details, see appendix). 516 *UNTS* 205; *ND I*, p. 1

Art.		Art.	
1	75, 81	2	76, 77
3	32, 33, 53	4	32, 35–7, 53, 118, 263
5	32, 60, 61	6	32
7	32, 41–3, 45	8	32, 47–8
9	32, 48	10	32, 49
11	32, 48	12	183
13	32, 46–7	14	81–2, 84–5, 89, 91, 435
15	81, 95, 100, 271	16	82, 87, 99, 102, 104, 111, 263
17	93, 95, 97, 267, 401	18	82, 95, 271
19	97, 98, 137, 268, 345	20	97
21	98	22	99
23	99	24	49, 135, 136, 137, 139, 264
Generally 1, 6, 15			

Convention on the High Seas, Geneva, 29 April 1958. In force 30 September 1962. Sixty-two ratifications* (for further details, see appendix). 450 *UNTS* 11; *ND I*, p. 257.

Art.		Art.	
1	203	2	204, 205, 264, 286, 332, 401, 435, 436
3	442	5	257–8, 260
4	435	7	262
6	208, 214, 263	11	209
10	209, 264–5		

Convention on Fishing and Conservation of the Living Resources of the High Seas, Geneva, 29 April 1958. In force 20 March 1966. Thirty-seven ratifications* (for further details, see appendix). 559 *UNTS* 285; *ND I*, p. 353 1, 15, 287, 297

Convention on the Continental Shelf, Geneva, 29 April 1958. In force 10 June 1964. Fifty-seven ratifications* (for further details, see appendix). 499 *UNTS* 311; *ND I*, p. 101

Optional Protocol of Signature concerning the Compulsory Settlement of Disputes arising from the Law of the Sea Conventions, Geneva, 29 April 1958. In force 30 September 1962. Thirty-seven ratifications*. 450 *UNTS* 169; *ND I*, p. 268 15, 453

1959 Antarctic Treaty, Washington, 1 December 1959. In force 23 June 1961. Forty-three ratifications. 402 *UNTS* 71 165
Protocol on Environmental Protection, Madrid, 4 October 1991. In force 14 January 1998. Thirty-seven ratifications. 30 *ILM* 1461 (1991) 335, 343, 358

1960 Convention on Third Party Liability in the Field of Nuclear Energy, Paris, 29 July 1960. In force 1 April 1968. Sixteen ratifications (as of March 1997). 1968 *UKTS* 69 362

1961 Argentina–Uruguay. Declaration on the Outer Limit of the River Plate, Montevideo, 30 January 1961. *Limits in the Seas* No. 44 (1972) 47

Iceland–United Kingdom. Agreement settling the Fisheries Dispute, Reykjavik, 11 March 1961. In force 11 March 1961. 397 *UNTS* 275 453

1962 International Agreement regarding the Maintenance of Certain Lights in the Red Sea, London, 20 February 1962. In force 28 October 1966. Sixteen ratifications. 1967 *UKTS* 8 271

Convention on the Liability of Operators of Nuclear Ships, Brussels, 25 May 1962. Not in force. Seven ratifications (as of February 1997). 57 *AJIL* 268 (1963) 362

1963 Convention on Civil Liability for Nuclear Damage, Vienna, 21 May 1963. In force 12 November 1977. Thirty-one ratifications (as of June 1998). 2 *ILM* 727 (1963) 23, 362

Treaty banning Nuclear Weapon Tests in the Atmosphere, in Outer Space and under Water, Moscow, 5 August 1963. In force 10 October 1963. 134 ratifications. 480 *UNTS* 43; *ND I*, p. 285 392, 428

Act regarding Navigation and Economic Co-operation between the States of the Niger Basin, Niamey, 26 October 1963. In force 1 February 1966. Nine ratifications. 587 *UNTS* 9 443

1964 Fisheries Convention, London, 9 March 1964. In force 15 March 1966. Eleven ratifications. 581 *UNTS* 57; *ND I*, p. 41 54, 284

UK–USA. Agreement relating to the Use of United Kingdom Ports and Territorial Waters by the N.S. *Savannah*, London, 19 June 1964. In force 19 June 1964. 530 *UNTS* 99; *ND II*, p. 654 63, 91, 343, 363

Agreement concerning the Niger River Commission and the Navigation and Transport on the River Niger, Niamey, 25 November 1964. In force 12 April 1966. Nine ratifications. 587 *UNTS* 19 443

1965 European Agreement for the Prevention of Broadcasts transmitted from Stations outside National Territories, Strasbourg, 22 January 1965. In force 19 October 1967. Eighteen ratifications (as of 28 October 1998). 634 *UNTS* 239; *ND I*, p. 270 211, 212

Convention on Facilitation of International Maritime Traffic, London, 9 April 1965. In force 5 March 1967. Eighty-two ratifications.# 591 *UNTS* 265 276

Convention on Transit Trade of Land-locked States, New York, 8 July 1965. In force 9 June 1967. Thirty-six ratifications.* 597 *UNTS* 3 442–3, 444

1966 International Convention on Load Lines, London, 5 April 1966. In force 21 July 1968. 141 ratifications.# 640 *UNTS* 133 266, 272, 273

Protocol, London, 11 November 1988. Not in force. Twenty-nine ratifications.# 272

International Convention for the Conservation of Atlantic Tuna, Rio de Janeiro, 14 May 1966. In force 21 March 1969. Eight ratifications, 23 adherences. 673 *UNTS* 63 314

1967 Treaty for the Prohibition of Nuclear Weapons in Latin America, Mexico, 14 February 1967. In force 22 April 1968. Thirty-two ratifications (as of March 1997). 634 *UNTS* 281 429

Convention on Conduct of Fishing Operations in the North Atlantic, London, 1 June 1967. In force 26 September 1976. Fourteen ratifications. 1977 *UKTS* 40; ND *I*, p. 468 287

1968 Convention on Road Traffic, Vienna, 8 November 1968. In force 21 May 1977. Fifty-eight ratifications.* Cmnd. 4032 443

1969 Convention on the Law of Treaties, Vienna, 23 May 1969. In force 27 January 1980. Eighty-seven ratifications.* 1980 *UKTS* 58 6, 24, 112, 460

Agreement for Co-operation in Dealing with Pollution of the North Sea by Oil, Bonn, 9 June 1969. In force 9 August 1969. Eight ratifications. Terminated 1 September 1989. 704 *UNTS* 3; *ND II*, p. 632 334, 357

International Convention on Tonnage Measurement of Ships, London, 23 June 1969. In force 18 July 1982. 120 ratifications.# 1982 *UKTS* 50 276

International Convention relating to Intervention on the High Seas in Cases of Oil Pollution Casualties, Brussels, 29 November 1969. In force 6 May 1975. Seventy-two ratifications.# 1975 *UKTS* 77; *ND II*, p. 592 169, 216, 354–5, 450

Protocol relating to Intervention on the High Seas in Cases of Marine Pollution by Substances other than Oil, London, 2 November 1973. In force 30 March 1983. Forty-one ratifications.# 1313 *UNTS* 3; *ND IV*, p. 451 354–5

International Convention on Civil Liability for Oil Pollution Damage, Brussels, 29 November 1969. In force 19 June 1975. Seventy-six ratifications.# 1975 *UKTS* 106; *ND II*, p. 602 359–61, 376, 377

Protocol, London, 19 November 1976. In force 8 April 1981. Fifty-four ratifications.# 1981 *UKTS* 26 359

Protocol, London, 25 May 1984. Not in force. Nine ratifications (as of January, 1994). Cmnd. 9927 360

Protocol, London, 27 November 1992. In force 30 May 1996. Thirty-eight ratifications.# 1996 *UKTS* 86 360–1

Abu Dhabi–Qatar. Agreement on Settlement of Maritime Boundary Lines and Sovereign Rights over Islands, 20 March 1969. In force 20 March 1969. *UN Leg. Ser.* B/16, p. 403 200

Convention on the Conservation of the Living Resources of the Southeast Atlantic, Rome, 3 October 1969. In force 24 October 1971. Eighteen ratifications. 801 *UNTS* 101 297

Protocol of Termination, Madrid, 19 July 1990. Not in force. Two acceptances. 297

1970 Federal Republic of Germany–Liberia. Treaty on the Use of Liberian Waters and Ports by N.S. *Otto Hahn*, Bonn, 27 May 1970. No information on date of entry into force. *UN Leg. Ser.* B/18, p. 408 363

ILO Convention No. 133 concerning Crew Accommodation on Board Ship (Supplementary Provisions), Geneva, 30 October 1970. In force 27 August 1991. Twenty-six ratifications. 1997 *UKTS* 25 270

1971 Treaty on the Prohibition of the Emplacement of Nuclear Weapons and other Weapons of Mass Destruction on the Seabed and Ocean Floor and in the Subsoil thereof, London, Moscow and Washington, 11 February 1971. In force 18 May 1972. 100 ratifications (as of 1 January 1997). 1973 *UKTS* 13; *ND I*, p. 288 54, 428

Portugal–Spain. Agreement concerning Oceanographic Co-operation, Lisbon, 27 May 1971. In force 27 May 1971. *UN Leg. Ser.* B/16, p. 475 416

Nordic Agreement concerning Co-operation in Measures to deal with Pollution of the Sea by Oil, Copenhagen, 16 September 1971. In force 16 October 1971. Four ratifications. 822 *UNTS* 311; *ND II*, p. 637 337, 358

Agreement on Special Trade Passenger Ships, London, 6 October 1971. In force 2 January 1974. Sixteen ratifications.# 1980 *UKTS* 7 266, 273

Protocol on Space Requirements for Special Trade Passenger Ships, London, 13 July 1973. In force 2 June 1977. Fifteen ratifications.# 1980 *UKTS* 7 266, 273

Convention relating to Civil Liability in the Field of Maritime Carriage of Nuclear Material, Brussels, 17 December 1971. In force 15 July 1975. Fourteen ratifications.# *ND II*, p. 664 362

International Convention on the Establishment of an International Fund for Compensation for Oil Pollution Damage, Brussels, 18 December 1971. In force 16 October 1978. Fifty-two ratifications.# 1978 *UKTS* 95; *ND II*, p. 611 359–61, 377

Protocol, London, 19 November 1976. In force 22 November 1994. Thirty-four ratifications.# Cmnd. 7029 359

Protocol, London, 25 May 1984. Not in force. Four ratifications (as of January 1994). Cmnd. 9926 360

Protocol, London, 27 November 1992. In force 30 May 1996. Thirty-six ratifications.# 1996 *UKTS* 87 360–1

1972 Convention for the Prevention of Marine Pollution by Dumping from Ships and Aircraft, Oslo, 15 February 1972. In force 7 April 1974. Thirteen ratifications. Terminated 25 March 1998. 1975 *UKTS* 119; *ND II*, p. 670 334, 367–8, 372

Protocol, Oslo, 2 March 1983. In force 1 September 1989. Thirteen ratifications. 1989 *UKTS* 59 334, 367

USSR–USA. Agreement on the Prevention of Incidents on and over the High Seas, Moscow, 25 May 1972. In force 25 May 1972. 852 *UNTS* 151; *ND II*, p. 529. Protocol to the Agreement, Washington, 22 May 1973. In force 22 May 1973. 24 *UST* 1063; *ND IV*, p. 285 430

USSR–USA. Interim Agreement on Certain Measures with respect to Limitation of Strategic Offensive Arms, Moscow, 26 May 1972. In force 3 October 1972. 23 *UST* 3462; *ND I*, p. 296 428

Brazil–Uruguay. Agreement on the Final Establishment of the Chuy River Bank and the Lateral Sea Limit, Montevideo, 21 July 1972. In force 12 June 1975. *ND V*, p. 9 182

Convention on the International Regulations for Preventing Collisions at Sea, London, 20 October 1972. In force 15 July 1977. 131 ratifications.# 1977 *UKTS* 77; *ND IV*, p. 245 95, 175, 267, 272, 273

International Convention for Safe Containers, Geneva, 2 December 1972. In force 6 September 1977. Sixty-four ratifications.# 1979 *UKTS* 40 276

Convention on the Prevention of Marine Pollution by Dumping of Wastes and Other Matter, London, Mexico City, Moscow, Washington, 29 December 1972. In force 30 August 1975. Seventy-seven ratifications.# 1976 *UKTS* 43; *ND IV*, p. 331 363–7, 372, 379, 390

Amendments to the Convention, London, 1 December 1978. Not in force. Twenty ratifications.# 18 *ILM* 517 (1979) 366

Amendments to the Annexes of the Convention, London, 1 December 1978. In force 12 March 1979. 1979 *UKTS* 71 364

Amendments to the Annexes of the Convention, London, 12 November 1993. In force 20 February 1994. 1995 *UKTS* 89–91 366, 368

Protocol to the Convention, London, 8 November 1996. Not in force. One ratification.# 34 *LOSB* 71 (1997) 155, 366, 368, 370

Convention for the Conservation of Antarctic Seals, London, 1 June 1972. In force 11 March 1978. Seventeen ratifications (as of March 1997). 11 *ILM* 251 (1972) 320

1973 Norway–United Kingdom. Agreement relating to the Transmission of Petroleum by Pipeline from the Ekofisk Field and Neighbouring Areas to the United Kingdom, Oslo, 22 May 1973. In force 22 May 1973. 1973 *UKTS* 101; *ND IV*, p. 137 375

International Convention for the Prevention of Pollution from Ships, London, 2 November 1973, as amended by the Protocol, London, 1 June 1978. In force 2 October 1983. 105 ratifications.# 1340 *UNTS* 61; *ND IV*, p. 345 and X, p. 32 6, 63, 274, 339–45, 347, 351, 353, 355, 372, 379, 390, 394

Argentina–Uruguay. Treaty concerning the Rio de la Plata and the Corresponding Maritime Boundary, Montivedeo, 19 November 1973. In force 12 February 1974. 13 *ILM* 251 (1974) 295

Convention on Fishing and Conservation of the Living Resources of the Baltic Sea and Belts, Gdansk, 13 September 1973. In force 28 July 1974. Six ratifications. 1090 *UNTS* 54 296

Convention on International Trade in Endangered Species of Wild Fauna and Flora, Washington, 3 March 1973. In force 1 July 1975. 137 ratifications.* 1976 *UKTS* 101 319

1974 Japan–Korea. Agreement concerning Joint Development of the Southern Part of the Continental Shelf adjacent to the Two Countries, Seoul, 30 January 1974. In force 22 June 1978. *ND IV*, p. 117 199

Italy–Yugoslavia. Agreement on Co-operation for the Protection of the Waters of the Adriatic Sea and Coastal Zones from Pollution, Belgrade, 14 February 1974. In force 20 April 1977. *ND VI*, p. 456 337

Nordic Convention on the Protection of the Environment, Stockholm, 19 February 1974. In force 5 October 1976. Four ratifications. *ND IV*, p. 514 337, 389, 460

Convention on the Protection of the Marine Environment of the Baltic Sea Area, Helsinki, 22 March 1974. In force 3 May 1980. Seven ratifications. *ND IV*, p. 455 333, 335, 343, 357, 368, 373, 375, 384–5, 390, 393

Denmark–Sweden. Agreement concerning the Protection of the Sound from Pollution, Copenhagen, 5 April 1974. In force 13 December 1974. 1272 *UNTS* 420; *ND VI*, p. 459 337

Convention for the Prevention of Marine Pollution from Landbased Sources, Paris, 4 June 1974. In force 6 May 1978. Thirteen ratifications. Terminated 25 March 1998. 1978 *UKTS* 64; *ND IV*, p. 499 334, 372, 381–3

Protocol, Paris, 26 March 1986. In force 1 September 1989. Twelve ratifications (as of March 1997). Cm. 87 334, 390

Canada–USA. Agreement relating to the Establishment of Joint Pollution Contingency Plans for Spills of Oil and Other Noxious Substances, Ottawa, 19 June 1974. In force 19 June 1974. *ND VI*, p. 464 337, 358

India–Sri Lanka. Agreement on the Boundary in Historic Waters between the Two Countries and Related Matters, New Delhi, 26 June 1974. In force 8 July 1974. *ND V*, p. 326 183

International Convention for the Safety of Life at Sea, London, 1 November 1974. In force 25 May 1980. 137 ratifications.# 1184 *UNTS* 2; 1980 *UKTS* 46. Protocol to the Convention, London, 1 June 1978. In force 1 May 1981. Ninety ratifications.# 1981 *UKTS* 40 63, 91, 107–8, 265–73 *passim*, 342.

Protocol to the Convention, London, 11 November, 1988. Not in force. Thirty ratifications.# IMO Doc. HSSC/Conf/11 265

Amendments, 17 June 1983. In force 1 July 1986. 1998 *UKTS* 13–15 266

Amendments, 24 May 1994. In force 1 July 1995 266, 268, 271–2

Amendments, 16 May 1995. In force 1 January 1997. 1997 *UKTS* 15 268

Amendments, 4 June 1997. In force 1 July 1999 269

Convention relating to the Carriage of Passenges and their Luggage by Sea, Athens, 13 December 1974. In force 28 April 1987. Twenty-six ratifications.# Cmnd. 6326 277

Protocol, London, 1 June 1990. Not in force. Three ratifications.# 277

Japan–Korea. Agreement concerning the Establishment of Boundary in the Northern Part of the Continental Shelf Adjacent to the Two Countries, Seoul, 30 January 1974. In force 22 June 1978. 1225 *UNTS* 103 199

France–Spain. Convention on the Delimitation of the Continental Shelves of the Two States in the Bay of Biscay, Paris, 29 January 1974. In force 5 April 1975. *ND V*, p. 251 200

1975 Gambia–Senegal. Agreement delimiting Maritime Boundaries, Banjul, 4 June 1975. In force 27 August 1976. *Limits in the Seas* No. 85 (1979) 197

Colombia–Ecuador. Agreement on Delimiting Marine and Submarine Areas and on Maritime Co-operation, Quito, 23 August 1975. In force 22 December 1975. *UN Leg. Ser.* B/19, p. 398; *ND V*, p. 12 182, 197, 296

1976 Convention for the Protection of the Mediterranean Sea against Pollution, Barcelona, 16 February 1976. In force 12 February 1978. Twenty-one ratifications (as of 1 September 1998). 1102 *UNTS* 27 333, 335–7, 343, 357, 389, 395, 451

Amendments, Barcelona, 10 June 1995. Not in force. Two ratifications (as of 1 September 1998). 31 *LOSB* 65 (1996) 333, 370

Protocol for the Prevention of Pollution of the Mediterranean Sea by Dumping from Ships and Aircraft, Barcelona, 16 February 1976. In force 12 February 1978. Twenty-one ratifications (as of 1 September 1998). 1102 *UNTS* 92 333, 368, 372, 374

Amendments, Barcelona, 10 June 1995. Not in force. Two ratifications (as of 1 September 1998). 31 *LOSB* 72 (1996) 368, 374

EC–Senegal. Agreement on Fishing off the Coast of Senegal, Brussels, 15 June 1979. No information on date of entry into force. *OJEC* 1980 L226/18 417

USSR–USA. Treaty on the Limitation of Strategic Offensive Arms, Vienna, 18 June 1979. Not in force. 18 *ILM* 1138 (1979) 428

International Convention on Maritime Search and Rescue, London, 1 November 1979. In force 22 June 1985. Fifty-nine ratifications.# 1986 *UKTS* 59 271

Amendments, May 1998. In force January 2000 271

Convention on Long-range Transboundary Air Pollution, Geneva, 13 November 1979. In force 16 March 1983. Forty-three ratifications.* 18 *ILM* 1442 (1979) 391

Protocol, Helsinki, 8 July 1985. In force 2 February 1987. Twenty-one ratifications.* 1480 *UNTS* 215 391

Protocol concerning the Control of Emissions of Nitrogen Oxides or their Trans-boundary Fluxes, Sofia, 31 October 1988. In force 14 February 1991. Twenty-six ratifications.* 1992 *UKTS* 1 391

Protocol concerning the Emissions of Volatile Organic Compounds or their Fluxes, Geneva, 18 November 1991. In force 29 September 1997. Seventeen ratifications.* 31 *ILM* 568 (1992) 391

Protocol on Further Reductions of Sulphur Emissions, Oslo, 14 June 1994. In force 5 August 1998. Twenty-one ratifications.* 33 *ILM* 1540 (1994) 391

South Pacific Forum Fisheries Agency Convention, Honiara, 10 July 1979. In force 9 August 1979. Sixteen ratifications. FAO Fisheries Report No. 293 (1983), p. 201 293

Convention on the Conservation of Migratory Species of Wild Animals, Bonn, 23 June 1979. In force 1 November 1983. Fifty-six ratifications.* 1990 *UKTS* 87 318–19

Convention on the Conservation of European Wildlife and Natural Habitats, Bern, 19 September 1979. In force 1 June 1982. Thirty-three ratifications (as of March 1997). 1982 *UKTS* 56 319

1980 France–Tonga. Convention concerning the Delimitation of Economic Zones, Nuku' Alofu, 11 January 1980. In force 11 January 1980. 84 *RGDIP* 986 (1980) 197

EC–Norway. Agreement on Fisheries, Brussels, 27 February 1980. In force 16 June 1981. *OJEC* 1980 L226/48 295

EC–Guinea Bissau. Agreement on Fishing off the Coast of Guinea Bissau, Brussels, 27 February 1980. No information on date of entry into force. *OJEC* 1980 L226/34 417

Mexico–USA. Agreement of Co-operation regarding Pollution of the Marine Environment by Discharges of Hydrocarbons and Other Hazardous Substances, Mexico City, 24 July 1980. In force 30 March 1981. 20 *ILM* 696 (1981) 358

Convention on Future Multilateral Co-operation in the North-east Atlantic Fisheries, London, 18 November 1980. In force 17 March 1982. Six ratifications. Cmnd. 8474 297

Convention creating the Niger Basin Authority, Faranah, 21 November 1980. In force 3 December 1982. Eight ratifications. 1346 *UNTS* 207 443

Table of conventions

Joint Declaration on the Protection of the Wadden Sea, Copenhagen, 9 December 1982. In force 9 December 1982. D. Freestone and T. Ijlstra (eds), *The North Sea: Basic Legal Documents in Regional Environmental Co-Operation* (1991), p. 259 337

Nauru Agreement concerning Co-operation in the Management of Fisheries of Common Interest, Yaren, 11 February 1982. In force 2 December 1982. Seven ratifications. FAO Fisheries Report No. 293 (1983), pp. 206–9 293, 296

1983 Eastern Pacific Ocean Tuna Fishing Agreement, San José, 15 March 1983. Not in force. One ratification. *FAO Fisheries Report* No. 293 (1983), p. 189 331

Convention for the Protection and Development of the Marine Environment of the Wider Caribbean Region, Cartagena de Indias, 24 March 1983. In force 30 March 1986. Twenty ratifications (as of March 1997). 1988 *UKTS* 38 333, 385, 391

Protocol concerning Co-Operation in Combating Oil Spills in the Wider Caribbean Region, Cartagena de Indias, 24 March 1983. In force 17 January 1987. Eighteen ratifications (as of March 1997). 1988 *UKTS* 38 333

Protocol concerning Specially Protected Areas and Wildlife, January 1990. Not in force. Six ratifications (as of March 1997). Cm. 3161 333, 393

Canada–Denmark. Agreement for Co-operation relating to the Marine Environment, Copenhagen, 26 August 1983. In force 26 August 1983. 23 *ILM* 269 (1984) 337, 358, 375

Agreement for Co-Operation in Dealing with Pollution of the North Sea by Oil and Other Harmful Substances, Bonn, 13 September 1983. In force 1 September 1989. Nine ratifications (as of January 1994). Cmnd. 9104 334, 357–8

1987 Certain Pacific Island States–USA. Treaty on Fisheries, Port Moresby, 2 April 1987. In force 15 June 1988. No information on number of ratifications. 26 *ILM* 1048 (1987) 312

Convention concerning Seafarers' Welfare at Sea and in Port (No. 163), Geneva, 8 October 1987. In force 3 October 1990. Eleven ratifications (as of May 1998). Cm. 658 270

Agreement on the Resolution of Practical Problems with Respect to Deep Seabed Mining Areas, and Exchange of Notes between the US and the Parties to the Agreement, New York, 14 August 1987. In force 14 August, 1987. 26 *ILM* 1502 (1987) 233, 237

1988 United Kingdom–France. Joint Declaration of 2 November 1988, 14 *LOSB* 14 (1989) 113

USA–Canada. Agreement on Arctic Co-operation, Ottawa, 11 January 1988. In force 10 October 1988. 28 *ILM* 141 (1989) 106

United Kingdom–Ireland. Agreement concerning the Delimitation of Areas of the Continental Shelf between the Two Countries, Dublin, 7 November 1988. In force 11 January 1990. 1990 *UKTS* 20 150

Mozambique–Tanzania. Agreement regarding the Tanzania/ Mozambique Boundary, Maputo, 28 December 1988. In force 29 July 1993. 9 *IJMCL* 404 (1994) 46

United Nations Convention against Illicit Traffic in Narcotic Drugs and Psychotropic Substances, Vienna, 20 December 1988. In force 11 November 1990. 149 ratifications.* 1992 *UKTS* 26 171, 215, 219

Convention for the Suppression of Unlawful Acts against the Safety of Maritime Navigation, 10 March 1988. In force 1 March 1992. Thirty-seven ratifications.# 211, 277

Protocol for the Suppression of Unlawful Acts Against the Safety of Fixed Platforms Located on the Continental Shelf, 10 March 1988. In force 1 March 1992. Thirty-four ratifications.# 211

1989 USA–USSR. Uniform Interpretation of Norms of International Law Governing Innocent Passage, Jackson Hole, 23 September 1989. 14 *LOSB* 12–13 (1989) 86, 89

Australia–Indonesia. Treaty on the Zone of Co-operation in an Area between the Indonesian Province of East Timor and Northern Australia, 6 December 1989. In force 9 February 1991. 29 *ILM* 469 (1990) 199

Liberia–United Kingdom. Exchange of Notes concerning the Use of United Kingdom Controlled Ships registered in Liberia, Monrovia, 16 February and 17 March 1989. In force 17 March 1989. 1989 *UKTS* 39 261

United Kingdom–Vanuatu. Exchange of Notes concerning the Use of British Controlled Ships registered in Vanuatu, Port Vila, 20 February 1989. In force 20 February 1989. 1989 *UKTS* 48 261

International Convention on Salvage, London, 28 April 1989. In force 14 July 1996. Twenty-six ratifications.# 1996 *UKTS* 93; 14 *LOSB* 77 (1990) 277, 356

Basel Convention on the Control of Transboundary Movement of Hazardous Wastes and their Disposal, Basel, 22 March 1989. In force 5 May 1992. 122 ratifications.* 1995 *UKTS* 100 92, 208, 342, 356–7

Agreement between Denmark, Iceland and Norway concerning Capelin Stocks in the Waters between Greenland, Iceland and Jan Mayen, Copenhagen, 12 June 1989. In force 1 July 1989. [1989] *Overenskomster med fremmede Stater* (Norwegian Treaty Series) 904 295

Convention for the Prohibition of Fishing with Long Driftnets in the South Pacific, Wellington, 23 November 1989. In force 17 May 1991. Twelve ratifications (as of 9 March 1998). 29 *ILM* 1449 (1990) 300

Protocol I, Noumea, 20 October 1990. In force 28 February 1992. One ratification. 29 *ILM* 1449 (1990) 300

Protocol II, Noumea, 20 October 1990. In force 5 October 1993. Two ratifications. 29 *ILM* 1449 (1990) 300

USA–South Korea. Agreement regarding the High Seas Squid Driftnet Fisheries in the North Pacific Ocean, Washington, 13 September 1989. In force 26 September 1989. 29 *ILM* 464 (1990) 220, 300

USA–Taiwan. Agreement in Driftnet Fisheries, 30 June 1989. No further information 220, 300

Eastern Pacific Ocean Tuna Fishing Agreement, Lima, 21 July 1989. Not in force. Two ratifications. FAO, *Compendium of Basic Texts Concerning International Management and Development of Tuna Fisheries* (1992), p. 135 311

1990 Belgium–France. Agreement on the Delimitation of the Territorial Sea, Brussels, 8 October 1990. In force 7 April 1993. 19 *LOSB* 27 (1991) 197

Belgium–France. Agreement on the Delimitation of the Continental Shelf, Brussels, 8 October 1990. In force 7 April 1993. 19 *LOSB* 29 (1991) 197

Trinidad and Tobago–Venezuela. Treaty on the Delimitation of Marine and Submarine Areas, Caracas, 18 April 1990. In force 23 July 1991. 19 *LOSB* 22 (1991) 113, 197

Agreement on the Organisation for Indian Ocean Marine Affairs Co-operation, Arusha, 7 September 1990. No information on date of entry into force or ratifications. 16 *LOSB* 57 (1990) 416

Agreement establishing the South Pacific Applied Geoscience Commission, Tarawa, October 1990. No information on date of entry into force, ratifications or source. 416

Convention establishing the North Pacific Marine Science Organisation, Ottawa, 12 December 1990. In force 24 March 1992. Six ratifications *Canada TS* 1992/8. 416

International Convention on Oil Pollution Preparedness, Response and Co-Operation, London, 30 November 1990. In force 13 May 1995. Forty ratifications. # 18 *LOSB* 37 (1991) 355–6, 376

Accord of Co-Operation for the Protection of the Coasts and Waters of the North-east Atlantic against Pollution due to Hydrocarbons or Other Harmful Substances,

LOSB 54 (1993) 155, 333, 335–7, 343, 357, 368, 373, 375, 376, 385, 386, 390, 393, 395

Convention on the Protection of the Black Sea against Pollution, Bucharest, 21 April 1992. In force 15 January 1994. Six ratifications. 22 *LOSB* 31 (1993) 334, 391

Protocol on Protection of the Black Sea Marine Environment against Pollution from Land-based Sources, Bucharest, 21 April 1992. In force 15 January 1994. Six ratifications. 22 *LOSB* 41 (1993) 334, 386–7, 391

Protocol on Co-Operation in Combating Pollution of the Black Sea Marine Environment by Oil and Other Harmful Substances in Emergency, Bucharest, 21 April 1992. In force 15 January 1994. Six ratifications. 22 *LOSB* 4 (1993) 334

Protocol on Protection of the Black Sea Marine Environment against Pollution by Dumping, Bucharest, 21 April 1992. Not in force. No ratifications (as of 31 March 1998). 22 *LOSB* 47 (1993) 334, 368–9, 370

Convention for the Protection of the Marine Environment of the North-East Atlantic, Paris, 22 September 1992. In force 25 March 1998. Sixteen ratifications Cm. 2265; 23 *LOSB* 32 (1993) 155, 334, 335–7, 367–8, 370, 372–3, 383–4, 385, 386, 390, 394, 395, 451

Framework Convention on Biological Diversity, 5 June 1992. In force 29 December 1993. 174 ratifications.* 1995 *UKTS* 51 000, 000

Niue Treaty on Co-operation in Fisheries Surveillance and Law Enforcement in the South Pacific Region, Honiara, 9 July 1992. In force 20 May 1993. No information on number of ratifications. 32 *ILM* 136 (1993) 293

Palau Arrangement for the Management of the Western Pacific Island Purse Seine Fishery, Sura, 28 October 1992. In force 8 December 1995. Five ratifications. 312

Agreement on Co-operation on Research, Conservation and Management of Marine Mammals in the North Atlantic, Nuuk, 9 April 1992. In force 8 July 1992. 26 *LOSB* (1994) 318

Agreement on the Conservation of Small Cetaceans of the Baltic and North Seas, New York, 17 March 1992. In force 29 March 1994. Six ratifications.* 1995 *UKTS* 52 318

Agreement for the Reduction of Dolphin Mortality in the Eastern Pacific Ocean, La Jolla, 23 April 1992. In force 23 April 1992. No information on number of ratifications. 33 *ILM* 935 (1994) 319

1993 Cape Verde–Senegal. Treaty on the Delimitation of the Maritime Frontier between the Republic of Cape Verde and the Republic of Senegal, 17 February 1993. No information on date of entry into force. 26 *LOSB* 45 (1994) 130

Convention on Sub-Regional Co-operation in the Exercise of Maritime Hot Pursuit, Country, 1 September 1993. No information on date of entry into force or ratifications. 10 *African Journal of International and Comparative Law* 183 (1998) 216

Colombia–Jamaica. Maritime Delimitation Treaty, 12 November 1993. No information on date of entry into force. 26 *LOSB* 50 (1994) 200

Agreement to Promote Compliance with International Conservation and Management Measures by Fishing Vessels on the High Seas, Rome, 24 November 1993. Not in force. Nine ratifications (as of March 1997). 33 *ILM* 968 (1994) 260, 303–5, 309, 310, 322

Convention on Maritime Liens and Mortgages, Geneva, 6 May 1993. Not in force. Three ratifications.* 33 *ILM* 353 (1995) 277

Agreement for the Establishment of the Indian Ocean Tuna Commission, Rome, 25 November 1993. In force 27 March 1996. Fifteen ratifications. Cm. 2695 (1994) 313, 323, 450

Convention for the Conservation of Southern Bluefin Tuna, Canberra, 10 May, 1993. In force 20 May 1994. 26 *LOSB* 57 (1994) 313–14

1994 Agreement on the Implementation of Part XI of the 1982 Law of the Sea Convention, 28 July, 1994. In force 28 July 1996. Ninety-one ratifications.* *LOSB* Special Issue IV (1994); 33 *ILM* 1309 (1994) 20–1, 230, 238

Annex

Section 1 231, 238, 240, 243, 247–8, 249, 250, 251, 253, 378–9	Section 2 244, 248, 250
5 249, 417	3 241, 242, 245, 246, 247, 252, 437
6 251	7 240, 241, 243, 246
8 248, 253	9 240, 243, 246

General Agreement on Tariffs and Trade, Marrakesh, 15 April 1994. Entry into force and ratifications as for the following Agreement. 33 *ILM* 1154 (1994) 113, 441

Agreement establishing the World Trade Organisation, Marrakesh, 15 April 1994. In force 1 January 1995. 134 ratification (as of 10 February 1999). 33 *ILM* 1144 (1994) 113

Convention on Co-operation for the Protection and Sustainable Use of the Danube River, Sofia, 29 June 1994. In force 22 October 1998. Nine ratifications. 388

Convention for the Protection of the Meuse, Charleville-Mezieres, 26 April 1994. No information on date of entry into force or number of ratifications. 34 *ILM* 854 (1995) 388

Convention for the Protection of the Scheldt, Charleville-Mezieres, 26 April 1994. No information on date of entry into force or number of ratifications. 34 *ILM* 859 (1995) 388

Convention on the Conservation and Management of Pollock Resources in the Central Bering Sea, Washington, 16 June 1994. In force 8 December 1995. Six ratifications. 34 *ILM* 67 (1995) 306–7

1995 Agreement for the Implementation of the Provisions of the United Nations Convention on the Law of the Sea of 10 December 1982 relating to the Conservation and Management of Straddling Fish Stocks and Highly Migratory Fish Stocks, New York, 4 August 1995. Not in force. Eighteen ratifications.* 34 *ILM* 1542 (1995); 29 *LOSB* 25 (1996) 21, 207, 308–11, 322, 323, 456

Estonia–Finland–Sweden. Agreement regarding the M/S Estonia, Tallinn, 23 February 1995. No information on date of entry into force. 31 *LOSB* 62 (1996) 152

Council of Europe Agreement on Illicit Traffic by Sea, implementing Article 17 of the United Nations Convention against Illicit Traffic in Narcotic Drugs and Psychotropic Substances, Strasbourg, 31 January 1995. Not in force (as of 6 January 1999). Two ratifications. 29 *LOSB* 62 (1995); Cm. 2979 170–1, 219

International Convention on Standards of Training, Certification and Watchkeeping for Fishing Vessel Personnel, 7 July 1995. Not in force. Two ratifications.# 270

Netherlands–Venezuela. Agreement establishing a Bilateral Oil Spill Contingency Plan to Protect the Coastal and Marine Environment, 21 February 1995. In force 13 March 1996. *Tractatenblad* 1996, No. 101 337

Waigani Convention to Ban Importation into Forum Island Countries and to Control the Transboundary Movement and Management of Hazardous Wastes within the South Pacific Region, Waigani, 16 September 1995. Not in force (as of 30 March 1999). Four ratifications. 6 *Yearbook of International Environmental Law* (1995) (diskette) 343

African Nuclear-Weapon-Free Zone Treaty, Addis Ababa, 21–23 June 1995. Not in force. Three ratifications (as of 17 February 1998). 35 *ILM* 705 (1996) 369, 429

Treaty on the Southeast Asia Nuclear-Weapon-Free Zone, Bangkok, 15 December 1995. In force 1997. Ten ratifications. 35 *ILM* 635 (1996) 369, 429

EC–Canada. Fisheries Agreement, Brussels, 20 April 1995. In force 20 April 1995. *OJEC* 1995 L327/20 306

1996 Eritrea–Yemen. Arbitration Agreement, 3 October 1996. In force 2 November 1996. 100 *RGDIP* 1125 (1996) 192

Convention concerning Seafarers' Hours of Work and the Manning of Ships (No. 180), Geneva, 22 October 1996. Not in force. No ratifications (as of May 1998). *Lloyds of London Press, Ratification of Maritime Conventions*, Vol. II, p. 6. 410 270

International Convention on Liability and Compensation for Damage in Connection with the Carriage of Hazardous and Noxious Substances (HNS) by Sea, London, 3 May 1996. Not in force. No ratifications.# Cm. 3580 361–2

Convention on the Collection, Deposit and Disposal of Waste generated during Navigation on the Rhine and Inland Waterways, Strasbourg, 9 September 1996. No information on date of entry into force or number of ratifications. *Traetatenblad*, 1996, No. 293 388

USA–Trinidad and Tobago. Agreement concerning Maritime Counter-Drug Operations, Port of Spain, 4 March 1996. In force 4 March 1996. 220

Agreement on the Conservation of Cetaceans of the Black Sea, Mediterranean Sea and Contiguous Atlantic Area, Monaco, 24 November 1996. Not in force. One ratification.* 36 *ILM* 777 (1997) 319

1997 Australia–Indonesia. Treaty establishing an Exclusive Economic Zone Boundary and Certain Seabed Boundaries, Perth, 14 March 1997. No information on date of entry into force. 35 *LOSB* 107 (1997) 196

Convention on the Law of the Non-Navigational Uses of International Watercourses, Adopted by United Nations General Assembly, New York, 21 May 1997. Not in force. Four ratifications.* 36 *ILM* 700 (1997) 387

1

Introduction

Scope of the book

This book is concerned with the public international law of the sea – that is to say, with the rules and principles that bind States in their international relations concerning maritime matters. Accordingly, it does not discuss, except incidentally, the rules of private maritime law, which concern such matters as marine insurance, carriage of goods by sea and maritime liens; nor does it provide a survey of the municipal law of the United Kingdom, or of any other country, relating to the law of the sea. Furthermore, it is concerned with the laws of peace and not with the matters that have traditionally been considered under the heading of the laws of war, and consequently topics such as maritime neutrality and prize law fall beyond its scope. Nonetheless, this leaves a considerable body of law within the purview of the book.

Our treatment of the subject falls into two broad divisions. First, we take each of the major maritime zones recognised in contemporary international law, and explain the rules presently applicable to that zone against the background of the main stages of the historical development of those rules. Increasingly, however, the law of the sea is being developed along functional, rather than zonal, lines. For example, whereas the 1958 United Nations Conference on the Law of the Sea concentrated mainly on producing a framework of rules governing States' rights and duties in the territorial sea, continental shelf and high seas, many of the more recent international agreements have been concerned not with particular zones but with particular uses of the seas, such as pollution, fishing (which was in fact also the subject of one of the conventions produced by the 1958 conference) and navigation. We have, therefore, thought it necessary, in order to bring together the many rules of international law relating to the various uses of the seas, to provide separate surveys of each of the main activities carried out in the seas. These functional surveys appear in the later chapters of the book.

Although the international law of the sea is in principle limited in its application to States and other entities having international personality, it has immediate significance for individuals. Thus, for instance, individuals may be arrested in coastal waters on charges of illegal fishing, or find that their ships are denied passage through the waters of an archipelago. In both cases they are immediately involved in questions of international law which may be discussed with the local authorities 'on the spot', or arise in subsequent proceedings in a municipal court, or be taken up on the international plane by their government. In the last chapter we discuss the ways in which such disputes arise and are handled, and the inter-relationship between international and municipal law.

Laws, whether international or municipal, do not grow up in isolation, but influence and are moulded by the politics, economics and geography of the 'real world' to which they apply. This is particularly apparent in relation to the law of the sea. From the early eighteenth century up to the end of the nineteenth cen-tury the seas were largely subject to a *laissez-faire* regime. Beyond the narrow belt of coastal seas, the high seas were open to free and unrestricted use by all. Such a regime reflected the interests of the dominant European powers of the period in promoting seaborne trade and maintaining communications with their colonies. This *laissez-faire* regime was adequate for the two main uses of the sea – navigation and fishing – which prevailed during this period, since ships were small and relatively few in number compared with today, and fish stocks were thought to be inexhaustible.

In the second half of the twentieth century the premises upon which the *laissez-faire* regime rested underwent a fundamental change. The traditional hegemony of the European States was challenged both by the emergence of the two Superpowers, the USA and the USSR (which, as major naval powers, shared an interest in maximising the freedom of maritime communication), and by the nationalism and demands for economic autonomy of the developing countries, most of which gained their independence after the Second World War. The uses of the seas multiplied and intensified as a result of developments in technology and an increasing demand for resources, with increased possibilities for conflict. Developments in scientific research and understanding made it clear that the seas are by no means an inexhaustible resource. Offshore oil, gas and mineral deposits are plainly finite resources; but even the ability of marine fisheries to produce a sustainable yield is dependent upon the effective implementation of measures to protect them from overfishing, pollution and other threats to the delicate balance of the marine ecosystems.

These changes in the way that the seas are used, and in the ways that the uses of the seas are perceived, produced considerable stresses within the interna-tional community and strong pressures for changes in the law. This, in turn, led to some radical developments in the law. Some of those developments followed clearly from particular circumstances. For example, the threat of pollution from tankers – especially the generation of supertankers built to maximise efficiency on the long sea routes adopted between 1967 and 1975 when the Suez Canal was closed by the Arab–Israel conflict – led to pressure from coastal States for tighter controls over vessels passing near their coasts. Such control was thought neces-sary to protect both coastal fisheries and the tourist and other interests in the foreshore. Episodes of over-fishing threatening the existence of commercial fish stocks off Latin America and in the North Atlantic similarly led to demands from States for extended coastal jurisdiction over resources adjacent to their coasts. Those pressures found expression in the massive extension of coastal jurisdiction in the 1970s.

Other changes have had a more diffuse effect. Technology has developed which permits, for example, the abstraction of energy from the tides, the bridging of ever-wider straits, and the building of artificial islands on which industries can be sited offshore. It has made possible the recovery of mineral resources from ever-deeper parts of the oceans, and the electronic location of commercial fish stocks with pin-point accuracy. The irresistible lure of profits from the exploitation of marine resources, coupled with the inescapable constraints of geography and technological possibility, have led States to develop a range of pragmatic legal solutions to facilitate the orderly utilisation of the seas across a wide range of activities. The agreements on cross-boundary continental shelf resources, and on the exploitation of the resources of the deep sea bed, are examples.

These developments in the law have been brought about by peaceful diplomacy; but in practically every case, there is an underlying conflict between the interests of different users of the seas. The strengthening of anti-pollution laws inevitably increases the cost of moving cargoes by sea. Fishery conservation measures necessarily limit the right of fishermen to take their catch. Great bridges and offshore installations may impede the passage of ships. The range of conflicting interests is immense. Plainly, States have differing kinds and degrees of interests in the seas, ranging from major maritime powers such as the United States and Russia to small landlocked countries such as Bolivia and Nepal. Some States fish exclusively off their coasts, but others have important distant-water fishing fleets. Some States have broad continental shelves rich in mineral resources, but others do not. While these differences have a strong influence on the maritime policies of the States concerned, it should not be forgotten that even within States there are conflicting interests at work. The United Kingdom, for instance, is an island State and is both a significant shipping nation and one of the major victims of oil pollution from tanker casualties. Each nation's maritime policy represents a compromise between such divergent interests.

It is the task of the law both to accommodate these uses and to provide a framework for resolving conflicts between them. This book attempts to show how that balance has been struck.

Early development of the subject

The development of the law of the sea is inseparable from the development of international law in general. While there have over the centuries been many documented systems of relations between independent polities, in Africa and Asia and Europe, 'international law' as it exists today is the body of law initially generated by the relations between the European States during the period known as 'modern' (i.e., post-medieval) history. Cultural imperialism that may be; but it is an inescapable fact. International law in this sense grew up only when the emergence of independent, territorially-defined States made possible truly international relations, instead of the network of imperial relations based upon personal allegiances which subsisted throughout the effective life of the Holy Roman Empire. This change, while commonly said to be epitomised by the Treaty of Westphalia in 1648, was not an event, but rather a slow and subtle evolution. It was clearly discernible in Europe from the sixteenth century onwards.

In the early phases of international law, rules were drawn partly from the canons of Roman law, which underwent a revival in Western Europe beginning in the late eleventh century, partly from State practice, which gave rise to customary rules concerning, for example, the exchange of legations and conduct of war, and partly (and perhaps mainly) from what those who articulated the rules believed to be the dictates of common sense. The articulation and refinement of rules appropriate to international relations underlying Roman law and custom was largely the province of jurists who, under the general intellectual influence of the Renaissance and Reformation, drew on many sources in their work. For example, the Dutchman Hugo Grotius (1583–1645), commonly regarded as the father of modern international law (which reflects rather unfairly upon his distinguished predecessors, such as the Spaniards Vitoria, 1480–1546, and Suarez, 1548–1617, and the Italian Gentilis, 1552–1608), drew on reason and the law of nature, supported by references to scripture and a wide range of classical Greek and Roman writers, for his statements of the law. State practice was, at this stage, given a subsidiary role. Grotius regarded it as generating a 'voluntary law of nations', of lesser weight than the rules of natural law. Though this was undoubtedly in large measure a reflection of the intellectual climate of the time it was also practically inevitable, because it was not until the seventeenth century that European States made serious efforts to maintain records of diplomatic dealings (and so, of State practice) in public archives.[1]

Early treatises on the law of the sea were often written in the context of particular disputes, as were tracts on other subjects of international law. For instance, Grotius's great work *Mare Liberum*, published in 1609, was written in order to vindicate the claims of the Dutch East India Company, by whom he was employed, to trade in the Far East despite the monopoly on trade in the area claimed by the Portuguese at that time. That book upheld the doctrine of the freedom of the seas, and was seen as threatening contemporary British claims to control the seas around Great Britain. It was met by spirited responses from writers such as the Scot Welwood in his *Abridgment of all Sea Lawes* (1613) and the Englishman Selden in his *Mare Clausum* (1635). Such literary exchanges did much to clarify understanding of the issues involved in the law of the sea, and to refine the concepts upon which it was based. Modern international law has almost

---

[1] See the classic study by Garrett Mattingly, *Renaissance Diplomacy* (London, Jonathan Cape), 1955.

wholly abandoned the intellectual foundations upon which many of the early writers built, but their work remains of continuing importance both because it enshrines the prevailing views of their day upon the law of the sea and because the modern law has developed, by a continuing process of modification and refinement, from those foundations.

What is loosely called the 'natural law tradition' persisted throughout the eighteenth century, although the most influential writers, such as Wolff (1679–1754) and Vattel (1714–67), attached to customary law an importance equal to that of natural law. But natural law, as a political doctrine, was losing its influence in the course of struggles against royal absolutism, and was being steadily displaced by political theories based upon the notion of consensual government, exemplified by Rousseau's 'social contract'. In international law this development found expression in the rise of the positivist school, which regarded the voluntary assumption of obligations by States, as evidenced by their practice and contained in the rules of customary and treaty law, as being of more immediate importance than the dictates of natural law.

Schools of legal thought do not have the coherence and defined life-spans of movements in fields such as art history. The rise of positivism is more a matter of a shift in the balance of the range of rhetorical tools employed by jurists than it is of the replacement of one intellectual structure by another. The positivist approach, with its emphasis upon what States actually do rather than upon what Greeks, Romans, Prophets and common reason might have thought that States should do, can be traced at least as far back as the great English lawyer Richard Zouche (1590–1660); but as the conceptual framework of international law, it is pre-eminently a child of the Enlightenment. It had many distinguished followers, such as Bynkershoek (1673–1743) and Martens (1756–1821), and has been overwhelmingly dominant in international law since the nineteenth century. Although there are signs that the age of positivism is passing, and that the rigour with which positivist theory tested putative rules of law against the recorded practice of States is giving way to an altogether looser approach to determinations of normativity, positivism remains the official creed of international lawyers, and the place from which we must begin.

Sources of the modern law of the sea

This positivist approach to international law is reflected in article 38 of the Statute of the International Court of Justice, which directs the Court to apply, in deciding international disputes brought before it:

(a) international conventions, whether general or particular, establishing rules expressly recognised by the contesting States;
(b) international custom, as evidence of a general practice accepted as law;
(c) the general principles of law recognised by civilised nations;

(d) . . . judicial decisions and the teachings of the most highly qualified publicists of the various nations, as subsidiary means for the determination of rules of law.

Article 38 is as much concerned with the establishment of authority and legitimacy in the international legal system as it is with the identification of the kinds of rule that may be made. It does not merely stipulate what the sources of law are: it also stipulates who may make those rules and how they may make them. Only States may make those rules, and only by the modalities falling within paragraphs (a) to (c) of article 38. The prescription in article 38 is, strictly, a direction to the International Court alone; but it is widely accepted as an authoritative statement of the sources of international law applicable more generally. It is necessary to say a little about each of them in turn.

International conventions

Conventions (or treaties or agreements, as they are often called) are the clearest expression of legal undertakings made by States. Furthermore, States are, in general, allowed to modify by treaty rights and duties attaching to them under customary law (there is an exception in the case of customary law rules of *jus cogens,* such as the rules forbidding genocide or the waging of aggressive war, but this controversial category of 'peremptory norms' allowing of no derogations has little relevance to the law of the sea). Accordingly, the existence of a treaty relating to any particular matter will usually provide a clear and conclusive statement of the rights of the States Parties to it in their relations with each other. Treaties are binding only upon the States Parties to them. The relations between a State Party to a treaty and non-Party States continue to be regulated by customary law. However, the provisions of treaties may, as we shall see, become binding upon other States if they pass into customary law.

Treaties often require, in addition to signature, ratification by the parties before they enter into force. Multilateral treaties may require ratification by a prescribed minimum number of States. Treaties remain binding until any time limit set down in them expires or, if the parties intended to allow denunciation, until they are denounced, or until the parties conclude a later treaty relating to the same subject matter. These and other rules concerning the conclusion, interpretation, termination and suspension of treaties are set out in the 1969 Vienna Convention on the Law of Treaties, which codified and in some respects added to the customary international law on the subject.[2]

There are many treaties dealing with various aspects of the law of the sea. Some are multilateral, such as the 1958 Conventions on the territorial sea, high seas and continental shelf, and the 1973 Convention on the Prevention of Pollution from Ships. Many others, dealing with matters such as access to ports,

[2] See Sir I. Sinclair, *The Vienna Convention on the Law of Treaties*, 2nd edn (Manchester, Manchester University Press), 1984.

fishing rights and maritime boundary delimitations, are bilateral. Details of the main collections of treaties can be found in 'Further reading' at the end of this chapter, and the contents of the treaties themselves are described in the following chapters of this book.

Customary international law

The International Court's Statute refers to 'international custom, as evidence of a general practice accepted as law', as a source of international law. This formula is, however, in some ways misleading. It would be better phrased, 'international custom, as evidenced by a practice generally accepted as law'.

Orthodox legal theory requires proof of two elements in order to establish the existence of a rule of customary international law. The first is a general and consistent practice adopted by States. This practice need not be universally adopted, and in assessing its generality special weight will be given to the practice of States most directly concerned – for example, the practice of coastal States in the case of claims to maritime zones, or of the major shipping States in claims to jurisdiction over merchant ships. The second element is the so-called *opinio juris* – the conviction that the practice is one which is either required or allowed by customary international law, or more generally that the practice concerns a matter which is the subject of legal regulation and is consistent with international law. This second requirement prevents such consistent practices as the provision of red carpets for visiting heads of State and, as we shall see in chapter four, the exercise of restraint in certain cases in enforcing coastal State laws against foreign ships in passage through the territorial sea, from becoming rules of law: they remain merely 'rules' of comity or courtesy.

The combination of these two elements in the formation of customary law can be seen, for instance, in the emergence of the continental shelf as a legal concept. In 1945 President Truman claimed for the United States ownership of the resources of the sea bed adjacent to the coast of the United States, and this was followed by similar claims made by many other States. These claims, coupled with the belief that they were permissible in international law, provided the basis of a customary rule recognising coastal States' ownership of continental shelf resources, which emerged by the late 1950s. This example has an added interest because these rights were, in 1958, set out in articles 1–3 of the Continental Shelf Convention; and in the *North Sea Continental Shelf* cases (1969) the International Court regarded those articles in the 1958 Convention as 'reflecting, or as crystallising, received or at least emergent rules of customary international law'.[3]

This illustrates the point that conventional provisions having a 'norm-creating character' – that is, provisions purporting to lay down rules of law of general applicability, rather than merely settling issues between the particular States Parties on the basis of expediency – may arise from or pass into customary law,

---

[3] [1969] *ICJ Rep.* 3 at 39.

and so be or become binding upon States not party to the convention. There is nothing mystical about this transformation. Customary law requires only practice coupled with *opinio juris*. The practice may be prompted by and crystallise around a proposition set out in a treaty in the same way that it may do so in relation to a putative rule of law set out anywhere else. If there is a sufficiently general acceptance of treaty rules by non-Parties, coupled with the necessary *opinio juris*, or by Parties acting in a manner evidencing a belief that the treaty rules represent not merely treaty obligations but also customary law, those rules may become binding as a matter of customary law.[4]

Customary international law is, in principle, binding upon all States. However, the essential role of consent in the formation of customary law has two important consequences as far as this general principle is concerned. First, if a State persistently objects to an emerging rule of customary law, as a matter of strict law it will not be bound by that rule. The objection must be persistent: States will not be permitted to acquiesce in rules of law and later claim exemption from them at will. This point arose in the *Anglo-Norwegian Fisheries* case (1951), in which the United Kingdom attempted to show that State practice had established a customary rule imposing a ten-mile limit upon lines drawn across the mouth of bays where such lines served as the baselines from which the territorial sea is measured. The United Kingdom failed to prove sufficient generality in the practice of adopting a ten-mile limit to establish it as a rule of customary law, but the International Court added:

> In any event the ten-mile rule would appear to be inapplicable as against Norway inasmuch as she has always opposed any attempt to apply it to the Norwegian coast.[5]

The alleged rule would not, therefore, have been 'opposable' (to use the common term) to Norway anyway. Thus, even if a general practice has generated a rule of customary law, which is in principle binding upon all States, particular States may be able to claim the status of persistent objectors, with the result that they will not be bound by the rule. For instance, at least until 1980, the United States consistently refused to accept the legality of territorial sea claims in excess of three miles, and consequently it was not bound by such claims even though the overwhelming majority of States made or recognised claims to a twelve-mile territorial sea so that customary law could be said to have admitted such wider claims. The general rule of customary law was not opposable to the United States as long as it maintained its persistent opposition.

---

[4] The relationship between treaty and custom has been discussed at length in the International Court: see the judgments (including the Separate and Dissenting Opinions) in the *Nicaragua (Merits)* case, [1986] *ICJ Rep.* 3. Cf. R. Bernhardt, 'Custom and treaty in the Law of the Sea', 205 *Recueil des cours* (1989.vi) 167–412; M. Mendelson, 'The International Court of Justice and the sources of international law', in V. Lowe and M. Fitzmaurice (eds), *Fifty Years of the International Court of Justice* (Cambridge, Cambridge University Press), 1996, pp. 63–89.

[5] [1951] *ICJ Rep.* 116 at 131.

Viewed in this light, it will be readily understood that the primary function of proof of a 'general practice accepted as law' is to create a *presumption* that all States, whether or not they have contributed to that practice, are bound by the resultant rule. They are presumed to have assented to that to which States in general have assented. In this sense States are bound by customary rules even if they have not specifically assented to them. But this presumption is liable to be rebutted by proof of persistent objection, which may have prevented a State from becoming bound by the obligations contained in those rules. That, at least, is the position in legal theory. In practice, it becomes increasingly difficult (and in political and economic terms, increasingly costly) to hold out against a rule that is accepted by the overwhelming majority of other States. The pressure for conformity is likely to prove irresistible in the long run. The United States' opposition to claims in excess of three miles was for many years underlined by its 'Freedom of Navigation' programme,[6] in which US warships and military aircraft asserted their right to treat waters more than three miles from coastal baselines as high seas. However, that programme, which was a source of considerable friction in US relations with some States which took a different view of the law, was abandoned in the late 1970s; and by 1982 the United States had explicitly accepted the legality of territorial sea claims of up to twelve miles.

The second consequence of the determinative role of consent as the basis of obligation in customary law is that it is unnecessary to have recourse to the general practice of States in order to create a presumption that a particular State is bound by a rule if it can be proved that that State has in fact consented to the rule. Furthermore, individual States may consent to rules which have not been generally accepted, with the result that they become bound by them. So, for example, the first few States to claim a twelve-mile territorial sea were bound *inter se* to admit its legality, even though States in general did not at that time recognise claims of more than three miles in breadth. As we noted above, such twelve-mile claims would not have been opposable to States persistently objecting to them. This phenomenon is sometimes explained by writers and courts in terms of the existence of 'local' or 'regional' rules of customary international law. While it is often the case that States in a region will adopt similar positions on questions such as the breadth of the territorial sea, in reality the point is much more general than those terms imply, since there is no need for States consenting to the rule in question to come from the same locality or region. The rule is simply a sub-set of international legal obligations.

Consent to rules may be found in the form of legislative claims based upon the rule, declarations of Ministers and so on. In principle, there is no reason why support for United Nations resolutions should not evidence such consent. In practice most States do not intend – and intention is the crucial test – their support for a particular resolution to be taken as consent to any rule of law which the resolution may purport to lay down; and in the absence of such intention an

---

[6] See *DUSPIL 1979*, 997–8.

affirmative vote for a resolution is merely a declaration of political intent and not an assumption of legal obligation. But there are some resolutions that were clearly regarded as statements of customary international law, and their adoption by unanimous or overwhelming majority votes has been taken as a decisive step in the crystallisation of the rules that they contain. The most celebrated example is General Assembly resolution 2625 (XXV), the Declaration on Principles of International Law concerning Friendly Relations between States.[7] If the intention to accept a rule as binding is the key, there is no reason why such an intention should not operate to bind the State however it is expressed. The International Court pursued this reasoning to its logical conclusion in the *Nuclear Tests* cases (1974), by holding that even purely unilateral declarations, in which French Ministers undertook to cease atmospheric nuclear weapons tests, were, if made with the intention of binding France, binding upon France as a matter of international law.[8]

It will be apparent that customary international law is not a monolithic body of general rules uniformly binding upon all States alike. Rather, the existence of customary law obligations between particular States is ultimately a question of opposability. Thus customary law may develop by shifts in the patterns of opposability. For instance, at a time when most States claimed only three- or twelve-mile fishery zones, but a few Latin American States claimed 200-mile fishery zones, it could be said that the 'general' rule – using the term in a descriptive rather than a prescriptive sense – was that international law admitted fishery jurisdiction only up to three or twelve miles from shore, and that as an exception 200-mile claims were opposable to the Latin American States alone. But as more and more States have moved to the Latin American position and claimed 200-mile zones the balance has shifted, so that the 'general' rule now admits the legality of such claims, even though they would not be opposable to any States which have persistently objected to them.[9] It is in this sense that we refer in this book to 'general' rules and practices.

While the foregoing account is believed both to be correct and to represent a generally accepted view, the nature of customary law is a controversial matter.[10]

---

[7] See Sir I. Sinclair, 'The significance of the Friendly Relations Declaration', in V. Lowe and C. Warbrick (eds), *The United Nations and the Principles of International Law* (London, Routledge), 1994, pp. 1–32.

[8] *Nuclear Tests Cases* [1974] *ICJ Rep.* 253 at 267. The Court's later treatment of the point, in the Burkina Faso/Mali *Frontier Dispute* case, suggests that the *Nuclear Tests* statements on unilateral acts should be understood more narrowly than they were expressed: see [1986] *ICJ Rep.* 554 at 574.

[9] There are, in fact, no States now objecting to 200-mile fishery zones.

[10] For a fuller account of this aspect of the matter see A. V. Lowe , 'Do general rules of international law exist?', 9 *Review of International Studies* 207–13 (1983) and T. Stein, 'The approach of the different drummer: the principle of the persistent objector in international law', 26 *Harvard International Law Journal* 457–82 (1985). For another view see J. I. Charney, 'The persistent objector rule and the development of customary international law', 56 *BYIL* 1–24 (1985).

In particular, it has sometimes been argued that rules of customary law may create truly general obligations, which States cannot escape by persistent opposition. One example of such an argument of relevance to this book is the claim by Professor De Visscher that the legal concept of the continental shelf is not, strictly speaking, the product of customary law, developed according to the processes which we have described, but is rather the expression of the direct and irresistible operation of certain facts – the extension of a State's land mass below the adjacent waters – upon the formation of international law.[11] Although the International Court has occasionally given 'objective' force *erga omnes* to certain types of legal status, such as the legal personality of the United Nations in the *Reparations* case (1949), it is questionable how far this view may properly be adopted. Although it is arguable that De Visscher's approach, deriving universally applicable rules from the *effectiveness* of claims rather than from their recognition by other States, may be applicable to other maritime claims such as claims to archipelagic and historic waters,[12] this argument is at best highly controversial. Unfortunately, shortage of space precludes its further examination in this book.

Evidence of State practice, sought in connection with the proof of customary law, can be found in many places, including States' legislation, the decisions of their courts, and the statements of their official government and diplomatic representatives. Sometimes requests for statements of practice emanating from international organisations or conferences produce replies containing comprehensive statements of practice upon a particular point. Accordingly, national statute books, law reports, parliamentary debates, collections of diplomatic material and the records of international conferences will yield evidence of State practice. States involved in international litigation will also frequently explain their practice and opinions on the law in pleadings before the court or tribunal concerned, and support their arguments by extensive and detailed examinations of the practice of other States. Further details on these sources of materials will be found at the end of this chapter.

It is necessary to exercise some care when analysing State practice. Claims appearing on the statute book may have been quietly abandoned or may never have been enforced, and therefore may not represent the actual 'practice' of the State. In this context it is also necessary to bear in mind the basic distinction between two kinds of jurisdiction: legislative and enforcement jurisdiction. Legislative jurisdiction is the right to prescribe laws. It may be limited *ratione loci* (i.e., limited in the geographical area within which the law applies – for example, fisheries jurisdiction is in general limited to 200 miles from the coast), *ratione personae* (i.e., limited in its application to certain classes of person – for example, some customs laws may apply only to nationals and ships flying the flag of the

---

[11] C. De Visscher, *Problèmes de confins en droit international public* (Paris, Pedone), 1969, pp. 148ff., and *Les effectivités du droit international public* (Paris, Pedone), 1967.
[12] Indeed, were this not the case, the geographical shape of a State would vary as between States which have and States which have not persistently objected to its claims to maritime territory.

legislating State), and *ratione materiae* (i.e., limited to certain kinds of matter – for example, States have jurisdiction in respect of the natural resources of that part of the continental shelf which lies more than 200 miles from shore, but not over other uses of the sea in that area).

In the case of legislative jurisdiction, statutes can be taken more or less at face value. Thus, a claim to legislate for, say, customs matters in the waters adjacent to its coast but beyond its territorial sea is a claim to legislative jurisdiction whether or not the law is enforced in practice. A pattern of statutes of that kind could form the basis of a rule of customary international law permitting the exercise of legislative jurisdiction in customs matters. It is, however, always necessary to take account of the municipal rules of statutory interpretation which, for example, commonly provide that statutes be presumed to apply only within territorial limits. Enforcement jurisdiction, on the other hand, is the right actually to enforce laws. It often coexists with legislative jurisdiction. For example, a State may not only legislate for customs matters, but also actually enforce those laws against ships while they are outside its territorial sea. But they do not always go together. Although a State's customs laws may be stated to apply to all ships within, say, twenty-four miles of its coast, the State may enforce that law against foreign vessels only if the vessel subsequently comes into one of the State's ports. In such a case, it would be legitimate to infer a belief on the part of the State that it was entitled to exercise legislative jurisdiction over foreign vessels within twenty-four miles of its coasts, but not necessarily to infer a belief that it had enforcement jurisdiction over them there. Thus, legislation is a fallible guide to claims to enforcement jurisdiction.

General principles of international law

The rather vague category of 'general principles of international law' is not of great significance for the law of the sea. Its presence in article 38 of the International Court's Statute permits the Court to fill in gaps in treaty and customary law by applying principles of law which are common to the major legal systems of the world and are suitable for transposition into the international legal system. Estoppel is an example of such a principle. General principles of a slightly different kind have more relevance. Rules such as the freedom of the high seas and the exclusiveness of flag State jurisdiction over ships on the high seas are sometimes described as general principles of law, in the sense that in the absence of clear proof of, for example, a right under treaty for a State other than the flag State to exercise jurisdiction over ships on the high seas, no such right will exist. Here any doubt over the existence of the non-flag State's rights is settled in favour of the exclusiveness of the flag State's jurisdiction, by reference to the general principle. It thus functions as a residual presumption for the resolution of doubtful claims. But such principles are better regarded as rules, or more accurately principles, of customary law, albeit principles having a particular and fundamental importance.

Judicial decisions and the writings of publicists

The final paragraph of article 38(1) refers to judicial decisions and the writings of publicists as a subsidiary means for the determination of rules of law. This puts their role into a proper perspective. Judges and jurists cannot *create* law: only States can do that, through the formation of treaty and customary rules and general principles of law. Judicial decisions and the writings of jurists serve merely to aid the identification of rules created by States. The value of a statement by a judge or a legal author on a point of international law is dependent upon his or her standing, and the thoroughness with which he or she has researched the appropriate materials.

It will be clear that international law is a complex subject. The collection and analysis of State practice is a difficult task, compounded by the fact that States rarely feel it necessary to explain in legal terms why they act as they do. Writers have a crucial role in researching State practice and articulating the legal rules on which it is based and which it generates. In addition, they perform the service of tracing the development of the law and identifying divergences in State practice, and of describing the network of legal obligations resulting from the enormous body of overlapping rules of customary and treaty law. We refer at the end of each chapter to some of the most important specialist monographs and articles on individual topics within the law of the sea, but it is appropriate to mention here the classic work of writers such as Colombos, McDougal and Burke, O'Connell, and Dupuy and Vignes, who have prepared general expositions of the subject, and, towering above all, the monumental work of Gilbert Gidel, *Le droit international public de la mer* (3 vols, Paris, 1932–4), a book of outstanding scholarship which remains of great value and interest.

From time to time the enormous task of bringing together all the basic rules on the law of the sea has been essayed, and it is to these codification efforts that we now turn.

Attempts at codification

There have been many attempts to codify the rules of customary international law applicable to the seas. Most of these, especially in the decades preceding the establishment of the United Nations, were undertaken by non-governmental learned societies. Four such bodies have made particularly notable contributions.

The International Law Association has, since its inception in 1873, produced several reports and sets of resolutions, and held lengthy and detailed discussions, on various topics such as territorial waters, marine pollution, the sea bed and its resources, international waterways, deep-sea-bed mining, piracy, and port State jurisdiction. Apart from the participation of distinguished lawyers, which has preserved a high standard of legal scholarship, and of interest, in its work, the Association has also been enriched by the participation of non-lawyers, such as shipowners, politicians and economists, concerned with the topics under review.

The more prestigious (if only because its membership is strictly limited) Institute of International Law was also founded in 1873. Its members have included many of the most eminent international lawyers of the day, and its deliberations and reports are accorded great respect. It has adopted resolutions on such matters as international waterways, the high seas, the regime of merchant ships, submarine cables, marine resources, the territorial sea and internal waters, marine pollution, and, in a rare flight of fancy, the creation of an International Waters Office. Unlike the Association, whose main language is English, a large proportion of its business has been transacted, and reported, in French.

The third body is the Harvard Law School, which prepared notable reports on territorial waters and piracy in the first part of the twentieth century. The final body is the American Law Institute, whose *Restatement of the Law* includes a volume on the Foreign Relations Law of the United States. This occasionally idiosyncratic study is of enormous influence upon United States courts faced with questions of international law, and of considerable influence in the world beyond.

Several other organisations have produced draft articles on aspects of the international law of the sea, and in addition some individuals, such as Domin-Petrushevecz, Bluntschli, Fiore and Internoscia, have undertaken the codification of international law single-handedly – although enthusiasm for such projects seems to have died out after the First World War. Apart from the incidental interest which all model codes, collective and individual, have as reflections of prevailing approaches to the law of the sea, their main value lies in the careful collection and analysis of State practice which is (or at least should have been) associated with their preparation. It is this that gives the work of the Association and Institute, and the Harvard research, its especially influential position in the development of the law.

There have been four major inter-governmental attempts to codify the peacetime rules of the international law of the sea. The first was instigated by the League of Nations. In 1924 the League appointed a Committee of Experts to draw up a list of subjects ripe for codification. Territorial waters, piracy, exploitation of marine resources and the legal status of State-owned merchant ships were among the subjects considered, and the committee circulated 'Questionnaires' to governments on the first three of them. Subsequently, a Preparatory Commission was set up to prepare three topics – nationality, State responsibility and territorial waters – for codification. These preparations involved the circulation of a 'Schedule of Points' to governments and, after replies had been received from them, the drafting of 'Bases of Discussion' on which the Codification Conference could base its work. There were also reports drawn up for the Committee and Preparatory Commission, notably those prepared by the German lawyer, Schücking. These reports, and the replies of governments, are of enormous interest, and represent an unrivalled survey of State practice and policy of the period.

Unfortunately, the conference, which convened at The Hague in 1930 did not succeed in adopting a convention on territorial waters. A committee was set up to study the subject and its rapporteur, François, produced a report setting out such agreement as had been reached. This included draft articles on matters such as the nature and extent of coastal States' rights over the territorial sea, and of the right of innocent passage. However, it was not possible to reach agreement on the crucial question of the breadth of territorial waters. Accordingly, the conference decided to do no more than refer the draft articles to governments, in the hope that agreement could be reached at some later date.

The Hague draft articles were, however, not without influence. When the League of Nations was replaced by the United Nations in 1945, it was thought desirable to provide for the establishment of a body charged with the 'progressive codification' of international law. This body is the International Law Commission (hereafter, ILC), a body of thirty-four eminent lawyers, serving in individual capacities but nominated and elected by governments, whose first members were appointed in 1948. During its early years the ILC embarked on the preparation of draft articles on the high seas and the territorial sea. Its rapporteur, François, who had prepared the 1930 conference report, drew heavily on the Hague articles. By 1956 the ILC had, at the request of the UN General Assembly, produced a report covering most aspects of the law of the sea of contemporary importance. This report, the product of painstaking analysis and careful drafting and illuminated by the observations of governments on its early drafts, formed the basis of the work of the first United Nations Conference on the Law of the Sea (UNCLOS I), held at Geneva in 1958.

UNCLOS I was attended by eighty-six States – almost double the number at the 1930 conference. It succeeded in adopting four conventions: the Convention on the Territorial Sea and the Contiguous Zone; the Convention on the High Seas; the Convention on the Continental Shelf; and the Convention on Fishing and Conservation of the Living Resources of the High Seas. The first three of these were ratified by substantial numbers of States, and were also based in large measure upon customary international law, as presented in the ILC's reports. Consequently, these three conventions constituted the core of the generally accepted rules of the law of the sea concerning maritime zones. The fourth Geneva convention, and an optional Protocol on dispute settlement, proved less popular, perhaps partly because they went further than the existing obligations which customary law imposed on States.

The one major problem that the 1958 conference could not solve was that which had defeated the 1930 conference: the breadth of the territorial sea. Accordingly a second conference, UNCLOS II, was convened in 1960 to discuss that problem, and also the associated question of fishery limits. It failed, by only one vote, to adopt a compromise formula providing for a six-mile territorial sea plus a six-mile fishery zone. Agreement on the breadth of the territorial sea had to await the preparation of the Convention drawn up by the third United Nations Conference on the Law of the Sea (UNCLOS III), more than half a century after the first attempt at The Hague.

UNCLOS III had its origins in the Sea Bed Committee established in 1967 by the United Nations General Assembly to examine the question of the deep sea bed lying beyond the limits of national jurisdiction (i.e., beyond the continental shelf), following a proposal by Dr Arvid Pardo, the Maltese ambassador. The 1958 conference had not made any special provision for the legal regime of the deep sea bed, because at the time its great mineral wealth was not appreciated and the technology necessary for its exploitation did not exist. As we shall see in chapter twelve, many States were keen to have the deep sea bed and its resources internationalised and declared the 'common heritage of mankind', in order to avoid a 'land-grab' for its resources from which only the developed States would be in a position to benefit. Any internationalisation of the sea bed beyond national jurisdiction required a definition of the limits of national jurisdiction over the sea bed and the revision of parts of the 1958 Convention on the Continental Shelf and of the 1958 Convention on the High Seas. However, many States were reluctant to review the law of the sea, which had been so laboriously codified in the 1950s. Nonetheless, the presence in the United Nations of many newly independent States, which had had no say in the formulation of the 1958 Conventions, provided a substantial majority in favour of reviewing the earlier law. Moreover, many States were increasingly concerned about the problems of over-fishing and marine pollution off their coasts, neither of which could satisfactorily be controlled within the narrow jurisdictional limits upon which the 1958 regime was based. The existence of these factors, and the recognition that the various parts of the law of the sea were inextricably inter-related, led to widespread support for a review of the whole of the law of the sea. It was agreed in 1970, in General Assembly Resolution 2570, to convene a United Nations conference with the task of producing a comprehensive Convention on the Law of the Sea.

The conference, the third United Nations Conference on the Law of the Sea (UNCLOS III), held its first session in 1973, and worked for several months each year until it finally adopted a convention in 1982. The conference was divided into three main committees, as was the Sea Bed Committee, which had been engaged from 1971 to 1973 in preparatory work for the conference. Committee One dealt with the problem of the legal regime of the deep sea bed. Committee Two dealt with the regimes of the territorial sea and contiguous zone, the continental shelf, exclusive economic zone, the high seas, and fishing and conservation of the living resources of the high seas, as well as with specific aspects of these topics, such as the questions of straits and archipelagic States. Committee Three dealt with the questions of the preservation of the marine environment and scientific research. In addition, smaller *ad hoc* groups considered other detailed questions on behalf of the conference.[13]

[13] For an analysis of the conference procedure, see B. Buzan, 'Negotiating by consensus: developments in technique at the United Nations Conference on the Law of the Sea', 75 *AJIL* 324–48 (1981) and J. K. Sebenius, *Negotiating the Law of the Sea* (Cambridge, Mass., Harvard University Press), 1984. The *American Journal of International Law* published a series of useful articles reviewing the work of the sessions of UNCLOS III by B. H. Oxman and J. R. Stevenson. They appear as follows: Stevenson and Oxman, 68

In contrast with the 1930 Hague Conference and the first two UN Law of the Sea Conferences, UNCLOS III had no 'Bases of Discussion' or ILC report to aid its work. It was, from the time of the establishment of the Sea Bed Committee, seen as a political rather than a narrowly legal enterprise – indeed, the issue was from the outset assigned to the UN General Assembly's First (Political and Security) rather than Sixth (Legal) Committee. The attendance of about 150 States, each with its own interests to promote and defend, made negotiations difficult; but a number of loose groupings soon emerged. The most prominent were the 'Group of 77', as the group of developing States (in fact numbering around 120 States) is known, and the groups of Western capitalist and of east European socialist States. The Group of 77, whose coherence is remarkable in view of the diversity of its members, achieved a notable diplomatic triumph in leaving its imprint clearly upon the Convention text. But there were many other special interest groups coexisting with these broad blocs. For example, the groups of landlocked and geographically disadvantaged States, of archipelagic, and of straits States, and of 'coastal' and 'maritime' States, all played important roles during negotiations on at least some parts of the Convention.

The positions of States at the outset of UNCLOS III were too far apart on many issues for the preparation of even an agreed basis for discussion to have been a practical possibility. It was appreciated, however, that there was little point in adopting measures by votes, in which the major maritime States, on whose acceptance the efficacy of the Convention would in large measure depend, could be easily outvoted by other participants. It was therefore agreed to proceed by way of 'consensus' procedures, searching for areas of maximum agreement without formal votes. UNCLOS III worked for the whole of its time on this basis, except when it came to adopting the final text of the Convention. At that stage a vote was forced by the United States, which could not accept some of the Convention's provisions.

This 'consensus' approach led, from 1975 onwards, to the production of a series of 'negotiating texts', containing draft articles on all of the topics under consideration by the conference. The texts were prepared by the chairmen of the conference's three main committees. The early texts represented in part an emerging consensus among delegates, and in part the aspirations of their drafters. They were modified only if it was thought that an amendment would have greater support than the existing text. Consequently, the subsequent negotiating texts evidenced an increasing level of agreement on most of the essential issues, such as the extent of the territorial sea, the legal regimes of the territorial sea, contiguous zone, continental shelf, exclusive economic zone and high seas, and the regulation of scientific research and marine pollution. Provisions in these texts soon began to be incorporated into national legislation, and so to exert an influence

---

AJIL 1–32 (1974), 69 *AJIL* 1–30, 763–97 (1975); Oxman, 71 *AJIL* 247–69 (1977), 72 *AJIL* 57–83 (1978), 73 *AJIL* 1–41 (1979), 74 *AJIL* 1–47 (1980), 75 *AJIL* 211–56 (1981) and 76 *AJIL* 1–23 (1982).

upon the development of customary international law. Indeed, at least the broad principles of many of the innovations made by the 1982 Convention, such as the establishment of rights to 200-mile Exclusive Economic Zones (EEZs), had passed into customary law some years before the Convention itself entered into force.

Difficulties in securing agreement upon a few matters, chief among which were certain provisions of the legal regime of the deep sea bed, delayed the preparation of a final text until 1982. The text of the UN Convention on the Law of the Sea was finally adopted on 30 April 1982 by 130 votes to four, with seventeen abstentions.[14] Its failure to secure unanimous support illuminates the hybrid nature of the Convention. In part – principally in Part XI, dealing with the deep sea bed – it is an exceptionally precise, detailed instrument closer in appearance to a commercial contract or concession than to an international treaty. The unacceptability of some of these details was the main cause of negative votes and abstentions on the adoption of the Convention. The other parts are more in the nature of a framework treaty or *loi-cadre,* leaving the elaboration of precise rules to other bodies, such as national governments and international organisations, and to dispute settlement procedures or future international negotiations. Perhaps because of the flexibility inherent in this approach, these parts did command general support. On 10 December 1982 the United Nations Convention on the Law of the Sea (hereafter we refer to it as the Law of the Sea Convention or LOSC) was opened for signature at Montego Bay in Jamaica by States and by international organisations such as the EC to which States have delegated competence in matters touching upon the Convention (LOSC, arts 305–7).[15]

[14] Israel, Turkey the United States and Venezuela voted against. Belgium, Bulgaria, Byelorussia, Czechoslovakia, the German Democratic Republic, the Federal Republic of Germany, Hungary, Italy, Luxembourg, Mongolia, the Netherlands, Poland, Spain, Thailand, the Ukraine, the USSR and the United Kingdom abstained. Votes against and abstentions were explained by the delegations concerned at the meeting on 30 April 1982, and recorded in UNCLOS III, *Official Records*, Vol. XVI, pp. 152–67.

[15] Adherence by international organisations is governed by arts 305–7 and Annex IX. Organisations to which member States have transferred competence over matters governed by the Convention may sign the Convention if the majority of their member States have done so, and may ratify it under similar conditions. Participation of the organisation does not increase its member States' entitlement to representation by, for example, giving the organisation a separate vote in the International Sea Bed Authority; nor does such participation confer any rights on member States not party to the Law of the Sea Convention. In practice, art. 305 and Annex IX only apply at present to the EC, which gave formal confirmation of its adherence to the Convention in April 1998. Namibia, then represented by the UN Council for Namibia, and self-governing associated States and self-governing territories with treaty-making competence over matters governed by the Convention, were also entitled to become parties to the Convention (LOSC arts 305–7). Namibia became an independent State in 1990. National liberation movements which had participated in the work of UNCLOS III were entitled to sign the Final Act in their capacity as observers (LOSC Resolution IV), and to participate as observers in meetings arranged under the Convention, such as meetings of the Authority (LOSC art. 156 (3)); but they may not ratify the Convention.

The Convention was open for signature for a period of two years. At the end of that time it had been signed by 159 States and other entities (including the EC). Among the major non-signatories were the then Federal Republic of Germany, the United Kingdom and the United States, all of which were opposed essentially only to parts of the Convention's regime for the deep sea bed. In particular, they considered the machinery for the administration of the deep sea bed through the International Sea Bed Authority and the restrictions placed upon commercial companies engaged in the mining of deep-sea-bed resources to be unnecessarily cumbersome and expensive.

During the next ten years, two processes unfolded in parallel. On the one hand many States, both parties and non-parties, applied at least the main provisions of the 1982 Convention. Rights always pass into customary international law more readily than obligations, and this was reflected in the reception accorded to the 1982 Convention. Many States that had not previously done so moved swiftly to extend their territorial seas to twelve miles, and their fisheries jurisdiction to 200 miles, for example. The main features of the 1982 regime were steadily being consolidated as rules of customary international law.

Preparations for the implementation of the Convention continued. A Preparatory Commission for the International Sea Bed Authority and for the International Tribunal for the Law of the Sea (PREPCOM) had been established by Resolution I annexed to the Final Act of UNCLOS III, adopted on 10 December 1982. Meetings of PREPCOM, which was based in Kingston, Jamaica, were held from 1983 onwards. It operated through a number of Special Commissions, which drafted the detailed rules that would be necessary to bring the International Sea Bed Authority (ISA) and the regime for deep-sea-bed mining, and the International Tribunal for the Law of the Sea (ITLOS), into operation.[16]

The sixtieth ratification of the Convention was deposited by Guyana on 16 November 1993, and the Convention was therefore due to enter into force on 16 November 1994, as provided in article 308 of the Convention. The prospect of the Convention, with its elaborate machinery for the international governance of the deep sea bed, entering into force without the participation of major industrialised States such as the USA was unattractive. Efforts continued to find a way of accommodating the concerns of the States that remained outside the Convention, thus enabling them to ratify. Quite apart from the goal of securing the widest possible adherence to the Convention, the participation of the major industrialised States was desirable in order to spread the (considerable) costs which were expected to arise from the operation of the two main institutions associated with the Convention, the ISA and the ITLOS.

Concurrently, negotiations were under way to conclude a new agreement that would modify the effect of the provisions of Part XI of the 1982 Convention, so

---

[16] For an account of the establishment of PREPCOM, see W. Goralcyzyk, 'Preparatory measures for the implementation of the Convention on the Law of the Sea', XIV *Polish Yearbook of International Law* 7–42 (1985).

as to meet the concerns of the industrialised nations that remained outside the LOSC regime. Their concerns had already been met in part by the adoption by UNCLOS III at the last minute of Resolution II, annexed to the Final Act, which gave certain priorities and guarantees to the deep-sea-mining companies of industrialised States. Those guarantees did not, however, assuage the fears that the ISA would be an expensive and inefficient organisation which would impede, rather than promote, the rational exploitation of deep-sea-bed resources. With the prospect of the entry into force of the Convention looming, negotiations were conducted in particular earnest in 1990–4 in order to find a solution.[17] These negotiations bore fruit in the Agreement on the Implementation of Part XI of the Convention (the 'Implementation Agreement'), which was adopted by the General Assembly on 28 July 1994.

The 1994 Implementation Agreement is a curious creature. The 1982 LOSC does not permit reservations (arts 309, 310), and the procedures for its amendment are both protracted and open only to States Parties (arts 311–17). Neither route was suitable for modifications of the Convention sought by the industrialised States that remained outside the Convention. Instead, the 1994 Implementation Agreement was made, its title disingenuously implying that it was concerned to put into effect the 1982 provisions rather than to change them. In fact, it stipulates that several provisions of Part XI of the LOSC 'shall not apply' and modifies the effect of others. The provisions of the 1994 Implementation Agreement are designed to ensure that the ISA will be cost-effective, take decisions in a manner that does not override the interests of the industrialised nations, and approach the regulation of the exploitation of the resources of the deep sea bed in a sound commercial fashion. The Implementation Agreement, in an imaginative development of the Law of Treaties, stipulates that

1 After the adoption of this Agreement, any instrument of ratification or formal confirmation of or accession to the Convention shall also represent consent to be bound by this Agreement.
2 No State or entity may establish its consent to be bound by this Agreement unless it has previously established or establishes at the same time its consent to be bound by the Convention.

The intention was that the LOSC should take effect as modified by the Implementation Agreement. There is little doubt that this has been achieved in relation to States which ratified the LOSC after or at the same time as the Implementation Agreement, or which ratified the Implementation Agreement after they ratified the LOSC. According to the traditional law of treaties, it cannot have that effect in relation to States that ratified the LOSC before 28 July 1994 but have not ratified the Implementation Agreement. There are around two dozen such States.

---

[17] See, e.g., E. Riddell-Dixon, 'The Preparatory Commission on the International Sea-Bed Authority: "New Realism"?', 7 *IJECL* 195–216 (1992); G. J. Mangone, 'Negotiations on the 1982 LOSC given extra urgency by the 60th ratification', 9 *IJMCL* 57–71 (1994); L. D. M. Nelson. 'The new deep sea-bed mining regime', 10 *IJMCL* 189–203 (1995).

In theory, those States could choose to remain bound by the original LOSC rules on deep-sea-bed mining. But since any deep-sea-bed mining will in practice take place under the Implementation Agreement regime, that choice is illusory. The Implementation Agreement, which entered into force on 28 July 1996, has effectively modified the LOSC, however limited its effects might be in theory.

The modifications wrought by the 1994 Implementation Agreement opened the door for ratification by the industrialised States. The adoption of that Agreement seems also to have given added impetus to the move to persuade all States which had not yet ratified the LOSC to do so. Many major States ratified the LOSC in the wake of the Implementation Agreement, among them Australia, Chile, China, Finland, Germany (now unified), India, Japan, Malaysia, the Netherlands, Norway, the Russian Federation and the United Kingdom. A full table of parties appears at the end of this book.

The 1994 Implementation Agreement may be contrasted with a second agreement supplementing the 1982 LOSC. This is the Agreement on Straddling Fish Stocks and Highly Migratory Fish Stocks, concluded on 4 August 1995. The 'Straddling Stocks Agreement', as it is known (its official title is the United Nations Agreement for the Implementation of the United Nations Convention on the Law of the Sea of 10 December 1982 relating to the Conservation and Management of Straddling Fish Stocks and Highly Migratory Fish Stocks) may properly be called an 'implementation' agreement. As is explained in chapter fourteen below, it gives substance to the principles concerning the conservation and management of fish stocks, set out in Parts V (Exclusive Economic Zone) and VII (High Seas) of the LOSC. The Straddling Stocks Agreement concerns matters of real importance to many deep-water-fishing States. Nonetheless, by July 1998 it had attracted only fifty-nine signatures and eighteen ratifications or accessions. It will enter into force thirty days after the deposit of the thirtieth instrument of ratification or accession. This record may be compared with the seventy-nine signatures and ninety-one ratifications or accessions to the 1994 Implementation Agreement by July 1998. The 1994 Agreement entered into force on 28 July 1996. Tables of signatures, accessions and ratifications of the 1994 and 1995 Agreements are set out at the end of this book.

The 1994 and 1995 Agreements complete the UN Law of the Sea 'package' as it stands at present. The two instruments are inextricably linked with the LOSC, as is evident from their titles, their substance (discussed in chapters twelve and fourteen below), and the fact that disputes arising under them are subject to the dispute settlement provisions set out in Part XV of the LOSC. In the case of the Straddling Stocks Agreement, which may be signed and ratified by a State whether or not it is a Party to the LOSC, the Part XV provisions would apply even to States not Party to the LOSC. There is further work to be done on the implementation of certain parts of the LOSC[18] but the international community

---

[18] See the Special Issue, 'The Law of the Sea Convention: unfinished agendas and future challenges', *International Journal of Marine and Coastal Law*, Vol. 10, No. 2 (1995).

now has a more comprehensive, more detailed, and more widely accepted regime for the seas than at any time in the past.

The LOSC entered into force on 16 November 1994. As of July 1998, 127 States had ratified or acceded to it. Among the major maritime States, only the USA had not ratified the LOSC, and that for parochial reasons rather than any deliberate rejection of the LOSC regime;[19] and even the USA is among the twenty or so States that have signed but not yet ratified the 1994 Implementation Agreement (as are Belgium and Canada, also non-parties to the LOSC). The UN regime for the seas is already almost universally accepted, and is moving steadily closer to universal subscription. Such dissatisfaction as there is with the regime is now confined to relatively minor points of detail, which will be discussed in the following chapters. Some of these points of dissatisfaction have been manifested in the form of declarations made by States on signature, ratification or accession to the LOSC.[20] We noted above that no *reservations* to the LOSC are permitted. Yet some of these declarations look very much like reservations: only an authoritative ruling from an international tribunal will determine whether or not they are. These declarations are of great importance for an understanding of the current state of the Law of the Sea. They are discussed at appropriate points in the following chapters.

The familiarity of parts of the Law of the Sea system, and the fact that it is the product not only of the LOSC but of a large number of other instruments administered by a wide range of national and international authorities,[21] should not be allowed to conceal the extraordinary achievement that this immensely strong, complex regime represents, or the Herculean labours of the many distinguished lawyers and statesmen whose wisdom and persistence brought it into being.

International organisations

Finally, we must mention the role of international organisations in developing the law of the sea, beginning with those in the United Nations 'family'. As will be seen in subsequent chapters, many organisations make some contribution to the subject, although they are not primarily concerned with maritime matters.[22]

---

[19] See 'Law of the Sea Forum', 88 *AJIL* 687–714 (1994). For tables of signatures and ratifications, see the Appendix to this book.

[20] The Declarations are reprinted in *The Law of the Sea: Declarations and Statements with respect to the United Nations Convention on the Law of the Sea and to the Agreement relating to the Implementation of Part XI of the United Nations Convention on the Law of the Sea* (New York, United Nations), 1997. Updated lists appear at http://www.un.org/Depts/los/los_decl.htm.

[21] P. J. Allott, 'Power sharing in the law of the Sea', 77 *AJIL* 1–30 (1983).

[22] For a recent survey see ' "Competent or relevant international organizations" under the United Nations Convention on the Law of the Sea', 31 *LOSB* 79–95 (1996).

For example, the International Atomic Energy Agency was responsible for preparing a Convention on Civil Liability for Nuclear Damage, which is applicable to damage caused by nuclear-powered ships; and the World Health Organisation has prepared regulations concerning sanitary and quarantine matters affecting international shipping. Other organisations have clearer interests in maritime matters but, not being primarily regulatory agencies, have a less direct influence on the development of the law. Thus the UN Food and Agriculture Organisation, the FAO, has made a great contribution to fishery science and to the understanding of conservation techniques. Its activities include reviewing world fisheries generally, the establishment of regional fishery bodies to advise on fisheries management, and providing assistance to many poorer countries in developing their fishing industries.

The organisation that has probably had the most substantial direct effect upon the law of the sea is the IMO – the International Maritime Organisation. The IMO was established in 1958, when its constitutive treaty, signed in 1948, came into force. Until 1982 it was known as IMCO – the Intergovernmental Maritime Consultative Organisation. It has a wide competence in matters affecting shipping and has adopted a detailed and technical approach to its work. Its committees, such as the Maritime Safety Committee, the Legal Committee and the Marine Environment Protection Committee, have played a prominent role in drawing up regulations concerning navigation and pollution. Some of these regulations are presented to the IMO Council, composed of the representatives of thirty-two States with the largest interests in the provision of shipping and in international seaborne trade and other special interests in maritime transport or navigation. The Council in turn passes them on to the IMO Assembly, in which all member States – at present numbering about 156 – have a seat. The Assembly may then decide to recommend that members comply with the proposals. Such recommendations are not binding. Alternatively, the IMO may seek a more formal arrangement by having measures adopted in the form of a convention at a diplomatic conference convened under its auspices. Around forty conventions and protocols, many of which have attracted a high number of ratifications, have been concluded in this way (see table 3). Some of these conventions provide that they may be amended by resolutions adopted by the IMO Assembly or another IMO body (such as the Maritime Safety Comittee). Such amendments, in most cases, come into force after a specified time for a State, unless the State objects to them (the so-called 'tacit acceptance' procedure).

Organisations outside the UN 'family', whose competence is limited to certain matters and certain regions, fulfil a crucial role, and often have a much greater and more direct influence upon particular maritime activities within their competence than their more wide-ranging international counterparts. Notable examples are regional bodies such as the EC and wider alliances such as the OECD, both active in advancing the causes of resource management and environmental protection, and *ad hoc* bodies such as the Baltic Marine Environment Protection Commission (HELCOM), which are concerned with marine pollution. In the fisheries field, major contributions have been made by the regional fisheries commissions and the International Council for the Exploration of the Sea. These, and other, international organisations have a considerable part to play in the development of the law. The recommendations and conventions which they make or initiate, the constant and detailed surveillance which they exercise over maritime matters, and the reports which they prepare, all exert a great influence on States' perceptions of what is happening in the seas. They mould the formulation of national maritime policies, and hence State practice and the development of international law. We refer to the work of many of these organisations in the following chapters.

The present legal regime

From the description of various sources of the law of the sea, it will have become evident that there is no single text containing the whole of that law. The 1982 Law of the Sea Convention certainly provides a framework within which most uses of the seas are located. Apart from the 127 States and other entities that have ratified the Convention, those which have signed but not ratified it are nevertheless obliged to refrain from acts which would defeat its object and purpose unless they make clear that they do not intend to proceed to ratification;[23] and those intending to ratify will obviously tend, in general, to conform to its terms – or, at least, its spirit – before they do so. Furthermore, as we shall see, some parts of the Law of the Sea Convention reflect pre-existing customary international law, and many other parts which went beyond previous practice have already passed into customary law. In both cases such provisions may be binding on States as customary law, whether they are parties to the Convention or not.[24] The few States parties to the 1958 Conventions which have not ratified or acceded to the LOSC will remain bound by the 1958 Conventions until they lawfully denounce them or become parties to the LOSC, which is expressly stated to prevail over the 1958 conventions.[25]

In addition to the basic conventional framework described above, rules of customary law, such as those concerning historic bays, and other international conventions concerning, for example, pollution and navigation, are and will continue to be of enormous importance in determining the detailed rights and

---

[23] Vienna Convention on the Law of Treaties 1969, art. 18. See further G. M. White, 'UNCLOS and the modern law of treaties: selected issues', in W. E. Butler (ed.), *The Law of the Sea and International Shipping: Anglo-Soviet Post UNCLOS Perspectives* (New York, Oceana), 1985, pp. 15–37.

[24] Although some have argued that because the 1982 Convention represents a package deal States cannot take rights under it without also taking the duties, and consequently even consistent practice may not generate entitlements under customary law. See, e.g., the discussion in H. Caminos and M. R. Molitor, 'Progressive development of international law and the package deal', 79 *AJIL* 871–90 (1985); and cf. chapter five, footnote 25 below.

[25] Art. 311.

duties of States. In the following chapters we have sought to bring all these sources together, so as to give a bird's eye view of the present complex web of the law, and of the major developments that have brought it to its present state. Inevitably we have had to omit much detail. This is particularly the case, and particularly regrettable, in our accounts of customary law. We offer generalisations based on our knowledge of State practice, but in such a short book can give only examples to illustrate, rather than comprehensive surveys to justify, our statements.

Further reading

A convenient introduction to the materials of public international law can be found in J. Dane and P. A. Thomas, *How to Use a Law Library*, 3rd edn (London, Sweet & Maxwell), 1996. Searching for material on the law of the sea has become much easier with the arrival of the internet. New sites are being established all the time. There are good routes into this burgeoning mass of material from the 'links' pages on the web sites of the United Nations Division for Ocean Affairs and the Law of the Sea (http://www.un.org/Depts/los/index.html) and the International Maritime Organisation (http://www.imo.org/imo/links/lnkstart.htm).

Treaties

There are three main general collections of international treaties: the *Consolidated Treaty Series*, ed. C. Parry, covering the period from 1648 to the early years of the present century; the *League of Nations Treaty Series*, covering the period from 1920 to the Second World War; and the *United Nations Treaty Series*, covering post-war treaties. The United Nations is in the process of placing its treaty database on the internet: see http://www.un.org/Depts/Treaty/. Several States publish collections of treaties to which they are party, such as the *United Kingdom Treaty Series* and the *United States Treaty* series. Details of ratifications, signatures and other actions in relation to most multilateral and some bilateral treaties can be found by following the links from the United Nations Treaty web site or the International Maritime Organisation web link site, both given above.

Texts of major treaties on the law of the sea are reproduced in the volumes of *New Direction in the Law of the Sea*, 11 vols (Dobbs Ferry, N.Y., Oceana, 1973–81), its second loose-leaf edition, 2 vols (London, Oceana, 1983–), and the more recent volumes on *Global Developments* (New York, Oceana, 1996–) and on *Regional and National Developments* (New York, Oceana, 1995–). The bi-monthly *International Legal Materials* produced by the American Society of International Law (1962 to date) also reproduces major treaties. So, too, does the *Law of the Sea Bulletin* (1983–) published by the Division for Ocean Affairs and the Law of the Sea of the United Nations Office of Legal Affairs in New York. All three publications also include texts of significant national legislation, United Nations resolutions, etc.

Customary international law

State practice is often published in the form of the texts of decrees or statutes, law reports or volumes of diplomatic correspondence. Many States now publish selected texts, often in national international law journals or yearbooks, such as the section on *United Kingdom Materials in International Law* included in the *British Yearbook of International Law* from 1978 onwards. Some States collect their practice: the best-known collections include the *Digest of United States Practice in International Law* (1973–80) and the *Cumulative Digest of United States Practice in International Law 1981–88* (1993–5), published by the United States Government, which follow on from the digests of US practice prepared by M. M. Whiteman (15 vols, 1963–74), G. H. Hackworth (8 vols, 1940–4) and J. B. Moore (8 vols, 1906), and the *Répertoire de la pratique française en matière de droit international public* prepared by A. C. Kiss (5 vols, 1962). There is also much valuable material, drawn from the practice of all States, published in the *Chronique des faits* section of the *Revue générale de droit international public.*

In addition to *New Directions in the Law of the Sea* and *International Legal Materials*, much national practice is reprinted in the United Nations *Law of the Sea Bulletin*. The United Nations also publishes occasional volumes of *Law of the Sea: Current Developments in State Practice*. Older practice was collected in certain volumes of the *United Nations Legislative Series* (bearing the UN document code UN Doc. ST/LEG/SER.B/1, 2, 6, 8, 15, 16, 18, and 19 respectively).

Codification

Records of the proceedings of the conferences on the law of the sea, and of the committees which prepared for them, have been published by the League of Nations (in the case of the 1930 Hague Conference) and the United Nations (in the case of UNCLOS I, II and III). The Hague Papers have been conveniently reprinted in the *Progressive Codification of International Law (1925–28)* 2 vols (Dobbs Ferry, N.Y., Oceana, 1972) and *League of Nations Conference for the Codification of International Law (1930)* 4 vols (Dobbs Ferry, N.Y., Oceana, 1975), both edited by S. Rosenne. The proceedings of the International Law Commission are published in the Commission's annual *Yearbooks*. The papers of the UN Sea Bed Committee are published in the official records of the United Nations General Assembly. Concise accounts of the work of all United Nations bodies can be found in the annual *Yearbooks* of the United Nations.

The most important papers of UNCLOS I, II and III are published by the United Nations in the *Official Records* of those conferences. A fuller set of UNCLOS III papers is reprinted in R. Platzöder, *Third United Nations Conference on the Law of the Sea*, 18 vols (Dobbs Ferry, N.Y., Oceana, 1982–7). Its sequel, *The Law of the Sea (Second Series)*, 15 vols (Dobbs Ferry, N.Y., Oceana, 1989–93) reproduces documents of the Preparatory Commission, from 1983 onwards. The United Nations Division for Ocean Affairs and the Law of the Sea in New York publishes a good deal of extremely valuable material on the Law of the Sea. Apart from the *Law of the Sea Bulletin* (which includes not only State practice but also summaries of national claims, declarations and statements made by signatories of the Law of the Sea Convention and regular lists of States which have signed or ratified the key treaties), it has published a *Master File Containing References to Official Documents of the Third United Nations Conference on the Law of the Sea* (New York, 1985) and a list of *Multilateral Treaties Relevant to the United Nations Convention on the Law of the Sea* (New York, 1985). Other publications are mentioned at appropriate points in this text. Finally, mention must be made of the massive project undertaken by the University of Virginia under the general direction of M. H. Nordquist for the production of an article-by-article commentary and legislative history of the

Introduction

Convention under the title *United Nations Convention on the Law of the Sea 1982: A Commentary*, 6 vols projected (Dordrecht, Nijhoff. 1985–). In view of the relative paucity of *travaux préparatoires* of the Convention and the distinction of the contributors to that series, it enjoys an unusual authority on the subject.

It is convenient to note here that documents emanating from a wide range of organisations are reprinted in the *Annual Review of Oceans Affairs* (New York, United Nations. 1985–) and *International Organizations and the Law of the Sea: Documentary Yearbook* (Dordrecht, Nijhoff, 1985–).

Judicial decisions

Judgments of courts appear in the reports of the court concerned, notably those of the Permanent Court of International Justice and the International Court of Justice and national collections of law reports. Many arbitral tribunal awards are collected in the United Nations *Reports of International Arbitral Awards*. The *International Law Reports* reproduce notable decisions of international and municipal tribunals.

Publicists

The writings of publicists, which often contain valuable collections and analyses of State practice and treaty law, are manifold. Among the leading international law textbooks are Sir R. Jennings and Sir A. Watts, *Oppenheim's International Law*, 9th edn (London, Longman), 1992, and I. Brownlie, *Principles of Public International Law*, 5th edn (Oxford, Oxford University Press), 1998. Among the learned journals which frequently carry articles concerning the law of the sea are the *International Journal of Estuarine and Coastal Law* (which was renamed the *International Journal of Marine and Coastal Law* from 1993), *Marine Policy, Ocean Development and International Law, Ocean Management, Maritime Policy and Management, Ocean Yearbook* and, more generally, the *American Journal of International Law*, the *International and Comparative Law Quarterly* and the reports of the conference proceedings of the Law of the Sea Institute, the International Law Association and the Institut de droit international. Perhaps the best guide to this literature is the periodical bibliography, *Public International Law*, although the United Nations Division for Ocean Affairs and the Law of the Sea occasionally publishes bibliographies.

The classical literature on the law of the sea is well described in the monumental study by J. H. W. Verzijl, *International Law in Historical Perspective*, Vol. IV (Leyden, Sijthoff), 1971.

Modern monographs, etc. on the law of the sea

R. P. Anand, *Origin and Development of the Law of the Sea* (The Hague, Nijhoff), 1982.

D. Bardonnet and M. Virally (eds), *Le nouveau droit international de la mer* (Paris, Pedone), 1983.

D. Bowett, *Law of the Sea* (Manchester, Manchester University Press), 1967.

E. D. Brown, *The International Law of the Sea*, 2 vols (Aldershot, Dartmouth), 1994.

C. J. Colombos, *The International Law of the Sea*, 6th edn (London, Longman), 1967.

O. De Ferron, *Le droit international de la mer*, 2 vols (Paris, E. Droz), 1958.

R.-J. Dupuy and D. Vignes (eds), *Traité du Nouveau Droit de la Mer* (Paris, Economica), 1985.

——, *A Handbook of the New law of the Sea*, 2 vols (Dordrecht, Nijhoff), 1991 (an updated translation of the previous item).

G. Gidel, *Le droit international public de la mer*, 3 vols (Paris, 1932–4) (reprinted Vaduz, Topos Verlag), 1981.

Hague Academy of International Law/United Nations University, *The Management of Humanity's Resources, The Law of the Sea (Workshop 1981)* (The Hague, Nijhoff), 1982.

M. S. McDougal and W. T. Burke, *The Public Order of the Oceans* (New Haven, Conn., Yale University Press), 1962.

S. Oda, *The Law of the Sea in our Time. I: New Developments 1966–1975* (Leyden, Sijthoff), 1977 (Vol. II of this title, *The United Nations Seabed Committee 1968–73* (Leyden, Sijthoff), 1977, also by S. Oda, summarises the work of the UN Sea Bed Committee).

——, *International Control of Sea Resources* (Dordrecht, Nijhoff), 1989.

H. A. Smith, *The Law and Custom of the Sea*, 3rd edn (London, Stevens), 1959.

T. Treves, 'Codification du droit international et pratique des états dans le droit de la mer', 223 *Recueil des cours* (1990-IV), 9–302.

J. Wang, *Ocean Politics and Law* (New York, Greenwood), 1991.

——, *Handbook on Ocean Politics and Law* (New York, Greenwood), 1992.

National and regional studies and collections of documents

L. Bouony, 'Les Etats arabes et le nouveau droit de la mer', 90 *RDGIP* 849–75 (1986).

W. E. Butler, *The Soviet Union and the Law of the Sea* (Baltimore, Johns Hopkins Press), 1971

——, *The USSR, Eastern Europe and the Development of the Law of the Sea*, 3 vols (Dobbs Ferry, N.Y., Oceana), 1979.

J. Crawford and D. R. Rothwell (eds), *The Law of the Sea in the Asian-Pacific Region* (Dordrecht, Nijhoff), 1992.

E. C. Farrell, *The Socialist Republic of Vietnam and the Law of the Sea* (The Hague, Nijhoff), 1997.

J. Greenfield, *China's Practice in the Law of the Sea* (Oxford, Clarendon Press), 1992.

A. A. el-Hakim, *The Middle Eastern States and the Law of the Sea* (Manchester, Manchester University Press), 1979.

A. L. Hollick, *U.S. Foreign Policy and the Law of the Sea* (New Jersey, Princeton), 1981.

B. Johnson and M. W. Zacher (eds), *Canadian Foreign Policy and the Law of the Sea* (Vancouver, University of British Columbia Press), 1977.

C. C. Joyner, *Antarctica and the Law of the Sea* (Dordrecht, Nijhoff), 1992.

B. Kwiatkowska, 'Ocean affairs and the Law of the Sea in Africa: towards the 21st century', 17 *Marine Policy* 11–43 (1993).

R. D. Lumb, *The Law of the Sea and Australian Offshore Areas*, 2nd edn (St Lucia, Queensland, University of Queensland Press), 1978.

M. H. Nordquist and C. H. Park, *North America and Asia-Pacific and the Development of the Law of the Sea* (London, Oceana), 1981.

N. S. Rembe, *Africa and the International Law of the Sea* (Alphen aan den Rijn, Sijthoff), 1980.

J. A. Roach and R. W. Smith, *United States Responses to Excessive Maritime Claims* (The Hague, Nijhoff), 2nd edn, 1996.

V. Sebek, *The Eastern European States and the Development of the Law of the Sea*, 2 vols (Dobbs Ferry, N.Y., Oceana), 1977.

C. R. Symmons, *Ireland and the Law of the Sea* (Dublin, Round Hall Press), 1993.

A. Szekely, *Latin America and the Development of the Law of the Sea*, 2 vols (Dobbs Ferry, N.Y., Oceana), 1976.

P. Tangsubkul, *ASEAN and the Law of the Sea* (Singapore, Institute of Southeast Asian Studies), 1982.

T. Treves and L. Pineschi (eds), *The Law of the Sea. The European Union and its Member States* (The Hague, Nijhoff), 1997.

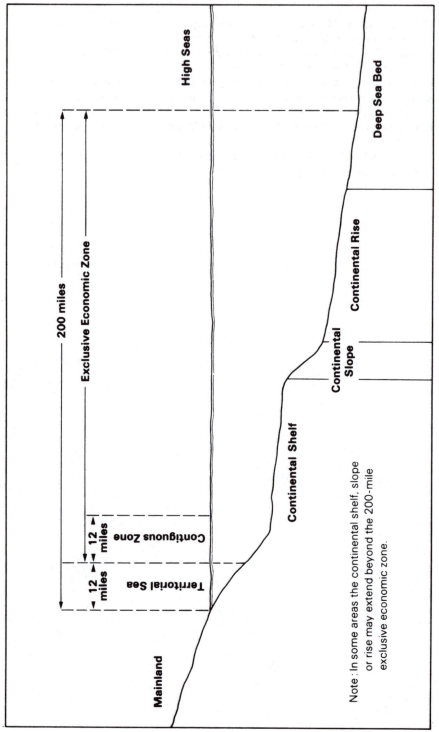

Maritime zones

Note: In some areas the continental shelf, slope or rise may extend beyond the 200-mile exclusive economic zone.

2

Baselines

Introduction

In determining the extent of a coastal State's territorial sea and other maritime zones, it is obviously necessary first of all to establish from what points on the coast the outer limits of such zones are to be measured. This is the function of baselines. The baseline is the line from which the outer limits of the territorial sea and other coastal State zones (the contiguous zone, the exclusive fishing zone and the exclusive economic zone (EEZ)) are measured.[1] The waters on the landward side of the baseline are known as internal waters (see chapter three). Thus the baseline also forms the boundary between internal waters and the territorial sea. While this boundary does not mark the outer limit of a State's territory, since in international law the territorial sea forms part of a State's territory, it does represent the demarcation between that maritime area (internal waters) where other States enjoy no general rights, and those maritime areas (the territorial sea and other zones) where other States do enjoy certain general rights. Baselines may also be relevant in drawing maritime boundaries: where two neighbouring States agree that the boundary between their maritime zones is to be a line equidistant from both States, it is from the baselines of each State that such equidistance is normally calculated.

Traditionally both writers and international conventions (including the Law of the Sea Convention) have treated the rules relating to baselines as part of the body of law relating to the territorial sea. This was justifiable at the time when the territorial sea was the only zone of coastal State jurisdiction. But since the baseline is now used to measure not only the outer limit of the territorial sea, but also the outer limits of the contiguous zone, the exclusive fishing zone and the EEZ, and in some circumstances the continental shelf, it no longer seems appropriate

---

[1] One relatively recent, and so far as is known unique, exception to using the baseline as the point from which the outer limit of maritime zones is measured, is the 150-mile Falkland Islands Interim [Fisheries] Conservation and Management Zone established in 1986, which is measured from a single point in the middle of the Falkland Islands. See Proclamation No. 4 of 1986 of the Governor of the Falkland Islands, 9 *LOSB* 19 (1987). The territorial sea, however, is measured from conventional baselines.

to consider baselines simply as part of the law relating to the territorial sea. Thus in this book we deal with baselines as a separate topic.

The question of baselines was considered at the 1930 Hague Codification Conference. As we saw in the previous chapter, this conference did not succeed in adopting any convention on the law of the sea.[2] Nevertheless the work done by the conference in respect of baselines formed a useful basis for the International Law Commission (ILC) when it came to consider the topic as part of its study of the law of the sea in the early 1950s. The Commission's deliberations resulted in a number of articles dealing with baselines being included in the 1958 Geneva Convention on the Territorial Sea and the Contiguous Zone. These provisions – articles 3 to 11 and 13 – were not only binding on parties to the Convention, but in most respects were also regarded, for reasons which will be explained later, as representing the rules of customary international law. Thus it is not surprising to find that the Law of the Sea Convention – in articles 4 to 14 and 16 – simply repeats most of the 1958 Convention's provisions *verbatim*, making only a few slight additions to cover geographical situations not considered by the ILC or the 1958 Geneva conference. At the same time it is regrettable that greater effort was not made in the Law of the Sea Convention to resolve the ambiguities and fill in the gaps in the 1958 rules: suggestions for improvements have not been lacking from commentators.[3]

If all coastlines were relatively straight and unindented, the question of ascertaining the baseline would be a simple one. All that would be necessary would be to select the high- or low-tide mark as the baseline. In practice, however, the position is not nearly so straightforward. Many coasts are not straight, but are indented or penetrated by bays, and have islands, sandbanks and harbour installations off them. It is necessary, therefore, to have rules on baselines which deal with a wide variety of geographical circumstances. At the same time, it is desirable that the rules should be formulated in as precise and objective a way as possible, so that two cartographers, asked to draw the baselines along a particular stretch of coast, would ideally both arrive at the same result. It is also desirable that the waters enclosed by baselines should be of such a nature that the regime of internal waters is as or more appropriate to them than the regime of the territorial sea or EEZ. These desiderata should be borne in mind in the discussion of the rules that follows. If the rules are not sufficiently precise, it may be possible for a State to draw its baselines in a generous manner, thus pushing the outer limit of its territorial sea and other zones farther seawards and bringing greater

[2] The report of the conference's Committee on Territorial Waters contained a set of draft articles on the territorial sea. Six of these articles were concerned with the problems of baselines and dealt with the low-water line, low-tide elevations, bays, harbour works, islands and river mouths. These draft articles are reproduced in S. Rosenne (ed.), *League of Nations Conference for the Codification of International Law [1930]* (Dobbs Ferry, N. Y., Oceana), 1975, pp. 833–6.

[3] See, for example, the works by Hodgson and Alexander, and Hodgson and Smith, referred to in 'Further reading' at the end of this chapter.

areas of sea within internal waters, thus reducing the areas of sea available for use by other States.

The normal baseline

Article 3 of the Territorial Sea Convention and article 5 of the Law of the Sea Convention provide in identical words that 'the normal baseline for measuring the breadth of the territorial sea is the low-water line along the coast as marked on large-scale charts officially recognised by the coastal State'. The effect of choosing the low-water line,[4] rather than the high-tide line, is to push the outer limit of the territorial sea and other zones seawards, particularly on coasts where there is an extensive tidal range.

The rules in articles 3 and 5 were drafted with coasts which are relatively straight and unindented particularly in mind. The low-water line is described in both the Territorial Sea and Law of the Sea Conventions as the 'normal baseline'; but the variety of geographical circumstances for which special provisions are laid down makes it doubtful whether in practice the low-water line is the normal baseline for most States. The Law of the Sea Convention appears to recognise this situation, for in article 14 it provides that 'the coastal State may determine baselines in turn by any of the methods provided for . . . to suit different conditions'.

The special geographical conditions for which particular rules are laid down in the Geneva and Law of the Sea Conventions are: (i) straight baselines for coasts deeply indented or fringed with islands; (ii) bays; (iii) river mouths; (iv) harbour works; (v) low-tide elevations; (vi) islands; and (vii) reefs.[5] Each of these will now be considered in turn. In the discussion of each type of baseline, it may be found useful to refer to the figure on p. 36.

Straight baselines

Customary rules

The law concerning straight baselines developed in the context of Norwegian baseline claims. Much of the coast of Norway is penetrated by fjords and fringed

---

[4] There appears to be no uniformity in State practice as to whether the low-water line is represented by the mean low-water spring tide, the lowest astronomical tide or some other low-water line. See *Whiteman*, Vol. IV, p. 141; and *O'Connell*, Vol. I, pp. 171–85, *op. cit.* in 'Further reading' at the end of this chapter, in the general section.

[5] One special geographical condition for which the Law of the Sea (and Territorial Sea) Conventions make no provision is permanent ice shelves, found in parts of the Arctic and Antarctic. Such shelves may be many miles in width. It is uncertain whether the baseline should be the outer edge of the ice shelf or the edge of the land. This issue was deliberately not discussed at UNCLOS III for fear of re-opening the question of the legal status of Antarctica. For further discussion of this issue, see *O'Connell, op. cit.*, Vol. I, pp. 197–8.

by countless islands, islets, rocks and reefs, known as the *skjaergaard* (a Norwegian word meaning literally rock rampart). In theory it would be possible to draw the baseline along the Norwegian coast by following the low-water mark around all the fjords, islands and rocks and by drawing lines across bays: but in practice this would be very cumbersome, and it would be difficult to ascertain the outer limit of the Norwegian territorial sea. Instead, from the mid-nineteenth century onwards, Norway used as the baseline a series of straight lines connecting the outermost points on the *skjaergaard*. In the 1930s the United Kingdom began to object to this method of drawing the baseline, arguing that it was contrary to international law. The United Kingdom's objections were motivated by the fact that the effect of using such straight lines, rather than the low-water mark, as the baseline was to extend farther seawards the outer limit of the Norwegian territorial sea, thus reducing the area of high seas open to fishing by British vessels. The ensuing dispute, which centred on a Norwegian decree of 1935 delimiting straight baselines north of 66°28.8' north, was referred by the United Kingdom to the International Court of Justice in 1949.

In its judgment in the *Anglo-Norwegian Fisheries* case (1951), the Court held that the Norwegian straight baseline system was in conformity with international law. The Court was much influenced by the geographical circumstances of the case. It observed that the *skjaergaard* was but an extension of the Norwegian mainland, and that it was the outer limit of the *skjaergaard*, not the mainland, that constituted the real dividing line between the land and the sea. The low-water mark to be used for constructing the baseline was therefore not that of the mainland, but the outer line of the *skjaergaard*. The Court then noted that 'three methods have been contemplated to effect the application of the low-water mark rule'[6] – the *tracé parallèle* (i.e., drawing the outer limit of the territorial sea by following the coast in all its sinuosities), the *courbe tangente* (i.e., drawing arcs of circles from points along the low-water line) and straight baselines. Where a coast was deeply indented or fringed by islands, then, according to the Court, neither the *tracé parallèle* nor the *courbe tangente* method was appropriate. Instead. 'the baseline becomes independent of the low-water mark, and can only be determined by means of a geometric construction'.[7] The straight baseline was such a geometrical construction, and had been used by several States without objection.[8] In this connection the Court considered it of some importance that no objection had been made to the Norwegian system by the United Kingdom or other States between 1869 (when Norway had first begun applying a detailed system of straight baselines) and 1933 (when the United Kingdom had first objected to the system).

[6] [1951] *ICJ Rep.* 116 at 128.
[7] *Ibid.*, at p. 129.
[8] The Court itself gave no examples of such States. States utilising straight baselines prior to the Court's judgment include Ecuador, Egypt, Iran, Saudi Arabia and Yugoslavia. See *Whiteman, op. cit.*, Vol. IV, p. 148 and Waldock, *op. cit.*, in the section entitled 'Straight baselines' in 'Further reading'.

Although it upheld the validity of straight baselines in international law, the Court made it clear that the coastal State does not have an unfettered discretion as to how it draws straight baselines, and it laid down a number of conditions governing the drawing of such baselines. First, such lines must be drawn so that they do 'not depart to any appreciable extent from the general direction of the coast'.[9] Secondly, they must be drawn so that the 'sea areas lying within these lines are sufficiently closely linked to the land domain to be subject to the regime of internal waters'.[10] Thirdly – and here the Court seems to have been considering the way in which individual lines are drawn rather than the system as a whole – it is legitimate to take into account 'certain economic interests peculiar to a region, the reality and importance of which are clearly evidenced by a long usage'.[11]

Conventional rules

At the time it was given, the Court's judgment was widely regarded as a piece of 'judicial legislation'. However, the rules enunciated by the Court were taken up by the ILC and eventually incorporated in the Territorial Sea Convention (art. 4), which closely followed the language of the Court's judgment. While the Court suggested that straight baselines were simply a special application of the low-water mark principle of constructing the baseline, the Territorial Sea and Law of the Sea Conventions more realistically recognise straight baselines as a distinct method of construction.

Under both Conventions a system of straight baselines 'may' be used 'in localities where the coastline is deeply indented and cut into, or if there is a fringe of islands along the coast in its immediate vicinity' (TSC, art. 4(1); LOSC, art. 7(1)). It is clear from the use of the word 'may' that even where a coast fulfils the requisite conditions a State has a choice as to whether it uses straight baselines or not. The USA, for example, does not use straight baselines on the coast of Alaska, although it is entitled to do so. In practice, however, most States do exercise their option and draw straight baselines, because the use of such lines is likely to place their baseline (and hence the outer limits of their various maritime zones) farther seawards than other methods of drawing the baseline, and makes the drawing of the outer limit of the territorial sea (and other zones) more straightforward.

Having established the situation where the use of straight baselines is permissible, the Territorial Sea and Law of the Sea Conventions go on to lay down a number of conditions governing the way in which straight baselines may be drawn. First:

---

[9] [1951] *ICJ Rep.* 116 at 133.
[10] *Ibid.*
[11] *Ibid.*, and cf. the Court's discussion of individual baselines of the Norwegian system at p. 142.

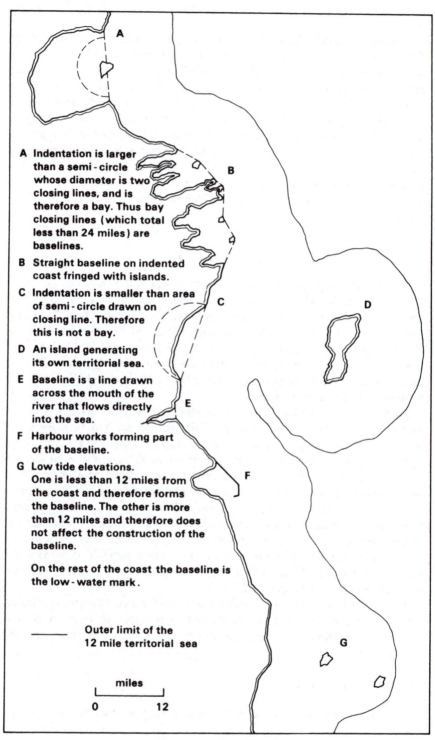

A **Indentation is larger than a semi-circle whose diameter is two closing lines, and is therefore a bay. Thus bay closing lines (which total less than 24 miles) are baselines.**

B **Straight baseline on indented coast fringed with islands.**

C **Indentation is smaller than area of semi-circle drawn on closing line. Therefore this is not a bay.**

D **An island generating its own territorial sea.**

E **Baseline is a line drawn across the mouth of the river that flows directly into the sea.**

F **Harbour works forming part of the baseline.**

G **Low tide elevations. One is less than 12 miles from the coast and therefore forms the baseline. The other is more than 12 miles and therefore does not affect the construction of the baseline.**

On the rest of the coast the baseline is the low-water mark.

——— **Outer limit of the 12 mile territorial sea**

miles

0   12

The construction of baselines

[straight] baselines must not depart to any appreciable extent from the general direction of the coast, and the sea areas lying within the lines must be sufficiently closely linked to the land domain to be subject to the regime of internal waters. (TSC, art. 4(2); LOSC, art. 7(3))

This provision follows the *Anglo-Norwegian Fisheries* case almost *verbatim*. Second, straight baselines may not be drawn to or from low-tide elevations unless lighthouses or similar installations which are permanently above sea level have been built on them, or, the Law of the Sea Convention adds, 'in instances where the drawing of baselines to and from such elevations has received general international recognition' (TSC, art. 4(3); LOSC, art. 7(4)). The point of this provision is presumably to prevent baselines being drawn too far seawards of the coast, and thus to reinforce the first condition. Third, a State may not draw straight baselines in such a way as to cut off from the high seas (or, the Law of the Sea Convention adds, the EEZ) the territorial sea of another State (TSC, art. 4(5); LOSC, art. 7(6)). This provision deals with highly exceptional situations, where a smaller territory is embedded in a larger territory (e.g., Monaco in France) or where small islands belonging to one State lie close to the coast of another State (e.g., Greek islands lying close to the coast of Turkey). Finally, a State utilising a straight baseline system must clearly indicate the lines on charts to which 'due publicity' must be given (TSC, art. 4(6); LOSC, art. 16).

Both the Territorial Sea and Law of the Sea Conventions follow the *Anglo-Norwegian Fisheries* case in providing that in determining particular baselines, 'account may be taken . . . of economic interests peculiar to the region concerned, the reality and the importance of which are clearly evidenced by a long usage' (TSC, art. 4(4); LOSC, art. 7(5)). The most obvious such economic interest, and the interest at issue in the *Anglo-Norwegian Fisheries* case, is fishing. Neither the Territorial Sea Convention nor the Law of the Sea Convention contains any provision limiting the length of individual baselines (apart from 'archipelagic' baselines: see chapter six), although an unsuccessful attempt was made at UNCLOS I to introduce a maximum length of fifteen miles for any one baseline. In the *Anglo-Norwegian Fisheries* case the longest line, whose validity was upheld by the Court, was forty-four miles. (In this chapter, as elsewhere in this book, all references to 'miles' are to nautical miles unless otherwise stated.) It would seem, therefore, that there is in principle no restriction on the length of individual baselines, although obviously in practice the necessity for compliance with the general conditions set out above will be a restraining factor.

The Law of the Sea Convention contains a provision, dealing with a rather exceptional geographical situation, which has no equivalent in the Territorial Sea Convention. Article 7(2) provides that, '[w]here because of the presence of a delta and other natural conditions the coastline is highly unstable, the appropriate points [between which straight baselines may be drawn] may be selected along the furthest seaward extent of the low-water line'. This provision, inspired by a Bangladeshi proposal, is not very well drafted. It is not clear if this provision is laying down a third type of coastline, in addition to deeply indented coasts and coasts fringed with islands, where straight baselines may be drawn, or whether it applies only to deltas on coasts which fall into the first two categories. The drafting history of the provision suggests the latter.[12] Nor is it wholly clear whether the use of the 'furthest seaward extent of the low-water line' is subject to the general rules about the use of low-tide elevations as basepoints for straight baselines, contained in article 7(4), or is an exception to such rules, although the better view is that it is subject to article 7(4). Furthermore, the meaning of the phrase 'and other natural conditions' is obscure, but appears to refer to causes of coastal instability other than deltas. Article 7(2) goes on to provide that where straight baselines are drawn along the furthest seaward extent of the low-water line of deltas, then 'notwithstanding subsequent regression of the low-water line, the straight baselines shall remain effective until changed by the coastal State in accordance with [the] Convention'. In general it is unlikely that this part of article 7(2) will have much practical application as most deltas advance rather than retreat: normally a retreating delta occurs only where heavy damming has taken place upstream. However, this provision may be important in the future if predictions of a significant rise in sea levels as a result of global climate change are fulfilled, although article 7(2) does, of course, require a State eventually to change its baselines. In practice there appears to be only one possible case of a State drawing straight baselines utilising article 7(2) (although some deltas are enclosed within straight baselines drawn on the basis of other criteria). In 1990 Egypt drew a system of straight baselines along its Mediterranean coast including the Nile delta (part of which is retreating at the rate of about forty metres a year). The baselines drawn around the Nile delta may be based on article 7(2). The USA objected to Egypt's action on the ground that the coastline concerned was neither deeply indented nor fringed with islands.[13]

State practice

Although both the International Court of Justice in the *Anglo-Norwegian Fisheries* case and the Territorial Sea and Law of the Sea Conventions regard the use of straight baselines as being limited to exceptional geographical circumstances, and although few States have a coastline that is anywhere near as indented or fringed with islands as that of Norway, some 55–65 States have in fact drawn straight baselines along all or part of their coasts,[14] and a further fifteen States

---

[12] Prescott and Bird, *op. cit.* in 'Further reading' under 'Straight baselines', pp. 289–91, 295–6.

[13] *Limits in the Seas* No. 116 (1994), see 'Further reading', under 'Straight baselines'.

[14] The reason for the lack of precision about the number is that it is not always possible to tell if the use by a State of a straight line as the baseline is intended to be a straight baseline *stricto sensu* or a bay or river closing line. Most straight baselines are depicted, and reference to their legislative source given, in *Atlas of the Straight Baselines* and/or *Limits in the Seas*, both in 'Further reading'.

have adopted enabling legislation to draw straight baselines but have not yet drawn them.[15]

As we have seen, the rules governing the use of straight baselines laid down in customary and conventional law are relatively imprecise, and thus allow States a considerable latitude in the way they draw straight baselines. A good many States, however, do appear to have gone beyond the spirit and the vague wording of these rules. Studies by the Geographer of the US Department of State (in the *Limits in the Seas* series) and by Prescott (*op. cit.* in 'Further reading') suggest that of the straight baseline systems so far drawn, about two-thirds depart from the rules of international law in one way or another. First, some States (such as Albania, Cuba, Italy, Senegal and Spain) have drawn straight baselines along coasts which are not deeply indented. A particularly good example is Colombia, which has drawn a single straight baseline 131 miles in length along part of its Caribbean coast and enclosed a smooth coast with no fringing islands.[16] A second form of departure is the drawing of straight baselines along coasts which possess some offshore islands but which do not form a fringe in the immediate vicinity of the coast. This has been done by, among others, Ecuador, Iceland, Iran, Italy, Malta and Thailand. Perhaps the most extreme example is Vietnam, which has used the isolated islet of Hon Hai, lying seventy-four miles from the mainland coast, as a basepoint for its straight baseline system, and connected it northwards to Hon Doi islet and southwestwards to Bay Canh islet, each of which is 161 miles away.[17] A third form of breach is to draw straight baselines which depart to a considerable extent from the general direction of the coast. For example the straight baselines of Myanmar and Ecuador are in some places at an angle of 60° to the general direction of the coast[18] (by comparison in the Norwegian baseline system, generally regarded as the standard model, the angle of deviation is never more than about 15°). Fourth, baselines are sometimes drawn so that the sea areas inside the lines are insufficiently closely linked to the land to be subject to the regime of internal waters. Again Myanmar's system is a good illustration: the 222-mile long line across the Gulf of Martaban is at one point seventy-five miles from the nearest land and encloses as internal waters an area the size of Denmark, and in Myanmar's system as a whole the ratio of land (i.e., islands lying within the baselines) to water is less than 1 : 50 (in comparison, the ratio in the Norwegian system is 1 : 3.5). Fifth, some States appear to accept the use of low-tide elevations as basepoints, regardless of whether lighthouses or similar installations have been built on them: see, for example, the enabling legislation

---

[15] For a list of both categories, see J. A. Roach and R. W. Smith, *United States Responses to Excessive Maritime Claims* (The Hague, Nijhoff), 2nd edn, 1996, pp. 77–81.

[16] See *Limits in the Seas* No. 103 (1985).

[17] See *Limits in the Seas* No. 99 (1983).

[18] See *Limits in the Seas* No. 14 (1970) (Burma – now Myanmar) and No. 42 (1972) (Ecuador). Minor amendments were made to Myanmar's system in 1977: see *UN Leg. Ser.* B/19, p. 42.

of Saudi Arabia and Syria.[19] Sixth, in spite of the obligation not to draw straight baselines in such a way as to cut off the territorial sea of another State from the high seas or EEZ, Morocco's straight baselines do just that in respect of Spain's North African enclaves of Ceuta and Melilla.[20] Seventh, in spite of the obligation to publicise baselines, Haiti, North Korea and Malaysia have drawn the outer limit of their territorial sea in a way which presupposes that it is measured from straight baselines, even though such lines have not been published. Finally, some States have located basepoints for straight baselines in the sea. The leading example here is Bangladesh, which has drawn a straight baseline system all of whose basepoints are in the sea. For most of its course the line lies close to the ten-fathom isobath and in places is fifty miles from the nearest land.[21] Less objectionable is the practice of some States in locating the terminus of their baseline system in the sea but on the boundary with the neighbouring State. Other anomalies in the drawing of straight baselines are the bizarre practice of locating the terminus of a system in another State's territory (as Ecuador has done in Colombia and Venezuela in Guyana); and not anchoring a straight baseline to the mainland coast, so that it is possible to sail into internal waters without crossing the baseline (as has been done by, amongst others, Bangladesh and Norway (in Spitsbergen)). Surveying State practice, Prescott concludes that abuse of the rules relating to straight baselines has been such that 'it would now be possible to draw a straight baseline along any section of coast in the world and cite an existing straight baseline as a precedent'.[22] On the other hand, it should be noted that some of the straight baselines referred to above have provoked objections from other States: for example, Myanmar and India have objected to Bangladesh's baselines; France, Singapore, Thailand and the USA to those of Vietnam; and the USA has protested against the straight baselines of a further twenty-six States.[23] The question of the legality of baselines which do not appear to conform to the rules is further considered at the end of this chapter. In 1987 the US State Department published a study proposing guidelines for evaluating straight baseline claims for their conformity with international law.[24] Admirable though this study is, it seems unlikely that the criteria which it sets

---

[19] See *Limits in the Seas* Nos 20 (1970) and 53 (1973), respectively.

[20] See *Atlas of the Straight Baselines*, p. 170.

[21] *Ibid.*, p. 86.

[22] Prescott, 'Straight and archipelagic baselines', *op. cit.* in 'Further reading' under 'Straight baselines', p. 38.

[23] Roach and Smith, *op. cit.* in footnote 15, pp. 18–19. For details see pp. 77–138, *passim.*

[24] *Limits in the Seas* No. 106 (1987). For a different approach to curbing straight baseline claims, see Reisman and Westerman, *op. cit.* in 'Further reading' under 'Straight baselines'. See also the US Government's view of the way in which art. 7 of LOSC should be applied, set out in its commentary on the Convention attached to the President's letter transmitting the Convention to the Senate for its advice and consent to ratification, reproduced in Roach and Smith, *op. cit.* in footnote 15, pp. 544–7 (and see also pp. 60–8).

forth (which relate to what is meant by a deeply indented coastline and fringing islands) have had or are likely to have any significant impact on the practice of States.

The effect of drawing straight baselines, even strictly in accordance with the rules, is often to enclose considerable bodies of sea as internal waters: for example, the whole of the Minches, lying between the Inner and Outer Hebrides off the west coast of Scotland, is enclosed by straight baselines and thus is internal waters. It should, however, be noted that in some such internal waters, including the Minches, there is a right of innocent passage given by the Conventions: see p. 61.

Bays

Pre-1958 customary rules

International law has always recognised that bays have a close connection with land and that it is more appropriate that they should be considered as internal waters than as territorial sea. Customary international law had, accordingly, recognised that the baseline could in principle be drawn across the mouth of bays, enclosing them as internal waters. But customary international law failed to provide clear rules on two essential points: the criteria by which an indentation of the coast would be recognised as a bay, and the maximum length of the closing line across a bay. As regards the first point, the deficiencies of customary international law can be seen in the *North Atlantic Coast Fisheries* case (1910), where the Permanent Court of Arbitration found that there was no general criterion of international law which defined a bay. Factors to be taken into account in deciding whether an indentation was a bay included the penetration of the bay inland and the security and economic interests of the coastal State therein. As regards the maximum length of closing lines for bays, the United Kingdom in the *Anglo-Norwegian Fisheries* case argued that customary international law had established ten miles as the maximum length for closing lines. This contention was rejected by the International Court on the ground that there was no uniformity of State practice on the question.

Conventional rules

The Territorial Sea Convention, in article 7, established clear and precise rules for determining both of these hitherto uncertain points, and these rules are repeated almost *verbatim* in the Law of the Sea Convention (art. 10). At the outset it should be noted that these rules do not apply to cases where straight baselines are used (see above), or to historic bays or bays whose coasts belong to more than one State (both of which are considered below). To establish whether an indentation is a bay in the legal sense the Conventions lay down a subjective description and an objective geometric test. As regards the former, a bay is described as 'a well-marked indentation whose penetration is in such proportion to the width of its mouth as to contain land-locked waters and constitute more than a mere curvature of the coast'. Such an indentation will nevertheless not be a bay in the legal sense unless it also fulfils the following geometric test (and see also points A and C in the figure in this chapter). First, a line should be drawn between the natural entrance points of the indentation. Next, a semi-circle having the diameter of this line should be constructed and its area measured. (Where the presence of islands means that an indentation has more than one mouth, the diameter of the semi-circle is a line as long as the sum total of the lengths of the lines across the different mouths.) Then the area of water between the line across the mouth of the indentation and the low-water mark around the indentation should be calculated: for this purpose any islands within the indentation are to be included in the area of water. If the area of water is larger than the area of the semi-circle, the indentation is a bay. Conversely, if the area of water is smaller, the indentation is not a bay. Once an indentation has been established as being a bay, a closing line can be drawn across it. If the length of the line between the natural entrance points of the bay (in the case of bays with more than one mouth, the total of the lengths of the lines across the different mouths) is less than twenty-four miles, this line is the closing line and, therefore, the baseline. If the line or lines are more than twenty-four miles in length, then a straight line of twenty-four miles is drawn within the bay in such a way as to enclose the greatest amount of water possible: this line then forms the baseline. Around the unenclosed part of the bay the baseline will be the low-water mark (unless any of the features that justify a different baseline are present).

These provisions, which the International Court of Justice in the *Land, Island and Maritime Frontier* case (1992) said 'might be found to express general customary law',[25] are obviously a great improvement on previous customary international law, but their practical application is not wholly free from difficulty. The main difficulty is that often it is not obvious which are the 'natural entrance points' of an indentation. An example of this problem can be seen in *Post Office v. Estuary Radio* (1968), where the English Court of Appeal had to decide whether the Thames estuary was legally a bay. Estuary Radio argued that the natural entrance points of the estuary were Orfordness and the North Foreland (in which case the estuary would not have been a bay because it would have failed the semi-circle test). The Post Office, on the other hand, argued that the natural entrance points were the Naze and Foreness (in which case the estuary was a bay). Although the Court of Appeal accepted the Post Office's contention, neither set of points seems very obviously to be the 'natural entrance points' of the estuary. Similarly, difficulties may arise in determining the extent to which rivers running into a bay, or other subsidiary features such as lagoons, should be taken into account in calculating the area of water within the bay. The application of

[25] [1992] *ICJ Rep.* 351 at 588.

the rules to bays with islands fringing, or lying just seaward of, the mouth may also be problematic.[26]

Even where the application of article 7 of the Territorial Sea Convention has been free from difficulty, some States parties to the Convention have nevertheless failed to act in conformity with it. Thus, the Dominican Republic has drawn closing lines across four bays which do not meet the semi-circle test while the closing line in a Portuguese bay exceeds twenty-four miles.[27]

Historic bays

We must now turn to consider the two types of bay to which the provisions of article 7 of the Territorial Sea Convention and article 10 of the Law of the Sea Convention do not apply – historic bays and bays whose coasts belong to more than one State. (The first of these will be dealt with in this section; the second in the next section.) Neither the Territorial Sea Convention nor the Law of the Sea Convention contains any provisions dealing with historic bays, although UNCLOS I had before it a memorandum on the subject prepared by the UN Secretariat (see the reference in 'Further reading' at the end of this chapter under 'Bays') and a draft article proposed by Japan,[28] and UNCLOS III had a draft article proposed by Colombia.[29] UNCLOS I did, however, adopt a resolution requesting the UN to arrange for the study of the juridical regime of historic waters, including historic bays.[30] Such a study was published by the UN Secretariat in 1962 (see the reference in 'Further reading'), but it has not led to any international legislative action. The position is therefore governed by customary international law. In the *Tunisia/Libya Continental Shelf* case the International Court stated that 'general international law . . . does not provide for a *single* "regime" for "historic waters" or "historic bays", but only for a particular regime for each of the concrete, recognised cases of "historic waters" or "historic bays" ':[31] thus, in one case only exclusive 'historic' fishing rights might exist, whereas in another the coastal State might enjoy full sovereignty. This approach was endorsed by the International Court in the *Land, Island and Maritime Frontier* case. Accordingly, claims to historic title must be approached with circumspection. However, the general criteria for the establishment of a historic title were addressed in the 1962 UN Secretariat study, according to which a State may validly claim title to a bay on historic grounds if it can show that it has for a considerable period of time

---

[26] For a discussion of these and other problems, see the works cited in the general section of 'Further reading' by Beazley (pp. 16–26), Hodgson and Alexander (pp. 3–21), Prescott (pp. 51–60), O'Connell (pp. 396–406) and United Nations (1989a) (pp. 28–31).

[27] See *Limits in the Seas* Nos 5 (1970) and 27 (1970), respectively. It is not clear whether these claims are still in force.

[28] UNCLOS I, *Official Records*, Vol. III, p. 241.

[29] UNCLOS III, *Official Records*, Vol. V, p. 202. Cf. also the discussion of historic bays in Vol. II, pp. 100–11 and Vol. IV, p. 196.

[30] *Op. cit.* in footnote 28, Vol. II, p. 145.

[31] [1982] *ICJ Rep.* 18 at 74 (emphasis in the original).

claimed the bay as internal waters and has effectively, openly and continuously exercised its authority therein, and that during this time the claim has received the acquiescence of other States. The United States Supreme Court has applied these criteria in *US* v. *Louisiana* (1969) and *US* v. *Alaska* (1975), and they were implicitly accepted by the International Court in the *Land, Island and Maritime Frontier* case. Where title to a historic bay has been acquired, a closing line may be drawn across the mouth of the bay which will then form the baseline. There appear to be no rules as to the maximum permissible length of such lines, and it would seem that if good title has been acquired, the closing line may be of any length.

The need for authority to have been effectively exercised over a claimed historic bay for a considerable period of time is a condition which is objected to by many recently independent developing States, which argue that it is impossible for them to produce evidence of an uninterrupted exercise of authority. While in fact it would seem possible for such States to cite the practice of both the colonial and pre-colonial period (Sri Lanka's claim to Palk Bay as historic waters is based not only on acts of the British, Dutch and Portuguese colonial administrations but also on authority exercised by the pre-colonial kings of Ceylon), some developing States have argued for a theory of 'vital bays' under which vital security or economic interests would justify title to a bay independently of any true historic title. Such a doctrine, whose origins can be traced back to the early part of the twentieth century, has naturally been rejected by the traditional maritime States, such as the United Kingdom and the USA, because of the ease with which it would allow a State to claim large areas of sea as internal waters, at the expense of the international community.

In the case of historic bays strictly so called, the question whether a State has acquired good title to a claimed historic bay is likely to depend largely on whether other States have acquiesced in its claim. At the present time some twenty States claim historic bays.[32] Examples of such claims include those by Russia to Peter the Great Bay (although several States, including the United Kingdom and the USA, do not accept it as a historic bay);[33] by Canada to Hudson Bay (although the USA does not accept it as a historic bay);[34] by Thailand to the inner part of the Gulf of Thailand;[35] and by Vietnam to parts of the Gulfs of Thailand and Tonkin (to which claims a number of States, including France, Thailand, China and the USA, have objected).[36] As these examples show, historic

---

[32] For a list of claimed historic bays, see Roach and Smith, *op. cit.* in footnote 15, pp. 33–4.

[33] See *Whiteman*, *op. cit.*, Vol. II, pp. 250–7 and Roach and Smith, *op. cit.* in footnote 15, pp. 49–50.

[34] *Ibid.*, pp. 236–7.

[35] Declaration of 22 September 1959. *UN Leg. Ser.* B/16, p. 34.

[36] See *Limits in the Seas* No. 99 (1983) and Roach and Smith, *op. cit.* in footnote 15, pp. 39–40, 52–3. For other historic bays which the USA has protested, see *ibid.*, pp. 35–53, *passim*.

bays are likely to be larger than bays governed by article 7 of the Territorial Sea Convention and article 10 of the Law of the Sea Convention, partly because in the case of smaller bays it is simpler for a State to close a bay under the conventional rules rather than risk a claim to historic status that may be disputed.

Perhaps the most controversial claim to a bay on historic grounds is that of Libya to the Gulf of Sidra (Sirte). In 1973 Libya claimed the Gulf as a historic bay and drew a closing line across it which is 296 miles in length. This action evoked protests from several States, including Australia, France, Norway, the United Kingdom, the USA and the USSR. The USA not only sent a note of protest but passed through the Gulf with a naval squadron. Further displays of naval strength by the USA to demonstrate its objections to the Libyan claim and its assertion that the Gulf remains high seas have taken place, notably in 1981 (when two Libyan aircraft were shot down by the USA) and in 1986. There seems little evidence to support Libya's claim to have exercised sovereignty over the Gulf 'through history' and much evidence of objections from other States. The conclusion must be, therefore, that the Gulf of Sidra is not a historic bay. Conceivably it might be claimed as a 'vital bay', but such a claim would only have any validity as against those States that accept the doctrine of vital bays.[37] Lest it be thought that such claims are confined to recently independent States, it may be noted that the Italian claim to the Gulf of Taranto is in many respects similar to this Libyan claim, and has elicited rejections from States such as the United Kingdom and the USA.[38]

Bays bordered by more than one State

As with historic bays, bays which are bordered by more than one State are not dealt with by either the Territorial Sea Convention or the Law of the Sea Convention. There are over forty such bays in the world. Examples include Lough Foyle (bordered by Ireland and the United Kingdom), the Bay of Figuier (France and Spain) and Passamaquoddy Bay (Canada and the USA). The normal rule of customary international law in relation to such bays would appear to be that unlike bays governed by article 7 of the Territorial Sea Convention and article 10 of the Law of the Sea Convention, or historic bays, they cannot be closed by a line drawn across their mouth. Instead the baseline is constituted by the low-water mark around the shores of the bay. The matter, however, is not free from

---

[37] For fuller discussion of Libya's claim, see F. Francioni, 'The Gulf of Sidra Incident (*United States* v *Libya*) and international law', 5 *Italian Yearbook of International Law* 85–109 (1980–1); Symposium on Historic Bays of the Mediterranean, *op. cit.* in 'Further reading' under 'Bays', pp. 311–26; and J. M. Spinnato, 'Historic and vital bays: an analysis of Libya's claim to the Gulf of Sidra', 13 *ODIL* 65–85 (1983). For a skilful defence of the Libyan position, see F. A. Ahnish, *The International Law of Maritime Boundaries and the Practice of States in the Mediterranean Sea* (Oxford, Clarendon Press), 1993, chapter 7.

[38] Roach and Smith, *op. cit.* in footnote 15, pp. 43–4.

controversy. Exceptionally it may be possible for the riparian States to show that the position is different by reason of historic title. Such is the case with the Gulf of Fonseca, bordered by El Salvador, Honduras and Nicaragua. In *El Salvador* v. *Nicaragua* (1917) the now defunct Central American Court of Justice held that the Gulf was a historic bay, thus having the character of internal waters, and that the three riparian States were co-owners of its waters except for the innermost three miles which was the exclusive property of each. In the *Land, Island and Maritime Frontier* case, decided some seventy-five years later, the International Court reached a similar conclusion as to the Gulf's status, observing that the juridical status of the waters subject to co-ownership was *sui generis*, although essentially that of internal waters, through which nevertheless third States had a right of innocent passage. On the other hand, in a dissenting opinion Judge Oda vigorously denied that it was possible for a multi-State bay to be treated as a historic bay. A more controversial treatment of a multi-State bay is the 1988 Boundary Agreement between Mozambique and Tanzania under which a closing line is drawn across Ruvuma Bay, which does not appear to have been claimed as a historic bay, with the Bay then being divided between the two States as internal waters.

River mouths

Article 13 of the Territorial Sea Convention and article 9 of the Law of the Sea Convention provide in almost identical wording that:

> If a river flows directly into the sea, the baseline shall be a straight line across the mouth of the river between points on the low-water line of its banks. [LOSC, art. 9. TSC has 'low-tide']

No limit is placed on the length of such a river closing line. The provision, in the absence of any qualification to the contrary, would appear to apply both to rivers with a single riparian State as well as to rivers with two riparian States, although the latter application is apparently not accepted by some States, such as the USA.[39]

Estuaries

It should be noted that articles 13 (TSC) and 9 (LOSC) apply only to rivers that flow 'directly' into the sea. Most large rivers do not flow directly into the sea but enter it via estuaries. In such cases the question of the baseline should be governed by the provisions concerning bays (as we earlier saw was done with the Thames estuary in *Post Office* v. *Estuary Radio*). The original ILC draft did in fact contain a specific provision to this effect, but it was deleted at UNCLOS I because of the difficulty of defining an estuary.

[39] See *Whiteman, op. cit.*, Vol. IV, pp. 250–7.

It may not always be easy to distinguish between a river entering the sea directly and one entering the sea via an estuary; and in any case the distinction is open to abuse. Nor is it always easy to determine exactly where the mouth of a river is located, especially on a coast with an extensive tidal range. An example of these problems can be seen in the action of Argentina and Uruguay in 1961 in drawing a line 120 miles in length across the mouth of the river Plate between Punta del Este in Uruguay and Cabo San Antonio in Argentina.[40] This action, which has met with protests from a number of other States, including the United Kingdom and the USA, is said by Argentina and Uruguay to be based on article 13,[41] although few cartographers would be likely to choose the location of the above line as the mouth of the river Plate or indeed say that the river entered the sea 'directly': furthermore, the river Plate estuary has in the past been claimed, inconsistently with the present claim, as a historic bay.[42]

Deltas

Where a river enters the sea via a delta, it is unlikely that articles 13 and 9 will be applicable. Instead the baseline is likely to be constituted by the low-water mark or in some cases by straight baselines (as the Law of the Sea Convention with its provision on deltas on highly unstable coastlines, referred to above, provides). In addition, in many instances, the provisions on low-tide elevations and islands (considered below) will be applicable.

Harbour works

Article 8 of the Territorial Sea Convention provided that the 'outermost permanent harbour works which form an integral part of the harbour system' (such as jetties and breakwaters) were to be regarded as forming part of the coast and thus could serve as the baseline. Article 11 of the Law of the Sea Convention repeats article 8 almost *verbatim*, but makes it clear that harbour works must be attached (or at least very close) to the coast if they are to be used as baselines, by adding that 'off-shore installations and artificial islands shall not be considered as permanent harbour works'. Although the Conventions do not make provision for such an eventuality, it would seem reasonable for coastal States to be able to draw a straight line across the mouth of a harbour (although such a line would normally have a negligible influence on the extent of the territorial sea). Support for such a position is provided by article 50 of the Law of the Sea Convention which permits archipelagic States to draw closing lines across harbours (see p. 125 below). In the *Dubai/Sharjah Border Arbitration* (1981) the

[40] Text of the Argentina–Uruguay Declaration in *Limits in the Seas* No. 44 (1972).
[41] In fact, however, neither Argentina nor Uruguay is a party to the Territorial Sea Convention, although both have signed it.
[42] See *Whiteman, op. cit.*, Vol. IV, pp. 240, 342–3.

tribunal implied that the provisions of articles 8 and 11 were part of customary international law.[43]

Where roadsteads which are 'normally used for the loading, unloading and anchoring of ships' lie not only beyond the baseline but also wholly or partly outside the territorial sea, they are included in the territorial sea, though they do not otherwise affect its delimitation (TSC, art. 9; LOSC, art. 12). Strictly speaking these provisions (which appear to have very limited practical application, a rare example being their probably illegitimate invocation by the Federal Republic of Germany in 1983 to justify extending its territorial sea to sixteen miles in one area[44]) have nothing to do with baselines, and are only included here for the sake of completeness.

Low-tide elevations

A low-tide elevation is defined in the Conventions as 'a naturally formed area of land which is surrounded by and above water at low tide but submerged at high tide' (TSC, art. 11(1); LOSC, art. 13(1)). Low-tide elevations are often referred to in older books and treaties as 'drying rocks' or 'banks'. The effect of low-tide elevations on the delimitation of the territorial sea was uncertain under customary international law before 1958, but clear rules were laid down in article 11 of the Territorial Sea Convention, which are repeated *verbatim* in article 13 of the Law of the Sea Convention. Under these provisions:

> Where a low-tide elevation is situated wholly or partly at a distance not exceeding the breadth of the territorial sea from the mainland or an island, the low-water line on that elevation may be used as the baseline for measuring the breadth ot the territorial sea.

Where, however:

> a low-tide elevation is wholly situated at a distance exceeding the breadth of the territorial sea from the mainland or an island, it has no territorial sea of its own.

This is so even if such a low-tide elevation is situated at a distance less than the breadth of the territorial sea from another low-tide elevation, which in turn is situated less than the breadth of the territorial sea from the mainland: i.e., it is not possible to 'leapfrog' from one low-tide elevation to another. The now-general recognition of a twelve-mile territorial sea gives low-tide elevations a much

---

[43] 91 *ILR* 543 at 661–2.

[44] J. Van Dyke *et al.* (eds), *International Navigation: Rocks and Shoals Ahead* (Honolulu, Hawaii, Law of the Sea Institute), 1988, pp. 103–5. In 1994 Germany modified its claim, enclosing the roadstead concerned as territorial sea, with the waters between that and the normal twelve-mile outer limit of the territorial sea reverting to EEZ: see Roach and Smith, *op. cit.* in footnote 15, pp. 126–8.

greater potential for extending the outer limit of the territorial sea seawards than when the territorial sea was more commonly three miles in breadth. Thus, in an extreme case, where a low-tide elevation is twelve miles from the mainland, the outer limit of the territorial sea will be twenty-four miles from the mainland.

Finally, it should be noted that in limited cases low-tide elevations can be used as basepoints in constructing a straight baseline system (see above).

Islands

An island is defined in the Conventions as 'a naturally formed area of land, surrounded by water, which is above water at high tide' (TSC, art. 10(1); LOSC, art. 121(1)). This definition removes the doubts which had existed in customary international law before 1958 as to whether in addition an island had to be capable of effective occupation, by making it clear that this is not a necessary condition. The Conventions go on to provide that the territorial sea of an island is measured in accordance with the general rules on baselines (TSC, art. 10(2); LOSC, art. 121(2)). This means that every island, no matter what its size has a territorial sea (which appears also to have been the position in customary international law before 1958). With large islands, such as Great Britain, Greenland and Madagascar, there are obviously no problems. But it also means that every islet or rock, no matter how small in size, has a territorial sea, i.e., the islet or rock, or rather the low-water mark around it, will serve as part of the baseline. The question then arises whether this is the baseline for the territorial sea only, or the baseline for all maritime zones.

The Territorial Sea Convention mentioned only the territorial sea specifically, but by implication it also included the contiguous zone (see TSC, art. 24(2)). State practice after 1958 suggested that it also included the twelve-mile exclusive fishing zone.[45] (The continental shelf, the only other kind of maritime zone in existence before UNCLOS III, was not, under customary international law or the Continental Shelf Convention, measured from the baseline.) The Law of the Sea Convention, on the other hand, specifically provides that all islands in principle can serve as the baseline for all maritime zones, viz. the territorial sea, contiguous zone, EEZ and continental shelf [46] (LOSC, art. 121(2)), but makes a partial exception for 'rocks which cannot sustain human habitation or economic life of their own': such 'rocks' can serve as the baseline only for the territorial sea and contiguous zone, but not for the EEZ or continental shelf (LOSC, art. 121(3)).

---

[45] Although Ireland objected to the United Kingdom claiming a twelve-mile fishing zone around the miniscule islet of Rockall. See Symmons, *op. cit.* in 'Further reading' under 'Islands', pp. 101–2.

[46] Under the Law of the Sea Convention, unlike the Continental Shelf Convention or pre-UNCLOS customary international law, the outer limit of the continental shelf is in many, but not all, cases measured from the baseline. See art. 76 and the discussion in chapter 8, pp. 148–9.

This provision is poorly drafted. It does not define what a 'rock' is or suggest any dividing line between 'rocks' and other islands. In addition, the question of whether any particular 'rock' can sustain 'human habitation' or 'economic life' is one that may admit of more than one answer because of the vagueness of the phrases used.[47] The effect of article 121(3), which is further analysed in chapters eight and nine (see pp. 150–1 and 163–4), is to create a situation – the one situation – where the baseline is not the same for all maritime zones. It also has the rather anomalous result that a low-tide elevation can sometimes generate an exclusive economic zone, whereas an uninhabitable 'rock' cannot, even though the latter will usually be a much more visible manifestation of land. On the other hand, as long as the other conditions for the drawing of straight and archipelagic baselines are satisfied, it would appear permissible to use an uninhahitable 'rock' as a basepoint in constructing a straight baseline or archipelagic baseline system, and in such a case the limitations of article 121(3) could be circumvented. In practice most 'rocks' lie immediately offshore, and thus if article 121(3) is applied and they are discounted as basepoints for delimitation of the EEZ and continental shelf, the extent of those zones will not be greatly affected. However, the few isolated oceanic 'uninhabitable rocks' that do exist (and exactly how many will depend on what criteria, if any, emerge as to the size and habitability of 'rocks') – such as Rockall (off the United Kingdom), St Peter and St Paul Rocks (off Brazil) and L'Esperance Rock (off New Zealand) (all less than 0.01 square miles in area) – are likely to give or have already given rise to difficulties and disputes (see further chapter nine).

Archipelagos

Where islands are grouped so as to form an archipelago, the Law of the Sea Convention provides that, in addition to any baselines drawn along individual islands to delimit internal waters, straight lines may be drawn around the outermost points of the archipelago itself (archipelagic baselines). Such archipelagic baselines form the baseline from which the territorial sea and other zones are measured. This matter is discussed more fully in chapter six.

Artificial islands

The definition in the Conventions of an island as being 'naturally-formed' excludes artificial islands, although the distinction between a 'naturally-formed' and an 'artificial' island may not always be easy to make in practice: for example, if a State constructs some kind of barrier in the sea so that sand being moved by currents piles up against it, with the result that eventually an island is formed, is

[47] For a fuller discussion of the meaning of art. 121(3), see E. D. Brown, 'Rockall and the limits of national jurisdiction of the UK', 2 *Marine Policy* 181 (1978) at 205–8 and Kwiatkowska and Soons, *op. cit.* in 'Further reading' under 'Islands', pp. 150–73.

this a 'naturally-formed' or an artificial island? The only provision on artificial islands in the 1958 Geneva Conventions was article 5(4) of the Continental Shelf Convention, which provided that installations connected with the exploration and exploitation of the shelf's natural resources and located on the continental shelf 'do not possess the status of islands. They have no territorial sea of their own, and their presence does not affect the delimitation of the territorial sea of the coastal State.' The implication would seem to be that no artificial island is entitled to a territorial sea or, therefore, to serve as a basepoint. The Law of the Sea Convention reinforces this conclusion. First, article 11 provides, as we have already seen, that 'offshore installations and artificial islands shall not be considered as permanent harbour works' and therefore do not, *qua* harbour works, form part of the baseline. Secondly, articles 60(8) and 80 provide that artificial islands and installations constructed in the EEZ or on the continental shelf have no territorial sea of their own nor does their presence affect the delimitation of the territorial sea, EEZ or continental shelf. Thirdly, even though the construction of artificial islands on the high seas is now recognised as a freedom of the high seas (LOSC, art. 87), the prohibition on States from subjecting any part of the high seas to their sovereignty (LOSC, art. 89) prevents the establishment of any maritime zones around artificial islands on the high seas. This principle is spelt out for that part of the high seas overlying the International Sea Bed Area. Under article 147(2) stationary installations used for the conduct of activities in the Area have no territorial sea of their own, nor do they affect the delimitation of the territorial sea, EEZ or continental shelf.

Reefs

The coral reefs of atolls present a problem in that they may be continuously submerged or, if exposed at low tide, may be situated at a distance greater than the breadth of the territorial sea from the islands of the atoll: in neither case, therefore, under the rules so far considered could such reefs serve as the baseline. And yet it is desirable for a variety of reasons, principally ecological, that the territorial sea should be measured from the outer limit of the reef so that the lagoon inside the reef, which normally constitutes the main source of food for the inhabitants of an atoll, has the status of internal waters. The problem of coral reefs was recognised and discussed by the ILC in the earlier stages of its work[48] but no provision on the subject was contained in its final draft, nor does the matter appear to have been discussed at UNCLOS I. With the emergence into independence since 1958 of many States formed of atolls in the Caribbean and Indian and Pacific Oceans, such as the Bahamas, the Maldives and Nauru, there has come greater political impetus for a specific rule for coral reefs, and such a rule is now contained in the Law of the Sea Convention. Article 6 provides that:

[48] See *Whiteman, op. cit.*, Vol. IV, pp. 297–300, 306.

In the case of islands situated on atolls or of islands having fringing reefs, the baseline for measuring the breadth of the territorial sea is the seaward low-water line of the reef, as shown by the appropriate symbol on charts officially recognized by the coastal State.

A number of points may be noted about this provision. First, it is not limited in its application to atolls or coral reefs (unlike an early draft provision in the ILC).[49] Secondly, it suggests that only reefs exposed at low tide, and not wholly submerged reefs, may be used as baselines (again unlike the early ILC draft, which had provided that 'the edge of the reef as marked on . . . charts should be accepted as the low-water line'): in practice, however, there is in most cases only a short distance between the low-water line and the seaward limit of the reef. Thirdly, it is not clear whether the term 'fringing reef' is used in its technical geomorphological sense as meaning a reef extending outwards from the shore from which it is not separated by a channel, or whether it also includes a barrier reef which lies parallel to the shore from which it is separated by a wide and deep lagoon. A UN study of baselines stated in 1989 that 'it may be assumed that the reference to fringing reefs in article 6 can be applied without distinction to any reefs, including barrier reefs, which are separated from the low-water line of the island and form a fringe along its shore'.[50] Even so, it is not clear whether there is any limit that should be placed on the distance a fringing reef which is to serve as a baseline may lie from the coast of an island. A further problem is that article 6 does not specify what is to happen where there is a gap in the fringing reef. The obvious solution is to draw a straight line across the gap, and this appears to be the growing practice of States: see, for example, the legislation of Fiji,[51] Nauru[52] and of New Zealand in respect of the Tokelau Islands.[53] This solution is more problematic, however, where the gap is extensive, and would not seem possible at all where the reef fringes only part of the island.[54] Finally, many atolls form part of archipelagos. In such cases it will often be simpler and more advantageous for the archipelagic State to use archipelagic baselines as the baseline (see chapter six) than to construct baselines in accordance with the provisions of article 6. Furthermore, as Beazley points out, with the now-general acceptance of a twelve-mile territorial sea, article 6 achieves little that could not be achieved by the provisions on low-tide elevations.[55]

---

[49] However, Beazley, *op. cit.* in 'Further reading' under 'Reefs', p. 298, argues that the terms 'atoll' and 'fringing reef' used in art. 6, together with the *travaux préparatoires*, point to art. 6 being limited in its application to coral reefs only.

[50] United Nations (1989a), *op. cit.* in 'Further reading', in the general section, p. 9.

[51] See *Limits in the Seas* No. 101 (1984), which, however, questions whether in some cases this has not been done somewhat arbitrarily, particularly because of the use of submerged reefs.

[52] Interpretation Act 1971. *UN Leg. Ser.* B/16, p. 19.

[53] Tokelau (Territorial Sea and Exclusive Economic Zone) Act 1977, s. 5. *ND VII*, p. 468.

[54] For suggestions as to what should be done in this situation, see United Nations, *op. cit.*, pp. 11–13.

[55] Beazley, *op. cit.*, pp. 303–4, 311.

Charts and publicity

Under the Territorial Sea Convention the only baselines which the coastal State was required to indicate on charts and publicise were straight baselines (TSC, art. 4(6)). Under the Law of the Sea Convention this obligation is extended to closing lines across river mouths and bays, and there is now an obligation to deposit a copy of a chart showing such baselines (or alternatively a list of geographical co-ordinates) with the UN Secretary General (LOSC, art. 16). Presumably the reason why the list of baselines to be indicated on charts and publicised has not been extended to the low-water line and low-tide elevations is partly that such features are constantly changing as the result of tides and currents, and partly that the low-water line is the normal baseline which the coastal State must adopt if it does not choose man-made baselines such as river and bay closing lines and straight baselines and which must be marked on 'large-scale charts officially recognised by the coastal State' (TSC, art. 3; LOSC art. 5).

Article 16 of the Law of the Sea Convention should introduce greater precision and certainty into the drawing of baselines. This is particularly important for mariners and fishermen wanting to know whether they are in any of a coastal State's maritime zones and, if so, which. The requirement of publicity may also help to reduce some of the past abuse of straight baselines and river mouth and bay closing lines which we have noted above.

It might seem that once a State has exercised the full range of options provided by the Conventions in drawing baselines and has duly charted and publicised such baselines, that would be the end of the matter. However, if there is a significant rise in sea levels over the coming decades as a result of global climate change, as is widely predicted, this is likely to cause a number of States to redraw their baselines as the low-water line on some coasts moves appreciably landwards, some low-tide elevations disappear, and some islands become low-tide elevations or disappear completely.[56]

Present-day customary international law relating to baselines

Given the number of States parties to the Territorial Sea Convention and/or the Law of the Sea Convention (and at the time of writing only twenty-seven coastal States did not come into one or other or both of these categories), the question of what is the customary international law relating to baselines is one of diminishing importance, although it may of course still be significant in the context of a specific dispute.

---

[56] For fuller discussion of this issue, see A. H. A. Soons, 'The effects of a rising sea level on maritime limits and baselines', 37 *NILR* 207–32 (1990), especially at 216–26, and D. Freestone and J. Pethick, 'Sea level rise and maritime boundaries' in G. H. Blake (ed.), *Maritime Boundaries* (London, Routledge), 1994, pp. 73–90.

We will begin by considering whether the provisions of the Territorial Sea Convention and the corresponding provisions of the Law of the Sea Convention have, to the extent that they differ from the customary rules before 1958, passed into customary international law. There is considerable evidence that this has indeed happened. There are three main arguments to support this view. First, the Territorial Sea Convention's provisions on baselines were incorporated *in toto* and unchanged into the Law of the Sea Convention, with little discussion and no opposition at UNCLOS. Secondly, the Territorial Sea Convention's rules on baselines have been incorporated by reference into other treaties, the parties to which include States which are not parties to the Territorial Sea Convention.[57] Thirdly, there is the legislation of States enacted at a time when they were not bound, *qua* parties, by either the Territorial Sea Convention or the Law of the Sea Convention. This legislation generally reflects the Conventions' provisions (practice on straight baselines reflects the provisions less faithfully than practice on other matters). We have discovered and examined some ninety pieces of such legislation. Of this legislation, only fourteen pieces (for example, the legislation of Ireland,[58] Kuwait,[59] New Zealand,[60] Samoa,[61] Sri Lanka[62] and Sudan[63]) refer to most or all of the types of baseline dealt with by the Conventions: in these cases the legislation is generally in accordance with the Conventions' provisions. The majority of States, however, simply refer in their legislation to the low-water mark and/or straight baselines, or, in one or two cases, to baselines being delimited in accordance with international law or the Conventions: a few States provide only for archipelagic baselines (on which see chapter six). Of individual types of baseline, we have already commented on the legislation relating to straight baselines earlier in this chapter. As regards bays, only four States (New Zealand,[64] Papua New Guinea,[65] Samoa[66] and Vanuatu[67]) have legislation reflecting the Conventions' provisions. In the case of the other twenty-four States whose legislation mentions bays, the legislation either fails to define a bay and/or fails

---

[57] For example, the 1962 and 1969 amendments to the International Convention for the Prevention of Pollution of the Sea by Oil, Annex A and art. II respectively; the 1964 European Fisheries Convention, art. 6; and the 1971 Treaty on the Prohibition of the Emplacement of Nuclear Weapons and Other Weapons of Mass Destruction on the Seabed and Ocean Floor, art. II.

[58] Maritime Jurisdiction Acts, 1959 and 1964. *UN Leg. Ser.* B/15, p. 90.

[59] Decree of 17 December 1967 regarding the Delimitation of the Breadth of the Territorial Sea of Kuwait. *UN Leg. Ser.* B/15, p. 96.

[60] Territorial Sea and Exclusive Economic Zone Act, 1977. *UN Leg. Ser.* B/19, p. 65.

[61] Territorial Sea Act, 1971. *UN Leg. Ser.* B/18, p. 33.

[62] Maritime Zones Law No. 22 of 1976 and Presidential Proclamation of 15 January 1977. *UN Leg. Ser.* B/19, pp. 120, 124.

[63] Territorial Waters and Continental Shelf Act, 1970, *UN Leg. Ser.* B/16, p. 30.

[64] *Op. cit.* in footnote 60, ss. 2 and 6.

[65] National Seas Act, 1977, Schedule 1. *ND VII*, p. 486.

[66] *Op. cit.* in footnote 61, ss. 2 and 6.

[67] Maritime Zones Act No 23 of 1981, ss. 1 and 4. *Smith, op. cit.* in the general section of 'Further reading', p. 471.

to prescribe the maximum limit of the closing line. One should not conclude from this, however, that the practice of these States is necessarily contrary to the Conventions. What is essential in determining this question is how these States in practice draw baselines across bay mouths, and on this we have very little information. Three cases, however, have come to our attention where closing lines appear to have been drawn across bays contrary to the rules of the Convention. These are certain of the bay closing lines utilised by Angola, Argentina and France.[68] In the case of river-mouth closing lines, only seven States have legislation referring to such baselines and all but possibly one of these pieces of legislation (that of Cameroon[69]) is in accordance with the Conventions. Nineteen States have legislation dealing with harbour works: in each case the legislation conforms to the Conventions. Of the fifteen States whose legislation refers to low-tide elevations, all but one follow the Conventions, the exception being Saudi Arabia,[70] which appears to allow low-tide elevations wherever situated to generate a territorial sea. Eighteen States have legislation dealing with islands: generally it follows the Conventions (although in some cases an island is not defined), but Saudi Arabia[71] allows artificial islands to generate a territorial sea, while Iran[72] provides that the waters between islands less than twenty-four miles apart have the status of internal waters and, in rather similar fashion, the United Arab Emirates[73] includes as internal waters the waters between islands less than twelve miles apart or between islands and the mainland where they are less than twelve miles apart. Lastly, in assessing whether the provisions of the Conventions have passed into customary law, it must not be forgotten that (as pointed out earlier) international courts and tribunals have suggested that the Conventions' provisions on bays and harbour works represent customary international law.

Finally, it remains to consider whether the two significant additions to the Territorial Sea Convention's provisions on baselines made by the Law of the Sea Convention – dealing with straight baselines on highly unstable coasts (art. 7(2)) and reefs (art. 6) – have passed into customary law. (The third principal change made – the inability of uninhabitable rocks to generate a continental shelf and

---

[68] *Limits in the Seas* No. 28 (1970) (Angola); J. R. V. Prescott, *The Maritime Boundaries of the World* (London, Methuen), 1985, pp. 279, 313 (Argentina and France).

[69] Decree No. 71/DF/416 of 26 August 1971, art. 1. *UN Leg. Ser.* B/19, p. 131. It is not clear whether the lines drawn across certain specified river mouths are river-mouth closing lines, bay closing lines, straight baselines or an illegitimate use of roadsteads as the baseline.

[70] Royal Decree concerning the Territorial Waters of the Kingdom of Saudi Arabia (Royal Decree No. 33 of 16 February 1958), arts. 1 and 5. *UN Leg. Ser.* B/15, p. 114.

[71] *Ibid.*

[72] Act on the Marine Areas of the Islamic Republic of Iran in the Persian Gulf and the Oman Sea, 1993, art. 3. 24 *LOSB* 10 (1993). For protests by the USA, the EU and Qatar, see 25 *LOSB* 101 (1994), 30 *LOSB* 60 (1996) and 32 *LOSB* 89 (1996), respectively. For Iran's responses, see 26 *LOSB* 35 (1994), 31 *LOSB* 37 (1996) and 33 *LOSB* 87 (1997).

[73] Federal Law No. 19 of 1993 in respect of the Delimitation of the Maritime Zones of the United Arab Emirates, art. 2. 23 *LOSB* 94 (1994).

EEZ – will be considered in chapters eight and nine.) As regards article 7(2), there is, as we saw earlier, little or no practice on this matter, and it would therefore seem that this provision has not (yet) passed into customary law. In the case of reefs, thirteen States – Belize,[74] Fiji,[75] Kiribati,[76] Maldives,[77] Marshall Islands,[78] Micronesia,[79] Nauru,[80] New Zealand (in respect of the Cook Islands, Niue and the Tokelau Islands),[81] Solomon Islands,[82] (Southern) Yemen,[83] Tonga,[84] Tuvalu[85] and the United Kingdom (in respect of Bermuda and the Cayman Islands)[86] – enacted legislation before the entry into force of the Law of the Sea Convention which is wholly or broadly in accord with article 6. Given the relatively limited number of States to which article 6 is potentially applicable and the fact that a number of these States have drawn archipelagic baselines in such a way as to obviate the need to invoke article 6, the above practice, coupled with the apparent absence of any protest, would suggest that article 6 has passed into customary law.

Validity of baselines

In those cases where a State either has a discretion as to which kind of baseline it chooses and/or has to construct an artificial line to serve as the baseline – namely, straight baselines, bay and river-mouth closing lines and low-tide elevations – the coastal State's action in exercising its discretion and constructing lines remains subject to international law. As the International Court of Justice put it in the *Anglo-Norwegian Fisheries* case in an oft-quoted dictum:

[74] Maritime Areas Act, 1992, s. 4(4). 21 *LOSB* 3 (1992).
[75] Marine Spaces (Archipelagic Baselines and Exclusive Economic Zone) Order, 1981, s. 4(c). *Smith*, p. 139.
[76] Maritime Zones (Declaration) Act, 1983, s. 2. *Smith, op. cit.*, p. 245.
[77] Constitution of the Republic, art. 1. *UN Leg. Ser.* B/18, p. 28.
[78] Maritime Zones Declaration Act, 1984, s. 2(1). United Nations, *The Law of the Sea. National Legislation on the Territorial Sea, the Right of Innocent Passage and the Contiguous Zone* (New York, United Nations), 1995, p. 210.
[79] Act of 1988 to amend title 18 of the Code of the Federated States of Micronesia, s. 1. *Ibid.*, p. 224.
[80] *Loc. cit.* in footnote 52.
[81] Territorial Sea and Exclusive Economic Zone Act, 1977, s. 4(5) (Cook Islands). *Smith, op. cit.*, p. 325; Territorial Sea and Exclusive Economic Zone Act, 1978, s. 6 (Niue). *Smith, op. cit.*, p. 335; *loc. cit.* in footnote 53 (Tokelau Islands).
[82] Delimitation of Marine Waters Act, 1978, s. 5(3). *Smith, op. cit.*, p. 143.
[83] Act No. 45 of 1977 concerning the Territorial Sea, Exclusive Economic Zone, Continental Shelf and Other Marine Areas, art. 5. *UN Leg. Ser.* B/19, p. 21.
[84] Territorial Sea and Exclusive Economic Zone Act, 1978, s. 5(1). *Smith, op. cit.*, p. 441.
[85] Marine Zones (Declaration) Ordinance, 1983, s. 2. *Smith, op. cit.*, p. 459.
[86] Bermuda (Territorial Sea) Order, 1988, S.I 1988, No. 1838; Cayman Islands (Territorial Sea) Order, 1989, S.I. 1989 No. 2397.

The delimitation of sea areas has always an international aspect; it cannot be dependent merely upon the will of the coastal State as expressed in its municipal law. Although it is true that the act of delimitation is necessarily a unilateral act because only the coastal State is competent to undertake it, the validity of the delimitation with regard to other States depends upon international law.[87]

Thus, where a baseline is clearly contrary to international law, it will not be valid, certainly in respect of States which have objected to it, although a State which has accepted the baseline (for example in a boundary treaty) might be estopped from later denying its validity. In border-line cases – for example, where there is doubt as to whether a State's straight baseline system conforms to all the criteria laid down in customary and conventional law – the attitude of other States in acquiescing in or objecting to the baseline is likely to prove crucial in determining its validity.[88] Having said this, it must, however, be pointed out that few doubtful baselines have encountered active opposition or led to serious disputes, the Norwegian straight baseline system prior to 1950 and the Gulf of Sidra closing line being notable exceptions. Most States, it seems, do not bother to protest against baseline claims which are not in conformity with international law, the major exception being the USA.[89] It may be that the widespread toleration of much of the practice described in this chapter which clearly appears to contravene the relevant rules of international law (particularly as regards straight baselines) will in time lead to a modification of those rules themselves.

Further reading

General

L. M. Alexander, 'Baseline delimitations and maritime boundaries', 23 *VJIL* 503–36 (1983).

P. B. Beazley, *Maritime Limits and Baselines* (London, Hydrographic Society, Special Publication No. 2), 3rd edn, 1987.

R. D. Hodgson and L. M. Alexander, *Towards an Objective Analysis of Special Circumstances. Bays, Rivers, Coastal and Oceanic Archipelagos and Atolls*, Law of the Sea Institute, University of Rhode Island, Occasional Paper No. 13, 1972.

—— and R. W. Smith, 'The informal single negotiating text (Committee II). A geographical perspective', 3 *ODIL* 225–59 (1976).

D. P. O'Connell, *The International Law of the Sea* (Oxford, Clarendon Press), Vol. I, 1982, chapters 5 and 9–11 [*O'Connell*].

J. R. V. Prescott, *The Maritime Political Boundaries of the World* (London, Methuen), 1985.

---

[87] [1951] *ICJ Rep.* 116 at 132.

[88] For an example of this, see the *Anglo-French Continental Shelf* case (1977), paras 121–44, where France was estopped from denying that Eddystone Rock (whose status as an island was in doubt) could be used as a basepoint because of its previous acquiescence in the use of the Rock as a basepoint.

[89] For US protests, see Roach and Smith, *op. cit.* in footnote 15, chapters 3 and 4, *passim*.

T. Scovazzi (ed.), *La Linea di Base del Mare Territoriale* (Milan, Giuffre), 1986.

R. W. Smith, *Exclusive Economic Zone Claims: An Analysis and Primary Documents* (Dordecht, Nijhoff), 1986 [*Smith*].

United Nations, *The Law of the Sea. Baselines: An Examination of the Relevant Provisions of the United Nations Convention on the Law of the Sea* (New York, United Nations), 1989a.

——, *The Law of the Sea. Baselines: National Legislation with Illustrative Maps* (New York, United Nations), 1989b.

M. Voelckel, 'Les lignes de base dans la Convention de Genève sur la mer territoriale', 19 *AFDI* 820–37 (1973).

M. M. Whiteman, *Digest of International Law*, 15 vols, 1963 [*Whiteman*]

Straight baselines

The Geographer, US Department of State, *Limits in the Seas*. The straight baselines legislation of about forty-five States has so far been reproduced and analysed in this series. No. 106 (1987) is on 'Developing standard guidelines for evaluating straight baselines'.

G. Marston, 'Low tide elevations and straight baselines', 46 *BYIL* 405–23 (1972–73).

J. R. V. Prescott, 'Straight and archipelagic baselines' in G. Blake (ed.), *Maritime Boundaries and Ocean Resources* (London, Croom Helm), 1987, pp. 38–51.

——, 'Straight baselines: theory and practice' in E. D. Brown and R. R. Churchill (eds), *The UN Convention on the Law of the Sea: Impact and Implementation* (Honolulu, Hawaii, Law of the Sea Institute), 1987, pp. 288–318.

V. Prescott and E. Bird, 'The influence of rising sea levels on baselines from which national maritime claims are measured and an assessment of the possibility of applying article 7(2) of the 1982 Convention on the Law of the Sea to offset any retreat of the baseline' in C. Grundy-Warr (ed.), *International Boundaries and Boundary Conflict Resolution* (Durham, University of Durham), 1990, pp. 279–300.

W. M. Reisman and G. S. Westerman, *Straight Baselines in International Maritime Boundary Delimitation* (London, Macmillan), 1992.

T. Scovazzi *et al.* (eds), *Atlas of the Straight Baselines* (Milan, Giuffre), 2nd edn, 1989.

C. H. M. Waldock, 'The Anglo-Norwegian Fisheries Case', 28 *BYIL* 114–71 (1951).

Bays

L. J. Bouchez, *The Regime of Bays in International Law* (Leiden, Sijthoff), 1963.

A. Gioia, *Titoli Storici e Linea di Base del Mare Territoriale* (Padua, Cedam), 1990.

I. Scobbie, 'The ICJ and the Gulf of Fonseca: when two implies three but entails one', 18 *Marine Policy* 249–62 (1994).

M. P. Strohl, *The International Law of Bays* (The Hague, Nijhoff), 1963.

Symposium on Historic Bays of the Mediterranean, 11 *Syracuse Journal of International Law and Commerce* 205–415 (1984).

UN Secretariat, 'Historic Bays', First UN Conference on the Law of the Sea, *Official Records*, Vol. I, pp. 1–38.

——, 'Juridical regime of historic waters including historic bays', *ILC Yearbook*, 1962, Vol. 2, pp. 1–26.

G. Westerman, *The Juridical Bay* (Oxford, OUP), 1987.

Islands

D. W. Bowett, *The Legal Regime of Islands in International Law* (Dobbs Ferry, N.Y., Oceana), 1979.

H. Dipla, *Le Régime Juridique des Iles dans le Droit International de la Mer* (Paris, Presses Universitaires de France), 1984.

H. W. Jayewardene, *The Regime of Islands in International Law* (Dordrecht, Nijhoff), 1990.

B. Kwiatkowska and A. H. A. Soons, 'Entitlement to maritime areas of rocks which cannot sustain human habitation or economic life of their own', 21 *NYIL* 139–81 (1990).

N. Papadakis, *The International Legal Regime of Artificial Islands* (Leiden, Sijthoff), 1977.

C. R. Symmons, *The Maritime Zones of Islands in International Law* (The Hague, Nijhoff), 1979.

United Nations, *The Law of the Sea. Regime of Islands: Legislative History of Part 8 (Article 121) of the United Nations Convention on the Law of the Sea* (New York, United Nations), 1987.

Reefs

P. B. Beazley, 'Reefs and the 1982 Convention on the Law of the Sea', 6 *IJECL* 281–312 (1991).

I. Kawaley, 'Delimitation of islands fringed with reefs: article 6 of the 1982 Law of the Sea Convention', 41 *ICLQ* 152–60 (1992).

3

Internal waters

Definition

Internal, or national, or interior, waters are those waters which lie landward of the baseline from which the territorial sea and other maritime zones are measured (LOSC, art. 8; TSC, art. 5(1); see chapter two). Thus, internal waters of a maritime character mostly comprise bays, estuaries and ports, and waters enclosed by straight baselines.[1] Waters enclosed by the baseline drawn around the outermost islands of an archipelagic State have a special status, which is considered in chapter six; but each separate island within the archipelago is entitled to its own baseline, drawn according to the normal principles, so that its ports, bays and so on may be constituted as internal waters (LOSC, art. 50).

Legal status

In the seventeenth century Hale set out a simple test for deciding whether as a matter of English law an area of water fell within 'the realm' and within the jurisdiction of the common law courts: 'That arm or branch of the sea which lies within the *fauces terrae*,[2] where a man may reasonably discern between shore and shore is or at least may be within the body of a county'. The same general approach, treating waters lying within notional lines drawn between distinct headlands as integral parts of the territory of the coastal State, was adopted in international practice.[3] The present conventional rules concerning the baseline fulfil the same function with greater precision. As a matter of international law the baseline divides a State's land territory and the internal waters which are assimilated to it from its territorial sea, which is the State's maritime territory.

---

[1] The great internal 'seas', such as the Caspian, which have no outlet to the oceans are not maritime areas, and are not governed by the international law of the sea.

[2] The 'jaws of the land'.

[3] See *Attorney-General of Canada* v. *Attorney-General of British Columbia* (Canada, 1984).

This approach implies that, just as the State is in principle free to deal with its land territory, so it should be free to deal with its internal waters as it chooses; and for this reason those waters have not been made the subject of detailed regulation in any of the Conventions on the Law of the Sea.

The coastal State enjoys full territorial sovereignty over its internal waters. Consequently, there is no right of innocent passage, such as exists in the territorial sea, through them. The single exception to this principle is that where straight baselines are drawn along a coastline that is deeply indented or fringed with islands, enclosing as internal waters areas which had not previously been considered as such, a right of innocent passage continues to exist through those newly enclosed waters, at least for parties to the Territorial Sea and Law of the Sea Conventions (LOSC, art. 8(2); TSC, art. 5 (2)).[4] That, at least, is the position under the Conventions: the position in cases where such lines are drawn in exercise of rights under customary law is less clear, the *Anglo-Norwegian Fisheries* case making no reference the preservation of rights of innocent passage in these circumstances.[5]

Two aspects of coastal States' sovereignty over internal waters have given rise to much discussion, and will be considered separately. These are the question of access to ports, and the question of the exercise of jurisdiction over foreign ships in ports.

The right of access to ports and other internal waters

The existence of sovereignty over internal waters and the absence of any general right of innocent passage through them logically implies the absence of any right in customary international law for foreign ships to enter a State's ports or other internal waters. There is, indeed, very little support in State practice for such a right. A much quoted dictum from the award in the *Aramco* arbitration in 1958 stated that 'According to a great principle of public international law, the ports of every State must be open to foreign vessels and can only be closed when the vital interests of the State so require.'[6] But that dictum itself is not supported by the authorities cited by the tribunal, and there is almost no other support for the proposition. While it is undoubtedly true that the international ports of a State are presumed to be open to international merchant traffic (the right to exclude foreign warships is undoubted), this presumption has not acquired the status of a

---

[4] The Minches, lying between the mainland of north-west Scotland and the islands of the Outer Hebrides, are an example: see *UKMIL 1993*, 660. Cf., the comment of the International Law Commission on this provision: *ILC Yearbook*, 1956, Vol. II, p. 268.

[5] See, e.g., T. L. McDorman, 'In the wake of the *Polar Sea*: Canadian jurisdiction and the Northwest Passage', 10 *Marine Policy* 243–57 (1986) at 247–9.

[6] 27 *ILR* 167 at 212. See further Lowe, *op. cit.* in 'Further reading'.

right in customary law.[7] Moreover, any such right would be subject to substantial restrictions.

First, it is clear that States have the right to nominate those of their ports which are to be open to international trade – that is, to those ships which the State chooses or binds itself by treaty to admit to its ports. This rule, which can be traced back at least as far as *Bates* case (England) in 1610, often finds expression in laws designating ports of entry for customs, immigration and international trade purposes.[8]

Secondly, it is generally admitted that a State may close even its international ports to protect its vital interests without thereby violating customary international law, and it would be difficult to establish that any interests invoked by a State were inadequate to justify closure. States have, on many occasions, closed their ports to foreign ships in order to defend important interests. Those interests have included the safeguarding of coastal State security and of good order on shore,[9] and the prevention of pollution;[10] and ports have also been closed in order to signal political displeasure.[11]

Furthermore, States have a wide right to prescribe conditions for access to their ports. The International Court in the *Nicaragua* case noted that internal waters are subject to the sovereignty of the State and that it is 'by virtue of its sovereignty that the coastal State may regulate access to its ports'.[12] Similarly, the US Supreme Court in *Patterson v. Bark Eudora* (1903), stated that 'the implied consent to enter our harbours may be withdrawn, and if this consent may be wholly withdrawn, it may be extended upon such term and conditions as the government sees fit to impose'.[13] There is a great deal of state practice setting out the conditions of entry to ports;[14] but more significant than the measures adopted unilaterally by States are the provisions in multilateral treaties that

---

[7] See the 1975 UNCTAD study, 'Economic Co-operation in Merchant Shipping, Treatment of Foreign Merchant Vessels in Ports', UN Doc. TD/BC.4/136 (9 September 1975); de La Fayette, *op. cit.* in 'Further reading'.

[8] See, for example, the Act of 8 July 1987 governing the Ocean Space of the People's Republic of Bulgaria, Chapter 2 ('Internal Waters'), 13 *LOSB* 8 (1989); the Statute of Ukraine concerning the State Frontier, 4 November 1991, art. 14, 25 *LOSB* 85 (1994).

[9] See, e.g., the incidents reported in the *Revue générale de droit international public*, vol. 73 (1969), p. 449 (Japan/PRC), and vol. 85 (1981), p. 894 and vol. 89 (1985), p. 1026 (France/USSR). Cf., the provisions of the US Magnuson Act of 1976, 50 USC, § 191, and of Danish law, noted in K. Bangert, 'Denmark and the law of the sea' in T. Treves and L. Pineschi (eds), *The Law of the Sea: The European Union and its Member States* (The Hague, Kluwer), 1997, pp. 97–125, at 103.

[10] See Kasoulides, *op. cit.* in 'Further reading', p. 22; cf., the practice reported at 89 *RGDIP* 169 (1985) (New Zealand/USA), and 26 *AFDI* 863–5 (1980) (France).

[11] See the examples cited in de La Fayette, *op. cit.* in 'Further reading'.

[12] [1986] ICJ Rep. 14 at 111.

[13] 190 *US* 169 at 178.

[14] For a good example see the 1995 Norwegian Regulations Governing Pilotage and Entry to Norwegian Waters, posted on the internet at http://www.state.gov/www/global/oes/oceans/ntrvol13.html.

envisage the refusal of entry to ports to ships that do not comply with measures adopted under the treaties: the SOLAS and MARPOL Conventions are examples.[15] Indeed, the 1982 LOSC itself quite clearly presupposes that States may set conditions for entry to their ports (see LOSC arts 25(2), 211(3), 255). It is, however, possible that closures or conditions of access which are patently unreasonable or discriminatory might be held to amount to an *abus de droit*, for which the coastal State might be internationally responsible even if there were no right of entry to the port.

The one case where there is a clear customary law right of entry to ports concerns ships in distress. If a ship needs to enter a port or internal waters to shelter in order to preserve human life, international law gives it a right of entry. This was recognised in cases such as the *Creole* (1853) and the *Rebecca* or *Kate A. Hoff* case (1929). It is, however, unsafe to extend that principle further. In particular, it is by no means clear that a ship has a right to enter ports or internal waters in order to save its cargo, where human life is not at risk. At least in circumstances where the condition of the ship carries a risk of serious pollution, the better view is that coastal States may forbid such ships to enter their internal waters if measures have been taken to save the lives of persons on board: the decision should be taken by weighing the gravity of the ship's situation against the probability, degree and kind of harm to the coastal State that would arise were the ship allowed to enter.[16]

While there is no general right of entry into ports for foreign merchant ships in customary law, the position in treaty law is very different, for many treaties confer rights of entry. Most commonly, such rights are found in bilateral treaties of 'Friendship, Commerce and Navigation', whose numbers run into many hundreds. Sometimes, more specific agreements have been concluded: for example, a dozen bilateral agreements giving rights of entry were made in connection with the voyages of the United States Nuclear Ship *Savannah* in 1964.[17] In addition, the multilateral Convention and Statute on the International Regime of Maritime Ports, 1923, provides for a reciprocal right of access to, and equality of treatment within, maritime ports; it has not, however, been widely ratified. The provisions of the EC Treaty on non-discrimination and free movement of goods would seem to give the Member States a similar reciprocal right of access to each other's ports.[18] The right of States to close their maritime ports may also

---

[15] See, e.g., the EU proposal to ban from its ports ships failing to comply with SOLAS ISM Code (on which, see chapter thirteen below), noted in the 1997 Report of the Secretary General, *Oceans and the Law of the Sea*, UN Doc. A/52/487 (20 October 1997), para.152; MARPOL, art. 5 (on which, see chapter fifteen).

[16] See the papers by D. J. Devine cited in 'Further reading'. See also the Netherlands decision in the *Long Lin* (1995), *Nederlands Juristenblad 1995*, p. 299, No. 23; noted in the *NILOS Newsletter*, No. 12, pp. 4–5 (1995).

[17] *ND* II p. 654. See further chapter fifteen below.

[18] See the *Mary Poppins* case, reported in I. von Münch, 'Freedom of navigation and trade unions', 19 *Jahrbuch für internationales Recht* 128 at 137–42 (1976) ; cf., *O'Connell*, Vol. II, p. 850.

be limited in certain circumstances by treaty obligations to permit free transit for trade purposes: Article V of the GATT is one example. Thus, despite the absence of any clearly established right of entry to ports in customary law, most States enjoy such rights under treaty.

Finally, it should be mentioned that although rights of access, to the extent that they exist, imply a right to leave ports, the right of exit is subject to important limitations. Thus States are entitled to arrest ships in port, in accordance with their normal legal processes. For example, vessels may be seized for customs offences. Similarly, ships in port are liable to arrest as security in civil actions or actions *in rem* against the ship itself, though under the 1952 Brussels Convention on the Arrest of Sea-going Ships, vessels of party States are subject to civil arrest only in the case of 'maritime claims' as defined in article 1 of that Convention. Furthermore, States may detain ships which are in an unseaworthy condition, or otherwise unfit to proceed to sea.[19] States may also require foreign ships to obtain clearing papers from the port authorities, certifying compliance with customs and health formalities, before they leave port. These rights flow from the sovereignty of the State in its ports, and submission to them is arguably an implied condition of admission to the ports.

Two specific points concerning port State jurisdiction over foreign ships, and the detention of such ships in port, should be noted. First, port State jurisdiction is considerably extended in the case of pollution offences by the Law of the Sea Convention: the relevant provisions are discussed in chapter fifteen.[20] Secondly, any ship that has been arrested for a violation of a State's EEZ laws must be promptly released (as must the crew) upon the posting of a reasonable bond or other security: it may not be detained in port (LOSC, arts 73(2), 226(1), 292).[21]

Foreign ships may also seek access to navigable rivers and canals in a State. These, too, constitute internal waters, but in practice are treated differently from ports. Thus, while there is no right of access to navigable rivers situated wholly within the boundaries of a single State, in the case of international rivers, which flow through the territory or constitute the boundary of more than one State, wider rights exist.

Following the precedent set in the Final Act of the Congress of Vienna in 1815, the major international rivers in Europe were subjected to a right of free navigation established by treaty; and during the nineteenth century the principle was extended to Africa and the Americas.[22] The regulation of river traffic was at

---

[19] See further chapters thirteen and fifteen.

[20] See further chapter thirteen, where the role of port States in the enforcement of safety conventions is discussed; and cf., *UKMIL 1994*, pp. 652–3.

[21] The first case before the International Tribunal for the Law of the Sea (*The M/V 'Saiga'*, December 1997) arose from an alleged violation of art. 73(2) by Guinea. See further chapter nineteen.

[22] See J. H. Verzijl, *International Law in Historical Perspective*, Vol. III (Leyden, Sijthoff), 1977, pp. 103–221; *Territorial Jurisdiction of the International Commission of the River Oder*, PCIJ, Ser. A, No. 23 (1929); and the works by Baxter, Teclaff, and Zacklin & Caflisch, in 'Further reading'.

one time largely in the hands of commissions, such as those responsible for the Rhine, the Elbe and the Oder – though these last two do not now exist.[23] For the Danube, the 1948 Belgrade Convention replaced the 1921 Definitive Statute of the Danube. It preserved freedom of navigation but deprived non-riparian users, among them the United Kingdom, the United States and France, of their participation in the control of river traffic, leading those States to withhold recognition of the reconstituted Danube Commission. However, in the case of boundary rivers which are the subject of bilateral treaties, commissions of representatives of the riparian States are common and continue to function satisfactorily.

Treaties or unilateral declarations allowing free navigation, subject always to regulations imposed by riparian States, have at various times been made in respect of many major rivers around the world, and a multilateral treaty to this effect – the Barcelona Convention on the Regime of Navigable Waterways of International Concern – was concluded in 1921, although it has not been widely ratified. Although the matter is not free of controversy, it seems that the predominant view is that, in the absence of a subsisting treaty right, ships of non-riparian States do not enjoy a right of access to any river, national or international.[24]

Canals are in principle to be treated in the same manner as natural waterways, but again the practical importance of the great inter-oceanic canals has resulted in their express 'internationalisation'. Thus, in the 1977 Panama Canal Treaties, and in the 1957 Declaration in which Egypt affirmed its intention to respect the terms of the 1888 Convention of Constantinople concerning the Suez Canal, all States are declared to have the right of free navigation through the canals, which remain, however, under the sovereignty of the State concerned – although in the case of the Panama Canal the United States of America has been given the right to manage the canal until the year 2000, in continuation of the extensive powers which it formerly enjoyed under the 1903 Hay–Bunau-Varilla Treaty.[25]

Jurisdiction in internal waters

By entering foreign ports and other internal waters, ships put themselves within the territorial jurisdiction of the coastal State. Accordingly, that State is entitled to enforce its laws against the ship and those on board, subject to the normal rules concerning sovereign and diplomatic immunities, which arise chiefly in the case of warships. But since ships are more or less self-contained units, having not only a comprehensive body of laws – that of the flag State – applicable to them while in foreign ports, but also a system for the enforcement of those flag

[23] For a concise account see Sir Robert Jennings and Sir Arthur Watts (eds), *Oppenheim's International Law*, 9th edn (Harlow, Longman), 1992, Vol. I, pp. 574–80.
[24] See Jennings and Watts, *op. cit.* in footnote 23, p. 580.
[25] For an entertaining account of the extraordinary circumstances surrounding the making of the Hay–Bunau-Varilla treaty, see D. Howarth, *The Golden Isthmus* (London, Collins), 1966, chapter 9.

State laws through the powers of the captain and the authority of the local consul, coastal States commonly enforce their laws only in cases where their interests are engaged. Matters relating solely to the 'internal economy' of the ship tend in practice to be left to the authorities of the flag State. [26]

While the details of enforcement policy may vary from State to State, the foregoing statement is a serviceable summary of the general practice of States. However, States have given different explanations for the adoption of this practice, and a distinction is commonly drawn between Anglo-American and French positions on the matter. The Anglo-American position, summarised in the United Kingdom reply to the Hague 'Questionnaire' of 1929 and in American cases such as *Cunard S. S. Co.* v. *Mellon* (1923), is that the coastal State's jurisdiction over foreign ships in its ports is complete, but that it may, as a matter of policy, choose to forgo the exercise of its jurisdiction. France, on the other hand, is said to adopt the system of 'partial désintéressement', according to which the coastal State has in law no jurisdiction over purely internal affairs on foreign ships in its ports. This view derives from the *Avis* of the Conseil d'État in the case of the *Sally* and the *Newton* in 1806, on which subsequent French practice was modelled.[27] It was held there that two inter-crew assaults were within the sole jurisdiction of the flag State consul. That *Avis* has been taken as setting out a general rule of customary international law, although, as Charteris pointed out, there was in force at the time a convention with the United States (under whose flag the *Sally* and the *Newton* sailed) which aimed to delimit coastal and consular jurisdiction, and gave consuls competence over incidents confined to the interiors of their ships. Moreover it should be remembered that this case, and almost all others cited in support of the 'French doctrine', were decided at a time when the sovereignty of the coastal State over internal and territorial waters was not a settled part of French jurisprudence.[28]

Despite any differences between the theoretical bases of French and Anglo-American practice, it is clear that the practice of these States, and of States in general, is remarkably consistent. Thus, local jurisdiction will be asserted when the offence affects the peace or good order of the port either literally (for example, customs or immigration offences), or in some constructive sense. A French court, no doubt a little more sensitive to violence than the court in 1806 had been,

---

[26] See the *Restatement (Third): Foreign Relations Law of the United States*, § 512 (1987). For a curious exception see the decision of the Seychelles Supreme Court in *R.* v. *Fayolle* (1971).

[27] See *Juris-Classeur de Droit International*, fasc. 553–1, para. 82 (1993); R.-J. Dupuy, 'The sea under national competence' in R.-J. Dupuy and D. Vignes, *A Handbook on the New Law of the Sea* (Dordrecht, Nijhoff), 1991, p. 247 at pp. 247–51 (also published as *Traité du Nouveau Droit de la Mer* (Paris, Economica), 1985, p. 219 at pp. 219–24). The 1806 *Avis* was still in force in 1979: see P. Daillier and A. Pellet, *Nguyen Quoc Dinh: Droit international public* (Paris, Librarie générale de droit et de jurisprudence), 1994, p. 1061.

[28] Cf. chapter four below, and the case of the *Johmo* (France, 1970).

decided in the *Tempest* (1859) that some crimes, such as homicide, had an intrinsic gravity which, apart from any actual disturbance to the port resulting from their commission, warranted local intervention. Other States have taken the same view: for example, the United States in the cases of *Wildenhus* (1887) (homicide) and *People* v. *Wong Cheng* (1922) (opium smoking), and Mexico in the case of *Public Minister* v. *Jensen* (1894) (shipwreck due to master's imprudence, even though it did not compromise tranquillity of port).

Coastal States will also assert jurisdiction where their intervention is requested by the captain, or the consul of the flag State, of the ship. The Belgian cases of *Watson* (1856) and *Sverre* (1907), both involving thefts on board foreign ships, illustrate this point; and the Costa Rican case of *State* v. *Dave Johnson Plazen* (1927), in which local authorities intervened after the victim of a murder on board a foreign ship was transferred to a hospital onshore, was decided on a similar ground, although it could equally well have been decided on the 'gravity' principle.

Thirdly, coastal authorities commonly intervene in cases where a non-crew member is involved. This ground was recognised in the decisions in the *Cordoba* (1912) in France and the *Redstart* (1895) in Italy, for instance. Some States, such as Japan, have asserted the right to intervene in cases involving their nationals. Others claim the right to remove 'wanted persons' from foreign ships in their ports. This was done in 1949 when one Eisler, wanted by the British police for extradition to the United States, was removed from a Polish ship lying off Southampton, despite protests by the captain and the flag State authorities; and in 1884 the United States, approving the removal of one Menez from an American ship of which he was a crew member, while it was in a Cuban port, noted that American police frequently went on board foreign ships in their ports to arrest people accused of crimes under United States law.[29]

The United States asserted an even wider right in the Medvid incident in 1985. Medvid, a crew member of a Soviet freighter, apparently tried to escape from the ship while it was in a United States port, in order to seek asylum. While the local immigration authorities released him for return to the ship after interviewing him and concluding that he was not seeking asylum, the United States government asserted that it had a clear right to remove him from the ship, by force if necessary, if it was suspected that he was being taken from the United States against his will.[30]

Coastal States will, of course, exercise their jurisdiction in matters which do not concern solely the 'internal economy' of foreign ships. Pollution, pilotage and navigation laws are routinely enforced against such vessels and, as we have noted, ships may be arrested in the course of civil proceedings in the coastal State. But, with the exception of the categories described above, States do not

[29] For the Eisler incident see R. Y. Jennings, 'Extradition and asylum', 26 *BYIL* 468 (1949); for the Menez incident, see Moore, *Digest*, Vol. II, p. 278.
[30] See 80 *AJIL* 622–7 (1986).

exercise their jurisdiction in respect of the internal affairs of foreign ships in their ports even though, as a matter of strict law, they would be entitled to do so because of the voluntary entry of those ships within their territorial jurisdiction. Indeed, it is common practice for States to conclude bilateral consular conventions providing for the reservation of jurisdiction over matters of internal discipline, etc. to the authorities of the flag State.[31]

This reasoning will clearly not apply to ships driven into internal waters by *force majeure* or distress, and accordingly international law demands that they be given a degree of immunity from coastal State jurisdiction. They are entitled to be excused liabilities which arise inevitably from their entry in distress – for example, liability to pay import duties on their cargoes, or liability to arrest (see, for example, the *Rebecca* or *Kate A . Hoff* case (1929), the *Brig Concord* (USA, 1815)). It has even been held, in the *Creole* arbitration (1853), that a coastal State had no right to release slaves on board a foreign ship driven into its ports by distress, even though its laws prohibited slavery; however it is most unlikely that the monstrous illegality of slavery would today be considered to be protected by the essentially humanitarian distress rule. Ships in distress must comply with some laws, which it is reasonable to expect them to observe once they reach the relative calm of the port. In the Canadian case of *Cushin and Lewis* v. *R.* (1935), for example, such ships were held bound to observe regulations concerning the reporting in of cargo on arrival at a port. There is also some authority, such as the *Carlo Alberto* case (France, 1832), for the view that vessels forced to seek refuge in the port of a State in which they had intended to made an unlawful landing enjoy no immunity at all from local jurisdiction.

The essential ground for the application of local law to visiting ships is their temporary presence within the territorial jurisdiction of the coastal State. Sometimes the coastal State has sought to impose on foreign ships obligations which, if they are to be complied with in the State's ports, must be complied with throughout the voyage. Notable examples that have arisen in the past include the United States liquor laws of the 1920s, prohibiting the carriage of alcohol in American waters; laws subjecting foreign shipping companies serving United States ports to a wide range of duties to disclose details of their trade, in America and elsewhere, and to American anti-trust laws; and laws regulating the employment of seamen on foreign ships frequenting American ports. All these exercises of jurisdiction have been vigorously protested by the flag States concerned, with varying degrees of success.[32] They are objectionable both on the ground that they offend against the rule of comity concerning the 'internal economy' of

---

[31] See, e.g., the British Consular Relations Act 1968 and Orders made thereunder implementing bilateral consular treaties.

[32] See, e.g., the discussion by the US Supreme Court in the context of the US National Labor Relations Act, in *McCulloch* v. *National Labor Relations Board* (1963). In *McCulloch* the Court affirmed the constitutional power of Congress to legislate for alien seamen on foreign ships in US waters, but held that in that case Congress had not exercised that power.

visiting ships and, more seriously, that in some respects at least they exceed the limits of jurisdiction which can properly be claimed on the basis of the temporary presence of foreign ships in ports.

Further reading

Ports and other internal waters

A. H. Charteris. 'The legal position of merchantmen in foreign ports and national waters', 1 *BYIL* 45–96 (1920).

D. P. O'Connell, *The International Law of the Sea* (Oxford, Clarendon Press), Vol. II, 1984 [*O'Connell*].

V. D. Degan, 'Internal waters', 17 *NYIL* 3–44 (1986).

D. J. Devine, 'The Cape's False Bay: a possible haven for ships in distress', 16 *South African Yearbook of International Law* 80–91 (1990–91).

——, 'Ships in distress – a judicial contribution from the South Atlantic', 20 *Marine Policy* 229–234 (1996).

P. Fedozzi, 'La condition juridique des navires de commerce', 10 *Recueil des Cours* 5–222 (1925).

F. Francioni, 'Criminal jurisdiction over foreign merchant vessels in territorial waters', 1 *Italian Yearbook of International Law* 27–41 (1975).

P. C. Jessup, *The Law of Territorial Waters and Maritime Jurisdiction* (New York, Jennings), 1927.

G. Kasoulides, *Port State Control and Jurisdiction – Evolution of the Port State Control Regime* (Dordrecht, Nijhoff), 1993.

L. de La Fayette, 'Access to ports in international law', 11 *IJMCL* 1–22 (1996).

R. Laun, 'Le régime international des ports', 15 *Recueil des Cours* 1–143 (1926).

J. L. Lenoir, 'Criminal jurisdiction over foreign merchant ships', 10 *Tulane Law Review* 13–35 (1935).

A. V. Lowe, 'The right of entry into maritime ports in international law', 14 *San Diego Law Review* 597–622 (1977).

D. Vignes, 'La juridiction de l'Etat du port et le navire en droit international', in Société Française pour le Droit International, *Colloque de Toulon: Le Navire en Droit International* (Paris, Pedone), 1992, pp. 127–50.

Rivers and canals

R. R. Baxter, *The Law of International Waterways, with particular regard to Interoceanic Canals* (Cambridge, Mass., Harvard University Press), 1964.

L. Caflisch, 'Règles générales du droit des cours d'eau internationaux', 219 *Recueil des Cours* (1989, vii) 9–226.

Centre for Studies and Research of the Hague Academy of International Law, *Rights and Duties of Riparian States of International Rivers* (Dordrecht, Nijhoff), 1991.

H. Fortuin, 'The regime of navigable waterways of international concern and the Statute of Barcelona', 7 *Netherlands International Law Review* 125–43 (1960).

S. Gorove, *Law and Politics of the Danube. An Interdisciplinary Study* (The Hague, Nijhoff), 1964.

International Law Association, *Reports* of the 46th–60th conferences (1954–82).

L. A. Teclaff, *The River Basin in History and Law* (The Hague, Nijhoff), 1985.

B. Vitányi, *The International Regime of River Navigation* (Alphen aan den Rijn, Sijthoff), 1979.

R. Zacklin and L. Caflisch (eds), *The Legal Regime of International Rivers and Lakes* (The Hague, Nijhoff), 1981.

4

The territorial sea

Development of the concept

In this section we outline the development of the concept of the territorial sea as a maritime zone. The questions of the status of the sea bed underlying the territorial sea and of the air space above it arose separately from the question of the status of the waters themselves, and accordingly we defer consideration of them to the following section.

Although the legislation of several States, such as Guyana, Pakistan and the Seychelles, declares that the State's sovereignty 'extends and has always extended' to its territorial sea,[1] such statements are historically incorrect: the true picture of the development of the concept is rather more complex.

Since the replacement of the Holy Roman Empire by a system of independent sovereign States having definite boundaries – what has been termed the 'birth of territoriality' during the sixteenth and seventeenth centuries – it has been generally accepted that coastal States enjoy some rights to regulate in their own interests activities in the seas adjoining their coasts. Even during the great debates in the seventeenth century between Grotius, as advocate of the freedom of the seas, and the proponents of 'closed seas' (see chapters one and eleven), this much was agreed. Grotius, for example, did not claim that all the seas were open to use by all men. Borrowing a distinction drawn by the Italian civil lawyer Baldus in the fourteenth century, between rights of property (dominium) and rights of jurisdiction or control (imperium) in the sea, Grotius argued that there could be no property rights in the high seas but seems to have admitted the existence of jurisdiction without property rights in those coastal waters that could be effectively controlled from the land.

Grotius' position was developed during the seventeenth century by writers such as Welwood (*De dominio maris*, 1615), who abandoned the distinction

---

[1] Guyana, Maritime Boundaries Act, 1977, s. 5, *UN Leg. Ser.* B/19, p. 33, *ND VII*, p. 112; Pakistan, Territorial Waters and Maritime Zones Act, 1976, s. 2(1), *UN Leg. Ser.* B/19, p. 185, *ND VII*, p. 478; Seychelles, Maritime Zones Act, 1977, s. 3(1), *UN Leg. Ser.* B/19, p. 102, *ND VIII*, p. 11.

between property and jurisdictional rights in the marginal belt. On the basis that property rights demand the existence of jurisdiction for their protection and that the right to exclude, for example, foreign fishermen by the exercise of jurisdiction is tantamount to the existence of property rights, the idea gained ground of a simple distinction between high seas, free and open to all, and coastal waters susceptible to appropriation by the adjacent State. By the end of that century this idea was well established. For instance, the influential work by Bynkershoek, *De dominio maris dissertatio*, published in 1702, was based upon the twin pillars of the freedom of the high seas and the 'sovereignty' of the coastal State over its adjacent sea.

Although Bynkershoek himself regarded this 'sovereignty' as complete, and as including the right to deny foreign ships passage through the territorial sea, his view was not generally shared and was not to survive. Vattel, whose treatise *Le droit des gens* was published in 1758, took the part of earlier writers such as Grotius and Gentilis, and declared that ships of all States enjoyed a right of innocent passage through the territorial sea. While the exact scope of this right has been questioned in several respects, such as its extension to warships, its existence has not been seriously challenged since the early nineteenth century.

As the distinction between high seas and the territorial sea (or 'territorial waters', as it was, and in some quarters still is, commonly known) crystallised, two matters remained unresolved: first, the question of the width of those waters, which we consider below, and secondly, the question of the precise juridical nature of coastal States' rights over the territorial sea. Some writers claimed that coastal States either had proprietorial rights in their territorial seas, or at least enjoyed sovereignty or plenary jurisdiction over them. The practice of many States supported this view. For example, by the early nineteenth century British and American jurisdictional claims were premised upon the existence of a belt of maritime territory surrounding a State, and the civil codes adopted in the middle of that century by several Latin American States treated territorial seas as integral parts of the State. On the other hand, States such as France and Spain did not claim ownership or sovereignty over the territorial sea, but merely jurisdictional competence over adjacent waters for specific purposes – notably defence and the regulation of customs and fishing. These claims had not then been consolidated into a single claim to maritime territory: indeed, the distances over which jurisdiction was claimed often varied according to the subject matter of the regulation (see chapter seven). This approach was more easily reconciled with the existence of a right of innocent passage than the sovereignty doctrine, and found some enthusiastic advocates. The theory was expounded in various forms[2] but found its classic exposition in an article by La Pradelle in 1898.[3] He

---

[2] Neatly summarised, along with other theories, in P. Fauchille's *Traité de droit international public* (1925).

[3] A. G. De Lapradelle, 'Le droit de l'Etat sur la mer territoriale', 5 *RGDIP* 264–84, 309–47 (1898).

argued that States enjoyed only a 'bundle of servitudes' (*faisceau de servitudes*) over coastal waters, permitting them to exercise jurisdiction in the measure necessary for the protection of their interests, and he accepted the corollary that if the existence of a right of jurisdiction were to be questioned the burden lay upon the coastal State to prove that it did exist – quite the opposite of the presumption flowing from the 'sovereignty' doctrine.

These two broad approaches coexisted for several decades. They were considered by the English Court for Crown Cases Reserved in the *Franconia* case (*R.* v. *Keyn* (1876)), in which the question of the status of the territorial sea arose. Keyn was the commander of the German ship *Franconia*, which collided with the British ship *Strathclyde* two and a half miles off Dover beach,[4] causing the death of thirty-eight of the *Strathclyde*'s passengers. Keyn was prosecuted for manslaughter and convicted by an English court. He appealed on the ground that the court lacked jurisdiction to try him, because he was a foreigner and at the material time sailing on a foreign ship on the high seas. The Crown maintained that the collision, having occurred within three miles of the shore, had occurred within the realm and so within British jurisdiction. After an extensive review of the conflicting authorities, contained in a set of judgments of great learning, the Court of Crown Cases Reserved decided, by a majority of seven to six (a fourteenth judge would have joined the majority, but died before judgment was given), to allow the appeal. The common thread running through the majority judgments was the view that even though Great Britain might be entitled to claim a territorial sea, it had not expressly done so, and until Parliament made that claim by legislation the courts were not entitled to hold that British jurisdiction extended to foreigners and foreign ships beyond British shores. Some judges went further and argued that Britain could not, consistently with international law, apply the whole of its criminal law to foreigners in the territorial sea.

The *Franconia* decision was clearly not expected by the British government, and two years later English law was brought back into line with the view of international law that Great Britain had taken throughout the nineteenth century, by the enactment of the Territorial Waters Jurisdiction Act, 1878. That Act reaffirmed the 'rightful jurisdiction' of the Crown over territorial waters, which were 'deemed by international law to be within the territorial sovereignty of Her Majesty'. This position has been consistently adhered to ever since, although, as will be seen, the Act was the subject of much critical comment, and there were occasional doubts on the question expressed privately within the British government.

Doubts concerning the juridical nature of the territorial sea survived into the present century. States such as France, Italy, Russia and the Ottoman Empire continued to maintain claims to separate jurisdictional zones for various purposes. On the other hand, a unified claim to sovereignty and plenary jurisdiction over a belt of maritime territory was made, for example, by the countries of the

---

[4] A fertile location for jurisdictional issues: cf. *The Parlement Belge* (1878–79) 4 *P.D.* 129, (1880) 5 *P.D.* 197.

British Empire (which had agreed upon a single three-mile limit for all jurisdictional purposes at the 1923 Imperial Conference), the United States, the Netherlands and the Scandinavian States. Jurists were similarly divided in their views, as is evident, for instance, from the debates of the International Law Association and of the Committee of Experts preparing for the Hague Codification Conference, both in the 1920s.

With hindsight it is possible to see that the trend in doctrine and State practice was steadily towards recognition of coastal States' sovereignty over their territorial seas. Governments had repeatedly been faced with the question of the juridical status of those waters, directly in the context of various diplomatic exchanges from the early nineteenth century onwards, and indirectly through the deliberations of influential bodies such as the Institute of International Law. And in the twenty years preceding the 1930 Hague Conference the question had arisen in several connections – notably in relation to the limits of neutrality and naval warfare during World War I; the work of the 1919 Conference on Aerial Navigation (see below); the dispute over the application of the United States' liquor laws to foreign ships (see chapter seven); and the preparation for the Hague Conference itself. In each case, it was evident that support for the principle of coastal State sovereignty over the territorial sea was growing.

The replies of governments to the Schedule of Points circulated before the 1930 Hague Conference showed that most respondents preferred the sovereignty doctrine. Some, such as France and Poland, considered the juridical status of the territorial sea unsettled; and other States which had not replied to the Schedule, such as Greece and Czechoslovakia, argued at the Conference against the ascription of sovereignty to the coastal State. But it was clear that, despite some reluctance to use a word so heavily burdened with implications and overtones deriving from its use in connection with land territory, there was general agreement that the principle of coastal sovereignty should be included in any draft treaty. The final text forwarded to the Hague Conference by its Territorial Waters Committee accordingly included a provision that:

> The territory of a State includes a belt of sea described in this Convention as the territorial sea. Sovereignty over this belt is exercised subject to the conditions prescribed by the present Convention and the other rules of international law.[5]

The text was not adopted as a convention, mainly because of a failure to agree on the vital question of the breadth of the territorial sea. Nonetheless, there has been no serious challenge to the principle of coastal sovereignty over the territorial sea since the Hague Conference, and the 1930 Conference may fairly be regarded as the occasion when the doubts over that sea's juridical status, which had persisted right up to the preceding decade, were finally dispelled.

---

[5] League of Nations Doc. C. 351(b). M. 145(b). 1930. v, p. 212. Reproduced in S. Rosenne, *League of Nations Conference for the Codification of International Law (1930)* (Dobbs Ferry, N.Y., Oceana), 1975, p. 1414.

In the years following the Hague Conference, the few States that had not espoused the sovereignty doctrine came to do so, as did States gaining their independence. That is not to say that the municipal law of every State treats the sea in the same way as the land so that, for example, municipal laws automatically apply there. Thus, British territorial waters remain as a matter of domestic law outside the 'realm', and British laws apply therein only to the extent specifically provided.[6] But for the purposes of international law, States have sovereignty, and the plenary jurisdiction which is its concomitant, over the territorial sea. This principle was sufficiently well established in State practice for François to adopt it in his first report to the ILC in 1950, and for it to survive, almost unquestioned, throughout the ILC debates and the 1958 Geneva Conference. Such discussion as there was centred upon the relationship between coastal State sovereignty and the right of innocent passage, which we consider below.

In order to emphasise that the right of innocent passage rendered coastal States' rights over the territorial sea less extensive than those over their land territory, the Hague formula was amended so as to provide that:

(1) The sovereignty of a State extends, beyond its land territory and its internal waters, to a belt of sea adjacent to its coast, described as the territorial sea.
(2) This sovereignty is exercised subject to the provisions of these articles and to other rules of international law. (TSC, art. 1)

A substantially similar provision, in which a reference to archipelagic waters was inserted after that to internal waters, appears in the Law of the Sea Convention (art. 2(1), (3)).

Legal status of the bed, subsoil and superjacent air space of the territorial sea

We have seen that during the first three decades of this century the sovereignty of States over their territorial seas, subject to the right of innocent passage for foreign ships through those seas, gained general acceptance. Although claims to sovereignty over the superjacent air space and subjacent sea bed gained acceptance at about the same time, this development was distinct from the consolidation of the sovereignty theory in respect of the waters themselves. States that had for many years claimed sovereignty over the waters did not at first claim sovereignty over the superjacent air space and sea bed in the zone.

The question of the status of the air space above States' territory and territorial sea arose following the use of balloons during the Franco-Prussian war in 1870–1. In the period following that war, jurists divided in their views on the

---

[6] See *R. v. Keyn* (1876). See, too, the French case of *Minister of Defence et al. v. Starr and the British Commonwealth Insurance Co.* (the *Johmo*) (1970); B. E. Alexander, 'The territorial sea of the United States: is it twelve miles or not?', 20 *JMLC* 305–22 (1997).

question. Some, such as Fauchille, proposed that the air be treated in a manner similar to the high seas, free for the use of all, but subject to rights of 'conservation' for the subjacent State up to a height of 1,500 m. Others, such as Merighnac, thought that States should enjoy sovereignty in their air space. This division mirrored the contemporary doctrinal dispute over the status of the territorial sea itself. Although an international congress in 1910 failed to resolve the question, the practice during the First World War was to treat the air space as subject to the sovereignty of the subjacent State. Some States had taken this position earlier, such as the United Kingdom in its Aerial Navigation Act of 1911. International agreement was reached at the 1919 Paris Conference on a Convention for the Regulation of Aerial Navigation, article 1 of which provided that:

> The High Contracting Parties recognise that every Power has complete and exclusive sovereignty over the air space above its territory.
> For the purpose of the present Convention, the territory of a State shall be understood as including the national territory . . . and the territorial waters adjacent thereto.

This Convention was also a significant step towards the general recognition of sovereignty over the territorial sea itself. Since 1919, sovereignty over the superjacent air space has been a firm principle of international law, enshrined in article 2 of the 1944 Convention on International Civil Aviation, article 2 of the Territorial Sea Convention, and article 2(2) of the Law of the Sea Convention. No right of innocent passage for aircraft has ever been admitted, the dangers to the coastal State inherent in the speed of aircraft and their ability to avoid detection being considered to preclude any such right.

The question of the status of the bed of the territorial sea was ignored for the most part until the present century, it being assumed either that the bed was subject to the coastal State's sovereignty, or that it was not, according to each writer's views concerning the status of the waters of the territorial sea. The lack of any significant interest in use of the sea bed (apart from the construction of piers and submarine mines at relatively short distances from the shore) resulted in there being little attention paid to the sea bed as a separate legal concept and little State practice from which rules of international law concerning the sea bed might have been deduced.[7]

While this shortage of practice was recognised by the drafters of the 1930 Hague Conference text on the territorial sea, it was agreed that an article should be included stating that 'the territory of a coastal State includes also the air space above the territorial sea, as well as the bed of the sea, and the subsoil'.[8] Again, no provision was made for a right of 'innocent passage' through the subsoil, for

---

[7] But see *UKMIL 1992*, pp. 745–6, and the magnificently scholarly analysis in G. Marston, *The Marginal Seabed: United Kingdom Legal Practice* (Oxford, Oxford University Press), 1981, for references to some of the early practice.

[8] League of Nations Doc. C. 351(b). M. 145(b) 1930. v, p. 213; Rosenne, *op. cit.* in footnote 5, p. 1415.

the obvious reason that such a right would amount to a freedom to mine and tunnel the subsoil. Sovereignty over the sea bed and subsoil, once articulated and accepted at the Hague Conference, was readily incorporated into international law, and was reiterated without opposition in the Territorial Sea Convention (art. 2) and the Law of the Sea Convention (art. 2(2)). Nevertheless, the question of the time at which this right of sovereignty became established for particular States has arisen in a number of cases in federal jurisdictions where ownership of the bed has been disputed between the federal and provincial governments. Such cases have not, however, provided definitive answers to the question.[9]

Thus, although the extension of sovereignty to sea bed, waters and air space alike was recognised by 1930, and is now taken as one of the basic rules of the law of the sea, the process by which this came about was more complex. As Marston has put it:

> the rule for the bed and subsoil of the territorial sea was conceived later than the corresponding rule for the superjacent waters and later even than that for the superjacent airspace, although the subsequent crystallisation process resulted in a unitary customary rule and not three separate rules.[10]

The breadth of the territorial sea

Through much of the history of the territorial sea, the question of its breadth has been a matter of controversy. Early practice and doctrine, in the sixteenth and seventeenth centuries, employed vague criteria, such as the limits of visibility, to determine the extent of the waters over which control was claimed. Later, writers such as Grotius and Bynkershoek did much to promote the tendency, already evident in the practice of some States, to replace such unsatisfactory criteria with the rule that coastal States' rights over marginal waters extended up to the point at which those waters could be controlled by shore-based cannon. This 'cannon-shot' doctrine was probably not intended to support the establishment of a continuous belt of maritime territory along the whole coast, but rather to acknowledge the possibility of 'pockets' of control by actual cannon present at various places on shore, this being in accordance with Dutch and Mediterranean State practice of the day. Scandinavian States, on the other hand, did not employ the cannon-shot rule, but claimed maritime *dominium* over fixed distances from the shore

---

[9] Cf. the cases of *US* v. *California* (1947); *US* v. *Louisiana* (1950); *US* v. *Texas* (1950); *US* v. *Maine* (1975); *Reference re Offshore Mineral Rights of British Columbia* (Canada, 1967); *New South Wales* v. *The Commonwealth* (Australia, 1975); *Reference re Mineral and Other Natural Resources of the Continental Shelf* (Canada, Newfoundland, 1983); *Re Attorney-General of Canada and Attorney-General of British Columbia* (Canada, 1984).

[10] G. Marston, 'The evolution of the concept of sovereignty over the bed and subsoil of the territorial sea', 48 *BYIL* 321 (1976–7), at 332.

along the whole coastline, regardless of the actual presence or absence of shore batteries. These distances were progressively reduced from those claimed around the sixteenth century, and had largely settled at the four-mile Scandinavian 'league' by the mid-eighteenth century.

The 'cannon-shot' and 'fixed distance' approaches coexisted for several generations, and eventually converged. The decisive move towards fusion of the two approaches came at the end of the eighteenth century. In 1782 Galiani suggested that it would be reasonable to adopt a three-mile limit along the whole coast, rather than await the establishment of coastal batteries at any particular point. The distance was chosen as a matter of reasonableness and convenience, cannon of the day having a range of under three miles: it was not chosen as the precise range of actual cannon. The three-mile limit was adopted for neutrality purposes by the United States at the beginning of the War of the Coalition in 1793. Thenceforward the 'cannon-shot' principle was commonly treated as generating a continuous belt of maritime territory three miles in breadth, although this belied its origin. The three-mile rule gained rapid and widespread acceptance. It was recognised, for example, by Lord Stowell in *The Anna* (Great Britain, 1805). The survival of this distance throughout the nineteenth century, despite increases in the range of artillery, is explicable by the interest of the major naval powers, which were its main supporters, in preserving the maximum freedom of navigation for their merchant fleets and warships.

Although the three-mile limit was adhered to by most of the major powers throughout the nineteenth century, it was never unanimously accepted. The Scandinavian countries consistently claimed four miles, and several other countries, such as Spain, claimed zones of more than three miles for specific purposes (see chapter seven). Indeed, shortly before the First World War, France, Italy, Russia, Spain and the Ottoman Empire all claimed the right to jurisdiction up to any distance from shore reasonable for the control of specific activities such as fishing or smuggling, within the overall limit of the actual range of coastal artillery. These claims evidenced growing dissatisfaction with the three-mile limit, and the British Foreign Office thought that they might lead to its demise as a rule of law. But these wider claims were not publicly admitted by States claiming only three miles. For example, until the late 1960s, when the practice seems to have been abandoned, the United Kingdom often issued protests saying that 'His Majesty's Government are obliged to place firmly on record that they do not recognise territorial jurisdiction over waters outside the limit of three miles from the coast; nor will they regard British vessels engaged in their lawful pursuits on the high seas as being subject to any measures which the [coastal State] Government may see fit to promulgate,'[11] or something similar.

The effect of such 'persistent objection' was that the wider claims were not 'opposable' to objecting States. Consequently, it is meaningless to speak of a

---

[11] See the example quoted in A. V. Lowe, 'The development of the concept of the contiguous zone', 51 *BYIL* 109 (1981), at 149.

single limit for territorial sea claims existing at any one time. Between three-mile States, the three-mile rule operated; between States claiming, say, six miles that distance was recognised. Between different groups many disputes arose, of which the Anglo-Spanish dispute, which ran throughout most of the nineteenth and early twentieth centuries,[12] is but one of many examples. This difficulty persists to the present day, and we return to it below.

The 1930 Hague Conference attempted to reach agreement upon the width of the territorial sea, and failed. At the final meeting of its Territorial Waters Committee, twenty States sought territorial seas of three miles, twelve sought six miles, and the four Scandinavian States sought recognition of their own historic four-mile claim. Moreover, several States wanted the right to claim contiguous zones beyond the territorial sea. No general agreement was reached. Consequently Gidel, writing four years later, expressed the view that there was no rule of international law fixing the limit of the territorial sea, except in the negative sense that the validity of claims of up to three miles could not be denied.[13] Subsequently, both the First (1958) and the Second (1960) UN Conferences on the Law of the Sea tried to agree upon a limit, again without success.

Although a proposal for a six-mile territorial sea coupled with an additional six-mile fishery limit failed by only one vote to be adopted at the Second UN conference, it is evident that such a compromise would have been short-lived even if it had been adopted. Whereas in 1960 the great majority of States claimed territorial seas of less than twelve miles, by the closing stages of UNCLOS III the position was dramatically reversed, and the great majority of States claimed territorial seas of twelve miles or more (see the Appendix for current claims). It should, however, be noted that some of the wider 'territorial sea' claims have a juridical content different from that embodied in the Territorial Sea Convention. For example, Uruguay allows full freedom of navigation and overflight in the outer 188 miles of its 200-mile territorial sea.[14] The steady shift towards twelve-mile territorial seas, especially among newly independent States, was a reflection of the desire to bring coastal waters – and the fishing, pollution and so on conducted, often by foreign vessels, within them – under national control. Indeed, many of the States claiming three- or twelve-mile territorial seas also claimed jurisdiction over matters such as fishing and pollution out to much greater distances. The consensus in favour of a twelve-mile territorial sea was, however, perfectly clear by the time that UNCLOS III finished its work.

The Law of the Sea Convention sets the limit of the territorial sea at twelve miles (art. 3). Accordingly, the present position in international law appears to

---

[12] See Masterson, *op. cit.* in 'Further reading'.

[13] G. Gidel, *Le droit international public de la mer* (Paris, 1932–34) (reprinted Vaduz, Topos Verlag), 1981, Vol. 3/1, p. 134.

[14] Executive Decree D. 604/1969, 3 December 1969, *UN Leg. Ser.* B/19, p. 90. The claim was protested by the USA: Roach and Smith, *op. cit.* in 'Further reading', p. 158. See further the discussion in L. D. M. Nelson, 'The patrimonial sea', 22 *ICLQ* 668 (1973), at 679.

be as follows. For parties to the Law of the Sea Convention, and all other States recognising the lawfulness of territorial sea claims up to at least twelve miles, the twelve-mile limit will prevail. Wider claims (of which around fifteen still exist: see Appendix) will not be recognised, except as between States making or otherwise recognising such claims. Thus, for example, 200-mile claims would be opposable to Ecuador and Somalia, both of which claim 200-mile territorial seas, but not to, say, India, which claims only twelve miles. In fact, several of the States that had previously claimed territorial seas in excess of twelve miles have pulled back their claims and adopted the twelve-mile limit. Argentina and Brazil, for example, pulled back from 200-miles to twelve miles in the early 1990s when they ratified the 1982 Convention, as Ghana and Senegal had done some years before.[15] In theory, the few non-LOSC States making territorial sea claims narrower than twelve miles would not be bound even by the twelve-mile claims in so far as they have persistently objected to them. However, since the United States announced in 1983 that it would respect claims of up to twelve miles which accord to other States their rights and freedoms under international law[16] – chiefly rights of passage – it seems highly unlikely that there is any State in the position of a persistent objector in this matter. The twelve-mile limit is now firmly established in international law, and the practice, if not always the legislation, of all States is converging upon acceptance of that limit.[17]

One legal aspect of this development is the existence of duties owed by coastal States to foreign vessels in their territorial seas. Thus Judge Fitzmaurice in his separate opinion in the *Fisheries Jurisdiction* case (1973) said:

> The territorial sea involves responsibilities as well as rights . . . for example policing and maintaining order; buoying and marking channels and reefs, sandbanks and other obstacles; keeping navigable channels clear and giving notice of danger of navigation; providing rescue services, lighthouses, lightships, bell-buoys, etc.[18]

Such reasoning had earlier led Judge McNair to state, in his dissenting opinion in the *Anglo-Norwegian Fisheries* case (1951):

> International law does not say to a State: 'You are entitled to claim territorial waters if you want them.' No maritime State can refuse them. International law imposes upon a maritime State certain obligations and confers upon it certain rights arising out of the sovereignty which it exercises over its maritime territory.

---

[15] See the list of such States in Roach and Smith, *op. cit.* in 'Further reading', pp. 151–3.

[16] Presidential Proclamation of 10 March 1983, 22 *ILM* 461 (1983).

[17] The previous edition of this book (p. 68) recorded the anomalous German claim, motivated by the desire to control tanker traffic in an exceptionally busy area, establishing the 'Heligoland box', which extended at one point up to sixteen miles from the shore. See 7 *LOSB* 9–22 (1986). That claim was overtaken by the 1994 legislation which adopted a twelve-mile limit for German territorial waters, as the GDR had claimed prior to German unification: see 27 *LOSB* 55 (1995).

[18] [1973] *ICJ Rep.* 3 at 27 n. 8.

The possession of this territory is not optional, not dependent upon the will of the State, but compulsory.[19]

This notion of a territorial sea automatically appurtenant to coastal States, which had been expressed by the Permanent Court of Arbitration in the *Grisbådarna* case as early as 1909, is implicit in both the 1958 Territorial Sea Convention (article 1 of which, as we have seen, prescribes the extension of sovereignty to that sea, rather than simply leaving it to States to claim such sovereignty) and the Law of the Sea Convention (art. 2) which follows the 1958 text. Similarly, the requirement that a State 'give appropriate publicity to any danger to navigation, of which it has knowledge, within its territorial sea' (TSC, art. 15(2); LOSC, art. 24(2)), by imposing duties in respect of the territorial sea, suggests that there is a zone within which this duty must be discharged. It follows, therefore, that international law should lay down a *minimum* breadth for the territorial sea within which coastal States must fulfil their duties towards foreign shipping. While the theoretical basis of this view has not been adequately explored, it is evident that the many jurists who subscribe to it regard three miles as the minimum breadth, that distance being the smallest claimed for the territorial sea during modern times. The time may soon come, however, when customary international law moves beyond the Law of the Sea Convention and regards twelve miles not merely as the maximum, but as the minimum, mandatory limit for the territorial sea.

The right of innocent passage

The existence of a right of innocent passage through the territorial sea for foreign ships was, as we noted above, widely conceded throughout the period during which the concept of the territorial sea began to crystallise, and particularly since the time of Vattel. This was no well-defined right, around which notions of coastal sovereignty collected, as it were: rather, the concepts of innocent passage and coastal sovereignty developed in parallel, each helping to mould the other.

'Passage'

The definition of 'passage' is a relatively easy matter. It includes not only actual passage through the territorial sea, but also stopping and anchoring in so far as this is incidental to ordinary navigation or rendered necessary by *force majeure* or distress (TSC, art. 14(3); LOSC, art. 18(2)). The Law of the Sea Convention expressly extends the distress exception to cases where one ship seeks to assist another ship, person or aircraft in danger or distress (LOSC, art. 18(2)).

[19] [1951] *ICJ Rep.* 116 at 160.

Otherwise, ships are not allowed to 'hover' or cruise around in the territorial sea, because, regardless of whether or not they are 'innocent', they would not be engaged in passage: passage must be 'continuous and expeditious' (LOSC, art. 18(2)). All submarines and other underwater vehicles must navigate on the surface (TSC, art. 14(6); LOSC, art. 20). These conventional definitions are in accordance with a long and consistent general practice among States.

The 1930 Hague Conference articles introduced a new element into the definition of passage, not previously adopted in State practice, by including ships travelling through the territorial sea to or from internal waters within the scope of the right of innocent passage. This was not because there was considered to be any right, analogous to innocent passage, to enter or leave internal waters; thus, coastal States retained the right to take, impose and enforce conditions for admission to internal waters (TSC, art. 16(2); LOSC, art. 25(2)). Rather, it was done for the convenience of bringing such ships within the legal regime of ships in innocent passage, for general purposes of coastal State control and jurisdiction. The Territorial Sea Convention adopted the same position, in article 14(2); and that article was carried over into the Law of the Sea Convention, modified slightly so as to include within the scope of 'passage' the voyages of ships navigating the territorial sea in order to call at roadsteads or port facilities outside internal waters (LOSC, art. 18(1)). The extension of the right of innocent passage to voyages to and from ports was regarded by the International Court in the *Nicaragua* case (1986) as being established in customary law.[20]

'Innocence'

For a long time the criterion of 'innocence' lacked any clear definition, and probably any clear meaning. During the nineteenth and early twentieth centuries, Anglo-American practice and some jurists, such as Schücking, whose reports prepared the ground for the 1930 Hague Conference, appear to have regarded innocence as a question distinct from that of compliance with coastal State laws. From their point of view it was not necessary that any coastal law should have been violated in order that innocence be lost; it was enough that vital coastal interests, such as security, be prejudiced. Conversely, it would seem to follow that not all infractions of coastal laws would deprive passage of its innocent character, but only those which had such a prejudicial effect. Furthermore, if prejudice to coastal State interests were the criterion, it would not be necessary to point to any particular act of the foreign ship as being incompatible with innocence, and the mere presence of the ship could be enough to threaten the coastal State. On the other hand, other States, and most other jurists, drew no such distinction, either expounding the law as if the duty to comply with local laws was in essence the same as the duty to remain 'innocent' during passage, or taking no clear position on the question.

[20] [1986] *ICJ Rep.* 12 at 111.

The 1930 Hague Conference adopted a text somewhere between these views. It read:

> Passage is not *innocent* when a vessel makes use of the territorial sea of a coastal State for the purpose of doing any act prejudicial to the security, to the public policy or to the fiscal interests of that State.[21]

Here no breach of any coastal State law was required, but it was arguably necessary that the foreign ship commit some act other than merely passing through the territorial sea. State practice after 1930 (for example, the Bulgarian Decree Law of 25 August 1935,[22] and the Japanese case of *Japan* v. *Kulikov* (1954)) showed a tendency to follow the Hague formulation, tying the concept of innocence broadly to prejudice to security, public policy and fiscal interests of the coastal State.

The question of innocence received full discussion before the International Court of Justice in the *Corfu Channel* case (1949). The case concerned the denial of passage through the Corfu Channel to British warships, and is discussed in more detail in chapter five. The important point for present purposes is that, in defining the right of innocent passage, the Court referred to the *manner* of passage as the decisive criterion, holding that as long as the passage was conducted in a fashion which presented no threat to the coastal State it was to be regarded as innocent. The whole tenor of the judgment made clear that innocence was a quality capable of objective determination, and that a coastal State's view would not necessarily be conclusive. It followed that a breach of a coastal State's law would not *ipso facto* deprive passage of its innocent character. The Court's view was, therefore, close to that adopted in early Anglo-American practice.

Although the more flexible approach of the International Court was fresh in the minds of the International Law Commissioners when they began preparing draft articles on the territorial sea, most of them preferred the approach adopted in the 1930 Hague draft, in which non-innocence was defined by reference to *acts* prejudicing coastal State interests rather than to the *manner* of passage. Some disagreed. Lauterpacht, for instance, proposed that, except in the case of acts prejudicing coastal State security, only acts violating specific coastal State laws could deprive passage of its innocence. Fitzmaurice, on the other hand, suggested that passage could, where it prejudiced coastal security, be non-innocent irrespective of any act of the vessel. However, the final Commission text provided that passage was innocent so long as the ship did not commit 'any acts prejudicial to the security of the coastal State or contrary to the present rules, or to other rules of international law'.[23] The term 'present rules' was understood, as the Commission's commentary makes clear, to refer to the duty which was imposed by another of the draft articles to comply with coastal State legislation

---

[21] League of Nations Doc. C. 351(b). M. 145(b). 1930. v, p. 213; Rosenne, *op. cit.* in footnote 5, p. 1415.

[22] *UN Leg. Ser.* B/1, p. 53 (art. 4).

[23] *ILC Yearbook 1956*, Vol. II, p. 272.

on matters such as public health, immigration, customs and fiscal matters, navigation, fishing and the protection of the products of the territorial sea, these being the interests which the coastal State was entitled to protect in its territorial sea.

The Commission's draft article was not accepted by the 1958 conference. The United States proposed an amendment stating that 'passage is innocent so long as it is not prejudicial to the security of the coastal State . . .' Other States objected to this on two main grounds: first, that deletion of the reference to acts of the passing ship gave too much latitude to the coastal State in the determination of innocence, and (which is more difficult to accept) was contrary to existing international law; and secondly, that interests other than security deserved protection. A compromise text was eventually adopted as article 14(4) of the Territorial Sea Convention, which read:

> (4) Passage is innocent so long as it is not prejudicial to the peace, good order or security of the coastal State. Such passage shall take place in conformity with these articles and with other rules of international law.

Unlike the 1930 Hague draft, which stipulated the circumstances in which passage was *not* innocent, article 14(4) stipulated the circumstances in which passage *was* innocent. The 1958 provision, which was broadly compatible with the actual practice of States (however their legislation may have been framed), and so with customary law, clearly does not require the commission of any particular act, or the violation of any law, before innocence is lost. Nor does violation of a coastal law *ipso facto* deprive a passage of its innocence, unless the violation actually prejudices the coastal interests. This latter rule is subject to one exception. According to article 14(5):

> Passage of foreign fishing vessels shall not be considered innocent if they do not observe such laws and regulations as the coastal State may make and publish in order to prevent these vessels from fishing in the territorial sea.

Such laws could deal not only with actual fishing but also with, for example, storage of nets while the vessel was in transit. This provision was adopted at the 1958 conference with the express purpose of introducing an additional element into the criterion of innocence applicable to fishing vessels. It represents the only case in which breach of a coastal State law *ipso facto* deprives passage of its innocent character.

Despite the acceptance of the Territorial Sea Convention by around fifty States, and the incorporation of the terms of its 'innocent passage' provisions in several municipal laws, such as the Territorial Sea and Maritime Zones Law 1977 of Burma (as it then was),[24] the Pakistan Territorial Waters and Maritime Zones Act 1977[25] and the Yugoslav Law of 22 May 1965,[26] the definition of innocent passage was substantially amended in the Law of the Sea Convention.

[24] *UN Leg. Ser.* B/19, p. 8, *ND VII*, p. 356 (chapter 2).
[25] *UN Leg. Ser.* B/19, p. 85, *ND VII*, p. 478 (s. 3).
[26] *UN Leg. Ser.* B/15, p. 188, *ND I*, p. 35 (art. 12).

Article 19 of the 1982 Convention retains, as paragraph 1, the text of the 1958 article 14(4), quoted above. But article 19 goes on to provide in paragraph 2 that 'passage of a foreign ship shall be considered to be prejudicial to the peace, good order or security of the coastal State if in the territorial sea it engages in any of the following activities', and there follows a list including weapons practice; spying; propaganda; launching or taking on board aircraft or military devices; embarking or disembarking persons or goods contrary to customs, fiscal, immigration or sanitary regulations; wilful and serious pollution; fishing; research or survey activities; and interference with coastal communication or other facilities. The list is completed by two rather wider categories of activity:

(a) any threat or use of force against the sovereignty, territorial integrity or political independence of the coastal State, or in any other manner in violation of the principles of international law embodied in the Charter of the United Nations; ...

(1) any other activity not having a direct bearing on passage. (LOSC, art. 19(2)(a), (l))

The comparatively simple definition of innocence in the 1958 Convention was replaced by these detailed provisions in the 1982 Convention in the hope of producing a more objective definition, allowing coastal States less scope for interpretation and so less opportunity for abuse of their right to prevent non-innocent passage. The precise significance of the changes is, however, not clear from the text of article 19. On the one hand, the reference to *activities* suggests that the mere presence or passage of a ship could not, under the 1982 Convention, be characterised as prejudicial to the coastal State, unless the ship were to engage in some activity. This would, at least in theory, widen the scope of the right of innocent passage. On the other hand, the addition of a list of proscribed activities, if it is non-exhaustive (as the retention of the general 1958 formula as article 19(1) and the phrasing of article 19(2)(1) imply), would seem to have narrowed the right of innocent passage, if it has changed the law at all. Under article 19(2) commission of any of the listed acts – which include *any* activity not having a direct bearing on passage – will automatically render the passage non-innocent, whereas under the 1958 rules it would have been necessary to show that such activities actually prejudiced the peace, good order or security of the coastal State.

Furthermore the reference in paragraph (2)(a) of article 19 to threats of force is wide enough to encompass threats directed against States other than the coastal State, although the 1958 formula would not have rendered such threats incompatible with innocence, at least in the absence of some link, such as a mutual defence treaty, between the coastal State and the threatened State. This, too, would narrow the right of innocent passage. Otherwise the list of 'protected interests' appears to be little more than an express statement of the protected interests which were implicit in the 1958 obligation to conduct passage in accordance with 'these articles and other rules of international law' (TSC, art. 14(4)). The

1958 provision concerning fishing vessels has become subsumed within this general scheme, and has anyway lost much of its importance following the massive extension of fisheries jurisdiction since the time of the first Law of the Sea Conference.

Thus, while the 1982 definition of innocence adheres to the basic approach in the 1958 Territorial Sea Convention of defining innocence by reference to prejudice to coastal State interests, whether or not it involves any violation of coastal State law, it also introduces doubts as to whether or not non-innocence must turn on activities of the ship, and whether or not certain activities may automatically deprive passage of its innocence. Those doubts were addressed in a bilateral agreement of peculiar importance.

In 1989 the USA and the USSR (as it then was) signed a Uniform Interpretation of Norms of International Law Governing Innocent Passage.[27] Paragraph 3 of the Uniform Interpretation states

> 3. Article 19 of the Convention of 1982 sets out in paragraph 2 an exhaustive list of activities that would render passage not innocent. A ship passing through the territorial sea that does not engage in any of those activities is in innocent passage.

The Uniform Interpretation makes plain the understanding of the USA and the former USSR concerning the proper interpretation of innocence. In view of the importance of those two States as maritime powers, and the consonance of the interpretation with the UNCLOS text, the agreement is likely to prove very influential, although it cannot, of course, be binding upon States not party to it.

State practice quickly reflected the influence of the reformulation of innocent passage. Lists of activities incompatible with innocence, based on earlier drafts prepared by UNCLOS III, appeared in municipal laws as early as the Act Concerning the Territorial Sea and Other Maritime Zones enacted by the then South Yemen in 1977.[28] Other States have since incorporated the substance of the definition in the 1982 Convention into their laws: for example, the French decree of 1985,[29] the Romanian Act of 1990,[30] the remarkably comprehensive Belize legislation of 1992,[31] and the Jamaican Act of 1996.[32] In the few cases where States have adopted legislation at variance with article 19, other States

---

[27] 14 *LOSB* 12–13 (1989). The Uniform Interpretation was signed at Jackson Hole, Wyoming.

[28] *UN Leg. Ser.* B/19, p. 21, *ND VIII*, p. 57 (art. 6). The People's Republic of South Yemen and the Yemen Arab Republic merged in 1990, becoming the Republic of Yemen. See also, for example, the 1977 Korean legislation (art. 5): *UN Leg. Ser.* B/19, p. 95, and, as amended, 33 *LOSB* 45 (1997).

[29] Decree No. 85/185: see 6 *LOSB* 14 (1985).

[30] Act concerning the Legal Regime of the Internal Waters, the Territorial Sea and the Contiguous Zone of Romania, 7 August 1990 (art. 9): 19 *LOSB* 9 (1991).

[31] An Act to make provision with respect to the Territorial Sea, Internal Waters and the Exclusive Economic Zone of Belize, 24 January 1992 (Part IV): 21 *LOSB* 3 (1992).

[32] Maritime Areas Act, 1996 (s. 18): 34 *LOSB* 31 (1997).

have protested: the objections to the 1993 Iranian legislation[33] are an example.[34] These developments are rapidly transforming article 19 of the 1982 Convention into a rule of customary international law.

The right to deny and suspend passage

The territorial sea is subject to the sovereignty of the coastal State, and the only right which foreign ships enjoy there, apart from any right given by a specific treaty, is the right of innocent passage. In consequence, if the foreign ship ceases to be innocent or steps outside the scope of passage it may be excluded from the territorial sea. Accordingly, it is provided that 'the coastal State may take the necessary steps in its territorial sea to prevent passage which is not innocent' (TSC, art. 16(1); LOSC, art. 25(1)). There is no express provision setting out the right to exclude vessels not engaged in passage, but this right undoubtedly exists in customary international law,[35] and hovering vessels would almost certainly be deemed non-innocent, so providing a further justification for their exclusion. In addition, as we shall see below, ships that have stepped outside the right of innocent passage are subject to the full jurisdiction of the coastal State and may (subject to the usual exception for warships and other vessels enjoying sovereign immunity) be arrested by the coastal State for any violation of its laws.

It is a logical consequence of this right that States should have the right to suspend passage altogether in areas where the passage of *any* ship would prejudice its peace, good order or security. States have commonly exercised this right so as to exclude foreign ships from zones in front of naval dockyards, for example.[36] The right appeared in the Territorial Sea Convention in the following form:

> the coastal State may, without discrimination amongst foreign ships, suspend temporarily in specified areas of its territorial sea the innocent passage of foreign ships if such suspension is essential for the protection of its security. (TSC, art. 16(3))

The right has been interpreted liberally, as is often the case where rights protect security interests.[37] This liberality is reflected in the corresponding provision in

---

[33] An Act on the Marine Areas of the Islamic Republic of Iran in the Persian Gulf and the Oman Sea, 1993 (arts 5–9): 24 *LOSB* 10 (1993).

[34] See, e.g., the US protest of 11 January 1994, 25 *LOSB* 101 (1994), and the German (for the EU) démarche of 14 December 1994, 30 *LOSB* 60 (1996). And see the Iranian reply of 3 May 1995, 31 *LOSB* 37 (1996).

[35] For an example of its application by the UK, see *UKMIL 1991*, p. 633.

[36] For a typically broad enabling provision, see art. 17 of the Statute of Ukraine concerning the State frontier, 4 November 1991: 25 *LOSB* 85 (1994).

[37] And see the unusual inversion of this principle, in which the USA banned US ships entering *Cuban* waters and enforced the ban by action taken in the US territorial sea: 90 *AJIL* 448 (1996).

the Law of the Sea Convention, which adds to the quoted words: 'including weapons exercises' (LOSC, art. 25(3)). This inelegant formula underlines the fact that it is not only that which is necessary, but also that which is expedient for the protection of coastal security, which is seen as justifying the temporary suspension of passage.

States may not suspend, even temporarily, innocent passage through straits. We consider this point in chapter five.

Warships and ships carrying hazardous materials

The question of the right of warships to engage in innocent passage has long been one of the most controversial aspects of the law of the sea. The argument against their enjoying this right was succinctly put by Elihu Root, counsel for the United States in the *North Atlantic Coast Fisheries* arbitration in 1910:

> Warships may not pass without consent into this zone, because they threaten. Merchant ships may pass and repass because they do not threaten.[38]

Ironically, Root had previously been the Secretary of State of the country that, in recent times, has been one of the stoutest defenders of the right of innocent passage for warships. The source of the controversy is clear. The major naval powers (among which the United States could not be counted before the First World War) seek maximum freedom of manoeuvre for their warships in order to secure their interests, whereas other States seek to deny foreign warships close access to their shores precisely in order to protect their own security.

This stark conflict of interests has prevented the adoption of any clear rules on the matter. The 1930 Hague Conference text provided:

> As a general rule, a coastal State will not forbid the passage of foreign warships in its territorial sea and will not require a previous authorisation or notification.[39]

While the *Corfu Channel* case settled the right of warships to innocent passage through straits, it did not deal expressly with their rights in the territorial sea *simpliciter*. Accordingly, the question remained open at the 1958 Geneva conference. The International Law Commission, noting that the laws of many States required previous authorisation or notification, proposed that the Convention should allow such requirements. The proposed text was adopted by one of the conference's committees, being supported by States that sought a requirement of authorisation and by those that, though not seeking authorisation, did demand prior notification. In plenary session the latter group joined with those States seeking an unrestricted right of innocent passage for warships and secured the deletion of the authorisation requirement, leaving a text under which only prior

[38] North Atlantic Coast Fisheries Arbitration, *Proceedings*. Vol. II, p. 2007.
[39] League of Nations Doc. C. 351(b). M. 145(b). 1930. v, p. 217; Rosenne, *op. cit.* in footnote 5, p. 1418.

notification could be required. However, this resulted in those States demanding authorisation joining with those objecting even to prior notification in voting to reject the amended article, with the consequence that the Territorial Sea Convention contained no express provision on the matter.

Different conclusions are drawn from this background to the 1958 Convention. Some argue that since article 14(1), which reads:

> Subject to the provisions of these articles, ships of all States, whether coastal or not, shall enjoy the right of innocent passage through the territorial sea

appears under the rubric 'Rules applicable to all ships', both merchant and warships enjoy the right. It is also argued that because it is expressly provided in article 14 of the Territorial Sea Convention, which is concerned with innocent passage, that submarines must navigate on the surface (art. 14(6)) and because at present all submarines are warships, it follows that warships are intended to have a right of innocent passage. The same arguments can be made out in relation to the 1982 Convention (LOSC arts 17, 20).

On the other hand, others regarded the matter as unregulated by the 1958 Convention, and some States, such as Czechoslovakia, Hungary, Romania and the USSR, entered declarations accompanying their ratifications of the Territorial Sea Convention to this effect,[40] claiming the right to require prior authorisation for the passage of foreign warships. That view has persisted under the 1982 Convention. A sizeable minority of States – around forty – currently demands prior authorisation or notification of the passage of warships,[41] although the demands have been opposed by the major western naval powers[42] and in a significant number of cases those powers have countered the claims by the physical assertion of a right of passage without seeking authorisation from, or notifying, the coastal State.[43] One of the most important developments was the agreement between the USA and the former Soviet Union that, as they put it in the bilateral 1989 Uniform Interpretation of Norms of International Law Governing Innocent Passage,

---

[40] See the entry for the Territorial Sea Convention in the *Lists of Signatures, Ratifications, Accessions etc., of Multilateral Treaties in Respect of which the Secretary-General Performs Depositary Functions*, published by the United Nations and at http://www.un.org/Depts/Treaty.

[41] See the lists of such States in *UKMIL 1995*, pp. 677–81, and in Roach and Smith, *op. cit.* in 'Further reading', pp. 266–7. And see the lists of declarations made on signature or ratification of the 1982 Convention, in the UN paper, *The Law of the Sea. Declarations and statements with respect to the United Nations Convention on the Law of the Sea* (New York, United Nations), 1997, p. 84, and at http://www.un.org/Depts/los/los_decl.htm.

[42] See, e.g., the statements by Germany, 27 *LOSB* 7 (1995); Italy, 27 *LOSB* 5 (1995); the Netherlands, 32 *LOSB* 8 (1996); and the note concerning the UK position in *UKMIL 1995*, p. 682.

[43] Roach and Smith, *op. cit.* in 'Further reading', pp. 266–7, lists the dates of US protests and assertions of the right of innocent passage.

> All ships, including warships, regardless of cargo, armament or means of propulsion, enjoy the right of innocent passage through the territorial sea in accordance with international law, for which neither prior notification nor authorisation is required.[44]

That agreement, which marked a major shift from the earlier Soviet position, appears to have been part of a wider package of agreements, in accordance with which the US agreed to refrain from sending its warships into the Black Sea to assert (contrary to the wishes of the USSR) a right of innocent passage there.[45] Nonetheless, despite this accord between the two main naval powers[46] there is no sign that the adoption or renewal of laws requiring prior notification or authorisation of passage for warships has ceased, or even slowed down.[47]

Untidy as this result is, it appears to have the virtue of acceptability. State practice has contrived to avoid most direct confrontations over the question of rights of passage for warships. Where a coastal State requires no authorisation or notification, it seems that the naval powers give none. Where some requirement is laid down, low-level contacts between naval attachés and local navy officers, on a rather informal basis, seem to be favoured. Any such contact occurs against a general diplomatic background of consistent denials by 'naval' States of the legality of requirements of prior authorisation or notification for passage. In this way the principles of both sides remain intact because neither side is willing to force the issue.[48] Given this background of unenthusiastically enforced laws and of the determination to preserve rights of passage for warships, it is not wholly surprising that UNCLOS III decided to adopt the ambiguous 1958 'solution' and leave the matter open once more. Although the emergence of many new States since 1958 might well have produced a majority in favour of authorisation or notification, there seems to be a general sense that the question is, for all practical purposes, best left without a clear answer.

One point that is clear is that submarines passing through the territorial sea must navigate on the surface. This rule has been accepted for as long as submarines

---

[44] 14 *LOSB* 12–13 (1989), 24 *ILM* 1444 (1989), paragraph 2. Cf. the 1984 Rules for Navigation and Sojourn of Foreign Warships in the Territorial Waters (Territorial Sea) of the USSR and the Internal Waters and Ports of the USSR, 24 *ILM* 1715 (1985).

[45] The instrument setting out that part of the agreement was not reproduced in the *LOSB* or in *ILM*, but can be found in 6 *IJECL* 73–6 (1991). For an account of the Black Sea incidents, see Roach and Smith, *op. cit.* in 'Further reading', pp. 243–51.

[46] Cf. the abandonment of the requirement of prior authorisation by Poland: Act concerning the maritime areas of the Polish Republic, 1991, 21 *LOSB* 66 (1992). Similar steps have been taken by Bulgaria, Slovenia, Sweden and Turkey: see Roach and Smith, *op. cit.* in 'Further reading', pp. 276–8.

[47] See, e.g., the claims by China, Law on the Territorial Sea and the Contiguous Zone of 25 February 1992 (art. 6), 21 *LOSB* 24 (1992); the UAE, Federal Law No. 19 of 1993 (art. 5), 25 *LOSB* 94 (1994). And see the statements by, e.g., Malta, 25 *LOSB* 16 (1994); Yemen, 25 *LOSB* 8 (1994); Croatia, 27 *LOSB* 9 (1995); Algeria, 31 *LOSB* 7 (1996); Iran, 33 *LOSB* 88 (1997).

[48] Although, as was noted above, the USA has asserted its rights of passage.

have been used as naval vessels. Needless to say, this rule, though included in both the Territorial Sea Convention, as article 14(6), and the Law of the Sea Convention, as article 20, is not always observed. In the 1980s submerged foreign submarines were located and pursued on several occasions in Swedish and other territorial waters. Depth-charges were used against them after warnings to leave the area had been given, in exercise of the right to take necessary steps to prevent non-innocent passage. In October 1981 one such submarine ran aground near a Swedish naval base. It was Russian: despite the position taken by the USSR at the 1958 conference, it seems that no notification was given or authorisation sought before the submarine entered Swedish waters.[49]

A problem analogous to that of warships has arisen in the form of nuclear-powered ships and ships carrying hazardous cargoes. Some States regard these vessels as inherently threatening to their peace and good order, and consequently not entitled to a right of innocent passage. The early claims concerned nuclear-powered vessels, and were motivated by the voyages of the first nuclear-powered merchant ship, the United States Nuclear Ship *Savannah*. Spain, for example, enacted legislation in 1964 stating that the passage of nuclear ships through territorial waters was to be considered an exception to the right of innocent passage.[50] For their part the flag States of nuclear-powered vessels have been cautious in sending them through foreign waters. Before the *Savannah* visited the United Kingdom in 1964, for instance, an elaborate agreement regulating its passage through British territorial waters had been concluded by the British and US governments. Similar agreements were made with other States whose waters the *Savannah* entered.[51]

The fears of coastal States seem to have diminished, since the right of passage for nuclear-powered ships is recognised in the Law of the Sea Convention, article 23 of which requires them, and ships carrying nuclear or other inherently dangerous or noxious substances, to carry documents and observe internationally agreed precautionary measures (such as those included in the 1974 SOLAS Convention, discussed in chapter thirteen) when exercising their right to innocent passage. Coastal States are also specifically authorised to require such ships to confine their passage to any sea lanes that they might have designated in their territorial seas (LOSC, art. 22(2)).[52] Nonetheless, States have continued to enact laws and make statements claiming the right to demand prior notification or

---

[49] See M. Jacobsen, 'Sweden and the law of the sea' in T. Treves and L. Pineschi (eds), *The Law of the Sea: The European Union and its Member States* (The Hague, Nijhoff), 1997, p. 495 at pp. 499–500, 513–18.

[50] Act No. 25/64, 29 April 1964, art. 7, *UN Leg. Ser.* B/16, p. 45.

[51] *ND II*, p. 654. See also the agreements relating to the voyages of the German NS *Otto Hahn*: K. Hakapää, *Marine Pollution in International Law* (Helsinki, Suomalainen Tiedeakatemia), 1981, p. 165.

[52] See, e.g., Jamaica's Maritime Areas Act of 1996 (s. 17), 34 *LOSB* 29 (1997); and Lithuania's legislation on the territorial sea of 25 June 1992 (prefatory note), 25 *LOSB* 75 (1994).

authorisation for the passage of nuclear-powered ships.[53] Some States have asserted the right to require prior notification or authorisation for the passage of ships carrying inherently dangerous or noxious cargoes.[54] There have, however, been objections from several, mainly western, States to such limitations upon the right of innocent passage for certain classes of ships and their cargoes.[55] Perhaps because of the common interest that shipowner and coastal State alike will generally have in arranging a safe and expeditious passage for such vessels, these national claims to impose additional restrictions upon the innocent passage of 'dangerous' ships have not led to major difficulties in practice.[56]

Rights and duties of the coastal State

Coastal States' legislative jurisdiction

We turn next to the rights of the coastal State to make laws for its territorial sea and to enforce them. State practice and doctrine on the question of the extent of a coastal State's rights to enact legislation – its legislative, as opposed to its enforcement, jurisdiction – varied according to whether the territorial sea was regarded as a mere 'bundle of servitudes' or as a belt of maritime territory under the plenary jurisdiction of the State. The aim, in all cases, was to reconcile the right of innocent passage with the legitimate interests of coastal States in the enforcement of their laws in the territorial sea.

Those adhering to the former view considered that States had jurisdiction only in respect of certain specific matters, of which the most commonly accepted were navigation, customs, fishing, sanitation and security. The general criminal and civil laws of a State were not regarded as extending to foreign ships in the territorial sea. This view was close to that taken in respect of ships in port under the 'internal economy' doctrine, which we considered in chapter three, according to which only acts on foreign ships which had effect beyond the ship were subject to the coastal State's law. Indeed, it is arguable that the real concern of States

[53] See, e.g., the statements made by Egypt, 25 *LOSB* 12 (1994); Malaysia, 33 *LOSB* 8 (1997); Malta, 25 *LOSB* 15 (1994); Oman, 25 *LOSB* 17 (1994); Saudi Arabia, 31 *LOSB* 10 (1996); Yemen, 25 *LOSB* 38 (1994); and see the legislation of, e.g., Estonia (8 *IJMCL* 422 (1993)) and the UAE (25 *LOSB* 94 (1994)).

[54] See, e.g., the statements made by Egypt, 25 *LOSB* 13 (1994); Malta, 25 *LOSB* 16 (1994); Oman, 25 *LOSB* 17 (1994); and see the legislation of, e.g., Estonia (8 *IJMCL* 422 (1993)) and the UAE (25 *LOSB* 94 (1994)).

[55] See, e.g., the objections made by Germany, 27 *LOSB* 6 (1995); the Netherlands, 32 *LOSB* 8 (1996); the UK, *UKMIL 1995*, p. 683, and the USA, 31 *LOSB* 39 (1996). And see *UKMIL 1991*, p. 632, and 31 *LOSB* 39 (1996), and A. Nollkaemper, 'Laws of the sea: transboundary movement of hazardous wastes', 22 *Marine Pollution Bulletin* 428–31 (1991), on the application of this point to the Basel Convention on the Control of Transboundary Movements of Hazardous Wastes and their Disposal.

[56] The claim by Costa Rica to require prior authorisation for the passage of fishing vessels is less likely to be tolerated. It was protested by the EU: see 28 *LOSB* 31 (1995).

and jurists adopting this position was to limit the occasions for coastal State interference with foreign vessels, which is a question of enforcement, rather than legislative, jurisdiction. Nonetheless, the laws of several States incorporated limitations upon their actual application to foreign vessels, suggesting a limitation upon legislative jurisdiction proper: Cuba, Romania and Spain,[57] among others, incorporated such limitations in their laws. For such States, matters that belonged to the internal economy of foreign ships were for the flag State alone to deal with, although it should be noted that there is a curious ambivalence in this position. These States accepted the right to intervene in matters of internal economy when requested to do so by the authorities of the flag State, and it would therefore seem that they must have accepted that their laws *could* be applied in full to foreign ships when a request was made, again suggesting that the limitation sounded only in enforcement jurisdiction.

States claiming plenary jurisdiction, as a consequence of their claims to sovereignty over the territorial sea, allowed no such limitations upon coastal State legislative jurisdiction as a matter of law. The United Kingdom has held to this position throughout the nineteenth and twentieth centuries, giving it clear expression in the Territorial Waters Jurisdiction Act of 1878, which extended the ambit of all indictable offences (that is, offences triable by jury, rather than triable summarily before magistrates) to all vessels in the territorial sea. That Act met with considerable opposition within Parliament, and from other States and jurists, who regarded it as exceeding the limited jurisdiction allowed to coastal States under international law. But the British government held fast to its view that there was no limit on States' legislative jurisdiction in law, and the Act was passed. Thus, for example, during the dispute with the United States in the 1920s arising from the enforcement of American prohibition laws against British ships in the American territorial sea, the British government was careful not to challenge the ultimate right of the United States to legislate for those ships. However, this attitude was tempered in two ways. First, the consequences of the British view, which was also adopted by some other Sates, were not always insisted upon. For instance, although children born on foreign ships in British ports automatically acquired British nationality under British law, the Law Officers of the Crown advised, in an opinion of 10 November 1897, that this would not apply to a child born of foreign parents on a foreign ship merely passing through British waters. Similarly, during discussions arising from the case of the *Savarkar* in 1910 the Lord Chancellor stated that where a prisoner was carried on a foreign ship into British waters the British government would not be entitled, or at least would not choose, to demand that extradition procedures be complied with before the ship and its prisoner left British waters.[58] This latter example

[57] Cuba, Code of Social Defence, 1936, art. 7, *UN Leg. Ser.* B/2, p. 29; Romania, Penal Code, 1936, art. 7, *UN Leg. Ser.* B/2, p. 99; Spain, Code of Military Justice, 1945, art. 9(1), *UN Leg. Ser.* B/2, p. 108.

[58] Lord Loreburn's opinion of 10 September 1910 in *Law Officers' Opinions to the Foreign Office*, microfilm (Dobbs Ferry, N.Y., Oceana).

overlaps with the second concession, which is that, even where legislative jurisdiction does exist, its exercise or enforcement will be restrained where interests
of comity so demand. In these ways the more inconvenient implications of plenary
jurisdictional claims were largely avoided.

Attempts at the codification of the law applicable to the territorial sea have
failed to resolve this divergence in State practice, except perhaps by implication.
The 1930 Hague Draft included an article obliging foreign ships to 'comply with
the laws and regulations enacted in conformity with international usage by the
coastal State', and in particular those regarding 'navigation, pollution and the
resources of the territorial sea' (Hague Draft article 6). The presence of a list
might be taken to have implied that legislative jurisdiction was limited to specific purposes, but it will be recalled that the Hague Draft upheld the principle of
sovereignty over territorial waters, and this, coupled with the absence of any
specific limitations on legislative jurisdiction apart from the provisions prohibiting discriminatory laws (Hague Draft article 6) and the levying of charges upon
ships for merely passing through the territorial sea (Hague Draft article 7),
suggests that no such limitations were intended to be imposed as a matter of
international law. Again, considerations of international comity would nevertheless have engendered some restraint in the exercise of jurisdiction, especially in
respect of ships in innocent passage.

The International Law Commission adopted a similarly uncertain position.
Noting that no list of matters on which States might legislate could be exhaustive, it proposed an article providing:

> Foreign ships exercising the right of innocent passage shall comply with the laws
> and regulations enacted by the coastal State in conformity with these articles and
> other rules of international law and, in particular, with such laws and regulations
> relating to transport and navigation.

This provision was eventually adopted as article 17 of the Territorial Sea Convention, but without it being made clear in the process whether there were any
limitations *ratione materiae* on legislative jurisdiction implicit in the article.

The Law of the Sea Convention has modified the coastal State's legislative
competence. Article 21 allows the coastal State to adopt laws 'in respect of all or
any of the following' – the following topics being, broadly, navigation, protection of cables and pipelines, fisheries, pollution, scientific research, and customs,
fiscal, immigration and sanitary regulations. The coastal State must give due publicity to all such laws (LOSC, art. 21(3)). These laws may not affect the design,
construction, manning or equipment of foreign vessels unless they conform to
generally accepted international standards. This novel and significant limitation
upon the legislative competence that coastal States previously enjoyed in theory
is intended to balance coastal and flag State interests. This solution allows the
coastal State to legislate but removes the risk of divergent design, construction,
manning and equipment standards, to which ships cannot adjust during a voyage.
Foreign ships are bound to comply with coastal State laws enacted consistently

with the Convention, as they are with sea lanes designated by the coastal State (LOSC, arts 21(4), 22).[59] In addition, foreign ships must comply with 'all generally accepted international regulations relating to the prevention of collisions at sea', apparently whether or not the flag State or the coastal State is a party to the conventions containing those regulations (LOSC, art. 21(4)). The most important regulations are those in the 1972 Collisions Regulations Convention (see chapter thirteen).

Although the Law of the Sea Convention strongly suggests that coastal State legislative jurisdiction is limited, since the listed topics are not even presented as examples, as they had been in the 1930 and 1958 texts, there is still some doubt. As we shall see, the Law of the Sea Convention provides for the enforcement of general criminal jurisdiction in some circumstances, under article 27, and the existence of general enforcement jurisdiction clearly presupposes the existence of general legislative jurisdiction.

In the light of this uncertainty, it seems that the present legal position can best be put as follows. States may not legislate so as to hamper (TSC, art. 15(1); LOSC, art. 24(1)) or levy charges upon innocent passage (TSC, art. 18(1); LOSC, art. 26). They may charge for specific services rendered, such as rescue or pilotage services, but not in a manner that discriminates between ships of different foreign flags (TSC, art. 18(2); LOSC, art. 26(2)). Similarly, other legislation may not discriminate against ships of any State or against ships carrying cargoes to, from or on behalf of any State (LOSC, art. 24(1)(b)). They may legislate for such matters as navigation, pollution, fishing, etc. listed in article 21 of the Law of the Sea Convention and implicit in article 17 of the Territorial Sea Convention; and all ships, whether in innocent passage or not, must comply with such laws while in the territorial sea. It is also well established in State practice that ships not engaged in innocent passage, either because they are not passing, or are passing but are not innocent, are subject to all coastal State laws. Beyond this, it seems a legitimate inference from the principle of coastal State sovereignty over the territorial sea that States retain the right to extend any other legislation apart from that dealing with navigation and so on, to foreign ships in their waters, but that they will normally be expected, as a matter of comity, to refrain from doing so.

Coastal States' enforcement jurisdiction

The question of the extent of coastal States' rights of enforcement jurisdiction has many parallels with the question of their legislative jurisdiction, the two being commonly, though wrongly, regarded as covered by the single question of the extent of coastal State control over foreign vessels. Thus, the same basic division

---

[59] But coastal States must take account of the recommendations of the competent international organisation (the IMO) when prescribing sea lanes: LOSC, art. 22.

exists in the doctrine and State practice between States such as the United Kingdom, which has regarded itself for well over a century as entitled in strict law to enforce any of its laws against foreign vessels in its waters, and States which considered themselves entitled only to enforce specific laws on matters such as customs and fishing against foreign ships.

Both views admitted of exceptions. States claiming full enforcement jurisdiction were conscious that comity required restraint in its exercise. It was, for instance, mainly on the basis of comity and usage that the enforcement of the American liquor laws was challenged by other States, rather than on the basis of any legal limits upon American rights to enforce those laws. Generally, indeed, enforcement jurisdiction was in practice only exercised in limited circumstances: primarily when the offence disturbed the peace of the port or involved a stranger to the crew of the foreign ship; where coastal State intervention was requested by the flag State; in order to arrest a person sought by the coastal State; or where a specific law applying to the conduct of the ship in customs, navigation, fishing, etc. matters was breached. Ships in innocent passage were otherwise not the object of enforcement measures. These limitations, accepted as a matter of comity by Great Britain and similarly minded States, were regarded by States claiming only limited jurisdiction as defining as a matter of law the only occasions on which coastal States might intervene.

This doctrinal divergence was evident in the replies of governments to the Schedule of Points circulated before the 1930 Hague Conference. But it was also evident that the actual enforcement practice of States was more or less uniform, and that the difference between the British doctrine of plenary jurisdiction and the doctrine of limited jurisdiction espoused by Belgium, France, Norway and others was of theoretical rather than practical significance. Accordingly, it was not difficult to reach agreement on draft articles which provided that States must not exercise enforcement jurisdiction on board foreign passing vessels unless the peace of the coastal State was compromised, or the flag State requested coastal State intervention. In addition, the draft articles provided that States could enforce laws concerning navigation, pollution and fishing, even against passing vessels, and could enforce other laws where the ship was lying in the territorial sea or passing through it having left the internal waters of that State.[60] Otherwise, no enforcement jurisdiction existed although violations of coastal State laws in the territorial sea could, of course, be prosecuted if the violator subsequently appeared in the internal waters or land territory of the State concerned.

In the years between the 1930 and 1958 conferences State practice adhered broadly to the Hague formula, but without the underlying doctrinal dispute being resolved. The case of *The David,* before the US-Panama Claims Commission in 1933, shows this continuing uncertainty, with a majority of the arbitrators holding that innocent passage conferred, in the absence of any clear preponderance

---

[60] League of Nations Doc. C. 351(b). M. 145(b). 1930. v, pp. 214–15; Rosenne, *op. cit.* in footnote 5, pp. 1416–17.

of authority, no immunity from coastal State enforcement jurisdiction, and the minority holding that such immunity did exist.

The International Law Commission proposed draft articles on the matter, which followed the 1930 articles in excluding as a matter of law coastal State rights of enforcement except in certain circumstances where enforcement was permitted. The main exception was that States had a right to enforce laws of particular concern to the territorial sea as a consequence of the legislative juris- diction that they were given under what became article 17 of the Territorial Sea Convention. This was accepted by the 1958 conference, and there is no doubt that States may enforce these laws against foreign ships, whether passing or stationary, in the territorial sea.

Other laws could, according to the International Law Commission's proposal, be enforced on foreign ships only if their violation had disturbed the peace of the coastal State or local intervention was requested. But this was not accepted by the 1958 conference. The United States proposed an amendment with the spe- cific purpose of reasserting the full jurisdiction of the coastal State by replacing the mandatory requirement that States 'may not' exercise jurisdiction except in the stated circumstances with the exhortatory suggestion that they 'should not' do so. This was accepted, with the result that although States were expected, as a matter of comity, not to enforce their laws in respect of crimes committed on passing ships unless the consequences extended to the coastal State, or disturbed the peace of the country or the good order of the territorial sea, or coastal State intervention was requested by the flag State, or (an exception not then evident in State practice, but added by the conference) to suppress drug trafficking, they nonetheless retained the ultimate legal right to do so if they so wished (TSC, art. 19(1)).

Enforcement jurisdiction was, under the Territorial Sea Convention, excluded as a matter of international law in only one case: where the crime was committed before the ship entered the territorial sea and the ship is merely passing through the sea without entering internal waters (TSC, art. 19(5)). Coastal States were expressly given the right to take enforcement measures in respect of crimes com- mitted on ships passing through the territorial sea after leaving internal waters (TSC, art. 19(2)), and impliedly retained the right, which flows from their sover- eignty, to enforcement jurisdiction over ships not engaged in passage but lying in the territorial sea. Where it was proposed that jurisdiction be exercised, it was required that due regard be paid to the interests of navigation (TSC, art. 19(4)), and, if the action was to be taken under the 'peace of the port' provisions of article 19(1)(a) and (b), it was required that the flag State authorities be notified if the captain of the foreign ship so requested.

Civil jurisdiction was treated similarly in the 1958 Convention. Article 20(1) provided that passing ships should not be stopped or diverted in order to exer- cise civil jurisdiction against a person on board. Paragraph 2 of that article pro- hibited the arrest of ships for civil proceedings, except in relation to obligations or liabilities assumed by the ship itself in the course of, or for the purpose of, its voyage through the territorial sea; but here coastal State jurisdiction was expressly reserved in the case of ships lying in the territorial sea or passing through it after leaving internal waters.

The 1982 Law of the Sea Convention took over, almost *verbatim* and without any serious debate on their substance, the 1958 provisions. They became articles 27 and 28 of the 1982 Convention. The present position under treaty law is, therefore, that coastal State enforcement jurisdiction in the territorial sea is in principle complete, except for (a) jurisdiction over crimes committed before a ship, merely passing through the territorial sea, entered that sea; and (b) jurisdiction in civil matters to arrest a ship in connection with liabilities not incurred in connection with its voyage through the territorial sea. The Law of the Sea Convention requires that coastal State laws should not discriminate in form or in fact – that is, as a matter of legislative or enforcement jurisdiction – against ships of any State or ships carrying cargoes to, from or on behalf of any State (art. 24(1)(b)). In addition, rules of comity require that jurisdiction should not be exercised over passing ships except in the circumstances set out in article 19 of the Territorial Sea Convention and article 27 of the Law of the Sea Convention. The Law of the Sea Convention provisions on pollution (art. 220) have also resulted in minor limitations upon coastal State enforcement jurisdiction, as we shall see in chapter fifteen.

It should be noted that for the States, now numbering more than sixty, parties to the 1952 Brussels Conventions on Penal Jurisdiction in Matters of Collision, and on the Arrest of Sea-going Ships, this basic jurisdictional framework is overlain by more specific rules. The Convention on Penal Jurisdiction, for example, accords exclusive jurisdiction in collisions to the authorities of the flag State: unless a State party exercises its right to declare that the Convention will not apply to its territorial sea, the jurisdiction allowed to it under the Territorial Sea or Law of the Sea Conventions will clearly be limited by the 1952 Convention. On the other hand, the 1958/1982 rules on the exercise of civil jurisdiction appear to be more restrictive that those of the 1952 Convention on the Arrest of Sea-going Ships, which allow arrest for the purpose of any maritime claim, and not merely those claims arising from the voyage through the territorial sea.

The rules on coastal State jurisdiction outlined above apply to all foreign merchant vessels, but specific provision is made for ships operated by foreign governments and foreign warships, to take account of their right to sovereign immunity. Government ships operated for commercial purposes are treated like all other merchant ships (TSC, art. 21; such ships are included in the general jurisdictional provisions of Part II, section 3(B) of the Law of the Sea Convention). This follows the approach of the 1926 Brussels Convention on the Immunity of State-owned Ships, and current trends in the law of State immunity. Nonetheless, several East European States entered reservations when ratifying the Territorial Sea Convention, claiming full immunity for all government-operated ships, whether or not commercial. Those reservations will, however, be of no effect for States which have ratified the Law of the Sea Convention (see LOSC, arts 309, 311(1)).

Government ships operated for non-commercial purposes, such as warships, are not subject to the enforcement jurisdiction of the coastal State, because of the immunity that they enjoy under customary international law (TSC, art. 22(2); LOSC, art. 32). However, both warships and other government-operated non-commercial ships are subject to the legislative jurisdiction of the coastal State, it being only the enforcement of law against them which is precluded by reason of their immunity. Hence they are under an obligation to respect coastal State laws; and under customary law, and under article 31 of the Law of the Sea Convention, the flag State is responsible for loss to the coastal State arising from non-compliance by such ships with laws concerning passage through the territorial sea. Responsibility would also attach, under customary law, to the flag State for breach of any other laws that the ship was obliged to obey.

Warships which violate coastal State laws concerning passage through the territorial sea and which ignore requests for compliance may be required to leave the territorial sea (TSC, art. 23; LOSC, art. 30), and the coastal State may use any force necessary to compel them to do so. This will allow the upholding of laws on matters such as customs, navigation and pollution. Laws not 'concerning passage', such as the general criminal law of the coastal State, cannot be upheld in this way under the treaty provisions, the warship retaining its right to pursue its passage unmolested. Though the treaties are silent, and there is a dearth of State practice on the point, it seems reasonable to extend this right of exclusion to non-commercial government-operated ships, since their legal status can, for these purposes, be assimilated to that of warships.

It should also be recalled that some breaches of coastal State laws may involve a loss of innocence, depriving the ship of its right of innocent passage and entitling the coastal State to take any necessary steps to prevent what has become non-innocent passage through its territorial sea (TSC, art. 16(1); LOSC, art. 25(1)). In some cases this right to exclude the offending vessel from the territorial sea may be a convenient alternative to arresting it and instituting proceedings before municipal courts.[61] It also offers a remedy where the ship has not violated a coastal law, but has gone outside its right of innocent passage by threatening coastal interests in the manner described above. Finally, it may be noted in passing that States enjoy a general right of self-defence in international law: thus, if they are facing an imminent attack from foreign vessels in their territorial sea and have no other means of protection, they may use any necessary force against the vessels in order to defend themselves.

The regime concerning coastal State jurisdiction established by the 1958 and 1982 Conventions is, at least in broad terms, reflected in contemporary State practice. In recent years a number of States have adopted unusually detailed laws concerning their legislative and enforcement jurisdiction in the territorial

---

[61] See, e.g., the *Attican Unity* (Netherlands, 1986), 101 *ILR* 436.

sea, and most of these laws follow the terms of the Conventions closely.[62] There are, however, some exceptional cases in which States have asserted a rather wider jurisdiction than is envisaged by the Conventions: Romania, for example, adds to the list of occasions for the assertion of criminal jurisdiction cases where crimes are directed against the interests of Romania or a Romanian national or resident, or are committed by a Romanian national.[63]

Coastal States' duties

We have already discussed the most important duties incumbent upon coastal States in respect of their territorial seas. In the discussion concerning the breadth of the territorial sea it was noted that States must give notice of known navigational hazards. This duty exists both in customary law, as was recognised in the *Corfu Channel* case (1949) and under treaty (TSC, art. 15(2); LOSC, art. 24(2)). The coastal State must also provide basic navigational services such as lighthouses and rescue facilities.

States must not hamper innocent passage (TSC, art. 15(1); LOSC, art. 24(1). This rule has been seen in the context of limitations upon coastal State jurisdiction, but it is of general application and would, for example, operate so as to prevent unreasonable interference with innocent passage by the establishment of installations in the territorial sea.

In addition to these specific duties States are, of course, subject to all the other rules of international law that may apply to their dealings with the territorial sea. For example, disputes over the delimitation of maritime boundaries must be settled by peaceful means, and no unnecessary force must be used in enforcing coastal State rights against foreign ships in the territorial sea. These general rules apply equally to other States concerned.

Further reading

P. Allott, 'Language, method and the nature of international law', 45 *BYIL* 79–135 (1971).

W. E. Butler, 'Innocent passage and the 1982 Convention: the influence of Soviet law and policy', 81 *AJIL* 331–47 (1987).

C. C. Emanuelli, 'La pollution maritime et la notion de passage inoffensif', 11 *Canadian Yearbook of International Law* 13–36 (1973).

P. T. Fenn, 'Origins of the theory of territorial waters', 20 *AJIL* 465–82 (1926).

[62] See, e.g., the Belize law of 24 January 1992 (Part VI), 21 *LOSB* 3 (1992); Poland, Act concerning the Maritime Areas of the Polish Republic and the Marine Administration, 21 March 1991 (arts 12, 13), 21 *LOSB* 66 (1992).

[63] Act concerning the Legal Regime of the Internal Waters, the Territorial Sea and the Contiguous Zone of Romania, 7 August 1990 (art. 17), 19 *LOSB* 9 (1991). Cf. the Bulgarian Act of 8 July 1987 governing the Ocean Space of the People's Republic of Bulgaria (art. 32), 13 *LOSB* 8 (1989).

E. Franckx, 'The USSR position on the issue of innocent passage of warships through foreign territorial waters', 18 *JMLC* 33–65 (1987).

——, 'Innocent passage of warships: recent developments in US-Soviet relations', 14 *Marine Policy* 484–90 (1990).

T. W. Fulton, *Sovereignty of the Seas. An Historical Account of the Claims of England to the Dominion of the British Seas* (Edinburgh, Blackwood), 1911.

P. C. Jessup, *The Law of Territorial Waters and Maritime Jurisdiction* (New York, Jennings), 1927.

H. S. K. Kent, 'Historical origins of the three-mile limit' 48 *AJIL* 537–53 (1954).

L. T. Lee, 'Jurisdiction over foreign merchant ships in the territorial sea. An analysis of the Geneva Convention on the Law of the Sea', 55 *AJIL* 77–96 (1961).

L. Lucchini and M. Voelckel, *Droit de la Mer*, Vol. 2 (Paris, Pedone), 1996, pp. 202–303.

A. Manin, 'L'échouement du Whisky 137 dans les eaux suédoises', 27 *AFDI* 689–710 (1981).

W. E. Masterson, *Jurisdiction in Marginal Seas* (New York, Macmillan), 1929.

F. Ngantcha, *The Right of Innocent Passage and the Evolution of the Law of the Sea* (London, Pinter), 1990.

D. P. O'Connell, 'The juridical status of the territorial sea', 45 *BYIL* 303–83 (1971).

J. K. Oudendijk, *Status and Extent of Adjacent Waters* (Leyden, Sijthoff), 1970.

J. A. Roach and R. W. Smith, *United States Responses to Excessive Maritime Claims* (The Hague, Nijhoff), 2nd edn, 1996.

D. R. Rothwell, 'Coastal State sovereignty and innocent passage: the voyage of the *Lusitania Expresso*', 16 *Marine Policy* 427–37 (1992).

S. A. Swartztrauber, *The Three-Mile Limit of Territorial Seas* (Annapolis, Naval Institute Press), 1972.

T. Treves, 'Navigation', chapter 17 of R.-J. Dupuy and D. Vignes, *A Handbook of the New Law of the Sea*, Vol. 2 (Dordrecht, Nijhoff), 1991.

United Nations, *The Law of the Sea. National Legislation on the Territorial Sea, the Right of Innocent Passage and the Contiguous Zone* (New York, United Nations), 1995.

5

Straits

Definition

'Strait' is not a term of art, and it is not defined in any of the conventions produced by the United Nations Conferences on the Law of the Sea. It bears its ordinary meaning, describing a narrow natural passage or arm of water connecting two larger bodies of water. It is the legal status of the waters constituting the strait and their use by international shipping, rather than any definition of 'strait' as such, that determines the rights of coastal and flag States. Because the legal regime of straits was substantially revised in the Law of the Sea Convention, and because a number of important 'straits States' such as Turkey (in relation to the Dardanelles and the Bosphorus) and Iran (in relation to the Strait of Hormuz) are not yet parties to the 1982 Convention, the pre-LOSC rules will be first considered separately.

The regime under customary law and the Territorial Sea Convention

Under pre-1958 customary international law, and indeed under the 1958 Territorial Sea Convention, the rights of passage through straits depended primarily upon whether the waters of the strait were high seas or territorial sea. If they were high seas, then foreign ships enjoyed the same freedom of navigation, free from coastal jurisdiction or control, through the strait as they enjoyed in any other part of the high seas. If, on the other hand, the strait was comprised of territorial waters of one or more States, then foreign ships enjoyed the right of innocent passage through the strait. That position was reflected in article 16(4) of the 1958 Territorial Sea Convention. In principle, as has been seen in chapter four, the right of innocent passage can be suspended temporarily by the coastal State if that is essential for the protection of its security. But were passage to be suspended in straits connecting areas of the high seas, such as the Straits of Gibraltar or Malacca, the freedom of navigation which exists on the high seas would be undermined, as Vattel had pointed out in the eighteenth century. Accordingly, a rule of customary international law emerged providing that innocent passage could not be suspended in straits used for international navigation between one part of the high seas and another. This rule was recognised by the International Court of Justice in the *Corfu Channel* case in 1949, and was subsequently incorporated in article 16(4) of the Territorial Sea Convention, which provides:

> There shall be no suspension of the innocent passage of foreign ships through straits which are used for international navigation between one part of the high seas and another part of the high seas or the territorial sea of a foreign State.

The characterisation of a strait as one 'used for international navigation' was considered in the *Corfu Channel* case. As we saw in the previous chapter, the United Kingdom asserted its right of passage through international straits by sending a naval force through the Corfu Channel, without complying with Albanian regulations requiring prior authorisation. Albania claimed that its sovereignty had been violated by the passage. It argued that the channel was not a strait used for international navigation, because it was only an alternative route between the Adriatic and the Aegean Seas and it was used almost exclusively by local traffic. This argument was rejected by the Court, which held that 'the decisive criterion is rather its geographical situation as connecting two parts of the high seas and the fact of its being used for international navigation', and noted its 'special importance to Greece by reason of the traffic to and from the port of Corfu'. The Channel's secondary importance as a sea route and the actual volume of traffic through the Channel (and, it seems, the precise legal status of the waters), were irrelevant to the right of passage through it.

As far as the rights of the coastal State and of third States in the Corfu Channel were concerned, the International Court held that, although the high degree of tension in Greco-Albanian relations (Greece considered itself technically at war with Albania) would have justified the regulation of the passage of warships for security reasons, passage through the strait could not actually be prohibited. Thus, either of the coastal States could, for example, have limited the number of foreign ships traversing its waters within the strait at any one time, or have prohibited passage during hours of darkness, had such measures been necessary for the protection of its security in the prevailing circumstances. But neither State was entitled to suspend passage through the strait completely, or to deny the existence of the right of passage by subjecting it to a requirement of special authorisation.[1]

The *Corfu Channel* case itself established that, as a matter of customary law, warships (and hence, *a fortiori*, merchant ships) had a right of innocent passage through international straits which could not be suspended by the coastal State. Some jurists[2] and, indeed, delegates of some of the maritime powers to UNCLOS

---

[1] [1949] *ICJ Rep.* 4, at 28–9.

[2] See, e.g., *O'Connell, op. cit.* in 'Further reading', Vol. I, p. 327; S. N. Nandan and D. H. Anderson, 'Straits used for international navigation: A commentary on Part III of the United Nations Convention on the Law of the Sea 1982', 60 *BYIL* 159–204 (1989).

III argued that under customary law there was through international straits a rather wider right of passage, amounting to a freedom of navigation unlimited by any criterion of 'innocence' and, unlike innocent passage (which extends only to ships), including a right of overflight for foreign aircraft. This argument, which is controversial and contains an element of hindsight, is better examined in detail later, after we have outlined the LOSC regime.

We have noted that article 16(4) of the Territorial Sea Convention reflected the position generally understood to obtain in customary international law. In one respect, however, the precise wording of article 16(4) went beyond customary law as it stood in 1958. While the nature of the right of passage followed customary law, the definition of straits within which that right subsists did not. The article refers to:

> straits which are used for international navigation between one part of the high seas and another part of the high seas or the territorial sea of a foreign State.

In rejecting the ILC proposal that only straits '*normally* used for international navigation' should be included, the 1958 conference was simply reflecting the decision in the *Corfu Channel* case; but in extending the article to include not only straits connecting two areas of the high seas, as the ILC had proposed, but also straits connecting the high seas with the territorial sea of another State, the conference was moving beyond mere codification.

It is clear that article 16(4) was primarily intended to secure the right of access to the Israeli port of Eilat, situated at the head of the Gulf of Aqaba, through the Straits of Tiran, which were then under Arab control. It did not achieve this aim because the Arab States, reluctant to accept the article, did not sign the Territorial Sea Convention. Nonetheless, western States have declared on several occasions, in the face of an actual or threatened closure of the Straits of Tiran to Israeli shipping, that those Straits (and, indeed, the waters of the Gulf of Aqaba, the whole of which consists of territorial waters of the littoral States) constitute an international waterway in which no State has the right to prevent free and innocent passage. This view implies that customary law includes a right of passage through those straits at least as wide as that in article 16(4); and support for this can be drawn from the unanimous Resolution 242 of the UN Security Council in 1967 affirming the necessity for guaranteeing freedom of navigation through international waterways in the Middle East. Nonetheless, the status of the customary law right of passage through straits leading to the territorial sea of a third State remains controversial.

The regime under the Law of the Sea Convention

In the years between UNCLOS I and the close of UNCLOS III many States made claims to wider coastal jurisdiction, notably in the form of extended territorial seas, economic zones and the enclosure of archipelagic waters. While these claims were not necessarily incompatible with the preservation of rights of passage through international straits, they signalled a growing reluctance to regard passing foreign ships as beyond the jurisdictional reach of coastal States whose security, environmental or economic interests those ships might adversely affect. The major maritime States, on the other hand, considered that their economic well-being and security – particularly in relation to the deployment, and pursuit, of submarines, some of which now carried strategic nuclear missiles – depended upon continuing guarantees of passage through international straits such as Dover, Gibraltar, Hormuz, Bab el Mandeb and Malacca. A compromise was reached at UNCLOS III, based on the creation of two new legal rights of passage: 'transit passage' through international straits, which is discussed below, and 'archipelagic sea lanes passage' through archipelagic waters (and through international straits within archipelagic waters), which is discussed in chapter six. Both new rights allow less coastal State control over passing vessels than does innocent passage, but both also fall far short of granting the same freedom of navigation as would exist if the waters of the straits constituted high seas.

The regime of transit passage applies to 'straits which are used for international navigation between one part of the high seas or an exclusive economic zone and another part of the high seas or an exclusive economic zone' (LOSC, art. 37). Three categories of strait are excluded from this definition. The first is the category of straits through which there is a high-seas route, or a route through an exclusive economic zone, of similar convenience with respect to its navigational and hydrographical characteristics (LOSC, art. 36: the so-called Florida Strait between the USA and Cuba would be an example). The second category is that of straits formed by an island bordering the strait and its mainland, where a route of similar navigational and hydrographic convenience exists through the exclusive economic zone or high seas seaward of the island (LOSC, art. 38(1): the Straits of Messina between Italy and Sicily, and the Pemba Channel off Tanzania are examples).[3] The third category is that of straits connecting an area of the high seas or an exclusive economic zone with the territorial sea of a third State, as in the Straits of Tiran (LOSC, art. 45).

In the first of these exceptional cases, which can apply only in straits more than twenty-four miles wide, there exists freedom of navigation through the economic zone or high-seas route, and the right of innocent passage through the bands of territorial seas which lie on either side of it. In the second and third cases, there exists a non-suspendable right of innocent passage under the 1982 Convention. In all three cases, States may regulate innocent passage through the parts of the strait falling within their territorial seas in the same way that they

---

[3] It is not wholly clear whether the Corfu Channel, part of which lies between the Greek island of Corfu and Albania (and thus not between an island and its mainland), falls into this category.

regulate innocent passage through other parts of their territorial seas.[4] In all other straits used for international navigation, unless they are the subject of some special treaty (such as the Montreux Convention, which regulates the Dardanelles and Bosphorus), Part Three of the Law of the Sea Convention establishes a right of transit passage.

In some cases there may be real doubt as to whether or not a strait is a 'transit passage' strait. The Northwest Passage through the Canadian archipelago, for example, is considered by Canada to fall within its internal waters (Canada having drawn straight baselines around its Arctic archipelago in 1985) and to be subject to no rights of passage whatever, whereas the United States considers the Passage to be subject to a right of transit passage. That dispute was circumvented in 1988 by means of the bilateral Agreement on Arctic Co-operation which obliges the United States to obtain Canadian consent for voyages of US ice-breakers through the Passage while expressly preserving the views and rights of both parties on the question.[5] Somewhat similar doubts arise in relation to the Northeast Passage north of Russia. Here, apart from some of the individual straits making up the Passage being enclosed by straight baselines drawn in 1985, there are doubts as to whether the straits can be said to be 'used for international navigation', and thus attract a right of transit passage, in the light of the handful of sailings through the (often ice-bound) straits that have actually taken place.

It has been suggested that the LOSC scheme for passage through straits, as described above, is subject to two modifications. First, Iraq[6] and Saudi Arabia[7] take the view that the transit passage regime also applies to passage between islands situated near to international straits if the IMO has designated shipping lanes lying near such islands (as it has in the Straits of Hormuz). This may often involve no more than a clarification of where the international strait is considered to lie; but if there were a case where ships are directed by an IMO traffic scheme away from a high-seas or EEZ route through a strait and into a coastal State's territorial sea,[8] the nature of the right of passage might appear to be put in question. Secondly, Greece has stated that where the presence of many islands creates

---

[4] See, e.g., the 1985 Italian prohibition on ships of over 50,000 grt carrying oil or other noxious cargoes through the Straits of Messina, and the consequent exchange of diplomatic notes with the USA: J. A. Roach and R. W. Smith, *United States Responses to Excessive Maritime Claims* (The Hague, Nijhoff), 2nd edn, 1996, pp. 323–7. See further chapter four and 10 *IJMCL* 272–5 (1995).

[5] See Roach and Smith, *op. cit.* in footnote 4, pp. 339–53, at 348.

[6] 5 *LOSB* 15 (1985).

[7] 31 *LOSB* 10 (1996).

[8] It must surely be the case, however, that the right of transit passage extends not only to areas where the shores are less than twenty-four miles apart, but also to the approaches to the strait: see J. R. B. Langdon, 'The extent of transit passage: some practical anomalies', 14 *Marine Policy* 130–6 (1990); and cf. Roach and Smith, *op. cit.* in footnote 4, pp. 286–7.

a multiplicity of potential straits (as, for example, in the Aegean), the coastal State may designate those in which the right of transit passage is to exist[9] – much as it may designate passages through archipelagic waters. Turkey has objected to this interpretation of the Convention, even though it is not a party to the Convention.[10]

Transit passage is the exercise of freedom of navigation and overflight solely for the continuous and expeditious transit of the strait between one area of high seas or economic zone and another, or in order to enter or leave a State bordering the strait (LOSC, art. 38(2)). While there is no criterion of 'innocence' to be satisfied, ships and aircraft exercising this right are bound to refrain from the threat or use of force, whether directed against States bordering the straits or in any other manner that violates the principles of international law embodied in the UN Charter (LOSC, art. 39(1)(b); UN Charter, art. 2(4)). This is, however, not a *condition* of the right of transit passage but rather an obligation ancillary to it.[11] Moreover, there is an obligation to refrain from any activities other than those incidental to their normal modes of continuous and expeditious transit unless rendered necessary by *force majeure* or distress (LOSC, art. 39(1)(c)). It is provided that any activity that is not an exercise of the right of transit passage remains subject to the 'other applicable provisions' of the Convention (LOSC, art. 38(3)). Accordingly, any activity threatening a coastal State would bring the ship or aircraft under the general regime of innocent passage, in which case passage could be denied for want of innocence. In the absence of such 'activity', the only remedy for any threat of force – for example, a threat which may be implicit in the mere fact of the passage of a large number of warships – would appear to be to pursue the matter as a breach of international law through diplomatic channels and dispute settlement procedures: there is no right to impede the passage. Similarly, transit passage cannot be suspended for security or any other reasons (LOSC, art. 44). Of course, in extreme cases coastal State action might be justifiable on the basis of the right of self-defence or the somewhat wider rights to take counter-measures apparently admitted by the International Court in the *Nicaragua* case.[12]

While in transit ships must comply with generally accepted international regulations, procedures and practices for safety at sea and for the prevention of pollution from ships (LOSC, art. 39(2)). Thus standards in, for example, SOLAS

[9] 5 *LOSB* 13 (1985), and 29 *LOSB* 7 (1995). Cf. the statement by Yugoslavia, 25 *LOSB* 20 (1994), and the exchanges between the USA and Yugoslavia in Roach and Smith, *op. cit.* in footnote 4, pp. 291–2.

[10] A/CONF.62/WS/26, May 1982, and 30 *LOSB* 9 (1996).

[11] Cf. the Netherlands' Declaration made upon ratification of the 1982 Convention, which asserts that '[c]onsiderations with respect to domestic security and public order shall not affect navigation in straits used for international navigation': 32 *LOSB* 9 (1996).

[12] [1986] *ICJ Rep.* 14, at 102–4, 110–11. See further J. Hargrove, 'The *Nicaragua* judgment and the future of the law of force and self-defence', 81 *AJIL* 135–43 (1987).

conventions and the IMO pollution conventions would be applicable to ships in the strait even if their flag States were not parties to those conventions. Aircraft, too, must comply with international standards whilst exercising their right of overflight (LOSC, art. 39(3)).[13] In this way coastal State interests can be protected without imposing unreasonable burdens on passing ships and aircraft, for although the coastal State may legislate for passing craft in these matters, it may only apply internationally agreed standards in its legislation (LOSC, art. 42(1)). This precludes the exposure of merchant ships to a mass of differing, and possibly inconsistent, regulations as they sail around the world. In the same way coastal States may prescribe sea lanes and traffic separation schemes in the strait, but these must first have been adopted by the competent international organisation – that is, the IMO (LOSC, art. 41). The duty to comply with international safety and pollution standards is independent of coastal legislation: the advantage of implementing them in such legislation is that they then become directly enforceable by the coastal State authorities as a matter of municipal law, whereas the international law duty of compliance would allow only an international claim through diplomatic channels for breach of the treaty obligation, and the international conventions themselves leave enforcement in the hands of the flag State. There is, in addition, a specific duty to refrain from research and survey activities during passage unless the prior authorisation of the States bordering the strait is obtained – even, it seems, if the passage is entirely within the waters of only one of them (LOSC, art. 40).

Apart from the right to implement international safety and pollution standards, coastal States may legislate for passing vessels only in respect of fishing and the taking on board or putting overboard for any commodity, currency or person in violation of local customs, fiscal, immigration or sanitary regulations (LOSC, art. 42(1)). No international standards are imposed here but these laws, like all others, must not be applied in a manner that discriminates in form or in fact between foreign ships or denies, hampers or impairs their right of transit passage (LOSC, art. 42(2)).[14] Laws on other matters may not be extended to passing ships. In this respect, coastal State jurisdiction over ships in transit passage is considerably narrower than is jurisdiction over ships in innocent passage (on which, see chapter four above).

So far, we have been concerned with the right to extend the geographical ambit of coastal laws to vessels in transit passage – that is, with legislative jurisdiction. The 1982 Convention is silent on the question of the enforcement of these laws against such ships. Accordingly the general territorial sea rules apply (LOSC, art. 34), under which enforcement *should*, as was seen in chapter four, only be exercised where the good order of the territorial sea or coastal State is

---

[13] See the exchanges between the USA and Spain concerning air traffic regulations applicable in the Strait of Gibraltar for a discussion of the scope of coastal States' regulatory rights: Roach and Smith, *op. cit.* in footnote 4, pp. 301–9.

[14] See further, on the obligation of non-discrimination, the remarks on the WTO/GATT at p. 113 below.

disturbed or competent authorities of the flag State request assistance. On the other hand, the express provision for the exercise of enforcement jurisdiction in case of pollution causing or threatening major pollution (LOSC, art. 233) may be evidence of a general understanding that exercises of enforcement jurisdiction against ships in transit passage *must* be confined to this case, notwithstanding the wider coastal State powers enjoyed under the territorial sea regime. Were this latter interpretation to prove correct, coastal State laws could in general be enforced in respect of the acts of foreign ships in transit passage only when the ships put into the State's ports.[15] There is, however, a general duty to comply with all laws made within the legislative competence allowed under the Convention to straits States (LOSC, art. 42(3)).[16]

The rights of transit passage described above extend to all ships and aircraft, both military and commercial. As far as submarines are concerned, their apparently common practice of transiting some international straits while submerged seems to be recognised in the requirement that passing vessels engage only in activities 'incident to their *normal mode* of continuous and expeditious transit' (LOSC, art. 39(1)(c); emphasis added). This, at least, is the interpretation adopted by the maritime States, and it is consistent with the *travaux préparatoires* of UNCLOS III. It underlines the importance of transit passage for submarines, which must normally pass through the territorial sea on the surface. Similarly, transit passage is of great importance to military aircraft, which have no right of innocent passage over the territorial sea and which are not covered by the air services agreements that typically permit the overflight of States' territories by scheduled civil aircraft.

A difficult question arose in the case concerning *Passage through the Great Belt*. Denmark began to build a road bridge across the Great Belt, which lies between two Danish islands and is the principal strait connecting the Baltic with the North Sea. The planned height of the bridge permitted all existing ships, and most offshore drilling platforms, to pass underneath it. The very largest such platforms, which can and do make trans-oceanic voyages under their own power, could not pass under the bridge, and some such platforms were built in Finnish shipyards. In the case brought by Finland against Denmark in 1991, the International Court was called upon to decide whether such platforms enjoyed the same rights of passage as do ships, and whether that right could be unilaterally

---

[15] The ambiguity concerning the scope of strait States' enforcement jurisdiction is not resolved in the declaration made by the States bordering the straits of Malacca and Singapore in 1982: see M. H. Nordquist, S. Rosenne and A. Yankov, *UN Convention on the Law of the Sea 1982: A Commentary*, vol. IV (Dordrecht, Nijhoff), 1991, pp. 388–9.

[16] Although here again, the obligation appears not to be a *condition* of transit passage, so that a ship violating a coastal State law does not *ipso facto* cease to be in the course of transit passage. Were it otherwise such ships would always be exposed to the full competence of the coastal State to enforce its laws against ships in innocent passage, which would deprive transit passage of one of the key characteristics that it was intended to have.

curtailed by States building structures such as the Great Belt bridge across international straits. The case was, however, withdrawn from the Court before a decision was given on the merits, Denmark and Finland having reached a compromise.[17] The bridge has now been built and provides a direct road link between Copenhagen and the Danish mainland (Jutland).

The LOSC regime and customary law

Since the end of UNCLOS III, it has been argued by some of the major maritime States, notably the United States and the United Kingdom,[18] that the rights of transit passage given by the Convention are part of customary international law. Several arguments have been advanced in support of this view.[19]

First, it is argued that a right of passage similar to transit passage existed in customary law before the Convention was drawn up. Undoubtedly, the ships of the main maritime States have sailed, and continue to sail, through major straits in what was, and is, intended to be an exercise of a right substantially correspond-ing to the now conventional right of transit passage.[20] Overflight and submerged passage, both of which fall outside the scope of innocent passage, have long taken place in straits such as Gibraltar, apparently without the prior consent or sub-sequent protests of the littoral States. In addition to the practice of the physical exercise of passage through certain straits, treaty practice lends some support to this contention. For example, article 23 of the 1923 Treaty of Lausanne *recog-nises* (rather than establishes) the 'principle of freedom and transit and naviga-tion by sea and by air' in the Dardanelles and the Bosphorus, and the freedom of transit by sea is reaffirmed in the 1936 Montreux Convention. Similarly, the 1979 Treaty of Peace between Egypt and Israel refers to the right of all nations

---

[17] See M. Koskenniemi, Note, 32 *ILM* 101–5 (1993), and 'L'affaire du passage par le Grand-Belt', 38 *AFDI* 905–47 (1992). The alternative route, through the Sound, was too shallow for passage by the affected drilling platforms and drill ships.

[18] See the statement of the President on United States Ocean Policy, 10 March 1983, 22 *ILM* 464 (1983), and the US Diplomatic Note to Algeria (as protecting power for Iran), 12 July 1984, 78 *AJIL* 884 (1984). And see the British *Parliamentary Debates* (Hansard), House of Lords, Vol. 484, col. 382, 5 February 1987, reprinted in 10 *LOSB* 11 (1987).

[19] See, for instance, Mahmoudi, *op. cit.* in 'Further reading', and the various papers in R. B. Krueger and S. A. Riesenfeld (eds), *The Developing Order of the Oceans* (Honolulu, Law of the Sea Institute), 1985, pp. 661–730, and in J. M. Van Dyke (ed.), *Consensus and Confrontation: The United States and the Law of the Sea Convention* (Honolulu, Law of the Sea Institute), 1985, pp. 292–301. Not all contributors took the same view.

[20] See, for example, the practice of the USA: Roach and Smith, *op. cit.* in footnote 4, pp. 284–365. Note, too, the French and Italian measures prohibiting passage through the Bouches de Bonifacio to ships carrying dangerous cargoes, which apply only to French and Italian ships: Roach and Smith, *op. cit.*, pp. 299–300 and 25 *LOSB* 65, 66 (1994). Passage by foreign flag ships is not prohibited under the measures.

to 'unimpeded and non-suspendable freedom of navigation and overflight' through the Strait of Tiran and Gulf of Aqaba.[21]

While it is true that the 1958 Territorial Sea Convention (art. 16(4)) provided only for a non-suspendable right of innocent passage for ships through straits, that provision must be viewed in its historical context. In the 1950s, when the ILC and UNCLOS I were preparing the text of what became article 16(4), and when three-mile territorial sea claims were (even if far from undisputed) still the norm, most major international straits still had a high-seas corridor down the middle. Moreover, neither the ILC nor UNCLOS I was given the task of pre-scribing rules for aerial navigation, and the omission of any reference to rights of overflight is therefore not surprising. Furthermore, submarines were at that time perceived as warships fulfilling their classic World War Two role, as means of launching stealthy attacks on foreign ships. They had not yet acquired their role as platforms for the 'nuclear deterrent'. There was, therefore, no good and 'peaceful' military reason for them to travel submerged. The absence of mention of any right of submerged passage is also not surprising. And since it was, and is, indisputable that vessels in the territorial sea (whether or not in a strait) are, within limits, subject to the jurisdiction of the coastal State, and that the coastal State has the right of self-defence, the requirement that the right of passage through straits must not prejudice the peace, good order or security of the coastal State might have appeared reasonable enough. It would, therefore, be unwise to read too much into the omission from the 1958 Convention of a separate right of freedom of navigation through international straits.

On the other hand, it must be said that several littoral States, both inside UNCLOS III and outside it in declarations such as the 1971 statement of Indo-nesia, Malaysia and Singapore on the Malacca Straits,[22] held to the view that the only right of passage through international straits was that of non-suspendable innocent passage. That view was opposed by several of the major maritime States, notably the USA.[23] This divergence of views was partly explicable on the basis that some maritime States had refused to recognise the extension by littoral States of their territorial waters so as to cover passages that were formerly high seas. The United States, for example, acted on the basis that a high-seas passage

---

[21] See further R. Lapidoth, 'The Strait of Tiran the Gulf of Aqaba and the 1979 Treaty of Peace between Egypt and Israel', 77 *AJIL* 84–108 (1983); M. Elbareidi, 'The Egyptian-Israeli Peace Treaty and access to the Gulf of Aqaba: a new legal regime', 76 *AJIL* 532–54 (1982). Note, too, the statements by Egypt and Israel that the provisions of the 1979 Peace Treaty concerning passage through the Strait of Tiran and Gulf of Aqaba come within the framework of the general regime of waters forming straits referred to in LOSC Part III: 25 *LOSB* 13 (Egypt) and 46 (Israel) (1994).

[22] *ND IV*, p. 330.

[23] Although many of the delegates at UNCLOS III, including those of the United States, considered transit passage to be a new concept in international law: see *DUSPIL 1974*, 374–52; *DUSPIL 1975*, 421–2.

existed through the Strait of Gibraltar, which narrows to a width of only eight miles, despite the historic six-mile claim by Spain and the extension of Moroccan territorial waters from three to twelve miles in 1973. Neither claim was recognised by the United States, which at that time adhered to the old three-mile rule. There was, nonetheless, a real difference of opinion as to the juridical nature and extent of the right of passage through international straits.

In relation to this core of disagreement over the precise legal status of international straits and rights of passage through them, the balance of juristic opinion seemed to favour the conclusion that customary law prior to UNCLOS III accorded only a non-suspendable right of innocent passage through them. It is possible, however, that while this opinion was correct as regards international straits in general, a good case could have been made out for the existence of a wider right of freedom of navigation in relation to certain key international straits, such as the Straits of Dover, Gibraltar and Hormuz.

A second argument is that the provisions of the Law of the Sea Convention relating to navigation represent a consensus among participating States as to what State practice is or should be. For example, a German declaration characterises the right of transit passage as the prerequisite for recognition of the right of States to extend their territorial seas to twelve miles.[24] But while there was by the end of UNCLOS III a consensus on the navigational provisions, that consensus would seem to relate to the provisions as components of the Convention, rather than as components of customary law. This view, that the right of transit passage is a 'contractual' right, available only to the parties to the Convention, is reflected in the Iranian declaration made on signing the Convention,[25] and is borne out by the package-deal nature of UNCLOS III.

A third argument is that since the Convention asserts that 'all' ships and aircraft enjoy the right of transit passage (art. 38(1)), ships and aircraft of non-Party States must enjoy the right. It is doubtful, however, whether the drafters of the Convention actually did intend to accord such rights to third States, as article 36(1) of the Vienna Convention on the Law of Treaties requires if third parties are to enjoy rights under treaties.

It remains possible that the transit passage regime has passed into customary law by virtue of State practice since the adoption of the Convention. This practice has, however, a certain ambivalence. It may not be possible to establish whether a State party to the Convention permits passage because it considers itself obliged by customary law to do so (i.e., whether the State acts with *opinio juris*) or because it is bound by the Convention to so. Moreover, as far as surface vessels are concerned, it will usually be impossible to tell merely by observing their conduct whether they are engaging in innocent passage or transit passage. In the case of a submarine transiting a strait submerged, the strait State(s) will

---

[24] 27 *LOSB* 7 (1995).
[25] 5 *LOSB* 42 (1985); 26 *LOSB* 35 (1994); 33 *LOSB* 87 (1997). And cf. chapter one, footnote 24 above.

often be unaware of its presence. In some cases it is probably reasonable to assume that straits States, especially where these are allies of the flag State in question, have acquiesced in such passage or accepted that passage through the strait was indeed transit passage. Some strait States have, however, explicitly granted a right of transit passage to ships of all States. For example, the United Kingdom and France announced (at the time that the United Kingdom extended its territorial sea from three to twelve miles, so abolishing the high-seas corridor in straits such as the Straits of Dover), that rights equivalent to a right of transit passage would be afforded to other States in the Straits of Dover.[26] Similarly, Thailand, while not a party to the Convention, affirmed that

> according to the well-established rules of customary international law and State practice as recognised and codified by the 1982 United Nations Convention on the Law of the Sea, ships of all States have the right . . . of transit passage in the strait (*sic*) used for international navigation.[27]

The conclusion which emerges is that through certain straits of particular importance to international navigation, such as the Straits of Dover and probably the Straits of Gibraltar, a customary law right akin to transit passage does exist, either because the States bordering the straits have explicitly granted such a right to third States, or because they have acquiesced in the exercise of such a right. However, a general right of transit passage may not yet have become established in customary international law.[28]

In the case of merchant ships this residual doubt is of less importance than might at first appear. Under international trade agreements, bilateral, regional, and (in the case of the WTO/GATT) global, there is an ever-increasing range of trade-related obligations not to discriminate between foreign States. Since the membership of the WTO is fast approaching the universal, the scope for a 'straits State' lawfully to discriminate between foreign merchant ships is steadily diminishing. Nonetheless, the issue remains important in the context of passage by military vessels.

[26] Joint declaration of 2 November 1988, 14 *LOSB* 14 (1989). See also the UK statements in *Parliamentary Debates* (Hansard), *loc. cit.* in footnote 18; D. H. Anderson, 'The Strait of Dover and the Southern North Sea – some recent legal developments', 7 *IJECL* 85–98 (1992). See also the French Law No. 71–1060 of 1971, which enables regulations to be made for 'free maritime and aerial navigation' through the straits bordered by France (English translation in 11 *ILM* 153 (1972)).

[27] 23 *LOSB* 108 (1993). See also the Korean Enforcement Decree of Territorial Sea and Contiguous Zone Act 1978–1996, article 4, which clearly distinguishes between rights of passage in the territorial sea and through international straits: 33 *LOSB* 48 (1997).

[28] Note, for example, the ambivalence of the provision by which Trinidad accords or recognises rights of transit passage for Venezuelan vessels through straits under Trinidadian sovereignty: Agreement between the Republic of Trinidad and Tobago and the Republic of Venezuela on the delimitation of marine and submarine areas, 18 April 1990, art. VI. But cf. art. 4 of the Venezuela–Netherlands Maritime Boundary Treaty, 1978, which accords a 'right of passage in transit'.

Special regimes

The Law of the Sea Convention rules on transit passage do not oust the rules applicable under long-standing international conventions which regulate passage through particular straits in whole or in part (LOSC, art. 35(c)). Though this principle is simply stated, the implications of its application are more complicated. For example, a treaty made in 1881 between Argentina and Chile provides that 'the Straits of Magellan are neutralised for ever, and free navigation is guaranteed to the flags of all nations', but does not elaborate upon the nature of this right of 'free navigation'.[29] Similarly, the 1904 Anglo-French Declaration respecting Egypt and Morocco speaks of the securing of the 'free passage of the Straits of Gibraltar' – although that declaration is arguably concerned only with the neutralisation of the shore, and not with the regime of passage at all. Since 'free navigation' and 'free passage' were not terms of art clearly distinguished from, for example, non-suspendable innocent passage, it seems that the best interpretation of the Law of the Sea Convention is that its straits regime would apply to these straits, there being no special rules on passage to oust it, but that the neutrality obligations under the special conventions would survive.

More difficult are conventions such as the 1857 Treaty of Copenhagen, stated by Sweden to fall within the scope of article 35(c). That Treaty includes in relation to the Baltic the provision that 'No vessel shall henceforth, under any pretext whatsoever, be subjected, in its passage of the Sound or Belts, to any detention or hindrance'. Here the right of passage appears to be supplemented by an immunity from coastal State enforcement jurisdiction. In this case the effect would seem to be that rules in the Law of the Sea Convention dealing with, for example, the scope of coastal States' legislative competence would be applicable, but that the rules on enforcement jurisdiction would not. The Finnish and Swedish governments have similarly stated that the straits off the Aaland Islands fall within article 35(c), the applicable conventions in this case being the 1921 Convention on the Non-Fortification and Neutrality of the Aaland Islands, which limits the access of warships to the territorial seas of the islands, and the 1940 Agreement on the demilitarisation of the islands concluded by Finland and the Soviet Union. Apart from the constraints upon warships, these conventions would have very little practical impact upon the general regime set out in the 1982 Convention.[30]

---

[29] See now art. 10 of the Argentina-Chile Treaty of Peace and Friendship 1984, under which the parties agree that their boundary in the Straits in no way affects the 1881 Treaty, and Argentina 'assumes the obligation to maintain at all times and under any circumstances the right of ships of all flags to navigate expeditiously and without obstacles through the jurisdictional waters towards and away from the Straits of Magellan'. See also the declarations concerning the 1984 Treaty made by Argentina (30 *LOSB* 6 (1996), 35 *LOSB* 101 (1997)) and Chile (33 *LOSB* 83–4 (1997)).

[30] 5 *LOSB* 10 (Finland) and 22 (Sweden) (1985); 32 LOSB 11 (Sweden) (1996).

The most detailed of the specific international conventions is the Montreux Convention of 1936 concerning the Bosphorus and Dardanelles. This Convention, the latest of a series concerning the straits beginning with a Russo-Turkish treaty of 1774, gives during peacetime 'complete freedom of transit and navigation' to merchant vessels, and 'freedom of transit' during daylight hours for certain light warships which give prior notification to the Turkish government. The provisions concerning warships are detailed. Broadly speaking, they must be under 10,000 tons, and no more than nine warships, which must not exceed 15,000 tons in all, may pass at any one time; however, the Black Sea littoral States have wider rights and may send capital ships of any tonnage through the straits, one at a time, and may in some circumstances send submarines through. These provisions confining the right of passage to certain classes of ship, and imposing conditions such as prior notification on that right, would continue to apply despite the entry into force of the Law of the Sea Convention. But again, the Law of the Sea Convention provisions on coastal State legislative jurisdiction would apply to the Bosphorus and the Dardanelles, since the Montreux Convention does not deal with this question.

The restrictive rules of the Montreux Convention are, however, under some pressure. Aircraft carriers are expressly excluded from the right of passage under the Convention, but in 1976 the USSR sent the warship *Kiev* through the straits. The *Kiev* is equipped with a dozen aircraft, two dozen helicopters and a flight deck six hundred feet long, but was said by the Soviet Union to be an 'anti-submarine cruiser' and not an aircraft carrier. In fact warships are permitted by the Montreux Convention to carry flight decks as long as they are not 'designed or adapted primarily for the purpose of carrying and operating aircraft at sea'; but it is difficult to accept that this was not the intended role of the *Kiev*. The episode has been repeated since, for example in 1991 when the *Admiral Flota SSSR Kuznetzov* transited the straits.[31] These ships have been allowed through by Turkey, which asserts that it alone is entitled to decide upon the proper interpretation of the Convention. This underlines the need for the revision of the Montreux Convention (of which there is no immediate prospect) and may signal the practical demise of some of the limitations imposed by that Convention on the passage of warships. Similarly, there has been some concern that the regulations adopted by Turkey concerning passage through the straits are, or are being applied in a manner, not entirely compatible with the Montreux Convention.[32] However, this does not affect the present point, which is that as a matter of law the detailed rules of the Montreux Convention would (were Turkey to become bound by the Law of the Sea Convention) coexist with the provisions of the Law of the Sea Convention concerning matters outside the scope of the Montreux Convention.

[31] See *UKMIL 1991*, p. 636.
[32] See J. A. Thomas, 'Troubled waters in the Bosporus and Dardanelles', [1994] 10 *OGLTR* 297–306. The Turkish regulations, which differ from IMO regulations, are reprinted at 10 *IJMCL* 570 (1995).

Further reading

General

R. P. Anand, 'Transit passage and overflight in international straits', 26 *IJIL* 71–105 (1986).

R. R. Baxter, *The Law of International Waterways* (Cambridge, Mass., Harvard University Press), 1964.

E. Bruël, *International Straits*, 2 vols (Copenhagen, Busck), 1947.

H. Caminos, 'The legal regime of straits in the 1982 United Nations Convention on the Law of the Sea', 205 *Recueil des Cours* (1987, v) 9–246.

B. B. Jia, *The Regime of Straits in International Law* (Oxford, Clarendon), 1998.

K. L. Koh, *Straits in International Navigation: Contemporary Issues* (Dobbs Ferry, N.Y., Oceana), 1982.

R. Lapidoth-Eschelbacher, *Les détroits en droit international* (Paris, Pedone), 1972.

S. Mahmoudi, 'Customary international law and transit passage', 20 *ODIL* 157–74 (1989).

J. N. Moore, 'The regime of straits and the Third United Nations Conference on the Law of the Sea', 74 *AJIL* 77–121 (1980).

S. N. Nandan and D. H. Anderson, 'Straits used for international navigation: a commentary on Part III of the United Nations Convention on the Law of the Sea 1982', 60 *BYIL* 159–204 (1989).

D. P. O'Connell, *The International Law of the Sea*, 2 vols (Oxford, Clarendon), 1982, 1984 [*O'Connell*].

ODIL, Special Issue on Straits, 18 : 4 (pp. 391–491) (1987).

W. M. Reisman, 'The regime of straits and national security. An appraisal of international lawmaking', 74 *AJIL* 48–76 (1980).

W. L. Schachte and J. P. A. Bernhardt, 'International straits and navigational freedoms', 33 *Virginia JIL* 527–56 (1993).

M. C. Stelakatos-Loverdos, 'The contribution of channels to the definition of straits used for international navigation', 13 *IJMCL* 71–89 (1998).

United Nations, *Law of the Sea: Straits Used for International Navigation – Legislative History of Part III of the United Nations Convention on the Law of the Sea* (New York, United Nations), 2 vols, 1991, 1992.

J. A. de Yturriaga, *Straits used for International Navigation: a Spanish Perspective* (Dordrecht, Nijhoff), 1991.

Particular straits

A. R. Deluca, *Great Power Rivalry at the Turkish Straits: The Montreux Conference and Convention of 1936* (Boulder, Colo., East European Quarterly), 1981.

F. D. Froman, '*Kiev* and the Montreux Convention' 14 *San Diego Law Review* 681–717 (1977).

L. Gross, 'The Geneva Conference on the Law of the Sea and the right of innocent passage through the Gulf of Aqaba' 53 *AJIL* 564–94 (1959).

D. H. N. Johnson, 'Some legal problems of international waterways with particular reference to the Straits of Tiran and the Suez Canal', 31 *Modern Law Review* 152–64 (1968).

T. L. McDorman, 'In the wake of the *Polar Sea*: Canadian jurisdiction and the Northwest Passage', 10 *Marine Policy* 243–57 (1986).

D. Pharand, *Canada's Arctic Waters in International Law* (Cambridge, Cambridge University Press), 1988, Part 4 (pp. 185–257).

G. Plant, 'Navigation regime in the Turkish Straits for merchant ships in peacetime', 20 *Marine Policy* 15–27 (1996).

D. R. Rothwell, 'International straits and UNCLOS: an Australian case study', 23 *JMLC* 461–83 (1992).

T. Scovazzi, 'Management regimes and responsibility for international straits: with special reference to the Mediterranean Straits', 19 *Marine Policy* 137–52 (1995).

F. Vali, *The Turkish Straits and NATO* (Stanford, Cal., Hoover Institution Press), 1972.

A series of detailed monographs, each written by a specialist, is published by Kluwer (Aalphen aan den Rijn, and for volumes after 1986, Dordrecht) under the general editorship of G. J. Mangone. The following volumes have been published:

G. Alexandersson, *The Baltic Straits*, 1982.

W. E. Butler, *The Northeast Arctic Passage*, 1978.

L. Cuyvers, *The Straits of Dover*, 1986.

S. B. Kaye, *The Torres Strait*, 1997.

R. Lapidoth, *The Red Sea and the Gulf of Aden*, 1981.

M. Leifer, *Malacca, Singapore and Indonesia*, 1978.

M. A. Morris, *The Strait of Magellan*, 1989.

C.-Y. Pak, *The Korean Straits*, 1988.

D. Pharand and L. Legault, *Northwest Passage: Arctic Straits*, 1984.

R. K. Ramazani, *The Persian Gulf and the Strait of Hormuz*, 1979.

C. L. Rozakis and P. N. Stagos, *The Turkish Straits*, 1987.

S. K. Truver, *The Strait of Gibraltar and the Mediterranean*, 1980.

6

Archipelagos

Development of a special regime for archipelagos

We saw in chapter two that every island can generate a territorial sea and that most islands can generate all other maritime zones. In the case of an archipelago (that is, a group of islands), the question of whether this rule should apply, or whether an archipelago should enjoy a special regime which would recognise and reinforce its unitary nature (for example, by drawing baselines around and enclosing the archipelago), was debated extensively, but inconclusively, between 1930 and 1958. Thus neither the 1930 Hague Conference, nor the ILC in preparing its draft articles for the 1958 conference, nor that conference itself – in spite of having before it an excellent memorandum on the subject by the Norwegian jurist Jens Evensen (see the reference in 'Further reading') – were able to agree on any provisions dealing specifically and comprehensively with archipelagos.

The 1958 conference, however, did deal with one type of archipelago, the so-called 'coastal' archipelago. Article 4 of the Territorial Sea Convention, it may be recalled (see chapter two), provided that straight baselines might be drawn around islands fringing a coast. It is therefore possible, using this provision, to draw straight baselines around the outermost points of a coastal archipelago and 'tie' it to the mainland coast. This is what Norway had done, and the United Kingdom disputed, in the *Anglo-Norwegian Fisheries* case (1951); and since then similar action has been taken by other States, e.g., by the United Kingdom in respect of the Hebrides,[1] and by the Federal Republic of Germany in respect of the Frisian islands.[2]

It was unsuccessfully argued by some at the 1958 conference, notably Indonesia, the Philippines, Denmark and Yugoslavia, that the rules on straight baselines, which deal with coastal archipelagos, could be applied by analogy to 'mid-ocean' archipelagos such as Tonga and the Philippines. This distinction

---

[1] Territorial Waters Order in Council, 1964. S.I. 1965, p. 6452A; *UN Leg. Ser.* B/15, p. 129.

[2] *Limits in the Seas* No. 38 (1974).

between 'coastal' and 'mid-ocean' archipelagos is one that is commonly made, and although it is in general terms easy to see the difference between the two types, it is sometimes difficult in practice to apply the distinction: for example, is Iceland's straight baseline system in effect tying offshore islands to a mainland coast (and so governed by the rules on straight baselines), as Iceland claims, or is it in reality a system of straight lines drawn around the islands of a mid-ocean archipelago? This difficulty in distinguishing between the two broad categories of archipelago points to a further factor: the great geographical diversity of archipelagos, even within each broad group, which has made it difficult to draw up a set of agreed rules of general application.

The main advocates of a special regime for archipelagos at the 1958 conference were Indonesia and the Philippines. Shortly before the conference, in 1957 and 1955 respectively, these two States announced that they would enclose the whole of their archipelagos by straight lines and treat the waters thus enclosed as internal waters.[3] These claims were followed by detailed legislation in 1960 and 1961.[4] The reasons for these claims, which met with protests from a number of States (including the United Kingdom and the USA),[5] were primarily security and, in the case of Indonesia, to stress the unity and integrity of its vast and heterogeneous island territory.

The principal opposition at UNCLOS I to a special regime for archipelagos came from the major maritime States. They feared that such a regime would result in areas which had previously been high seas or territorial seas becoming internal waters, with the consequent loss of navigational rights for both their naval and commercial vessels, especially in the case of archipelagos such as the Bahamas, Fiji, Indonesia and the Philippines, which straddle important shipping routes. Until UNCLOS III these maritime States consistently took the view that the normal regime of islands should apply to mid-ocean archipelagos, thus leaving territorial sea or high-seas routes between most islands.

Since 1958 many archipelagic States in the Caribbean and Indian and Pacific Oceans have become independent, and this increased the pressure for the adoption of a special regime for mid-ocean archipelagos to meet the interests of archipelagic States. These interests are economic (fishing and the control of inter-island traffic); political (promoting the unity of the archipelago); security; preventing smuggling

[3] See Indonesian communiqué of 14 December 1957, *Whiteman, op. cit.* in 'Further reading' at the end of this chapter, Vol. IV, p. 284; and Philippine *note verbale* of 7 March 1955 to the UN Secretary General, UN Doc. A/2934 (1955), pp. 52–3. These were really the first specific claims to a special status for archipelagos, although rather unclearly formulated claims had been made earlier by Ecuador (in respect of the Galapagos Islands), Tonga and Bermuda. For details see O'Connell, *op. cit.* in 'Further reading', pp. 23–4, 45–7 and 51 and Munavvar, *op. cit.* in 'Further reading', pp. 54–65.

[4] Indonesia: Act No. 4. Concerning Indonesian Waters, 18 February 1960. *Limits in the Seas* No. 35 (1971). Philippines: Act No. 3046 of 17 June 1961 to define the Baselines of the Territorial Sea of the Philippines (as amended by Act No. 5446 of 18 September 1968). *ND I*, p. 27; *UN Leg. Ser.* B/15, p. 105; *Limits in the Seas* No. 33 (1971).

[5] See *Whiteman, op. cit.* in 'Further reading', Vol. IV, pp. 283–5.

and illegal entry; and the control of pollution. The question of a special archipelagic regime was taken up and vigorously pursued at UNCLOS III by a group of archipelagic States (Fiji, Indonesia, Mauritius and the Philippines), and as a result the Law of the Sea Convention contains a special regime for mid-ocean archipelagos in Part IV. Coastal archipelagos are covered by the provisions on straight baselines – although it should be noted that the Convention does not use the terms 'mid-ocean' or 'coastal', nor does it distinguish directly between the two.

The essential features of the new regime laid down in Part IV (which even before the entry into force of the Convention was being increasingly reflected in State practice, discussed below) are as follows. First, it permits straight 'archipelagic baselines' to be drawn around the outermost islands of archipelagos, thus meeting the wishes of archipelagic States. Secondly, it creates a new legal concept of 'archipelagic waters' for the waters thus enclosed of a nature designed to accommodate the navigational interests of maritime States. Before looking at these two aspects in detail, it is necessary to consider the definition of an archipelago and an archipelagic State.

Definition of an archipelago and an archipelagic State

Only an archipelagic *State* can draw archipelagic baselines around an archipelago (LOSC, art. 47). It is therefore important to know what an archipelagic State is. Article 46 defines an archipelagic State as 'a State constituted wholly by one or more archipelagos and may include other islands'. An archipelago is defined in the same article as:

> a group of islands, including parts of islands, interconnecting waters and other natural features which are so closely interrelated that such islands, waters and other natural features form an intrinsic geographical, economic and political entity, or which historically have been regarded as such.

A number of points should be noted about these definitions. First, archipelagic States do not include mainland States which possess non-coastal archipelagos, e.g., Denmark (with the Faroes), Ecuador (the Galapagos Islands), Norway (Svalbard), Portugal (the Azores) and Spain (the Canaries). This means that archipelagic baselines cannot be drawn around such archipelagos, nor in many cases would it appear to be justifiable under the Law of the Sea Convention to construct straight baselines around them. This seems an unnecessary and unreasonable restriction: the reason for it appears to have been a fear that extending the archipelagic regime to the non-coastal archipelagos of mainland States would lead to a proliferation of claims.[6] It may be noted, however, that some archipelagos of this type, such as the Faroes, the Galapagos and some of the Canary Islands, are bounded

---

[6] See Munavvar, *op. cit.* in 'Further reading', p. 85.

at present by a series of straight lines which serve as the baselines.[7] To the extent that such claims have been recognised by other States (as those of the Faroes have been, for example[8]), they must be regarded as being valid under customary international law.[9]

Secondly, the definition of an archipelagic State would appear to embrace a number of States which do not normally consider themselves to be archipelagic States, such as Japan, New Zealand and the United Kingdom. While it is not clear whether States have a choice as to whether they consider themselves as archipelagic States, they certainly do have an option as to whether they draw archipelagic baselines – and the capacity to draw such baselines appears to be the only consequence of a State being designated an archipelagic State – since article 47 says 'an archipelagic State *may* draw straight archipelagic baselines' (emphasis added). In any case most of these non-traditional archipelagic States will in practice be unable to draw archipelagic baselines because of the rules governing the drawing of such lines, discussed in the next section.

Even if we exclude States which would not consider themselves to be archipelagic States (like Japan and the United Kingdom), there are still quite a number of States – somewhere between twenty-five and thirty-five – which fall within the definition of an archipelagic State. Although the definition of an archipelago (and thus an archipelagic State) is rather wide and imprecise (for example, nothing is said about the number of islands or their size and proximity relative one to another), some of the difficulties which might arise as a result are in practice avoided by the fact that the extent to which archipelagic baselines may be drawn around archipelagos is, as we shall see in a moment, much more clearly and strictly formulated. The effect is to deprive some archipelagic States altogether of the possibility of drawing archipelagic baselines.

At the present time some seventeen States have formally claimed archipelagic status by enacting appropriate legislation, although not all of them appear

---

[7] For the Faroese legislation, see Order No. 598 of 21 December 1976 on the Fishing Territory of the Faroes. *ND V*, p. 111; *UN Leg. Ser.* B/19, p. 192. Order No. 599 of 21 December 1976 on the Boundary of the Sea Territory of the Faroes. *ND V*, p. 112. For the legislation relating to the Galapagos, see Ecuador Supreme Decree No. 959-A of 28 June 1971 prescribing Straight Baselines for the Measurement of the Territorial Sea. *UN Leg. Ser.* B/18, p.15; *Limits in the Seas* No. 42 (1972). For the legislation relating to the Canaries, see Law No. 15/78 of 20 February 1978 on the Economic Zone. *ND VIII*, p. 19; *UN Leg. Ser.* B/19, p. 250; *Smith, op. cit.* in 'Further reading', p. 425; and Royal Decree No. 2510/1977. *UN Leg. Ser.* B/19, p. 112.

[8] The EC, Norway and the former USSR appear to have recognised the Faroese claim when concluding agreements with Denmark permitting their vessels to fish in the Faroese 200-mile fishing zone. See Denmark–EC Agreement on Fisheries, 1977; Faroes–Norway Agreement on Mutual Fishery Rights, 1979; and Denmark–USSR Agreement on Mutual Fishery Relations between the Faroes and the USSR, 1977.

[9] The USA, on the other hand, has protested the claims relating to the Faroes and Galapagos, as well as those of Portugal (relating to the Azores) and Sudan. See J. A. Roach and R. W. Smith, *United States Responses to Excessive Maritime Claims* (The Hague, Nijhoff), 2nd edn, 1996, pp. 112–17.

yet to have drawn archipelagic baselines. These seventeen States are: Antigua and Barbuda,[10] Bahamas,[11] Cape Verde,[12] Comoros,[13] Fiji,[14] Indonesia,[15] Jamaica,[16] Kiribati,[17] Marshall Islands,[18] Papua New Guinea,[19] Philippines,[20] St Vincent and the Grenadines,[21] Sao Tomé e Principe,[22] Solomon Islands,[23] Trinidad and Tobago,[24] Tuvalu[25] and Vanuatu.[26] As can be appreciated (from the notes below), nearly all these claims pre-date the entry into force of the Law of the Sea Convention, and most pre-date the conclusion of UNCLOS III. Nevertheless, most of these claims are in accordance with the Convention (and most of the States concerned are parties to the Convention): to the extent that the legislation referred to is not in conformity with the Convention, this will be pointed out below.

[10] Maritime Areas Act, 1982. United Nations (1992), *op. cit.* in 'Further reading' (hereafter UN 1992), p. 1.

[11] Archipelagic Waters and Maritime Jurisdiction Act, 1993. 31 *LOSB* 31 (1996).

[12] Law No. 60/IV/92. 26 *LOSB* 24 (1994). This legislation replaces earlier legislation (Decree No. 126/77, *Smith, op. cit.*, p. 95), which was incompatible with the Law of the Sea Convention as regards both the drawing of archipelagic baselines and other States' navigational rights therein. The new legislation is still incompatible on the latter point – see below.

[13] Law No. 82–005. *Smith, op. cit.*, p. 103; UN 1992, *op. cit.*, p. 20.

[14] Marine Spaces Act, 1977. *Smith, op. cit.*, p. 103; UN 1992, *op. cit.*, p. 23; *Limits in the Seas* No. 101 (1984).

[15] Law No. 6 of 1996 concerning the Indonesian Territorial Waters. *State Gazette* (1996), No. 73; *Additional State Gazette* (1996), No. 3, 647. This legislation, which is discussed briefly in E. R. Agoes, 'Current issues of maritime and coastal affairs in Indonesia', 12 *IJMCL* 201–24 (1997), at 203–4, revises the legislation referred to in footnote 4 above, which was incompatible with the Convention as regards the navigational rights of other States.

[16] Maritime Areas Act, 1996. 34 *LOSB* 29 (1997).

[17] Maritime Zones (Declaration) Act, 1983. *Smith, op. cit.*, p. 245; UN 1992, *op. cit.*, p. 56.

[18] United Nations, *The Law of the Sea. Practice of States at the Time of the Entry into Force of the UN Convention on the Law of the Sea* (New York, United Nations), 1994, p. 9.

[19] National Seas Act, 1977. *Smith, op. cit.*, p. 363; UN 1992, *op. cit.*, p. 61.

[20] *Op. cit.* in footnote 4. Also UN 1992, *op. cit.*, p. 75.

[21] Maritime Areas Act, 1983. *Smith, op. cit.*, p. 399; UN 1992, *op. cit.*, p. 86.

[22] Decree-Law No. 14/78 of 16 June 1978. *ND VII*, p. 50; *UN Leg. Ser.* B/19, p. 101; as amended by Decree Law No. 48/82, 1 *LOSB* 39 (1983); *Limits in the Seas* No. 98 (1983). Both in UN 1992, *op. cit.*, p. 93.

[23] Delimitation of Marine Waters Act, 1978. *Smith, op. cit.*, p. 413; and Declaration of Archipelagos of Solomon Islands, 1979, and Declaration of Archipelagic Baselines, 1979. *UN Leg. Ser.* B/19, pp. 106, 107: UN 1992, *op. cit.*, p. 100.

[24] Archipelagic Waters and Exclusive Economic Zone Act, 1986. 9 *LOSB* 6 (1987); UN 1992, *op. cit.*, p. 109. Archipelagic Baselines of Trinidad and Tobago Order, 1988. *Legal Supplement*, Part B, Vol. 24, No. 281.

[25] Maritime Zones (Declaration) Ordinance, 1983. *Smith, op. cit.*, p. 459; UN 1992, *op. cit.*, p. 124.

[26] Maritime Zones Act, 1981. 1 *LOSB* 64 (1983); *Smith, op. cit.*, p. 471; UN 1992, *op. cit.*, p. 131.

It should also be noted that some States which are able to claim archipelagic status in conformity with the Convention (such as Grenada and Seychelles) have so far elected not to do so.

Archipelagic baselines

Article 47(1) provides that 'an archipelagic State may draw straight archipelagic baselines joining the outermost points of the outermost islands and drying reefs of the archipelago'. These lines then serve as the baseline from which the breadth of the archipelagic State's territorial sea, contiguous zone, exclusive economic zone and continental shelf is measured (LOSC, art. 48). The drawing of archipelagic baselines is subject to a number of conditions, of which two are precise and mathematical, and the remainder (many of which parallel the conditions governing the drawing of straight baselines) more general and less precise. These conditions are as follows:

1 Archipelagic baselines must be so drawn that the ratio of land to water within the lines is not more than 1 : 1 and not less than 1 : 9 (LOSC, art. 47(1)). For the purpose of computing this ratio, 'land' may include 'waters lying within the fringing reefs of islands and atolls, including that part of a steepsided oceanic plateau which is enclosed or nearly enclosed by a chain of limestone islands and drying reefs lying on the perimeter of the plateau' (LOSC, art. 47(7)). The maximum ratio of 1 : 1 prevents archipelagic States which consist predominantly of one large island or a few large islands close together (such as Cuba, Iceland, Madagascar, New Zealand and the United Kingdom) from drawing archipelagic baselines (although why this is thought to be necessary is unclear): often in such cases, however, it will be possible for the State concerned to draw straight baselines along all or part of the coast of the main island and tie in offshore islands in this way, as has been done notably by Cuba[27] and Iceland.[28] The minimum ratio of 1 : 9 prevents archipelagic baselines being drawn around very distant islands in an archipelago or around the whole of widely dispersed archipelagos consisting of small islands, such as Kiribati and Tuvalu. Nevertheless, these figures accommodate the main archipelagic claims – as they were intended to do. By way of illustration, the ratio of land to water in the Indonesian and Philippine claims is 1 : 1.2 and 1 : 1.8 respectively.

[27] Act of 24 February 1977 (Decree No. 1) concerning the Breadth of the Territorial Sea. *ND VII*, p. 23; *UN Leg. Ser.* B/19, p. 16; *Limits on the Seas* No. 76 (1977); *Smith, op. cit.*, p. 109.
[28] Law No. 41 of 1 June 1979 concerning the Territorial Sea, the Economic Zone and the Continental Shelf. *UN Leg. Ser.* B/19, p. 43; *Smith, op. cit.*, p. 209. But note that neither the Cuban nor the Icelandic baselines are wholly in conformity with the Convention's provisions on straight baselines: see J. R. V. Prescott, *The Maritime Political Boundaries of the World* (London, Methuen), 1985, pp. 260 and 337.

2 Archipelagic baselines must not exceed 100 miles in length, except that up to three per cent of the total number of lines may be between 100 and 125 miles in length (LOSC, art. 47(2)). These figures are generous to the archipelagic State, and the fact that they changed quite considerably during successive versions of the negotiating text suggests that their choice is not based on any objective geographical, ecological or oceanographical factors. By way of illustration again, it is of interest to note that the Indonesian system is made up of 196 lines, of which five are between 100 and 125 miles in length and the remainder less than 100 miles. On the other hand, the Philippine system does not fulfil the requirements of the Convention, having eighty lines, of which two are between 100 and 125 miles in length, one is 140 miles and the remainder less than 100 miles.

3 The 'main islands' of the archipelago must be included within the archipelagic baselines (LOSC, art. 47(1)). The meaning of 'main islands' is not altogether clear: it could refer to the largest islands, the most populous islands or the islands most prominent in some other way.

4 The drawing of archipelagic baselines must not 'depart to any appreciable extent from the general configuration of the archipelago' (LOSC, art. 47(3)). Whether most archipelagos have an ascertainable 'configuration' may be doubted. In any case, it is the archipelagic baselines themselves, by being drawn around the outermost islands of the group, which largely determine the configuration of the archipelago.

5 Archipelagic baselines 'shall not be drawn to and from low-tide elevations, unless lighthouses or similar installations which are permanently above sea level have been built on them or where a low-tide elevation is situated wholly or partly at a distance not exceeding the breadth of the territorial sea from the nearest island' (LOSC, art. 47(4)).

6 Archipelagic baselines must not be drawn in such a way as to cut off the territorial sea of another State from the high seas or its exclusive economic zone (LOSC, art. 47(5)). The Indonesian baseline system would seem to have this effect on the territorial sea of Singapore. On the other hand, even without the Indonesian system, it is doubtful whether Singapore would have been able to generate an exclusive economic zone because of the close proximity of several Indonesian islands. In a case like this, where the result appears to be the same whether the rule in article 47(5) is applied or not, it would seem not unreasonable for the archipelagic State to be allowed to draw archipelagic baselines, even though a strict reading of article 47(5) might suggest that no such baselines should be drawn in this situation.

7 The archipelagic State must clearly indicate its archipelagic baseline system on charts of an adequate scale. Alternatively, it may list the geographical co-ordinates of the points to and from which archipelagic baselines are drawn. In either case, due publicity must be given to such charts or lists. Furthermore, a copy of each chart or list must be deposited with the UN Secretary-General (LOSC, art. 47(8), (9)).

It is not necessary for an archipelagic State to attempt to enclose all the islands making up that State in a single system of archipelagic baselines, since, according to its definition in article 46, an archipelagic State can consist of a number of archipelagos (as, for example, is the case with the Solomon Islands and Mauritius) and other islands. In such cases, archipelagic baselines can be drawn around each of the archipelagos making up the archipelagic State (provided, of course, that the above conditions are fulfilled), as indeed the Solomon Islands have done; and outlying islands can be excluded from the archipelagic baseline system (as Fiji has done).

Archipelagic waters

Archipelagic waters comprise all the maritime waters within archipelagic baselines. One qualification must, however, be made. *Within* archipelagic baselines an archipelagic State can draw closing lines across river mouths, bays and harbours on individual islands in accordance with the normal rules on baselines. The waters so enclosed are internal waters, not archipelagic waters (LOSC, art. 50). Article 50 does not refer to the possibility of drawing closing lines across gaps in the coral reefs of atolls. Thus, lagoons lying within such reefs would appear to be archipelagic waters, rather than internal waters, notwithstanding the fact that they are regarded as 'land' for the purpose of calculating the land–water ratio within archipelagic baselines (LOSC, art. 47(7) – discussed above) and that under the ordinary rules on baselines they would be internal waters. It would seem logical that they should always be treated as internal waters and archipelagic States be permitted to draw closing lines across gaps in reefs, as in fact Fiji has done in its archipelagic baseline system.[29]

The concept of archipelagic waters is a new one in international law. Such waters are neither internal waters nor territorial sea, although they bear a number of resemblances to the latter. An archipelagic State has sovereignty over its archipelagic waters, including their superjacent air space, subjacent sea bed and subsoil, and 'the resources contained therein' (LOSC, art. 49). This sovereignty is, however, subject to a number of rights enjoyed by third States. First, an archipelagic State must 'respect' rights enjoyed by third States deriving from existing agreements (LOSC, art. 51(1)). This provision was presumably inserted to avoid any possible conflict between an archipelagic State's rights under the Law of the Sea Convention and its obligations under prior agreements, and is an exception to the general provision under article 311 dealing with the relationship of the Convention to prior treaties. Secondly, an archipelagic State must

> recognise traditional fishing rights and other legitimate activities of the immediately adjacent neighbouring States in certain areas falling within archipelagic waters. The terms and conditions for the exercise of such rights and activities, including

[29] See footnote 14.

the nature, the extent and the areas to which they apply, shall, at the request of any of the States concerned, be regulated by bilateral agreements between them. Such rights shall not be transferred to or shared with third States or their nationals. (LOSC, art. 51(1))

Furthermore, in circumstances such as exist in relation to Indonesia and Malaysia, where part of an archipelagic State's archipelagic waters

lies between two parts of an immediately adjacent neighbouring State, existing rights and all other legitimate interests which the latter State has traditionally exercised in such waters and all rights stipulated by agreement between those States shall continue and be respected. (LOSC, art. 47(6))

In implementation of article 47(6), for whose benefit and at whose prompting the provision was inserted in the Convention, Indonesia and Malaysia signed a bilateral agreement in 1982.[30] The agreement has provisions guaranteeing navigation and overflight between East and West Malaysia (discussed below), deals with cables linking East and West Malaysia and passing through Indonesian waters (also discussed below), and permits Malaysian fishermen to fish by traditional methods in part of Indonesia's archipelagic waters east of the Anambas Islands, an area where Malaysian fishermen have fished for decades.

The third obligation on an archipelagic State is to

respect existing submarine cables laid by other States and passing through its waters without making a landfall. An archipelagic State shall permit the maintenance and replacement of such cables upon receiving due notice of their location and the intention to repair or replace them. (LOSC, art. 51(2))

It should be noted that this provision applies only to cables, and not pipelines, and then only to existing cables. The laying of new cables and new pipelines by other States is thus totally dependent on the consent of the archipelagic State. As far as existing pipelines are concerned, the question arises as to whether an archipelagic State can require their removal. Where the State owning the pipeline is a party to the Law of the Sea Convention, articles 49 and 51(2) would appear to suggest that this is possible. Where the pipeline State is not a party, however, legal relations between the pipeline State and the archipelagic State will be based on customary international law. If the pipeline has been laid in an area that according to custom is high seas or was high seas at the time the pipeline was laid, then it would seem that the archipelagic State may not interfere with the pipeline and take away the other State's acquired rights. This point may, of course, be of only theoretical interest as far as pipelines passing through archipelagos are concerned, but the point is a general one which may have

---

[30] Treaty relating to the Legal Regime of Archipelagic State and the Rights of Malaysia in the Territorial Sea and Archipelagic Waters as well as in the Airspace above the Territorial Sea, Archipelagic Waters and the Territory of the Republic of Indonesia lying between East and West Malaysia. For a discussion of the Treaty, see Hamzah, *op. cit.* in 'Further reading'.

practical application in other areas. The Indonesia–Malaysia agreement, referred to above, in its provisions on cables essentially repeats the provisions of article 51(2), but in addition also permits Malaysia to lay new cables and pipelines through Indonesian waters provided that this does not interfere with the exploitation of sea-bed mineral resources by Indonesia within its territorial sea and archipelagic waters, and requires Indonesia to protect existing cables and pipelines, for example by establishing safety zones around them where appropriate.

Finally, and most important, there are the navigational rights of other States. The ships of all States enjoy in archipelagic waters the same right of innocent passage as they enjoy in the territorial sea (LOSC, art. 52(1)). This right may only be suspended, temporarily and in specified areas, for security reasons, after due notice has been given (LOSC, art. 52(2)). In addition, foreign ships and aircraft enjoy the rather more extensive right of 'archipelagic sea lanes passage' in sea lanes and air routes designated by the archipelagic State: sea lanes must be designated in consultation with the 'competent international organisation' (by which is meant the IMO)[31] (LOSC, art. 53(1), (2), (9)). Such lanes and routes, which may be up to fifty miles in width, shall cross both archipelagic waters and the territorial sea beyond, and shall include all normal passage routes used for international navigation or overflight (LOSC, art. 53(4), (5)). Archipelagic sea lanes passage is essentially the same as transit passage through straits (discussed in chapter five), and the rights and duties of foreign States and the archipelagic State in respect of archipelagic sea lanes passage are the same, *mutatis mutandis*, as the rights and duties of foreign States and straits States in respect of transit passage (LOSC, arts 53, 54). On this latter point the Convention simply cross-refers to the articles on transit passage through straits (LOSC, art. 54): a similar technique is also used earlier when dealing with innocent passage in archipelagic waters (LOSC, art. 52(1)). This may have one unfortunate effect as far as the jurisdiction of the archipelagic State over foreign shipping in archipelagic waters is concerned. While the general jurisdictional competence – both legislative and enforcement – of the coastal State is set out in the provisions of the Law of the Sea Convention on innocent passage and transit passage (and by cross-reference applies to innocent passage in archipelagic waters and archipelagic sea lanes passage), the Convention in its provisions on pollution gives the coastal State additional enforcement jurisdiction in respect of pollution over foreign vessels in its territorial sea and straits (see LOSC, arts 220, 233). This additional jurisdiction does not appear to apply in archipelagic waters. The result, therefore, seems to be that in its archipelagic waters an archipelagic State has less enforcement jurisdiction over foreign vessels in matters of pollution than a non-archipelagic State in its territorial sea or straits or than the archipelagic State itself has in its

---

[31] In 1997 the IMO agreed on a procedure for the designation of archipelagic sea lanes: see IMO Assembly Resolution A.858 (20). In May 1998 the Maritime Safety Committee of the IMO adopted General Provisions for the Adoption, Designation and Substitution of Archipelagic Sea Lanes.

own territorial sea lying *beyond* its archipelagic waters. This seems anomalous and undesirable, and may possibly be an oversight in drafting.[32]

Article 53(12) provides that 'if an archipelagic State does not designate sea lanes or air routes, the right of archipelagic sea lanes passage may be exercised through the routes normally used for international navigation'. This provision, assuming it applies to aircraft (and the wording is rather ambiguous because of the omission of a reference to overflight at the end of the sentence), is most important, especially for military aircraft,[33] for without it aircraft would have no guaranteed right to overfly archipelagos, since aircraft, unlike ships, enjoy no right of innocent passage. Article 53(12) also means that even if the archipelagic State does not designate sea lanes, submarines will be able to transit archipelagic waters submerged: normally submarines in innocent passage (which would apply if there were no article 53(12)) have to navigate on the surface. The importance of article 53(12) is underlined by the fact that it was not until May 1998 that the first (and so far only) sea lane (a partial system for Indonesian archipelagic waters) was approved by the IMO.[34]

Under the Indonesia–Malaysia agreement referred to above, Indonesia has designated two corridors of twenty miles in width for Malaysia to exercise archipelagic sea lanes passage between East and West Malaysia. Furthermore, in such sea lanes Malaysia has the right (not enjoyed by other States) to conduct naval or aerial manoeuvres so long as such manoeuvres do not infringe Indonesia's security. In addition, Malaysian civilian aircraft can continue to use existing air routes above Indonesia's archipelagic waters.

Not all the States that have enacted archipelagic legislation have done so in conformity with the Convention as far as other States' rights of navigation through archipelagic waters are concerned. The legislation of Cape Verde and Comoros accords foreign vessels a right of innocent passage through archipelagic waters, but makes no mention of archipelagic sea lanes passage, although the legislation of Cape Verde does provide that the Government is to prepare regulations with regard to sea lanes in archipelagic waters. Secondly, the Philippines has retained its original archipelagic legislation[35] which accords the waters enclosed by archipelagic baselines the status of internal waters and says nothing about other States' navigational rights therein, although according to a Philippine *note verbale* of 1955[36] there is a right of innocent passage. When ratifying the Law of the

---

[32] On the other hand, some commentators have argued that because art. 233 provides that the strait State may take enforcement action in respect of a violation of the anti-pollution legislation which it is permitted to enact under art. 42, and because art. 42 applies *mutatis mutandis* to archipelagic waters, therefore art. 233 is applicable to archipelagic waters. See, for example, M. H. Nordquist (ed.), *United Nations Convention on the Law of the Sea: A Commentary* (Dordrecht, Nijhoff), Vol. II, 1993, p. 487.

[33] Civilian aircraft will usually have a right of overflight by virtue of a pre-existing bilateral air services agreement.

[34] *IMO News*, 1998, No. 2, p. 27.

[35] See footnote 4.

[36] See footnote 3.

Sea Convention the Philippines made a declaration that the 'provisions of the Convention on archipelagic passage through sea lanes do not nullify or impair the sovereignty of the Philippines as an archipelagic State over the sea lanes and ... that the concept of archipelagic waters is similar to the concept of internal waters under the Constitution of the Philippines, and removes straits connecting these waters with the economic zone or high seas from the rights of foreign vessels to transit passage for international navigation'.[37] This declaration was objected to by Australia, Belarus, Bulgaria, Czechoslovakia, Russia, Ukraine and the USA on the grounds that it exceeded the permissible scope of declarations given by article 310 of the Convention and was in reality an impermissible reservation and that it indicated an intention by the Philippines to contravene the Convention.[38] In response the Philippines said that it intended to harmonise its domestic legislation with the provisions of the Convention and that 'the necessary steps are being under taken to enact legislation dealing with archipelagic sea lanes passage and the exercise of Philippine sovereign rights over archipelagic waters, in accordance with the Convention'.[39] As far as we are aware, such legislation has not yet been enacted.

Customary international law

With the entry into force in 1994 of the Law of the Sea Convention and an increasing number of States becoming parties to it, the question of how far the provisions of the Convention concerning archipelagos also represent customary international law is one of decreasing significance. There is, nevertheless, a good deal of evidence to suggest that the Convention's provisions have passed into custom. First, the claims of those States which have enacted archipelagic legislation in conformity with the Convention (and the vast majority of claims to archipelagic status come into this category), virtually all of which were made before the entry into force of the Convention, have been accepted by other States without apparent protest, and in particular by the major maritime States whose interests are most affected by such claims.[40] Secondly, certain elements of the Convention's archipelagic regime have been recognised in a number of treaties concluded before the entry into force of the Convention. Such treaties include the Indonesia–Malaysia agreement discussed above; the 1985 Treaty of Raratonga, which includes in its definition of 'territory' 'archipelagic waters' (art. 1) and

---

[37] United Nations, *Multilateral Treaties Deposited with the Secretary-General. Status as at 31 December 1996* (New York, United Nations), 1997, pp. 836–7.

[38] *Ibid.*, pp. 841–3 and Roach and Smith, *op. cit.* in footnote 9, pp. 221–2, 401–3 (USA).

[39] United Nations, *The Law of the Sea. Current Developments in State Practice*, II (1989), p. 96.

[40] For explicit recognition by the USA of the Convention regime as representing customary international law, see Kwiatkowska, *op. cit.* in 'Further reading', pp. 28–9 and Roach and Smith, *op. cit.* in footnote 9, pp. 210–12.

amongst various navigational rights mentioned refers to 'archipelagic sea lanes passage' (art. 5); the 1987 Pacific Island States–USA Treaty on Fisheries, which refers to the areas closed to US fishing as including the 'archipelagic waters' of certain Pacific island States (Schedule 2 of Annex I); and some twenty bilateral maritime boundary agreements where at least one of the parties is an archipelagic State, which implicitly or, in a few cases, explicitly[41] recognise the archipelagic baselines drawn by the archipelagic State concerned.

Conclusions

The development of a special regime for archipelagos by the Law of the Sea Convention, and now reflected in customary international law, has succeeded in meeting the aspirations of archipelagic States while at the same time satisfying the interests of maritime States. Hodgson and Smith, however, have questioned whether the concept of an archipelagic State is really necessary with the introduction of the exclusive economic zone. They point out that the use of archipelagic baselines will only marginally increase the size of the exclusive economic zone (compared with measuring the zone from each individual island), and that the gain in the waters enclosed by baselines becoming archipelagic rather than territorial sea or exclusive economic zone 'may be more psychological than real'.[42] On the other hand, these factors have probably helped to make the concept of an archipelagic State acceptable to the maritime States. And for an archipelagic State, as Anand points out,[43] 'the psychological feeling of its various islands and sea between them being universally accepted as one unit is no mean gain'.

Further reading

C. F. Amerasinghe, 'The problem of archipelagos in the international law of the sea', 23 *ICLQ* 539–75 (1974).

R. P. Anand, 'Mid-ocean archipelagos in international law. Theory and practice', 19 *IJIL* 228–56 (1979).

D. Andrew, 'Archipelagos and the law of the sea', 2 *Marine Policy* 45–64 (1978).

D. W. Bowett, *The Legal Regime of Islands in International law* (Dobbs Ferry, N.Y., Oceana), 1979, chapter 4.

J. Evensen, 'Certain legal aspects concerning the delimitation of the territorial waters of archipelagos', *First UN Conference on the Law of the Sea, Official Records*, Vol. I, pp. 289–302.

B. A. Hamzah, 'Indonesia's archipelagic regime. Implications for Malaysia', 8 *Marine Policy* 30–43 (1984).

---

[41] E.g., Cape Verde-Senegal Treaty, 1993.

[42] R. D. Hodgson and R. W. Smith, 'The informal single negotiating text (Committee II). A geographical perspective', 3 *ODIL* 225 (1976), at 244.

[43] Anand, *op. cit.* in 'Further reading', p. 254.

L. L. Herman, 'The modern concept of the off-lying archipelago in international law', XXIII *Canadian Yearbook of International Law* 172–200 (1985).

R. D. Hodgson and L. M. Alexander, *Towards an Objective Analysis of Special Circumstances, Bays, Rivers, Coastal and Oceanic Archipelagos and Atolls*, Law of the Sea Institute, University of Rhode Island, Occasional Paper No. 13, 1972, pp. 45–52.

The Geographer, US Department of State, *Limits in the Seas*.

H. W. Jayewardene, *The Regime of Islands in International Law* (Dordrecht, Nijhoff), 1990, chapter 5.

B. Kwiatkowska, 'The archipelagic regime in practice in the Philippines and Indonesia – making or breaking international law?', 6 *IJECL* 1–32 (1991).

—— and E. R. Agoes, 'Archipelagic waters – an assessment of national legislation' in R. Wolfrum (ed.), *Law of the Sea at the Crossroads* (Berlin, Dunker & Humblot), 1991, pp. 107–51.

R. Lattion, *L'archipel en droit international* (Lausanne, Payot), 1984.

M. Munavvar, *Ocean States: Archipelagic Regimes in the Law of the Sea* (Dordrecht, Nijhoff), 1995.

D. P. O'Connell, 'Mid-ocean archipelagos in international law', 45 BYIL 1–77 (1971).

J. R. V. Prescott, 'Straight and archipelagic baselines' in G. Blake (ed.), *Maritime Boundaries and Ocean Resources* (London, Croom Helm), 1987, pp. 38–51.

P. E. J. Rogers, *Midocean Archipelagos and International Law* (New York, Vantage Press), 1981.

R. W. Smith, *Exclusive Economic Zone Claims: An Analysis and Primary Documents* (Dordrecht, Nijhoff), 1986 [*Smith*].

P. Tangsubkul, *The Southeast Asian Archipelagic States: Concept, Evolution and Current Practice* (Honolulu, Hawaii, East-West Environment and Policy Institute), 1984.

United Nations, *The Law of the Sea. Archipelagic States: Legislative History of Part 4 of United Nations Convention on the Law of the Sea* (New York, United Nations), 1990.

——, *The Law of the Sea. Practice of Archipelagic States* (New York, United Nations), 1992.

P. de Vries Lentsch, 'The right of overflight over strait States and archipelagic States', XIV *NYIL* 165–225 (1983).

M. M. Whiteman, *Digest of International Law*, 15 vols, 1963 [*Whiteman*].

7

The contiguous zone

Development of the concept

The contiguous zone is a zone of sea contiguous to and seaward of the territorial sea in which States have limited powers for the enforcement of customs, fiscal, sanitary and immigration laws. It has its origins in functional legislation such as the eighteenth century 'Hovering Acts' enacted by Great Britain against foreign smuggling ships hovering within distances of up to eight leagues (i.e., twenty-four miles) from the shore. These Acts, which had effect from 1736 until their repeal by the 1876 Customs Consolidation Act, were at the time regarded as permitted by 'the common courtesy of nations for their convenience', as Lord Stowell put it in the case of *Le Louis* in 1817. However, this was at a time when practice had not yet given the three-mile limit for the territorial sea the force of a rule of law.

A dispute with Spain in the early years of the nineteenth century over seizures of British ships within the six-mile Spanish customs zone, among other incidents, focused attention on the extent of maritime claims. By mid-century the three-mile limit for the territorial sea, combined with the exclusivity of flag State jurisdiction on the high seas beyond, was well established in Anglo-American practice and served well the interests of free navigation. Great Britain recognised that its wider customs zones were inconsistent with the three-mile rule. The seizure of the French ship the *Petit Jules* twenty-three miles off the Isle of Wight in 1850 was the last occasion on which the Hovering Acts were enforced against a foreign vessel beyond the marine league.[1] Indeed, the British Law Officers advised that the seizure was impermissible under international law, and the one member of the crew who had been captured was set free. From then on, the three-mile rule was applied in Britain and its dominions and colonies. However, this rule was subject to two exceptions allowing the exercise of jurisdiction against foreign vessels at greater distances from shore.

[1] For details of and references to this and other cases and to pre-1958 legislation see Lowe, *op. cit.* in 'Further reading' at the end of this chapter.

First, according to the doctrine of constructive presence, where a ship beyond the marine league sent its boats within that limit (as occurred for the purpose of illegal fishing in the case of the *Araunah* (1888) and for the purpose of releasing prisoners in the *Catalpa* incident (1877) in Australia) no distinction was drawn between the ship and its boats, and the ship was liable to be seized for the violation of the local law.[2] According to later refinements of the doctrine, illustrated, for example, by some of the diplomatic exchanges concerning the seizure of the *Henry L. Marshall* for violation of the American liquor laws in 1922 and by the Italian case of the *Sito* in 1957, it had no application where a foreign ship communicated with the shore not by means of its own boats but by means of boats sent out from the shore. In such cases the exclusive jurisdiction of the flag State over its ships on the high seas was said to remain intact. This rejection of 'extensive' constructive presence (as distinct from 'simple' constructive presence, where the ship's own boats are involved) impedes action against drug traffickers. It is not surprising that some States have begun to take a more liberal view in cases such as *R. v. Sunila and Solayman* (Canada, 1986) extending the doctrine to instances where the communication was effected with a ship sent out from shore.[3]

The second exception was the doctrine of hot pursuit. This provided that when a ship was found within the territorial sea of a State, and there was good reason to believe that it had violated the local law, it could be pursued and arrested on the high seas. The doctrine, which was incorporated in the Geneva Conventions as article 23 of the High Seas Convention and in the LOSC as article 111, is discussed in more detail in chapter eleven. What is important for present purposes is the fact that it, like the doctrine of constructive presence, allowed a measure of enforcement jurisdiction beyond the three-mile limit, which was otherwise adhered to more or less strictly.

Other States adopted different approaches. Several, mostly in Europe, did not claim territorial seas as zones of unified jurisdiction but, as was noted in chapter four, claimed a variety of jurisdictional zones. The width of each zone was fixed at whatever distance the State concerned thought was necessary for the purpose for which that zone was established. For example, France maintained three-mile zones for fishery and general policing purposes, but a six-mile neutrality zone and a twenty-kilometre customs zone. Belgium, Italy, Greece and Spain and, outside Europe, Cuba and Turkey were among other States adopting similar positions. While exact widths varied from State to State, customs and security zones were usually more extensive than other zones.

The practice of a third group of States was much closer to the concept of the contiguous zone as it is recognised today. Several Latin American States claimed

---

[2] *Ibid.*
[3] *R. v. Sunila and Solayman* (Canada, 1986); W. C. Gilmore, 'Hot pursuit and constructive presence in Canadian law enforcement', 12 *Marine Policy* 105–11 (1988). Cf., e.g., *Re Pulos* (Italy, 1976); *R. v. Mills* (UK, 1995) noted by W. C. Gilmore, 'Hot Pursuit: The Case of *R. v. Mills and Others*', 44 *ICLQ* 949–58 (1995).

a one-league belt as the public property of the State, and beyond that zone of sovereignty a second zone, of a further three leagues, in which the State enjoyed the right of policing for customs and security purposes only. The 1855 Chilean Civil Code contained such a provision, as did the laws of, for example, Argentina, Ecuador, Honduras and Mexico. While some non-American States, such as Egypt, Latvia and Norway, followed this practice, the most notorious claims were those advanced by the United States in its 1922 Tariff Act. Under this Act, foreign ships within twelve miles of the United States' coasts were subjected to US laws on the prohibition of alcohol, which had been introduced by the Volstead Act in 1919. The US liquor laws provoked a great deal of opposition from foreign States, partly because they were apparently enforced with much more than the usual vigour against foreign ships, and partly because the policy enforced was not one shared by the States concerned. Sufficient wrath was raised in the British Foreign Office for it to be suggested that all US ships and all ships trading from US ports be barred from entering British ports. Wisely, no attempt was made to implement the suggestion.

Despite the strong opposition to the unilateral enforcement of US law beyond the marine league, there was some sympathy with the general aim of preventing hovering vessels from violating the prohibition laws. Both these sentiments were satisfied by the 1924 Anglo-American 'Liquor Treaty'. That treaty began by reaffirming the importance of the three-mile limit and went on to provide that the British government would raise no objection to the searching of British vessels within one hour's steaming of the US coast, thus satisfying the US demands without conceding its right to act in the absence of the specific treaty agreement. Similar treaties were concluded by the USA with most European States, as well as with Panama, Chile and Japan, and there was a comparable arrangement between the Baltic States in the 1925 Helsingfors Treaty. These agreements set a pattern which has found modern expression in the Anglo-American agreements on the interdiction of unlawful traffic in narcotics in the Caribbean, discussed in chapter eleven below.

By the early part of the twentieth century there were, therefore, three main approaches to the question of jurisdiction beyond the three-mile limit. First, there were States that denied that such jurisdiction existed, except where given by treaty or under the doctrines of hot pursuit and constructive presence. This group included Britain and the dominions, Germany, Denmark, Sweden, Japan and the Netherlands, as the replies to the Hague Codification Conference's 'Schedule of Points' in 1929 showed. Second, there were States that claimed a variety of jurisdictional zones; and, third, there were States that claimed a jurisdictional zone, usually for customs and security purposes, which was clearly distinct from the territorial sea.

The idea of using a distinct contiguous zone beyond a narrow territorial sea as a basis for compromise between such groups of States, and for facilitating agreement on the question of the breadth of the territorial sea, had been put forward by Renault during the discussion of neutrality zones by the Institute of

International Law as far back as 1894. The idea was taken up more generally by the learned societies in the years before the Hague conference; but despite the considerable interest shown in proposals to include a zone of extended customs, sanitary and security jurisdiction in the 1930 Hague conference text, none was in fact agreed upon, doubtless largely as a result of the same failure to agree upon the width of the territorial sea as prevented the text from being adopted as a treaty.

In the years between the Hague and Geneva conferences, State practice remained divided between those States, such as the United Kingdom, which did not recognise the validity of contiguous zone claims, and the increasing number of States which made such claims. During this period the notion of a territorial sea distinct from other jurisdictional zones became generally accepted, although a few States, such as Cuba, Spain and Greece, still kept to the idea of a 'territorial sea' whose width varied according to the purpose for which jurisdiction was exercised. Many States claimed special customs and security, and sometimes sanitary and immigration, zones on the high seas contiguous to their territorial sea. Claims to fishery zones also became commonplace, and State practice does not seem to have distinguished between the legal character of these fishery zones and that of other contiguous zones. However, one of the most eminent jurists of the period, Gidel, did distinguish between them, requiring the establishment of fishery zones by treaty but admitting the legality of unilateral claims to other contiguous zones. The distinction was preserved in the reports which François made to the International Law Commission during its consideration of the law of the sea, in the reports of the Commission itself, and at the Geneva conference, where the question of fishery zones was allotted to a special committee. With the establishment of 200-mile fishery jurisdiction in the LOSC, the distinction between the two kinds of zone was put beyond argument.

The 1958 (Geneva) conference eventually agreed upon the establishment of a contiguous zone within which the coastal State enjoys limited jurisdiction. That provision, which was set out in article 24 of the Territorial Sea Convention, was reproduced without significant debate or change as article 33(1) of the 1982 Convention. That article states that in the contiguous zone

the coastal State may exercise the control necessary to:
(a) Prevent infringement of its customs, fiscal, immigration or sanitary laws and regulations within its territory or territorial sea;
(b) Punish infringement of the above laws and regulations committed within its territory or territorial sea.

Breadth of the contiguous zone

States are not obliged to maintain contiguous zones, as they are to maintain territorial seas; and unlike the continental shelf, the contiguous zone is not automatically ascribed to the coastal State. Under both the 1958 and 1982 Conventions a State must choose whether to claim a contiguous zone, and just over one-third of coastal States have chosen to do so (see appendix).[4]

Under the Territorial Sea Convention the contiguous zone could not extend more than twelve miles from the baseline (TSC, art. 24(2)), or, unless there was agreement to the contrary between the States concerned, farther than the median line equidistant from the nearest points on the baselines where two States lay opposite or adjacent to each other (TSC, art. 24(3)). No agreement on the breadth of the territorial sea was reached at the 1958 conference, and the practice of States concerning contiguous zone claims in the years immediately following consequently varied, some claiming a three-mile territorial sea and nine-mile contiguous zone, others a six-mile territorial sea and six-mile contiguous zone, and so on. These claims, modelled on the wording of article 24 of the 1958 Convention, were overtaken by the move towards twelve-mile territorial sea claims. In the light of those claims, UNCLOS III decided to move the contiguous zone seaward, setting the outer limit at twenty-four miles from the baseline (LOSC, art. 33), so allowing a twelve-mile contiguous zone beyond the twelve-mile territorial sea. Since the purpose of the zone is essentially the protection of the shore, it must be doubted whether a contiguous zone is necessary if a twelve-mile territorial sea is established. It is, however, clear that many States wish to exercise their right to claim one.

The wave of new claims to maritime zones after the late 1970s included many to contiguous zones. As of 1997, approximately fifty-one States had claimed a twenty-four mile contiguous zone (although, as is noted below, some claims are for purposes wider than those set out in the conventions), and five other States had claimed a contiguous zone of between twelve and twenty-four miles. In addition, Syria maintains an eccentric claim to a six-mile contiguous zone beyond its thirty-five mile territorial sea. A claim by Namibia to exercise 'contiguous zone' rights of control throughout its entire 200-mile EEZ was amended, after a US protest, so as to confine the claim to a twenty-four mile contiguous zone.[5]

Unlike the Territorial Sea Convention, the 1982 Law of the Sea Convention contains no provision on the delimitation of the contiguous zone between opposite and adjacent States. This is possibly because its delimitation would (for States claiming an EEZ) amount to a delimitation of a part of the EEZ, and is therefore dealt with as such: see chapter ten below. Some, however, take the view that because the contiguous zone is not an area of sovereignty or exclusive jurisdiction, there is no reason why contiguous zones should not overlap, and

---

[4] The UN stated in 1996 that there were 151 coastal States, of which 145 had enacted maritime legislation: see *LOSB* 30, p. 79 (1996). In 1997 there were more than fifty contiguous zone claims.

[5] J. A. Roach and R. W. Smith, *United States Responses to Excessive Maritime Claims* (The Hague, Nijhoff), 2nd edn, 1996, pp. 170–1; Territorial Sea and Exclusive Economic Zone of Namibia Act No. 3 of 1990, 30 June 1990, 21 *LOSB* 59 (1992); Territorial Sea and Exclusive Economic Zone of Namibia Amendment Act, 1991, 21 *LOSB* 64 (1992).

hence no strict need for delimitation.[6] Others take a different view: for instance Yugoslavia, when ratifying the 1982 Convention, declared that delimitation of the contiguous zone should be governed by 'the principles of customary international law, codified in article 24, paragraph (3) of the 1958 Convention'.[7]

Legal status of the contiguous zone

The early unilateral claims had asserted both the right to prescribe regulations to operate in the extended zones and the right to enforce them; in other words, both legislative and enforcement jurisdiction. The literal wording of article 24 of the Territorial Sea Convention and of article 33 of the Law of the Sea Convention, however, ascribes only enforcement jurisdiction to the coastal State. Action may be taken only in respect of offences committed within the territory or territorial sea of a State, not in respect of anything done within the contiguous zone itself. This seems to have been the intention of the 1958 conference. The ILC had proposed a text identical to that adopted, but a Polish amendment which deleted the reference to infringements committed within the territory or territorial sea in order to 'make provision for action to deal with possible infringement within the contiguous zone' was adopted by the First Committee at Geneva. That proposed article also included a right to protect security interests. This was opposed, despite the prevalence of security zones in State practice, by some States which saw in such claims a danger to free navigation in the zone. The amended article was rejected in plenary session and replaced by the original ILC text, to which immigration had been added as a protected interest, and which had clearly been considered to create a zone of enforcement jurisdiction only. Indeed, this seems a necessary result of the 1958 scheme, for article 19(5) of the Territorial Sea Convention (and now article 27 of the Law of the Sea Convention) forbids the arrest of ships passing through the territorial sea for offences committed before they enter that sea. If legislative jurisdiction were to exist in the contiguous zone so that ships could commit offences there, they would be able to achieve a greater degree of immunity from coastal State jurisdiction by fleeing into the territorial sea than by fleeing to the high seas or economic zone, since in the latter case they could be seized after hot pursuit (HSC, art. 23; LOSC, art. 111).

Article 33 of the Law of the Sea Convention follows article 24 of the Territorial Sea Convention almost verbatim as far as the legal status of the contiguous zone and list of purposes are concerned. In addition, it should be noted that by a legal fiction the contiguous zone has been extended to archaeological and historical objects. Article 303(2) provides that

[6] See, e.g., M. Hayashi, 'Japan. New Law of the Sea legislation', 12 *IJMCL* 570–80, at 572 (1997).
[7] *LOSB*, Special Issue I (1987), p. 9; http://www.un.org/Depts/los/los_decl.htm.

in order to control traffic in such objects, the coastal State may, in applying article 33, presume that their removal from the sea-bed in the [contiguous] zone . . . without its approval would result in an infringement within its territory or territorial sea of the laws and regulations referred to in that article.

State practice since 1958 has not always followed the conventional provisions on the status of the zone. Many States have followed the Convention formula more or less closely, apparently limiting their claims to enforcement jurisdiction.[8] Some States quite clearly claimed both enforcement and legislative jurisdiction, although the laws in this category tend to date from the years prior to the adoption of the 1982 Convention.[9] Some States claim contiguous zones for purposes other than those listed in the conventions, notably for security purposes (see appendix). The claims to legislative jurisdiction in the contiguous zone do not appear to have evoked significant international opposition in practice. The claims to security jurisdiction, on the other hand, have been opposed. One study listed eighteen States whose claims to security jurisdiction in a contiguous zone have been protested by the USA.[10]

Opposition to the extension of contiguous zone rights to cover security interests should perhaps be seen as a reflection of the concern among maritime States that security zones represent a particular threat to the freedom of navigation. The extension of contiguous zone rights in other respects (as was done in relation to archaeological objects in article 303 of the 1982 Convention) may prove to be more acceptable to the international community.[11] Support for the view that States may enjoy contiguous zone rights in customary law wider than those set out in the conventional regime was given by a United States court in the controversial case of the *Taiyo Maru* (1974), a Japanese vessel pursued from the nine-mile

---

[8] See, e.g., Australia, Seas and Submerged Lands Act, 1973 as amended by the Maritime Legislation Amendment Act, 1994, 27 *LOSB* 49 (1995); Brazil, Law No. 8617 of 4 January 1993 on the territorial sea, the contiguous zone, the exclusive economic zone and the continental shelf, 23 *LOSB* 17 (1993); Republic of Korea, Territorial Sea and Contiguous Zone Act, 1977–95, 33 *LOSB* 45 (1997); South Africa, Maritime Zones Act, 1994, 32 *LOSB* 75 (1996).

[9] See, e.g., India, Territorial Waters Continental Shelf, Exclusive Economic Zone and Other Maritime Zones Act, 1976, *UN Leg. Ser.* B/19, p. 47, *ND V* p. 305, *Smith, op. cit.* in 'Further reading', p. 213; Pakistan, Territorial Waters and Maritime Zones Act, 1976, *UN Leg. Ser.* B/19, p. 85, *ND VII*, p. 478, *Smith, op. cit.*, p. 357; Sri Lanka, Maritime Zones Law, 1976, *UN Leg. Ser.* B/19, p. 120, *Smith, op. cit.*, p. 427.

[10] Roach and Smith, *op. cit. in* footnote 5, p. 172: The States listed are Bangladesh, Burma (now Myanmar), Cambodia, China, Egypt, Haiti, India, Iran, Nicaragua, Pakistan, Saudi Arabia, Sri Lanka, Sudan, Syria, United Arab Emirates, Venezuela, Vietnam and Yemen.

[11] Although only a few States, including Denmark, France, Tunisia and South Africa, have as yet taken advantage of the possibility afforded by LOSC, art. 303: see A. Strati, *The Protection of the Underwater Cultural Heritage: an emerging objective of the contemporary law of the sea* (The Hague, Nijhoff), 1995, at p. 185; cf. 16 *LOSB* 12 (1990) (French legislation of 1989), and 32 *LOSB* 75 (1996) (South African legislation of 1994). UNESCO is drafting a convention on the underwater cultural heritage: see further chapter eight.

fishery zone contiguous to the three-mile American territorial sea. The court held that article 24 of the Territorial Sea Convention was permissive, not exhaustive, and that contiguous zones, apparently including both enforcement and legislative jurisdiction, could be established for purposes other than those detailed in the article. Similarly, in the case of *U.S.* v. *Gonzalez* (1985), a United States court held that the 'protective principle' of jurisdiction in international law justified the exercise of jurisdiction over foreign ships on the high seas to enforce narcotics legislation, although in this case no limit *ratione materiae* was set to such jurisdiction: the case is discussed further in chapter eleven.[12] While the interdiction of traffic in illegal narcotics may in any event be said to fall within customs or sanitary legislation, it is likely that States will be tolerant of moves to extend national jurisdiction in order to repress such generally deplored activities.

The difficulty of resolving the problem of the legal status of the contiguous zone has, indeed, increased with the adoption of the Law of the Sea Convention. Under the Geneva rules and under the earlier practice, at least of those States which did not claim a 'variable' territorial sea, the contiguous zone was a part of the high seas. It followed that, unlike the case of the territorial sea, where the sovereignty of the coastal State resulted in a presumption in favour of the existence of that State's jurisdiction in case of doubt, the presumption in the contiguous zone was against the existence of coastal State jurisdiction over foreign ships: coastal State rights were to be strictly construed. But under the Law of the Sea Convention the contiguous zone falls not within the high seas but within the EEZ. The consequence is, in theory, that the presumption against coastal State jurisdiction is removed. In cases where a dispute arises concerning a claim by a coastal State to jurisdictional rights not expressly granted under the Convention, the question is to be resolved, as will be seen in chapter nine, 'on the basis of equity' and 'taking into account the respective importance of the interests' of the parties concerned and of the world at large. It is unclear what effect, if any, this change will have, but it is likely to make the extension of contiguous zone rights *ratione materiae*, and the inclusion of both enforcement and legislative jurisdiction, more easy to defend than formerly.

Further reading

L. Caflisch, 'Submarine antiquities and the law of the sea', 13 *NYIL* 3–32 (1982).
E. D. Dickinson, 'Jurisdiction at the maritime frontier', 40 *Harvard Law Review* 1–29 (1926).
Sir G. Fitzmaurice, 'Some results of the Geneva Conference on the Law of the Sea', 8 *ICLQ* 73–121 (1959).
A. M. Frommer, 'The British Hovering Acts: a contribution to the study of the contiguous zone', 16 *Revue belge de droit international* 434–58 (1981–2).

[12] Cf. the practice of the Italian courts reported in *O'Connell*, vol. II, *op. cit.* in 'Further reading', p. 1059.

G. Gidel, 'La mer territoriale et la zone contiguë', 48 *Recueil des Cours* 241–73 (1934).

P. C. Jessup, *The Law of Territorial Waters and Maritime Jurisdiction* (New York, Jennings), 1927.

A. V. Lowe, 'The development of the concept of the contiguous zone', 52 *BYIL* 109–69 (1981).

W. E. Masterson, *Jurisdiction in Marginal Seas* (New York, Macmillan), 1929.

D. P. O'Connell, *The International Law of the Sea*, 2 vols (Oxford, Clarendon), 1982, 1984 [*O'Connell*].

S. Oda, 'The concept of the contiguous zone', 11 *ICLQ* 131–53 (1962).

A. Pazarci, 'Le concept de zone contiguë dans la convention sur le droit de la mer de 1982', 18 *Revue belge de droit international* 249–71 (1984–5).

S. A. Riesenfeld, *Protection of Coastal Fisheries under International Law* (Washington, D.C., Carnegie), 1942.

R. W. Smith, *Exclusive Economic Zone Claims: An Analysis and Primary Documents* (Dordecht, Nijhoff), 1986 [*Smith*].

See also the further reading in chapter eleven.

8

The continental shelf

Introduction

Physically, the sea bed adjacent to a typical coast is usually considered to consist of three separate sections (as was illustrated in the figure at the end of chapter 1). First, the section that slopes down gradually from the low-water mark to the depth, averaging about 130 metres, at which the angle of declination increases markedly: this is the continental shelf proper. Second, the section bordering the shelf and having the steeper slope, going down to around 1,200 to 3,500 metres: this is known as the continental slope. Third, there is in many locations an area beyond the slope where the sea bed falls away more gradually and is composed mainly of sediments washed down from the continents. This is called the continental rise, and typically descends to a depth of around 3,500 to 5,500 metres. Together these three sections form the continental margin, which constitutes about one-fifth of the sea floor. (See the figure at the end of chapter 1 and the figure at the end of this chapter.)

In many places the continental margin – and especially the continental shelf – is rich in natural resources. Most important are the extensive oil and gas reserves, which represent something like ninety per cent of the total value of minerals taken from the sea bed. Offshore exploitation of oil and gas on a commercial scale did not begin until shortly before the Second World War, but it expanded rapidly as a result of developments in technology and increasing demand. By the mid-1990s offshore oil and gas production accounted for around one-third of total world production; and some estimated that around 70 per cent of the world's undiscovered reserves lie offshore. It is expected that by 2005 there will be around 4,100 offshore oil and gas fields on stream, and almost 9,000 offshore platforms associated with them. The main concentrations of production facilities lie in four areas: north-west Europe, west Africa, south-east Asia and north America. Attention is turning to new resources, such as the fields of methane hydrate deposits on the Japanese shelf.[1] Other minerals are also important. There

[1] Some estimates claim that methane hydrate deposits contain twice the organic carbon resources in all recyclable and unrecovered oil, gas and coal deposits on earth, and thirty

has long been interest in 'placer' deposits of heavy minerals containing metals such as tin, titanium, chromium and zirconium. In the 1970s, before world markets were upset by the collapse of the International Tin Agreement, around one-quarter of world tin production came from offshore casserite deposits dredged from the Indian Ocean.[2] Diamonds have been recovered commercially from the sea bed off Namibia. Pools of brine in the subsoil, notably under the Red Sea, contain concentrations of lead, zinc, gold and silver, and may become an important source of these metals, and perhaps of thermal energy. Volcanic springs yielding high concentrations of iron, zinc, copper, silver and gold have been found off Papua New Guinea, and at least one company has staked a claim to an offshore mine site to exploit them. While exploitation of all these offshore resources is likely to become easier and cheaper as marine technology develops, the commercial feasibility of exploitation depends upon the balance of supply and demand and the price that can be obtained for the resources.

As well as mineral resources, there are also important fisheries on the continental shelf for sedentary species, such as oysters and clams, and lobsters and crabs (although the classification of the two latter organisms as 'sedentary' is controversial). In some areas, notably the Pacific, these fisheries make an important contribution to the economies of the littoral States.

The existence of such a rich diversity of valuable resources makes the legal status of the continental shelf an important practical question. This chapter outlines the rules of international law relevant to the determination of that status. The delimitation of the continental shelf between neighbouring States is discussed in chapter ten.

The legal status of the continental shelf

In the early years of the twentieth century, in the period leading up to the Hague Codification Conference of 1930, it became generally accepted that possession of a territorial sea gave the coastal State proprietary rights over the resources of that sea, including its bed and subsoil. There were much older claims to the resources of the subsoil, exploited by tunnelling from the shore. The United Kingdom, for example, had long claimed such a right in relation to the submarine mines off Cornwall. But the significance of the twentieth-century development of the law on this matter was that it drew a clear distinction between the bed of the territorial sea, which automatically appertained to the coastal State, and the bed of the high seas, which did not. The bed of the high seas could, however, be the subject of effective occupation by a State; and such occupation was sufficient to give

---

times the amount of carbon dioxide in the atmosphere: 'Oceans and the Law of the Sea: Law of the Sea. Report of the Secretary General' (hereafter, 'Oceans and the Law of the Sea, 1997'), UN Doc. A/52/487 (20 October 1997), paras 252–3.

[2] J. Pernetta, *Atlas of the Oceans* (London, Philip), 1994, p. 147.

that State title to its resources. Mining from the coast was one way of achieving effective occupation, resulting in proprietorial rights to parts of the subsoil of the high seas. Regular exploitation of, and the assertion of rights of control over, specific areas of the surface of the sea bed could similarly give such rights to such areas. This was fairly common practice. The United Kingdom, for example, claimed sovereign rights in respect of pearl and chank fisheries off Ceylon, as did France in respect of sponge fisheries beyond the territorial sea off Tunis. Such claims were widely recognised, and did not significantly compromise the legal regime of the high seas, because the freedoms of fishing and navigation in the superjacent waters were unaffected. However, some authorities disputed the right of States to appropriate areas of the bed of the high seas, on the ground that it was in law *res communis* and therefore incapable of unilateral appropriation, rather than *res nullius*, in which case it would have been open for appropriation by the first State to establish effective occupation. Nevertheless, exclusive rights to harvest the resources of specific areas of the sea bed, as distinct from claims to ownership of the bed itself, seem to have been generally admitted.

The question of jurisdiction and property rights over marine resources was proposed for examination by the Hague conference, but not discussed by that conference. Nonetheless, the practical importance of sea-bed resources was such that it was inevitable that States would soon take action to arrogate to themselves the sea bed adjacent to their coasts. The first step was cautious. In 1942 the United Kingdom, on behalf of Trinidad, and Venezuela concluded a Treaty relating to the Submarine Areas of the Gulf of Paria.[3] Under this treaty the sea bed in the Gulf beyond the territorial waters of the two States was divided into two sectors. In one sector the United Kingdom agreed not to assert any claim to sovereignty or control and to recognise any rights of sovereignty or control lawfully acquired by Venezuela, while Venezuela gave a corresponding undertaking in respect of the other sector. Although the treaty bound only the two signatories, its effect was tantamount to the division of the sea bed of the Gulf of Paria between them, since it was most improbable that any other State would have sought to build up a title based on effective occupation of a zone which the coastal States were actively engaged in developing. Thus the treaty clearly defined the sectors within which each party was to make no claim to sovereignty, but did not itself assert the sovereignty of the other party over such sectors: sovereignty still had to arise from occupation. So the 1942 treaty succeeded, in effect, in delimiting the continental shelf before the legal concept of the continental shelf itself was established.

It is customary, however, to regard the proclamation made by President Truman of the USA in 1945 as the first clear assertion of the idea that a continental shelf belongs to the coastal State. The Truman proclamation stated that:

---

[3] See A. Francis, 'Treaty between the Republic of Trinidad and Tobago and the Republic of Venezuela on the delimitation of the marine and submarine areas: an analysis', 6 *IJECL* 169–98 (1991).

the Government of the United States regards the natural resources of the subsoil and seabed of the continental shelf beneath the high seas but contiguous to the coasts of the United States as appertaining to the United States, subject to its jurisdiction and control.[4]

In its preamble, the proclamation justified this claim on the basis of contiguity and reasonableness.

The Truman Proclamation was followed by similar claims on the part of many other States. These varied in their precise nature. Some claimed jurisdiction and control over the resources of the continental shelf, while others claimed sovereignty over the shelf as such. Yet other claims, made by a number of Latin American States, extended not only to the shelf but also to the superjacent waters, and in some cases even to the air space above those waters. The inconsistency of early practice, as regards both the nature and the geographical extent of the claims, was such that in 1951, in his award in the arbitration between Petroleum Development Ltd and the Sheikh of Abu Dhabi, Lord Asquith stated that the doctrine of the continental shelf could not claim to have 'assumed hitherto the hard lineaments or the definitive status of an established rule of international law'.[5]

Throughout the following years more and more States laid claim to some kind of rights over the shelf. By the time of the 1958 Geneva conference about twenty States, some acting both in their own right and on behalf of dependent territories, had made such claims. At the 1958 conference the idea that coastal States should enjoy certain rights over their continental shelves was generally accepted. The Continental Shelf Convention adopted by the conference provided that these rights should be 'sovereign rights for the purpose of exploring and exploiting' the resources of the continental shelf (CSC, art. 2). So firmly was the principle of coastal State rights over the continental shelf established that in 1969, only eighteen years after the *Abu Dhabi* award, the ICJ stated in its judgment in the *North Sea Continental Shelf* cases that:

> [T]he rights of the coastal State in respect of the area of continental shelf that constitutes a natural prolongation of its land territory into and under the sea exist *ipso facto* and *ab initio* by virtue of its sovereignty over the land, and as an extension of it in an exercise of sovereign rights for the purpose of exploring the seabed and exploiting its natural resources. In short there is here an inherent right.[6]

It is not clear whether or not the International Court intended to rewrite legal history, so that the *ab initio* appurtenance of the shelf of the coastal State would,

---

[4] *ND I*, p. 106. And see A. L. Hollick, 'US Oceans Policy: the Truman Proclamation', 17 *VJIL* 23–35 (1976–7).

[5] 18 *ILR* 144 at 155.

[6] [1969] *ICJ Rep.* 3, at 23. For an interesting application of this dictum in a domestic context see the 1983 decision of the Court of Appeals of Newfoundland, Canada, *Reference re Mineral and Other Offshore Resources of the Continental Shelf*, 90 *ILR* 234, at 262–5.

in retrospect, be said to have attached the continental shelf as a matter of inter-national law to Abu Dhabi by 1951, for example. But it is quite clear that the doctrine of the continental shelf was firmly established in international law by 1958, and that its position has not weakened since then.

While the doctrine of the continental shelf has not itself weakened, a certain amount of duplication and possible confusion arose with the emergence of the concept of the 200-mile exclusive economic zone (EEZ) at UNCLOS III. As we shall see in chapter nine, under the Law of the Sea Convention the coastal State has sovereign rights over all the natural resources of its EEZ, including the sea-bed resources (LOSC, art. 56). There are, accordingly, now two distinct legal bases for coastal State rights in relation to the sea bed. The first is the classical doctrine of the continental shelf, as formulated in the Continental Shelf Conven-tion and in customary international law, and as preserved in Part VI of the 1982 Law of the Sea Convention. The second is the newer concept of the EEZ, which is set out in Part V of the 1982 Convention and, as is explained in chapter nine, is also now established in customary international law. It is important to keep these two bases separate. Their origins are quite different, and, while they will usually apply concurrently to the same geographical area, this is by no means always the case. The EEZ has a breadth of 200 miles, which may be greater or less than the breadth of the 'physical' continental shelf under the classical doc-trine, although under the Law of the Sea Convention the minimum breadth of the continental shelf is 200 miles, and thus not less than the EEZ. It should also be borne in mind that while a continental shelf exists *ipso facto* and *ab initio* and therefore need not be claimed, an EEZ must always be claimed so that, as the International Court recognised in the *Libya/Malta Continental Shelf* case, there can be a continental shelf without an EEZ but there cannot be an EEZ without a continental shelf.[7] And although the continental shelf and EEZ represent differ-ent bases for rights to the sea bed, the Law of the Sea Convention does provide, in article 56(3) in Part V, that EEZ sea-bed sovereign rights are 'exercised in accordance with' the provisions of Part VI of the Convention, concerning the continental shelf.

In this chapter we approach the question of continental shelf rights primarily from the perspective of the classical continental shelf doctrine, looking first at the area to which it applies and secondly at the nature of coastal States' rights.

The seaward limit of the continental shelf

The inner or landward limit of the continental shelf has never been contenti-ous. It has always been regarded as being the outer limit of the territorial sea (even though the exact breadth of the territorial sea itself has been controver-sial). However, it has been less easy to attain an agreed definition of the outer

[7] [1985] *ICJ Rep.* 13, at 33.

limit of the continental shelf. The Truman Proclamation did not fix in terms of miles or depth a seaward limit for the claim which it advanced to the continental shelf (although an accompanying memorandum by the State Department Legal Advisor noted that 'The continental shelf is usually defined as that part of the undersea land mass adjacent to the coast, over which the sea is not more than 100 fathoms (600 feet) in depth'[8]). But by referring to the continental shelf as 'an extension of the land mass of the coastal State and thus naturally appurtenant to it' the Proclamation, like other claims which referred to rights over the 'continental shelf' to an unspecified distance, was clearly confined to the continental margin as the physical continuation of the land mass. It is, however, not clear whether the Truman Proclamation was intended to be more limited than that and confined, for example, to the continental shelf in the strict geomorphological sense.

The continental shelf claims were the first claims to jurisdiction extending beyond the comparatively modest belt of coastal waters to be made in time of peace since the abandonment of the grandiose claims over the high seas in the early nineteenth century (see chapter eleven). It was therefore natural that there should at some point be felt, among lawyers and governments alike, a desire to limit the extent to which these claims encroached upon the area of high seas and its traditional freedoms. Unfortunately, the few (Latin American) States among the early claimants which did fix seaward limits for their continental shelf claims often put the limit, usually of 200 miles, beyond the furthermost reach of their continental margins.

In the early stages of the development of the concept of the continental shelf the question of the seaward limit was less important than it became, as a result of developments in offshore technology, in later years. When the ILC first addressed the task of drafting an article establishing a conventional seaward limit, it proposed that the legal definition of the shelf should include all of the sea bed contiguous to the coast where the depth of the superjacent waters admitted of the exploitation of the resources of the sea bed and subsoil. A number of governments suggested that this 'exploitability' criterion was too vague, and might lead to international conflicts. In its 1953 report the ILC accordingly replaced it with the more precise limit of the 200-metre isobath. It was thought that, for practical purposes and for the foreseeable future, the 200-metre isobath limit would satisfy national interests in the shelf.[9] However, reconsidering the question in the light of the resolutions of the Inter-American Specialised Conference on Conservation of Natural Resources, held at Cuidad Trujillo in 1956, a majority of the ILC followed the lead of that conference in reintroducing the 'exploitability' criterion as an alternative limit in addition to the 200-metre isobath. This ensured

[8] A. L. Hollick, *U.S. Foreign Policy and the Law of the Sea* (New Jersey, Princeton), 1981, p. 49.
[9] By 1997 the offshore industry was envisaging the recovery of oil at depths of 10,000 feet (just over 3,000 metres) and distances of 250 miles from land: 'Oceans and the Law of the Sea, 1997', UN Doc. A/52/487 (20 October 1997), para. 245.

that in circumstances where exploitation was possible at depths greater than 200 metres the coastal State would retain its exclusive rights, and so prevented the possibility of pockets of deeper sea bed arising as lacunae in national continental shelves. Although there was considerable opposition to this dual criterion at the 1958 Geneva Conference, the ILC proposal was eventually approved. Thus, article 1 of the 1958 Continental Shelf Convention defined the continental shelf as being:

> the seabed and subsoil of the submarine areas adjacent to the coast but outside the area of the territorial sea, to a depth of 200 metres or, beyond that limit, to where the depth of the superjacent waters admits of the exploitation of the natural resources of the said areas . . .

In the *North Sea Continental Shelf* cases the International Court said that this article represented customary law (although the Court also laid much stress on the continental shelf being the 'natural prolongation' of the coastal State's land mass). The definition of the continental shelf contained in the 1958 Convention was adopted by many States, a number of which were not parties to the Convention, in their national legislation.

In spite of the widespread adoption of the 1958 Convention's definition of the continental shelf, that definition was not free from difficulty. Even at the 1958 conference it was recognised that the addition of the exploitability test rendered the seaward limit dangerously imprecise. It was clear that new technology would push the limit farther and farther from the shore, and that 'exploitability' – which could mean anything from the ability to drag up a basket of sedentary fish to the ability to establish a full-scale profit-making offshore oil complex – was itself an elusive criterion. Moreover, it was not clear whether it was the ability of the coastal State, or of any other State – or even of all other States – which was in question. The use of the word 'adjacent' also raised questions. Was it intended to operate so as to restrain the seaward limit of exploitability, holding it within some notional area of 'adjacency'? Or did it simply mean that, to qualify as continental shelf, the sea bed must be one continuous mass, unbroken by troughs or depressions, regardless of how far it extended?

In the years following the 1958 conference, attention was increasingly given to the resources of the deep sea bed beyond the physical continental shelf (see chapter twelve). It became clear that, given sufficient investment, there were few, if any, areas of the ocean bed which could not be exploited in some way. It was feared that the consequence of continued adherence to the exploitability test in the face of rapidly developing technology, rendering ever deeper areas 'exploitable', would be the eventual extension of coastal State 'continental shelf' claims so as to cover the entire ocean floor. This would in practice have benefited only those few States with the technology necessary to exploit the deep ocean bed, and as we note in chapter twelve the geographical distribution of States over the globe is such that, were national claims to be established into the mid-ocean and delimited by the use of median lines (see chapter ten), the developed

States would be the major beneficiaries of the carving up of the sea bed. This led to calls for the internationalisation of the deep sea bed, placing the mineral resources of that area beyond the reach of unilateral claims. However, this in turn necessitated the fixing of a definite outer limit for national claims to jurisdiction over the sea bed.

There was considerable difficulty in reaching agreement on this outer limit at UNCLOS III. The consolidation of the emergent rules on the EEZ automatically imported acceptance of an outer limit of at least 200 miles from coastal States' baselines. This brought about thirty-six per cent of the total sea bed within national jurisdiction, including in some areas parts of the sea bed lying beyond the physical continental margin. But a number of States, including the UK, USA and the then USSR, have continental margins which extend beyond the 200-mile limit, and were therefore reluctant to give up any claims to the resources in the outermost portions of their continental margins. On the other hand, States with narrow shelves wished to secure agreement on the 200-mile limit or some other basis which would maximise the area of sea bed beyond the permissible scope of national jurisdiction, because that sea bed would form the International Sea Bed Area, in the fruits of whose exploitation it was intended that all States should share.

The Law of the Sea Convention provides that:

> The continental shelf of a coastal State comprises the sea-bed and subsoil of the submarine areas that extend beyond its territorial sea throughout the natural prolongation of its land territory to the outer edge of the continental margin, or to a distance of 200 nautical miles from the baselines from which the breadth of the territorial sea is measured where the outer edge of the continental margin does not extend up to that distance. (LOSC, art. 76(1))

Thus, the legal definition of the shelf is quite distinct and different from the geological definition. Areas of the sea bed which lie beyond the physical continental margin are included, so long as they are within 200 miles of the coast. This principle is now a rule of customary international law.[10] Where the continental margin (defined in article 76(3) as consisting of the shelf, slope and rise, but excluding the deep oceanic floor with its oceanic ridges) extends beyond 200 miles, the outer limit of the legal continental shelf is determined by the application of a complex test known, after its architects, as the 'Irish formula'.[11] The limit is *either* a line connecting points not more than sixty miles apart, at

[10] See the *Libya/Malta Continental Shelf* case, [1985] *ICJ Rep*. 13, at 29–36. There is an implication in the *Greenland/Jan Mayen* case that the customary rule has modified art. 1 of the 1958 Continental Shelf Convention: see R. R. Churchill, 'The Greenland-Jan Mayen case and its significance for the international law of maritime boundary delimitation', 9 *IJMCL* 1–29, at 13 (1994).

[11] Cf. the discussion of the Irish continental shelf claim in C. R. Symmons, 'Ireland and the Law of the Sea' in T. Treves and L. Pineschi (eds), *The Law of the Sea: The European Union and its Member States* (The Hague, Kluwer), 1997, 261 at 286–91.

each of which points the thickness of sedimentary rocks is at least one per cent of the shortest distance from such point to the foot of the continental slope, *or* a line connecting points not more than sixty miles apart, which points are not more than sixty miles from the foot of the slope. In each case the points referred to are subject to a maximum seaward limit: they must be either within 350 miles of the baseline or within 100 miles of the 2,500-metre isobath (LOSC, art. 76(4), (5)). At the initiative of Sri Lanka, special provisions were made to apply to the Bay of Bengal, where the configuration of the sedimentary rocks is such that the application of the Irish formula would result in an inequitably small legal shelf (see Annex II of the Final Act of UNCLOS III).

In broad terms, therefore, a coastal State is entitled to a continental shelf consisting of (a) the sea bed reaching 200 miles from the baselines, and (b), subject to the 'Irish formula', any area of physical continental margin (often known as the 'outer' continental shelf) beyond it. The limits established by the 1982 Convention allow the inclusion within national jurisdiction of substantially the whole of the physical continental margin.

Despite its detail, the formula in the 1982 Convention leaves room for considerable uncertainty.[12] The sea-bed configuration may change over time, and many areas have not been charted recently (or at all). The isobaths may be difficult to locate; and they, too, may move as sea levels change. Similarly, the thickness of the sedimentary rocks may not be known, or may not be known sufficiently accurately to fix a limit under article 76. In an attempt to avoid disputes over the limits of the shelf, the 1982 Convention established a 21-person Commission on the Limits of the Continental Shelf (LOSC, Annex II). The first members were elected in 1997. States[13] proposing to establish an outer limit of their continental shelves beyond the 200-mile limit must notify the outer limits to the Commission within ten years of becoming bound by the Convention and deposit relevant oceanographic data with the Secretary General of the United Nations, who will give due publicity to them (LOSC, art. 76(7), (8), (9), and Annex II). The Commission may make recommendations to States concerning the delimitation; and 'the limits of the shelf established by a coastal State on the basis of these recommendations shall be final and binding' (LOSC, art. 76(8)). It is not clear how far delimitations not so based must or may be regarded as valid.

The provisions of the 1982 Convention on the outer limit of the continental shelf have been widely adopted in State practice. There is a clear trend in national legislation away from definitions based on the '200 metre isobath plus exploitability' criterion and towards definitions based on a '200 mile plus continental

---

[12] See the IOC study of the implications of preparing large-scale maps for UNCLOS III, UN Doc. A/CONF.62/L.99 (1979), UNCLOS III, OR, Vol. XI, p. 121; P. A. Verlaan, 'New seafloor mapping technology and article 76 of the United Nations Convention on the Law of the Sea', 21 *Marine Policy* 425–34 (1997).
[13] The Commission has sought a ruling as to whether non-party States may submit data to it: 'Oceans and the Law of the Sea, 1997', UN Doc. A/52/487 (20 October 1997), para. 50.

margin' criterion.[14] Newer claims tend to adopt the 1982 '200 mile plus margin' formula, in various forms and in some detail, whereas older claims generally do no more than reproduce or paraphrase the provisions of article 76(1).[15] Many of the older claims based on the 200-metre isobath relate to the shallow continental shelves of the Mediterranean, Baltic and North Sea, where there is no possibility of a State claiming more than 200 miles of shelf. Moreover, some States that retain the older formula have stated that they consider article 76 of the 1982 Convention to represent international law.[16] Claims inconsistent with article 76 are scarce: the most notable examples have been the claims by Ecuador, Chile and Iceland, which have been protested by other States.[17] It would be difficult to argue that any continental shelf claim consistent with the article 76 formula was not compatible with customary international law.

The continental shelves of islands

Under the Continental Shelf Convention, islands are entitled to their own continental shelves (CSC, art. 1(b)). While the term 'island' is not defined in that Convention, it is reasonable to assume that the draftsmen intended the term to have the same meaning as it has in the Territorial Sea Convention, i.e., 'a naturally-formed area of land,[18] surrounded by water, which is above water at high tide'. In order to overcome some of the inequities that might be thought to result from the capacity of small, isolated islands to generate possibly extensive continental shelves, the Law of the Sea Convention provides that:

> Rocks which cannot sustain human habitation or economic life of their own shall have no exclusive economic zone or continental shelf. (LOSC, art. 121(3))

---

[14] See the Appendix to this book. Cf. the summary tables of claims in 34 *LOSB* 47–63 (1997).

[15] See, e.g., the (Canadian) Oceans Act, 1996, s. 17, 35 *LOSB* 38, 45 (1997); (Japanese) Law on the Exclusive Economic Zone and the Continental Shelf (Law No. 74 of 1996), art. 2, 35 *LOSB* 94, 95 (1997) (and cf. Act No. 140 of 14 June 1996, art. 2, 33 *LOSB* 36 (1997)); (Jamaican) Maritime Areas Act, 1996, s. 21, 34 *LOSB* 29, 38 (1997); (Russian) Federal Law on the Continental Shelf of the Russian Federation, 25 October 1995, art. 1, 32 *LOSB* 43 (1996); (South African) Maritime Zones Act, No. 15 of 1994, s. 8, 32 *LOSB* 75, 77 (1996).

[16] See, e.g., the US policy concerning the continental shelf: J. A. Roach and R. W. Smith, *United States Responses to Excessive Maritime Claims* (The Hague, Nijhoff), 2nd edn, 1996, pp. 193–208. Cf. the 1988 UK–Ireland Continental Shelf Boundary Agreement, which extends the boundary to 60 miles beyond the foot of the slope in the south-west (point 94) and to 100 miles beyond the 2,500-metre isobath in the north-west (point 132): R. R. Churchill, 'Current Developments: The Law of the Sea', 38 *ICLQ* 413–17 (1989).

[17] Roach and Smith, *op. cit.* in footnote 16, pp. 203–8.

[18] See the statements asserting that the artificial island erected next to Venezuela's Aves island is not entitled to maritime zones: 35 *LOSB* 97–100 (1997). And see chapter two.

The poor drafting of this provision and the problems to which it gives rise were discussed in chapter two.[19] However, it may be noted that the report of the Conciliation Commission concerning the continental shelf of Jan Mayen island regarded the provisions of the article as 'reflecting the present status of international law on the subject',[20] although no evidence was given to support this statement.

The rights and duties of the coastal State

Since the continental shelf was originally the bed of an area that remained high seas (CSC, art. 3), it was inevitable that coastal-State rights in the area should be limited. This position has been modified by the establishment of the EEZ as an area of maritime jurisdiction, and at this point it is necessary to consider separately coastal State rights over the shelf within the 200-mile zone (where the continental shelf regime and EEZ regime coexist) and in the 'outer' continental shelf beyond the 200-mile zone (where only the continental shelf regime applies, as it does in cases where the coastal State does not claim an EEZ).

Rights and duties within the 200-mile zone

The basic principle that has always governed coastal State rights over the continental shelf is that these rights are limited to the exploration of the shelf and exploitation of its natural resources. In other words, the shelf is not regarded as part of the territory of the coastal State. In both the 1958 and the 1982 Conventions the coastal State's rights are described as 'sovereign'. According to the International Law Commission such rights include 'all rights necessary for and connected with the exploitation of the continental shelf . . . [including] jurisdiction in connection with the prevention and punishment of violations of the law'.[21] The 'sovereign rights' attaching to the coastal State cover all the natural resources of the shelf, that is:

> the mineral and other non-living resources of the sea bed and subsoil together with living organisms belonging to sedentary species, that is to say, organisms which, at the harvestable stage, either are immobile on or under the sea bed or are unable to move except in constant physical contact with the sea bed or the subsoil. (CSC, art. 2(4); LOSC, art. 77(4))

Thus oil and gas are included, as are sedentary species such as oysters, clams and abalone. It was, however, controversial whether crabs and lobsters fell within

[19] See also chapter nine.
[20] Report of the Conciliation Commission established by the Governments of Iceland and Norway concerning the continental shelf area between Iceland and Jan Mayen, 20 *ILM* 797 at 803 (1981).
[21] *ILC Yearbook*, 1956, Vol. II, p. 253 at 297.

the definition of sedentary species; and this controversy gave rise to several disputes, such as the USA–Japan dispute over the king crab fishery in the eastern Bering Sea and the Franco-Brazilian dispute over the lobster fishery off the Brazilian coast. In so far as the shelf within the 200-mile zone is concerned, that controversy is a thing of the past, because all rights to exploit resources (including fish) within the zone belong to the coastal State (LOSC, art. 56(1)). The former freedom to take non-sedentary species from what was originally the high seas has been supplanted by the coastal State's EEZ rights.

The coastal State's sovereign rights are limited to natural resources. Thus, *non*-natural 'resources' are not included in the ambit of these rights even if they are found on the continental shelf, so that, for example, wrecks lying on the shelf are excluded from the category of continental shelf resources. The fact that the continental shelf is not in law a part of the territory of a State, and that wrecks are not in law continental shelf 'resources', creates some difficulty. Certain wrecks have great importance, as graves or monuments or as archaeological sites. The 1982 Convention allows coastal States a limited jurisdiction over wrecks, out to the limits of the twenty-four-mile contiguous zone (LOSC, art. 303; and see chapter seven). No such rights exist over the rest of the continental shelf, or as part of States' EEZ rights:[22] indeed, a proposal to grant coastal States such rights was specifically rejected at UNCLOS III. Although there are problematic questions, such as the persistence of flag State jurisdiction over wrecks,[23] it is clear that as a matter of international law the effective regulation of wreck sites more than twenty-four miles from the baseline requires international agreement, because the coastal State does not have jurisdiction over foreign ships and nationals at the wreck site. A number of such agreements have been made, in which each State party agrees to exercise its own jurisdiction over its nationals and ships to forbid unauthorised interference with the site.[24] Such agreements

---

[22] Though if the wreck lies within the EEZ of a State, disputes relating to international law rights and jurisdiction over the wreck ought, strictly, to be settled according to the formula set out in art. 59 of the 1982 Convention. See chapter nine. Malaysia appears to assert rights over archaeological and historical objects found within its EEZ or on its continental shelf: see United Nations, *The Law of the Sea. Declarations and Statements with respect to the United Nations Convention on the Law of the Sea* (New York, United Nations), 1997, p. 33.

[23] And, indeed, the identification of the flag State. The wrecks may pre-date States, or have flown the flag of a State no longer existent (or much changed in its geographical scope). Similar problems attend the implementation of LOSC, art. 149, which requires the preservation or disposal of all objects of an archaeological or historical nature found in the International Sea Bed Area for the benefit of mankind as a whole, regard being had to the preferential rights of 'the State or country of origin, or the State of cultural origin, or the State of historical and archaeological origin'.

[24] See, e.g., the 1995 agreement made by Estonia, Finland and Sweden concerning the site of the wreck of the *M/S Estonia*, in which almost 900 people died: 31 *LOSB* 62 (1996). The wreck lies on Finland's continental shelf.

never have more than three or four parties and, of course, bind only those parties. They therefore provide only a limited solution to the problem. UNESCO is taking the lead in attempts to draft a multilateral international convention on the subject.[25] In the absence of a satisfactory international regime for the protection of continental shelf wreck and archaeological sites, however, several States have unilaterally asserted jurisdiction for this purpose.[26]

As was mentioned above, the coastal State has sovereign rights for the purpose of exploring the shelf[27] and exploiting its natural resources (CSC, art. 2(1); LOSC, arts 56(1), 77(1)). Such rights include the right to construct and authorise the use of artificial islands and installations and structures used for economic purposes (or which may interfere with economic activities), and to authorise drilling, on the continental shelf (LOSC, arts 60, 80, 81). These rights are exclusive in the sense that no State can undertake such activities without the coastal State's consent (CSC, art. 2(2); LOSC, art. 77(2)). These continental shelf rights do not depend on occupation or proclamation but automatically attach to the coastal State (CSC, art. 2(3); LOSC, art. 77(3)). It follows that it is for the coastal State, through its own laws and regulations, to define the conditions under which exploration and exploitation of the shelf may be conducted. A wealth of such legislation exists, particularly in relation to offshore oil and gas and sedentary fisheries. Furthermore, many standards, on matters such as safety and pollution, are enforced through the incorporation of terms in licences permitting the offshore activities in question. In circumstances where offshore oil or gas fields overlap the shelves of two or more States, arrangements have sometimes been made for the joint regulation or joint exploitation of the cross-boundary resources. We describe this practice briefly in chapter ten.

The coastal State's rights over the continental shelf are not unlimited. In earlier practice (and under the Continental Shelf Convention) the superjacent waters were high seas, and freedom of navigation and fishing were preserved. Now the latter freedom has disappeared in the EEZ, but it is still provided that:

---

[25] Much attention has been devoted to the legal protection of wreck sites. For recent discussions see the papers in the special issue on the protection of the underwater cultural heritage, 20 *Marine Policy* 283–356 (1996); A. Strati, *The Protection of the Underwater Cultural Heritage: an emerging objective of the contemporary law of the sea* (The Hague, Nijhoff), 1995. See also the *Report by the Director-General on action taken concerning the desirability of preparing an international instrument for the protection of the underwater cultural heritage*, UNESCO Doc. 29 C/22, 5 August 1997: available at http://unesdoc.unesco.org/.

[26] See B. Kwiatkowska, 'Creeping jurisdiction beyond 200 miles in the light of the 1982 Law of the Sea Convention and State practice', 22 *ODIL* 153, at 163 (1991); L. Migliorino, '*In situ* protection of the underwater cultural heritage under international treaties and national legislation', 10 *IJMCL* 483–95 (1995). For an illustration of the complex questions of municipal law that arise in this context see D. P. Larsen, 'Ownership of historic shipwreck in US law', 9 *IJMCL* 31–56 (1994).

[27] On the exploration of the shelf see further chapter sixteen.

The exercise of the rights of the coastal State over the continental shelf must not infringe or result in any unjustifiable interference with navigation and other rights and freedoms of other States as provided for in this Convention. (LOSC, art. 78(2))

Plainly it is inevitable that some interference with navigation will result. The establishment of drilling platforms and other installations for the exploitation of offshore resources, which the coastal State alone may authorise (CSC, art. 5(2); LOSC, arts 60(1), 80), must to some degree impede freedom of navigation. But as a right consequent upon the right to exploit, the establishment of such installations is expressly permitted (CSC, art. 5; LOSC, arts 60, 80). Furthermore, the 1958 and 1982 Conventions permit the coastal State to establish safety zones of up to 500 metres, measured from the outer limits of the installations, although some States, such as Norway, have forbidden certain navigational and fishing practices in wider areas.[28] In practice even a cluster of 500-metre zones can effectively curtail such activities in the interstitial waters. On the other hand, no installations may be erected 'where interference may be caused to the use of recognised sea lanes essential to international navigation' (CSC, art. 5(6); LOSC, art. 60(7)).

Coastal States have exclusive jurisdiction over artificial islands and 'economic' structures and installations on the continental shelf (LOSC, arts 60, 80. Cf. CSC, art. 5(4)), and the right to take 'appropriate measures' for the safety of the islands, structures and installations and for the safety of navigation in the safety zones that may be established around them (LOSC, art. 60(4),(5),(6). Cf. CSC, art. 5(2),(3)). In the case of fixed structures that provision is largely unproblematic, although there has been controversy over the kinds of legislation that coastal States may extend to offshore installations and the exact powers that they have over foreign vessels within safety zones. But many modern offshore structures are mobile (such as MODUs – Mobile Offshore Drilling Units), often moving from one location to another, and often navigating under their own power. Coastal State jurisdiction is plainly an inadequate basis for the regulation of such mobile units and activities upon them, yet neither the 1958 nor the 1982 Convention deals specifically with the issue. Canadian legislation contains a provision that is pragmatic and consistent with principle. Canadian laws apply

(a) on or under any marine installation or structure from the time it is attached or anchored to the continental shelf of Canada in connection with the exploration of that shelf or the exploitation of its mineral or other non-living resources until the marine installation or structure is removed from the waters above the continental shelf of Canada;

---

[28] See R. R. Churchill, *op. cit.* in 'Further reading'; G. Ulfstein, 'The conflict between petroleum production and fisheries in international law' in G. Ulfstein, P. Andersen, and R. R. Churchill (eds), *Proceedings of the European Workshop on the Regulation of Fisheries* (Strasbourg, Council of Europe), 1987, pp. 183–96.

(b) on or under any artificial island constructed, erected or placed on the continental shelf of Canada; and

(c) within such safety zone surrounding any marine installation or structure or artificial island referred to in paragraph (a) or (b) as is determined by or pursuant to the regulations.[29]

Once an offshore oil or gas field is exhausted, installations used in its exploitation no longer serve any immediately useful purpose but will constitute a potential hazard to navigation and an obstacle to fishing. The 1958 Convention required the complete removal of abandoned installations (CSC, art. 5(5)). Because of the cost and difficulty of removing certain installations (especially the massive concrete platforms used in the North Sea), the 1982 Convention does not require complete removal. It merely requires that abandoned or disused installations be removed 'to ensure safety of navigation' and taking account of generally accepted international standards (such as those developed by the IMO) and having due regard to other interests such as fishing and the marine environment, with appropriate publicity being given to installations only partly removed (LOSC, art. 60(3)). That partial removal obligation has been amplified in guidelines drawn up in 1989 by the IMO.[30] The question of the disposal of installations once removed is distinct, and has been treated as a question of pollution. This is reflected in the guidelines for the disposal of offshore installations at sea, adopted by the Oslo Commission in 1991 as a complement to the IMO guidelines in order to bring the disposal of installations at sea within the framework of controls on dumping[31] (see further, chapter fifteen).[32] State practice is clearly moving towards requiring partial removal only, even on the part of the few States Parties that remain bound by the 1958 Continental Shelf Convention.[33]

---

[29] Oceans Act, 1996, s. 20(1), 35 *LOSB* 38, 46 (1997). Cf. the position in Italian law: T. Treves, 'Italy and the Law of the Sea' in Treves and Pineschi (eds), *op. cit.* in footnote 11, 327 at 341.

[30] Guidelines and Standards for the Removal of Offshore Installations and Structures on the Continental Shelf and in the Exclusive Economic Zone, annexed to IMO Resolution A. 672(16), 19 October 1989. See E. D. Brown, *The International Law of the Sea* (Aldershot, Dartmouth), 1994, Vol. I, pp. 267–8; and for the text see *ibid.*, Vol. II, p. 117. See also Kasoulides, *op. cit.* in 'Further reading'.

[31] The definition of dumping in the 1982 Convention expressly includes the disposal at sea of installations: LOSC, art. 1(1)(5)(a)).

[32] There is some disagreement over the competence of the Oslo Commission in this regard, but there is no doubt that the disposal of installations at sea falls within the ambit of the 1992 Paris Convention for the Protection of the Marine Environment of the North-East Atlantic. See E. D. Brown, *op. cit.* in footnote 30, Vol. I, pp. 269–72; and for the text of the Oslo guidelines see *ibid.*, Vol. II, p. 121. Disposal of installations is dealt with in a number of regional pollution agreements: see, e.g., the 1992 Baltic Convention and 1994 Mediterranean Protocol (see chapter fifteen). Cf. E. A. Kirk, 'The 1996 Protocol to the London Dumping Convention and the *Brent Spar*', 46 *ICLQ* 957–64 (1997).

[33] The UK stated that the toppling of the *Piper Alpha* platform in 1989 was in accordance with the partial removal obligation and the IMO guidelines, although the UK was at that time bound by the 1958 Convention: see *UKMIL 1990*, p. 585.

A further limitation on coastal States' rights results from the obligation to permit, subject to measures to protect rights of exploration and exploitation and to other specified conditions, both the laying and the maintenance of submarine pipelines and cables by other States on the shelf (CSC, art. 4; LOSC, art. 79). Conditions which may be specified relate to the course of pipelines[34] and the prevention of pollution from or by them, and to other matters where the pipelines or cables enter the territorial sea of the coastal State or are used in connection with the exploration or exploitation of the shelf.[35]

For the sake of completeness, it should be noted that the coastal State is expressly given the right to exploit shelf resources by tunnelling (CSC, art. 7; LOSC, art. 85), although this provision is probably redundant in view of the wider rights given elsewhere.

Rights beyond the 200-mile zone

Coastal State rights over the 'outer' shelf beyond the 200-mile zone are slightly different, since the superjacent waters are in that area high seas, rather than part of the coastal State's EEZ. Generally, the same rights exist in relation to exploration and exploitation and the establishment of installations, and the same obligations apply regarding respect for the freedoms of pipeline and cable laying and of navigation. But there are significant differences nevertheless.

First, in relation to living resources, the question of what is comprised within the category of sedentary species becomes critical. While sedentary species remain under the exclusive control of the coastal State, non-sedentary species fall under the regime of free fishing, as one of the freedoms of the high seas. Accordingly, if commercial fisheries are found at such distances from land, disputes over whether a particular species is sedentary could arise as they have done in the past.[36] Secondly and more importantly, exploitation of non-living resources is subject to additional restrictions under the Law of the Sea Convention. Where such resources are exploited in this outer portion of the shelf, the coastal State – which, of course, has the exclusive right to engage in such exploitation – has to pay to the International Sea Bed Authority (on which see chapter twelve) a

---

[34] The 1982 Convention does not give the coastal State the right to dictate the course of submarine cables. Note in this respect the cautious terms of the Iranian letter of 18 October 1996, part (c), para. 6: 33 *LOSB* 87, 88 (1997). Some States, however, assert the right to authorise the course of cables on their shelves: see, e.g., the (Russian) Federal Law on the Continental Shelf of the Russian Federation, 25 October 1995, art. 22, 32 *LOSB* 43, 58 (1996); cf. B. Kwiatkowska, 'Creeping jurisdiction beyond 200 miles in the light of the 1982 Law of the Sea Convention and State practice', 22 *ODIL* 153 at 163 (1991).

[35] On the provisions for the protection of cables and pipelines, see E. Wagner, 'Submarine cables and protections provided by the law of the sea', 19 *Marine Policy* 127–36 (1995); and see further chapter eleven.

[36] In fact such a dispute arose in 1994 between Canada and the USA over the question of whether scallops (for which US fishermen were fishing on the Grand Banks beyond Canada's 200-mile fishing zone) were a sedentary species: see 10 *IJMCL* 221–2 (1995).

proportion of the value or volume of the production at the site after the first five years of exploitation. The proportion would rise from one per cent in the sixth year to seven per cent in the twelfth and following years. The Authority is to distribute any such payments to States Parties to the Convention:

> on the basis of equitable sharing criteria, taking into account the interests and needs of developing States, particularly the least developed and the land-locked among them. (LOSC, art. 82(4))

Developing countries that are net importers of the minerals exploited would be exempt from the obligation to pay (LOSC, art. 82(3)). This scheme is a kind of *quid pro quo* for the diminution of the resources of the International Sea Bed Area consequent upon allowing jurisdiction over the shelf beyond the 200-mile limit. A third difference is that the coastal State has somewhat more limited controls over research on its outer continental shelf: this point is discussed in chapter sixteen.

Non-independent territories

Special provision is made in the Law of the Sea Convention concerning the beneficial ownership of the resources of maritime zones of non-independent territories: this point is discussed in the next chapter.

Further reading

B. B. L. Auguste, *The Continental Shelf. The Practice and Policy of the Latin American States, with special reference to Chile, Ecuador and Peru* (Geneva, Librarie E. Droz), 1960.

E. D. Brown, *Sea-Bed Energy and Minerals: The International Legal Regime. Vol. 1, The Continental Shelf* (Dordrecht, Nijhoff), 1992.

R. R. Churchill 'The conflict between oil and fisheries: a survey of Norwegian and United Kingdom law and practice' in G. Ulfstein, P. Andersen and R. R. Churchill, *Proceedings of the European Workshop on the Regulation of Fisheries* (Strasbourg, Council of Europe), 1987, pp. 197–213.

T. C. Daintith and G. D. M. Willoughby, *A Manual of United Kingdom Oil and Gas Law* (London, Sweet & Maxwell), 1984.

L. F. E. Goldie, 'Sedentary fisheries and article 2(4) of the Continental Shelf Convention', 63 *AJIL* 86–97 (1969).

Sir C. J. B. Hurst, 'Whose is the bed of the sea?', 4 *BYIL* 34–43 (1923–4).

D. N. Hutchinson, 'The seaward limit to continental shelf jurisdiction in customary international law', 56 *BYIL* 133–87 (1985).

G. C. Kasoulides, 'Removal of offshore platforms and the development of international standards', 13 *Marine Policy* 249–65 (1989).

B. Kwiatkowska and A. H. A. Soons, 'Entitlement to maritime areas of rocks which cannot sustain human habitation or economic life of their own', XXI *NYIL* 139–81 (1990).

H. Lauterpacht, 'Sovereignty over submarine areas', 27 *BYIL* 376–433 (1950).

U. Leanza and L. Sico (eds), *Mediterranean Continental Shelf: Delimitations and Regime,* 4 vols, (Dobbs Ferry, N.Y., Oceana), 1988.

T. L. McDorman, 'The entry into force of the Law of the Sea Convention and the article 76 outer continental shelf regime', 10 *IJMCL* 165–87 (1995).

M. W. Mouton, *The Continental Shelf* (The Hague), 1952, and 85 *Recueil des Cours* 343–465 (1954).

B. H. Oxman, 'The preparation of article I of the Convention on the Continental Shelf', 3 *JMLC* 245–305, 445–72, 683–723 (1971–2).

K. Ramakrishna, R. E. Bowen and J. H Archer, 'Outer limits of continental shelf: a legal analysis of Chilean and Ecuadorean island claims and US responses', 11 *Marine Policy* 58–68 (1987).

A. Razavi, *Continental Shelf Delimitation and Related Maritime Issues in the Persian Gulf* (The Hague, Nijhoff), 1997.

A. Reynaud, *Le plateau continental de la France* (Paris, Librarie générale de droit et de jurisprudence), 1984.

M. Roelandt, *La condition juridique des pipelines dans le droit de la mer* (Paris, Presses Universitaires de France), 1990.

Z. J. Slouka, *International Custom and the Continental Shelf* (The Hague, Nijhoff), 1968.

United Nations, *The Law of the Sea: National Legislation on the Continental Shelf* (New York, United Nations), 1989.

——, *The Law of the Sea: Definition of the Continental Shelf. An Examination of the Relevant Provisions of the UN Convention on the Law of the* Sea (New York, United Nations), 1993.

D. Vallée, *Le plateau continental dans le droit positif actuel* (Paris, Pedone), 1971.

R. Young, 'The legal status of submarine areas beneath the high seas', 45 *AJIL* 225–39 (1951).

See also the further reading recommended in chapter ten.

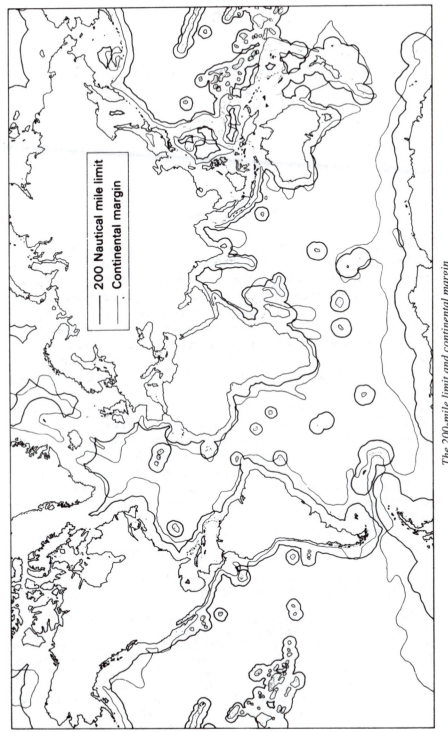

The legend in the image reads:

—— 200 Nautical mile limit
—— Continental margin

The 200-mile limit and continental margin

9

The exclusive economic zone

Evolution of the EEZ

The exclusive economic zone (EEZ) is a zone extending up to 200 miles from the baseline, within which the coastal State enjoys extensive rights in relation to natural resources and related jurisdictional rights, and third States enjoy the freedoms of navigation, overflight by aircraft and the laying of cables and pipelines. The EEZ is a concept of recent origin. While its historical roots lie in the trend since 1945 to extend the limits of coastal State jurisdiction ever seawards (particularly in the Truman and other continental shelf proclamations, and the resource-oriented claims of Latin American and African States to broad territorial seas and fishing zones), its more direct and immediate origins lie in the preparations for UNCLOS III. The concept of the EEZ was put forward for the first time by Kenya to the Asian-African Legal Consultative Committee in January 1971, and to the UN Sea Bed Committee in the following year. Kenya's proposal received active support from many Asian and African States.[1] At about the same time many of the Latin American States began to develop the similar concept of the patrimonial sea.[2] The two lines of approach had effectively merged by the time UNCLOS began, and the new concept – the EEZ being the preferred name – had attracted the support of most developing States and began to attract support from some developed coastal States such as Canada and Norway.

The EEZ is a reflection of the aspiration of the developing countries for economic development and their desire to gain greater control over the economic

[1] See, for example, the Conclusions in the General Report of the African States Regional Seminar on the Law of the Sea, held in Yaoundé, June 1972. *UN Leg. Ser.* B/16, p. 601; *ND I*, p. 250.

[2] Declaration of Santo Domingo, June 1972. *UN Leg. Ser.* B/16, p. 599; *ND I*, p. 247. Although this declaration is the first Latin American Declaration to refer to the patrimonial sea, it is the culmination of a series of earlier Latin American proclamations moving towards this concept, in particular the Montevideo Declaration on the Law of the Sea, 1970 and the Lima Declaration on the Law of the Sea, 1970. *UN Leg. Ser.* B/16, pp. 586 and 587; *ND I*, pp. 235 and 237. For the differences between the Latin-American and African positions, see G. Pontecorvo (ed.), *The New Order of the Oceans* (New York, Columbia University Press), 1986, chapters 6 and 7, especially at p. 140.

resources off their coasts, particularly fish stocks, which in many cases were largely exploited by the distant-water fleets of developed States. At the same time the EEZ could be seen as something of a compromise between those States that claimed a 200-mile territorial sea (some Latin American and African States) and those developed States (e.g., Japan, the then USSR and the USA) which were hostile to extended coastal State jurisdiction. The fact that the EEZ could be seen as a compromise proposal led to its rapid acceptance in principle at UNCLOS by most States, although many landlocked and geographically disadvantaged States were initially rather reserved towards the EEZ because it reduced the area of high seas open to use by all States. Thereafter negotiations on the EEZ at UNCLOS were limited to points of detail, and eventually led to the inclusion in the Law of the Sea Convention of a special section – Part V – dedicated to the EEZ.

Under the Convention there is no obligation on a State to claim an EEZ. Nevertheless most coastal States have in fact exercised their right to make such a claim (for details of such claims see the Table of Claims in Appendix 1). The major exceptions are the States bordering the Mediterranean and some States bordering other semi-enclosed seas, where it is impossible for geographical reasons to establish an EEZ of a full 200 miles breadth; a handful of States which still claim a 200-mile territorial sea (see Table of Claims); and one or two developed States such as the United Kingdom, which have preferred to claim a 200-mile exclusive fishing zone (EFZ) rather than a 200-mile EEZ because the former, together with the exclusive rights over sea-bed resources which they already have under the continental shelf regime, give these States all that they at present want from an EEZ.[3] The vast majority of States which have so far claimed an EEZ did so well before the entry into force of the Law of the Sea Convention, many of them in the late 1970s when UNCLOS III was still in progress. The volume of such claims, coupled with an almost complete absence of protest, has led most commentators to conclude that the EEZ had become part of customary international law long before the entry into force of the Convention, and indeed in the *Libya/Malta Continental Shelf* case (1985) the International Court said that it is 'incontestable that ... the EEZ ... is shown by the practice of States to have become part of customary law'.[4] It would seem that what is part of customary international law are the broad rights of coastal and other States enumerated in articles 56 and 58 of the Convention. It is much more doubtful whether the detailed obligations in the articles relating to the exercise of coastal

---

[3] Quite a number of developed States, such as Canada, Germany, Japan, the former USSR and the USA, in fact began by claiming a 200-mile EFZ in the late 1970s. These claims were one by one converted to EEZs in the years following the adoption of the Law of the Sea Convention.

[4] [1985] *ICJ Rep.* 13, at 33. Note, too, that in the *Franco-Canadian Fisheries* arbitration the tribunal acknowledged that the EEZ was part of customary law, at least as far as sovereign rights to natural resources was concerned (see para. 49), and in the *Franco-Canadian Maritime Boundary* arbitration the tribunal observed that article 58, providing for freedom of navigation in the EEZ, 'undoubtedly represents customary law as much as the institution of the 200 mile zone itself' (para. 88).

State jurisdiction over fisheries, pollution and research have passed or are likely quickly to pass into customary international law, partly because of a lack of claims embodying the duties of the Convention, partly because there is some divergence between State practice and the Convention, and partly because some of the conventional rules would not seem to have the 'fundamentally norm-creating character' necessary for the creation of a rule of customary international law (see chapter one). This reflects a tendency for rights to pass more quickly into custom than duties. Even in relation to the broad rights enumerated in articles 56 and 58, there is some divergence between State practice and the Convention. This will be referred to at appropriate points below.[5]

The universal establishment of 200-mile EEZs would embrace about thirty-six per cent of the total area of the sea. Although this is a relatively small proportion, the area falling within 200-mile limits contains over ninety per cent of all presently commercially exploitable fish stocks, about eighty-seven per cent of the world's known submarine oil deposits, and about ten per cent of manganese nodules (see, further, table 1 below). Furthermore, a large proportion of marine scientific research takes place within 200 miles of the coast, and virtually all the major shipping routes of the world pass through the EEZs of States other than those in which the ports of departure and destination are situated. In view of these extensive activities conducted within 200 miles of land, the legal regime of the EEZ provided for in the Law of the Sea Convention is obviously of crucial importance.

This chapter begins by looking at the way in which the EEZ is delimited. It then considers the legal nature of the EEZ, examining in turn the rights which coastal States enjoy therein, the rights of other States, and the relationship between these two groups of rights.

Delimitation of the EEZ

Outer limit

The inner limit of the EEZ is the outer limit of the territorial sea (LOSC, art. 55). The zone's outer limit 'shall not extend beyond 200 nautical miles from the baselines from which the breadth of the territorial sea is measured' (LOSC, art. 57). The wording of this provision suggests that, while 200 miles is the maximum extent of the EEZ, it would be quite possible for a State, if it so wished, to claim an EEZ of some lesser extent.[6] In many regions, of course, coastal States have

[5] For a much fuller discussion of national laws relating to the EEZ and their compatibility with the Convention, see works by Burke, Juda and Smith (pp. 32–40), *op. cit.* in 'Further reading'.

[6] Throughout this book we refer frequently, in common with nearly all other writers, to a 200-mile EEZ. Strictly speaking, this is not accurate. Because the inner part of the 200 miles consists of territorial sea, one ought to refer to a 188-mile EEZ (in the case of a twelve-mile territorial sea) or a 197-mile EEZ (in the case of a three-mile territorial sea).

no option but to claim less than 200 miles because of the presence of neighbouring States' EEZs. It may be wondered why the figure of 200 miles was chosen as the maximum breadth for the EEZ. The reasons are historical and political: 200 miles has no general geographical, ecological or biological significance. At the beginning of UNCLOS the most extensive zones claimed by coastal States were the 200-mile claims of some Latin American and African States. Since it would have been very difficult to persuade those States to accept some lesser limit than 200 miles, it was thought – correctly, as it turned out – that it would be easiest to reach agreement on the outer limit of the EEZ by choosing the figure that represented the broadest existing claims. However, there remains the question as to why the figure of 200 miles was originally chosen by the first State to claim a zone of this limit, namely Chile. According to Hollick,[7] the figure of 200 miles seems to have been something of an accident. Chile's claim was motivated by a desire to protect its then new offshore whaling operations. The whaling industry only wanted a fifty-mile zone, but was advised that some precedent was necessary. The most promising precedent appeared to be the security zone adopted in the 1939 Declaration of Panama. This zone was wrongly thought to have been 200 miles in breadth: in fact it varied and was nowhere less than 300 miles.

Boundaries

In many regions States are unable to claim a full 200-mile zone because of the presence of neighbouring States, and it is therefore necessary to delimit the EEZs of opposite and adjacent States. The international law governing such boundary delimitation is discussed in the next chapter.

Islands

In principle all land territory can generate an EEZ. However, three qualifications must be made to this statement. First, although islands normally generate an EEZ, article 121(3) of the Law of the Sea Convention provides that 'rocks which cannot sustain human habitation or economic life of their own shall have no exclusive economic zone or continental shelf'. The poor drafting of this provision was criticised in chapter two. So far the provision seems to have had limited impact in practice. As far as can be ascertained, only one State with an EEZ – Mexico[8] – has incorporated provisions modelled on article 121(3) in its domestic legislation. On the other hand, a number of States have claimed EEZs around islands which could conceivably be regarded as uninhabitable rocks,

[7] A. L. Hollick, 'The origins of 200 mile offshore zones', 71 *AJIL* 494–500 (1977).
[8] Law regulating the Eighth Paragraph of Article 27 of the Constitution relating to the Exclusive Economic Zone, 10 February 1976, art. 3. *UN Leg. Ser.* B/19, p. 233; *ND V*, p. 292; subsequently replaced by Federal Act relating to the Sea, 1985, arts 51 and 63. 7 *LOSB* 53 (1986); 25 *ILM* 889 (1986).

e.g., France (in respect of various tiny islands in the Pacific and Indian Ocean),[9] Fiji (in respect of the island of Ceva-i-Ra)[10] and Venezuela (in respect of Aves island, an action which has been recognised in various bilateral boundary agreements[11] but which has drawn protests from Antigua, St Kitts, St Lucia and St Vincent on the ground that the action is contrary to article 121(3)[12]). And even Mexico itself has claimed an EEZ around tiny islets, such as Clarion and Roca Portida in the Pacific (although not around the Roca Alijos).[13] The main impact which article 121(3) seems to have had so far has been to lead the United Kingdom to give up the 200-mile fishing zone which it established in 1976 around the minute islet of Rockall (and which met with protests form several States[14]) when it acceded to the Law of the Sea Convention in 1997.[15] This suggests that the United Kingdom, at least before 1997, did not regard article 121(3) as being part of customary international law. It has also been argued that apart from the lack of State practice, another reason why article 121(3) has not become a customary rule is because it is not of the necessary fundamental norm-creating character.[16]

Non-independent territories

The second qualification relates to territories which have not attained either full independence or some other self-governing status recognised by the UN, and to territories under colonial domination. Resolution III, adopted by UNCLOS III at the same time as the Convention text, declares that in the case of such territories 'provisions concerning rights and interests under the Convention shall be implemented for the benefit of the people of the territory with a view to promoting their well-being and development.' This resolution replaced a transitional article at the end of earlier drafts of the Convention text, which had proposed to vest the resources of the maritime zones of such territories in their inhabitants. The

---

[9] Decrees Nos 78–143, 78–144, 78–146 and 78–147 (relating to French Polynesia; French Southern and Antarctic Territories; the islands of the Mozambique Channel; and Clipperton Island, respectively). *Journal Officiel*, 11 February 1978, pp. 683–7; *Smith, op. cit.* in 'Further reading', p. 154 *et seq.*

[10] *Limits in the Seas* No. 101 (1984).

[11] USA–Venezuela Maritime Boundary Treaty, 1978; Netherlands–Venezuela Treaty of Delimitation, 1978; and France–Venezuela Convention relating to the Delimitation of Economic Zones, 1980.

[12] 35 *LOSB* 97–100 (1997).

[13] C. R. Symmons, *The Maritime Zones of Islands in International Law* (The Hague, Nijhoff), 1979, pp. 125–6. Further on Mexican practice, see W. Van Overbeek, 'Article 121(3) LOSC in Mexican State practice in the Pacific', 4 *IJECL* 252–67 (1989).

[14] C. R. Symmons, 'The Rockall dispute deepens: an analysis of recent Danish and Icelandic actions', 35 *ICLQ* 344–73 (1986).

[15] See further R. R. Churchill, 'United Kingdom accession to the UN Convention on the Law of the Sea', 13 *IJMCL* 263 (1998), at 271–3.

[16] B. Kwiatkowska and A. H. A. Soons, 'Entitlement to maritime areas of rocks which cannot sustain human habitation or economic life of their own', *21 Netherlands Yearbook of International Law* 139–81 (1990) at 174–81.

transitional article presented formidable legal and political difficulties, and was opposed by most States which are administering powers – although it is noteworthy that New Zealand adopted legislation for the Tokelau Islands which is in keeping with its spirit.[17] Resolution III avoids the major difficulties inherent in its predecessor, but it is still not entirely clear to which territories it applies, or what the precise obligations of the administering powers might be.[18] In practice 200-mile EEZs or fishing zones have been established by administering powers for nearly all dependent territories.

Antarctica

Finally, it should be noted that the effect of article IV of the 1959 Antarctic Treaty (which prohibits new territorial claims in the Antarctic and the assertion or enlargement of existing territorial claims) would seem to be that EEZs cannot be claimed off territory lying within the area to which that Treaty applies, namely the area south of 60° South. Notwithstanding the prohibition in article IV, Australia claimed an EEZ off its Antarctic territory in 1994.[19] This claim has not (yet) evoked any reaction from other States, apart from the USA which made a protest in 1995.[20]

The legal status of the EEZ

During the earlier stages of UNCLOS there was considerable discussion as to the exact legal nature of the EEZ. Many maritime States argued, because of a fear of 'creeping jurisdiction', that the EEZ should have a residual high seas character, i.e., any activity not falling within the clearly defined rights of the coastal State would be subject to the regime of the high seas. This approach did not find favour with the majority of UNCLOS participants, and articles 55 and 86 of the Law of the Sea Convention make it clear that the EEZ does not have a residual high seas character. Equally it is clear that the EEZ does not have a residual territorial sea character, which would have created a presumption that

[17] Tokelau (Territorial Sea and Exclusive Economic Zone) Act 1977, *ND VII*, p. 468; *Smith, op. cit.*, p. 341.
[18] For a discussion of these questions, see M. H. Nordquist (ed.) *United Nations Convention on the Law of the Sea 1982. A Commentary* (The Hague, Nijhoff), 1989, Vol. V, pp. 478–82 and R. R. Churchill, 'The Falkland Islands fishing zone: legal aspects', 12 *Marine Policy* 343–60 (1988) at 350–3.
[19] Maritime Legislation Amendment Act, 1994. 27 *LOSB* 49 (1995); Governor-General's Proclamation of 26 July 1994, 10 *IJMCL* 97 (1995).
[20] J. Green, 'Antarctic EEZ baselines', 11 *IJMCL* 333 (1996) at 341. For discussion of the Australian action, see S. Kaye and D. R. Rothwell, 'Australia's Antarctic maritime claims and boundaries', 26 *ODIL* 195–226 (1995), especially at 208–11, and C. C. Joyner, 'The Antarctic Treaty System and the Law of the Sea – competing regimes in the Southern Ocean?' 10 *IJMCL* 301–31 (1995) at 307–11.

any activity not falling within the clearly defined rights of non-coastal States would come under the jurisdiction of the coastal State – as was desired by some UNCLOS participants (notably those Latin American States claiming a 200-mile territorial sea). Instead, the EEZ must be regarded as a separate functional zone of a *sui generis* character, situated between the territorial sea and the high seas. The *sui generis* legal character of the EEZ has three principal elements: (1) the rights and duties which the Law of the Sea Convention accords to the coastal State; (2) the rights and duties which the Convention accords to other States; and (3) the formula provided by the Convention for regulating activities which do not fall within either of the two previous categories. We examine each of these three elements in turn.

The rights and duties of the coastal State in the EEZ

The coastal State's rights and duties are set out in broad terms in article 56 of the Law of the Sea Convention, and amplified in later articles. The coastal State's rights relate essentially to the natural resources of the EEZ, and fall under six broad headings.

1 Non-living resources

First, the coastal State has 'sovereign rights for the purpose of exploring and exploiting, conserving and managing' the non-living natural resources of the sea bed and subsoil and the superjacent waters. With the exception of the provisions relating to 'conserving and managing' and 'superjacent waters', the rights accorded to the coastal State are exactly the same as it enjoys in respect of sea-bed resources under the 1958 Geneva Convention on the Continental Shelf and customary international law (see chapter eight). Furthermore, these sea-bed rights are to be exercised in accordance with the provisions of the Law of the Sea Convention relating to the continental shelf (see chapter eight). Had it not been for a strong desire on the part of many coastal States, now reflected in the provisions of the Law of the Sea Convention, to include within the legal continental shelf those parts of the continental margin extending beyond 200 miles, the legal regime of the continental shelf could have been subsumed within the EEZ.

The reference to the coastal State 'conserving and managing' non-living resources seems to be a question of drafting rather than of substance. The whole phrase 'sovereign rights for the purpose of exploring and exploiting, conserving and managing' applies to both living and non-living resources: presumably the reference to 'conserving and managing' is intended to apply primarily, if not exclusively, to living resources, since the Convention contains no further provisions relating to the conservation or management of non-living resources. The reference to the non-living resources of the superjacent waters relates to the various minerals which can be extracted from sea water.

2 Living resources

Article 56 provides that the coastal State has 'sovereign rights for the purpose of exploring and exploiting, conserving and managing' the living natural resources of the sea bed and subsoil and the superjacent waters. These rights, together with certain duties imposed on the coastal State, are spelt out in detail in articles 61 to 73. We will examine these provisions in chapter fourteen. It may be noted here, however, that unlike the position in regard to non-living resources, the Convention gives the coastal State generally more extensive rights, exercisable in a greater area, than it enjoyed under customary international law in respect of its exclusive fishing zone.

3 Other economic resources

Article 56 gives the coastal State 'sovereign rights . . . with regard to other activities for the economic exploitation and exploration of the zone, such as the production of energy from the water, currents and winds'. This provision gives the coastal State quite new rights, and reflects – and is phrased so as to permit the coastal State to take advantage of – developments in technology. The production of energy will usually require the construction of installations of some kind (e.g., wave barrages), so that this aspect of the right must be read in conjunction with the next right.

4 Construction of artificial islands and installations

In respect of this and the following two rights the Law of the Sea Convention confers on the coastal State, not 'sovereign rights' (as with the first three rights), but the more limited 'jurisdiction'. Article 56 provides that the coastal State has 'jurisdiction as provided for in the relevant provisions of this Convention with regard to . . . the establishment and use of artificial islands, installations and structures'. The 'relevant provisions' referred to are to be found in article 60. This article gives the coastal State:

> the exclusive right to construct and to authorise and regulate the construction, operation and use of:
> (a) artificial islands;
> (b) installations and structures for the purposes provided for in article 56 and other economic purposes;
> (c) installations and structures which may interfere with the exercise of the rights of the coastal State in the zone.

The coastal State has exclusive jurisdiction over such artificial islands, installations and structures, and has the right to establish safety zones, which are normally not to exceed 500 metres in breadth, around them (LOSC, art. 60(2), (4), (5)). The distinction between the rights of the coastal State to construct 'artificial islands' for any purpose, and the right to construct 'installations and structures' for more limited purposes, seems tenuous, since, in the absence of a definition of an 'artificial island', an 'installation' or 'structure' could be regarded as being an 'artificial island'. On the other hand, since the Convention does make a distinction between 'artificial islands' and 'installations and structures', the categories are presumably not intended to overlap. It seems paradoxical that 'artificial islands' can be constructed for any purpose (such as deep-water ports, offshore airports or mining platforms) unlike 'installations and structures', when 'artificial islands' are normally larger and thus create a greater impediment to other uses of the EEZ. The reason for this distinction, it seems, is to prevent the coastal State having jurisdiction over installations and structures used for military purposes by other States.[21] Nevertheless, the distinction is frequently not maintained in national legislation.[22]

The rights of the coastal State in respect of artificial islands, installations and structures are subject to certain duties. Thus the coastal State must give due notice of the construction of artificial islands, installations and structures, must maintain permanent means for giving warning of their presence and must remove, in whole or in part, those installations and structures no longer in use, in order to ensure safety of navigation (LOSC, art. 60(3), and see further chapter eight). Furthermore, the coastal State must not construct artificial islands, installations and structures 'where interference may be caused to the use of recognised sea lanes essential to international navigation' (LOSC, art. 60(7)).

The rights which the coastal State is given in respect of artificial islands, installations and structures in its EEZ are similar to the rights the coastal State is given under the continental shelf regime in respect of structures for exploring and exploiting the natural resources of the continental shelf (see the previous chapter), but are wider, since they may be exercised for a broader range of purposes.

5 Marine scientific research

Article 56 gives the coastal State 'jurisdiction as provided for in the relevant provisions of this Convention with regard to . . . marine scientific research'. The 'relevant provisions' of the Convention are to be found in Part XIII. Article 246(1) provides that the coastal State has 'the right to regulate, authorise and conduct' scientific research in its EEZ. The coastal State must normally give its consent to pure research by other States in its EEZ, but it may withhold its consent to resource-oriented research (LOSC, art. 246(3), (5)). In either case, those wishing

---

[21] See Orrego Vicuña (1989), *op. cit.* in 'Further reading', pp. 74–5. See also chapter seventeen below, pp. 427–8.

[22] For examples of such legislation, see Kwiatkowska, *op. cit.* in 'Further reading', p. 114 and *Smith, op. cit.* in 'Further reading', pp. 34–8. See also J. A. Roach and R. W. Smith, *United States Responses to Excessive Maritime Claims* (The Hague, Nijhoff), 2nd edn, 1996, pp. 183–4, 189–91.

to undertake research in another State's EEZ are subject to various obligations. These provisions are discussed in more detail in chapter sixteen.

The powers of control over scientific research in its EEZ which the coastal State is given by the Law of the Sea Convention are broadly similar to the powers the coastal State is given by the 1958 Continental Shelf Convention to regulate research on its continental shelf, except that here, of course, the powers are wider, since they relate not just to the sea bed but also to the superjacent column of water.

6 Pollution control

Article 56 confers on the coastal State 'jurisdiction provided for in the relevant provisions of this Convention with regard to . . . the protection and preservation of the marine environment'. The 'relevant provisions' of the Convention are to be found in Part XII. This part gives the coastal State legislative and enforcement competence in its EEZ to deal with the dumping of waste (LOSC, arts 210(5), 216), other forms of pollution from vessels (LOSC, arts 211 ((5)–(6)), 220, 234), and pollution from sea-bed activities (LOSC, arts 208, 214). These provisions are discussed in detail in chapter fifteen.

Apart from its competence to regulate pollution from sea-bed activities which is broadly similar to the powers which a coastal State has hitherto enjoyed under the continental shelf regime, the powers to control pollution in the EEZ given to a coastal State by the Law of the Sea Convention are quite novel. Previously the only powers which coastal States enjoyed in areas beyond the territorial sea were those powers to take action against maritime casualties threatening or causing serious oil pollution which were given by the 1969 International Convention relating to Intervention on the High Seas in Cases of Oil Pollution Casualties (discussed in chapter fifteen).

The above six rights are set out in article 56(1), sub-paragraphs (a) and (b). Article 56(1) goes on, however, in sub-paragraph (c), to state that in addition to these rights the coastal State also has in its EEZ 'other rights and duties provided for in this Convention'. The principal rights which would appear to be referred to here are those which the coastal State has in its contiguous zone (LOSC. art. 33; and see chapter seven) – for the contiguous zone is coterminous with the inner twelve miles of the EEZ – and the right of hot pursuit (LOSC, art. 111; and see chapter eleven).

We have seen that, in relation to each of the six principal rights outlined above, the Convention imposes a number of duties on the coastal State. In addi-tion, article 56(2) lays down a general duty on a coastal State:

> in exercising its rights and performing its duties under this Convention in the exclusive economic zone . . . [to] have due regard to the rights and duties of other States and [to] act in a manner compatible with the provisions of this Convention.

The rights and duties of other States in the EEZ

The rights and duties of other States are set out in article 58 of the Law of the Sea Convention. They are all essentially concerned with international communications and are those high-seas freedoms that have survived the demands of coastal States. Of the four freedoms specifically mentioned in the 1958 High Seas Convention, fishing in the EEZ has come within the jurisdiction of the coastal State: the other three freedoms remain open to all States, although subject to greater limitations than on the high seas. We now consider each of these three rights of other States in turn.

1 Navigation

Article 58(1) provides that in the EEZ all States enjoy 'the freedoms referred to in article 87 of navigation' and 'other internationally lawful uses of the sea related to' this freedom compatible with the other provisions of the Convention. This freedom is subject to a number of limitations. First, the freedom may possibly be subject to the general limitation governing all freedoms of the high seas set out in article 87(2) – namely, that these freedoms must be exercised 'with due regard for the interests of other States in their exercise of the freedom of the high seas'. The uncertainty arises because of the rather oblique and ambiguous reference in article 58(1) to article 87, which is located in Part VII of the Convention dealing with the high seas. Secondly, under article 58(2) freedom of navigation in the EEZ is subject to the provisions of articles 88 to 115 of the Convention and the other relevant rules of international law which deal with navigation on the high seas (see chapters eleven and thirteen), in so far as they are not incompatible with the Convention's provisions on the EEZ.[23] There are two further limitations on freedom of navigation in the EEZ not explicitly mentioned in the Convention but which are implicit in its provisions. First, foreign shipping is subject to the coastal State's powers of pollution control (discussed above). Secondly, foreign ships may be affected by the presence of artificial islands and installations – although, as we have seen, such structures may not be placed in 'recognised sea lanes essential to international navigation'. It must also not be forgotten that shipping in the inner twelve miles of the EEZ will be in the coastal State's contiguous zone and therefore subject to the jurisdiction which the coastal State enjoys in that zone (and see chapter seven). Indeed, there are signs of an extension into the rest of the EEZ of a competence similar to that enjoyed in the contiguous zone. Where this is effected by treaty it is, as between the parties, not controversial. An example arises at the regional level under the Council of Europe's Agreement on Illicit Traffic by Sea, Implementing article 17 of the United Nations Convention against Illicit Traffic in Narcotic Drugs and

---

[23] For an explanation of the effects of this qualifying phrase on the provisions contained in arts 88–115, see Orrego Vicuña (1989), *op. cit.* in 'Further reading', pp. 99–102.

Psychotropic Substances. Under articles 6 to 10 of the Agreement a coastal State (or for that matter any other State) which suspects that a vessel of another party to the Agreement is engaging in drug trafficking in the coastal State's EEZ, may request the flag State for authorisation to stop and board the vessel, and, if appropriate, take enforcement measures. It is, however, very doubtful whether the coastal State has a general right to assert unilaterally enforcement jurisdiction in respect of narcotics throughout its EEZ. However, when signing or ratifying the 1988 UN Convention against Illicit Traffic in Narcotic Drugs and Psychotropic Substances, Brazil and Jamaica made declarations that the consent of the coastal State is necessary if the flag State under article 17 of the Convention authorises another State to stop and search in the EEZ one of its vessels suspected of engaging in drug trafficking. The Member States of the European Union have objected to Brazil's declaration as being contrary to international law.[24]

In general terms the provisions of the Law of the Sea Convention outlined above appear reasonably adequate for guaranteeing unhampered navigation by foreign merchant shipping through coastal States' EEZs. It may be wondered, however, exactly how extensive the rights of warships are. In particular, can warships engage in naval manoeuvres or practise using their weapons? Naval manoeuvres, and perhaps weapons practice, are clearly 'uses of the sea related to' navigation, but there might be argument over the extent to which they are 'internationally lawful' (a majority of writers take the view that such uses of the high seas have been lawful in the past), or compatible with other provisions of the Convention – notably article 88, which provides that the high seas 'shall be reserved for peaceful purposes'. This question is discussed further in chapter seventeen (see pp. 427–8).

The legislation of a number of States (nearly all of which are parties to the Law of the Sea Convention) is not in conformity with the Convention as far as the navigational rights of other States in the EEZ are concerned. Thus the Maldives[25] and Portugal[26] accord to foreign shipping the right, not of freedom of navigation, but of innocent passage. Possible unjustifiable interference with navigation may result from the legislation of Guyana,[27] India,[28] Mauritius,[29]

---

[24] United Nations, *Multilateral Treaties deposited with the Secretary-General. Status at 31 December 1995* (New York, United Nations), 1996, pp. 293–6. See also Roach and Smith, *op. cit.* in footnote 22, pp. 414–7; and see p. 219 below.

[25] Law No. 32/76 of 5 December 1976, s. 1. *UN Leg. Ser.* B/19, p. 134; *ND IX*, p. 295; Smith, *op. cit.* in 'Further reading', p. 278.

[26] Act No 33/77 of 28 May 1977, art. 3. *UN Leg. Ser.* B/19, p. 93; *ND VIII*, p. 1; *Smith, op. cit.*, p. 371. Article 3 is somewhat ambiguous on this point. It reads: 'Establishment of the exclusive economic zone shall take into account the rules of international law, namely those concerning innocent passage and overflight.'

[27] Maritime Zones Act, 1977, s. 18. *UN Leg. Ser.* B/19, p. 33; *Smith, op. cit.* in 'Further reading', p. 193.

[28] Territorial Waters, Continental Shelf, Exclusive Economic Zone and Other Maritime Zones Act, 1976, s. 7(6). *UN Leg. Ser.* B/19, p. 47; *ND V*, p. 305; *Smith, op. cit.*, p. 213.

[29] Maritime Zones Act, 1977, s. 9. *ND VII*, p. 414; *Smith, op. cit.*, p. 287.

Pakistan[30] and the Seychelles,[31] each of which claims the competence to designate certain areas of its EEZ for resource exploitation: within such areas provision may be made for 'entry into and passage through the designated area of foreign ships by the establishment of fairways, sealanes, traffic separation schemes or any other mode of ensuring freedom of navigation which is not prejudicial to the interests' of the coastal State concerned. Furthermore, these five States claim to be able to extend any law in force to the EEZ and to regulate the conduct of any person in the EEZ:[32] a somewhat similar claim is found in the legislation of Bangladesh,[33] Barbados,[34] Belize,[35] Grenada,[36] Jamaica,[37] Samoa,[38] St Kitts and Nevis,[39] Sri Lanka,[40] and Vanuatu.[41] Nigerian law provides that, to protect any installation in designated areas of its EEZ, the Nigerian authorities may prohibit ships from entering without consent a specific part of the zone.[42] Haiti claims to be able to exercise in its EEZ 'any control which it deems necessary to' ensure navigational safety, prevent violations of health, fiscal, customs and immigration laws, and prevent pollution.[43] Cape Verde claims to prohibit any activity by foreign shipping in its EEZ which causes pollution or is prejudicial to the marine environment or material resources of its EEZ,[44] while possible unjustifiable interference with shipping may result from Namibia's claim to exercise any powers which it may consider necessary to prevent the contravention of any law relating to the natural resources of the sea[45] and from Iran's claim to prohibit any activity

---

[30] Territorial Waters and Maritime Zones Act, 1976, s. 6(4). *UN Leg. Ser.* B/19, p. 85; *ND VII*, p. 478; *Smith, op. cit.,* p. 357.

[31] Maritime Zones Act, 1977, s. 9. *UN Leg. Ser.* B/19, p. 102; *ND VIII*, p. 11; *Smith, op. cit.,* p. 407.

[32] Guyana's Act, ss. 19 and 41; India's Act, ss. 7 and 15; Mauritius's Act, ss. 10 and 15; Pakistan's Act, ss. 6(5) and 14(2); Seychelles Act, ss. 10 and 15.

[33] Territorial Waters and Maritime Zones Act, 1974, s. 9. *UN Leg. Ser.* B/19, p. 4; *ND V*, p. 286; *Smith, op. cit.,* p. 69.

[34] Marine Boundaries and Jurisdiction Act, 1978, s. 8. *ND VII*, p. 335; *Smith, op. cit.,* p. 73.

[35] Maritime Areas Act, 1992, s. 23. 21 *LOSB* 3 (1992).

[36] Marine Boundaries Act, 1978, s. 8. *Smith, op. cit.,* p. 175.

[37] Exclusive Economic Zone Act, 1991, s. 9. 21 *LOSB* 28 (1992).

[38] Exclusive Economic Zone Act, 1977, s. 15, *ND VIII*, p. 38; *Smith, op. cit.,* p. 483.

[39] Maritime Areas Act, 1984, s. 28. United Nations (1993), *op. cit.* in 'Further reading', p. 303.

[40] Maritime Zones Law, 1976, s. 12. *UN Leg. Ser.* B/19, p. 120; *ND V*, p. 317; *Smith, op. cit.,* p. 427.

[41] Maritime Zones Act, 1981, s. 14. *Smith, op. cit.,* p. 471. Under s. 13(g) the Minister is also empowered to make regulations to provide for 'such other matters as may be required for giving full effect to the sovereignty of Vanuatu in relation to' the EEZ.

[42] Exclusive Economic Zone Decree, 1978, s. 3(2). *ND VII*, p. 474; *Smith, op. cit.,* p. 347.

[43] Decree No. 38 of 8 April 1977, art. 7. *Smith, op. cit.,* p. 201.

[44] Law No. 60/IV/92 delimiting the Maritime Areas of the Republic of Cape Verde, 1992, art. 16. 26 *LOSB* 24 (1994).

[45] Territorial Sea and Exclusive Economic Zone of Namibia Amendment Act, 1991, s. 2. 21 *LOSB* 64 (1992).

in its EEZ inconsistent with its rights.[46] These claims give rise to concern that what many hoped the Law of the Sea Convention would achieve, namely a clear demarcation of coastal States' rights and an end to 'creeping jurisdiction', will be undermined.

2 Overflight

Article 58 provides that all States enjoy freedom of overflight in the EEZ, and 'other internationally lawful uses of the sea related to' this freedom compatible with the provisions of the Convention. This freedom is subject to the first two limitations to which the freedom of navigation is subject, namely due regard for other States, and articles 88 to 115, etc. (although many of these articles have no application to aircraft). In addition, the freedom is implicitly subject to two further possible limitations. First, the coastal State's right to construct artificial islands and installations might effectively prevent low flying in the vicinity of such structures. Secondly, aircraft are subject to the coastal State's competence to regulate the dumping of waste. Given the attitude of some States, such as Brazil, to military activities in their EEZs, there may also be some uncertainty about the use of the EEZ by foreign military aircraft for the purpose of military exercises (and see further chapter seventeen).

There is one further matter of importance about which there is also uncertainty, and that is the rules of the air which apply to aircraft in the EEZ. Under article 12 of the Convention on International Civil Aviation 1944, aircraft over the 'high seas' must comply with the Rules of the Air laid down by the International Civil Aviation Organisation (ICAO). Over a State's territory and territorial sea, however, aircraft must comply with that State's regulations, which may diverge from ICAO rules (art. 38 of the 1944 Convention). In this context, is the EEZ to be regarded as high seas or territorial sea? The Law of the Sea Convention gives no direct answer, but it would seem reasonable to argue that article 12 is one of the 'pertinent rules of international law' which by virtue of article 58(2) apply to the EEZ. Furthermore, articles 39(3) and 54 of the Law of the Sea Convention provide that aircraft exercising a right of transit passage over straits or archipelagic sea-lanes passage over archipelagic waters, i.e., *landwards* of the EEZ, must observe ICAO rules: this also suggests that ICAO rules apply in the EEZ. A similar conclusion was put forward in a 1987 study by the ICAO secretariat.[47] If it is correct that ICAO rules do apply in the EEZ, this position might

---

[46] Act on the Marine Areas of the Islamic Republic of Iran in the Persian Gulf and Oman Sea, art. 16. 24 *LOSB* 10 (1993). For protest from the EU, see 30 *LOSB* 60 (1996): for Iran's response, see 31 *LOSB* 37 (1996). The USA has objected to many of the claims referred to above. See Roach and Smith, *op. cit.* in footnote 22, pp. 186–9.

[47] 'The United Nations Convention on the Law of the Sea – Implications, if any, for the Application of the Chicago Convention, its Annexes and other International Air Law Instruments', Doc. No. LC/26 – WP/5–1 of 4 February 1987, para. 11.12. Reproduced in 3 *International Organisations and the Law of the Sea Documentary Yearbook* 243 (1987).

require modification where a coastal State built an airport on an artificial island in its EEZ, because it would probably be thought necessary that the coastal State's regulations should apply, to some degree at least, in and around the airport.

3 Laying of submarine cables and pipelines

Finally, all States enjoy the freedom of laying submarine cables and pipelines in the EEZ, and 'other internationally lawful uses of the sea related to' this freedom compatible with the other provisions of the Convention. This freedom is subject to the first two limitations to which the freedom of navigation is subject, namely due consideration for the interests of other States and articles 88 to 115 of the Convention. While many of these articles have no application to cables and pipelines, articles 112 to 115 are specifically concerned with them, dealing principally with the question of their being broken or damaged. In addition, there is a further explicit limitation contained in article 79. Although this article is in the part of the Law of the Sea Convention dealing with the continental shelf, it must also apply to the EEZ, since the sea bed of the EEZ consists of the continental shelf. Article 79(3) provides that 'the delineation of the course for the laying of' pipelines (but not cables) is 'subject to the consent of the coastal State'. Article 79(4) empowers the coastal State to lay down conditions for cables and pipelines entering its territorial sea, and to establish its jurisdiction over cables and pipelines constructed on or used in connection with the exploration and exploitation of its continental shelf[48] or the operations of artificial islands and installations under its jurisdiction. How far article 79(3) is compatible with a freedom to lay pipelines may be questioned, and to use the term 'freedom' here is perhaps misleading. Furthermore, two States – Cape Verde[49] and Sao Tome e Principe[50] – purport to make the laying of both cables and pipelines as such, rather than simply the delineation of the course of pipelines, subject to their prior consent.

The effect of the above provisions is that the rights of other States to navigate, overfly and lay cables and pipelines in a coastal State's EEZ are less extensive than their corresponding rights on the high seas. Furthermore, article 58(3) obliges other States when exercising their rights in a coastal State's EEZ to

> have due regard to the rights and duties of the coastal State and . . . comply with laws and regulations adopted by the coastal State in accordance with the provisions of this Convention and other rules of international law in so far as they are not incompatible with Part V of the Convention (on the EEZ).

[48] In practice the coastal State and the State which is the owner of the pipeline may agree on a regime of concurrent jurisdiction. For an actual example, see the Agreement between Norway and the United Kingdom relating to the Exploitation of the Frigg Field Reservoir and the Transmission of Gas therefrom to the United Kingdom, 1976, arts 13–21.

[49] *Loc. cit.* in footnote 44, art. 21.

[50] Decree Law No. 15/78, art. 5. *Smith, op. cit.*, p. 405.

Relationship between the rights of the coastal State and the rights of other States

It is clear from the enumeration given above of the rights expressly attributed to the coastal State and to other States that there is considerable potential for conflict between these two groups of rights. The regulation of such conflict is in some cases expressly provided for in the Convention. Thus, for example, the provisions of article 60 (quoted above) are designed to avoid conflicts between the right of the coastal State to construct artificial islands or installations and the rights of foreign shipping. Similarly the coastal State's powers of pollution control are carefully spelt out in Part XII in order to minimise interference with foreign shipping. But in some cases the Convention contains no specific rules to avoid conflicts of use. For example, it is unclear whether and to what extent a coastal State may, as part of its sovereign rights to exploit and manage living resources, regulate foreign shipping in order to minimise conflicts with fishing in its EEZ, e.g. by requiring ships to avoid areas where there are standing nets or which are important spawning and nursery grounds for fish. In such cases the only guidance (if it can be called that) given by the Convention is the mutual obligation of coastal States and other States to have 'due regard' to each other's rights. In some cases other treaties will help to regulate conflicting uses: for example, the 1972 Convention on the International Regulations Preventing Collisions at Sea governs the relationship between vessels which are fishing and other vessels.[51]

The attribution of other rights in the EEZ

The Law of the Sea Convention, in attributing rights in the EEZ to the coastal State and other States, has covered most of the more obvious uses of the EEZ. There may, however, be some uses of the EEZ which do not fall within the rights of either the coastal State or other States. Possible examples include the emplacement of underwater listening devices for submarines (see chapter seventeen); the recovery of historic wrecks beyond the contiguous zone (for the position within the contiguous zone see article 303 of the Convention and chapter seven);[52] and

---

[51] For fuller discussion of these problems, see the articles by Brown and Robertson listed in 'Further reading' and W. T. Burke, 'Exclusive fisheries zones and freedom of navigation', 20 *San Diego Law Review* 595–623 (1983).

[52] But it should be noted that three States – Cape Verde, Jamaica and Morocco – require advance authorisation for archaeological exploration anywhere in their EEZs. See, respectively, Law No. 60/IV/92, *op. cit.* in footnote 44, art. 28; Exclusive Economic Zone Act, 1991, s. 7(1), 21 *LOSB* 20 (1992); and Decree No. 1–81–179 of 8 April 1981, art. 5, *Smith*, *op. cit.*, p. 303. In the declaration it made when ratifying the Convention Malaysia claimed that without prejudice to article 303, no archaeological or historical object should be removed from its maritime zones without its prior authorisation and consent. A similar declaration was made by Portugal. See also the literature referred to in notes 25 and 26 of the previous chapter.

jurisdiction over buoys used for pure scientific research (discussed in chapter sixteen): developments in technology may produce further examples. What is the position in relation to such uses? Which States are to have the competence to enjoy and regulate them? The Convention does not give a precise answer. Instead it provides, in article 59, a general formula for attributing rights in such cases. Article 59 reads as follows:

> In cases where this Convention does not attribute rights or jurisdiction to the coastal State or to other States within the exclusive economic zone, and a conflict arises between the interests of the coastal State and any other State or States, the conflict should be resolved on the basis of equity and in the light of all the relevant circumstances, taking into account the respective importance of the interests involved to the parties as well as to the international community as a whole.

Article 59 thus makes it clear that, in the case of unattributed rights, there is no presumption in favour of either the coastal State or other States: each case, as it arises, will have to be decided on its own merits on the basis of the criteria set out in article 59.[53] As far as the machinery for deciding such cases is concerned, this will be determined by the provisions of the Convention dealing with the settlement of disputes (discussed in detail in chapter nineteen). Essentially this means that there must first be an attempt at settlement by consensual means: if this is unsuccessful, the dispute must be referred to one of the judicial bodies listed in article 287, unless the dispute relates to military activities and one of the parties has made a declaration under article 298 exempting itself from settling such disputes by compulsory third-party means.

Significance of the EEZ

The extension of coastal State jurisdiction by means of 200-mile EEZs from what had previously generally been narrow coastal State limits to encompass areas which had formerly been high seas – areas containing the major proportion of the ocean's resources and being the site of most ocean activities – has represented a major change in the regulation of and access to ocean activities. It has meant a move away from open access to resources and regulation based primarily on flag State jurisdiction, to near-exclusive coastal State access to resources and regulation based primarily – though not exclusively – on coastal State jurisdiction. In chapters fourteen and fifteen we consider whether in practice the EEZ regime

[53] But note that Cape Verde, in clear contradiction of article 59, claims 'exclusive jurisdiction' with regard to any unattributed rights: see article 13 of Law No. 60/IV/92, *op. cit.* in footnote 44. A similar position was taken by Uruguay in the declaration it made when ratifying the Convention. Note also the comment of Nordquist, *op. cit.* in footnote 18, Vol. II (1993), p. 569: 'Given the functional nature of the exclusive economic zone, where economic interests are the principal concern, this formula [i.e., that in article 59] would normally favor the coastal State. Where conflicts arise on issues not involving the exploration for and exploitation of resources, the formula would tend to favor the interests of other States or of the international community as a whole.'

has been any better at managing fish stocks and preventing pollution than the previous narrow coastal State jurisdiction/high seas regime. Here it may be noted that in many cases the responsibility for managing the resources of the EEZ assumed by the coastal State, together with the necessary enforcement machinery, have represented for many coastal States a significant new undertaking as well as a new form of expenditure (which may, of course, be more than offset by an increase in revenue from the resources of the EEZ).

As regards the question of whether the EEZ has led to any fundamental redistribution of the ocean's resources – as many developing countries argued that it would and should – the following observations can be made. First, it seems that few developing countries are among the main beneficiaries of EEZs. Only about thirty States have gained significantly from establishing an EEZ, at least in terms of area (the resources of the area are not, of course, necessarily commensurate with its size), and these States are those that front the great oceans of the world. As a quick glance at an atlas will show, many such States are developed, not developing. African, Caribbean and Middle Eastern States, in particular, come off badly. Not only do most such States have small EEZs, their EEZs are poor in resources. The main developing States benefiting from an EEZ are China and many Latin American and Pacific island States. The fifteen leading beneficiaries of EEZs, together with some indication of the resources of their zones, are shown in table 1.

Secondly, one would have expected the widespread introduction of 200-mile EEZs and EFZs in the 1970s to have led to a reduction in the catches of distant-water fishing nations and an increase in the catches of the States off whose coasts they fished. This has to a considerable degree been the case, at least in relative terms. Distant-water catches peaked at a level of nearly sixteen per cent of the total world marine fish catch in 1972 and thereafter declined fairly steadily so that in 1994 the figure was no more than five per cent. On the other hand, in absolute terms the picture is less clear-cut. The distant-water catch amounted to about 8.5 million tonnes in 1972, declined to 6.5 in 1979, thereafter rose to 9 million in 1989, but declined to 4.5 million tonnes in 1994.[54] This reduction in catches has not been spread evenly among distant-water fishing States, however. Some, such as South Korea, Spain and Thailand, have been more successful in maintaining and obtaining fishing opportunities in distant waters than others, such as Bulgaria and Portugal, while the two leading distant-water fishing States, Japan and the former USSR/Russia, have to a considerable extent offset their losses by increased fishing in their own large EEZs. Many of those States which have successfully reduced foreign fishing off their coasts by the introduction of a 200-mile zone have significantly increased their catches (e.g., the USA, Canada, Iceland, Mexico and New Zealand). In the case of some developing countries which have substantially increased the size of their catch in recent years, e.g., Guinea-Bissau, Indonesia, Malaysia, Pakistan and Sri Lanka, the increase may

---

[54] FAO, *Yearbook of Fishery Statistics*, Vol. 78, 1994 (1997), p. xviii.

Table 1. *Leading EEZ beneficiaries*

State	Area of 200-mile zone (square nautical miles)[55]	Offshore oil production 1992 in '000 tonnes (proven reserves in million tonnes)		Offshore natural gas production 1992 in million cubic metres (proven reserves in billion cubic metres)		Fish catches or estimated potential (EP) in 200-mile zone (million tonnes)
1. USA	2,831,400	35,308	(707)	103,471	(1,189)	5.5 (1994)
2. France	2,083,400	0		0		Not available
3. Indonesia	1,577,300	57,270	(286)	7,236	(1,447)	6.7 (EP)
4. New Zealand	1,409,500	797	(18)	2,998	(82)	0.7 (1995)
5. Australia	1,310,900	24,153	(258)	16,952	(538)	2.5 (1995)
6. Russia	1,309,500	10,558	(41)	10,337	(17)	3.0 (1994)
7. Japan	1,126,000	697	(1)	286	(0)	6.5 (1994)
8. Brazil	924,000	26,145	(631)	7,236	(2)	0.6 (1995)
9. Canada	857,000	498	(162)	0	(298)	0.8 (1995)
10. Mexico	831,500	85,656	(5,712)	11,370	(1,926)	1.2 (1995)
11. Kiribati	770,000	Not available		Not available		Not available
12. Papua New Guinea	690,000	0	(37)	0	(314)	Not available
13. Chile	667,300	847	(54)	569	(65)	7.5 (1995)
14. Norway	590,500	89,640	(2,364)	32,044	(3,088)	3.0 (1995)
15. India	587,600	35,856	(1,047)	6,202	(430)	2.0 (EP)
Total all States	37,745,000	909,398	(37,276)	355,697	(25,393)	91.9 (1995)

Note: The figures for the areas of the EEZs of the USA and France include their overseas and dependent territories. There appear to be no separate figures for their metropolitan territories. The figure given for the area of Russia's EEZ is that given for the former Soviet Union: Russia's EEZ is unlikely to be significantly smaller. Micronesia and the Marshall Islands are almost certainly in the top fifteen States in terms of the area of their EEZs, but there appear to be no figures for these areas.
Source: Cols 1 and 2: *Limits in the Seas* No. 36, 4th revision (1981), p. 12; Cols 3 and 4: World Resources Institute, *World Resources 1994–95* (Oxford, Oxford University Press), 1994, pp. 354–5; Col 5: the figures (which are very approximate) have been calculated from a variety of EC, FAO and OECD publications.

be due as much to improvements in technology and greater investment in the fishing industry as to phasing out foreign fishing off their coasts. Even where a developing country has not reduced foreign fishing off its coasts, it may nevertheless have benefited economically from establishing a 200-mile zone through being able to impose licensing fees on foreign vessels fishing in the zone (although against this must be set the costs of managing its zone and enforcing its legislation). Many developing States, however, still lack the necessary capital and manpower to manage their EEZ properly and benefit from its resources.

[55] But note that *Smith, op. cit.* in 'Further reading', pp. 13–16 gives slightly different figures for the areas of some States' EEZs.

Overall, therefore, the establishment of 200-mile EEZs and EFZs has to some extent led to some redistribution of fishery resources.[56] This redistribution has largely been from distant-water fishing States to the States off whose coasts they fished. Although the former are nearly all developed States, the latter are by no means exclusively – and perhaps not even principally – developing States.[57] As regards resources other than fish, in the case of offshore oil and gas the introduction of the EEZ has effected no redistribution. Where the EEZ covers areas of sea bed that are continental shelf, any oil or gas there already belonged to the coastal State under the continental shelf doctrine. In areas of the EEZ where the sea bed is too deep to be continental shelf under the pre-LOSC regime, it is highly unlikely that there is any oil or gas. In the case of manganese nodules the establishment of the EEZ means that about ten per cent of the nodules are now under national jurisdiction rather than in the International Sea Bed Area. This represents a redistribution in favour of those States, such as Mexico and Papua New Guinea, whose EEZs contain manganese nodules, from the international community as a whole. Overall, therefore, it is likely that the introduction of the EEZ concept has not produced as much material gain for the developing countries as its original proponents suggested. Nevertheless, as a symbol of the control exercised by a State over its natural resources the introduction and acceptance of the EEZ was a considerable psychological gain for developing countries.

Further reading

D. Attard, *The Exclusive Economic Zone in International Law* (Oxford, Oxford University Press), 1987.

E. D. Brown, 'The exclusive economic zone. Criteria and machinery for the resolution of international conflicts between different users of the EEZ', 4 *Maritime Policy and Management* 325–50 (1977).

W. T. Burke, 'National legislation on ocean authority zones and the contemporary law of the sea', 9 *ODIL* 289–322 (1981).

J. I. Charney, 'The exclusive economic zone and public international law', 15 *ODIL* 233–88 (1985).

T. A. Clingan (ed.), *Law of the Sea: State Practice in Zones of Special Jurisdiction* (Honolulu, Hawaii, Law of the Sea Institute), 1982.

B. Conforti (ed.), *La Zona Economica Esclusiva* (Milan, Giuffre), 1983.

L. Juda, 'The exclusive economic zone and ocean management', 18 *ODIL* 305–31(1987).

B. Kwiatkowska, *The 200 Mile Exclusive Economic Zone in the New Law of the Sea* (Dordrecht, Nijhoff), 1989.

---

[56] For a fuller analysis, see L. Juda, 'World marine fish catch in the age of exclusive economic zones and exclusive fishery zones', 22 *ODIL* 1–32 (1991); and G. Pontecorvo, 'The enclosure of the marine commons: adjustment and redistribution in world fisheries', 12 *Marine Policy* 361–72 (1988).

[57] One calculation is that about two-thirds of the redistribution would go to developed States. See P. M. Wijkman, 'UNCLOS and the redistribution of ocean wealth', 16 *Journal of World Trade Law* 27 (1982), at 31–2.

B. Kwiatkowska, '200-mile exclusive economic/fishery zone and the continental shelf – an inventory of recent State practice', 9 *IJMCL* 199–234 and 337–88 (1994) and 10 *IJMCL* 53–93 (1995).

F. Orrego Vicuña, *The Exclusive Economic Zone* (Cambridge, Cambridge University Press), 1989.

—— (ed.), *The Exclusive Economic Zone: A Latin American Perspective* (Boulder, Colo, Westview), 1984.

F. H. Paolillo, 'The exclusive economic zone in Latin American practice and legislation', 26 *ODIL* 105–25 (1995).

H. B. Robertson, 'Navigation in the exclusive economic zone' 24 *VJIL* 865–915 (1984).

O. P. Sharma, 'Enforcement jurisdiction in the exclusive economic zone – the Indian experience', 24 *ODIL* 155–78 (1993).

R. W. Smith, *Exclusive Economic Zone Claims. An Analysis and Primary Documents* (Dordrecht, Nijhoff), 1986 [*Smith*].

United Nations, *The Law of the Sea. National Legislation on the Exclusive Economic Zone and the Exclusive Fishery Zone* (New York, United Nations), 1986.

——, *The Law of the Sea. Exclusive Economic Zone – Legislative History of Articles 56, 58 and 59 of the United Nations Convention on the Law of the Sea* (New York, United Nations), 1992.

——, *The Law of the Sea. National Legislation on the Exclusive Economic Zone and the Exclusive Fishery Zone* (New York, United Nations), 1993.

10

Delimitation of
maritime boundaries

Introduction

Because of the close geographical proximity of many States, their maritime zones often overlap to a greater or lesser extent. There is therefore a need for boundaries between such zones in order to avoid disputes and uncertainties over the right to exercise sovereignty, sovereign rights or jurisdiction and to exploit resources. When the only maritime zone was the territorial sea, in most cases of no more than three miles in breadth, the need for boundaries was limited and mainly confined to States adjacent to one another along the same stretch of coast. However, the tremendous extension of coastal State jurisdiction since 1945, expecially over the continental shelf and EEZ, has substantially increased the need for maritime boundaries, not only for more extensive boundaries seawards between adjacent States but also between States situated opposite one another.

The drawing of boundaries is essentially a task for the two (or sometimes three) States involved, and many bilateral treaties establishing maritime boundaries have been concluded which are examined later in this chapter. First, however, we look at the attempts to develop general rules and principles to guide States in the drawing of boundaries which have been made in both the 1958 Geneva Conventions and the 1982 Law of the Sea Convention. This has necessarily been a difficult task given the great diversity of coastal geography. In addition to the Conventions, customary law on this matter has been extensively developed through decisions of the International Court of Justice and various arbitral tribunals. There has been much more international litigation in this area of the Law of the Sea than any other – and indeed it has arguably been the most fertile area in the whole of international law for judicial dispute settlement in recent years.

In theory, each maritime zone demands a separate delimitation, yielding boundaries for the territorial sea, the EEZ or exclusive fisheries zone (in which the contiguous zone is commonly subsumed) and the continental shelf. In practice, there is an increasing tendency to parcel these delimitations together, both in judicial settlements and in bilateral agreements, by laying down a single maritime boundary without distinguishing between the different zones. Nonetheless, although there is a growing tendency for the principles on the delimitation of the various maritime zones to come together, it is convenient to consider them separately, and we do so here.

At the outset it should be emphasised that the principles of delimitation which have been laid down in the Conventions and by courts and arbitral tribunals have been formulated at a high level of generality. For this reason it is extremely difficult to offer any precise account of the principles of delimitation, such as might be applied in future to unresolved boundaries. Quite apart from the inherent generality and vagueness of the principles, each delimitation involves a situation which has its own unique characteristics which will have to be taken into account. Previous practice and decisions will at best point to the kind of factors to be considered and approach to be adopted, but will not permit the deduction of a precise boundary line which must be established.

Territorial sea boundaries

In the case of territorial sea delimitations between opposite States (i.e., two States facing each other) the normal practice has been to agree upon the median line, equidistant from the nearest points of the opposing States' shores, as the boundary. This was done, for example, in the 1932 Danish-Swedish Declaration concerning the Sound, for a large part of the boundary between the two States. Sometimes States have employed instead the centre line of the main deep-water channel passing between their shores: an instance of this is the 1928 Agreement between Great Britain and the Sultan of Johore concerning the Johore Strait.[1]

Practice in delimiting the territorial seas of adjacent States has been less consistent. Considerable use has been made of the equidistance principle, drawing a median line outwards from the boundary on the shore: the 1976 Colombia–Panama delimitation agreement is one of many examples. But other criteria have also been used. Thus the Permanent Court of Arbitration, in its award in the *Grisbådarna* case in 1909, favoured a line drawn perpendicular to the general direction of the coast. While that case turned in part upon use of the perpendicular in seventeenth-century practice, made relevant by a treaty of 1661 concerning the Norwegian-Swedish boundary, the perpendicular line is still occasionally referred to in delimitations, such as the 1958 Poland–USSR delimitation agreement and the 1972 Brazil–Uruguay Agreement on the Chuy River Bank and the Lateral Sea Limit. In addition, some maritime boundaries between adjacent States follow the line of latitude passing through the point where the land boundary meets the sea. This method was used, for example, in the 1975 delimitation agreement between Ecuador and Colombia.

---

[1] See the (UK) Straits Settlement and Johore Territorial Waters (Agreement) Act, 1928. This is, strictly, a colonial rather than an international delimitation.

In all cases it is possible that special circumstances, such as the presence of offshore islands or the general configuration of the coast, or claims to water areas based upon an historic title, will demand the adoption of some other boundary line by agreement between the States concerned. In the 1974 Agreement between India and Sri Lanka on the Boundary in Historic Waters between the Two Countries, for instance, a modified median line was used, to take account of 'historical' factors. Indeed, it is the common practice at present to set boundaries by reference to geographical co-ordinates for the sake of certainty and simplicity, and such determinations almost inevitably demand some departure from the exact median line or other criterion. The particularity of the circumstances of each case make generalisation upon these delimitations difficult, and since they are motivated primarily by expediency and a spirit of compromise it is probably wrong in any event to attempt to infer any rules of international law from them. Indeed, in the *Guinea/Guinea-Bissau* case (1985) the tribunal decided that all delimitations had to be measured against the single goal of producing an equitable solution in the circumstances of each case. Many examples of recent agreements have been collected and analysed in the series *Limits in the Seas*, published by the Geographer of the US Department of State and in the three-volume work edited by Charney and Alexander referred to in 'Further reading'.

The conventional rules concerning delimitation are consistent with the pattern of State practice described above. Article 12 of the 1958 Territorial Sea Convention and article 15 of the Law of the Sea Convention, which deal with the matter, are in substance identical. The latter reads:

> Where the coasts of two States are opposite or adjacent to each other, neither of the two States is entitled, failing agreement between them to the contrary, to extend its territorial sea beyond the median line every point of which is equidistant from the nearest points on the baselines from which the breadth of the territorial seas of each of the two States is measured. The above provision does not apply, however, where it is necessary by reason of historic title or other special circumstances to delimit the territorial seas of the two States in a way which is at variance therewith.

In the *Dubai/Sharjah Border Arbitration* (1981) part of the task of the tribunal was to draw a territorial sea boundary between two parts of the United Arab Emirates adjacent to each other along what was essentially a straight coast. The tribunal, applying customary international law, drew a 'lateral equidistance line from the coastal terminus which divides the two territorial seas according to the principles laid down in' article 12 of the Territorial Sea Convention and the draft of what became article 15 of the Law of the Sea Convention, and it regarded this line as 'in all respects equitable'.[2] The tribunal would seem thereby to have equated the customary and the conventional rules.

[2] 91 *ILR* 543 at 663.

Continental shelf and EEZ boundaries

Continental shelf

Early practice

Early delimitations of the continental shelf evidenced the application of no clear principles. The first ever agreed delimitation, in 1942 between the then British colony of Trinidad and Venezuela in the Gulf of Paria, for example, was said to have secured an 'equitable division' between the two territories concerned. Similarly, the Truman Proclamation in 1945 referred to the application of 'equitable principles' in determining boundaries.

1958 Convention

In the 1950s more specific principles emerged. Arguments for the adoption of the equidistance principle were pressed strongly in the ILC during this period. That solution had the advantages of simplicity and certainty. It was, however, evident from the outset that inflexible application of the equidistance principle was undesirable. For example, since islands could generate their own continental shelves, a single small offshore island could create massive distortions in the line of equidistance that would be produced by considering only the coast of the mainland. Again, the configuration of the mainland coast itself might render equidistance an inequitable principle. This was the source of the dispute litigated in the *North Sea Continental Shelf* cases (1969): under the equidistance principle the concavity of the coastline of the Federal Republic of Germany and the adjacent States, Denmark and the Netherlands, resulted in Germany being allotted an exceptionally small part of the North Sea shelf. There may be other special circumstances which would justify divergences from the equidistance principle. For these reasons the principle was from the first coupled with a reservation allowing such special circumstances to be accommodated. Thus the 1958 Continental Shelf Convention provided that the boundary of the continental shelf should be determined by agreement between the States concerned. However:

> In the absence of agreement, and unless another boundary line is justified by special circumstances, the boundary shall be determined by application of the principle of equidistance. (CSC, art. 6(2); cf. art. 6(I))

Thus, States shall first seek to agree on a boundary. If they are unable to do so, the boundary will be a line equidistant from the baselines of the parties (the median line), unless another line is justified by special circumstances.

Custom

Article 6 of the Continental Shelf Convention represents a rule of treaty law only, applying 'equidistance plus special circumstances' in the absence of agreement – and most continental shelf boundaries have been settled by agreement, as is explained below – in relations between States Parties to the Convention.

Thus the provision was not applicable in the *North Sea Continental Shelf* cases because Germany had not ratified the Convention. Prior to the entry into force of the Law of the Sea Convention, in situations where one or more of the States concerned was not a party to the Continental Shelf Convention customary international law applied. Such law has been developed by decisions of the International Court of Justice[3] and a number of arbitral tribunals.[4] In doing so the International Court and tribunals have not adopted the conventional approach to ascertaining rules of customary international law, which is to examine State practice and see whether there is the necessary degree of uniformity coupled with *opinio iuris* (cf. p. 7 above). Instead they have simply declared what customary law is. We are therefore here dealing with what is essentially judge-made law. In stating what customary law is, the International Court and tribunals have been faced with the almost impossible task of trying to formulate rules of sufficient generality to be applicable to a wide variety of geographical circumstances, while at the same time being of sufficient precision to allow the boundary to be reasonably easily determined in the particular case.[5] It has to be said that the Court and tribunals have not been very successful in this task. The rules of customary law they have enunciated are, as will be seen, very general and imprecise, while it has often been difficult to see how the boundary they have determined in the particular case follows from the principles of customary law stated in the case.

In the first case in which it had to deal with customary law, the *North Sea Continental Shelf* cases, the Court, after observing that there was no single method

---

[3] In the following cases: *North Sea Continental Shelf* cases (1969); *Continental Shelf (Tunisia/Libya)* case (1982); *Continental Shelf (Libya/Malta)* case (1985); and *Case concerning Maritime Delimitation in the Area between Greenland and Jan Mayen (Denmark v. Norway)* (1993), which concerned the boundary between the continental shelves and 200-mile fishing zones of the Danish island of Greenland and the Norwegian island of Jan Mayen. In the *Aegean Sea Continental Shelf* case (1978) the Court found that it lacked jurisdiction. The *Gulf of Maine* case (1984) also concerned delimitation of the continental shelf, as part of the delimitation of a single maritime boundary between both the continental shelves and the 200-mile fishing and economic zones of Canada and the USA in the Gulf of Maine. For reasons which will become apparent later, cases involving delimitation of a single maritime boundary are not directly relevant to delimitation of the continental shelf only.

[4] The main cases are the *Anglo-French Continental Shelf* case (1977) and the *Dubai/Sharjah Border Arbitration* (1981). The *Guinea/Guinea Bissau Maritime Boundary* case (1985) and the *Case concerning the Delimitation of Maritime Areas between Canada and the French Republic* (1992) both concerned a single maritime boundary between the continental shelves and the 200-mile fishing zones/EEZs of the States concerned, and therefore like the *Gulf of Maine* case are not directly relevant in the present context.

[5] But cf. the *Gulf of Maine* case, where the International Court made a distinction between principles of delimitation and practical methods for determining a boundary. According to the Court, only the former could be the subject of customary international law. See [1984] *ICJ Rep.* 246, at 290. This distinction has not been pursued by either the Court or tribunals in later cases.

of delimitation the use of which was compulsory, stated that under customary international law:

> delimitation is to be effected by agreement in accordance with equitable principles, and taking account of all the relevant circumstances, in such a way as to leave as much as possible to each Party all those parts of the continental shelf that constitute a natural prolongation of its land territory into and under the sea, without encroachment on the natural prolongation of the land territory of the other.[6]

This was accordingly achieved, following the Court's judgment in the case, through the negotiation of a series of treaties between the littoral States concerned, the Court having been asked only to indicate the principles of delimitation and not to determine the actual boundary, in such a way as to give Germany a larger share of the shelf than it would have enjoyed under a delimitation employing only the equidistance principle.

The International Court's dictum in the *North Sea Continental Shelf* cases that under customary international law delimitation is to be effected by agreement in accordance with equitable principles and taking account of all the relevant circumstances has been reiterated in all subsequent cases. Since the *Tunisia/Libya* case the Court has stressed, in addition, that the goal of the delimitation process is an equitable result, although this does not mean a judgment *ex aequo et bono*.

Although the delimitation rule in article 6 of the Continental Shelf Convention and the customary rules are rather differently formulated, and although the Court in the *North Sea Continental Shelf* cases stressed that the rule in article 6 had not passed into customary law, there has been a tendency to see them as leading to much the same effect. Thus, the arbitral tribunal in the *Anglo-French Continental Shelf* case in 1977, dealing with delimitation of the Western Approaches between France and the United Kingdom (both parties to the 1958 Convention), stated that the equidistance–special circumstances rule of article 6, which the tribunal saw as a single rule rather than (as suggested above) two rules (the main rule and an exception to it), 'in effect gives particular expression to a general norm that, failing agreement, the boundary between States abutting on the same continental shelf is to be determined on equitable principles'.[7] In the *Greenland/Jan Mayen* case the International Court went further and added:

> If the equidistance-special circumstances rule of the 1958 Convention is, in the light of this 1977 Decision, to be regarded as expressing a general norm based on equitable principles, it must be difficult to find any material difference – at any rate in regard to delimitation between opposite coasts – between the effect of Article 6 and the effect of the customary rule which also requires a delimitation based on equitable principles.[8]

---

[6] [1969] *ICJ Rep.* 3, at 54.
[7] 18 *ILM* 398 (1979), at 421.
[8] [1993] *ICJ Rep.* 38, at 58.

The Court thus appears to have equated article 6 with the customary international law rules on continental shelf delimitation, at least as far as opposite coasts are concerned. In doing so, it appears to have gone further than the *Anglo-French Continental Shelf* case where the tribunal noted that 'under article 6 the equidistance principle ultimately possesses an obligatory force which it does not have in the same measure under the rules of customary law' and that 'the rules of customary law are a relevant and even essential means for both interpreting and completing the provisions of article 6'.[9]

Although courts and tribunals have been reluctant to enumerate principles of delimitation under customary law, a number of such principles do seem to have emerged through consistent utilisation in a number of cases. First, in the case of delimitations between opposite (as opposed to adjacent) coasts, there is an increasing tendency for courts and tribunals, even when applying customary law, to begin the delimitation process by drawing an equidistance line as a provisional boundary and then considering whether it requires modification in the light of the relevant circumstances in order to achieve an equitable solution. This was done, for example, in the *Libya/Malta*[10] and *Greenland/Jan Mayen*[11] cases. Secondly, a court or tribunal will not choose as a boundary a line that encroaches on or cuts off areas that more naturally belong to one party than the other. This, perhaps somewhat question-begging, principle was applied in the *North Sea Continental Shelf*[12] and *Tunisia/Libya*[13] cases. Thirdly, courts and tribunals have emphasised that in carrying out a boundary delimitation, they are not engaged in an exercise in distributive justice and dividing the delimitation area into just and equitable shares.[14] Finally, a court or tribunal may limit the area in which the boundary is drawn because of the presence of continental shelves claimed by third States: this happened, for example, in the *Libya/Malta* case.

As we have seen, article 6 of the Continental Shelf Convention requires consideration of any 'special circumstances' which might justify a departure from the median line when drawing a continental shelf boundary, whereas customary international law requires 'relevant circumstances' to be taken into account. 'Special circumstances' have traditionally been regarded as being fairly narrow in scope: for example, the principal drafters of article 6, the International Law Commission, considered 'special circumstances' as embracing (and apparently being limited to) exceptional configurations of the coast, and the presence of islands and navigable channels.[15] 'Relevant circumstances', on the other hand, have been regarded as being much wider in scope: indeed, in the *North Sea*

---

[9] *Op. cit.* in footnote 7, pp. 421 and 422.
[10] [1985] *ICJ Rep.* 13, at 47 *et seq.*
[11] *Op. cit.* in footnote 8, pp. 61–2.
[12] *Op. cit.* in footnote 6, p. 47.
[13] [1982] *ICJ Rep.* 18, at 61–2.
[14] See, for example, the *Greenland/Jan Mayen* case, *op. cit.* in footnote 8, pp. 66–7 where the International Court quotes from its previous case law.
[15] See *ILC Yearbook*, 1956, Vol. II, p. 300.

Continental Shelf cases the International Court suggested that there was no limit to the kind of circumstances that might be taken into account in effecting an equitable delimitation.[16] Subsequent cases, however, have tended to narrow such circumstances to those that are relevant to the continental shelf and are primarily geographical in character. In the *Greenland/Jan Mayen* case the International Court, having (as we have already seen) effectively equated article 6 of the 1958 Convention with customary law, went on to point out that although special circumstances and relevant circumstances were different in origin and in name, there was a tendency to assimilate the two because 'they both are intended to enable the achievement of an equitable result', especially in the case of opposite coasts.[17] As regards the question of how particular relevant or special circumstances are to be weighted, it seems, especially from the *Libya/Malta* and *Greenland/Jan Mayen*[18] cases, that a court has a broad discretion to determine the relative weight of any particular circumstances, subject only to the need for some consistency with previous cases.

In fact a number of relevant or special circumstances can be identified with some confidence as there has been a degree of consistency in the case law. One relevant circumstance is the configuration of the coast. One example, the concavity of the German coast in the *North Sea Continental Shelf* cases, has already been mentioned. A second example is in the *Tunisia/Libya* case, where the Court noted that the marked change in the direction of the Tunisian coastline to the west of the terminus of the land frontier modified the situation of lateral adjacency of the parties.[19] A second relevant circumstance is the presence of islands. Small islands are usually given less than full effect: where a court is minded to utilise an equidistance line as the boundary it will be modified so that the boundary is not equidistant between the island and the opposite coast. An example is the *Anglo-French Continental Shelf* case, where the tribunal gave the Scilly Isles 'half effect', i.e., the boundary line was the line which bisected (i.e. was halfway between) an equidistance line between the mainland coasts of the United Kingdom and France (i.e., ignoring the Scilly Isles completely) and an equidistance line between the Scilly Isles and France. (In drawing both these lines the French island of Ushant was given full effect because of its size and proximity to the French mainland.[20]) Other examples are the *Tunisia/Libya* case, where the Tunisian Kerkennah islands were given half effect,[21] and the *Dubai/Sharjah* case, where the island of Abu Musa (belonging to Sharjah) was given no continental shelf beyond its twelve-mile territorial sea in order to achieve an equitable solution.[22] On the other hand, where even relatively small islands lie a long way

---

[16] *Op. cit.* in footnote 6, p. 50.
[17] *Op. cit.* in footnote 8, p. 62.
[18] *Op. cit.* in footnote 10, p. 39 and footnote 8, pp. 63–4.
[19] *Op. cit.* in footnote 13, p. 62–3.
[20] *Op. cit.* in footnote 7, pp. 454–6.
[21] *Op. cit.* in footnote 13, pp. 63–4 and 89–90.
[22] *Op. cit.* in footnote 2, p. 677.

from their metropolitan territory or constitute a single State, they will in principle be given full effect. This is illustrated by the *Greenland/Jan Mayen* case (in respect of Jan Mayen) and the *Libya/Malta* case (in respect of Malta). Where islands lie on the 'wrong' side of a line which a court is minded to choose as a boundary, they may be given their own small enclaves of continental shelf without the provisional boundary line being modified. This was done with the Channel Islands in the *Anglo-French Continental Shelf* case,[23] where the islands were each given a twelve-mile wide enclave of continental shelf, with the boundary in this area otherwise being a line down the middle of the English Channel equidistant from the coasts of England and France.

Thirdly, differences in the lengths of the relevant coastlines are a relevant circumstance, especially (perhaps only) in the case of opposite coasts. Where an equidistance line is drawn as the provisional boundary between two coastlines of markedly different lengths, there will be a considerable degree of disparity between the ratio of the coastlines to each other and the ratio of the areas of continental shelf attaching provisionally to each party. This is thought to be inequitable. In such cases, therefore, a court will adjust the provisional boundary line so that there is a reasonable degree of proportionality, or at least not excessive disproportionality, between the length of each party's coastline and the area of continental shelf attaching to it. Thus, for example, in the *Libya/Malta* case the fact that the ratio of the length of the Libyan coastline to the Maltese coastline was eight to one was a reason for adjusting a median line as the provisional boundary closer to Malta.[24] A similar exercise was carried out in the *Greenland/ Jan Mayen* case.[25] In the *Tunisia/Libya*[26] case the principle of proportionality was used in a somewhat different way, in order to confirm the equitableness of the court's proposed solution, rather than to modify an equidistance line.

Fourthly, the prior conduct of the parties, such as having agreed a provisional boundary line, may be a relevant circumstance. Thus, in the *Tunisia/ Libya* case the Court regarded a line extending seawards from the terminus of the land boundary which neither party had crossed when granting offshore oil and gas concessions as a highly relevant circumstance, and used it as the first segment of the boundary line.[27] The relevance of prior conduct was also recognised in the *Libya/Malta*[28] and *Greenland/Jan Mayen*[29] cases, although in neither case did the Court find that there was sufficient concordance of conduct for it to be relevant. Fifthly, security considerations may be a relevant circumstance. They were recognised in principle as relevant in the *Libya/Malta* and

---

[23] *Op. cit.* in footnote 7, pp. 444–5.
[24] *Op. cit.* in footnote 10, pp. 43–6, 49–50, but note the limitation of using proportionality expressed at pp. 45–6.
[25] *Op. cit.* in footnote 8, pp. 65–70.
[26] *Op. cit.* in footnote 13, p. 75.
[27] *Ibid.*, pp. 71 and 80–6.
[28] *Op. cit.* in footnote 10, pp. 28–9.
[29] *Op. cit.* in footnote 8, pp. 75–7.

Greenland/Jan Mayen cases;[30] but in practice they did not affect the course of the boundary line.

In the *North Sea Continental Shelf* cases the International Court placed great emphasis on the concept of the natural prolongation of land territory as a factor in continental shelf boundary delimitation.[31] Thus, geological and geomorphological features, such as a deep trench amounting to a discontinuity in the sea bed, would constitute relevant circumstances. However, in later cases courts and tribunals have severely downgraded such circumstances. In the *Libya/Malta* case the International Court, after noting that the EEZ gave the same rights over the sea bed and its subsoil as the continental shelf and that the EEZ was now incontestably part of customary law, concluded that under customary law the minimum breadth of the continental shelf must be 200 miles. In other words title to the continental shelf is now based on a distance criterion.[32] The consequence of this must be that geological and geomorphological factors are all but irrelevant, at least in the case of States opposite each other and less than 400 miles apart. They could be relevant where opposite States are more than 400 miles apart.[33] They could possibly also be relevant in the case of adjacent States, although in the *Tunisia/Libya* case[34] arguments based on geomorphology were effectively ignored by the International Court. Courts and tribunals have also been consistent in holding a variety of other factors to be irrelevant. These include socio-economic factors, such as disparities in the wealth and size of population of each party; differences in the area of land territory belonging to each party; and normally the natural resources and ecology of the delimitation area.[35]

Although the principles and circumstances relevant to continental shelf delimitation can now be identified with some confidence from the case law, the fact that courts and tribunals have a wide discretion as to which of these criteria are selected and how they are weighted means that in any particular case it is very difficult to predict what line will be chosen as the boundary by the court or tribunal concerned. It is largely this that has led a number of writers, and perhaps also even one or two judges of the International Court, to deny that courts and tribunals are applying rules of law when they engage in boundary delimitation: instead, it is suggested, they are in effect making a judgment *ex aequo et bono*. There is certainly some force in such arguments. The more cynical might observe

---

[30] *Op. cit.* in footnote 10, p. 42 and footnote 8, pp. 74–5, respectively.

[31] *Op. cit.* in footnote 6, pp. 51 and 53.

[32] *Op. cit.* in footnote 10, pp. 33–5.

[33] However, it should be noted that in the *Canada/France* case the tribunal held that it had no competence to delimit the continental shelf beyond 200 miles because of the interests of the international community, in particular the International Sea Bed Authority and the Commission on the Limits of the Continental Shelf, in the question of the seaward limit of the shelf beyond 200 miles: 31 *ILM* 1145 (1992), at 1172.

[34] *Op. cit.* in footnote 13, pp. 41–58.

[35] See, for example, the *Tunisia/Libya* case, *op. cit.* in footnote 13, pp. 77–8; the *Libya/Malta* case, *op. cit.* in footnote 10, pp. 40–1; and the *Greenland/Jan Mayen* case, *op. cit.* in footnote 8, pp. 73–4.

that in most cases the boundary line chosen by the court or tribunal more or less represents a splitting of the difference between what each party has claimed should be the boundary.

The Law of the Sea Convention

UNCLOS III had great difficulty in finding acceptable provisions concerning the delimitation of the continental shelf and EEZ. Participants at the Conference divided into two broad camps, those who favoured equidistance (with an exception for special circumstances) as the primary principle of delimitation and those who wanted the emphasis placed on equitable principles, with no mention being made of equidistance. Negotiations on the matter were very protracted, and the resulting compromise is not very meaningful, article 83(1) of the Convention providing simply:

> The delimitation of the continental shelf between States with opposite or adjacent coasts shall be effected by agreement on the basis of international law, as referred to in Article 38 of the Statute of the International Court of Justice, in order to achieve an equitable solution.

As can be seen, the article contains no specific reference to either equidistance or equitable principles. Strictly speaking, it deals only with delimitation by agreement. The phrase 'effected by agreement' is the same as that used in the *North Sea Continental Shelf* cases, in the passage quoted on p. 186. Of this phrase the International Court said in that case that it implied an obligation to enter into meaningful negotiations in good faith.[36] In seeking to negotiate an agreement the parties to a continental shelf delimitation are enjoined by article 83(1) to apply any rule of international law that may be binding upon them (which in practice is likely to be limited to customary rules[37]), although they probably remain free to agree to disregard any such rule, in order to reach an 'equitable solution'. It would, of course, be very odd if they succeeded in agreeing on a solution which they did not consider to be equitable. Taken literally, article 83(1) does not itself contain any provisions on delimitation where the parties are unable to reach agreement, let alone indicate to any competent tribunal any principles or methods to be used to settle the dispute. Article 83 does go on, however, in paragraph 2 to say something about procedures if the parties are unable to agree. It provides that if agreement on the boundary is not possible 'within a reasonable period of time', the matter is to be referred to the dispute settlement procedure set out in Part XV of the Convention, unless there is a special treaty in force between the States concerned which covers the matter, in which case the dispute is to

---

[36] *Op. cit.* in footnote 6, p. 47.
[37] Even if both States were parties to the Continental Shelf Convention, article 6 of the Convention would not be applicable. This is because article 311(1) of the Law of the Sea Convention provides that that Convention prevails over the 1958 Conventions. See further chapter one, p. 24.

be resolved according to the provisions of such treaty (art. 83(4)). It should be noted that States may choose to except boundary delimitation from the Convention's provisions on compulsory dispute settlement, apart from compulsory conciliation.

Pending settlement of delimitation disputes, the States concerned are to make every effort to enter into provisional arrangements of a practical nature (art. 83(3)). An example of such an arrangement might be the 1985 France–Tuvalu agreement, under which the equidistance line is used as a temporary boundary pending agreement upon a permanent boundary. Article 83(3) goes on to provide that pending the reaching of a definitive agreement on a boundary, the parties are to make every effort not to 'jeopardise or hamper the reaching of the final agreement'. This suggests that neither party should take any action in the area subject to delimitation, such as engaging in exploratory drilling for oil or gas, which might be regarded as prejudicial by the other party. Arguably such a rule exists also in customary international law.[38]

EEZ and fishing zone

Custom

Customary international law relating to the delimitation of the EEZ and/or fishing zone between neighbouring States has been developed by the International Court and arbitral tribunals in much the same way as they have done for continental shelf delimitation. So far only one case, the *Greenland/Jan Mayen* case (1993), has been concerned with an EEZ/fishing zone boundary as such. The other three cases so far decided, the *Gulf of Maine* (1984), *Guinea/Guinea Bissau* (1985) and *Canada/France* (1992) cases, were all concerned with delimitation of a single maritime boundary between both the continental shelves and the 200-mile EEZs/fishing zones of the States concerned.[39] Since the continental shelf and EEZ are coterminous within 200 miles of the coast and since there is a general trend in treaty practice to draw a single continental shelf/EEZ boundary within this area (as explained below), it seems legitimate to regard the single maritime boundary cases as relevant to EEZ delimitation. In practice, as will be seen,

[38] For discussion of this point, see R. R. Churchill and G. Ulfstein, *Marine Management in Disputed Areas: the Case of the Barents Sea* (London, Routledge), 1992, pp. 85–9.

[39] Two further cases concerning a single maritime boundary are currently pending before the International Court – *Case concerning Maritime Delimitation and Territorial Questions between Qatar and Bahrain*, which was referred to the Court in 1991 and for which the Court found that it had jurisdiction in 1994 and 1995, and *Case concerning the Land and Maritime Boundary between Cameroon and Nigeria*, referred to the Court in 1994 and for which the Court found that it had jurisdiction in 1998. One arbitration is also pending, between Eritrea and Yemen: see their Arbitration Agreement, 1996. Proceedings before the International Court in the *Case concerning the Maritime Delimitation between Guinea Bissau and Senegal*, which had been referred to the Court in 1991, were discontinued in 1995 when the parties reached an agreement settling their dispute.

courts and tribunals have applied many of the principles which they have laid down for continental shelf delimitation to delimitation of single maritime boundaries. All four cases mentioned were decided after the Law of the Sea Convention was signed but before its entry into force.

In the *Gulf of Maine* case the International Court was asked to draw a single boundary between the continental shelves and the 200-mile fishing zones of Canada and the USA. Although both States were parties to the Continental Shelf Convention, the Court held that this was not relevant to the drawing of a single boundary since the Convention related only to the sea bed and was not concerned with the superjacent waters. The Court then enunciated a two-stage fundamental norm of maritime delimitation:

(1) No maritime delimitation between States with opposite or adjacent coasts may be effected unilaterally by one of those States. Such delimitation must be sought and effected by means of an agreement, following negotiations conducted in good faith and with the genuine intention of achieving a positive result. Where, however, such agreement cannot be achieved, delimitation should be effected by recourse to a third party possessing the necessary competence.

(2) In either case, delimitation is to be effected by the application of equitable criteria and by the use of practical methods capable of ensuring, with regard to the geographic configuration of the area and other relevant circumstances, an equitable result.[40]

The Court then went on to decide that the criteria and methods of delimitation it should use were those that were appropriate for both the sea bed and water column, and that criteria which related to only one of these zones (such as geological criteria) should be ignored. The criteria that were most likely to be suitable for a multi-purpose delimitation were those of geography. The Court's emphasis on geographical criteria as the most appropriate for delimitation means that most, if not all, of those factors identified earlier as relevant to continental shelf delimitation, such as the principle of non-encroachment, coastal configuration, islands and proportionality, will be equally relevant to a single maritime boundary.

In the *Gulf of Maine* case the Court constructed a boundary in three segments. In the inner part of the Gulf of Maine, where the parties are adjacent, the boundary was a line which effected an equal division of the area where the parties' maritime zones overlapped. In the outer part of the Gulf, where Canada and the USA are opposite each other, the boundary was a median line in principle, adjusted and moved closer to Canada to take account of the greater length of the US coastline in the Gulf and to give only half effect to Canada's Seal Island. From the mouth of the Gulf the boundary was a line perpendicular to the closing line of the Gulf. The Court then checked to see whether this overall result was equitable. At this stage economic and other factors (*in casu* the long history of fishing on the resource-rich Georges Bank) could be relevant

---

[40] *Op. cit.* in footnote 5, pp. 229–300.

(even if irrelevant as delimitation criteria), but they would only disturb the boundary line which the Court had provisionally arrived at if they showed that result to be 'radically inequitable, that is to say, as likely to entail catastrophic repercussions for the livelihood and economic well-being of the countries concerned'.[41] This was not, however, the case here.

The International Court's approach in the *Gulf of Maine* case was broadly followed in the *Guinea/Guinea Bissau* and *Canada/France* cases. In the former case, in which the arbitral tribunal was asked to draw a single boundary between the territorial seas, continental shelves and EEZs of Guinea and Guinea Bissau, the main factors which the tribunal found to be relevant were the configuration and respective lengths of the parties' coasts, the principle of non-encroachment, security interests and the prior conduct of the two colonial powers before the parties' independence. In the *Canada/France* case, in which the tribunal was asked to draw a single boundary between the continental shelf and the 200-mile fishing zone of Canada and the continental shelf and the EEZ of the French islands of St Pierre and Miquelon which lie close to the coast of Newfoundland, the principal relevant factor was the principle of non-encroachment, with St Pierre and Miquelon being awarded a zone only twelve miles in breadth beyond its twelve-mile territorial sea in areas close to the Canadian coast, but a small corridor of maritime zone out to a full 200 miles to the south where this did not cut off seaward projections of the Canadian zone. Interestingly, part of this area had not been included by France in its proposed solution as part of the maritime zone of St Pierre and Miquelon. Proportionality was then used to check that the tribunal's solution was equitable (which it was).

In the *Greenland/Jan Mayen* case, unlike in the three cases just discussed, the International Court had not been asked by both parties to draw a single maritime boundary. The case had been referred to it unilaterally by Denmark, invoking its own and Norway's declarations under article 36(2) of the Court's Statute. Although Denmark had asked the Court to draw a single boundary, the Court decided, although without really explaining why, that it could not do so without the consent of Norway. It therefore engaged in two separate delimitation exercises, one for the continental shelf and the other in respect of the 200-mile fishing zones of Greenland and Jan Mayen, although ultimately the two boundaries drawn by the Court coincided. As regards the fishing zone boundary, the Court decided as a first step to determine such a boundary by applying the customary law governing EEZ delimitation. The Court asserted that this customary law was the same as the provisions of the Law of the Sea Convention governing EEZ delimitation (art. 74(1)), which are the same, *mutatis mutandis*, as those governing continental shelf delimitation (art. 83(1)) and which are discussed below. The Court then decided that it would follow the *Libya/Malta* and *Gulf of Maine* cases (neither of which, of course, was concerned with an EEZ boundary *simpliciter*) and draw a median line as the provisional boundary and then adjust it in the light of any

[41] *Ibid.*, p. 342.

relevant circumstances in order to achieve an equitable result. The circumstances which were found to be relevant were the great difference in the lengths of the relevant coasts of Greenland and Jan Mayen (the former was about nine times longer than the latter) and the fishery resources of the area. The provisional boundary was therefore moved eastwards towards Jan Mayen to take account of these circumstances and so as to give fishing vessels from Greenland 'equitable access to the capelin stock', the main fishery resource of the area.[42] It will be noted that the question of fishery resources played a greater role in the delimitation process here than in the *Gulf of Maine* and *Canada/France* cases, where they were held to be relevant only if the Court's provisional boundary was radically inequitable. The difference may be explained by the fact that in the *Greenland/Jan Mayen* case the Court was concerned with a separate fishing zone boundary whereas the other two cases were concerned with a multipurpose boundary. In the case of the continental shelf boundary the Court also drew a median line as the provisional boundary which it then adjusted (for reasons which are not entirely clear) so as to coincide with the fishing zone boundary.

Thus, it would seem that under customary law States are free to agree on any boundary for their overlapping EEZs that they like. Where they are unable to agree, and the matter is referred for third party settlement, the boundary should be drawn applying equitable criteria and taking account of all the relevant circumstances in order to produce an equitable result. Where the EEZ boundary is part of a multi-purpose boundary, the relevant circumstances will primarily be geographical features. Where, on the other hand, an EEZ boundary only is to be drawn, the circumstances that will be considered relevant are likely to be wider and would seem potentially to include any factors connected to the rights which coastal States enjoy in their EEZs. Given, however, the clear trend towards single maritime boundaries, the principles enunciated by the International Court and arbitral tribunals peculiar to delimitations concerned with the boundary for only one maritime zone, be it the continental shelf or the EEZ, are likely to be of decreasing significance.

The Law of the Sea Convention

At UNCLOS III there was a feeling that in general it is desirable for continental shelf and EEZ boundaries to coincide, and during the later sessions of the Conference negotiations on delimitation of continental shelf and EEZ boundaries were conducted together. Not surprisingly, therefore, the wording of the provisions of the Convention on the delimitation of EEZ boundaries, in article 74, is the same, *mutatis mutandis*, as that of article 83 on continental shelf delimitation. Thus, delimitation of EEZ boundaries is to be effected by agreement on the basis of international law in order to achieve an equitable solution (art. 74(1)), about which the same comments can be made as were made above in relation to the

---

[42] *Op. cit.* in footnote 8, p. 72 and see also pp. 79–81.

equivalent provision concerning the continental shelf. Procedures are set out where the parties cannot agree (art. 74(3)); and provisional arrangements called for in the interim (art. 74(3)). An example of such a provisional arrangement might be the 1977 Denmark–Sweden agreement, which provided that until a permanent boundary was agreed (as it was in 1984) the exclusive fishing zones in the area of the Kattegat lying beyond twelve miles from the coasts should be placed under joint Danish-Swedish fisheries jurisdiction.

Although the provisions of the Convention governing continental shelf and EEZ delimitation are the same, their wording is sufficiently imprecise for the provisions to be capable of application in more than one way, and thus for the continental shelf and EEZ boundaries to differ – a situation fraught with the potential for conflict (for example, if one State wanted to exploit its continental shelf underlying an area of another State's EEZ rich in fish stocks). In practice, of the EEZ boundaries that have so far been agreed, the EEZ boundary is the same as the continental shelf boundary in all but two cases. The first is the Australia–Papua New Guinea Maritime Boundaries Treaty of 1978, which provides for a divergence between the fisheries jurisdiction and the sea-bed jurisdiction boundaries in the Torres Strait, partly in order to recognise the importance of fishing to the inhabitants of certain Australian islands close to Papua New Guinea, and partly to avoid establishing Australian-inhabited enclaves north of a general maritime boundary between the two States.[43] The second instance is the Australia–Indonesia Maritime Boundaries Treaty of 1997, which provides for part of the EEZ boundary between the two States to diverge from the continental shelf boundary and regulates possible conflicts of use and jurisdiction in areas where the boundaries diverge. Although State practice exhibits an overwhelming trend towards EEZ and continental shelf boundaries coinciding, the practice is not such as to require a single boundary. Nevertheless, it is generally desirable that EEZ and continental shelf boundaries should coincide. However, the fact that articles 74 and 83 of the Law of the Sea Convention stipulate that such boundaries should represent an 'equitable solution' will in many cases make it more difficult to agree on a common boundary. A boundary that might be equitable for EEZ purposes might not be equitable for continental shelf purposes because of the different considerations that are relevant to achieving an equitable solution in each case – for example, the location of fish stocks in the case of the EEZ, the geological characteristics of the sea bed and the location of sea-bed mineral deposits in the case of continental shelf. The approach of the International Court in the *Gulf of Maine* case was, as we have seen, to sidestep this problem by concentrating upon the equity of the delimitation from the geographical point of view, paying scant attention to the equity of the resulting division of the economic resources of the area. That is not, however, to say that

---

[43] See Burmester, *op. cit.* in 'Further reading' at pp. 333–4. In relation to matters other than the sea bed and fisheries in the area of divergence, the treaty provides that no party may exercise jurisdiction without the concurrence of the other (art. 4(3)).

such economic factors will not figure more prominently in negotiated settlements of boundary lines.

State practice on delimitation

The principles described above will be applied, unless excluded or modified by the agreement of the parties, in judicial and arbitral determinations of maritime boundaries, and will also have a considerable influence on negotiated settlements as those principles considered particularly apposite will be invoked by a State to support its negotiating position. Most maritime boundaries so far have been settled by agreement rather than by a judicial or arbitral body. Currently about 140 such boundaries have been agreed, out of an estimated 400 or so potential boundaries.[44] In the case of territorial sea and continental shelf boundary agreements, the equidistance principle, modified to take account of special circumstances, has tended to predominate as the basis of the delimitation, although some recent agreements, such as the Belgium–France territorial sea and continental shelf boundary agreements of 1990, refer to the desire of the parties to arrive at an equitable solution. Few EEZ/fishing zone-only boundaries have been agreed. Since the late 1970s the trend, particularly outside Europe, has been to conclude agreements establishing a single maritime boundary for all zones. Within Europe there have been a few EEZ and fishing zone boundary agreements, but in many cases existing continental shelf boundaries agreed in the 1960s and early 1970s have been treated as *de facto* boundaries for the EEZ/fishing zone. Of the single maritime boundaries that have so far been agreed, many, particularly in the case of opposite coasts, are based on the equidistance principle, sometimes with modifications to simplify what would otherwise be an unduly complicated line or to take account of special circumstances (e.g., the India–Sri Lanka Maritime Boundary Agreement of 1976, the Colombia–Haiti Maritime Limits Agreement of 1978 and the France–Tonga Convention of 1980). A few agreements (e.g., the Colombia–Costa Rica Maritime Delimitation Treaty of 1977 and the Trinidad and Tobago–Venezuela Maritime Delimitation Treaty of 1990) appear to be based on equitable principles, while in two cases (the Colombia–Ecuador Marine Delimitation Agreement of 1975 and the Gambia–Senegal Maritime Boundaries Agreement of 1975) the boundary has been chosen, presumably for reasons of simplicity, as the line of latitude extending seawards from the terminus

---

[44] Such computations have been done, *inter alia*, by Blake, *op. cit.* in 'Further reading', chapter 1 and Charney, *op. cit.*, footnote 45 (see below). The statistics appear to treat territorial sea, continental shelf and EEZ boundaries between two States in the same sea as one boundary, but where two States have boundaries in more than one sea, this counts as more than one boundary: e.g., Canada and the USA have four potential boundaries – in the Atlantic, Pacific, Bering and Beaufort seas. For a list of boundary agreements concluded up to 1990, see Brown, *op. cit.* in 'Further reading', Vol. I, pp. 439–75. See also the UN volumes referred to in 'Further reading'.

of the land boundary. The American Society of International Law Maritime Boundary Project, which analysed all existing maritime boundary agreements, found such a diversity of practice, both as to the method of delimitation and the factors taken into account in the delimitation and the weight attached to them, that it concluded that 'no normative principle of international law has developed that would mandate the specific location of any maritime boundary line'.[45]

As regards State practice in the form of national legislation, of the many States which have legislated on the continental shelf and the EEZ, well over one-third include in their legislation reference to the equidistance principle, commonly as an interim solution pending the settlement of boundaries by agreement.[46] While this practice is, in view of the divergent practice of other States, probably insufficient to establish a rule of law of general application, the principle of opposability (see chapter one) is likely to secure the utilisation of the equidistance principle as a starting point for delimitations in several areas.

Co-operative arrangements

Attempts to delimit overlapping EEZs and continental shelves need not necessarily involve, or only involve, the drawing of a boundary line. The States concerned may decide to establish co-operative arrangements for the exploitation and management of the resources of the delimitation area either in place of a boundary line or to facilitate the drawing or continuing operation of a boundary. Four types of arrangement may be distinguished: (1) co-operative arrangements for the exploitation of sea-bed and/or fishing resources in place of a boundary line; (2) the establishment of a joint exploitation zone for sea-bed and/or fishing resources which straddles the boundary and is part of the boundary settlement; (3) arrangements for the exploitation of oil and gas fields found to be lying across the boundary line; and (4) co-operative arrangements to facilitate the management of transboundary fish stocks.

Turning to the first of these, States unable to agree, or reach agreement easily, on a maritime boundary (and the generality and vagueness of the rules surveyed above do not exactly help States to reach agreement) may decide instead to establish, either provisionally or on a longer-term basis, a zone in all or part of the area where their zones overlap, in which the sea-bed and/or fishery resources are to be jointly exploited and managed. The advantage of doing this is that in

[45] J. I. Charney, 'The American Society of International Law Maritime Boundary Project' in G. H. Blake (ed.), *Maritime Boundaries* (London, Routledge), 1994, 1 at 9. The results of the Project are published as Charney and Alexander (eds), *op. cit.* in 'Further reading', *passim*.

[46] See *Smith, op. cit.* in 'Further reading', *passim*. Barbados, Fiji, Iceland, India, Indonesia, Morocco, Mozambique, New Zealand, Nigeria, Oman, Qatar, Spain, Tonga and Western Samoa are among the States concerned. See also Brown, *op. cit.* in footnote 44, pp. 167–200, 305–19.

the absence of a boundary and without such a zone the exploitation of sea-bed resources is unlikely to take place because oil companies are usually unwilling to invest in disputed areas and in any case there is (as we have seen) probably a rule of international law that prohibits unilateral exploitation in such areas. As far as fishery resources are concerned, there is likely to be exploitation in such areas (there being no equivalent rule against unilateral exploitation, unless article 74(3) of the Law of the Sea Convention can be read as restraining such action), but such exploitation cannot be properly regulated and thus the resources are likely to become over-exploited.

In the case of sea-bed resources there are about half-a-dozen agreements establishing joint development zones. A good example is the agreement between Japan and South Korea. In 1974 the two States succeeded in reaching agreement on a continental shelf boundary in the northern part of the area where their continental shelves overlap, but were unable to agree on a boundary in the southern part of this area. Instead, in the same year they signed an Agreement concerning Joint Development of the Southern Part of the Continental Shelf Adjacent to the Two Countries. The Agreement, which is to last for fifty years and applies to an area of some 24,000 square nautical miles, provides that concessionaires from each party are to enter into operating agreements to carry out jointly exploration and exploitation of the area and are to appoint an operator and share the resources equally. A joint commission is established to oversee activities in the area.[47] Turning to co-operative arrangements for fisheries resources, there are several such arrangements, of which the best example is probably the 1978 Agreement between Norway and the then USSR on an Interim Practical Arrangement for Fishing in an Adjoining Area in the Barents Sea. The Agreement applies to an area of 67,500 square kilometres in the southern part of the Barents Sea where the EEZs of Norway and Russia overlap. Within this area total allowable catches, quotas and other regulatory measures are adopted by a Norwegian/Russian Fishery Commission. Each party has jurisdiction in the area only in respect of its own fishing vessels and such third State vessels as it has licensed to fish against its quota. Although described as 'interim' and originally concluded for one year only, the Agreement has subsequently been renewed annually, and this is likely to continue until the parties agree on an EEZ and/or continental shelf boundary.[48] Finally, there are also one or two instances where States have established a zone

---

[47] For fuller details of this and most of the other examples of co-operative sea-bed arrangements, see Fox (ed.), *op. cit.* in 'Further reading', *passim*. One of these examples is the Treaty between Australia and Indonesia on the Zone of Cooperation in an Area between the Indonesian Province of East Timor and Northern Australia, 1989. This treaty was challenged by Portugal before the International Court of Justice on the ground that it was a denial of East Timor's right to self-determination. The Court held that it could not rule on this question because Indonesia was not a party to the case: see the *East Timor* case (1995).

[48] For fuller details of this and other examples, see R. R. Churchill, 'Fisheries issues in maritime boundary delimitation', 17 *Marine Policy* 44 (1993) at 45–51.

for the joint management of both living and non-living resources. An example is the zone created by the Colombia–Jamaica Maritime Delimitation Treaty of 1993.

The second category concerns co-operative arrangements as part of a boundary settlement. The inclusion of such arrangements may facilitate the drawing of a boundary line because it may enable a more equitable sharing of resources to take place than would happen with a boundary *tout court* and may increase the number of variables involved in a boundary negotiation, thus promoting possibilities for trade-offs and compromises. Again there are a number of examples of such co-operative arrangements, both for sea-bed resources and for fisheries resources. An example of a sea-bed arrangement is the 1974 Continental Shelf Boundary Convention between France and Spain which establishes a zone of some 814 square nautical miles straddling these countries' continental shelf boundary in the Bay of Biscay. The aim of this arrangement is an equal division of resources between the two States which is to be achieved by encouraging companies from each State to participate in partnership agreements on an equal basis.[49] Similar zones straddling the boundary have been established for co-operation over the exploitation and management of fisheries, such as that between Argentina and Uruguay. These are discussed in chapter fourteen, in the context of the management of shared fish stocks (see pp. 294–6).

The third type of arrangement concerns co-operation over the exploitation of oil and gas fields found to be straddling a previously agreed boundary line. In the North Sea there are a number of fields in this situation. Several bilateral treaties, principally between the United Kingdom and Norway, have been concluded under which production from the cross-boundary reservoir is apportioned between the two States and arrangements for co-ordinated administration of the field are established. An example is the agreement between Norway and the United Kingdom concerning the Frigg gas field (1976). Another example, from outside the North Sea, is the 1969 Maritime Boundary Agreement between Abu Dhabi and Qatar which provides for the Al Bunduq field, which straddles the continental shelf boundary, to be exploited by a concessionaire of Abu Dhabi and all revenues to be shared equally between the two parties. The system adopted in such cross-boundary agreements is entirely a matter for the agreement of the parties. Customary international law does not yet seem to yield any precise rules applicable in the absence of such agreement, although some writers have advanced general solutions based on a mixture of basic principles of law, previous treaty practice and robust expediency.

Finally, in the fourth category mentioned above, there are various arrangements that have been agreed for fisheries in the context of boundary negotiations. They include such matters as access by fishermen from one State to the zones of the other State and the management of transboundary fish stocks. These are discussed in chapter fourteen.[50]

---

[49] For fuller details of this and other examples, see Fox, *op. cit.* in footnote 47.
[50] See also Churchill, *op. cit.* in footnote 48, pp. 55–7.

Further reading

G. Blake (ed.), *Maritime Boundaries and Ocean Resources* (London, Croom Helm), 1987.

E. D. Brown, *Sea-Bed Energy and Mineral Resources and the Law of the Sea* (Dordrecht, Nijhoff), 2nd edn, Vol. I (1992).

H. Burmester, 'The Torres Strait Treaty', 76 *AJIL* 321–49 (1982).

L. Caflisch, 'Les zones maritimes sous juridiction nationale, leurs limites et leur délimitation', 84 *RGDIP* 68–119 (1980) (and see D. Bardonnet and M. Virally (eds), *Le Nouveau Droit International de la Mer* (Paris, Pedone), 1983, for a later version).

J. I. Charney, 'Progress on international maritime boundary delimitation law', 88 *AJIL* 227–56 (1994).

——, 'The delimitation of ocean boundaries', 18 *ODIL* 497–531 (1987).

—— and L. M. Alexander (eds), *International Maritime Boundaries* (Dordrecht, Nijhoff), Vols I and II, 1991; Vol. III, 1997.

R. R. Churchill, 'The Greenland/Jan Mayen case and its significance for the international law of maritime boundary delimitation', 9 *IJMCL* 1–29 (1994).

D. A. Colson, 'The United Kingdom–France continental shelf arbitration', 72 *AJIL* 95–112 (1978), and 73 *AJIL* 112–20 (1979).

B. Conforti and G. Francalanci (eds), *Atlas of the Seabed Boundaries* (Milan, Giuffre), Part I, 1979; Part II, 1987.

M. D. Evans, *Relevant Circumstances and Maritime Delimitation* (Oxford, Clarendon), 1989.

——, 'Delimitation and the common maritime boundary', 64 *BYIL* 283–332 (1993).

M. B. Feldman, 'The Tunisia–Libya continental shelf case: geographic justice or judicial compromise?', 77 *AJIL* 219–38 (1983).

H. Fox (ed.), *Joint Development of Offshore Oil and Gas* (London, British Institute of International and Comparative Law), Vol. I, 1989; Vol. II, 1990.

W. Friedmann, 'The North Sea continental shelf cases – a critique', 64 *AJIL* 229–40 (1970).

L. Gross, 'The dispute between Greece and Turkey concerning the continental shelf in the Aegean', 71 *AJIL* 31–59 (1977).

L. L. Herman, 'The court giveth and the court taketh away: an analysis of the *Tunisia–Libya Continental Shelf* case', 33 *ICLQ* 825–58 (1984).

S. P. Jagota, *Maritime Boundary* (Dordrecht, Nijhoff), 1985.

D. M. Johnston, *The Theory and History of Ocean Boundary Making* (Kingston and Montreal, McGill-Queen's University Press), 1988.

—— and P. M. Saunders, *Ocean Boundary Making: Regional Issues and Development* (London, Croom Helm), 1988.

—— and M. J. Valencia, *Pacific Ocean Boundary Problems: Status and Solutions* (Dordrecht, Nijhoff), 1990.

L. de La Fayette, 'The award in the Canada–France maritime boundary arbitration', 8 *IJMCL* 77–103 (1993).

R. Lagoni, 'Interim measures pending maritime delimitation agreements', 78 *AJIL* 345–68 (1984).

L. H. Legault and B. Hankey, 'From sea to seabed: the single maritime boundary in the Gulf of Maine', 79 *AJIL* 961–91 (1985).

W. T. Onorato, 'Apportionment of an international common petroleum deposit', 17 *ICLQ* 85–102 (1968), and 26 *ICLQ* 324–37 (1977).

C. H. Park,. 'Oil under troubled waters: the Northeast Asia seabed controversy', 14 *Harvard International Law Journal* 212–60 (1973).

J. R. V. Prescott, *The Maritime Political Boundaries of the World* (London, Methuen), 1985.

S.-M. Rhee, 'Seabed boundary delimitation between States before World War II', 76 *AJIL* 555–88 (1982).

F. Rigaldies. 'L'affaire de la délimitation du plateau continental entre la République Française et le Royaume-Uni de Grande Bretagne et d'Irlande du Nord', 106 *JDI* 506–31 (1979).

D. R. Robinson, D. A. Colson and B. C. Rashkow, 'Some perspectives on adjudicating before the world court: the Gulf of Maine case', 79 *AJIL* 578–97 (1985).

J. Schneider. 'The Gulf of Maine Case: the nature of an equitable result', 79 *AJIL* 539–77 (1985).

R. W. Smith, *Exclusive Economic Zone Claims: An Analysis and Primary Documents* (Dordecht, Nijhoff), 1986 [*Smith*].

United Nations, *The Law of the Sea: Maritime Boundary Agreements (1970–84)* (New York, United Nations), 1987.

——, *The Law of the Sea: Maritime Boundary Agreements (1942–69)* (New York, United Nations), 1991.

——, *The Law of the Sea: Maritime Boundary Agreements (1985–91)* (New York, United Nations), 1992.

P. Weil, *Perspectives du Droit de la Délimitation Maritime* (Paris, Pedone), 1988. Published in English as *The Law of Maritime Delimitation – Reflections* (Cambridge, Grotius), 1989.

L. A. Willis, 'From precedent to precedent: the triumph of pragmatism in the law of maritime boundaries', 24 *Canadian Yearbook of International Law* 3–60 (1986).

J. C. Woodliffe, 'International unitisation of an offshore gas field', 26 *ICLQ* 338–53 (1977).

11

High seas

Introduction

The legal regime of the high seas has traditionally been characterised by the dominance of the principles of free use and the exclusivity of flag State jurisdiction, in sharp contrast to the powers of States over their coastal waters. The High Seas Convention which, alone among the 1958 Conventions, purported to codify customary international law, gave four examples of the freedom of the high seas: the freedoms of navigation, fishing, laying of submarine cables and pipelines, and overflight. The list of examples set out in the 1958 Convention has been extended in article 87 of the Law of the Sea Convention so as to include the freedom to construct artificial islands and other installations, and the freedom of scientific research. Some aspects of the high-seas freedoms have received close attention and have generated a considerable body of legal material of their own. Accordingly, we have reserved for treatment in later chapters some specific topics, such as high-seas fisheries (see chapter fourteen) and marine pollution (see chapter fifteen). Here we discuss only the general regime of the high seas.

Definition

The high seas were defined in the 1958 High Seas Convention as 'all parts of the sea not included in the territorial sea or in the internal waters of a state' (HSC, art. 1). With the advent of the EEZ and of the concept of archipelagic waters (see above, chapters nine and six respectively), this definition had to be modified. Article 86 of the Law of the Sea Convention, while strictly speaking not offering a *definition* of the high seas, states that the high-seas rules in the Convention apply to:

> all parts of the sea that are not included in the exclusive economic zone, in the territorial sea or in the internal waters of a State, or in the archipelagic waters of an archipelagic State.

In the case of exclusive fishery zones therefore, which a few States still claim, the zone remains a part of the high seas (because such zones are not mentioned in article 86 and are not equivalent to an EEZ), although of course the high-seas freedom of fishing will not apply there. The legal concept of the high seas includes not only the water column but also the superjacent air space. It also extends to the sea bed and subsoil subject, in the case of the 'outer' continental shelf beyond the EEZ, to the coastal State's sovereign rights to explore and exploit its resources (see chapter eight), and, in the case of activities to explore and exploit the resources of the International Sea Bed Area, to the provisions of Part XI of the 1982 Convention (art. 134(2); and see chapter twelve).

The legal status of the high seas

The high seas are open to all States, and no State may validly purport to subject any part of them to its sovereignty (HSC, art. 2; LOSC, arts 87, 89). This rule of customary law, codified in the conventions prepared by UNCLOS I and UNCLOS III, is a cornerstone of modern international law. But it has not always been so. In the fifteenth century there were many claims to sovereignty over extensive areas of the oceans: for example, by Sweden and Denmark in the Baltic and Norwegian Seas; by Venice in the Adriatic and Genoa and Pisa in the Ligurian Sea; and by Britain in the ill-defined 'British seas' around its coasts. Though sometimes cited as extreme examples of such claims, the divisions of the Atlantic Ocean between Spain and Portugal by Pope Alexander VI in 1493, modified in the Treaty of Tordesillas in 1494, were really no more than delimitations of spheres of influence in the Americas, then being colonised. Nonetheless, some States did claim the right to levy tolls as a condition of passage through these extensive areas of waters off their coasts, to license fishermen and to demand salutes from foreign ships to the warships of the coastal State in those waters.[1]

It was inevitable that during the great period of maritime exploration that began in the sixteenth century opposition to the notion of closed seas would mount. The doctrinal battle was fought in the seventeenth century, in the first decade of which Grotius published his *Mare Liberum*.[2] He was opposed by jurists such as the Italian, Gentili, and (as we noted in chapter one) the Englishman, Selden, whose book *Mare clausum, seu de dominio maris*, written in 1618 to counter Grotius' arguments, was published in 1635. The battle was eventually won by the advocates of the open seas, as the importance of free navigation in the service of overseas and colonial trade came to overshadow national interests in coastal fisheries, and as the development of real naval power displaced notional

---

[1] See J. H. W. Verzijl, *op. cit.* in 'Further reading', pp. 5–39.

[2] The learned editors of *Oppenheim* trace the principle of *mare liberum* back to the response of the English Queen Elizabeth I in 1580 to Spanish ambassador Mendoza's complaint that Sir Francis Drake had sailed across the Pacific, in defiance of Spanish claims: *Oppenheim I*, *op. cit.* in 'Further reading', p. 720.

claims to sovereignty over the seas. Most of the extravagant claims to maritime sovereignty were abandoned during the eighteenth century. By the first half of the nineteenth the conception of the high seas as an area juridically distinct from national waters and not susceptible to appropriation by any State had become clearly established. Nevertheless a few exceptional cases of claims to historic bays, and later to archipelagic waters, were admitted in derogation of this principle (see chapters two and six). More recently, the *laissez-faire* principles upon which the regime of the high seas is built gave rise to increasing criticism that the regime was incapable of dealing with the problems of controlling pollution and over-fishing. This criticism led eventually to the modification of the legal regime of a large part of what had been high seas, in the form of the EEZ, as established in the Law of the Sea Convention.

From the rule that no State can subject areas of the high seas to its sovereignty, or indeed to its jurisdiction, it follows that no State has the right to prevent ships of other States from using the high seas for any 'lawful purpose'. We examine the scope of this permissible use under the heading of 'Freedom of the high seas' in the next section. A second corollary of the status of the high seas is that apart from a few special cases, mostly created by treaty, no State has jurisdiction over foreign ships on the high seas: this aspect we consider in the final section below.

Freedom of the high seas

Precisely because States cannot in principle control the activities of other States on the high seas, so that users of the seas remain at liberty to do as they please apart from a few restrictive rules, and also because new ocean technology is constantly developing, the freedoms of the high seas cannot be exhaustively listed. This was recognised in the 1958 High Seas Convention, which claimed to be 'generally declaratory of established principles of international law'. Article 2 of the 1958 Convention listed the freedoms of navigation, fishing, laying and maintenance of submarine cables and pipelines (the 'right of immersion', which, unlike the other listed freedoms, involves use of the bed of the high seas), and overflight as examples of high-seas freedoms. It went on to state that:

> These freedoms, and others which are recognised by the general principles of international law, shall be exercised by all States with reasonable regard to the interests of other States in their exercise of the freedom of the high seas. (HSC, art. 2)

As we noted above, article 87 of the Law of the Sea Convention added to the (still non-exhaustive) list of high-seas freedoms the freedom to construct artificial islands and other installations permitted under international law and freedom of scientific research.

The fact that the 1958 High Seas Convention and the 1982 Law of the Sea Convention purport to give only non-exhaustive lists of examples of high-seas freedoms leaves room for controversies. There are high-seas activities alleged by some States to constitute freedoms, but denied this status by other States. The principle on which such disputes should be resolved is that any use compatible with the status of the high seas – that is, a use which involves no claim to appropriation of parts of the high seas – should be admitted as a freedom unless it is excluded by some specific rule of law.

All States, whether coastal or not, have the right to exercise high-seas freedoms. All exercises of the freedom of the high seas remain subject to the 'due regard' obligation, as the 'reasonable regard' obligation is now termed. The 'due regard' obligation is itself amended so as to protect the interests of others exercising not only the freedom of the high seas but also 'the rights under this Convention with respect to activities in the Area' – that is, activities covered by the international sea-bed regime (LOSC, art. 87(2); see chapter twelve).[3]

The requirement of 'due regard' seems to require that where there is a potential conflict between two uses of the high seas, there should be a case-by-case weighing of the actual interests involved in the circumstances in question, in order to determine which use is the more reasonable in that particular case. For example, the stringing out of long lines of fishing nets across a busy shipping lane would not be permissible, although the use of such nets elsewhere might be reasonable and permissible. Arguably, there is a presumption in favour of an established use as against a new use. Such a weighing of interests will normally occur through negotiations between the States concerned, although exceptionally third-party dispute settlement might be involved (on which, see chapter nineteen). What has been said so far is perhaps more a description of the ideal than of what actually happens. In practice stronger States have often been able to insist upon their own uses of the high seas even if such uses may appear unreasonable to other States.

This point may be illustrated by the example of weapons testing. It is generally accepted that some naval manoeuvres and conventional weapons testing may be conducted on the high seas.[4] Mariners are notified of the areas and times at which these take place, and although usually they are not actually forbidden to enter those areas and care is taken to avoid busy regions of the sea, there is a clear expectation that foreign vessels should keep out of these areas. While this practice is often acquiesced in, when France (which is not a party to the 1963 Treaty banning Nuclear Weapon Tests in the Atmosphere, in Outer Space and under Water, a treaty which prohibits such testing anywhere in the atmosphere or in territorial waters or high seas) declared a vast area of the Pacific closed to foreign shipping in 1974, and used force to prevent the entry into the zone of a vessel protesting against the French atmospheric nuclear tests therein, strong protests were made. Australia and New Zealand took the matter to the International

---

[3] Though not expressly stated, 'due regard' must clearly be paid also to those exercising rights over the continental shelf, which underlies parts of the high seas.

[4] On weapons testing, see the anonymous note, and the articles by Margolis, McDougal and Schlei, and Swan, listed in 'Further reading' below.

Court arguing that 'the interference with ships and aircraft on the high seas and in the superjacent air space, and the pollution of the high seas by radioactive fall-out, constitute infringements of the freedom of the high seas'. However, the *Nuclear Test* cases (1974) ended without a judgment on the merits of this contention, the Court holding that French announcements of a termination of atmospheric testing had effectively brought an end to the dispute.[5] Nonetheless, it is clear that in such cases the main criterion that the Court would use to determine whether or not the use fell within the freedom of the high seas would be that of reasonableness.[6]

The greater detail of the Law of the Sea Convention has also led to the subjection of some high-seas freedoms to certain additional constraints. Some constraints follow from the fact that ten per cent or so of the high seas overlie those parts of the continental shelf protruding beyond the 200-mile EEZ (the 'outer' continental shelf). For example, the right of immersion is subject to the rights of States to regulate the laying of pipelines across their continental shelves (LOSC, art. 79; cf. HSC, art. 26, and chapter eight). Here the freedom of immersion exists, even on the shelf, but its exercise may be regulated.[7] The right to establish structures on the bed of the high seas is more completely constrained. The construction, operation and use of artificial islands, of installations and structures established for economic purposes, and of installations and structures which may interfere with the exercise of coastal State rights on the continental shelf, are subject to the authorisation and regulation of the coastal State (LOSC, arts 80, 60). Similarly, freedom of research is limited by the rights of coastal States in respect of their continental shelves, and the rights of the International Sea Bed Authority in respect of the rest of the sea bed (see chapters eight, twelve and sixteen). Indeed, all activities relating to the sea bed beyond the limits of national jurisdiction are subject to the provisions concerning the International Sea Bed Area (LOSC, arts 134, 138, 141; and see chapter twelve).

Freedom of fishing is subject to a general duty to negotiate and agree upon measures necessary for the conservation of high-seas fisheries (LOSC, arts 63, 64, 116–20), amplified in the 1995 Agreement for the Implementation of the Provisions of the United Nations Convention on the Law of the Sea of 10 December 1982 Relating to the Conservation and Management of Straddling Fish Stocks and Highly Migratory Fish Stocks (the 'Straddling Stocks' Agreement). It is also subject to limited derogations in favour of the home States of anadromous and catadromous species, and coastal State rights over sedentary species on the

---

[5] An attempt by New Zealand to re-open the proceedings when France engaged in underground testing in the Pacific in 1995 failed: see the *Request for an Examination of the Situation in accordance with Paragraph 63 of the Court's Judgment of 20 December 1974 in the Nuclear Tests (New Zealand v. France) Case.*

[6] On which see O. Corten, *L'utilisation du 'raisonnable' par le juge international* (Bruxelles, Bruylant), 1997.

[7] Article 79 requires the consent of the coastal State to the delineation of the course of such pipelines but not, it seems, to the course of cables.

continental shelf (LOSC, arts 66, 67, 68). All these questions are discussed in detail in chapter fourteen.

The exercise of high-seas freedoms is also, of course, subject to general rules of international law, such as those governing the use of force. There is an explicit requirement that the high seas 'be reserved for peaceful purposes' (LOSC, art. 88; cf. art. 301), which is widely regarded as prohibiting only acts of aggression on the high seas, and will certainly be interpreted in that way by naval powers (see, further, chapter seventeen). Apart from the specific constraints imposed by the law of the sea, States may be bound by many other obligations deriving from general international law. Bilateral or multilateral treaties may bind States not to use areas of the high seas for the dumping of certain kinds of waste or the deployment of certain kinds of weapon, for example. There may, furthermore, be certain obligations that are related to the exercise of high-seas freedoms but do not diminish them. The reporting requirements on transboundary waste movements envisaged in the Basel and Bamako Conventions would be examples, in so far as they apply to ships on the high seas.[8]

Jurisdiction on the high seas

In general, the flag State, that is, the State which has granted to a ship the right to sail under its flag (see further, chapter thirteen), has the exclusive right to exercise legislative and enforcement jurisdiction over its ships on the high seas (HSC, art. 6; LOSC, art. 92).

This exclusiveness of flag State jurisdiction is illustrated by the way in which international law deals with the attribution of jurisdiction in the case of collisions between ships. Collisions may involve two States, each of which considers the collision and those responsible for it to be within its jurisdiction. The existence of such concurrent jurisdiction was upheld in 1927 by the Permanent Court of International Justice in the case of the French ship *Lotus*, which had collided with a Turkish vessel, causing loss of life. The narrow, and best, ground of the decision was that the collision had 'taken place' on the Turkish ship and that the officer responsible could therefore be prosecuted in Turkey as well as by France. The *Lotus* decision was much criticised, and the rule that it adopted was reversed by the 1952 Brussels Convention for the Unification of Certain Rules relating to Penal Jurisdiction.[9] The Brussels Convention rule was adopted in the 1958 High Seas Convention and in the Law of the Sea Convention, both of which reserve

---

[8] See E. B. Weinstein, 'The impact of regulation of transport of hazardous waste on freedom of navigation', 9 *IJMCL* 135–72 (1994); and see further chapter fifteen. US opposition to reporting requirements as infringements of the freedom of the high seas seems to regard (wrongly) reporting requirements as establishing *conditions* for the exercise of the freedom, rather than distinct ancillary obligations.

[9] The Convention was complemented by the Brussels Convention on Certain Rules concerning Civil Jurisdiction in Matters of Collision, adopted on the same date (10 May 1952).

penal and disciplinary proceedings in cases of collision or other navigational incidents to the authorities of the State in whose ship the defendant served or (if that be different) the State of which he is a national (HSC, art. 11; LOSC, art. 97). The latter alternative underlines the fact that a State retains jurisdiction over its nationals wherever they might be, whether on foreign ships or anywhere else; but the expectation is that in this case of concurrent jurisdiction it is the flag State whose jurisdiction has primacy (see, e.g., LOSC, art. 94).

Flag State jurisdiction also entails responsibilities. States Parties to the 1958 and 1982 Conventions must legislate to make it an offence for their nationals, or ships flying their flags, culpably to break or injure submarine cables and pipelines under the high seas (HSC, art. 27; LOSC, art. 113); and they must provide for compensation to be available for such damage to pipelines and cables (HSC, art. 28; LOSC, art. 114). As a complement to this duty they must also ensure that compensation is available from cable and pipeline owners for ships that are obliged to sacrifice anchors or fishing gear in order to avoid damaging the cable or pipeline (HSC, art. 29; LOSC, art. 115).[10] Similarly, compliance with international duties concerning matters such as safety at sea and the rendering of assistance to ships in distress is sought by imposing on flag States the duty to adopt and enforce legislation dealing with those matters (HSC, arts 10, 11; LOSC. arts 94, 98; see chapter thirteen).

The exclusiveness of the flag State's jurisdiction is not absolute. It admits of several exceptions, in which third States share legislative or enforcement jurisdiction, or both, with the flag State; and it is to these exceptions that we now turn.

Piracy

The first exception is the long established right – and, indeed, duty (HSC, art. 14; LOSC, art. 100) – of every State to act against piracy. This exception arose from the common interest of the European powers in protecting the fleets that were the lifelines of their trade and their colonial empires.[11] Piracy remains a serious, and increasing, problem, notably off parts of south-east Asia, South America and Africa, and in the Mediterranean and the Indian Ocean. It is a problem constantly under consideration by the IMO[12] and by the international shipping industry, which maintains a centre in Kuala Lumpur to monitor incidents of piracy.

Piracy includes any illegal act of violence, detention or depredation committed for private ends by the crew or passengers of a private ship (or aircraft) against

---

[10] See also, in respect of cables but not pipelines, the 1884 Convention for the Protection of Submarine Cables. Cf. E. Wagner, 'Submarine cables and protections provided by the law of the sea', 19 *Marine Policy* 127–36 (1995).

[11] Indeed, it was the policing of coastal waters against pirates that underlay the medieval claims to dominion over the seas: see T. A. Walker, *A History of the Law of Nations*, Vol. 1 (Cambridge, Cambridge University Press), 1899, pp. 118, 162–70.

[12] See *IMO News*, 1993, No. 1, pp. 4, 9–11, and 1998, No. 2, pp. 29–30.

another ship (or aircraft) or persons or property on board it, on (or over) the high seas[13] (HSC, art. 15; LOSC, art. 101). If a ship or aircraft is intended to be or has been used for such purpose by the persons in dominant control of it, it is a pirate ship or aircraft (HSC, art. 17; LOSC, art. 103). Piratical acts committed by warships or government ships and aircraft are assimilated to those committed by private ships if the crew has mutinied and taken control: otherwise, the 'official' nature of actions by such ships precludes their classification as piracy, as does the fact that such actions are not committed for private ends (HSC, art. 16; LOSC, art. 102).[14] The requirement that two vessels – pirate and victim – be involved distinguishes piracy from hijacking, and explains why attempts by passengers to gain control of ships, as happened on the Portuguese vessel *Santa Maria* in 1961, and on the Italian liner *Achille Lauro* in 1985, are not acts of piracy. Unless the law of the flag State provides otherwise, a ship retains its nationality even when it becomes a pirate ship (HSC, art. 18; LOSC, art. 104).

Article 22 of the High Seas Convention, which purports to codify the customary law concerning the high seas, and article 110 of the Law of the Sea Convention allow the visiting and boarding of any ship, of whatever flag, reasonably suspected of being engaged in piracy. If, however, the suspicions prove unfounded and the ship had done nothing to justify them, it must be compensated for any loss or damage which it has sustained (HSC, art. 22; LOSC, art. 110). Pirate ships on the high seas may be seized (HSC, art. 19; LOSC, art. 105), though only by clearly marked warships (or aircraft) or other authorised vessels on government service (HSC, art. 21; LOSC, art. 107). Where the seizure is wrongfully effected without adequate grounds the ship's flag State is entitled to compensation for any loss or damage caused from the State of the warship (HSC, art. 20; LOSC, art. 106). Those on board a pirate vessel may be arrested by the seizing vessel (HSC, art. 19; LOSC, art. 105). As a matter of international law, pirates may be tried by any State before whose courts they are brought, and that State may determine by its laws the penalties to be imposed (HSC, art. 19; LOSC, art. 105).[15]

Concerned at the rising incidence of acts of piracy and of terrorist acts threatening the safety of navigation, the IMO prepared the Convention for the

[13] Most of the 252 incidents of 'piracy' reported to the IMO in 1997 in fact took place within the territorial sea and are not, as a matter of international law, piracy.

[14] It is said that in some parts of the world government-owned launches are taken out unofficially to engage in piratical acts. It seems reasonable to assimilate such circumstances to a mutiny. In practice, however, no State is likely to attempt to arrest a foreign government ship for piracy unless the flag State has at least disavowed the actions of the ship. For a rare example of a public complaint of 'governmental' piracy, see the UAE complaint against Iran, 2 January 1997: 33 *LOSB* 91 (1997).

[15] It will, of course, depend upon the law of each State whether this competence permitted by international law has in fact been implemented. For example, see the account of the early treatment of piracy in English and US law, A. P. Rubin, *Ethics and Authority in International Law* (Cambridge, Cambridge University Press), 1997; and see also the (UK) Merchant Shipping and Maritime Security Act 1997, s. 26, and the note thereon in *Current Law Statutes* (London, Sweet & Maxwell), 1997.

Suppression of Unlawful Acts Against the Safety of Maritime Navigation (known in IMO *argot* as the 'SUA' Convention) in 1988. The Convention entered into force in 1992. The SUA Convention, which does not apply to warships or other military or police ships (art. 1), specifies as offences certain acts against shipping, including the seizure of ships, and (broadly speaking) the endangering of safe navigation by the use of violence against persons on board or by damage to the ship, its cargo or equipment, and attempts to commit those acts (art. 3). States Parties must make Convention offences punishable under their laws (art. 5), and establish their jurisdiction over offences committed on or against their ships, or in their territory, or by their nationals (art. 6(1)); and States may also assert their jurisdiction over offences committed by stateless persons habitually resident in their territory, offences involving their nationals as victims, and offences aimed at compelling the State to do or abstain from doing some act (art. 6(2)). Convention offences are deemed to be included as extraditable offences in extradition treaties between the States Parties (art. 11). A State in whose territory an alleged offender is found is obliged either to extradite him to any State Party asserting jurisdiction on the bases set out in article 6(1) and (2) or to submit the case to its own competent authorities with a view to its prosecution (arts 6(4), 7, 10). States Parties must, accordingly, establish their jurisdiction over all offenders found within their territory whom they decide not to extradite (art. 6(4)). The Convention also provides for co-operation between the parties in the repression of acts against the safety of navigation. A Protocol to the SUA Convention adopted in 1989 extends these principles to acts against fixed platforms located on the continental shelf.

Unauthorised broadcasting

The second exception to the exclusiveness of flag State jurisdiction concerns unauthorised broadcasting on the high seas. In the early 1960s a number of ships anchored in the North Sea and began to broadcast, for profit, without a licence from the States where the transmissions were received. Since these 'pirate' radio stations were based on foreign ships on the high seas, the view was taken that coastal States had no jurisdiction over them. Under the European Agreement for the Prevention of Broadcasting transmitted from Stations outside National Territories, signed in 1965, several European States agreed to punish their nationals engaged in or assisting unauthorised broadcasting, as well as anyone, of whatever nationality, on ships flying their flag from which unauthorised broadcasts were being made. This forced most stations to close down. Thus far, action against pirate broadcasting had not exceeded the general principle of exclusive flag State jurisdiction.

The Law of the Sea Convention goes further, however, allowing States where unauthorised transmissions either are received or cause interference with authorised radio communication to exercise jurisdiction over unauthorised broadcasters: flag States and national States of broadcasters retain a concurrent jurisdiction

(LOSC, art. 109). Rights of visiting, boarding and seizing ships, and of arresting and prosecuting persons on board, are vested in those States which have jurisdiction over unauthorised broadcasting, and are exercised under the conditions described above in relation to piracy (LOSC, art. 110). Although the original 'pirate' radio stations broadcasting popular music seem to have disappeared, as much perhaps as a result of the deregulation of the air-waves and rise of 'official' commercial radio stations as of repression under the 1965 Agreement, the provisions in the law of the Sea Convention retain their importance: they may, for instance, be applied to unofficial propaganda broadcasts from the high seas.

In the case of piracy and unauthorised broadcasting, States other than the flag State are given under the Law of the Sea Convention both legislative jurisdiction and enforcement jurisdiction over ships on the high seas (which exist anyway as a matter of customary international law in the case of piracy). In a number of other cases States enjoy extended control and enforcement jurisdiction over foreign ships on the high seas, unaccompanied by the legislative jurisdiction to prescribe rules which such ships are obliged to obey there. These cases we consider next.

Slave trading

Where a ship is reasonably suspected of being engaged in the slave trade, it may be visited and boarded (HSC, art. 22; LOSC, art. 110). However, despite a British proposal in 1956 to make it so, slave trading is not in international law analogous to piracy (although it is in English municipal law):[16] only the flag State may actually proceed to seize the ship or arrest those on board, if the suspicion that the ship is engaged in slavery is well founded. Other States may only report their findings to the flag State, which is, however, obliged to adopt effective measures for the repression of slave trading by its ships (HSC, art. 13; LOSC, art. 99). If any slave succeeds in escaping and taking refuge on board any ship, of whatever flag, he becomes, *ipso facto*, free (*ibid.*). Several international agreements, such as the 1890 General Act for the Suppression of the Slave Trade, include provisions for international co-operation in action against slave traders, and some provide for reciprocal rights of visit and search over vessels in parts of the high seas. No such rights of visit and search were expressly included in the 1926 International Slavery Convention or the 1956 Supplementary Slavery Convention, although those rights persist, of course, under the High Seas Convention and the 1982 Convention, which are generally regarded as codifying customary international law in this respect (HSC, art. 22; LOSC, art. 110).

---

[16] For an earlier (1854) proposal to that end, and a valuable account of the suppression of the slave trade generally, see C. Lloyd, *The Navy and the Slave Trade* (London, Frank Cass), 1968, p. 60 and *passim*.

Drug trafficking

Under the Law of the Sea Convention, few powers exist in the case of ships suspected of illicitly trafficking in narcotic and psychotropic drugs, despite the obligation on States to co-operate in suppressing that trade (LOSC, art. 108(1)). All that is allowed is that States with reasonable grounds for suspecting that their own ships are engaged in the trade may request the co-operation of other States in suppressing the traffic, although presumably there is an implication that other States should normally accede to such a request (LOSC, art. 108(2)). The position is, however, greatly modified in practice by the provisions of treaties dealing specifically with drug trafficking. These we consider below, under the heading 'Rights under special treaties'.

Ships of uncertain nationality

States may visit and enforce their laws against their own ships on the high seas. Consequently, where a ship, though flying a foreign flag (or refusing to show a flag), is reasonably suspected of being of the same nationality as a warship which encounters it on the high seas, the warship may visit and board it, check its documents and proceed to a further examination on board if necessary, in order to verify its right to fly the foreign flag.[17] As before, if the suspicions are unfounded and unjustified by the conduct of the ship visited, the ship is to be compensated for any loss or damage sustained (HSC, art. 22; LOSC, art. 110). If a ship is found to be flying the same flag as the inspecting warship, but not to be entitled to fly it, the ship may be seized and taken to a flag State port for punishment.[18]

Stateless ships

Some ships have, as a matter of international law, no nationality.[19] Ships may have been deprived of the right to sail under a particular flag (for example, Taiwan has revoked the rights of fishing vessels violating its laws on drift-net fishing);[20] or their purported flag may not be recognised.[21] To such ships are

---

[17] This is sometimes known as the *droit d'enquête* or *vérification du pavillon*.

[18] This rule is not set out in the conventions, but is said to be 'universally recognised': *Oppenheim I, op. cit.* in 'Further reading', p. 737.

[19] That is not the same as not being registered: a State may not require, or permit, the registration of ships below a certain size, for example, but may nonetheless regard such ships as having its nationality if they are owned by its nationals: see T. L. McDorman, *op. cit.* in 'Further reading'.

[20] *Ibid.*, at 532. If States revoke the right to fly their flag in order to escape international responsibility for the actions of the ships, the revocation may be ineffective: H. Meyers, *The Nationality of Ships* (The Hague, Nijhoff), 1967, p. 314.

[21] Cf. S. Talmon, *Recognition of Governments in International Law* (Oxford, Clarendon Press), 1998, p. 213.

assimilated those that sail under two or more flags, using them according to convenience (HSC, art. 6(2); LOSC, art. 92).

Ships without nationality are in a curious position. Their 'statelessness' will not, of itself, entitle each and every State to assert jurisdiction over them, for there is not in every case any recognised basis upon which jurisdiction could be asserted over stateless ships on the high seas. Thus, jurisdiction could clearly be asserted over stateless ships in a coastal State's maritime zones, on the basis of territoriality; and it could probably be exercised by the national State of the owners if such ships are outside the territorial seas of third States.[22] On the other hand it has been held, for example in the case of *Molvan* v. *A. G. for Palestine* (UK, 1948), that such ships enjoy the protection of no State,[23] the implication being that if jurisdiction *were* asserted no State would be competent to complain of a violation of international law. Widely accepted as this view is, it ignores the possibility of diplomatic protection being exercised by the national State of the individuals on such stateless ships. The better view appears to be that there is a need for some jurisdictional nexus in order that a State may extend its laws to those on board a stateless ship and enforce the laws against them. As has been seen, the Law of the Sea Convention establishes that such a nexus exists in favour of all States in relation to piracy – a kind of universal jurisdiction – and in relation to certain specially affected States as regards unauthorised broadcasting. Some States, notably the USA, have made a similar claim in relation to drug trafficking, which is regarded as constituting a grave threat to targeted States of importation; and this reasonable claim would therefore include the assertion of jurisdiction over stateless ships on the high seas engaged in the trafficking of drugs destined for the State asserting jurisdiction.[24] No right to visit and board stateless ships was expressly given under the High Seas Convention; this right is, however, given by article 110 of the Law of the Sea Convention, and is implicit in the status of stateless ships.

Hot pursuit and constructive presence

It has long been recognised under customary law, in cases such as the *I'm Alone* (1935), that the right of hot pursuit allows a warship or military aircraft of a State to pursue a foreign ship which has violated that State's laws within its internal waters or territorial sea and to arrest it on the high seas. This principle is recognised in both the High Seas Convention and the Law of the Sea Convention.

[22] *O'Connell, op. cit.* in 'Further reading', Vol. 2, p. 756.
[23] But see T. L. McDorman, *op. cit.* in 'Further reading', at 540 (1994).
[24] See the (US) Maritime Drug Law Enforcement Act 1986, 46 USCA § 1903; and see further below. The US has also asserted jurisdiction over stateless ships engaged in driftnet fishing on the high seas: see 23 *LOSB* 107 (1993). Some US courts have asserted a general jurisdiction over stateless ships: see *US* v. *Marino-Garcia* 679 F. 2d 1373 (1982), *cert. denied* 459 *US* 1114 (1983).

Pursuit must be begun while the ship or one of its boats is within the territorial sea (or, in the case of customs, fiscal, immigration or sanitary laws, within the contiguous zone), by the giving within range of the ship of a visual or auditory signal to stop, although the signalling ship or aircraft need not itself be within the territorial sea or contiguous zone at the time. The Law of the Sea Convention has extended the right to include hot pursuit from archipelagic waters, and also hot pursuit from the EEZ or the waters above the continental shelf in cases where a violation of the laws which the coastal State is entitled to make in respect of the zone or shelf has occurred. It may be noted in passing that the right to enforce laws respecting the continental shelf will itself involve a right to exercise legislative and enforcement jurisdiction over foreign ships on the high seas in cases where the shelf extends beyond the 200-mile zone. Pursuit must be hot and continuous. Although it is provided that a ship or aircraft may take over pursuit from the aircraft that began it, there is no express provision allowing one ship to take over from another subsequently. It would, however, seem reasonable to allow this. The pursuing vessel may use any necessary and reasonable force to effect the arrest, even if this results in the unavoidable sinking of the ship. Compensation is payable for loss or damage resulting from unjustified pursuit or for the exercise of unjustified force. The right of pursuit ceases as soon as the ship enters the territorial sea of its own or a third State, because to continue it therein would be to violate the sovereignty of the other State (HSC, art. 23; LOSC, art. 111).[25] There is no reason why the right of pursuit should cease when the vessel pursued enters the EEZ of its own or a third State.[26]

There is also, in customary international law, a right to arrest foreign ships which use their boats to commit offences within the territorial sea (and, perhaps, now the EEZ) while themselves remaining on the high seas. This is the doctrine of constructive presence, implicitly recognised in the provisions of the High Seas and Law of the Sea Conventions relating to hot pursuit, and which we considered in chapter seven. The doctrine of constructive presence may operate together with the right of hot pursuit, so as to give coastal States some flexibility in the manner in which they enforce their laws. For instance, in the case of *R.* v. *Mills* (1995), a right of hot pursuit was asserted by the United Kingdom against the *Poseidon*, a ship registered in St Vincent that was smuggling cannabis into the United Kingdom by transferring it on the high seas to a British trawler which came from an Irish port and subsequently put in to a British port.[27] The judge

---

[25] The coastal State may, of course, consent to pursuit within its territorial sea, and this is done in some bilateral agreements: see further chapter four.

[26] Though some States, such as Brazil (in the context of the 1988 UN Convention against Illicit Traffic in Narcotic Drugs, discussed below), have taken the view that arrests of ships within the EEZ need the consent of the coastal State. Brazil's statement was the subject of an objection by EC member States. See Kwiatkowska, *op. cit.* in 'Further reading', at p. 162.

[27] See W. C. Gilmore, 'Hot Pursuit: The Case of *R.* v. *Mills and Others*', 44 *ICLQ* 949–58 (1995).

was not troubled by the fact that the second ship was not one of the boats of the ship pursued, nor even a boat that had put out from and returned to British shores. A similar willingness to adopt a liberal approach to the detailed requirements of the conventional right of hot pursuit is evident elsewhere, for instance in the willingness to accept that the order to stop can be given by radio (though perhaps not by a ship or aircraft at any great distance from the pursued ship).[28]

Developing technology is making it possible to detect and track offending vessels using radar, sea-bed sensors and transponders, and satellite surveillance. It seems both inevitable and desirable that the conditions for the exercise of the right of hot pursuit be given a flexible interpretation in order to permit the effective exercise of police powers on the high seas.[29] In the meantime, States are beginning to conclude treaties providing for international co-operation to facilitate the exercise of the right of hot pursuit.[30]

Major pollution incidents

A further exception to the exclusiveness of flag State jurisdiction is often said to exist in favour of States whose coastline is threatened with serious pollution from a foreign shipping casualty on the high seas. This right, which gained rapid recognition after the British action against the *Torrey Canyon* in 1967, was the subject of the 1969 'Intervention' Convention, and is included in the Law of the Sea Convention as article 221. It is also widely suggested that such a right exists in customary international law, and there are several instances of the assertion of the right in national legislation.[31] This matter is discussed more fully in chapter fifteen.

Exceptional measures

States have sometimes justified interference with foreign ships on the high seas on the grounds of self-defence or necessity.[32] One classic incident, the *Virginius*, arose in 1873. There Spain seized on the high seas a US ship carrying US and British nationals and many weapons which they intended to use in the Cuban insurrection against Spain. Great Britain, but not the USA, accepted that the arrest

---

[28] See *R.* v. *Mills and Others* (1995); *R.* v. *Sunila and Soleyman* (1986); W. C. Gilmore, 'Hot pursuit and constructive presence in Canadian law enforcement', 12 *Marine Policy* 105–11 (1988). But see *US* v. *Postal* (1979).

[29] See C. H. Allen, *op. cit.* in 'Further reading'.

[30] See, e.g., the 1993 (Conakry) Convention on Sub-regional Co-operation in the Exercise of Maritime Hot Pursuit, and the accompanying Protocol regarding practical modalities of co-ordination of surveillance activities in the member States of the Sub-regional Fisheries Commission, which establishes such a system in west Africa.

[31] See Kwiatkowska, *op. cit.* in 'Further reading', at p. 173. Cf. ss. 137 and 141 of the (UK) Merchant Shipping Act, 1995.

[32] Cf. arts 33–34 of the ILC Draft Articles on State Responsibility, in the *ILC Yearbook*, 1980, Vol. II (Part Two), pp. 30–61.

of the ship was justified on the grounds of self-defence. More recently France asserted a right to visit and search on the high seas ships suspected of carrying arms to Algeria during the emergency of 1956 – 62. The Ministry of Defence argued in the case of the *Duizar* (1966) that this was justified by France's right of self-defence, but the French action was vigorously opposed by many of the States whose ships were affected. The explanation of the distinction between the responses to the *Virginius* and the Algerian incidents probably lies partly in the scale of the French operation – 4,775 ships were searched in the first year alone – and partly in the emergence during the intervening period of rules limiting the use of force generally, and notably article 51 of the UN Charter, which arguably limits the right of self-defence to cases of armed attack. It is notable that when, during the 1982 Argentina–UK Falklands/Malvinas conflict, a French ship was carrying weapons across the Atlantic to Argentina, the British government took the view that it had no right to intercept it on the high seas.[33]

One of the most notorious examples of interference with foreign shipping on the high seas is the Cuban 'quarantine' of 1962. Warships of the United States, and later Argentina, Dominican Republic and Venezuela, inspected ships bound for Cuba to determine whether they were carrying 'offensive military equipment' to the island.[34] The primary justification given for the quarantine was not the right of self-defence but the decision of the Organisation of American States, purportedly acting under Chapter VIII of the UN Charter (which it clearly was not), to institute the measure. The question of the legality of the quarantine, which remains controversial, is closely bound up with questions of the competence of international organisations and of the scope of self-defence in general, which are beyond the range of this book (but see chapter seventeen). And if the intention to create a precedent for future behaviour is a desirable quality in State practice called in evidence to support the existence of a rule of customary law, then the incident is perhaps best forgotten. But it, and other cases such as the US interdiction of refugees fleeing from Haiti in 1992,[35] demonstrate that even in peacetime States do unilaterally take exceptional measures of enforcement jurisdiction on the high seas, any opposition from other States being insufficient to deter them. States have also acted under the terms of United Nations Security Council resolutions to stop and search vessels on the high seas, in order to prevent the circumvention of sanctions imposed against Iraq, Haiti and Serbia. The international legality of such UN-authorised actions is not in doubt (see further chapter seventeen).

Perhaps the most notable claim to exceptional jurisdiction over foreign ships on the high seas will come to be seen in the development exemplified by the

---

[33] *UKMIL 1982*, 469.

[34] By contrast the 200-mile exclusion zone declared by the UK in the Falklands/Malvinas conflict in 1982 was generally respected, and no forcible interdictions occurred. See further chapter seventeen.

[35] See *Haitian Centers Council Inc.* v. *McNary* (US, 1992), noted in 87 *AJIL* 112–17 (1993).

case of *U.S.* v. *Gonzalez* and the US drug trafficking laws referred to above[36] and in chapter seven. It will be recalled that in that case jurisdiction over a foreign ship engaged in attempts to smuggle drugs into the United States was based on the protective principle of jurisdiction in international law. That, in the view of the court, justified the seizure and prosecution by the USA of ships and persons on the high seas 'to such an extent and to so great a distance as is reasonable and necessary to protect itself and its citizens from injury'. The court went on to speak of the requirement that the conduct punished should be 'generally recognised as a crime under the laws of States that have reasonably developed legal systems'; but the absence of any other limiting criterion *ratione loci* or *ratione materiae* makes this principle one of enormous potential scope, capable of subsuming and considerably extending not only the rules on the contiguous zone, but also the rules on visit and search on the high seas. In the context of the control of drug trafficking, such claims are being received by other States with apparent equanimity. Arrests are taking place against a background of increasing international co-operation in the repression of drug smuggling (discussed further below). Though it still seems unlikely that drug smuggling will become assimilated to piracy in international law, and so subject to universal jurisdiction, it seems quite possible that the law will develop so as to give to States a jurisdiction over ships engaged in drug smuggling similar to that which they enjoy over unauthorised broadcasters on the high seas.

Rights under special treaties

With the exceptions outlined above, and with the further exception of rights in contiguous zones, which were discussed in chapter seven, the exclusiveness of flag State jurisdiction on the high seas remains, in principle, intact. But the principle can be varied by specific agreement, and is indeed departed from in a wide variety of treaties.

Some, such as the joint inspection and surveillance scheme of the Northwest Atlantic Fisheries Organisation (NAFO – see chapter fourteen), grant only rights to visit and search or, like the 1884 Convention for the Protection of Submarine Cables, merely the right to approach, but not to board, suspected offenders in order to determine their nationality. In these instances only enforcement jurisdiction is extended, the capacity to prescribe rules and also to punish violations of them remaining with the flag State alone, to which third States' inspecting vessels would report.

In a few instances both enforcement and legislative jurisdiction has been extended. For instance, in 1974, before it claimed a 200-mile EEZ, the United States concluded a series of agreements subjecting to US jurisdiction vessels calling at the deep-water port facility located in the high seas about eighteen

---

[36] See footnote 24.

miles off Louisiana. United States legislation provided that foreign vessels might not use the facility unless their flag State had concluded such an agreement with the United States, which regarded the operation of deep-water ports as an exercise of the freedom of the high seas.[37]

The most significant developments of this kind have arisen in relation to the repression of drug smuggling. The United Kingdom and the United States concluded an agreement in 1981 to facilitate the interdiction by the United States in defined areas of the Caribbean and Gulf of Mexico and up to 150 miles off the eastern seaboard of the United States of British-flag vessels suspected of trafficking in drugs.[38] The agreement provided for the visit, search and seizure of such vessels on the high seas, and is comparable with the liquor treaties of the 1920s discussed in chapter seven. In 1988 the (UN) Vienna Convention Against Illicit Traffic in Narcotic Drugs and Psychotropic Substances was concluded: it entered into force in 1990. Article 17 of that Convention provides that States Parties may request each other's help in the repression of illicit traffic. A State Party may request permission to board 'a vessel exercising freedom of navigation' (and therefore, by definition, beyond the territorial sea) of another State Party. Such authorisation may be given on an *ad hoc* basis or by means of agreements such as that of the 1981 UK–USA agreement just described.[39]

The 1988 Vienna Convention was followed in 1995 by a Council of Europe Agreement on Illicit Traffic by Sea, implementing article 17 of the 1988 Convention. Under the 1995 Agreement, flag State authorisation is still required before one of its ships is boarded by another State Party (the 'intervening State') (art. 6).[40] The boarding and inspection having taken place, however, either the intervening State or the flag State (or, indeed, a third State Party to whose ports the ship is taken) may prosecute offences detected, the flag State having preferential jurisdiction (arts 3, 10, 14).[41] In their requirement for authorisation before ships of other States Parties are boarded, the 1988 and 1995 treaties are less adventurous than the 1981 UK–US Agreement, which itself gives such authorisation. That more progressive approach is being pursued at the bilateral level. Authorisation for the boarding of ships on the high seas appears, for example, in the Spanish-

---

[37] See, for example, the UK–USA Exchange of Notes concerning the Use of the Louisiana Offshore Oil Port, 14/25 May 1979. Cf. *DUSPIL 1974*, pp. 356–60, where the provisions of the US Deepwater Port Act of 1974 are noted, and *DUSPIL 1981–8*, Vol. II, pp. 2078–9, where other bilateral agreements are listed; R. B. Krueger, M. H. Nordquist and R. P. Wessely, 'New technology and international law: the case of deep-water ports', 17 *VJIL* 597–643 (1976–7).

[38] See Siddle, *op. cit.* in 'Further reading'. Cf. W. C. Gilmore, 'Narcotics interdiction at sea: UK–US co-operation', 13 *Marine Policy* 218–30 (1989).

[39] See W. C. Gilmore, 'Drug trafficking by sea: the 1988 United Nations Convention Against Illicit Traffic in Narcotic Drugs and Psychotropic Substances', 15 *Marine Policy* 183–92 (1991).

[40] See further chapter nine.

[41] See W. C. Gilmore, 'Narcotics interdiction at sea: the 1995 Council of Europe Agreement', 20 *Marine Policy* 3–14 (1996).

Italian treaty of 23 March 1990 to combat illicit drug trafficking at sea,[42] and in the US–Trinidad 'shiprider' agreement of 4 March 1996.[43]

Creeping jurisdiction on the high seas?

We began this chapter by noting the diminution in the area of the high seas that has resulted from the emergence of the EEZ and archipelagic waters. We end it by considering briefly whether the bounds of the high seas are now firmly fixed.

It is true that some States are claiming excessive jurisdiction over their 'outer' continental shelves. Several Indian Ocean States, for instance, assert jurisdiction over all installations and structures, and not just 'economic' installations and structures, on their outer continental shelves.[44] Furthermore, as we note in chapter fourteen, pressure on high-seas fisheries has led to unilateral action against foreign fishing vessels outside States' EEZs: the *Estai* case in 1995, in which Spain took Canada to the International Court, typifies this phenomenon.[45] More dramatically, there have been a number of attempts to stamp a particular juridical regime upon vast areas of the high seas. In chapter seventeen we refer to the creation of 'zones of peace' and nuclear-free zones in various parts of the oceans. But those zones are multilateral institutions: they have been established by the agreement of the neighbouring States, and do not purport to impose legal duties or liabilities upon non-party States. There have also been occasional suggestions of a return to what are best described as zones of influence in the oceans, established unilaterally by States. The best known is the Chilean proposal for a 'Presential Sea' (*mar presencial*) in the southern Pacific.[46] Yet that, too, has not as yet been pressed as far as a claim to impose obligations on third States. It seems to be confined to an assertion of Chile's interest in the area and its claim to a certain priority in relation to the resources (particularly the fisheries) of the area. All in all, the balance struck by UNCLOS III between the high seas and the zones of national jurisdiction appears to be holding.

---

[42] Each State is given the right to intervene as agent for the other: art. 5.

[43] The term 'shiprider' refers to the provision in treaties of this kind for law enforcement officers of one State to ride on law enforcement vessels of the other. See further W. C. Gilmore, 'Narcotics interdiction at sea: the 1995 Council of Europe Agreement', 20 *Marine Policy* 3–14 (1996). Comparable arrangements have been made in other contexts, such as the 1989 Agreements made by the USA with Taiwan and South Korea for the inspection of fishing vessels on the high seas: see Kwiatkowska, *op. cit.* in 'Further reading', at p. 171.

[44] See Kwiatkowska, *op. cit.* in 'Further reading', at p. 161.

[45] See 26 *LOSB* 19, 20 (1994); 28 *LOSB* 32, 45 (1995). See also the US announcement of 8 March 1993 on the enforcement of a moratorium on driftnet fishing on the high seas: 23 *LOSB* 107 (1993).

[46] See the articles by Joyner and De Cola, and by Dalton, in 'Further reading'. Cf. F. Orrego Vicuña, 'Toward an effective management of high seas fisheries and the settlement of the pending issues of the law of the sea', 24 *ODIL* 81–92, at 87–9 (1993).

Further reading

C. H. Alexandrowicz, 'Freitas versus Grotius'. 35 *BYIL* 162–82 (1959).

C. H. Allen, 'Doctrine of hot pursuit: a functional interpretation adaptable to emerging maritime law enforcement technologies and practices', 20 *ODIL* 309–41 (1989).

Anon., 'Exclusion of ships from non-territorial weapons testing zones', 99 *Harvard Law Review* 1040–58 (1986).

J. G. Dalton, 'The Chilean *Mar Presencial*: a harmless concept or a dangerous precedent?', 8 *IJMCL* 397–418 (1993).

B. H. Dubner, *The Law of International Sea Piracy* (The Hague, Nijhoff), 1979.

A. De Smet, 'Policing on the high seas; with special reference to the North Sea', *ND III*, pp. 193–205.

W. C. Gilmore, 'Drug trafficking by sea: the 1988 United Nations Convention Against Illicit Traffic in Narcotic Drugs and Psychotropic Substances', 15 *Marine Policy* 183–92 (1991).

——, 'Hot pursuit and constructive presence in Canadian law enforcement', 12 *Marine Policy* 105–11 (1988).

——, 'Hot Pursuit: The Case of *R.* v. *Mills and Others*', 44 *ICLQ* 949–58 (1995).

——, 'Narcotics interdiction at sea: the 1995 Council of Europe Agreement', 20 *Marine Policy* 3–14 (1996).

——, 'Narcotics interdiction at sea: UK–US co-operation', 13 *Marine Policy* 218–30 (1989).

N. Grief, *Public International Law in the Airspace of the High Seas* (Dordrecht, Nijhoff), 1994.

M. Halberstam, 'Terrorism on the high seas: the *Achille Lauro*, piracy and the IMO Convention on Maritime Safety'. 82 *AJIL* 269–319 (1988).

N. M. Hunnings, 'Pirate broadcasting in European waters', 14 *ICLQ* 410–36 (1965).

Sir Robert Jennings and Sir Arthur Watts (eds), *Oppenheim's International Law* (Harlow, Longman), 1992, 9th edn, Vol. I, *Peace* [*Oppenheim I*].

C. C. Joyner and P. N. De Cola, 'Chile's Presential Sea proposal: implications for straddling stocks and the international law of fisheries', 24 *ODIL* 99–121 (1993).

B. Kwiatkowska, 'Creeping jurisdiction beyond 200 miles in the light of the 1982 Law of the Sea Convention and State practice', 22 *ODIL* 153–87 (1991).

E. Margolis, 'The hydrogen bomb experiments and international law', 64 *Yale Law Journal* 629–48 (1955).

T. L. McDorman, 'Stateless fishing vessels, international law and the UN high seas fisheries conference', 25 *JMLC* 531–55 (1994).

M. S. McDougal and N. A. Schlei. 'Hydrogen bomb tests in perspective: lawful measures for security', 64 *Yale Law Journal* 648–710 (1955).

D. P. O'Connell, *The International Law of the Sea*, 2 vols (Oxford, Clarendon), 1982, 1984 [*O'Connell*].

J. P. Pancracio, 'L'affaire de *l'Achille Lauro* et le droit international', 31 *AFDI* 221–36 (1985).

N. M. Poulantzas, *The Right of Hot Pursuit in International Law* (Leyden, Sijthoff), 1969.

R. C. Reuland, 'The customary right of hot pursuit onto the high seas: annotations to article 111 of the Law of the Sea Convention', 33 *VJIL* 557–89 (1993).

N. Ronzitti (ed.), *Maritime Terrorism and International Law* (Dordrecht, Nijhoff), 1990.

A. P. Rubin, *Ethics and Authority in International Law* (Cambridge, Cambridge University Press), 1997.

——, *The Law of Piracy* (Newport, Rhode Island, Naval War College), 1988.

I. A. Shearer, 'Problems of jurisdiction and law enforcement against delinquent vessels', 35 *ICLQ* 320–43 (1986).

J. Siddle, 'Anglo-American co-operation in the suppression of drug smuggling', 31 *ICLQ* 726–47 (1982).

G. Starkle, 'Les épaves de navires en haute mer et le droit international: le cas du *Mont Louis*', 18 *Revue belge de droit international* 496–528 (1984–5).

J. D. Stieb, 'Survey of United States jurisdiction over high seas narcotic trafficking', 19 *Georgia J. Int. L.* 119–47 (1989).

J. W. L. Swan, 'An explosive issue in international law: the French nuclear tests', 9 *Melbourne University Law Review* 296–306 (1973–4).

T. Treves, 'Intervention en haute mer et navires étrangers', 41 *AFDI* 651–75 (1995).

Y. van der Mensbrugghe, 'Le pouvoir de police et des états en haute mer', 11 *Revue belge de droit international* 58–102 (1975).

A. van Swanenberg, 'Interference with ships on the high seas', 10 *ICLQ* 785–817 (1961).

United Nations, *The Law of the Sea: Navigation on the High Seas – Legislative History of Part VII, Section 1 of the UN Convention on the Law of the Sea* (New York, United Nations), 1989.

J. H. W. Verzijl, *International Law in Historical Perspective*, Vol. IV (Leyden, Sijthoff) 1971.

J. C. Woodliffe, 'The demise of unauthorised broadcasting from ships in international waters', 1 *IJECL* 402–6 (1986).

12

The international sea bed area

Introduction

In 1873 the *Challenger* expedition discovered the presence of potato-sized nodules scattered across large areas of the sea bed, mainly beyond the geological continental shelf at depths of around 3,500 metres. These manganese nodules, as they are known, are composed of high-grade metal ores. Their precise composition varies from site to site, but for those in the sites of main commercial interest, most of which lie in the deep ocean around the Clarion-Clipperton fracture zones in the north central Pacific,[1] it is typically about 26 per cent manganese, 7 per cent iron, 1.3 per cent nickel, 1.1 per cent copper and 0.27 per cent cobalt. Nodule deposits, which form by ill-understood processes of accretion, are estimated to be of the order of many thousands of millions of tons, although much of this is composed of deposits which, because of their low grade or the configuration of the sea bed on which they lie, are not commercially attractive. Nonetheless, there are sufficient recoverable deposits to offer a high level of self-sufficiency in the main minerals derived from them to States capable of exploiting them, with consequent benefits to the balance of payments of those States, and the strategic advantages of lessening dependence upon foreign land-based deposits.

When the commercial exploitation of the nodules was first seriously discussed in the 1960s and 1970s, it was recognised that if unrestricted sea-bed mining were to proceed, the economic advantages to sea-bed mining States would have corresponding disadvantages for land-based exporters of the minerals in question, especially those which are developing States. For example, the Democratic Republic of Congo (formerly Zaire), which produces copper and has about two-thirds of world cobalt reserves, expected a substantial fall in export revenues if sea-bed mining were to begin on a significant scale. Similarly Gabon, which at that time derived a significant part of its export income from manganese,[2] expected adverse economic effects. Nickel production, however

---

[1] The other main location is the deep sea bed in the Indian Ocean.
[2] The position has changed as a result of the development of the Gabonese oil industry.

was (and is)[3] dominated by Canada, Russia, France (through its possession of New Caledonia) and Australia, which are also major consumers of nickel and better able to withstand the impact of sea-bed mining on their economies.

Sea-bed mining is an expensive industry. The recovery of nodules from such great depths presents formidable technical problems.[4] Plans for commercial exploitation that were developed during the 1970s envisaged automated dredge-heads moving slowly across the sea bed, collecting nodules at rates of around 60 tons per hour, and piping them up to the mother ship. Control of the dredge-head is crucial, both in order to avoid submarine obstacles and to ensure that the collection path neither misses nodule deposits nor tracks over previously harvested areas. Anticipating world shortages of copper, nickel and manganese at the end of the century, industries began developing the necessary technology during the 1970s. With investment costs for mining vessels alone then of the order $150–200 million, rising to $0.8–1.5 billion for a full system covering all stages from prospecting to processing and marketing of minerals, companies came together in consortia in order to pool funds and expertise.

At present there are about half a dozen such consortia established by pri-vate companies. The composition of the consortia is somewhat fluid, but they have a substantial participation by United States companies, and British, French, Canadian, Japanese, Belgian, German, Italian and Dutch companies are or have been involved. States, too, have become actively involved in the develop-ment of the capacity to mine the deep sea bed. They include China, through the China Ocean Mineral Research and Development Association (COMRA); India, through its Department of Ocean Development; Russia, through the state enterprise Yuzhmorgeologiya; a consortium of what used to be called socialist States,[5] through the joint venture INTEROCEANMETAL; France and Japan, which were among the very first States to become involved; and the Republic of Korea.

The background to the Law of the Sea Convention provisions

As soon as it was realised that sea-bed mining was a commercial possibility, over thirty years ago, it was recognised that as international law then stood the main benefit of mining would accrue to a handful of developed States. Three different interpretations of the law, as it was at that time, each led to this con-clusion. First, as technology for the exploitation of the sea bed improved, so, under the 'exploitability' criterion for the outer limit of the continental shelf

---

[3] Though the pattern is changing with the discovery of new land-based reserves. Indo-nesia, for instance, has become a prominent supplier.

[4] See the summary of the seminar on developments in deep sea-bed mining technology, held in New York in 1988: 12 *LOSB* 57 (1988).

[5] Bulgaria, Cuba, the Czech Republic, Poland, Russia and Slovakia.

(CSC, art. 1; see chapter eight), it was arguable that the seaward limit of States' continental shelves itself moved into deeper and deeper waters. It was foreseeable that eventually the whole ocean floor would be divided up among coastal States; and, as accidents of geography and colonial history would have it, if the equidistance principle were to be used in delimitation in such circumstances a handful of rich developed States would end up with the lion's share. In the case of the United Kingdom, for instance, possession of the islands off Scotland and of the Falklands Islands would generate an entitlement to vast areas of the bed of the north and south Atlantic.

On a second view of the law, continental shelf limits could not properly be pushed out so far, but must be confined to areas corresponding roughly to the geological shelf. It would then have followed, in the absence of any special rules modifying the principles set out in the 1958 Geneva Conventions, that the abyssal plains of the ocean beds would be subject to the freedoms of the high seas. This view of the law was usually presented as giving to the deep sea bed the status of *res communis*: that is to say, the area and its resources could be used by any State, but no State could gain an exclusive title to any part of the area. Manganese nodules could therefore have been freely taken by any State able to do so, and that State would have had good title to them. This interpretation of the law derived some support from the preparatory work for the 1958 High Seas Convention. The ILC had noted in its final report in 1956 that it put forward no specific provision for the regulation of the exploration and exploitation of the bed of the high seas, considering the question to have insufficient practical importance. It seems, however, that the Commission regarded these activities as subject to the general principle of the freedom of the high seas and that, in so far as the question was considered at all, this view was generally accepted at the 1958 Geneva Conference itself.

The practical result of this second interpretation was not greatly different from that of the first. Here, too, the developed, mainly western, capitalist States, which were best placed to muster the necessary investment and technology, would be the main beneficiaries of sea-bed mining. The same result would have followed from the adoption of the third possible interpretation, under which the deep sea bed would be treated as an area of *res nullius*. On this view, title could have been gained to areas of the sea bed by their occupation through use, so that mining States would have become owners of parcels of the ocean floor and not, as under the previous interpretation, simply of the resources recovered from them (see further chapter eight).

Although the first of these possibilities was considered in the abstract,[6] the second interpretation was regarded by western States as the correct one. In 1974 the American company, Deep Sea Ventures Inc., filed a 'Notice of Discovery

---

[6] See the map reproduced in M. W. Zacher and J. G. McConnell, 'Down to the sea with stakes: the evolving law of the sea and the future of the deep seabed regime', 21 *ODIL* 71–103, at 92–3 (1990).

and Claim of Exclusive Mining Rights, and Request for Diplomatic Protection and Protection of Investment' with the US Department of State.[7] The company sought a promise of diplomatic protection against any attempt to interfere with the exclusive mining rights it claimed in respect of a specified nodule deposit in the Clarion fracture zone of the Pacific. The US State Department replied that it did not grant or recognise exclusive mining rights to the mineral resources of any area of the sea beyond the limits of national jurisdiction, but that pending the outcome of UNCLOS III such mining could proceed as a freedom of the high seas under existing international law.[8] The governments of Canada, the United Kingdom and Australia stated that they did not recognise the claim to exclusive rights, or even to any priority in rights of exploitation of the deposit as a result of publication of Deep Sea Ventures' claim.[9] However, these and other western States repeatedly affirmed that they regarded the actual mining of the sea bed as a permissible exercise of the freedom of the high seas.

While most western States held this view, it was not the view to which the majority of States subscribed. The history of the sea-bed question in the United Nations makes this apparent. The issue was first brought before the General Assembly in 1967 by the Maltese ambassador, Dr Avid Pardo, who proposed that there should be drawn up a 'Declaration and Treaty concerning the reservation exclusively for peaceful purposes of the sea-bed and ocean floor underlying the seas beyond the present limits of national jurisdiction, and the use of their resources in the interests of mankind'. As the title suggests, this proposal was motivated by the desire to secure both the demilitarisation of the sea bed (on which see chapter seventeen) and the prevention of a 'land grab' for sea-bed minerals. Significantly, the proposal was referred to the General Assembly's First (Political) rather than Sixth (Legal) Committee, and its first result was the establishment of a thirty-five-State *ad hoc* committee, replaced in 1968 by the larger and 'permanent' Committee on the Peaceful Uses of the Sea-bed and Ocean Floor beyond the Limits of National Jurisdiction.

From the outset it was clear that most industrialised States, both capitalist and communist, wanted the committee's work to move at a different pace and in a different direction to that sought by most developing States. The former, wishing to build upon the 1958 Conventions, which they considered to be broadly satisfactory, favoured a cautious approach to the question with a view to the eventual enunciation of agreed principles concerning the exploitation of the deep sea bed. The latter preferred more rapid progress towards the establishment not only of agreed principles but also of an international organisation with wide powers to regulate sea-bed mining. The developing States had a sufficient majority to

---

[7] *ND V*, p. 376; 14 *ILM* 51 (1975).

[8] *Ibid.*, p. 390; *ibid.* at 66 (1975).

[9] *Ibid.*, p. 391; and *ibid.* at 67 (Canadian response), 795 (Australian response), 796 (UK response) (1975).

secure the passage, during the 1969 debate on the Sea Bed Committee's report, of General Assembly Resolution 2574,[10] the so-called 'Moratorium Resolution', which declared that:

> pending the establishment of [an international regime including appropriate machinery]
> (a) States and persons, physical or juridical, are bound to refrain from all activities of exploitation of the resources of the area of the sea-bed and ocean floor, and the subsoil thereof, beyond the limits of national jurisdiction;
> (b) No claim to any part of that area or its resources shall be recognised.

Some, especially the Islamic States, asserted that this resolution was binding upon all States in international law. Western States vigorously denied this, and voted against the resolution, which was passed by sixty-two votes to twenty-eight, with twenty-eight abstentions.

Even if unanimous or near-unanimous General Assembly resolutions are regarded as having some quasi-legislative effect, there is no good argument for holding that a resolution passed, as here, by a modest majority vote is binding upon those who voted against it or abstained. It might, however, be argued that those States that voted for the resolution in the belief that they were establishing or declaring a rule of law – that is, States possessing the *opinio juris* necessary for the creation of a rule of customary international law – had bound themselves by the resolution.[11]

Despite continuing disagreement over the kind of regime envisaged for the sea bed, it was possible to produce, in 1970, a 'Declaration of Principles Governing the Sea Bed and Ocean Floor, and the Subsoil Thereof, beyond the Limits of National Jurisdiction', adopted by 108 votes to nil with fourteen abstentions, as General Assembly Resolution 2749.[12] The main reason for its general acceptability was its delphic construction. It solemnly declared, *inter alia*, that:

> (1) The sea bed and ocean floor, and the subsoil thereof, beyond the limits of national jurisdiction (hereinafter referred to as the Area), as well as the resources of the Area, are the common heritage of mankind.
> (2) The Area shall not be subject to appropriation by any means by States or persons, natural or juridical, and no State shall claim or exercise sovereignty or sovereign rights over any part thereof.
> (3) No State or person, natural or juridical, shall claim, exercise or acquire rights with respect to the Area or its resources incompatible with the international regime to be established and the principles of this Declaration.

[10] *ND II*, p. 737; 9 *ILM* 419 (1970).
[11] See the comments of the International Court of Justice on the legal effects of unilateral declarations in the *Nuclear Tests* cases [1974] *ICJ Rep.* 253, at 267–70, and in the Burkina Faso/Mali *Frontier Dispute* case, [1986] *ICJ Rep.* 554, at 573–4.
[12] *ND II*, p. 740; 10 *ILM* 220 (1971).

(4) All activities regarding the exploration and exploitation of the resources of the Area and other related activities shall be governed by the international regime to be established.

The 'Group of 77' developing States (which even at the time of UNCLOS III in fact included around 120 States) regarded this resolution as a binding statement of law rendering unilateral sea-bed mining unlawful. Western States, in accordance with their sound and consistent opinion that voting for United Nations resolutions does not of itself create legal obligations, regarded the resolution as merely a statement of political principle and intent. In any event, Resolution 2749 admitted of a wide range of interpretations, from that supporting open access to sea-bed resources under the freedom of the high seas until such time as the 'international regime' was established,[13] to that supporting a moratorium on unilateral development of sea-bed resources pending the establishment of an international organisation to govern the Area. The resolution bought acceptability at the cost of certainty.

Throughout the proceedings of the Sea Bed Committee and, from 1973 onwards, of Committee I of UNCLOS III, to which the sea-bed question was allocated, the divergence between the views of developed and developing States was evident. The Group of 77 sought the establishment of an international sea-bed authority itself having the power to engage in sea-bed mining, and to control mining by other licensees, who would pay it royalties which, along with its own profits, would be distributed among all States as the 'common heritage of mankind'. The developed States, in contrast, proposed initially that the authority should be established as little more than a registry of national claims to sea-bed mining sites, having few, if any, powers to interfere with the exploitation of the Area by the mining companies. There were divisions within both camps. The group of landlocked and other geographically disadvantaged States (see further, chapter eighteen), for example, which included both developed and developing States, pressed hard for guarantees concerning their representation in the authority and their share in the benefits of sea-bed mining.[14] Similarly those States, from both north and south, which have wide continental shelves opposed the efforts of the geographically disadvantaged States, among others, to establish narrow limits to national sea-bed jurisdiction in order to maximise the area constituting the common heritage of mankind.

These proceedings have inspired a vast and detailed literature,[15] rendering further discussion here otiose. Suffice it to say that there was a steady movement away from the position of the western States and towards that of the Group of 77. In an attempt to address the fears that an international authority having

---

[13] The regime was eventually established in 1994 with the entry into force of the 1982 Convention: see below.
[14] See S. C. Vasciannie, *Land-Locked and Geographically Disadvantaged States in the International Law of the Sea* (Oxford, Clarendon), 1990, chapters 5, 6.
[15] See the bibliography in E. D. Brown, *op. cit.* in 'Further reading', Vol. 3.

extensive regulatory powers would interfere for purely political reasons in mining operations, detailed provisions were drafted confining such discretion as was left to the authority within closely defined limits, and establishing an elaborate system of decision-making in which the interests of various groups of States were carefully balanced.

The result, Part XI of the Law of the Sea Convention and its associated annexes, was an extraordinarily complicated legal regime.[16] It provided for an International Sea Bed Authority with powers to control access to sea-bed mine sites and the recovery of minerals from them. Broadly speaking, the rate of recovery was to be limited so as to ensure that sea-bed minerals did no more than supply a certain proportion (some way over 60 per cent) of the growth in world demand for nickel, and whatever quantities of other metals were recovered along with the nickel.[17] That provision was originally motivated by the desire to protect land-based economies, and it is paradoxical that nickel, which is produced primarily by developed States, was taken as the bench-mark.[18] Levies on miners were to be distributed among States as the 'common heritage of mankind'. The Authority itself was to engage in sea-bed exploitation through its mining arm, the Enterprise. Miners seeking approval for operations in the Area would have been obliged to make an application in respect of two sites of equal value. The Authority would have chosen one for which it would have given approval and would have 'banked' the other, which the Authority would itself have exploited, either through the Enterprise or in association with developing States. The Convention thus envisaged a 'parallel system', in which both the Enterprise and individual States and mining ventures would have exploited the sea bed side-by-side. The Authority would have had the power to compel the transfer to it on fair commercial terms (set, if necessary, by commercial arbitration) of mining technology that it could not obtain on the open market, in order to enable it to engage in sea-bed mining.[19]

---

[16] For a fuller account of the regime as it stood in the original 1982 Convention text, see R.-J. Dupuy and D. Vignes (eds), *A Handbook on the New Law of the Sea* (Dordrecht, Nijhoff), 1991, Vol. 1, chapters 12–16; F. H. Paolillo, 'The institutional arrangements for the international sea-bed and their impact on the evolution of international organizations', 188 *Recueil des cours* 135–338 (1984, Vol. 4).

[17] The nickel ceiling was to be the whole of the increase in world nickel consumption during a five-year period ending in the year before the earliest commercial production under the Convention, plus 60 per cent of the increase during the period between the year before the earliest commercial production and the year for which authorisation was sought. Provision was made for a minimum rate of deemed growth (LOSC, art. 151(4)).

[18] The shortcomings of the 'nickel ceiling' were clearly illustrated by the falls in demand for metals in the 1970s and 1980s, and by the fact that when demand for nickel increased markedly in the 1990s nickel prices nonetheless fell sharply.

[19] The principle of compulsory transfer of technology was a major obstacle to acceptance of the regime by the United States, although it is hard to distinguish the principle from the practice of compulsory patent licensing, for which provision is commonly made in patent laws.

Resolutions I and II: preparatory investment protection

One of the major obstacles to the acceptance of these provisions by the United States and certain other industrialised States was the lack of protection said to exist for the very substantial investments which had already taken place in sea-bed mining prior to the adoption of the Convention. Accordingly, in a final effort to find a compromise acceptable to all, the spring 1982 session of UNCLOS III prepared special rules for 'pioneer investors', which amounted to an almost complete rewriting of the Convention's rules on sea-bed mining in their favour. These rules were set out in two Resolutions appended to the Final Act of UNCLOS III. Resolution I provided for the establishment of a Preparatory Commission (known as PrepCom), composed of representatives of States which had signed the Convention. PrepCom was given the task of preparing for the establishment of the International Sea Bed Authority, drafting its rules and procedures, and undertaking studies of the economic problems expected to arise from sea-bed mining. In addition, it was made responsible for the administration of the 'preparatory investment protection' ('PIP') provisions.

The rules designed to accommodate the demands of the mining ventures which had, by 1982, invested heavily in deep-sea-bed mining were set out in Resolution II. A number of mining ventures had been established by this time: Association Française pour l'étude et la recherche des nodules (AFERNOD) (France); Deep Ocean Resources Development Company (DORD) (Japan); the Kennecott consortium (USA, UK, Canada, Japan); Ocean Mining Associates (OMA) (USA, Belgium, Italy); Ocean Management Inc. (OMI) (Canada, USA, Federal Republic of Germany, Japan); and Ocean Minerals Company (USA, Netherlands). They were joined by the Indian Department of Ocean Development, and the Soviet state enterprise, Yuzhmorgeologiya.

Resolution II allowed for eight 'pioneer investors'. Four were to come from the four named pioneer investor States: France (now represented by the Institut Français de Recherche pour l'Exploitation de la Mer (IFREMER), Japan (DORD), India (the Government of the Republic of India) and the USSR (Yuzhmorgeologiya).[20] The other four were to be multinational consortia composed of companies from Belgium, Canada, the Federal Republic of Germany, Italy, Japan, the Netherlands, the UK and the USA,[21] and possibly others from developing States,[22] to be given 'pioneer status'. Each investor was required to be certified by its sponsoring State to have invested at least $30 million in preparation for sea-bed mining, of which at least ten per cent must have been invested in a specific site.

The provisions of Resolution II, which were themselves subsequently much modified by the 1994 Implementation Agreement,[23] were complex. They obliged certifying States to detail two sites, each of up to 150,000 square kilometres,

---

[20] Paragraph 1(a)(i).
[21] Paragraph 1(a)(ii).
[22] Paragraph 1(a)(iii).
[23] The current position is described below.

having resolved between themselves any competing or overlapping claims. One site was to be allocated by PrepCom to the pioneer, and the other banked for eventual use by the International Sea Bed Authority. In their sites, pioneers were to have immediate and exclusive rights to conduct exploratory activities short of commercial production. Pioneers were obliged to submit plans of work to the Authority as soon as the Convention entered into force.[24] The national States of all companies involved in the pioneer consortia had to have become parties to the Convention by that stage: if they had not, the companies concerned had to change their nationality if they were not to lose their pioneer status. Pioneers had also to apply for production authorisation, which meant that no actual commercial mining could take place until the Convention entered into force. Pioneers were to have priority, within the nickel-related production ceiling, over all other applicants, apart from the Enterprise. No other miners could be given production authorisations until the pioneers had, perhaps only after several years during which the production ceiling would have risen, had all their demands for authorisation met.

In return for this preferential treatment pioneers were obliged to pay an initial fee of $250,000 and an annual fixed fee of $1 million (and the production levy when they began production), to maintain investment in their site at levels to be prescribed by PrepCom, and to undertake to perform the obligations concerning technology transfer. And in order to advance the progress of the Authority's involvement in sea-bed mining, each pioneer could be obliged by the Authority to explore one of the 'banked' sites reserved to the Authority, on a cost-plus-ten-per-cent basis, and also to train designated personnel. Certifying States were, in addition, obliged to ensure that the Enterprise was provided with the funds necessary to begin operations when the Convention entered into force.

The main consideration for this privileged treatment of pioneer investors was intended to be the adherence of the western mining States to the Law of the Sea Convention regime. It was hoped, when the final components of this elaborate regime were put in place during the closing sessions of UNCLOS III, that the Part XI regime, coupled with the Resolutions, would be seen as a careful and reasonable compromise which could be accepted by all States. Part XI came very close indeed to achieving that aim. But the *zeitgeist* was against it. Conservative, free-market governments in a number of western States, including the United States and the United Kingdom, considered that the text still allowed an unacceptable degree of interference with intellectual property rights and the activities of mining companies by an unnecessarily complex, cumbersome and expensive international organisation.[25] The compromise was rejected by these States, though accepted by many other western States.

---

[24] In fact, they were allowed thirty-six months after its entry into force to make the application: 1994 IA, Annex, Section 1, paragraph 6.
[25] The full complexity of the system can only be fully appreciated by reading through the provisions of Part XI, Annexes III and IV, and the two Resolutions. No sketch can do its baroque architecture justice.

The Reciprocating States Regime

Multilateral agreements commonly take five to ten years to attract enough ratifications to enter into force, and there was no reason to suppose that this would not be true of the Law of the Sea Convention. Faced with this possible delay, during which domestic industries which had already invested hundreds of millions of dollars in preparations for sea-bed mining could get no direct return on their investments, a number of western States decided to set up an interim regime to permit and regulate mining before the Convention entered into force. And of course the States which remained so dissatisfied with the Part XI provisions that they were unlikely ever to ratify the 1982 Convention as it then stood had an even more pressing need to establish a workable legal regime for deep-sea-bed mining.

These 'Like-minded States' established the 'Reciprocating States Regime' in which each State adopted similar national legislation, which interlocked so as to provide for comprehensive regulation of sea-bed mining. The United States led the way with its Deep Sea Bed Hard Mineral Resources Act of 1980, followed by the Federal Republic of Germany's Act on the Interim Regulation of Deep Sea Bed Mining in the same year. In 1981 Britain, with its Deep Sea Mining (Temporary Provisions) Act, and France followed suit, as did Japan in 1982 and Italy in 1985.[26] The Soviet Union also adopted, in 1982, legislation very similar in many respects to that of the western States.[27]

The Reciprocating States Regime was sometimes known as the 'mini-treaty' regime, and although there was originally no published treaty underlying it, an Agreement concerning Interim Arrangements relating to Polymetallic Nodules of the Deep Sea Bed, made between France, the Federal Republic of Germany, the United Kingdom and the United States, was published in September 1982.[28] That agreement provided for consultations in order to avoid overlapping claims being made under the national laws of the parties, and made provision for arbitration in case of disputes and for consultation between the parties before any of them entered into any other international arrangements with respect to deep-sea-bed operations. However, the agreement was not concerned with the substantive rules governing sea-bed exploitation. In this respect, the Reciprocating States Regime depended entirely upon the provisions of the national laws, all of which followed the same basic pattern.

Under each national law, citizens of, and companies incorporated in, the State concerned were prohibited from engaging in exploration or exploitation of

---

[26] For the position of other States whose companies participated in the consortia, see T. Treves (ed.), *The Law of the Sea: The European Union and its Member States* (The Hague, Kluwer), 1997, pp. 69 (Belgium), 397 (Netherlands).

[27] The legislation has been reproduced as follows: Federal Republic of Germany, 20 *ILM* 393 (1981), 21 *ILM* 832 (1982); France, 21 *ILM* 808 (1982); UK, 20 *ILM* 1219 (1981); USA, 19 *ILM* 1003 (1980), 20 *ILM* 1228 (1981), 21 *ILM* 867 (1982); USSR, 21 *ILM* 551 (1982); Japan, 22 *ILM* 102 (1983); Italy, 24 *ILM* 983 (1985).

[28] 21 *ILM* 950 (1982).

deep-sea-bed resources unless they were licensed by that State or by one of the other reciprocating States. Equally, such citizens and companies were prohibited from interfering with the licensed operations of others. Detailed regulations and licence terms governed the conduct of activities in the area, and dealt with matters such as the prevention of pollution, the safety of employees, and the orderly development of the nodule 'mine'. Licensees were obliged to pay a levy, which would be transferred to the International Sea Bed Authority if and when the Law of the Sea Convention entered into force for them: otherwise the funds would be distributed as the State saw fit, although the German law required their use for development aid purposes.

These laws differed from the Law of the Sea Convention regime in important respects. The levy was only about half that envisaged in the Convention, and no provision was made for the 'banking' of reserved sites for eventual use by the Enterprise or developing States. Nor was there any requirement concerning the transfer of technology. The reciprocating States emphasised, however, that this legislation was interim, and would apply only pending the entry into force for them of the Law of the Sea Convention; and each law allowed the modification of licence terms so as to bring them into line with that Convention.

The Reciprocating States Regime was faced with the problem of overlaps between the sites claimed by the consortia. Efforts to resolve this problem resulted in the conclusion in August 1983 of a Draft Memorandum of Understanding on the Settlement of Conflicting Claims with Respect to Seabed Areas,[29] and in August 1984 of a Provisional Understanding Regarding Deep Seabed Matters (the cautious terminology reflected the insistence of the parties that the Regime was a purely interim scheme) to which Belgium, France, the Federal Republic of Germany, Italy, Japan, the Netherlands, the United Kingdom and the United States were parties.[30] The 1984 Provisional Understanding laid down procedures for avoiding overlapping licences, the consortia having entered in 1983 into voluntary agreements for resolving overlapping claims. It also provided a framework for the harmonisation of national laws and procedures regulating sea-bed mining.[31] On 14 August 1987 the so-called 'Midnight Agreement' eliminated overlaps between the claims of the Reciprocating States and of the then Soviet Union, clearing the way for the registration of the pioneer investors by PrepCom.[32]

The Reciprocating States regarded their legislation as an exercise of the undoubted right of States to regulate the activities of their nationals on the high seas. Between these States, and their nationals, the legislation was effective

---

[29] See 3 *LOSB* 37 (1984).

[30] See 4 *LOSB* 101 (1985); 23 *ILM* 1365 (1984).

[31] For full details and texts see E. D. Brown, *op. cit.* in 'Further reading'. See also E. D. Brown, '"Neither necessary nor prudent at this stage": the regime of seabed mining and its impact on the universality of the UN Convention on the Law of the Sea', 17 *Marine Policy* 81–107 (1993).

[32] See 26 *ILM* 1502 (1987), 11 *LOSB* 29 (1988). See also the agreements with China (1991 *UKTS* 52) and with the eastern European States (1995 *UKTS* 4, 5).

in awarding and protecting exclusive rights of exploration and exploitation of deep-sea-bed sites. But, while the Reciprocating States would claim that sea-bed miners were entitled to 'reasonable regard' from other users of the high seas of any nationality (see chapter eleven), so that there should be no wilful interference with mining vessels, their laws did not – and, in so far as they were based on the freedom of the high seas, could not – create exclusive rights over sea-bed sites enforceable against other States outside the Reciprocating States Regime. There was nothing to stop any other State, or the Authority, issuing licences overlapping with those issued by the Reciprocating States; nor could nationals of other States be prevented from exploiting parts of licensed sites, as long as they did not 'unreasonably' interfere with mining by the licensee or any other operators.[33] In short, third States would, in theory, retain much the same rights to exploit the sea bed, licensed areas included, as they would to share in the exploitation of unregulated high-seas fisheries.

This is not how the Group of 77 saw the position. In their view the unilateral legislation and any mining under it contravened customary international law, as evidenced in the Declaration of Principles governing the Sea Bed and other United Nations resolutions. These, and other declarations adopted at various international conferences, were seen as having constituted a rule of customary international law establishing that the deep sea bed is not subject to the legal regime of the high seas and prohibiting the appropriation and the exploitation of deep-sea-bed resources except under the regime contained in the Law of the Sea Convention. PrepCom endorsed this view. It criticised the Reciprocating States Regime strongly. In its view the recognition under that regime of 'non-Convention' licences was tantamount to a recognition of dispositions of parts of the Area, incompatible with article 137 of the Convention and with customary law. A PrepCom resolution of 30 August 1985 affirmed that the Convention regime is 'the only regime' for sea-bed mining, and rejected all other claims, agreements and actions regarding the Area and its resources as being incompatible with the Convention and its related Resolutions and 'wholly illegal'.[34]

That view had some force. Although customary international law is usually created by State practice coupled with *opinio juris*, it is difficult to see what 'practice' there can be in the case of a prohibitive rule. The alleged rule concerning the deep sea bed stipulated precisely that there should be *no* practice of sea-bed mining. Since customary law is quite clearly capable of including prohibitive rules, such as that alleged to prohibit unilateral sea-bed mining, abstract declarations of the law must be sufficient to generate such rules. There seems to be no good reason for denying that a series of resolutions, inside and outside the United Nations, which purported to declare the unlawfulness of unilateral legislation

---

[33] It is an interesting question whether commercial exploitation by a third-State national of a designated site of known commercial value licensed to another operator could ever be said to be a 'reasonable' exercise of a high-seas freedom.

[34] See 6 *LOSB* 74, 85–6 (1985). The statement was reiterated in 1986: 8 *LOSB* 36 (1986).

could have this effect.[35] But even if a rule had been established in this way, it would not necessarily follow that it had become binding upon all States. Those which had persistently objected to such a rule throughout the period of its emergence would not have been bound by it – as we saw, for example, when the application of the alleged 'ten-mile rule' on bay closing lines to Norway was discussed in chapter one. The Reciprocating States had persistently objected to the view that international law prohibited unilateral mining, and so could not have been bound by any such rule. To meet this objection, the Group of 77 argued that the rule in question was a rule of *jus cogens*, a peremptory norm of international law which is universally binding and does not permit 'opting out'. The Reciprocating States, for their part, did not accept that the sea-bed rules belong to that highly controversial category.

Even if a rule had been shown to be binding upon the Reciprocating States, they would have argued that their legislation did not violate it. It is arguable that the 1970 Declaration of Principles could be read so as to permit unilateral mining pending the entry into force of the Law of the Sea Convention, although the Group of 77 regarded licensing as tantamount to an assertion of sovereignty over the Area incompatible with the principle of the 'common heritage'. The unilateral legislation does not, however, seem capable of reconciliation with the terms of some of the other declarations.

This legal dispute was intractable, both positions being defensible, and both sincerely and tenaciously held. The Group of 77 at one stage suggested that the matter be referred to the International Court of Justice, which could have given an Advisory Opinion at the request of the United Nations General Assembly. The outcome of such a reference would have been unpredictable, and much would have depended upon the exact questions posed. Asked if the unilateral legislation was consistent with the various declarations on the deep sea bed, the Court would probably have had to say, no. But asked if those declarations bound, in law, the reciprocating States not to enact and operate such legislation the Court would probably have again to have answered, no.

In the event, no reference was made to the International Court, and during the 1980s the international community moved along parallel tracks. The Reciprocating States held in place their unilateral laws; and in March 1983 PrepCom began work on the implementation of the LOSC regime.[36]

---

[35] Cf. the prohibition on the acquisition of sovereignty over the moon and other celestial bodies: B. Cheng, 'United Nations resolutions on outer space: "instant" customary law?', 5 *Indian Journal of International Law* 23–48 (1965).

[36] See the report of the first PrepCom session, which describes the Statement of Understanding concerning the manner in which PrepCom was to operate: 3 *LOSB* 28, 31 (1984). PrepCom established four Special Commissions: I, on the problems that could be encountered by developing land-based producer States likely to be most seriously affected by the production of minerals derived from the Area; II, on the Enterprise, for the adoption of all measures necessary for the early entry into effective operation of the Enterprise; III, for the preparation of rules, regulations and procedures for the exploration and exploitation of the Area; and IV, to prepare recommendations regarding practical

PrepCom, the LOSC regime and the 1994 Implementation Agreement

PrepCom soon had to address practical problems in the implementation of Resolution II. In February 1986 the four States that had by then made applications for registration of pioneer investors – France, India, Japan and the USSR – concluded the Arusha Understanding. This Understanding dealt with (but did not entirely resolve) overlaps between the French, Japanese and Soviet claims in the Pacific: there was no overlap with an Indian claim in the Indian Ocean.[37] The distribution of the sites was such that the applicants found it difficult to conform with the obligation to indicate two sites of equal commercial value, from which the Authority would bank one. The applicants sought various concessions from PrepCom, and after extensive and delicate consultations PrepCom unanimously adopted an Understanding on new procedures and mechanisms (the 'New York Understanding') in September 1986.[38]

The New York Understanding made significant 'adjustments' to the Convention rules on sea-bed mining. For example, the time limit within which the $30 million investment had to be made in order to qualify as a pioneer investor, originally 1 January 1983 for the consortia and 1 January 1985 for developing States, was extended by the New York Understanding in the case of developing States (and, in addition, for the eastern European States, which were given the right to apply for one pioneer area) up to the date of entry into force of the Convention: and the provisions concerning the nomination of two sites to the Authority, one of which would be licensed and the other 'banked', were modified so as to give pioneer investors the right to specify a part of the sea bed 'that shall form part of the total area to be allocated to it'. The New York Understanding also provided that the four pioneer investors (the mining ventures of France, India, Japan and the then USSR) would assist PrepCom and the Authority in exploring a mine site for the first operation of the Enterprise.[39] Other potential applicants for pioneer status were to be offered the same terms as the first four pioneer investors; and investors from China, South Korea and a group of eastern European States were subsequently registered.

Perhaps surprisingly, given the focus on western mining companies pursuing the riches of the Clarion-Clipperton zone, the first pioneer investor to be registered was India, whose application in respect of a 150,000 square kilometre site in the south-central Indian Ocean basin was approved in the summer of 1987.[40]

---

arrangements for the establishment of the International Tribunal for the Law of the Sea: 3 *LOSB* 33 (1984).

[37] See 8 *LOSB* 35 (1986), and 10 *LOSB* 115–17 (1987). For notes on the applications see 3 *LOSB* 35 (1984) and 4 *LOSB* 102 (1985).

[38] 8 *LOSB* 38–9 (1986). It is not clear what legal authority PrepCom had to make these changes.

[39] The text of the New York Understanding appears at 8 *LOSB* 48 (1986). See also 8 *LOSB* 38 (1986) and 10 *LOSB* 115 (1987) for background information.

[40] 10 *LOSB* 121 (1987).

France, Japan and the USSR were not registered until later that year, after the 'Midnight Agreement' had resolved the last conflicts between their claims.[41] Three years later, and after some difficult negotiations, PrepCom adopted the Understanding on the Fulfilment of Obligations by the Registered Pioneer Investors and their Certifying States.[42] This again made pragmatic adjustments to the Convention rules, such as the waiver of the $1 million per annum fee payable by the pioneer investors in return for their participation in agreed training programmes and the exploration of an 'Authority' site. Similar terms were available to any other pioneer investors.

It was hoped that the accommodations to the exigencies of commercial life made by PrepCom might achieve the original purpose of the pioneer investor regime by producing a sea-bed mining regime sufficiently attractive to induce the Federal Republic of Germany, the United Kingdom and the United States to accede to the Convention. They did not have that effect. Efforts to secure universal agreement on an international regime for deep-sea-bed mining were not, however, abandoned. The decline in world metal markets in the 1980s, which rendered sea-bed mining commercially unattractive, averted the head-on clash which would almost certainly have arisen between the LOSC regime and the Reciprocating States Regime had sea-bed mining begun. The fall of Communist regimes in several east European States and the collapse of their economies gave added credibility to claims that the free-market approach to sea-bed mining was the most practical. States had the opportunity to reconsider their positions.

The States which had felt unable to accept Part XI were willing – or even keen – to accept the rest of the 1982 Convention. There was some genuine regret at their inability to ratify the Convention, both on their own part and on the part of other States,[43] which hoped that the LOSC would establish a truly universal public order for the oceans. At the same time, the States which had succeeded in their demands for a powerful international authority and regime to regulate sea-bed mining became increasingly concerned by the financial implications, as the number of ratifications of the Convention approached the number (sixty) needed to bring the Convention and the sea-bed regime into force. In the absence of major budget contributors such as the United States, Germany and the United Kingdom, either other, poorer States would have to pick up the bill for the Authority, or the Authority would be obliged to scale down its operations dramatically. States of various political and economic complexions therefore continued to search for a compromise, and informal negotiations were launched in 1990 under the auspices of the UN Secretary General.

---

[41] 12 *LOSB* 37 (1988). The certificates of registration as pioneer investors, which identify the registered sites, are reproduced in 12 *LOSB* 39–46 (1988). See also the *LOSB* Special Issues II (1988) and III (1991).
[42] The text is reproduced at 17 *LOSB* 31 (1991). See 17 *LOSB* 25 (1991) for background.
[43] See, e.g., the Group of 77 statement made at the 1989 PrepCom session: 15 *LOSB* 55 (1990).

By August 1993 the outlines of a possible compromise were emerging. A group of representatives of developed and developing States circulated a consultation paper, known as the 'Boat Paper', which formed the focus of the ensuing discussions. The following year agreement was reached. On 28 July 1994 the Agreement Relating to the Implementation of Part XI of the United Nations Convention on the Law of the Sea of 10 December 1982 (the '1994 IA') was adopted by 121 votes to none with seven abstentions.[44] That extraordinary Agreement[45] made substantial modifications to the manner in which the 'Part XI regime' would operate. Broadly speaking, those modifications sought to meet the objections to Part XI made by the major western States, and to provide a mechanism by which both 'latecomers' and States that had already ratified the original 1982 Convention could quickly integrate themselves into a single legal regime. They simplified the structure of the Authority, adopting an 'evolutionary approach'[46] to its structure, according to which the Authority begins life as a small, cost-effective and relatively simple organisation[47] but may develop in response to changing circumstances. They also provided greater safeguards for the interests of the sea-bed mining community. The 1994 Implementation Agreement is a very imaginative solution to a difficult problem, which demonstrates the flexibility of international law at its best. The Agreement was a considerable success. As we noted in chapter one, many States that had not ratified the 1982 Convention ratified the 1994 Agreement and at the same time became parties to the 1982 Convention as well.[48]

The international law of the deep sea bed has a complexity which readers could be forgiven for thinking is out of proportion to its current practical importance. Given the purpose of this book, and the plethora of detailed treatments of the subject, we will do no more than outline the regime as it stands at present under the 1982 Convention as modified by the 1994 Implementation Agreement.

Principles of the Law of the Sea Convention regime

The regime governs all activities connected with exploration and exploitation of mineral resources in the Area (LOSC, art. 134(2)). The latter is defined as the 'sea bed and ocean floor and subsoil thereof beyond national jurisdiction' (LOSC, art. 1). It was explained in chapter eight that 'national jurisdiction' for

---

[44] 33 *ILM* 1309 (1994). The States abstaining were Colombia, Nicaragua, Panama, Peru, the Russian Federation, Thailand and Venezuela.

[45] As was noted in chapter one, the Agreement gives rise to many complex questions of treaty law, modifying as it does the effect of the LOSC in a manner clearly not envisaged by LOSC arts 310–14, and purporting to prevail over the LOSC (1994 IA, art. 2).

[46] 1994 IA, Annex, Section 1, paragraphs 2, 3.

[47] It began life with a budget of about $4.25 million, which provided for a staff of 44. PrepCom was formally wound up in 1994 when the ISA began work.

[48] 1994 IA, art. 4(2).

these purposes extends, broadly speaking, to the outer edge of the continental margin, or to a distance of 200 miles from the baseline where the margin does not extend up to that distance. Both the Area itself, which comprises about sixty per cent of the whole sea bed, and its resources (limited by article 133 to mineral resources)[49] are the 'common heritage of mankind'. As such they are not susceptible of unilateral national appropriation. Rights in the Area and to its resources can be obtained only in accordance with the provisions of the Convention, which is to say, only with the authorisation of the International Sea Bed Authority established by the 1982 Convention (LOSC, arts 136, 137).

All activities in the Area, which in principle may be conducted both by the Authority itself through its mining arm, the 'Enterprise', and by commercial operators, are to be carried out for the benefit of mankind as a whole, taking into particular consideration the interests of developing States and peoples who have not attained self-governing status (LOSC, art. 140). Furthermore, since the superjacent waters and air space remain high seas, reasonable regard must be had to other legitimate uses of those waters and of the Area itself (LOSC, art. 147). A succinct (if ungrammatical) account of the core of the regime can be found in article 155(2), which states that any revision of Part XI

> shall ensure the maintenance of the principle of the common heritage of mankind, the international régime designed to ensure equitable exploitation of the resources of the Area for the benefit of all countries, especially the developing States, and an Authority to organize, conduct and control activities in the Area. It shall also ensure the maintenance of the principles laid down in this Part with regard to the exclusion of claims or exercise of sovereignty over any part of the Area, the rights of States and their general conduct in relation to the Area, and their participation in activities in the Area in conformity with this Convention, the prevention of monopolization of activities in the Area, the use of the Area exclusively for peaceful purposes, economic aspects of activities in the Area, marine scientific research, transfer of technology, protection of the marine environment, protection of human life, rights of coastal States, the legal status of the waters superjacent to the Area and that of the air space above those waters and accommodation between activities in the Area and other activities in the marine environment.

These, and other general principles (LOSC, arts 138–49), are elaborated upon in the Convention and the 1994 Implementation Agreement.

The International Sea Bed Authority[50]

It would be wrong to say that the Area is 'governed' by the Authority, because many uses of the Area, such as pipeline and cable laying and scientific research

---

[49] Living resources and other non-mineral resources (e.g., thermal energy) remain subject to the regime of the high seas.

[50] Documents concerning the Authority, and lists of current members of its various organs, are set out on its web site: http://www.isa.org.jm.

unconnected with the exploitation of sea-bed resources, may be carried out without the need for the Authority's permission (LOSC, arts 112, 143, 256). But the Authority is the body through which States Parties are to organise and control all activities concerned with sea-bed minerals beyond national jurisdiction (LOSC, arts 156, 157; 1994 IA, Annex, Section 1, paragraph 1).

Part XI of the 1982 Convention provides that the Authority has three principal organs: the plenary Assembly, the thirty-six-State Council, and the Secretariat (LOSC, art. 158). The Authority is served by two specialised bodies, the Legal and Technical Commission (LOSC, art. 163) and the Finance Committee (1994 IA, Annex, Section 1, paragraph 4, and Section 9).[51] In addition, there is the Authority's mining arm, the Enterprise. Each component of this system has a particular role to play, but it is the Council that is the most important organ, particularly after the amendments effected by the 1994 Implementation Agreement.

The Assembly

All States Parties to the Convention[52] are *ipso facto* members of the Authority and so, too, of the Assembly, wherein each State has one vote (LOSC arts 156(2), 159; 1994 IA, Annex, Section 1, paragraph 12). The Assembly is said to be 'the supreme organ of the Authority to which the other principal organs shall be accountable', but by depriving it of the power to act alone in crucial areas the 1994 Implementation Agreement has significantly reduced the power of the Assembly, and increased that of the Council, as we explain below when we discuss the decision-making process. The Assembly formally elects members of the Council, the Governing Body of the Enterprise, and other subsidiary organs of the Authority, and is the forum within which Authority decisions are formally adopted on matters such as the budget and sharing of the costs of the Authority, the rules governing sea-bed mining, and the distribution of the economic benefits of sea-bed mining (LOSC art. 160(2); 1994 IA, Annex, Section 7).

The Council

The Council is responsible for the implementation of the Convention regime within the limits set by the Convention and the general policies established by the Authority, and the establishment of the specific policies of the Authority. Its main specific tasks, listed in article 162, include the supervision of the implementation of Part XI of the Convention; the approval of plans of work submitted by sea-bed miners; the making of recommendations on economic assistance to

---

[51] The Legal and Technical Commission has for the time being been given responsibility for performing the functions previously assigned to the Economic Planning Commission, which was envisaged by LOSC article 163 but no longer forms part of the scheme.

[52] And initially also those States provisionally applying the 1994 Implementation Agreement. Provisional membership was due to end in November 1998.

developing countries which suffer serious adverse effects on their export earnings or economies resulting from a reduction in the price of an affected mineral or in the volume of exports of that mineral, to the extent that such reduction is caused by activities in the Area;[53] the recommendation of rules concerning the equitable sharing of economic benefits of sea-bed mining; and the adoption and provisional application (pending Assembly approval) of rules for the Authority.

The Council has thirty-six members. Its membership is carefully designed both to be representative of the main interest groups concerned with sea-bed mining and to establish a broadly equitable geographical distribution of Council members. According to Section 3, paragraph 15 of the Implementation Agreement (which complements LOSC, art. 161), members of the Council are to be elected by the Assembly in the following order:

(a) Four members from among those States Parties which during the last five years for which statistics are available, have either consumed more than 2 per cent in value terms of total world consumption or have had net imports of more than 2 per cent in value terms of total world imports of the commodities produced from the categories of minerals to be derived from the Area, provided that the four members shall include one State from the Eastern European region having the largest economy in that region in terms of gross domestic product and the State, on the date of entry into force of the Convention, having the largest economy in terms of gross domestic product, if such States wish to be represented in this group;

(b) Four members from among the eight States Parties which have made the largest investments in preparation for and in the conduct of activities in the Area, either directly or through their nationals;

(c) Four members from among States Parties which on the basis of production in areas under their jurisdiction, are major net exporters of the categories of minerals to be derived from the Area, including at least two developing States whose exports of such minerals have a substantial bearing upon their economies;

(d) Six members from among developing States Parties, representing special interests. The special interests to be represented shall include those of States with large populations, States which are land-locked or geographically disadvantaged, States which are major importers of the categories of minerals to be derived from the Area, States which are potential producers of such minerals and least developed States;

(e) Eighteen members elected according to the principle of ensuring an equitable geographical distribution of seats in the Council as a whole, provided that each geographical region shall have at least one member elected under this subparagraph. For this purpose, the geographical regions shall be Africa, Asia, Eastern Europe, Latin America and the Caribbean and Western Europe and Others.

It is further provided in Part XI that the numbers of landlocked and geographically disadvantaged States, and of coastal (especially developing) States, on the

---

[53] This provision has been modified by the 1994 IA, Annex, Section 7.

Council should be reasonably proportionate to their representation in the Assembly; and that each of the listed groups of States is to be represented on the Council by the members nominated by that group (LOSC, art. 161(2) and 1994 IA, Annex, Section 3, paragraph 10). Seats for Russia and the USA are guaranteed under the 'largest economy' provisions of sub-paragraph (a).[54] Each of the groups in sub-paragraphs (a), (b) and (c) is referred to as a 'chamber' of the Council; and the developing States members of the groups in sub-paragraphs (d) and (e) together form the fourth 'chamber' of the Council (1994 IA, Annex, Section 3, paragraph 9).[55] The significance of the chambers relates to decision-making in the Council, as will be explained below.

The Secretariat

The Secretariat of the Authority has the responsibility for the administration of the Authority and the maintenance of contacts with other international and non-governmental organisations recognised by ECOSOC whose work is relevant to the Authority (LOSC, arts 166–9). The first Secretary General, Mr Satya N. Nandan (Fiji), was elected in 1996 for four years.

The Legal and Technical Commission

The Legal and Technical Commission has a wide competence, including the supervision (at the request of the Council) of activities in the Area; the making of recommendations to the Council on such matters as the acceptance of applications for sea-bed mining, environmental protection, the establishment of an inspectorate for day-to-day supervision of sea-bed mining, the institution of cases before the Sea Bed Disputes Chamber, and measures to enforce decisions of the Chamber (LOSC, arts 163, 165). In addition, the Commission drafts the rules and regulations of the Authority (LOSC, art. 165). Members of the Commission must be persons with appropriate qualifications, such as

[54] It may be difficult to establish which other States are eligible in which category. Criteria such as the '2 per cent consumption' and 'largest investor' tests are more difficult to apply than might at first appear. The Assembly is responsible for settling the list of States eligible in each category: 1994 IA, Annex, Section 3, paragraph 9.

[55] At the first election the following States were elected: *Group A* Japan, United Kingdom, Russia, USA; *Group B* China, France, Germany, India; *Group C* Australia, Chile, Indonesia, Zambia; *Group D* Cameroon, Nigeria, Bangladesh, Oman, Brazil, Trinidad & Tobago; *Group E* Kenya, Namibia, Senegal, Tunisia, Egypt, South Africa, Sudan, Philippines, Malaysia, Republic of Korea, Argentina, Paraguay, Cuba, Italy, Austria, Netherlands, Ukraine and Poland. States may be eligible for election in a number of categories, and the 'principle of rotation' envisaged in the Implementation Agreement may require a certain amount of shuffling between categories. For example, it is intended that in 1999 the Netherlands should be a Group B member, Poland a Group C member, Sudan a Group D member, and Trinidad & Tobago a Group E member.

economists, mineral resource managers, oceanographers, mining engineers, environmentalists and, of course, lawyers. However, while the Council is to endeavour to ensure that the Commission includes all necessary skills, it is also required to take due account of the need for equitable geographical distribution and the representation of special interests when electing members. According to LOSC, article 163(2), the Commission should have fifteen members, but its size may be increased 'having due regard to economy and efficiency'. In fact, all twenty-two candidates nominated to the Commission were elected in the first election in 1996.[56]

The 1982 Convention originally provided for a second commission, the Economic Planning Commission (LOSC, arts 163, 164). Its task was to advise the Council on economic matters, and in particular to review trends of and factors affecting supply, demand and prices concerning raw materials which might be obtained from the Area. In the 1982 text it was also required to propose to the Council, for submission to the Assembly, a system of compensation for developing countries whose economies were adversely affected by sea-bed mining; but this function has been replaced by the provision of 'economic assistance', rather than compensation, to such States (LOSC, art. 164(2)(d); 1994 IA, Annex, Section 7). In accordance with the 'evolutionary approach' and the desire for efficiency and economy, the functions of the Economic Planning Commission are to be performed by the Legal and Technical Commission until either the Council decides otherwise or the first plan for the exploitation of a deep-sea-bed site is approved by the Authority (1994 IA, Annex, Section 1, paragraph 4).

The Finance Committee

The 1994 Implementation Agreement (Annex, Section 9) established a Finance Committee, for which the 1982 Convention had made no specific provision.[57] As in the case of the other organs, the election of its fifteen members, who must have appropriate financial qualifications, must take due account of the need for equitable geographical distribution and the representation of special interests. Each of the Council groups in sub-paragraphs (a), (b), (c) and (d) (see above under 'The Council') must have at least one member; and until the Authority is able to support itself financially from mining licence income its members must include the five largest contributors to its budget.[58] The Committee is responsible for making recommendations concerning the drafting of the financial rules of the Authority, the Authority's budget and the contributions of Member

---

[56] The first members came from the following States: Bahamas, Cameroon, China, Costa Rica, Côte d'Ivoire, Cuba, Egypt, Fiji, Finland, France, Gabon, Germany, India, Italy, Japan, Namibia, Norway, Poland, Republic of Korea, Russia, Ukraine, USA.

[57] Though LOSC, art. 162(2)(y) contemplates the establishment of such a body.

[58] The first members elected, in 1996, came from the following States: China, France, Germany, India, Italy, Jamaica, Japan, Mexico, Russia, South Africa, Tunisia, Uganda, United Kingdom, Uruguay, USA.

States to it, and the equitable sharing of the economic benefits of sea-bed mining activities.

The Enterprise

In the early days of UNCLOS III it was hoped by many that the mining of the riches of the deep sea bed would be primarily the privilege and responsibility of an international mining corporation, the Enterprise, to be established under the auspices of the Authority. The 1982 Convention provided for the establishment of the Enterprise as a separate organ of the Authority, and empowered it to engage in prospecting and mining the Area, and in the transportation, processing and marketing of the minerals recovered from it. Day-to-day control of its affairs was to be in the hands of the Director General, appointed by the Assembly and responsible to, but not a member of, the fifteen-member Governing Board of the Enterprise. Subject to obligations to comply with the Assembly's general policies and the Council's directives and to report to the Authority, the Enterprise was an autonomous organisation, and so would have stood in much the same relationship to the Authority as would commercial operators. Thus mining by the Enterprise would have been dependent upon authorisation by the Authority, following applications made by the Governing Board. The intention was that the Enterprise would gain the necessary mining technology by buying it from commercial operators, or entering into joint ventures with them. Its 'profits' would then be distributed, as part of the 'common heritage of mankind', by the Authority (LOSC, art. 170 and Annex IV).

That plan has been radically revised in the face of the commercial realities of sea-bed mining. No commercial mining of the Area is likely in the near future, and there is therefore no immediate need to establish the Enterprise. Moreover, the Enterprise is required by the 1994 Implementation Agreement to conduct its initial mining operations through joint ventures, not as an independent mining operator. Accordingly, the Secretariat will perform the functions of the Enterprise until the Council decides that the Enterprise should begin to operate independently of the Secretariat. Those functions are, in the first instance, extremely modest: they include the monitoring of sea-bed mining trends and developments, the assessment of research and prospecting data, and the assessment of approaches to joint-venture arrangements. Sea-bed mining is, conspicuously, not made a priority (1994 IA, Annex, Section 2).

Decision-making in the International Sea Bed Authority

The provisions on the composition of the Authority's organs go some way towards safeguarding the interests of the various constituencies concerned with sea-bed mining. It was, however, thought necessary to provide safeguards for the interests of those who might find themselves in a minority in those organs. The powers of the various organs are therefore closely defined, and a complex decision-making procedure has been established. The Council 'chambers' are given a crucial role in that procedure, which prevents simple majorities in the Authority from overriding the interests of the special groups. Broadly speaking, the more important a decision is for sea-bed mining interests the more it is insulated from simple majority decision-making within the Authority.

The Assembly was initially given 'the power to establish general policies in conformity with the relevant provisions of this Convention on any question or matter within the competence of the Authority' (LOSC, art. 160(1)). That position was, in theory, fundamentally changed by the 1994 Implementation Agreement, which brought the law into line with the political realities of the situation by stipulating that 'the general policies of the Authority shall be established by the Assembly in collaboration with the Council' (Annex, Section 3, paragraph 1). The implication of that is spelled out:

> Decisions of the Assembly on any matter for which the Council also has competence or on any administrative, budgetary or financial matter shall be based on the recommendations of the Council. If the Assembly does not accept the recommendation of the Council on any matter, it shall return the matter to the Council for further consideration. (1994 IA, Annex, Section 3, paragraph 4)

The practical result is that the Council is given the pivotal role in the formation of Authority policy. The Assembly can do no more than refuse to confirm decisions on these matters taken by other organs; and, as we will see, the procedure is designed so that this power cannot be used to frustrate certain key stages of the approval of sea-bed mining operations.

The Implementation Agreement stipulates that 'as a general rule, decision-making in the organs of the Authority should be by consensus' (Annex, Section 3, paragraph 2). Consensus means the absence of formal objection. In cases where a consensus cannot be achieved, the organ may have to fall back on a majority vote.[59] The Assembly, for example, decides questions of substance by a two-thirds majority, and questions of procedure by simple majority, in such circumstances. But the hope, and expectation, is that consensus will be the norm. In order to facilitate the achievement of consensus in the Assembly, two procedural devices were established by the Convention. First, when any matter of substance is first raised, the President of the Assembly may on his own initiative defer a vote on the question for up to five days, and must do so if requested by one-fifth of the members of the Assembly. This allows a 'cooling off' period, during which a compromise may be sought on divisive issues (LOSC, art. 159(9)). The second provision allows one-quarter of the members of the Authority to require the deferral of a vote pending the receipt of an advisory opinion from the Sea Bed Disputes Chamber (on which, see further chapter nineteen) on the conformity with the provisions of the Convention of any action proposed before

---

[59] Subject to the exceptional cases, described below, in which decisions *must* be taken by consensus.

the Assembly (LOSC, art. 159(10)). The intention here is to offer a means of testing the constitutionality of proposed action, rather than challenging an exercise of the Authority's powers after the fact, by which time the challenge may be too late to be effective (LOSC, art. 159(7)–(10)). The consensus principle is, however, quite general: it applies to all Authority organs, including the Council. Votes are not to be taken until all efforts to reach a consensus have been exhausted (1994 IA, Annex, Section 3, paragraphs 3, 5, 6).

Some substantive decisions to be taken by the Council *must* be taken by consensus: they cannot be taken by majority vote. These include the adoption of measures to protect the economies of developing countries from adverse effects of sea-bed mining; recommendations to the Assembly on the sharing of the benefits of sea-bed mining; the adoption of rules concerning sea-bed mining; and the adoption of amendments to Part XI of the Convention.[60] The necessity for proceeding in these four cases by consensus, and the veto power possessed by each State that it implies, creates a danger that the Authority may be unable to act. Accordingly a 'conciliation procedure' was built in to facilitate progress. Within fourteen days of submission of a proposal to the Council, the President of the Council is to determine whether or not any objection will be raised, and if so he has three days within which to establish a nine-man conciliation committee, which he chairs. That committee has fourteen days within which to recommend a proposal which will be adopted by consensus or, if it cannot make such a recommendation, to set out in its report to the Council the grounds on which the proposal is being opposed. This procedure is intended to minimise the risk of dissent flowing from misunderstandings of proposed actions (LOSC, art. 161(8)).

The risk of dissent precluding Council action in the case of the decisions requiring consensus is further reduced by other procedural devices. In the case of decisions on the protection of developing land-based producers and the sharing of benefits, the Council must act on the basis of a recommendation from the Finance Committee (1994 IA, Annex, Section 3, paragraph 7). The Finance Committee is directed as to the principles on which it must base the scheme for assisting land-based producers, so that room for dissent is greatly reduced at this stage (1994 IA, Annex, Section 7). Moreover, the Finance Committee must itself take its decisions by consensus (1994 IA, Annex, Section 9, paragraph 8).[61] The fifteen-person Finance Committee, described above, therefore becomes the crucial element in the decision-making procedure on assistance to land-based producers and sharing of benefits. In the case of mining regulations (known as the 'Mining Code'), it is specifically provided that if the Authority fails to adopt regulations in due time, it 'shall none the less consider and approve' plans of work submitted to it on the basis of such rules as it may have adopted, the norms in the 1982 Convention and 1994 Implementation

---

[60] LOSC, art. 161(8)(d). On the amendment procedure, see also LOSC, arts 312–16.
[61] Questions of procedure are decided by a majority of members present and voting.

Agreement, and the principle of non-discrimination among contractors (1994 IA, Annex, Section 1, paragraph 15).[62] As far as amendments to Part XI are concerned, the 1994 Implementation Agreement disapplied the provisions in article 155 of the Convention, which required a Review Conference to be convened fifteen years after commercial production begins under the LOSC sea-bed mining regime. Instead, the Assembly may undertake a review at any time, but only on the recommendation of the Council, which in turn is bound to maintain the principles set out in article 155(2) and rights acquired under then-existing mining contracts. Here, too, the opportunity for dissent is reduced by constraints upon the freedom of States Parties to effect significant changes in the character of the sea-bed mining regime.

Council decisions on other questions of substance require a two-thirds majority. In addition, it is necessary that the decision be not opposed by a majority in any one of the four chambers into which the members of the Council are divided (1994 IA, Annex, Section 3, paragraph 5).[63] The latter requirement offers added protection to the interests of the major consumers, investors and land-based exporters who, as has been seen, constitute chambers (a) to (c) of the Council. This procedure applies to decisions on matters such as the establishment of specific policies for the Authority; the exercise of control over activities in the Area; the institution of proceedings before the Sea Bed Disputes Chamber for non-compliance with the Authority's rules (see chapter nineteen), and the requesting of advisory opinions from the Sea Bed Disputes Chamber (LOSC, arts 161(8), 162; 1994 IA, Annex, Section 3, paragraphs 5, 8). Council decisions on procedural questions are taken by a simple majority of members present and voting (1994 IA, Annex, Section 3, paragraph 5).

These procedural safeguards were important in winning the confidence of the developed States and assuaging their fears that the developing States, with their large majority in the Assembly, might override the developed States' interests; but their practical importance should not be overstated. As Ambassador Engo, chairman of the First Committee at UNCLOS III, observed, 'neither group is without diversity of concrete interests given the factor of uneven development within each. We should bear in mind the manifold, the divergent interests, and abandon the false assumption of a bipolarized situation'.[64]

Financing the Authority

Up to the end of 1997 the Authority was funded out of the regular UN budget. Thereafter it will be funded by contributions from its members until it is able

---

[62] Draft regulations were proposed by the Legal and Technical Commission in March 1998: see ISBA/4/C/4*, 2 April 1998 (available on the ISA website, http://www.isa.org.jm/).
[63] This provision amends LOSC, art. 161, which previously required two-thirds majorities for some decisions and three-quarters majorities for others.
[64] UNCLOS III, *Official Records*, Vol. VII. Doc. A/Conf.62/C.I/L.20.

to fund itself from 'other sources' – the payments received from deep-sea-bed miners (LOSC, arts 171, 173; 1994 IA, Annex, Section 1, paragraph 14). The Secretary General submits a draft annual budget to the Finance Committee, which then reports to the Council, which passes it on to the Assembly for approval. Contributions are raised from member States in accordance with a scale based on that used for the regular UN budget: given universal membership of the Authority, this would result in the EC and the USA each providing about a quarter of the total contributions. These contributions may be supplemented by borrowing, and by voluntary contributions. The intention is that as sea-bed mining gets under way the Authority should move steadily towards being self-financing. Funding will come from the payments made to the Authority by commercial operators and the Enterprise (LOSC, arts 160(2), 162(2), 171, 172, 174, and Annex IV; 1994 IA, Annex, Sections 1, 2, 8).

The financing of the Enterprise is quite distinct from that of the Authority. It was originally intended that States Parties would provide the funds required for the development by the Enterprise of one mine site, through all stages from exploration to processing and marketing recovered minerals (LOSC, Annex IV, art. 11). Later, the Enterprise would generate its own funds from its mining activities, become self-supporting, and eventually become profitable (LOSC, Annex IV, and arts 170, 173(2)). That plan has been much modified. The 1994 Implementation Agreement stipulates that the obligation to fund one mine site no longer applies: indeed, States Parties are 'under no obligation to finance any of the operations in any mine site of the Enterprise or under its joint-venture arrangements' (Annex, Section 2, paragraph 3). That is one instance of the general principle adopted in the 1994 Agreement, that the Enterprise and commercial miners should stand on an equal footing, neither being subsidised (Annex, Section 2, paragraph 4, and Section 6). The present intention is, therefore, that the Enterprise should become an independent mining operator only when it is able to do so on a self-supporting commercial basis.

The system of exploitation

Attention can now be turned from the institutions to the substantive provisions of the deep-sea-bed mining regime. They are based on the 'parallel system', under which the Area may be exploited both by the Enterprise and by commercial operators.

Prospecting is the first stage of exploitation under this system. Although the term is not defined, it seems to connote general searches for sea-bed resources, rather than the detailed pre-production surveying which appears to be covered by the term 'exploration'. Prospecting is essentially free, requiring only notification to the Authority of the broad areas where it is being carried out and a written undertaking to observe the Convention rules on environmental protection and co-operation in programmes for training personnel from developing

States. Two or more prospectors may be active in the same area simultaneously. No exclusive rights arise from such notification (LOSC, Annex III, art. 2).

Exploration and exploitation, in contrast, require specific authorisation by the Authority, which authorisation carries with it exclusive rights. Qualified applicants may submit plans of work for the approval of the Authority. Applicants are 'qualified' if they are entities possessing the nationality of a State Party (or a State that is provisionally applying the 1994 Implementation Agreement) and effectively controlled by them or by their nationals: if control lies elsewhere, the controlling State or national State of the controllers must co-sponsor the application. In the case of multinational consortia, the national (and controlling) States of all the members must be parties. The applicants must also be sponsored by those States, and meet the qualification standards set out by the Authority. These standards 'shall relate to the financial and technical capabilities of the applicant and his performance under any previous contracts with the Authority', permitting the disqualification of applicants who have broken the terms of previous contracts but precluding discrimination against applicants on national or other grounds. Applicants are also obliged to undertake to comply with the Convention and rules made under it, to accept the control of the Authority over activities in the Area, and to give a written assurance of good faith in fulfilling contractual obligations (LOSC, art. 153, and Annex III, arts 3, 4; 1994 IA, Annex, Section 1, paragraph 12).

Applicants were formerly required to accept the Convention provisions concerning the mandatory transfer of technology. Those provisions were one of the main obstacles to ratification by certain western States, which considered them an unacceptable undermining of the principles of intellectual property ownership. The provisions stipulated that the applicant had to undertake to make available to the Enterprise and developing States wishing to engage in sea-bed mining, on fair and reasonable commercial terms and conditions, any technology which it used in sea-bed activities which it was legally entitled to transfer, if the Enterprise could not obtain such technology or equally efficient and useful technology on reasonable commercial terms on the open market (LOSC art. 188(2), and Annex III, arts 4, 5). Those provisions were disapplied by the 1994 Implementation Agreement, and replaced with a much simpler provision. It amplifies the general exhortation in article 144 of the 1982 Convention to promote technology transfer and obliges contractors and their sponsoring States to co-operate with the Authority in obtaining technology for the Enterprise and developing States 'on fair and reasonable commercial terms and conditions, consistent with the effective protection of intellectual property rights' (1994 IA, Annex, Section 5).

The plans of work submitted by qualified applicants (not by the Enterprise) must specify two sites of equal estimated commercial value which may or may not be contiguous, each large enough to support a mining operation. Data concerning both sites and their resources must also be submitted. The Authority may then approve a plan of work relating to one of the two sites, and enter into a contract with the applicant incorporating that plan. If it does so, it must designate the other site as a 'reserved site'. There is an initial period of fifteen years from the date of the site's 'reservation' (or, if that is later, fifteen years from the time that the Enterprise becomes independent of the Secretariat) during which reserved sites are available only for development by the Authority, acting through the Enterprise or in association with developing States. The Enterprise may choose to exploit such a site at any time during that period, but must decide within a reasonable time whether it wishes to proceed if a developing State announces that it intends to submit a plan of work in respect of that site. Where joint ventures are sought (as they must be by the Enterprise in its early days) the contractor that 'contributed' the reserved area has the right of first refusal to enter the joint venture arrangement (1994 IA, Annex, Section 2, paragraph 2). If the Enterprise does not submit a plan for a reserved site within the fifteen-year period the contractor that contributed the reserved area may submit a plan of work for it, as long as it offers in good faith to include the Enterprise as a joint-venture partner (LOSC, Annex III, arts 8, 9; 1994 IA, Annex, Section 2, paragraph 5).

Applications are to be dealt with by the Authority in order of receipt. To preclude any possibility of the Authority unreasonably impeding development of the sea bed, it is provided that approval of plans can be refused only in certain specified circumstances. These are, first, that all or part of the proposed site falls in a plan already approved, or awaiting final decision, by the Authority; second, that all or part of the proposed area is disapproved by the Authority because substantial evidence indicates the risk of serious harm to the marine environment from activities therein. The third ground is the 'anti-monopoly clause', allowing disapproval where the plan is sponsored by a State which either already holds approved plans for sites which, together with either site in the proposed plan, would amount to more than thirty per cent of the area of a circle of 400,000 square kilometres surrounding the centre of either of those sites, or alternatively has had plans approved for sites whose area exceeds two per cent of the Area, excluding reserved sites and areas disallowed on environmental grounds. Where proposals are submitted by consortia sponsored by several States, areas are computed on a pro rata basis. Even where the anti-monopoly criteria are met, the Authority may still approve the plan if it determines that approval would not in fact permit the State Party or its sponsored entities to monopolise activities in the Area (LOSC, Annex III, art. 6).

In all cases it is the Legal and Technical Commission which first reviews the proposed plan (1994 IA, Annex, Section 1, paragraph 6; LOSC, Annex III). The policies that it is to adopt have been spelled out in the 1994 Implementation Agreement. Deep-sea-bed resources are to be developed in accordance with sound commercial principles; there is to be no subsidisation of sea-bed mining (a provision backed up by the linking of the LOSC regime to the GATT/World Trade Organisation regime and its provisions on subsidies, procurement, and so on);[65] and there must be no discrimination, such as preferential access to markets, between minerals derived from the deep sea bed and those from other sources (1994 IA, Annex, Section 6, paragraphs 1 to 6).

Plans must indicate the maximum mineral production expected, year by year. Under the original 1982 provisions the Authority was required to limit production authorisations to levels that would permit sea-bed minerals to meet a certain proportion of the growth in world nickel demand.[66] That elaborate production ceiling, and the preferential treatment enjoyed by the Enterprise under it, was regarded as objectionable in principle by many western States. It was abandoned in the 1994 Implementation Agreement (Annex, Section 6, paragraph 7): regulation of production is left to the market. One of the chief advantages accorded to pioneer investors – priority in the allocation of production authorisations within the 'nickel ceiling' – has therefore gone. Pioneer investors do, however, benefit from the near-automatic approval of their applications for plans of work for their chosen sites; and that benefit extends under the 1994 Implementation Agreement to any State or entity that has invested over $30 million in deep-sea-bed research and development, at least 10 per cent of which is specific to the site for which approval is sought (1994 IA, Annex, Section 1, paragraph 6(a)).[67]

The applications by pioneer investors were dealt with in 1998. In August 1997 plans of work were submitted by the Government of India; the Institut Français de recherche pour l'exploitation de la mer (IFREMER)/Association Française pour l'étude et la recherche des nodules (AFERNOD) (France); Deep Ocean Resources Development Company (DORD) (Japan); Yuzhmorgeologiya (Russian Federation); China Ocean Mineral Research and Development Association (COMRA) (China); INTEROCEANMETAL Joint Organization (IOM) (Bulgaria, Cuba, Czech Republic, Poland, Russian Federation and Slovakia); and the Government of the Republic of Korea. The applicants were certified to have complied with their obligations under the Convention, including the obligations to put on training programmes for developing State nationals, to submit data on the deep sea bed (collected by the Authority in its POLYDAT database), and to relinquish half of the original site (which reverts to the Area) as required by Resolution II.[68] These conditions being satisfied, according to the 1994 Implementation Agreement the plans of work of these pioneer investors were 'considered to be approved', and the Secretary General of the Authority was requested to issue contracts to the investors (Annex, Section 1, paragraph 6(a)(ii)).[69]

---

[65] 1994 IA, Annex, Section 6, paragraph 1. Sea-bed mining is thus brought within the GATT/WTO dispute settlement procedures, on which see E.-U. Petersmann, *The GATT/WTO Dispute Settlement System* (London, Kluwer), 1997.

[66] See footnote 17 above.

[67] This applies whether or not they had previously registered as pioneer investors.

[68] Paragraph 1(e).

[69] See Docs ISBA/3/C/6, 11 August 1997; ISBA/3/C/7, 22 August 1997; and ISBA/4/A/1/Rev.1, 2 April 1998.

The next generation of miners will apply to the Authority for mining contracts. Again, the applications will be considered by the Legal and Technical
Commission, and if it recommends approval, the plan will be deemed to be
approved unless it is rejected on specified grounds[70] by two-thirds of the Council,
including majorities in each of the four Council 'chambers'. If the Commission
recommends disapproval or makes no recommendation, the Council may nonetheless approve it by a two-thirds majority, including majorities in each of the
chambers (1994 IA, Annex, Section 3, paragraph 11). There is, therefore, a
strong bias in favour of the approval of plans of work.

The financial terms of contracts concluded pursuant to approved plans of work
and production authorisations were very complicated in the 1982 text (LOSC,
Annex III, art. 13), and have been greatly simplified by the 1994 Implementation
Agreement. There is an initial fee of $250,000 payable for the processing of the
plan application. There will also be an annual fee payable by the contractor once
commercial exploitation begins; and the Authority is required to devise a payment system, of which the annual fee is a part, that 'should not be complicated',
sets rates within the range prevailing in respect of land-based mineral recovery
and is 'fair both to the contractors and to the Authority' (1994 IA, Annex,
Section 8, paragraph 1).

Throughout the contract period the Authority will supervise operations, and
may require operators to transfer to it any data necessary for the performance of
its functions. Thus compliance with the terms of plans of work and production
authorisations, to which miners are contractually bound, can be checked, as can
compliance with other regulations concerning, for example, environmental matters and the obligation of operators to establish training schemes for personnel
from the Authority or developing States. In cases of non-compliance the Authority may impose monetary penalties, and, in serious cases, suspend or terminate
the contract, although in all cases the contractor has the right to take the matter
through the dispute settlement procedure (LOSC, arts 186–91, and Annex III,
arts 14–19; see also chapter nineteen). That procedure ensures that rights and
duties provided for in the Convention are enforced. Neither the Authority nor
the contractor has the right to modify the terms of a contract without the other's
consent, although if circumstances arise in which the contract becomes inequitable or the achievement of objectives in the contract or Convention becomes
impracticable or impossible, there is a duty to negotiate an adjustment (LOSC,
Annex III, art. 19).

The common heritage

The 'common heritage' will be exploited for the benefit of 'mankind as a whole',
and not simply of the industrialised States, in a number of ways. The collection

[70] See LOSC, Annex III, art. 6.

and distribution among States – in particular, developing States and peoples – of payments made to the Authority by the commercial operators and perhaps later by the Enterprise is the most obvious. The Convention does not stipulate the manner in which the financial benefits are to be shared out; only that the sharing should be 'equitable' (LOSC, art. 140). Precise rules will be decided upon by the Authority. In fact some States will, in effect, have a preferential claim on the monies. These are the developing States that suffer adverse effects on their export earnings or economies as a result of falls in mineral prices caused by sea-bed mining, for whose benefit the Convention requires the Authority to establish a system of economic assistance (LOSC, art. 151(10); 1994 IA, Annex, Section 7). But it seems clear that the financial benefits of sea-bed exploitation are likely to be modest and not immediate. Commercial mining is still some way off; and the discoveries of substantial new land-based reserves of nickel, copper and cobalt in Canada and elsewhere and of manganese nodules within the coastal waters of Papua New Guinea are likely to postpone even further resort to the complex, expensive technologies for recovering minerals from the abyssal depths. The claims made in the 1960s of unimaginable wealth seem unlikely ever to be realised. Certainly, for the foreseeable future the most concrete dividend from the deep sea bed is likely to be in the form of knowledge and expertise channelled through the databases and training programmes organised by the Authority and the mining companies.

Further reading

D. H. Anderson, 'Resolution and Agreement Relating to the Implementation of Part XI of the UN Convention on the Law of the Sea: a general assessment', 55 *ZAOVR* 275–89 (1995).

E. D. Brown, *Sea-Bed Energy and Mineral Resources and the Law of the Sea*, Vol. 2, *The Area Beyond the Limits of National Jurisdiction* (London, Graham & Trotman), 1986; *ibid.*, Vol. 3, *Tables and Bibiliography* (London, Graham & Trotman), 1986.

E. R. Dixon, 'The Preparatory Commission in the International Seabed Authority', 7 *IJECL* 195–216 (1992).

M. Hayashi, 'Registration of the first group of pioneer investors by the Preparatory Commission for the International Sea-Bed Authority and for the International Tribunal for the Law of the Sea', 20 *ODIL* 1–33 (1989).

T. G. Kronmiller, *The Lawfulness of Deep Seabed Mining*, 2 vols (London, Oceana), 1980.

S. Mahmoudi, *The Law of Deep Sea-bed Mining: A Study of the Progressive Development of International Law Concerning the Management of the Polymetallic Nodules of the Deep Sea-bed* (Stockholm, Almqvist), 1987.

L. D. M. Nelson, 'The new deep sea-bed mining regime', 10 *IJMCL* 189–203 (1995).

M. G. Schmidt, *Common Heritage or Common Burden? The United States Position on the Development of a Regime for Deep Sea-bed Mining in the Law of the Sea Convention* (Oxford, Clarendon Press), 1989.

J. K. Sebenius, *Negotiating the Law of the Sea* (Cambridge, Mass., Harvard University Press), 1984.

United Nations, *The Law of the Sea: Concept of the Common Heritage of Mankind. Legislative History of Articles 131–150 and 311(6) of the United Nations Convention on the Law of the Sea* (New York, United Nations), 1996.

M. W. Zacher and J. G. McConnell, 'Down to the sea with stakes: the evolving law of the sea and the future of the deep seabed regime', 21 *ODIL* 71–103 (1990).

Zeitschrift für ausländisches öffentliches Recht und Völkerrecht, Symposium, The entry into force of the Convention on the Law of the Sea, Vol. 55 (pp. 273–420) (1995).

13

Navigation

Introduction

Along with fishing, navigation is the oldest use of the sea, and it remains one of the most important. While aircraft may have replaced ships as the prime means of conveying people across the oceans, ships are still the most important means of transporting goods on such routes: ninety-five per cent, by weight, of all international trade is seaborne. On the military side, during the Cold War the uneasy balance of terror between the two superpowers was heavily dependent upon the strategic qualities of nuclear submarines, and navies still remain an important element in the strategies of the major military powers (see further chapter seventeen). While almost all coastal States and some landlocked ones have a merchant navy of some description, one of the remarkable features of the international shipping industry is the degree to which ships are concentrated under the flags of relatively few States – although this does not necessarily indicate a similar distribution of ownership, since the beneficial owners of the ships[1] may not be nationals of or resident in the flag States concerned. Table 2 shows the distribution of ships between the major flag States in 1997. It will be seen that the ten leading flag States accounted for 63.4 per cent of world merchant shipping tonnage, and the next ten States for a further 17.2 per cent. Although ships are concentrated under the flags of relatively few States, in recent years the distribution of ships has become slightly less uneven. Thus, in 1978 the leading ten States accounted for no less than 72.9 per cent of all shipping and the leading twenty States for 88.2 per cent, compared with 80.6 per cent in 1997. Moreover the number of States possessing fleets totalling in excess of one million tons has gone up from forty-one in 1978 to forty-seven in 1997. Looking at the distribution of the world fleet among different categories of States, in 1997 the flags of OECD (i.e., developed market economy) States accounted for 26.0 per cent (54.1 per cent in 1978); flags of convenience (a term explained below) for 46.3 per

---

[1] The beneficial owner of a ship is defined by UNCTAD as the person or company which gains the pecuniary benefits from the operation of the ship. See UNCTAD, *Review of Maritime Transport 1978* (New York, United Nations), 1981, p. 11.

Table 2. *Distribution of world merchant shipping tonnage as at 31 December 1997:
leading twenty States ('000 gross tons)*

Panama	91,128		United Kingdom[c]	14,046
Liberia	60,058		Russia	12,282
Bahamas	25,523		USA	11,789
Greece	25,288		Philippines	8,849
Cyprus	23,653		St Vincent	8,374
Malta	22,984		South Korea	7,430
Norway[a]	22,839		Germany	6,950
China[b]	22,110		India	6,934
Singapore	18,875		Turkey	6,567
Japan	18,516		Marshall Islands	6,314
			Other States	101,688
			Total, all States	522,197

Notes

[a] Includes 19.780 million gross tons on the Norwegian International Ship Register.

[b] Includes 5.771 million gross tons registered in Hong Kong, but excludes Taiwan.

[c] Includes 4.759 million gross tons registered in the Isle of Man, 4.610 registered in Bermuda and 1.191 registered in other UK dependent territories.

Source: Lloyd's Register of Shipping, *World Fleet Statistics 1997*, London, 1998, pp. 13–15.

cent (27.3 per cent in 1978); developing States other than flags of convenience, 23.4 per cent (10.6 per cent in 1978); and the former Communist State-trading States of Eastern Europe, 4.3 per cent (8.0 per cent in 1978). Thus the change in the distribution of flag State ownership between 1978 and 1997 has been largely from developed market economy States to flags of convenience and other developing States.

In the rest of this chapter we look at the different rights of navigation enjoyed by ships on the high seas and in the various maritime zones subject to the jurisdiction of the coastal State, and then at the network of international conventions imposing safety standards and regulations which has arisen in order to try to ensure that these navigational rights are exercised in an orderly and safe manner. The need for such standards and regulations has been particularly apparent since the Second World War as a result of a number factors. First, there has been a tremendous increase in the number of ships (total world tonnage increased sixfold between 1948 and 1995), creating serious traffic problems in the busiest waterways. Secondly, the size of ships has increased enormously, with consequent reductions in manoeuvrability: for example, a supertanker travelling at full speed takes several miles to stop. Thirdly, ships now carry more dangerous cargoes, such as oil, liquefied natural gas, toxic chemicals and radioactive matter, thus making the consequences of any accident more serious. Lastly, the economic recession of the 1970s and 1980s led to a decline in shipbuilding, with the result that the average age of ships has increased (the average age in 1995 being 16.4 years): older ships are inherently less seaworthy.

Before we turn to look at navigation rights and safety obligations, we must first consider the question of the nationality of ships. This is necessary because these various rights and obligations, being imposed by international law, cannot be enjoyed by or imposed on ships as such, since ships are not subjects of international law. Instead, ships derive their rights and obligations from the State whose flag they fly and whose nationality they accordingly bear.

Nationality of ships

The ascription of nationality to ships is one of the most important means by which public order is maintained at sea. As well as indicating what rights a ship enjoys and to what obligations it is subject, the nationality of a vessel indicates which State is to exercise flag State jurisdiction over the vessel. Nationality also indicates which State is responsible in international law for the vessel in cases where an act or omission of the vessel is attributable to the State, and which State is entitled to exercise diplomatic protection on behalf of the vessel.

States usually grant their nationality to vessels by means of registration and by authorising vessels to fly their flag. Thus expressions such as 'the State of registration' or the 'flag State' are synonyms for the State whose nationality the vessels bears.[2] In view of the importance of nationality, it is desirable to know whether international law lays down any rules which govern the circumstances in which a State may grant its nationality to a vessel. Originally it seems that States had complete discretion in this matter. In the *Muscat Dhows* case (1905), where France had permitted subjects of the Sultan of Muscat to fly the French flag, the Permanent Court of Arbitration said that 'Generally speaking it belongs to every sovereign to decide to whom he will accord the right to fly his flag and to prescribe the rules covering such grants.'[3] This approach appears at first sight to have been followed in the 1958 Convention on the High Seas. Article 5 began

---

[2] Not all writers accept that the three terms are synonymous: see, for example, Johnson, *op. cit.* in 'Further reading' at the end of the chapter, under 'Nationality of ships'. Other writers have gone further and argued that the concept of nationality is inapplicable to ships and creates unnecessary difficulties: see, for example, R. Pinto, 'Flags of convenience', 87 *Journal du Droit International* 344–69 (1960). *O'Connell, op. cit.* in the section 'Nationality of ships' in 'Further reading', goes in the same direction, arguing that it is difficult to attribute a coherent meaning to the expression 'nationality of a ship': see Vol. II, pp. 750–69, especially at pp. 751–5. On the other hand the High Seas Convention (art. 5(1)), the Law of the Sea Convention (art. 91) and the UN Convention on Conditions for Registration of Ships (discussed below) (art. 4(2)) treat the flag State and State of nationality as synonymous and the last-mentioned convention treats the flag State and State of registration as generally being identical (see, in particular, arts 4 and 11).

[3] 2 *AJIL* 921 (1908) at 924. Cf. the similar approach adopted in the 1930 Hague Convention on Certain Questions relating to the Conflict of Nationality Laws.

by providing that 'Each State shall fix the conditions for the grant of its nationality to ships, for the registration of ships in its territory, and for the right to fly its flag.' However, the article went on to limit the discretion enjoyed by States by providing that:

> There must exist a genuine link between the State and the ship; in particular, the State must effectively exercise its jurisdiction and control in administrative, technical and social matters over ships flying its flag.

In adding this requirement of a 'genuine link' the draftsmen of the Convention (principally the ILC) were strongly influenced by the then recent judgment of the International Court of Justice in the *Nottebohm* case (1955). The decision of the Court in that case was widely interpreted as requiring that where a State claimed to exercise diplomatic protection in respect of one of its nationals in the circumstances there in question, nationality should be the legal reflection of a factual link – a 'genuine link' – between the individual and the State. The introduction of the requirement of a 'genuine link' as far as the nationality of ships is concerned gives rise to the difficulty of knowing what exactly comprises such a link. In its 1955 draft the ILC laid down objective criteria for determining the existence of a genuine link, but in its final draft the Commission felt that it was not practicable to suggest specific criteria. The position therefore remains unclear. Equally, it is uncertain what consequences follow when there is no genuine link between a vessel and the State whose nationality it purports to bear.

In spite of the fact that the Preamble to the High Seas Convention spoke of its provisions as being 'generally declaratory' of established principles of international law, it seems unlikely, in the light of the background to article 5 described above, that the requirement in that article of a 'genuine link' between the vessel and the State purporting to confer its nationality on it represented customary international law. This helps to explain why the requirement of a genuine link has not been widely observed in practice. While a number of States (e.g., Portugal and France) do require a genuine link with the ship, usually expressed in the requirement that all or a fixed proportion of the ship's owners and/or crew must have the nationality of the State concerned, other States require very little or virtually no link. This latter group of States, none of which became a party to the High Seas Convention, is generally known as the 'flag of convenience' or 'open registry' States. These expressions refer to States that permit foreign shipowners having no real connection with those States (in practice such shipowners come mainly from Greece, Japan, United Kingdom, USA, Hong Kong and Norway) to register their ships under the flags of those States. The low fees and taxation levied by such States, together with lower crew costs (which result from low wages and manning levels), and in some cases savings from not having to comply with international safety standards, reduce the shipowner's operating costs and therefore often give him a significant competitive advantage over shipowners whose vessels are not registered under flags of convenience. Flags of convenience, which have been prevalent since the 1950s, include Panama, which has the largest merchant fleet in the world under its flag, Liberia, Cyprus, Bahamas, Malta, St Vincent and the Marshall Islands. These States are often said to be lax in the qualifications required of the crews of their ships, and to be unwilling or unable to exercise effective jurisdiction over their ships in matters of pollution control and shipping safety. Their past record certainly gives some support to this point of view,[4] and some flag of convenience States lack adequate personnel to enforce safety standards on their ships: for example, in 1991 Bahamas had only fifteen full-time surveyors for the 973 ships on its register while Cyprus had nine for 1,350 ships.[5] It must, however, be stressed that substandard ships can be found under most, if not all, flags: they are by no means peculiar to flags of convenience. In fact, the establishment of a genuine link in the case of ships owned by companies, which can be freely incorporated in States other than the State where the majority of shareholders are resident, is difficult to determine. A British ship, for instance, may be owned by a British company, itself a subsidiary of other British companies, members of a corporate group whose ultimate holding company may be registered in another State and whose shareholders are resident in a third State. The distinction between 'convenience' and other flags, based on the existence of a genuine registration, is by no means clear-cut, and is of less practical importance than the question of the vigour with which the flag State exercises its jurisdiction and control over ships after registration.

An opportunity to give the requirement of a genuine link more substance was offered to the International Court of Justice in 1960 in the *Constitution of the Maritime Safety Committee of IMCO* case. There the Court was asked the meaning of the phrase 'the largest ship-owning nations' in article 28(a) of the Convention of IMCO (the Intergovernmental Maritime Consultative Organisation, as the IMO was then known), which at that time required that the eight 'largest ship-owning nations' be elected to the Maritime Safety Committee. The Court held that the concept of the genuine link was irrelevant for determining the meaning of this phrase in the IMCO Convention and that the nations with the largest registered tonnage fell within the terms of the phrase whether or not they were flags of convenience. That the Court refused this opportunity of giving its support to the requirement of a genuine link is understandable in view of the controversy over flags of convenience both within and outside IMCO.

In spite of the fact that the 'genuine link' requirement appears to have had little influence on State practice since the High Seas Convention came into force, the requirement is repeated in the Law of the Sea Convention (art. 91),

---

[4] For example, in the period 1980–3 the four largest flags of convenience accounted for twenty-seven per cent of the world shipping fleet but for thirty-seven per cent of lost tonnage: see *The Guardian*, 5 January 1987. This record continues. In 1994 flags of convenience accounted for 42.9 per cent of the world fleet but 66 per cent of total lost tonnage: see ISL, *Shipping Statistics Yearbook 1995*, Bremen, 1995, p. 51.

[5] *The Guardian*, 16 December 1993. However, in some cases the low number of surveyors may be misleading as some flag States contract out the work of surveying to classification societies.

although the requirement is not linked to the effective exercise of jurisdiction by the flag State, as it was in article 5 of the High Seas Convention. (The effective exercise of flag State jurisdiction is dealt with by article 94, discussed below.) There seems little reason for supposing that article 91 will have any more influence on State practice than article 5 of the High Seas Convention.

In the late 1970s UNCTAD began to deal with the problem of flags of convenience. Following a number of reports by the UNCTAD Secretariat and the labours of various working groups, UNCTAD sponsored a diplomatic conference which met from 1984 to 1986 and which adopted the United Nations Convention on Conditions for Registration of Ships, 1986. The Convention aims to strengthen the link between a ship and its flag State, and to ensure that States effectively exercise jurisdiction and control over their ships, not only in relation to administrative, technical, economic and social matters, but also with regard to the identification and accountability of shipowners and operators who, in the past, have sometimes hidden behind a complex and artificial veil of interconnecting companies. The Convention requires the adoption of laws requiring a clear link with the State, in the form of an appropriate level of participation (a matter on which each State is left with considerable discretion) by its nationals in the ownership or crewing of the ship (arts 8, 9). It further requires the maintenance of a detailed register from which the owners and operators, and a resident agent of the owner, can be readily identified, and the adoption of measures to ensure that the owner or operator can meet financial obligations to third parties (arts 6, 10, 11). In addition, the Convention requires States to maintain a competent and effective maritime administration in order to secure compliance with national and international shipping standards. The Convention would secure some tightening of flag State control over ships if it entered into force, but given that a decade after its adoption it had received only ten of the forty ratifications necessary for its entry into force, and that these ten ratifications accounted for less than one per cent of world shipping when entry into force also requires ratifying States to own not less than twenty-five per cent of world tonnage, it seems that it will be a long time, if ever, before the Convention enters into force. Even if it does, there is no guarantee that flag of convenience States will become parties to it, and indeed there seems little incentive for them to ratify the Convention.

The FAO has also sought to attack the use of flags of convenience in the case of fishing vessels. Concerned at the practice of some fishermen in re-registering their vessels under flags of convenience in order to evade obligations under regional fishery conservation treaties to which their original flag States were parties, the FAO, in the early stages of drafting what eventually became the 1993 Agreement to Promote Compliance with International Conservation and Management Measures by Fishing Vessels on the High Seas (discussed in chapter fourteen), sought to curb this practice by requiring a genuine link (criteria for which were indicated) between the vessel and the flag State. However, it became clear during the negotiations that no agreement would be reached on provisions dealing with the registration of fishing vessels or the allocation of flag, and the proposals for a genuine link requirement were therefore dropped.[6]

Some States have sought to curb the growth of flags of convenience and to discourage their vessels from re-registering under such flags by the adoption of unilateral measures. In the late 1980s Denmark, Germany and Norway set up 'international registers' parallel to their existing national registers. Conditions for being placed on the international register are more relaxed than those of the ordinary register, as are operating conditions (particularly as regards crewing). In effect the international register is a kind of semi-open registry. In the case of Norway this strategy has been particularly effective: the tonnage of vessels flying the Norwegian flag more than doubled between 1987, when the Norwegian International Ship Register was introduced, and 1995, when nearly ninety per cent were on the international register. To the same ends as international registers has been the practice of States such as France, Netherlands and the United Kingdom in using dependent territories instead of the metropolitan territory for registering ships. These developments underline the point made earlier that it is often not easy to say whether the link between a vessel and its flag State is 'genuine'. In addition to the developments just described, the United Kingdom, concerned that the rapid decline in the British fleet (which, excluding that registered in dependent territories, more than halved between 1978 and 1986) might affect its ability to requisition vessels in the event of armed conflict (and no doubt mindful of the considerable number of civilian vessels requisitioned during the Falklands hostilities in 1982), in 1989 signed agreements with two flag of convenience States – Liberia and Vanuatu – whereby in the event of war or other hostilities the latter States would 'waive the exercise of [their] sovereign authority' over British-controlled ships registered in those States where there was in force a 'contract of commitment' between the ship owner and the UK authorities.

Where the link between a vessel and its flag State clearly was not 'genuine', it would of course be open to the courts and other public authorities of other States to do the equivalent of lifting the corporate veil and not recognise the nationality of the ship concerned. Indeed, this was envisaged in the ILC's proposals for what became article 5 of the High Seas Convention. However, courts and other public bodies have traditionally refrained from doing this. Recent practice is a little more equivocal. While the European Court of Justice in two recent cases followed the traditional approach of refusing to look behind the flag of two EC-beneficially owned fishing vessels registered under flags of convenience,[7] the UN Security Council, in Resolution 787 of 1992 providing for the

---

[6] Further on this matter see G. Moore, 'The Food and Agriculture Organisation of the United Nations Compliance Agreement', 10 *IJMCL* 412–25 (1995) at 412–13. For the text of the draft containing the genuine link provision, see 9 *International Organisations and the Law of the Sea. Documentary Yearbook* 639 (1993).

[7] Case C-280/89, *Commission* v. *Ireland*; Case C-286/90, *Anklagemyndigheden* v. *Poulsen*.

enforcement of sanctions against Serbia and Montenegro, stipulated that any vessel in which the majority or controlling interest was held by a person operating from Serbia and Montenegro should be considered a vessel of Serbia and Montenegro for the purposes of implementation of Security Council resolutions, regardless of the flag under which the vessel sailed.[8]

The picture that emerges from the above discussion is of a rather confused situation. While in principle international law requires a genuine link between a vessel and the State whose flag it flies, there is no agreement as to what constitutes such a link. In practice links between a vessel and its flag State are often tenuous, and the authorities of other States are disinclined to challenge such links. To this rather confused situation further complexity has been added by the recent and increasingly widespread practice of bareboat chartering, whereby a vessel registered in one State is chartered to nationals of another State and during the period of the charter the vessel flies the flag of the second State while its registration in the first State is cancelled or suspended. By no means all States permit this practice, however.

So far we have discussed only the right of States to confer their nationality and flag upon ships. The question arises whether ships can sail under the flag of subjects of international law other than States, notably international organisations. In preparing the draft articles which eventually became the High Seas Convention, the ILC rejected the idea of including a provision recognising the right of the UN, and possibly other international organisations, to sail ships exclusively under their own flags, on the ground that the legal system of the flag State applied to a ship authorised to fly its flag and in this context the UN could not be assimilated to a State. Notwithstanding the negative approach of the ILC, the 1958 Geneva Conference inserted an article dealing with the question. Article 7 of the High Seas Convention stated that the provisions of the Convention 'do not prejudice the question of ships employed on the official service of an intergovernmental organisation flying the flag of the organisation'. The exact meaning of this provision is not really clear, but it would seem to leave the question open. In practice, ships have on a few occasions sailed under the flag of the UN (usually flown in conjunction with a national flag but occasionally flown alone): e.g., some of the vessels used in the UN Emergency Force in Egypt 1956–7.[9] Article 93 of the Law of the Sea Convention contains a provision very similar to article

---

[8] S/Res/787 (1992) of 16 November 1992, para. 10.
[9] For details of this and other examples, see UNCLOS I, *Official Records*, Vol. IV, p. 138. It is also of interest to note that in December 1983 the UN Secretary General sought the views of the Security Council on his intention to authorise the flying of the UN flag by ships evacuating members of the Palestine Liberation Organisation from Tripoli. In response the President of the Council confirmed that the Secretary General's proposal had the support of the Council. See *Resolutions and Decisions of the Security Council 1983*, pp. 5–6. For further discussion of the use of the UN flag, see M. H. Nordquist (ed.), *United Nations Convention on the Law of the Sea. A Commentary* (The Hague, Nijhoff), Vol. III, 1995, pp. 132–4.

7 of the High Seas Convention, except that it limits inter-governmental organ-isations to the UN, its specialised agencies and the IAEA. It is difficult to see why the article should be limited in its application to these intergovernmental organisations, when there are other, more developed organisations such as the EC which, since they have embryonic legal systems of their own, would pose fewer legal problems were their flags flown by vessels, and which, furthermore, can become parties to the Law of the Sea Convention. In fact in 1989 the EC Commission made a proposal for a Community ship register and flag, which would operate alongside, rather than instead of, the registers and flags of Member States.[10] However, the Commission withdrew this proposal in 1996, following a lack of support from Member States. It is also worth noting in this context that EC law restricts the discretion of Member States in granting their nationality to vessels.[11]

Finally, it should be noted that a vessel flying two or more flags is regarded as having no nationality (HSC, art. 6; LOSC, art. 92; and see chapter eleven).

Rights of navigation

We have described in earlier chapters the different navigational rights enjoyed by the ships of foreign States in the various zones of coastal States and on the high seas, and here we therefore do no more than briefly recapitulate them. In internal waters foreign vessels normally enjoy no rights of navigation, in the absence of a right given by treaty–for example, a treaty of friendship, commerce and navigation which might confer a right of access to ports, as was explained in chapter three. The major exception to this rule is that in those internal waters which, before their enclosure by straight baselines drawn under article 4 of the Territorial Sea Convention or article 7 of the Law of the Sea Convention, were part of the territorial sea or high seas, the right of innocent passage for foreign vessels is preserved (TSC, art. 5(2); LOSC, art. 8(2)). In the territorial sea itself foreign vessels enjoy the right of innocent passage, the meaning and scope of which were discussed in chapter four, although the coastal State may tempor-arily suspend that right in limited areas where necessary for its security. In straits consisting of territorial sea, this right of innocent passage may not, under the Territorial Sea Convention, be suspended (TSC, art. 16(4)). As we saw in chapter five, some of the existing special treaty regimes for particular straits (e.g. the 1936 Montreux Convention) give foreign vessels greater navigational rights, and the Law of the Sea Convention provides a general regime of transit passage

[10] For details see Churchill, *op. cit.* in 'Further reading' under 'Nationality of ships', pp. 602–5; and B. Helding, 'The Euros flag and related issues', 28 *European Transport Law* 389–404 (1993).

[11] For details see Churchill, *ibid.*, pp. 595–602. See also Case C-334/94, *Commission* v. *France*.

for many international straits (LOSC, arts 37–44). In archipelagic waters, foreign vessels, under the Law of the Sea Convention, enjoy the right of innocent passage: and they also enjoy a more extensive right of archipelagic sea lanes passage in sea lanes designated by the archipelagic State in its archipelagic waters and territorial sea (LOSC, arts 52 and 53; and see chapter six).

Beyond the territorial sea all vessels enjoy, in principle, freedom of navigation under the exclusive jurisdiction of their flag State. This freedom is, however, subject to a number of limitations. In a coastal State's contiguous zone it is subject to the right of the coastal State to exercise the control necessary to prevent and punish infringements of its customs, fiscal, immigration or sanitary regulations committed within its territory or territorial sea (TSC, art. 24; LOSC, art. 33, and see chapter seven). In the exclusive economic zone, freedom of navigation is subject to the coastal State's jurisdiction relating to pollution and resource control (see chapter nine); and in both the exclusive economic zone and in waters over the continental shelf it is subject to the obligation to 'respect' safety zones around artificial islands and installations. However, the coastal State is under a duty not to erect artificial islands and installations 'where interference may be caused to the use of recognised sea lanes essential to international navigation' (CSC, art. 5(3) and (6); LOSC, arts 60(6) and (7), 80). On the high seas the freedom of navigation is subject to the general obligation to have 'due regard' ('reasonable regard' in the High Seas Convention) 'to the interests of other States in their exercise of the freedom of the high seas' (HSC, art. 2; LOSC, art. 87(2)).

Finally, wherever a vessel may be, whether in one of a coastal State's zones or on the high seas, it will be subject to any relevant international obligations which have been undertaken by its flag State; for example, in relation to pollution control or shipping safety. The question of pollution is dealt with separately (see chapter fifteen): here we now turn to consider the scope of such obligations in relation to the safety of shipping.

Safety of shipping

It is obviously in the interests of shipowners, seafarers and the community at large that the transportation of people and goods by ships should be made as safe as possible, and that accidents such as foundering, stranding or collision should be kept to a minimum. Recognising this, article 10 of the High Seas Convention provided that every State shall take such measures for its vessels as are necessary to ensure safety at sea with regard to communications, the prevention of collisions, crew conditions and the construction, equipment and seaworthiness of ships, in conformity with 'generally accepted international standards'. The Law of the Sea Convention adopts the same basic approach, but sets out in more detail the duties of the flag State – including, for example, the duty to maintain regular checks upon the seaworthiness of ships, to ensure that crews are properly qualified and to hold inquiries into shipping casualties (LOSC, art. 94).

The emphasis upon internationally accepted standards in article 10 of the High Seas Convention and article 94 of the Law of the Sea Convention is dictated by practical necessity. While each State remains free in theory to apply its own legal standards relating to such matters as seaworthiness and crew qualifications to ships flying its flag and, to a more limited extent, to ships entering its ports or territorial sea, there would be chaos if these standards varied widely or were incompatible. Furthermore, because safety measures usually involve extra costs for shipowners, and because shipping is a very competitive industry, most States are reluctant to impose stricter safety legislation on their shipowners than other States impose upon theirs. For these reasons, therefore, the international community has developed a set of uniform international standards to promote the safety of shipping. These standards are contained in a number of international conventions, most of which are the work of IMO. The shipping safety standards dealt with by these conventions can be considered under four main headings: seaworthiness of ships, collision avoidance and ships' routeing, crewing standards, and the establishment of navigational aids.

Seaworthiness of ships

The main convention dealing with the seaworthiness of ships is the 1974 International Convention for the Safety of Life at Sea (SOLAS Convention), the latest in a succession of SOLAS Conventions, the first of which was prompted by the sinking of the *Titanic*. The Convention contains a large number of complex regulations laying down standards relating to the construction of ships, fire-safety measures, life-saving appliances, the carriage of navigational equipment and other aspects of the safety of navigation, the carriage of goods, special rules for nuclear ships and high speed craft, management for the safe operations of ships, and special measures to enhance maritime safety. The Convention has been amended from time to time, most extensively by Protocols of 1978 and 1988. In recent years amendments have become more frequent, partly in response to developments in technology and partly in response to major shipping casualties, such as the *Herald of Free Enterprise* (1987) and the *Estonia* (1994), both roll-on, roll-off (ro-ro) ferries. Thus, in the period 1990–5 inclusive, the Convention was amended on no less than nine occasions.

States Parties to the SOLAS Convention are obliged to impose, through their own legislation, the standards laid down in the Convention upon the vessels sailing under their flags. Enforcement lies largely with the flag State, but port States have a degree of control. They are entitled to see that ships flying the flag of other contracting parties which are present in their ports have on board valid certificates of the kind required by the SOLAS Convention. Where 'there are clear grounds for believing that the condition of the ship or of its equipment does not correspond substantially with the particulars of any of the certificates', or where a certificate has expired or where the ship and its equipment do not comply with the provisions of Regulation 11 of Chapter I of the Convention (which requires the condition of a ship and its equipment to be maintained after a survey), the authorities of the port State 'shall take steps to ensure that the ship shall not sail until it can proceed to sea or leave the port for the purpose of proceeding to the appropriate repair yard without danger to the ship or persons on board' (Chapter I, Regulation 19, as amended). In 1994 the Convention was amended to extend port State control to the checking of operational requirements 'when there are clear grounds for believing that the master or crew are not familiar with essential shipboard procedures relating to the safety of ships' (Chapter XI, Regulation 4).

As well as the SOLAS Convention, there are three other IMO conventions which are concerned with the seaworthiness of ships. The International Convention on Load Lines of 1966 deals with the problem of overloading, often the cause of shipping casualties, by prescribing the minimum freeboard (or the minimum draught) to which the ship is permitted to be loaded. Enforcement of the Convention is very similar to that of the SOLAS Convention, including the power of port States to detain ships which lack an appropriate and valid certificate. The Load Lines Convention is currently the subject of major revision, which is expected to be completed by 2000. The 1971 Agreement on Special Trade Passenger Ships, together with its Protocol of 1973, deals with the safety of ships carrying large numbers of unberthed passengers in special trades, such as the pilgrim trade. Finally, the 1977 International Convention for the Safety of Fishing Vessels (which is still not in force) lays down regulations governing the construction and equipment of fishing vessels. Because the Convention had not entered into force and had become outdated, a Protocol to the Convention was adopted in 1993. The Protocol amends and absorbs the parent Convention, updating it to take into account technological developments and eliminating those provisions which have discouraged States from ratifying the original Convention. The Protocol is not yet in force (see table 3).

In addition to conventions, the IMO (largely through its Assembly) has adopted numerous recommendations, guidelines and codes relating to the seaworthiness of ships. Such measures, being usually in the form of resolutions of the Assembly, are not as such legally binding. Nevertheless some of these measures, especially the codes, do make a transition from 'soft' to 'hard' law. For example, the Code for the Construction and Equipment of Ships carrying Dangerous Chemicals in Bulk, originally adopted by the IMO Assembly in 1971 as a non-binding resolution,[12] was subsequently incorporated in the legislation of at least a dozen States (and thus legally binding on the municipal level in those States), and finally was incorporated in the SOLAS Convention by the 1983 amendments to the Convention, thus becoming legally binding on the international plane.

[12] Resolution A.212 (VII) (1971).

Collision avoidance and ships' routeing

There has been a series of regulations designed to prevent collisions at sea. The current regulations are annexed to the Convention on the International Regulations for Preventing Collisions at Sea of 1972. The Regulations are principally concerned with a vessel's conduct and movements in relation to other vessels, particularly when visibility is poor, for the purposes of collision avoidance, and with the establishment of common standards in relation to sound and light signals. While the 1972 Convention is less than precise about the legal effects of these Regulations in so far as the relationship between breach of the Regulations and civil liability for collisions is concerned (breach does not necessarily result in civil liability, it seems), breach is commonly made an offence under the criminal law of the flag State party to the Convention. Prosecutions are, however, rare because in many legal systems substantial discretion rests with the master, and also because in many cases the identity of offending vessels is not known. Under the Law of the Sea Convention ships exercising their right of innocent passage through the territorial sea or their right of transit passage through straits must observe the Regulations, regardless of whether the flag State or the coastal State is a party to the 1972 Convention (LOSC, arts 21(4), 39(2)).

An important means of reducing the risk of collisions between ships is the use of traffic separation schemes to separate shipping in congested areas into one-way-only lanes. Early examples of such schemes can be found in agreements on routeing made by shipowners trading on certain routes (for example, in the China Sea) in the nineteenth century. They are now prescribed by the IMO, which began recommending such schemes in 1967. There are now over 100 routeing schemes laid down. At first compliance with IMO-recommended schemes was voluntary: flag States were not obliged to order their ships to follow them. But since the entry into force of the Collisions Regulations Convention in 1977 their observance has been mandatory for the ships of parties to that Convention (Rule 10). The introduction of traffic separation schemes is thought to be responsible for the general decrease in the number of collisions at sea. For example, in north-west European waters, where there are many separation schemes, the number of collisions dropped from 156 in the period 1956–61 to forty-five between 1976 and 1981.[13]

While the IMO is recognised as the only international body competent to prescribe traffic separation schemes (SOLAS Convention, Chapter V, Regulation 8), coastal States also have some competence in this area. Thus article 17 of the Territorial Sea Convention provided that in its territorial sea a coastal State may enact regulations relating to the navigation of foreign vessels exercising their right of innocent passage. The Law of the Sea Convention contains a similar provision (LOSC, art. 21), but adds that a coastal State prescribing a traffic separation scheme in its territorial sea must take into account any IMO recommendations and such factors as the special characteristics of particular ships and the density

[13] *IMCO News*, 1981, No. 4, p. 3.

of traffic (LOSC, art. 22). The IMO itself recommends coastal States wishing to establish routeing systems in their territorial sea to 'design them in accordance with IMO criteria for such schemes and submit them to IMO for adoption'.[14]

Coastal States may exercise enforcement jurisdiction against foreign vessels infringing prescribed schemes (TSC, art. 19; LOSC, art. 27). In practice enforcement is usually limited to requesting vessels to rejoin the separation scheme or, in more serious cases, reporting the infringement to the authorities of the flag State, although if an offending vessel put into one of the coastal State's ports it could be prosecuted. In straits subject to the regime of transit passage, the Law of the Sea Convention provides that the coastal State's competence is more limited. While the coastal State may still prescribe traffic separation schemes, proposed schemes must 'conform to generally accepted international regulations' and must be referred to the IMO 'with a view to their adoption' before being prescribed by the coastal State (LOSC, art. 41). The controversial question as to what enforcement jurisdiction coastal States have in straits subject to transit passage is discussed in chapter five. Finally, the limited competence which States enjoy to prescribe anti-pollution regulations in their EEZ includes the competence to prescribe regulations relating to 'navigational practices' (LOSC, art. 211(6), discussed in chapter fifteen).

As well as traffic separation schemes, the IMO also recommends deep water routes, areas to be avoided (which are areas in which either navigation is particularly hazardous or it is exceptionally important, especially for environmental reasons, to avoid casualties), and other routeing measures. The observance of such measures is mandatory under amendments to the SOLAS Convention adopted in 1995.

The management of marine traffic has begun to go beyond traffic separation and other routeing schemes and become more comprehensive, although it seems unlikely that it will reach the precision or sophistication of air traffic control. First, in both the Baltic Straits and the Straits of Malacca the IMO has recommended such measures as speed restrictions, the reporting by vessels of their position and the use of pilots.[15] Secondly, amendments to the SOLAS Convention adopted in 1994 make it possible to introduce mandatory ship reporting systems. Such systems are mandatory where they have been adopted and implemented in accordance with IMO guidelines and criteria. Ships must give their position, identity and other information. This will enable their journey through the system to be tracked. If the ship goes off course, or if there is a risk of collision or grounding, the shore authority will be able to warn the ship and take other necessary action. Reporting systems and actions taken to enforce them must be 'consistent' with the Law of the Sea Convention. In 1996 the IMO approved the first two mandatory reporting systems – the first in the Torres Strait and the

---

[14] IMO Assembly Resolution A.572 (XIV) (1985), Annex, para. 3.12.
[15] IMO Assembly Resolutions, A.480 (XII) (1981), A.579 (XIV) (1985) and A.620 (XV)(1987) on the Baltic; and A.375 (X) (1977) and A.476 (XII) (1981) on the Straits of Malacca.

Inner Route of the Great Barrier Reef, the second off Ushant.[16] In addition to such international measures, there are many national schemes, mainly in the form of Vessel Traffic Services in the approaches to ports and harbours.[17] The IMO has recommended 'Guidelines for Vessel Traffic Services', which national authorities are urged to follow 'in the interests of international harmonisation and improving maritime safety'.[18]

Crewing standards

Inadequately trained or qualified crews are a major factor in the cause of shipping accidents. It should therefore follow that an improvement in the quality of crews would lead to a reduction of accidents. The 1974 SOLAS Convention requires that all ships shall be 'sufficiently and efficiently-manned' (Chapter V, Regulation 13), while under ILO Convention No. 147 of 1976 concerning Minimum Standards in Merchant Ships each contracting State must 'ensure that seafarers employed on ships registered in its territory are properly qualified or trained for the duties for which they are engaged' (art. 2(e)). Similarly, article 94(4) of the Law of the Sea Convention provides that flag States must ensure that each of their ships 'is in the charge of a master and officers who possess appropriate qualifications . . . and that the crew is appropriate in qualification and numbers for the type, size, machinery and equipment of the ship'. More precise content is given to these rather vague and general obligations by the International Convention on Standards of Training, Certification and Watchkeeping for Seafarers (the 'STCW' Convention), adopted under the IMO's auspices in 1978. This Convention lays down mandatory minimum requirements for the certification of masters and other officers and prescribes basic principles for keeping

---

[16] *IMO News*, 1996, No. 3, p. 5. Three further systems, for the Great Belt, off Finisterre and in the Strait of Gibraltar, were adopted at the end of 1996: see *IMO News*, 1997, No. 1, p. 4. For a discussion of the legal issues involved, see E. Franckx, 'Coastal State jurisdiction with respect to marine pollution – some recent developments and future challenges', 10 *IJMCL* 253 (1995) at 266–72. Note also EC Council Directive 93/75/EC of September 1993 (*Official Journal of the European Communities* (OJEC), 1993, L247/ 19), which is aimed at ensuring that EC Member States are notified of the presence of dangerous or polluting goods on board vessels using their ports so that they can take appropriate measures. In addition some States prescribe reporting requirements for vessels in their territorial seas: for examples, see Plant, *op. cit.* in 'Further reading' under the heading 'Safety of shipping', pp. 261–2.

[17] For examples see Abecassis and Jarashow, *op. cit.* in 'Further reading' under 'Safety of shipping', pp. 446–7; E. Gold and D. M. Johnson, 'Ship-generated pollution: the creator of regulated navigation' in T. A. Clingan (ed.), *Law of the Sea: State Practice in Zones of Special Jurisdiction* (Honolulu, Hawaii, Law of the Sea Institute), 1982, p. 156 at 169–74; J. K. Kemp and A. F. M. De Bievre, 'A regional vessel traffic service for the North Sea', 5 *IJECL* 167–78 (1990); and Plant, *op. cit.*, pp. 260–3.

[18] IMO Assembly Resolution A.578 (XIV) (1985). Subsequently replaced by IMO Assembly Resolution A.857 (20) (1997). See also amendments to Regulation 8 of Chapter V of the SOLAS Convention, adopted in 1997, which provide that Vessel Traffic Services may be made mandatory only within the territorial sea.

navigational and engineering watches. Enforcement of the STCW Convention's provisions rests essentially with the flag State, although port States have certain powers of control for the purpose of verifying that seafarers required by the Convention to be certificated are so certificated (art. X). The Convention was extensively amended in 1995 in order to bring it up to date with technical developments and to introduce greater uniformity in its implementation by tightening up some of the rather loose language of the original Convention. In addition, the amendments require parties to provide detailed reports on their implementation of the Convention to the IMO, enhance port State control by allowing port States to intervene in the case of deficiencies deemed to pose a danger to persons, property or the environment, and require States to penalise those to whom they have issued certificates who do not comply with the Convention. At the same time as amending the STCW Convention, the IMO adopted an International Convention on Standards of Training, Certification and Watchkeeping for Fishing Vessel Personnel. The provisions of the STCW Convention do not apply to fishing vessels because of their specialised nature, so the 1995 Convention marks the first attempt to make mandatory standards of safety for crews of fishing vessels, such standards having been previously contained in non-binding IMO Assembly resolutions.

The working conditions of crews have been the subject of thirty-nine conventions and thirty recommendations adopted by the ILO, which make up the International Seafarers' Code. The most important of these conventions include: Convention concerning Seafarers' Hours of Work and the Manning of Ships (No. 180 (1996), revising earlier conventions), Convention concerning Crew Accommodation on Board Ship (No. 92 (1949), supplemented by No. 133 (1970)), Convention concerning Continuity of Employment of Seafarers (No. 145 (1976)) and Convention concerning Seafarers' Welfare at Sea and in Port (No. 163 (1987)). The ILO has also adopted a number of non-binding recommendations on the working conditions of seafarers, notably the Social Conditions and Safety (Seafarers) Recommendation, 1958 (No. 108). In addition, ILO Convention No. 147 (referred to above) requires States Parties to it to prescribe for their ships and effectively to enforce safety standards, social security measures, and shipboard conditions of employment equivalent to the provisions of various ILO conventions listed in the annex to the Convention.

Finally, it should be noted that article 9 of the 1986 UN Convention on Conditions for Registration of Ships requires flag States to promote, in co-operation with shipowners, the education and training of seamen, and to ensure that manning levels and competence and working conditions on ships conform to international rules and standards.

Establishment of navigational aids

Of obvious importance to the safety of shipping is the establishment of navigational aids such as lighthouses, lightships, buoys and radar beacons. An obligation is laid down by the SOLAS Convention on States Parties to arrange for the establishment and maintenance of such aids to navigation as, in their opinion, the volume of traffic justifies and the degree of risk requires, and to arrange for information relating to these aids to be made available to all concerned. (Chapter V, Regulation 14)

It may also be noted that under the Territorial Sea and Law of the Sea Conventions there is an obligation on every coastal State to 'give appropriate publicity to any dangers to navigation, of which it has knowledge within its territorial sea' (TSC, art. 15(2); LOSC, art. 24(2)). Similar obligations arise under customary law (see chapter four, pp. 81, 100). The cost of installing and maintaining navigational aids is normally borne solely by the coastal State, and it is not entitled to demand a contribution from ships sailing through its territorial sea (TSC, art. 18; LOSC, art. 26). However, there are one or two instances where States have entered into an agreement to share the cost of navigational aids, e.g., the 1962 International Agreement regarding the Maintenance of Certain Lights in the Red Sea. Under article 43 of the Law of the Sea Convention States bordering a strait subject to transit passage and user States are to co-operate 'in the establishment and maintenance in [the] strait of necessary navigational and safety aids', although nothing is said about how the costs of this are to be borne. Presumably local agreements or arrangements will allocate the sharing of costs.

Miscellaneous safety measures

Finally there are a number of miscellaneous initiatives taken by the IMO that bear on maritime safety and which are worthy of brief mention. First, the Convention on the International Maritime Satellite Organisation (INMARSAT) of 1976 provides for a world-wide maritime communications satellite system, which, since it began operations in 1982, has led, for the several thousand ships connected to the system, to a significant increase in the speed, reliability and quality of maritime communications, thus making for increased efficiency of navigation and safety at sea. Secondly, in 1977 the IMO Assembly adopted a Plan for the Establishment of a World-wide Navigational Warning Service.[19] The plan provides for shipping to be given information required for safe navigation and meteorological warnings through a number of regional authorities responsible for broadcasting such information. Thirdly, the 1979 International Convention on Maritime Search and Rescue facilitates international co-operation in search and rescue operations at sea by establishing an international search and rescue plan. The Convention was extensively revised in 1998. Fourthly, concerned by the evidence of poor management in shipping and its implications for safety, the IMO in 1993 adopted an International Safety Management Code which was subsequently incorporated in the SOLAS Convention by amendments adopted

---

[19] IMO Assembly Resolution A.381 (X) (1977). Subsequently replaced by IMO Assembly Resolution A.419 (XI) (1979), which in turn was replaced by Resolution A.706 (17) (1991).

in 1994. The Code requires every ship-owning company to establish a safety management system to ensure compliance with IMO regulations and to implement a policy the objectives of which are to provide for safe practices in ship operation, establish safeguards against all identified risks and to improve safety management skills of personnel. Flag States are to ensure that their companies comply with the Code. Fifthly, in 1987 the IMO adopted a voluntary Ship Identification Number Scheme. The aim of the Scheme is to give every ship a number which always remains the same, regardless of change of name, owner or flag, the idea being that this will help combat fraud and enable a record to be kept of substandard ships. Because few States put the Scheme into operation in its original form, the Scheme was made mandatory by amendments adopted to the SOLAS Convention in 1994. Finally, as part of its task of constantly seeking to improve shipping safety and to reduce dangers of whatever kind, the IMO is preparing a convention concerning the removal of wrecks and sunken or drifting cargo that may pose a hazard to navigation or a threat to the marine environment.

Evaluation of IMO conventions

In general, it must be said that the IMO has performed a very useful service in drafting the above conventions. While the criticism may be made that the conventions have been rather slow to enter into force and are not always widely ratified, this is scarcely the fault of the IMO, since ratification of conventions is entirely a matter within the discretion of its member States. Furthermore, it should be pointed out that the most important conventions –SOLAS, the Collision Regulations and Load Lines – have been ratified by virtually all the major shipping nations (see Table 3). As far as speed of entry into force is concerned, the use of the tacit amendment procedure for the technical annexes of all IMO Convention concluded since 1972, whereby amendments enter into force unless objected to, rather than – as formerly – requiring positive approval by a certain number of States, means that it is easier and quicker to amend the annexes of IMO Conventions in order to keep them abreast of technical developments than was at one time the case. The one major Convention which is not currently covered by this procedure is the Load Lines Convention, with the result that nearly all amendments to it have never entered into force. This situation will be improved if and when the 1988 Protocol to the Convention enters into force, as this introduces the tacit amendment procedure. In addition to bringing amendments (which are normally adopted by consensus) into force more quickly, another advantage of the tacit amendment procedure is that the date of entry into force of the amendment is known from the outset, thus allowing shipowners and others to plan in advance. In fact the tacit amendment procedure has almost become the victim of its own success. The frequency and volume of amendments has now become so great that it is causing difficulties in implementation and the IMO is accused in some quarters of going too fast. To this end, therefore,

Table 3. *Ratification of IMO maritime safety conventions*

Convention	Date of signature	Date of entry into force	Number of ratifications	Fleets of ratifying States as percentage of world merchant shipping fleet
SOLAS 1974	1.11.1974	25.5.1980	137	98.36
Load Lines	5. 4.1966	21.7.1968	141	98.34
Collision Regulations	20.10.1972	15.7.1977	131	96.43
Special trade passenger ships	6.10.1971	2.1.1974	16	22.78
Protocol	13. 7.1973	2.6.1977	15	21.08
Fishing vessels	2. 4.1993	Not in force (fifteen ratifications required representing an aggregate fleet of at least 14,000 fishing vessels)	6	6.10
Seafarers certification, etc.	1.12.1978	28.4.1984	132	98.04

Source: IMO Home Page on the World Wide Web (information correct as at 1 August 1998).

there is now an understanding that the SOLAS Convention should not normally be amended more often than once every four years.

There is no shortage of legislation on ship safety. The problem today is with the implementation and enforcement of this legislation. The primary responsibility for such implementation and enforcement lies with flag States. It is a widely held view that a number of flag States (some, but by no means all, of them flags of convenience) are unable or unwilling to enforce the provisions of IMO Conventions to which they are parties: evidence for this view is the fact that the casualty rate for ships of some States is much greater (up to one hundredfold in some cases) than for ships of other States. The IMO has begun to address the problems of inadequate flag State implementation and enforcement. In 1992 it set up a special committee to monitor implementation of IMO Conventions by flag States and to identify the measures necessary to ensure effective and consistent global implementation. Based on the preliminary work of this committee, the IMO Assembly in 1993 adopted a set of Interim Guidelines to Assist Flag States, replaced by definitive Guidelines in 1997, which set out the means for flag States to establish and maintain measures for the effective application and enforcement of the relevant conventions.[20] The IMO also helps flag States to fulfil their responsibilities through its Technical Co-Operation Programme, particularly through the provision of training, although the Programme's resources are limited. The problems of flag State jurisdiction, which are compounded by the proliferation in recent years of classification societies, many of questionable competence, which often undertake surveying and inspection on behalf of flag States, and by the use of multilingual crews who often do not stay together or on the same ship for long, might also be improved if the UN Convention on Conditions for Registration of Ships were to enter into force and be widely ratified, since article 5 of the Convention requires flag States to implement, and ensure compliance by their vessels with, international rules and standards concerning safety of shipping.

The current drawbacks of flag State enforcement are to some extent overcome by the powers of control given to the port State by some of the IMO Conventions, as has been seen above (and see chapter fifteen for the use of port State jurisdiction in controlling pollution). A similar, but more comprehensive, approach is found in ILO Convention No. 147 of 1976 concerning Minimum Standards in Merchant Ships. Under this convention and a protocol to it adopted in 1996, a State which believes that a foreign vessel in one of its ports does not conform to certain specified safety and labour standards may inform the flag State and 'may take measures necessary to rectify any conditions on board which are clearly hazardous to safety or health', provided that it does not 'unnecessarily detain or delay the ship' (art. 4). It would seem that under customary international law port States have – and in practice exercise – the competence to inspect foreign vessels in their ports and detain them if unsafe, so that the ILO and IMO Conventions essentially do no more than consolidate and clarify existing law and encourage port States to use their powers. Going somewhat further than the Conventions, but still in accordance with customary international law, the maritime authorities of fourteen European States signed a Memorandum of Understanding on Port State Control in 1982 (often known as the Paris Memorandum).[21] Under this Memorandum, each authority undertakes to maintain an effective system of port State control to ensure that vessels visiting its ports comply with the main IMO safety conventions discussed above, ILO Convention No. 147 and the International Convention for the Prevention of Pollution from Ships, 1973, as modified by a Protocol of 1978, to the extent that such conventions and their

---

[20] IMO Assembly Resolutions A.740 (18) (1993) and A.847 (20) (1997). The Assembly also adopted a Code for the Investigation of Marine Casualties and Incidents, which requests flag States to conduct an investigation of all serious casualties: Resolution A.849 (20) (1997).

[21] 21 *ILM* 1 (1982). The text of the memorandum has been amended several times since 1982. This memorandum replaces an earlier and less comprehensive memorandum of understanding signed at The Hague in March 1978. The number of parties to the 1982 memorandum has subsequently grown to seventeen and expanded from Western Europe to include Canada, Poland and Russia. Croatia, Japan and the USA co-operate with the Paris Memorandum parties.

amendments are in force and the port State is a party – but regardless of whether the flag State of the ship concerned is a party. The powers of control of each authority are those given by the various conventions. Each authority must inspect a minimum of twenty-five per cent of the ships using its ports each year: the idea behind this figure is that since most ships call at ports of more than one West European State in a year, it should lead to about ninety per cent of all ships visiting such ports being inspected each year. Guidelines for inspection are set out in Annex 1. Where an inspection reveals deficiencies that are clearly hazardous to safety, health or the environment, the hazard must be removed before the ship is allowed to proceed to sea. Arrangements are made for a regular exchange of information relating to inspections between the authorities parties to the memorandum. During the first eleven years of operation of the Memorandum about 130,000 inspections took place. In about 3.5 per cent of cases ships (the majority from developing countries) were found to have deficiencies serious enough to result in their being delayed or detained.[22] Between 1982 and 1989 the percentage of ships detained gradually declined, but since 1989 the percentage has increased, with 5.6 per cent being detained in 1992.[23] This suggests that the Memorandum has so far had a rather limited impact on substandard ships, although it may also reflect the fact that inspections (which have never overall reached the twenty-five per cent figure) are now targeted more closely at vessels which are thought might be deficient.

In recent years schemes of port State control, closely modelled on the Paris Memorandum, have been adopted for other regions of the world. These cover Latin America (the Viña Del Mar agreement, with eleven participating maritime administrations, signed in 1992); Asia-Pacific (Tokyo Memorandum of Understanding, signed in 1993, with eighteen parties); the Caribbean (Memorandum of Understanding on Port State Control in the Caribbean Region, signed in 1996, with twenty parties[24]); the Mediterranean (Memorandum of Understanding on Port State Control in the Mediterranean Region, signed in 1997, with ten parties); and the Indian Ocean (Memorandum of Understanding on Port State Control for the Indian Ocean Region, signed in 1998, with fifteen parties).[25] Finally, in 1995 the EC adopted a directive on port State control.[26] This is similar to, but more stringent than, the Paris Memorandum. As all EC coastal States are parties to the

---

[22] *IMO News*, 1994, No. 1, p. 19.

[23] *Ibid*. In 1994 the United Kingdom detained just over ten per cent of the ships inspected in its ports: *The Guardian*, 30 June 1995.

[24] The text of the Caribbean Memorandum is reproduced in 12 *IJMCL* 81 (1997) and 36 *ILM* 231 (1997).

[25] In February 1998 nineteen west and central African States agreed on a draft memorandum of understanding on port State control for that region, which is expected to be finalised in 1999. A similar scheme is planned for the Arabian/Persian Gulf. In March 1998 States signatory to the Paris and Tokyo memoranda signed a joint declaration on inter-regional action to eliminate substandard shipping. See *IMO News*, 1998, No. 2, p. 31.

[26] Council Directive 95/21/EC of 19 June 1995, *OJEC*, 1995, L157/1.

latter, there is obviously much overlap, which may cause confusion. The justification given by the EC for its own measure is that the Paris Memorandum has not been applied in a uniform way, the principal evidence for this assertion being wide differences in the proportion of ships detained by different States: the directive, it is argued, will be applied more consistently since, unlike the Memorandum, it is a formally legally binding instrument which can be strictly enforced.

Finally, going much less far than any of the provisions mentioned above, but similarly motivated, article 94(6) of the Law of the Sea Convention provides that a State which has clear grounds for believing that a flag State has not exercised proper jurisdiction and control over one of its ships may report the facts to the flag State, and that 'upon receiving such a report, the flag State shall investigate the matter and, if appropriate, take any action necessary to remedy the situation'.

It should be noted that neither under the Conventions nor under the various memoranda are port States given the right to prosecute foreign vessels for failure to comply with the required standards. However, it follows from the jurisdiction which States enjoy in their internal waters under customary international law (on which see chapter three) that a port State may make breach of an international standard by a foreign ship committed in its port, or committed before the ship entered the port but continuing there, an offence under its municipal law, and prosecute offenders. In practice it seems that many States do not make such breaches offences under their local law, and even when they do, rarely prosecute, being satisfied once the breach is remedied following detention of the vessel.

Other IMO conventions

Most of the conventions adopted under the auspices of the IMO are concerned with maritime safety (discussed above) or marine pollution (discussed in chapter fifteen). There are, however a few IMO conventions which deal with neither of these topics and it may be appropriate to make brief mention of them here. First, the Convention on Facilitation of International Maritime Traffic of 1965 reduces and simplifies government formalities, documentary requirements and procedures connected with the arrival, stay and departure of ships engaged in international voyages. Secondly, the 1969 International Convention on Tonnage Measurement of Ships establishes a unified system of tonnage measurement. Such a system had not existed prior to the entry into force of the Convention in 1982. The system laid down by the Convention, in comparison with previous tonnage measurement regulations, greatly simplifies the calculation of tonnages. Thirdly, the International Convention for Safe Containers of 1972 facilitates the international inter-modal transport of containers, while seeking to maintain a high level of safety in their handling. Fourthly, there are two conventions concerned with questions of liability: the 1976 Convention on Limitation of Liability for Maritime Claims (which, on its entry into force in 1986, replaced, as between parties to the Convention, the 1957 International Convention relating to the Limitation of the Liability of Owners of Sea-going Ships (which allowed a shipowner to limit his liability in relation to a variety of possible claims), in particular increasing the limits of shipowners' liability and making clear the circumstances in which a shipowner is not entitled to limit his liability), and the 1974 Convention relating to the Carriage of Passengers and their Luggage by Sea (which lays down uniform rules governing the liability of maritime carriers for death or injury of passengers and for damage or loss of luggage: in general liability is strict but limited). The limits of liability under the 1974 Convention were increased by a Protocol of 1990: a Protocol of 1996 performs a similar exercise for the 1976 Convention. Fifthly, the 1989 International Convention on Salvage, which replaces the 1910 Convention on Salvage and Assistance at Sea, changes the traditional system of salvage of 'no cure, no pay' by allowing salvors to obtain compensation where their action prevents a major pollution incident even though it does not save the ship. Sixthly, the 1993 Convention on Maritime Liens and Mortgages, adopted under the joint auspices of the IMO and UNCTAD, is intended to improve conditions for ship financing and the development of national merchant fleets and to promote international uniformity in the field of maritime liens and mortgages. Lastly, it must not be forgotten that the 1988 Convention for the Suppression of Unlawful Acts against the Safety of Navigation, which was discussed in chapter eleven, is the work of the IMO. In addition, the IMO is currently elaborating a convention on the arrest of ships.

It should not be forgotten that there are also many non-IMO international conventions relating to shipping, the majority of which are concerned with private law aspects and thus are beyond the scope of this book. Many of these private law conventions have been adopted under the auspices of the International Maritime Committee.

Further reading

General

E. Gold, *Maritime Transport* (Lexington, Mass., Lexington Books), 1981.
G. C. Kasoulides, *Port State Control and Jurisdiction* (Dordrecht, Nijhoff), 1993.

Nationality of ships

R. R. Churchill, 'European Community Law and the nationality of ships and crews', 26 *European Transport Law* 591–617 (1991).
D. H. N. Johnson, 'The nationality of ships', 8 *Indian Yearbook of International Affairs* 3–15 (1959).
M. L. McConnell, ' "Darkening confusion mounted upon darkening confusion": the search for the elusive genuine link', 16 *Journal of Maritime Law and Commerce* 365–96 (1985).

——, '"Business as usual": an evaluation of the 1986 United Nations Convention on Conditions for Registration of Ships', 18 *Journal of Maritime Law and Commerce* 435–49 (1987).

H. Meyers, *The Nationality of Ships* (The Hague, Nijhoff), 1967.

D. P. O'Connell, *The International Law of the Sea*, 2 vols (Oxford, Clarendon), 1982, 1984 [*O'Connell*].

OECD, 'Study on flags of convenience', 4 *JMLC* 231–54 (1972).

N. P. Ready, *Ship Registration* (London, Lloyds of London Press), 2nd edn, 1994.

H. W. Wefers Bettink, 'Open registry, the genuine link and the 1986 Convention on Registration Conditions for Ships', 18 *NYIL* 69–119 (1987).

Rights of navigation

R. J. Dupuy and D. Vignes (eds), *Traité du Nouveau Droit de la Mer* (Brussels, Bruylant), 1985, chapter 15 (and corresponding chapter in English translation).

W. Riphagen, 'La navigation dans le nouveau droit de la mer' in D. Bardonnet and M. Virally (eds), *Le Nouveau Droit International de la Mer* (Paris, Pedone), 1983, pp. 141–76.

I. A. Shearer, 'Problems of jurisdiction and law enforcement against delinquent vessels', 35 *ICLQ* 320–43 (1986).

J. M Van Dyke *et al.* (eds), *International Navigation: Rocks and Shoals Ahead* (Honolulu, Hawaii, Law of the Sea Institute), 1988.

Safety of shipping

D. W. Abecassis and R. L. Jarashow, *Oil Pollution from Ships* (London, Stevens), 2nd ed, 1985, chapter 4.

A. Cockcroft and J. F. Lameijer, *A Guide to the Collision Avoidance Rules* (London, Heinemann Newnes), 4th ed, 1990.

J. Hare, 'Port State control: strong medicine to cure a sick industry', 26 *Georgia Journal of International and Comparative Law* 571–94 (1997).

S. Mankabady, *The International Maritime Organisation* (London, Croom Helm), 2nd ed, 1986.

E. Molenaar, 'The EC directive on port State control in context', 11 *IJMCL* 241–88 (1996).

E. Osieke, 'The International Labour Organisation and the control of sub-standard merchant vessels', 30 *ICLQ* 497–512 (1981).

G. Plant, 'Legal environmental retraints upon navigation post-*Braer*', 10 *OGLTR* 245–68 (1992).

Safer Ships, Cleaner Seas. Report of Lord Donaldson's Inquiry into the Prevention of Pollution from Merchant Shipping (London, HMSO), 1994, Cm. 2560. For the British Government's response, see Cm. 2766 (1995).

IMO News, published quarterly, is a useful source of information on developments at the IMO.

14

Fishing

Background to the international law of fisheries

In the period 1993–5 (the latest years for which figures were available at the time of writing) the total world marine fish catch averaged 89.8 million metric tonnes a year. A further 19.1 million metric tonnes were caught in inland waters. In the period 1948–52 the annual total world marine catch averaged 19.4 million tonnes, from 1958 to 1962 34.0, from 1968 to 1972 57.5 and from 1978 to 1982 65.3 million. Thus, since the Second World War there has been a steady increase. This increase is mainly due to two factors: technical improvements, such as the development of sophisticated electronic fish-finding equipment, larger vessels (including factory freezers) and larger and stronger nets, and secondly greater investment in the fisheries of developing countries. While the rate of increase in the world catch has slowed down in recent years, mainly because most commercially exploitable fish stocks are now fully- or over-exploited, it has been estimated by the FAO that with proper management the total sustainable catch could be increased to about 100 million tonnes a year.

The twenty leading fishing States by weight of catch for the period 1993–5 are shown in table 4. The catches in the period 1973–5, the last three years before the general expansion to 200-mile fishing limits, are also shown by way of comparison. It is important to realise, however, that the weight of the catch does not tell one everything about relative wealth since the monetary value of a catch is not necessarily proportionate to its weight. As with most areas of economic activity, fishing shows marked inequalities between States. The leading twenty States in the period 1993–5 account for about eighty-one per cent of the total world catch, whereas the remaining nineteen per cent is shared between about 130 other coastal States. Among the twenty leading States, developed States are less dominant than in, for example, shipping. As developing countries have increased their investment in fisheries and improved their technology, so their share of the world catch has risen, while the catches of distant-water fishing States (i.e., those that fish predominantly off the coasts of other States, rather than their own coasts), which are mainly developed, have decreased as the States off whose coasts they fish have gained greater control over the fish stocks by

Table 4. *Catches of the twenty leading fishing States*

	Average annual catch 1993–5 inclusive ('000 metric tonnes)	Average annual catch 1973–5 inclusive ('000 metric tonnes)
1. China	11,796	3,166[a]
2. Peru	9,939	3,301
3. Japan	7,241	10,506
4. Chile	7,152	926
5. USA	5,514	2,854
6. Russia	3,919	8,428[b]
7. Thailand	3,148	1,429
8. Indonesia	3,109	944
9. India	2,683	1,388
10. S. Korea	2,672	1,943
11. Norway	2,640	2,732
12. Denmark[c]	2,192	1,982
13. Philippines	1,703	1,162
14. N. Korea	1,696[a]	1,400[a]
15. Iceland	1,630	947
16. Spain	1,284[a]	1,521
17. Malaysia	1,173	478
18. Taiwan	1,132[a]	N/A
19. Mexico	1,111	458
20. Canada	1,025	1,034
Total, all States	89,786	60,433[a]

Notes
[a] FAO estimate.
[b] The figure is for the former USSR: no separate figure is available for Russia.
[c] Including the Faroes and Greenland.
Source: FAO Yearbook of Fishery Statistics. Catches and Landings, Vols 80, 1995 (1997), pp. 103–5 and 46, 1978 (1979), pp. 17–19.

means of 200-mile exclusive fishing zones (EFZs) or EEZs. Nevertheless, for basic geographical and biological reasons, there will always remain substantial differences between the fish catches of States. First, the offshore zones of States, such as EFZs and EEZs, are of varying sizes. Second, fish are found in greatest abundance in the areas where there is most zooplankton, on which many species feed, directly or indirectly: these areas are the sub-tropical western coasts of America and Africa, along the Equator, temperate and sub-Arctic waters and shallow continental shelf waters.

The principal and most obvious use of fish is as food for human consumption. Fish is an important source of animal protein, accounting for about twenty per cent of the total world supply, and contains important vitamins and minerals.

Not all fish goes to human consumption, however. Just under thirty per cent is converted into fishmeal or oil and used as fertiliser or animal feed. This is particularly the case with small species such as sand eels, capelin and Peruvian anchoveta, which are not easily processed for human consumption.

One of the most important characteristics of fish is their migratory nature. Most fish stocks migrate often considerable distances during the course of their life cycle. This has important implications as far as jurisdictional boundaries in the sea are concerned. Furthermore, few, if any, fish stocks exist in isolation: most stocks are inter-related, either in the sense that one stock feeds on another (as cod do upon herring), or in that they inhabit the same area, so that fishermen intending to fish for one species will often take other species as by-catches. Thus regulations designed to deal with one particular stock may well have consequences for other stocks.

Before looking at the international law of fisheries it is necessary to examine a basic characteristic of marine fisheries which has profoundly influenced their regulation, both at the national and the international level. Fisheries are a common property natural resource. In other words, free-swimming fish in the sea are not owned by anyone: property rights only arise when the fish are caught and reduced into the possession of an individual fisherman. It therefore follows that anyone can, in principle, fish in the sea. From the common property nature of marine fish, there follow four consequences of particular note as far as the regulation of marine fisheries is concerned – a tendency for fish stocks to be fished above biologically optimum levels; a tendency for more fishermen to engage in a fishery than is economically justified; a likelihood of competition and conflict between different groups of fishermen; and the necessity for any regulation of marine fisheries to have a substantial international component. Each of these consequences needs to be examined in a little more detail.

Because fish are a common property resource, anyone can enter a particular fishery. It obviously follows that as more fishermen enter the fishery, more and more fish will – initially at least – be caught. If the quantity of fish caught, together with fish lost through natural mortality, exceeds the amount of fish being added to the stock through reproduction, then the size of the stock will start to decrease: in extreme cases the stock may even collapse, as has happened with the Antarctic whales and the California sardine. This phenomenon is known as over-fishing. Moreover, in the absence of any regulation, an individual fisherman has no incentive to restrain his activities in order to prevent over-fishing because there is no guarantee that other fishermen will follow his example: indeed the opposite is more likely to occur, for with one competitor removed there is more fish for those that remain. Thus, just as common land was over-grazed before the enclosure movement, so an unregulated fishery will normally lead to over-fishing.

Thus to prevent over-fishing it is usually necessary to regulate the amount of fish to be caught. To do this effectively, it is necessary to know how much fish can be caught without over-fishing resulting. As the result of research done by fisheries biologists, it is known that the growth of a particular fish stock is limited by environmental factors, such as the availability of food and the presence of natural predators, and that the stock will thus reach a particular size that cannot be exceeded. A stock which is not fished at all will tend to remain at this maximum size, and natural mortality and reproduction will balance out. Once the stock begins to be fished, however, its size will decrease. To recover its losses, the stock then starts growing at a rapid rate in an attempt to reach its original level. This rate of increase is greatest when a stock has been reduced to a particular size (which varies from stock to stock). It is at this level, which is known as the maximum sustainable yield (MSY), that the greatest quantity of fish can be caught year after year without the total size of the stock being adversely affected (assuming that environmental factors do not upset the balance).

Until forty or so years ago MSY was frequently suggested as the principal objective of fisheries management, but over the past four decades its limitations have been increasingly revealed. First, ascertaining the MSY for a particular stock is by no means an easy task, even where the data exists (which is not always the case). Secondly, because of the inter-relationship of stocks (as explained above), it makes little sense to determine the MSY for each stock in isolation: if one stock is fished at the level of MSY, it may be impossible to achieve the level of MSY for a related stock. Thus it is desirable to establish fishing levels for inter-related stocks as a single exercise.

A second consequence of the common property nature of fish is that it leads to economic inefficiency. Typically a fishery will begin with few entrants, each of whom will make a profit. Other fishermen, seeing these profits, will be attracted to the fishery. As the number of fishermen participating in the fishery increases, so the size of catch – and hence economic return – per vessel will decrease. Thus, in the absence of any limitation on the number of fishermen entering a fishery, the economic return for each vessel will be below the optimum (or maximum economic yield (MEY), as it is known) and indeed in the long term total revenue from the fishery will tend to equal the total cost of fishing. In other words, the same quantity of fish is caught as could be caught with substantially fewer vessels than those actually employed. This phenomenon is known as over-capacity (or over-capitalisation) and is found in most of the world's fisheries.

The third notable consequence of the fact that marine fish are a common property resource is the likelihood of competition and conflict between different groups of fishermen. It follows from the open access nature of fisheries that competition between fishermen is inevitable. Nor is such competition in itself necessarily harmful. However, it raises problems and may produce conflict where it is at such a level as to lead to over-fishing and economic inefficiency. More directly, conflict may also arise between fishermen using different types of gear, notably where trawlers seek to fish in areas where there is stationary gear such as standing nets. Conflict may also arise between fishing and other uses of the sea, such as the offshore oil and gas industry and dredging for sand and gravel.

Finally, because much fishing takes place outside what has traditionally been regarded as the territory of States it follows that the problems discussed above must be regulated – in part at least – on the international level through co-operation between States and through the medium of international law. The international law regulating marine fisheries falls into two very distinct phases. The first is the period up to the middle 1970s, which was characterised by generally narrow coastal State maritime zones and a considerable amount of international co-operation in fisheries management through a score of international fishery commissions. The second phase is the period since the mid-1970s when broad coastal State zones in the form of 200-mile EFZs and EEZs, inspired by the work of UNCLOS III and embracing most commercially exploitable fish stocks, have become the norm, while the role of international fishery commissions has been significantly reduced.

We will examine each of these phases in turn, the first briefly, the second in more detail. But before doing so it may be useful to outline the main kinds of measures employed to regulate fisheries, both at the national and the international level. First, there is the setting of a total allowable catch (TAC) which prescribes how much fish may be caught from a particular stock of fish over a specified period: such a TAC may then be divided into quotas to be allocated to individual States (in an internationally managed fishery) or individual vessels (in a nationally managed fishery). The purpose of the TAC is to try to ensure that no more fish are caught from a stock than is biologically justifiable. Secondly, gear regulations (such as minimum mesh sizes) and the minimum size of fish permitted to be caught may be prescribed in order to prevent the catching of immature fish. A third type of measure is closing certain areas to fishing and/or closing certain seasons to fishing in order to protect spawning and immature fish. Fourthly, by-catch levels may be specified in order to prevent too many fish of one species being incidentally caught when a vessel is directing its fishing at another species. The above measures are all essentially biological in nature, but there are also measures of a more economic character, most of which are only really possible in a nationally managed fishery or in a highly integrated international organisation such as the EC. Such measures include limiting the number of vessels which may fish, limiting their size, or limiting the number of days they may fish. The first such measure is aimed at increasing economic efficiency, i.e., the rate of return per vessel: the other two are more concerned with preventing over-fishing. All of the various measures mentioned have drawbacks. The biological measures require large quantities of reliable data in order to operate (which is often missing), they often militate against economic efficiency, and are usually difficult and costly to enforce. The economic measures often have adverse social and safety side-effects, and the second and third type of measures referred to may also work against economic efficiency.

International fisheries law prior to the mid-1970s

International fisheries law in this period was concerned mainly with three questions – access to resources, conservation, and the avoidance of conflicts between different types of fishing gear.

Access to resources

The way in which international law regulated access to fishery resources during this period is best understood by considering, first, the various jurisdictional zones of coastal States and, secondly, the regime of the high seas.

Internal waters and territorial sea

As we saw in chapters three and four, internal waters and the territorial sea form part of a State's territory and the only right which other States enjoy under general international law in these waters is a right of innocent passage in the territorial sea and, in very limited circumstances, in internal waters. It therefore follows that a State enjoys exclusive access to the fish stocks in its internal waters and territorial sea, unless another State is accorded access by agreement (as under the EC's Common Fisheries Policy): this, however, is most unusual in practice.

The exclusive fishing zone

The exclusive fishing zone (EFZ) is a concept of relatively recent origin in the international law of the sea. There had been a few claims to EFZs before 1958, notably the claims made in the late 1940s and early 1950s by some of the Pacific coast Latin American States to 200-mile zones, but these claims were vigorously challenged by the USA (in part to protect the interests of its tuna-fishing fleets), leading to a number of disputes following the arrest of US vessels. However, the more widespread claims to EFZs were largely the result of the failure of UNCLOS I and II to agree on the breadth of the territorial sea or to accord coastal States any special rights of access to fish stocks beyond the territorial sea. This failure led to a wave of unilateral claims by coastal States to twelve-mile EFZs (and some zones of greater breadth). Some of these claims were, initially, challenged. Thus, for example, the United Kingdom contested Iceland's proclamation of a twelve-mile EFZ in 1958, leading to a 'cod war' between the two States. However, by the early 1960s the United Kingdom and other States abandoned their opposition to such claims. There followed the conclusion of a number of bilateral agreements, and at a regional level in western Europe the Fisheries Convention of 1964, which recognised claims to a twelve-mile EFZ. These developments were such that, in the 1974 *Fisheries Jurisdiction* cases, the International Court of Justice had no hesitation in pronouncing that the twelve-mile EFZ had become established as a rule of customary international law. Within the EFZ the coastal State had exclusive or priority access to the resources of the zone, although in most cases States whose vessels had traditionally fished in the waters embraced by the new zones were given a period of time in which to phase out their activities and in some cases indefinite, though limited, continued access.

The continental shelf

Articles 1 to 3 of the Convention on the Continental Shelf, which the International Court of Justice in the *North Sea Continental Shelf* cases (1969) said also represent customary international law, gave the coastal State exclusive access to the natural resources of its continental shelf. These include 'living organisms belonging to sedentary species, that is to say, organisms which, at the harvestable stage, either are immobile on or under the seabed or are unable to move except in constant physical contact with the seabed or the subsoil' (CSC, art. 2(4)). While these sedentary species clearly include such things as oysters, clams and mussels, there has been considerable controversy as to whether they include creatures such as crabs and lobsters. Reference was made in chapter eight to some of the disputes that have arisen in this area.

High seas

As we saw in chapter eleven, the high seas are not susceptible to appropriation and are open to use by all States. Thus the vessels of all States have access to the fish stocks of the high seas. However, this freedom of access was clearly of most benefit to those States that had the capital and technology to take advantage of it, that is, in the main, developed distant-water fishing nations. While access to the fishery resources of the high seas was in principle free and unrestricted, in practice many States agreed, through arrangements regulating high-seas fisheries, to limit their access. These arrangements will be considered in the next section. A common consequence of freedom of fishing on the high seas, particularly where access was not limited through agreement, was that more vessels engaged in fishing than was economically justifiable, i.e., fishing was often at a level considerably above the MEY.

In the *Fisheries Jurisdiction* cases, where the International Court of Justice was faced with determining the validity of Iceland's extension of its fishing limits in 1972 from twelve to fifty miles, the Court held that under customary international law a coastal State particularly dependent on fishing for its economic livelihood in certain circumstances enjoyed preferential rights of access to the high-seas fishery resources in the waters adjacent to its coasts. This finding by the International Court has been criticised because of the lack of evidence for and the imprecision of the alleged rule, and, as far as we are aware, in practice no coastal State, either before or since the Court's judgment, has sought to rely on it.

Conservation

As regards conservation (i.e., the prevention of over-fishing), the concern of international law was originally largely limited to allocating the competence to adopt conservation measures, but it later became directly and increasingly concerned with substantive rules of conservation through the establishment of international fishery commissions and a number of *ad hoc* agreements regulating fishing.

As far as the competence to adopt conservation measures was concerned, this was distributed between coastal States, flag States and international fishery commissions. By virtue of the fact that internal waters and the territorial sea form part of its territory, a State had the competence to prescribe regulations governing fishing in those waters by vessels of whatever nationality and the competence to enforce such regulations. The coastal State had a similar competence in its EFZ and in respect of the sedentary species of its continental shelf. A flag State had the competence to prescribe fishery regulations for vessels flying its flag, wherever they might be. However, the flag State could take action to enforce such regulations only on the high seas or in its own internal waters, territorial sea or EFZ. It thus followed that, in the absence of international agreement to the contrary, the only way in which regulations could (and still can) be prescribed and enforced in respect of vessels fishing on the high seas was (and still is) through flag States.

This division of jurisdictional competence between coastal States and flag States did not provide an adequate framework for effective conservation. Since in most areas of the world territorial seas and EFZs formed a rather narrow band of waters, coastal States had in practice control only over a comparatively small area containing rather limited fish stocks: furthermore, in many cases fish stocks which were found within their areas of control migrated outside those areas at certain times of the year. As far as flag States were concerned, while they alone could regulate fishing on the high seas, there was in practice little incentive for them to take conservation measures. If a flag State took measures to conserve a particular fish stock, those measures would not have any beneficial effect unless other flag States fishing the same stock took similar measures; but there was no way in which other flag States could be compelled to do so. The fact that article 2 of the High Seas Convention provides that the freedom of fishing on the high seas 'shall be exercised by all States with reasonable regard to the interests of other States in their exercise of the freedom of the high seas' appears in practice not to have been a factor encouraging flag States to take conservation measures, either singly or in concert, or restraining them from excessive fishing.

In order to try to overcome some of the drawbacks of flag State jurisdiction and narrow coastal State jurisdiction – although, it must be emphasised, without attempting to change the basic nature of the jurisdiction enjoyed by coastal and flag States or the distribution of jurisdiction between them – some twenty or more international fishery commissions were established, the vast majority after 1945. These commissions were either set up to regulate particular species (e.g., whales, seals, tuna) or to regulate fisheries in particular regions (e.g., the North Atlantic, the North Pacific, the Baltic, the Mediterranean, etc.). The functions and powers of these commissions varied considerably, but they all tended to have the same shortcomings: the inability to agree on conservation measures recommended by scientists as essential; the possibility of opting out of any conservation measures adopted; and poor enforcement of such measures. The last two tended to be self-perpetuating in the sense that if one State saw another not accepting a recommendation, or not properly enforcing it, there was no incentive for it to adhere to its obligations, since this would put its fishermen at a disadvantage compared with the fishermen of the defaulting State. Finally, an international fishery commission could not control the fishing activities of those States which were unwilling to become members of it.

Apart from international fishery commissions, there were a number of international agreements, largely of an *ad hoc* character, which attempted to conserve fisheries on the high seas. Most of these agreements were bilateral or regional, as well as often being short-term, in character, but there was one general multilateral agreement – the 1958 Convention on Fishing and Conservation of the Living Resources of the High Seas, adopted at UNCLOS I. This Convention required States Parties to it to agree upon measures to conserve the fishery resources of the high seas: in certain very limited circumstances it gave a coastal State the right unilaterally to adopt conservation measures for areas of the high seas adjacent to its territorial sea. However, the Convention proved largely to be a dead letter. Many major fishing nations did not ratify it, because it did not correspond to the interests of coastal States, and because in many regions international fishery commissions had already been set up to take conservation measures.

Avoidance of gear conflicts

The avoidance and resolution of conflicts arising out of fishing activities, particularly conflicts between different types of gear, such as the interference and damage trawling may cause to standing nets, were the subject of a number of bilateral treaties and one regional agreement. The latter was the 1967 Convention on Conduct of Fishing Operations in the North Atlantic which was aimed at preventing collisions between vessels while fishing and conflicts between trawling and the users of fixed gear, and at facilitating the resolution of disputes arising out of such collisions and conflicts. These kinds of agreement are still important and many are still in force, although as the amount of foreign fishing in the 200-mile zones of coastal States has decreased, so has the practical application of these agreements.

Developments since the mid-1970s

In spite of the considerable body of international fisheries law which had evolved by the early 1970s, there was much dissatisfaction with the regime for fisheries which this law had established. Most developing coastal States were resentful of the fact that the vessels of distant developed States, equipped with the latest technology, were catching fish on the high seas a comparatively short distance from their coasts. Even if these States did not have adequate vessels of their own to fish their offshore waters, they wished at least to be able to control the activities of foreign operators and to be able to obtain some revenue through licence fees and to gain access to technological know-how. At the same time some developed coastal States were not happy with the existing legal regime, either because they wanted greater access to or control over their offshore fishery resources, or because they were sceptical of the ability of international fishery commissions effectively to regulate fishing in the face of the increasing pressure on stocks resulting from ever-more intensive methods of fishing. There was also a more general desire to try to put an end to disputes over the extent of coastal State jurisdiction relating to fisheries which had erupted at frequent intervals over the previous twenty years. Many States therefore seized the opportunity presented by the decision to convene UNCLOS III to press for a radical revision of the international legal regime governing fisheries.

The Sea Bed Committee and the earlier stages of UNCLOS III revealed three broad approaches to the question of fisheries. First, the developing countries, supported later by some developed countries such as Australia, Canada, New Zealand and Norway, advocated broad coastal State jurisdiction for fisheries, an idea which was subsequently developed and incorporated in proposals concerning the EEZ. The USA, and initially Canada, proposed an approach to fisheries management based on the migratory characteristics of different species. This proposal categorised fish into sedentary species, coastal species (i.e., non-sedentary species which inhabit nutrient-rich areas adjacent to the coast), anadromous species and wide-ranging species. Access to and management of the first three of these would vest exclusively or primarily in the coastal State, but wide-ranging species would be regulated by international fishery organisations. Finally, the two greatest traditional distant-water fishing nations, Japan and the then USSR, wanted as little change in the *status quo* as possible, and proposed that only developing coastal States should enjoy preferential rights in the waters adjacent to their coasts.

The Law of the Sea Convention's provisions on fisheries generally reflect the first of these approaches, although elements of the species approach can also be seen. By 1976 the fisheries provisions of the UNCLOS negotiating texts had received very wide support, and before the conference ended had inspired a large amount of State practice in the form of claims to 200-mile EEZs and EFZs and bilateral and regional agreements. Thus although the Law of the Sea Convention entered into force only in 1994, its provisions concerning fisheries had already had an enormous impact on State practice long before that date.

The core of the fisheries provisions of the Law of the Sea Convention is to be found in the articles dealing with the EEZ. The universal establishment of 200-mile EEZs and EFZs would embrace an area where about ninety per cent of commercial fishing currently takes place. Thus the regime for this area is obviously crucial to the proper management of marine fisheries. We therefore examine this regime first. This will be followed by a consideration of the regime governing fisheries on the high seas, and we end with a discussion of the rules governing the various species for which the law of the sea makes particular provision (highly migratory, anadromous, catadromous, marine mammals and sedentary).

The fisheries regime of the EEZ

The coastal State's rights and duties

Within the EEZ the coastal State has 'sovereign rights for the purpose of exploring and exploiting, conserving and managing' the fish stocks of the zone (LOSC, art. 56(1)). These rights are subject to a number of duties. The coastal State must take such conservation and management measures as will ensure that fish stocks in its EEZ are not endangered by over-exploitation, and that such stocks are maintained at or restored to 'levels which can produce the maximum sustainable yield, as qualified by relevant environmental and economic factors . . . and taking into account fishing patterns, the interdependence of stocks and any generally recommended' sub-regional, regional or global minimum standards (LOSC, art. 61(3)). Subject to this, the coastal State is required to promote the objective of optimum utilisation of the living resources of its EEZ (LOSC, art. 62(1)). Finally, the coastal State is to establish the allowable catch (often referred to as the total allowable catch: TAC) for each fish stock within its EEZ (LOSC, art. 61(1)).

It can be seen that these duties are formulated in very wide and general terms and that the coastal State is given a very broad discretion, particularly in relation to setting the allowable catch, where the management objective of MSY is so heavily qualified that a coastal State could legitimately set practically any size of allowable catch, as long as it did not lead to over-exploitation which endangered fish stocks. This, and the fact that the coastal State's management duties are exempted from the provisions of the Convention dealing with compulsory settlement of disputes (except for compulsory conciliation in certain cases, see p. 455), has significant implications for the access of foreign fishermen, as will shortly be seen. On the other hand, the breadth of a coastal State's discretion is not necessarily a bad thing, as it enables it to adopt the fishing management strategy best suited to its needs.

As can be seen from the Appendix, over ninety States currently claim a 200-mile EEZ and a further nine States a 200-mile EFZ (as well as some claims to lesser breadths, and ten 200-mile territorial sea claims). This practice, most of which long pre-dates the entry into force of the Law of the Sea Convention, coupled with the absence of protest, indicates that there is now in customary international law a right to claim a 200-mile EEZ or EFZ within which the coastal State has the broad rights set out in article 56(1) (quoted above) (and see chapter nine, p. 161). What is much less certain is whether the coastal State's fishery management duties set out in articles 61 and 62 have become part of customary law.[1] Relatively few States' national legislation refers to these duties.[2] This may be, not because the duties are not accepted, but because these duties are not considered as an appropriate matter for legislation, since they relate to administrative practices. On the other hand, the duties may be too vague and insufficiently of a 'norm-creating character' to pass into customary law. In any case, even if the duties were customary rules, their vagueness, coupled with the possibility of factual disputes over such matters as the state of fish stocks, means that it would be very difficult, if not impossible, to tell whether in any particular case the duties had been observed.

Access of other States to the EEZ

Article 62(2) provides that where the fishermen of the coastal State are not capable of taking the whole of the allowable catch, the coastal State is to permit the fishermen of other States to fish for the balance between what its fishermen take and the allowable catch. This obligation supports the objective of optimum utilisation mentioned above. The coastal State is given a broad discretion in deciding which other States' fishermen are to be given access to this surplus. Article 62(3) provides that in giving access,

> the coastal State shall take into account all relevant factors, including *inter alia*, the significance of the living resources of the area to the economy of the coastal State concerned and its other national interests, the provisions of articles 69 and 70, the requirements of developing States in the subregion or region in harvesting part of the surplus and the need to minimise economic dislocation in States whose nationals have habitually fished in the zone or which have made substantial efforts in research and identification of stocks.

Articles 69 and 70, which deal with landlocked and geographically disadvantaged States and are discussed in detail in chapter eighteen, in principle give a guaranteed access for such States to a portion of any surplus. Other States are completely subject to the coastal State's discretion (which again is exempted from compulsory dispute settlement). This discretion is particularly broad, since by having the latitude described above in determining the allowable catch, the coastal State can also determine the size of the surplus (if any).

State practice concerning the access of foreign fishermen to the EEZ, found not only in national legislation but also in over 300 bilateral agreements (virtually

---

[1] The views of writers differ quite widely on this question. For a succinct survey, see F. Orrego Vicuña, *The Exclusive Economic Zone* (Cambridge, Cambridge University Press), 1989, pp. 244–6.

[2] For details of such legislation, see Kwiatkowska (1989), *op. cit.* in 'Further reading' in the section entitled 'The EEZ regime', pp. 52–3 and 57–8.

all of which were concluded before the entry into force of the Law of the Sea Convention), reflects the Convention scheme to some extent, but it also displays considerable diversity and some divergence from the Convention's provisions.[3] In some cases foreign vessels are given access even where there is no surplus: thus, for example, the EC (which has the exclusive competence to negotiate and conclude bilateral fisheries agreements in place of its Member States[4]) and Norway give each other reciprocal access to their waters in order that previous fishing patterns should not be disrupted too severely by the introduction of 200-mile limits. Some States make access contingent upon being granted trade concessions (as Canada has done with the EC, and the USA with a number of States); or upon the payment of financial compensation in addition to licence fees (as several African States do with the EC); or upon the establishment of joint ventures with coastal State companies or other forms of economic co-operation (as some Latin American and African States do). In many of these cases the agreements concerned make no reference to the existence of any surplus. While there may be a rule of customary international law that coastal States must give foreign vessels access where there is a surplus (academic opinion is divided on this question), the diversity of practice is such that it is unlikely that there is any customary rule requiring coastal States to give access to any particular category of State (which, indeed, is also the position under the Convention).

Where the fishermen of other States are given access to its EEZ, the coastal State can prescribe conditions to govern such fishing. Article 62(4) of the Convention provides that these conditions may, for example, require foreign fishermen to have licences, to observe the coastal State's conservation measures, to carry out research programmes, to land part or all of their catches in the coastal State, and to train coastal State personnel. In the *Franco-Canadian Fisheries* arbitration (1986) the tribunal suggested that the coastal State's competence to prescribe legislation for foreign fishing vessels in its EEZ was limited to conservation measures *stricto sensu* and therefore could not include measures to regulate fish processing. This seems an unjustifiably narrow reading of article 62(4), which speaks of foreign vessels complying with the coastal State's 'conservation measures and the other terms and conditions established in [its] laws and regulations', and many of the illustrative list of eleven permissible types of measure go

---

[3] For detailed surveys of agreements and national legislation on access, see the following works referred to in 'Further reading': Attard, under 'The EEZ regime', pp. 161–72; Carroz and Savini, under 'The EEZ regime'; Churchill, under 'General works', pp. 176–84 (on EC practice); and Dahmani, under 'The EEZ regime', pp. 74–81. See also United Nations, *The Law of the Sea: Practice of States at the Time of Entry into Force of the United Nations Convention on the Law of the Sea* (New York, United Nations), 1994, pp. 39–40, 45–6, 71, 131 and 180.

[4] For a discussion of the EC's competence in relation to treaty-making concerning fisheries, see R. R. Churchill, 'The European Community and its role in some issues of international fisheries law' in Hey (ed.), *op. cit.* under 'General works' in 'Further reading'. See also the declaration made by the EC when confirming its signature of the Law of the Sea Convention.

beyond conservation. In any case the point was not central to the tribunal's decision. Whether permissible coastal State measures include legislation requiring foreign fishing vessels to have gear stowed when passing through the coastal State's EEZ without fishing there, a requirement found in the legislation of a number of States, is perhaps less certain. Certainly the claims of Costa Rica and the Maldives that such vessels require prior authorisation to transit their EEZ would seem to be contrary to the Convention.[5] A coastal State's measures must also, it would seem, be compatible with its other treaty obligations. This is suggested by the decision of a panel set up under the 1989 Canada–USA Free Trade Agreement which found that Canadian measures requiring salmon and herring caught within its EFZ in the Pacific to be landed in Canada before being exported, were contrary to the Agreement (and by implication to the GATT).[6] However, it should be noted that at the time the decision was given the Law of the Sea Convention was not in force. In the case of such a dispute between parties to the Convention the outcome might be less certain in the light of article 311 (see p. 24 above).

Where the coastal State has prescribed regulations in conformity with the Convention for foreign vessels fishing in its EEZ, it may enforce them by measures including 'boarding, inspection, arrest and judicial proceedings' (art. 73(1)). It must also be remembered that hot pursuit is possible in the case of those vessels that attempt to evade enforcement measures (see further chapter eleven). When a foreign vessel has been arrested, its flag State must be notified immediately and the vessel and crew 'promptly released upon the posting of reasonable bond or other security' (art. 73(2)(4)). Article 73(3) provides that where violations of its regulations are established, the penalties which the coastal State may impose may not include 'imprisonment, in the absence of agreements to the contrary by the States concerned, or any other form of corporal punishment'. Notwithstanding this prohibition, some thirty-two States, a number of which are parties to the Convention, do provide in their legislation for imprisonment, even in the absence of agreements with other States.[7]

---

[5] Costa Rica, Law No. 6267 of 1978, art. 7 and Decree No. 10404 of 1991, art. 2, discussed in J. A. Roach and R. W. Smith, *United States Responses to Excessive Maritime Claims* (The Hague, Nijhoff), 2nd edn, 1996, pp. 417–21. Maldives, Law No. 32/76 of 5 December 1976, art. 1. *Smith, op. cit.* in 'Further reading' under 'The EEZ regime', p. 278. For an excellent discussion of the permissible scope of coastal State legislative jurisdiction, see Burke (1994), *op. cit.* in 'Further reading' under 'General works', pp. 315–35. See also chapter nine above, p. 175. Note also that in its first decision in the *M/V Saiga* case (1997) (on the prompt release of the vessel) the International Tribunal for the Law of the Sea was faced with the question of whether the refuelling of fishing vessels from an accompanying tanker fell within the permissible scope of coastal State measures. The Tribunal decided that it did not need to answer this question, but briefly discussed the arguments either way. See paras 56–9 of its judgment.

[6] Referred to in United Nations, *op. cit.* in footnote 3, p. 132.

[7] Kwiatkowska, *op. cit.* in footnote 2, p. 87. A figure of twenty-one States is given in Roach and Smith, *op. cit.* in footnote 5, pp. 191–2.

For any coastal State with a sizeable EEZ proper enforcement of its fishery regulations in its EEZ presents a considerable challenge in terms of resources (vessels, aircraft, personnel, etc.) and technology (use of satellites to track vessels, computers, etc.). For developing countries these problems are particularly acute, none more so than for the tiny island States of the South Pacific with their vast EEZs. The latter States have engaged in increasing co-operation in surveillance and enforcement of their EEZs through an organisation known as the Forum Fisheries Agency (FFA), set up by the South Pacific Forum Fisheries Convention of 1979, whose members also include Australia and New Zealand. In 1982 seven of the smallest FFA members concluded the Nauru Agreement concerning Co-operation in the Management of Fisheries of Common Interest under which the parties agreed to establish uniform licence conditions for foreign distant-water vessels fishing for common stocks (mainly tuna) in their EEZs, to explore the possibility of establishing a centralised licensing system, and to co-operate in the monitoring and surveillance of foreign fishing by exchanging information and exploring the possibility of joint surveillance and reciprocal enforcement. In the following year a register was set up of all foreign distant-water vessels licensed to fish in the EEZs/EFZs of all seventeen FFA members – foreign vessels take ninety per cent of tuna caught in the South Pacific, the main fishery resource of the region. A vessel on this register which loses its 'good standing' (e.g., by committing a serious offence) is blacklisted and is not allowed to fish in any FFA EEZ. The FFA operates a database on the activities of foreign vessels. Minimum terms and conditions to be included in any agreement permitting distant-water vessels to fish in the EEZ/EFZ of an FFA member have also been agreed. Such terms and conditions include *inter alia* uniform catch and position reporting requirements, provisions for the placement of observers on foreign vessels and obligations on flag States to ensure that their vessels comply with coastal State laws and to take effective action against vessels that do not so comply. In 1992 FFA members signed the Niue Treaty on Co-operation in Fisheries Surveillance and Law Enforcement in the South Pacific Region, under which the parties agree to co-operate in developing regional procedures for fisheries surveillance and enforcement. Apart from putting the regional register and minimum terms and conditions already referred to on a treaty footing and requiring parties to provide the FFA with information on the activities of foreign fishing vessels and their surveillance and enforcement actions, the Niue Treaty encourages its parties to conclude subsidiary agreements to provide for one party to stop, board, search and seize foreign fishing vessels in the waters of another party, and to co-operate in prosecutions and enforcement of penalties. Pursuant to these provisions a subsidiary agreement has been concluded between Tonga and Tuvalu and further agreements are under elaboration.[8] In addition Australia and New Zealand routinely carry out aerial surveillance for other FFA members of their EEZs. Outside the Pacific an agreement similar to the Niue

---

[8] Bergin, *op. cit.* in 'Further reading' under 'The EEZ regime', pp. 305–6.

Treaty, the Agreement establishing Common Fisheries Surveillance Zones of Participating Member States of the Organisation of Eastern Caribbean States, was signed by the members of that organisation in 1991.[9]

The management of shared stocks

The Law of the Sea Convention conveys the impression that most fish stocks confine themselves to the EEZ of a single coastal State. In fact in some areas, such as the North-East and East Central Atlantic, this is very far from being the case. Many stocks migrate between the EEZs of two or more States (usually known as shared or joint stocks) and/or between the EEZ(s) and the waters beyond (straddling stocks). Straddling stocks are considered below. In relation to shared stocks, the Convention contains one brief provision. Article 63(1) exhorts the States concerned 'to seek . . . to agree upon the measures necessary to co-ordinate and ensure the conservation and development of such stocks'. Nothing further is said, for example, about management objectives or allocation of the catch among interested States, which are the kinds of things that the States concerned need to agree on if there is to be effective management of shared stocks. While it follows from article 63(1) and the case law of international courts and tribunals on the duty to negotiate[10] that the States concerned are required to negotiate arrangements for the management of shared stocks in good faith and in a meaningful way, there is no obligation on such States to reach agreement. If no agreement is reached, each State will manage that part of the shared stock occurring in its EEZ in accordance with the general rights and duties relating to fisheries management by a coastal State in its EEZ. The result may well be mismanagement of a shared stock and inequity in the allocation of benefits from it, for example if one State takes strict conservation measures with a view to maximising yield in the long term but thereby reducing its catch substantially in the short term, whereas the other State fishes the stock heavily in order to maximise short-term gain.

In practice States have been able to agree on co-operative arrangements for the management of shared stocks to a considerable extent. Excluding agreements concerned solely with the particular species identified by the Law of the Sea Convention which are considered below, there are currently at least twenty agreements in force dealing with the management of shared stocks, some of which have operated successfully for a decade or more, even though in some of these cases the position has been made more complicated by the absence of

[9] *Ibid.*, p. 305 and United Nations, *op. cit.* in footnote 3, pp. 180–1. For discussion of other co-operative arrangements in enforcement, see United Nations, pp. 42–8 and Kwiatkowska, *op. cit.* in footnote 2, pp. 68 and 88.

[10] See, for example, the *North Sea Continental Shelf* cases, [1969] *ICJ Rep.* 1, at 47, and the *Fisheries Jurisdiction* case, [1974] *ICJ Rep.* 3, at 32. See also Hayashi, *op. cit.* in 'Further reading' under 'Shared stocks', pp. 251–2.

agreement on the maritime boundary between the EEZs of the States concerned. While these agreements vary quite widely in the kinds of management measures adopted, from the point of view of form and institutions they fall into four main categories.

A first group of agreements takes the form of a periodic (usually annual) arrangement negotiated under a pre-existing framework treaty. Examples include the series of annual arrangements agreed between the EC and Norway under their 1980 Fisheries Agreement, whereby they set TACs for shared stocks, based on the recommendations of the International Council for the Exploration of the Sea, which are then allocated between them on the basis of zonal attachment; the 1989 Agreement between Denmark, Iceland and Norway concerning Capelin Stocks in the Waters between Greenland, Iceland and Jan Mayen, under which the three parties are to agree on a TAC for capelin in the waters concerned each year (if no agreement can be reached, Iceland is to set the TAC unilaterally), with the Agreement itself specifying the percentage of the TAC each party is to receive; and the 1978 Treaty between Australia and Papua New Guinea on Sovereignty and Maritime Boundaries, under which the parties are to adopt management measures for the fisheries of the Protected Zone in the Torres Strait, including the setting of TACs allocated between the parties in fixed percentages (the figure depending on the area concerned).

A second type of arrangement is where measures for the management of shared stocks are taken by a bilateral commission set up especially for this purpose. Examples include the Iceland-Norway Fisheries Commission set up by the 1980 Agreement concerning Fishery and Continental Shelf Questions, which sets TACs each year for stocks in the waters between Iceland and the Norwegian island of Jan Mayen and allocates TACs between the parties (except for capelin, the most important species, where allocation is determined by the agreement itself); the Norway-Russia (formerly Soviet Union) Commission established by their 1976 Fisheries Agreement, which each year sets TACs for shared stocks in the Barents Sea, allocating them in fixed percentages, the figure varying from one species to another; the International Pacific Halibut Commission, set up by the 1953 Convention for the Preservation of the Halibut Fishery of the Northern Pacific Ocean and Bering Sea as amended by a Protocol of 1979, which adopts management measures (including TACs, closed seasons, minimum fish sizes and gear regulations) for halibut stocks shared by Canada and the USA in the North Pacific and Bering Sea; the Mixed Technical Commission set up by the 1973 River Plate Treaty which adopts conservation and management measures for a large common fisheries zone straddling the boundary between the 200-mile zones of Argentina and Uruguay; and the South Atlantic Fisheries Commission, set up by Argentina and the United Kingdom in 1990 (but not by a treaty), which makes recommendations relating to conservation in the Argentina/Falklands area.

A third type of arrangement is measures adopted by a regional fisheries organisation. The main example of this type of arrangement, which makes particular sense in enclosed or semi-enclosed seas where fish migrate between the zones of several States, is the International Baltic Sea Fisheries Commission, established by the 1973 Convention on Fishing and Conservation of the Living Resources of the Baltic Sea and Belts, which adopts TACs, gear regulations, closed seasons, closed areas, etc. A somewhat analogous situation is the Common Fisheries Policy of the EC, where a wide range of management measures has been adopted by the Council.

Finally, there is a group of agreements where the parties undertake in a general way to co-operate over the management of shared fish stocks on an *ad hoc* basis but where (as far as we are aware) no detailed arrangements have yet been adopted. Examples include a number of boundary agreements which Colombia has included with its neighbours[11] (as well as some other Caribbean boundary agreements[12]); the 1984 Convention relating to the Regional Development of Fisheries in the Gulf of Guinea; the 1991 Convention on Fisheries Co-operation among States bordering the Atlantic Ocean (whose parties are the Atlantic coastal States of Africa); and the 1982 Nauru Agreement concerning Co-operation in the Management of Fisheries of Common Interest.

In spite of this not inconsiderable practice, it must also be admitted that there still exist many shared stocks for which no co-operative arrangements have yet been agreed by the States concerned.

The regulation of fishing on the high seas

While the overwhelming proportion of the world's commercial fishing takes place within 200 miles of land, the Law of the Sea Convention also contains provisions governing fishing on the high seas. This is important as many fish stocks spend part of their life cycle on the high seas and a few spend their whole life cycle there. The Convention provides that on the high seas fishing is in principle open to all States, subject to the restrictions arising out of the rules relating to straddling stocks and particular species discussed below (arts 87 and 116). Nevertheless, articles 117 to 120 lay down a duty on interested States to co-operate in the management and conservation of high-seas fishery resources, making use, where appropriate, of international fishery commissions. The aim of such management should be to 'maintain or restore populations of harvested species at levels which can produce the maximum sustainable yield, as qualified

---

[11] Colombia–Haiti Agreement on the Delimitation of the Maritime Boundaries, 1978; Colombia–Dominican Republic Agreement on Delimitation of Marine and Submarine Areas and Maritime Co-operation, 1978; Colombia–Costa Rica Treaty on Delimitation of Marine and Submarine Areas and Maritime Co-operation, 1977; Colombia–Panama Treaty on the Delimitation of Marine and Submarine Areas and Related Matters, 1976; and Columbia–Ecuador Agreement concerning Delimitation of Marine and Submarine Areas and Maritime Co-operation, 1975.

[12] Netherlands–Venezuela Boundary Delimitation Treaty, 1978 and Costa Rica–Panama Treaty concerning Delimitation of Marine Areas and Maritime Co-operation, 1980.

by relevant environmental and economic factors, including the special requirements of developing States, and taking into account fishing patterns, the interdependence of stocks and any generally recommended international minimum
standards' (art. 119(1)(a)). In adopting conservation measures States shall also
take into consideration 'the effects on species associated with or dependent upon
harvested species with a view to maintaining or restoring populations of such
associated or dependent species above levels at which their reproduction may
become seriously threatened' (art. 119(1)(b)). Any conservation measures adopted
should not discriminate in form or in fact against the fishermen of any State.

These provisions, which are modelled on part of the 1958 Geneva Convention
on Fishing and Conservation of the Living Resources of the High Seas, do not
really address the inherent weaknesses of the high-seas fisheries regime identified
earlier in this chapter. As with the position before the general establishment of
200-mile EEZs and EFZs, the only way in which meaningful management of
high-seas fisheries is possible is through international co-operation, especially
through regional fisheries commissions. Apart from commissions concerned solely
with particular species, which are considered later, there are currently four commissions whose task is to manage the high-seas fisheries of a particular region.
These bodies are the Northwest Atlantic Fisheries Organisation (NAFO), established by the 1978 Convention on Future Multilateral Co-operation in the North-
west Atlantic Fisheries; the North-East Atlantic Fisheries Commission, established
by the 1980 Convention on Future Multilateral Co-operation in the North-East
Atlantic Fisheries; the General Fisheries Council for the Mediterranean, established by the 1949 Agreement for the Establishment of the General Fisheries
Council for the Mediterranean as amended in 1976 and 1997; and the Commission for the Conservation of Antarctic Marine Living Resources (CCAMLR),
established by the 1980 Convention on the Conservation of Antarctic Marine
Living Resources. A fifth body – the International North Pacific Fisheries Commission set up by the 1952 International Convention for the High Seas Fisheries
of the North Pacific Ocean as amended by a Protocol of 1978 – ceased to exist
in 1993 when it was effectively replaced by the North Pacific Anadromous Fish
Commission (discussed below); and a sixth body, the International Commission
for the Southeast Atlantic Fisheries (set up by the 1969 Convention on the Conservation of the Living Resources of the Southeast Atlantic) has effectively
ceased to function, although a protocol of 1990 formally terminating its existence has not yet entered into force. Thus there are many regions where no high-
seas fisheries commissions exist. It is true that for some areas there are FAO
regional bodies such as the Western Central Atlantic Fisheries Commission and
the Indian Ocean Fishery Commission, but such bodies are purely advisory and
have no regulatory powers.

For reasons of space no detailed account can be given of the present four
regulatory high seas commissions. Instead a thumbnail sketch will be given of
what appear to be the two most significant in practice, NAFO and CCAMLR.
NAFO's role is to manage the fishery resources of the high seas of the Northwest

Atlantic, including straddling stocks (on which more below), and to co-ordinate scientific research. To the former end NAFO establishes each year TACs, which are then divided into quotas allocated to individual members of NAFO, and from time to time adopts other conservation measures such as minimum mesh sizes and by-catch levels. As was usual with the pre-UNCLOS commissions, it is possible for any member which does not like a NAFO measure to object to it within certain time limits and so not be bound. In order to promote greater compliance with its measures, NAFO has adopted a scheme of joint international inspection and surveillance,[13] under which an authorised inspector of one NAFO member may board and inspect a fishing vessel of any other member to see if that vessel is complying with NAFO measures. The inspector must notify the flag State of any apparent infringement and may prohibit the vessel from further fishing. The flag State must investigate allegations of illegal fishing promptly (including ordering the vessel to a nearby port if justified). Criminal proceedings against the vessel may be taken only by the flag State. To complement this scheme NAFO in 1995 adopted an observer scheme under which each vessel fishing in the NAFO area must carry an observer on board whose task is to monitor the vessel's compliance with NAFO measures. Apparent infringements are to be reported to a NAFO inspector and a report on the period of observation sent to NAFO and the flag State. Under a measure adopted in 1991 vessels must also report their movements into, within and out of the NAFO area; and in 1995 NAFO introduced a pilot project under which a certain proportion of vessels must carry satellite-tracking devices.

CCAMLR's area of competence is a huge one – all waters south of 60° South (including waters within 200 miles of land) as well as areas north of 60° South which are within the Antarctic Convergence (i.e., where the cold waters of the Antarctic meet the warmer waters of other oceans). Within this area, where commercial fishing began only in the 1970s, CCAMLR is responsible for co-ordinating research on Antarctic marine living resources (which are not limited to fish but include, for example, birds) and adopting conservation and management measures for these resources, such as the establishment of quantities to be harvested, the designation of protected species and closed seasons and the regulation of gear. In adopting such measures CCAMLR is charged with taking an ecosystem approach: for example, in regulating the catch of a particular fish species CCAMLR must also take into account the effect of its proposed measure on the populations of birds for which that fish species is a source of food. In this respect CCAMLR is the most advanced fisheries organisation in existence, but there are nevertheless significant limitations on its ecosystem approach, as marine mammals fall outside its competence and are regulated by other organisations (discussed below). In practice CCAMLR has adopted a number of

---

[13] The present scheme, replacing earlier schemes, dates from 1991 and was amended in 1995. Text in *Official Journal of the European Communities*, 1992, L54/2 and 1995, L329/1.

conservation and management measures such as precautionary catch limits for certain species of fish and crustaceans, including krill, which is the cornerstone of the Antarctic food chain, mesh size regulations, closed areas and closed seasons. In carrying out this task CCAMLR has been hampered by a lack of scientific knowledge of the Antarctic ecosystem, and in its early years by the lack of political consensus to take effective measures. As with NAFO, parties are not bound by measures to which they object. There is also an inspection and observer scheme to aid enforcement of CCAMLR measures which is broadly similar to that of NAFO.

Since the late 1970s fishing on the high seas has increased considerably as distant-water fishing vessels have been displaced from their traditional fishing grounds as a result of coastal States phasing out much foreign fishing from their 200-mile zones. Since the mid- to late 1980s high-seas fishing has given rise to three specific problems and sources of conflict – the exploitation of straddling stocks, the use of large-scale driftnets and the free rider problem – and has revealed the general inadequacy of the UNCLOS provisions. The problem of straddling stocks is considered separately below: the other issues we consider here.

As fishing on the high seas has grown and become more competitive and as technology has developed, so the size of some types of fishing gear, including driftnets, has increased. By the late 1980s driftnets up to thirty miles in length were being used. Such nets, suspended vertically to a depth of about thirty feet, caught not only their target species (usually tuna, salmon or squid), but also large numbers of other fish species, marine mammals (particularly dolphins), turtles and some sea birds. For this reason such nets, which were used mainly by Japanese, South Korean and Taiwanese vessels in the Indian and Pacific Oceans, were often dubbed 'walls of death'. Concern at the indiscriminate loss of marine life and the over-fishing of tuna and salmon caused by the use of such driftnets has prompted a considerable amount of diplomatic and legislative (both national and international) activity. In July 1989 the members of the South Pacific Forum adopted the Tarawa Declaration on Driftnet Fishing.[14] After expressing concern at the damage done by driftnet fishing and 'recognising' that such fishing 'is not consistent with international legal requirements in relation to rights and obligations of high seas fisheries conservation and management and environmental principles', the Declaration resolved to seek a ban on such fishing and to develop a convention to this end. Four months later the Organisation of Eastern Caribbean States adopted a similar declaration.[15] This was followed a month later by the adoption of UN General Assembly Resolution 44/225,[16] which recommended the cessation of large-scale pelagic driftnet fishing in the South Pacific by 1 July 1991 and a moratorium on such fishing elsewhere by 30 June 1992 unless it could be shown for a particular region that effective conservation and

---

[14] 14 *LOSB* 29 (1989).
[15] Castries Declaration on Driftnet Fishing, *ibid.*, p. 28.
[16] 15 *LOSB* 15 (1990).

management measures had been taken to prevent the unacceptable impact of such fishing. This recommendation has been re-affirmed in later General Assembly Resolutions.[17]

Following their call in the Tarawa Declaration, and only four months later, the South Pacific countries concluded the Wellington Convention for the Prohibition of Fishing with Long Driftnets in the South Pacific, 1989. The Convention applies to the high seas and EEZ/EFZ of the area between 10° North and and 50° South and between 130° East and 120° West, and requires its parties, who may be either members of the South Pacific Forum Fisheries Agency or other States with territory in the Convention area, to ban fishing by their nationals and vessels with driftnets in excess of 2.5 kilometres in length, to prohibit the use or carrying of such nets in their EEZs/EFZs, to prohibit the landing or import of fish caught with such nets, and to restrict port access and facilities for driftnet fishing vessels. Any vessel breaching the Convention loses its position of good standing under the FFA's regional register of foreign fishing vessels (referred to above). Under Protocol I, adopted in 1990, States from outside the Convention area whose vessels fish in the area agree to prohibit the use of driftnets proscribed under the Convention. Under Protocol II, adopted at the same time, States with waters adjacent to the Convention area undertake to prohibit their vessels from using proscribed driftnets in the Convention area and to take the same measures for their waters as Convention Parties. The USA has ratified Protocol I, and Canada and Chile have signed Protocol II. Although no States which have used driftnets are party to the Convention or its Protocols, driftnet fishing for tuna has ceased in the South Pacific.[18]

In the North Pacific the International North Pacific Fisheries Commission in 1989 imposed controls on Japanese driftnet fishing through the use of international observers on board vessels, and restrictions on numbers of vessels, fishing zones and seasons. In the case of South Korea and Taiwan, which were not members of the Commission, the USA concluded bilateral agreements with them in 1989 embodying similar measures. In March 1993 the USA announced the action it would take where it had reasonable grounds to believe that a vessel was conducting large-scale pelagic driftnetting operations on the high seas.[19] In such a case the USA would inform the flag State and then take 'appropriate action in accordance with' any agreements in force: 'if there are no pre-existing arrangements, the United States will seek a special arrangement to take law enforcement, or other appropriate action, on behalf of the authorities in whose territory the vessel is registered'. If the vessel turned out to be stateless, it would be 'subject to

---

[17] Resolutions 45/197 of 21 December 1990 and 46/215 of 20 December 1991, 17 *LOSB* 7 (1991) and 20 *LOSB* 14 (1992). The latter resolution puts back the date for implementation of a global moratorium to the end of 1992. Since 1991 the General Assembly has adopted a decision or resolution on driftnet fishing every year, while the Secretary General has produced an annual report on the question.

[18] Bergin, *op. cit.* in 'Further reading' under 'The EEZ regime', p. 301.

[19] Text of the announcement in 23 *LOSB* 107 (1993).

penalty' in the USA. In addition, the Driftnet Impact, Monitoring, Assessment and Control Act 1987, as amended in 1990, provides for trade sanctions against States that do not comply with international agreements regarding driftnets, while under the Marine Mammals Act 1988 vessels catching excessive numbers of marine mammals in driftnets can be excluded from the USA's EEZ. Finally, it is worth noting that in 1992 the EC prohibited EC vessels from fishing with nets longer than 2.5 kilometres, both on the high seas and in zones of national jurisdiction;[20] and in June 1998 it adopted a complete ban on driftnets which becomes fully effective at the beginning of 2002.[21]

The result of the above action has been a substantial decrease in large-scale driftnet fishing on the high seas, although it has not ceased completely. The main fishery where it persists (contrary to EC rules) is the Italian swordfish fishery in the Mediterranean, but as a result of a combination of the threat of economic sanctions by the USA and the provision of financial aid by the EC to enable the Italian fleet to be restructured, this form of high-seas driftnet fishing is in the course of being phased out. The UN resolutions on driftnet fishing are not, of course, formally binding, but it has been argued that the actions of nearly all States in complying with them has resulted in their provisions becoming customary international law.[22] At the same time the action taken against driftnet fishing has been criticised on the grounds that it is based on insufficient knowledge of the impact and effects of driftnets and it is pointed out that other types of fishing gear, such as purse-seine nets, trawls, and long-lines, are at least as indiscriminate in what they catch as driftnets.[23] On the other hand the action taken can be regarded as an example of the precautionary approach (discussed further below).

As mentioned above, a further concern with high-seas fisheries is the free rider problem. This refers to the situation where conservation measures for a particular stock or stocks on the high seas have been agreed by a number of States (often through a regional fisheries organisation) and vessels from States not parties to the agreement fish for the stock(s) concerned, thereby usually undermining the conservation measures that have been agreed. In recent years the free rider problem has been particularly acute for NAFO, CCAMLR and the North Atlantic Salmon Conservation Organisation (NASCO) (discussed further below). Here free riders have often been vessels which are beneficially owned by nationals of member States of NAFO, CCAMLR and NASCO who have re-registered their vessels in non-member States (e.g., Belize, Panama) precisely in order to evade NAFO, CCAMLR and NASCO restrictions on fishing. The free rider problem is a major example of the inadequacy of the UNCLOS high-seas

---

[20] Regulation 345/92, *Official Journal of the European Communities*, 1992, L42/15.

[21] Regulation 1239/98, *ibid.*, 1998, L171/1.

[22] G. J. Hewison, 'The legally binding nature of the moratorium on large-scale high seas driftnet fishing', 25 *JMLC* 557–79 (1994).

[23] Burke (1994), *op. cit.* in 'Further reading' under 'General works', pp. 86–7, 103–7, 117–21 and 270–1.

regime. Over the past few years a number of steps, in the form of both 'soft' and 'hard' law, have been taken to address this inadequacy. These steps will now be briefly surveyed chronologically.

In July 1991 the UN Secretary General convened a meeting of a Group of Technical Experts on High Seas Fisheries which produced a set of suggested Guidelines.[24] After emphasising the duties of co-operation in relation to the conservation and management of high-seas fisheries resources laid down in the Law of the Sea Convention and pointing out that failure to observe this duty could be a breach of the Convention, the Guidelines state that the right to fish on the high seas 'should generally be exercised in accordance with the terms of a fisheries conservation and management regime established by the States concerned' (para. 5). Fisheries commissions and organisation should be open to all States with an interest in the fishery concerned, and such bodies need to articulate more clearly 'the procedural and institutional steps and enforcement measures consequent upon failure by a State to take conservation measures or to co-operate with other States in the taking of such measures' (para. 10). Members of such bodies have a duty to ensure that their nationals comply with conservation measures taken by such bodies and that they 'do not resort to techniques, such as the reflagging of vessels, to escape controls' (para. 11). The Guidelines conclude by calling for increased multilateral discussion of common international standards for high-seas fisheries management.

In May 1992 an International Conference on Responsible Fishing was held at Cancun, Mexico and adopted the Cancun Declaration which called on the FAO to draft an International Code of Conduct on Responsible Fishing.[25] The FAO's response to this is considered below. A month after the Cancun Conference the UN Conference on Environment and Development (popularly known as the Earth Summit) met at Rio and amongst other things adopted Agenda 21, chapter 17 of which is concerned with the oceans.[26] Programme Area C of chapter 17 deals with 'Sustainable Use and Conservation of Marine Living Resources of the High Seas'. This section begins by observing that management of high-seas fisheries is 'inadequate in many areas and some resources are overutilised. There are problems of unregulated fishing, overcapitalisation, excessive fleet size, vessel reflagging to escape controls, insufficiently selective gear, unreliable databases and lack of sufficient co-operation between States' (para. 17.45). To redress these problems Agenda 21 calls for, *inter alia*, the negotiation, where appropriate, of international agreements for the effective management and conservation of high-seas fish stocks; the promotion of the development and use of selective fishing gear and practices that minimise waste in the catch of target species and minimise by-catch of non-target species; effective monitoring and enforcement with

[24] Reproduced in United Nations, *op. cit.* in 'Further reading' under the heading 'High seas', pp. 40–1.

[25] UN Doc. A/CONF. 151/15, annex.

[26] Chapter 17 is reproduced in 7 *IJECL* 296–329 (1992) and 8 *International Organisations and the Law of the Sea. Documentary Yearbook* 400–32 (1992).

respect to fishing activities; the promotion of scientific research and exchange of data in order to obtain better knowledge of high-seas fish stocks; and effective action to deter reflagging of vessels.

The FAO responded to the Cancun Declaration and the concerns expressed in Agenda 21 by holding a Technical Consultation on High Seas Fishing in September 1992[27] and followed this up by producing two instruments: the Agreement to promote Compliance with International Conservation and Management Measures by Fishing Vessels on the High Seas in 1993 and the Code of Conduct for Responsible Fisheries[28] in 1995. The Compliance Agreement has two main elements: setting out the responsibilities of flag States, and maximising information about high-seas fishing activities, the lack of which has been an obstacle to effective fisheries management in the past. As regards the former, article III(1) provides that 'each Party shall take such measures as may be necessary to ensure that fishing vessels entitled to fly its flag do not engage in any activity that undermines the effectiveness of international conservation and management measures'. To this end a flag State shall prohibit its vessels from fishing on the high seas unless it has authorised them to do so, and shall not so authorise a vessel unless it is satisfied that 'it is able, taking into account the links that exist between it and the fishing vessel concerned, to exercise effectively its responsibilities under this Agreement in respect of that fishing vessel' (art. III(3)). No party shall authorise any vessel, previously registered in another State, that has undermined the effectiveness of international conservation and management measures unless the period of suspension by the previous flag State has expired and no authorisation has been withdrawn in the previous three years. This provision therefore limits the ability of vessels with a bad compliance record to shop around for a new flag. An authorised vessel may only fish in accordance with the conditions laid down in its authorisation, must be marked in a way that permits ready identification, and must provide its flag State with such information on its operations as will enable the latter to fulfil its obligations under the Agreement. Flag States must enforce the Agreement in respect of their vessels and provide sanctions for breaches of the Agreement of sufficient gravity to be effective in securing compliance and to deprive offenders of the benefits of their illegal activities: in the case of serious breaches sanctions must include suspension or withdrawal of the authorisation to fish. Other parties shall assist the flag State in exercising its enforcement responsibilities, e.g., by providing evidentiary material. This includes, for the first time in a multilateral fisheries agreement, a degree of port State control. Where a party reasonably believes that a fishing vessel voluntarily in one of its ports has been used for an activity that undermines the effectiveness of international conservation and management measures, it shall

---

[27] *Report of the Technical Consultation on High Seas Fishing*, FAO Fisheries Report No. 484 (1992).
[28] FAO Doc. 95/20/Rev. 1 (1995). Reproduced in 11 *International Organisations and the Law of the Sea. Documentary Yearbook* 700–34 (1995).

promptly notify the flag State. 'Parties may make arrangements regarding the undertaking by port States of such investigatory measures as may be considered necessary to establish whether the fishing vessel has indeed been used contrary to the provisions of this Agreement' (art. V(2)).

Turning now to the second aspect of the Compliance Agreement, promoting the free flow of information about high-seas fishing activities, the Agreement provides that a flag State must provide certain information to the FAO about its vessels authorised to fish on the high seas, including action taken against its vessels engaging in activities that undermine the effectiveness of international conservation and management measures. The FAO shall circulate this information to other parties and to international fisheries organisations. Such information could, for example, be used by a coastal State to exclude a vessel with a poor record from its EEZ. The parties are also to exchange such information as they have about the activities of the vessels of non-parties.

In the early stages of negotiating the Compliance Agreement, an attempt was made to deal directly with the problem of reflagging by providing that a State should not grant the right to fly its flag to a vessel unless there was a genuine link between that State and the vessel, and the State believed that the vessel would not be used to undermine the effectiveness of international conservation and management measures. However, no agreement could be reached on this question. Instead the preamble to the Agreement recalls the request of Agenda 21 (quoted earlier) that States should deter reflagging.

Two years after concluding the Compliance Agreement, the FAO adopted the Code of Conduct for Responsible Fisheries mentioned above. The Code is a non-binding instrument, and partly because of this is very wide-ranging in its scope, dealing not just with high-seas fisheries but with all aspects of fishing, from catching to trade. The main articles of the Code deal with fisheries management (covering objectives, framework and procedures, data gathering, the precautionary approach, management measures and implementation), fishing operations (including duties of flag and port States, the encouragement of sustainable development, protection of the marine environment, the maintenance of biodiversity, and the safety of fishermen), aquaculture development, the integration of fisheries into coastal area management, post-harvest practices and trade, and fisheries research. It is intended that the articles of the Code will be supplemented by technical guidelines prepared by the FAO.

Except in the case of straddling stocks and highly migratory species (considered shortly below), the various measures just described have so far had little impact in practice on redressing the fundamental problems of high-seas fisheries. The FAO Compliance Agreement certainly has the potential to do so when it enters into force, provided that it is ratified not only by the main high-seas fishing States but also by the traditional and would-be free riders. The Agreement is also dependent on there being international conservation and management measures in place, something that is not the case with all high-seas fisheries at present. Where such measures are in place, however, the Agreement should not only improve enforcement and reduce the free rider problem, but should also make it difficult for States to opt out of measures where this is currently permitted.

Straddling stocks

As explained earlier, straddling stocks are stocks of fish that migrate between, or occur in both, the EEZ of one or more States and the high seas. Straddling stocks raise various problems. The first problem is how such stocks are to be managed: there is a risk, for example, that any management measures taken by a coastal State in its EEZ will be undermined by the activities of vessels fishing on the high seas. A second problem is how catches for such stocks are to be allocated between vessels fishing for such stocks in the EEZ and vessels fishing for those stocks on the high seas. The Law of the Sea Convention has only one brief provision dealing with straddling stocks. Article 63(2) provides as follows:

> Where the same stock or stocks of associated species occur both within the exclusive economic zone and in an area beyond and adjacent to the zone, the coastal State and the States fishing for such stocks in the adjacent area shall seek, either directly or through appropriate subregional or regional organisations, to agree upon the measures necessary for the conservation of these stocks in the adjacent area.

Clearly, this provision does not provide any substantive guidance as to how the problems involved with regulating straddling stocks are to be addressed, but it is significant that the co-operation called for relates only to measures to be taken in respect of the high seas, and not in respect of the EEZ. It should also be noted that under article 116(2) the freedom of fishing on the high seas is subject to the 'rights and duties as well as the interests of coastal States provided for, *inter alia*, in article 63, paragraph 2'. This provision has led some coastal States to argue that their interest in straddling stocks takes priority over that of States fishing on the high seas where there is no agreement on management measures for the stocks concerned and that in such circumstances they may regulate fishing for such stocks on the high seas[29] – a view rejected by high-seas fishing States.

In practice, in most of the relatively few areas where straddling stocks exist in commercially attractive quantities, there have been problems. One of the most significant areas for straddling stocks is the North-West Atlantic, where the fishery-rich Grand Banks off Newfoundland extend beyond Canada's 200-mile EEZ (formerly EFZ). Since 1979 straddling stocks on the high seas in this area have been managed by the Northwest Atlantic Fisheries Organisation (NAFO), referred to above. Under the NAFO Convention, NAFO is to co-ordinate and seek to ensure consistency of its management measures for straddling stocks

---

[29] See, for example, the declarations made by Cape Verde, São Tomé e Principe and Uruguay on signature or ratification of the Law of the Sea Convention. See also Burke (1994), *op. cit.* in 'Further reading', pp. 132–6.

with those of Canada. In the first few years of its existence, management of these straddling stocks by NAFO worked reasonably well, but problems arose after 1986 when Spain and Portugal, two significant distant-water fishing States, became members of the EC. From 1986 onwards the EC, under pressure from Spain, objected to the quotas allocated to it by NAFO, as it was legitimately entitled to do so under the NAFO Convention, and unilaterally set its own, considerably higher, quotas. Canada argued that this action, coupled with evasion of NAFO controls by an increasing number of flag of convenience fishing vessels registered in States not members of NAFO, was undermining its own conservation measures taken in its EFZ, reducing the amount of fish available for harvesting by its own vessels, and threatening the long-term well-being of the stocks concerned which by the early 1990s were in a severely depleted state. As a consequence Canada enacted legislation in 1994 which made it an offence for non-Canadian vessels to fish for straddling stocks on the high seas in contravention of NAFO conservation and management measures and conferred on the Canadian authorities the power to enforce this legislation.[30] A serious dispute arose in March 1995 when, acting under this legislation, the Canadian authorities arrested a Spanish vessel, the *Estai*, on the high seas. Spain referred the dispute to the International Court of Justice under article 36(2) of the Court's Statute,[31] where the case is pending. Even though it would seem difficult to argue that the Canadian legislation was not contrary to international law, it is unlikely that the Court will find that it has jurisdiction because Canada has made a reservation to its declaration under article 36(2) excluding its 1994 legislation from the Court's purview. In the meantime the dispute has effectively been settled by an agreement between Canada and the EC, concluded in April 1995, under which Canada and the EC agreed to put forward to NAFO proposals to strengthen NAFO conservation and enforcement measures and agreed on quotas for 1995. In addition, Canada agreed not to apply its legislation in respect of EC vessels. The proposed measures were subsequently adopted by NAFO in September 1995, and were summarised when discussing NAFO earlier.

A second significant area for straddling stocks is the so-called 'Donut Hole', an enclave of high seas in the Bering Sea surrounded by the EEZs of Russia and the USA. From the mid-1980s vessels from distant-water fishing States (principally China, Korea, Japan and Poland) began increasingly to fish in the Donut Hole as they were excluded from the Russian and US EEZs. Serious over-fishing, especially of pollock, resulted, as well as illegal incursions into the EEZs. These problems have now hopefully been resolved with the signing in 1994 by the two coastal States and the four distant-water fishing States mentioned of the Convention on the Conservation and Management of Pollock Resources in the Central

---

[30] An Act to amend the Coastal Fisheries Protection Act, 26 *LOSB* 20 (1994). The Act was accompanied by Regulations which have not been reproduced in *LOSB*, but which may be found in *Canada Gazette*, 15 June 1994, p. 2216 *et seq.*
[31] *Fisheries Jurisdiction* case, referred to the Court on 28 March 1995.

Bering Sea. The aim of the Convention is to establish an international regime for the conservation, management and optimum utilisation of the pollock resources of the Donut Hole which will restore and maintain pollock resources at a level that will permit maximum sustainable yield (MSY). This is to be done by Annual Conferences of the parties, advised by a Scientific and Technical Committee, setting the allowable harvest level, which is then to be divided into individual national quotas, and adopting such other conservation and management measures as are deemed appropriate. The Convention contains elaborate fall-back measures for determining the allowable harvest level where agreement cannot be reached in the Annual Conference, and, unlike most international fishery commission treaties, does not permit the parties to opt out of measures with which they do not agree. Apart from the usual flag State enforcement, the Convention also provides for any vessel, if requested, to carry an observer from a State other than the flag State to monitor its operations, and permits any party to board and inspect the vessel of any other party, although where an infraction is suspected, criminal proceedings may be taken only by the flag State. In relation to the possible undermining of the Convention by vessels registered in non-parties, the Convention provides that its parties shall encourage non-parties to respect the Convention's provisions. If this is not sufficient, the parties 'shall take measures, individually or collectively, which are consistent with international law, and which they deem necessary and appropriate, to deter' the adverse operations of non-parties. In addition, the parties are to try to prevent their fishing vessels from transferring their registration in order to avoid compliance with the Convention.

A third area for straddling stocks is the so-called 'Peanut Hole', an enclave of high seas in the Sea of Okhotsk entirely surrounded by the EEZ of Russia. From 1991 fishing in the Peanut Hole by distant-water fishing States (principally the same four as in the Donut Hole) was at such a level that it was having major deleterious effects on stocks both in the Hole and in the Russian EEZ. Although negotiations have been held between the States concerned, no agreement on management of the Peanut Hole fish stocks has yet been reached. Instead Russia in 1993, asserting that it was responsible for the conservation of fishery resources of the Peanut Hole, claimed to impose a moratorium on fishing activities in the Hole until an international agreement on this issue was reached. Some distant-water fishing States have voluntarily complied with the ban: those that have not have lost their quotas to fish in Russia's EEZ. Significantly, Russia has not sought to enforce its proclaimed moratorium against foreign vessels fishing in the Peanut Hole.[32]

Finally, mention may be made of another enclave of high seas, this time in the Barents Sea, known as the 'Loop Hole', which is surrounded by the EEZs of Russia and Norway. Before 1991 no fishing of any significance took place in

---

[32] See further A. G. Oude Elferink, 'Fisheries in the Sea of Okhotsk high seas enclave – the Russian Federation's attempts at coastal State control', 10 *IJMCL* 1–18 (1995).

this area. Since then fishing has taken place on an increasing scale, especially by Icelandic vessels (some of which operate under flags of convenience), to the irritation of Norway and Russia, which see the management measures they have adopted jointly for the rest of the Barents Sea (see above) undermined by this practice. So far this problem is unresolved.

Canada is not the only coastal State which has sought to overcome the problems posed by straddling stocks by claiming to extend its jurisdiction beyond the 200-mile limit. In the South-West Atlantic, where significant stocks straddle the 200-mile limits of Argentina and the Falkland Islands and the high seas beyond, Argentina, in enacting its EEZ legislation in 1991, included a provision under which 'national provisions concerning the conservation of resources shall apply beyond' the EEZ 'in the case of migratory species or species which form part of the food chain of species of' its EEZ.[33] Whether Argentina has sought in practice to enforce this claim, we have been unable to discover. A second Latin-American claim is that of Chile. In 1991 it enacted legislation[34] establishing what was called *mar presencial* (literally 'presential sea', 'the sea in which we are present'), embracing a huge area of high seas in the southeast Pacific. While the legal content of this concept is not very clear, it seems to include surveillance by Chile of activities by other States on the high seas which may affect the well-being of fish stocks in its EEZ, without affecting the regime of the high seas. Chile also enacted legislation in the same year which provided that conservation measures could be adopted for straddling stocks on the high seas: failure by other States to comply with such measures could lead to a ban on the landing of catches in Chile and the denial of port facilities.[35] Finally, Peru in 1992 enacted similar legislation to that of Argentina.[36]

Concern about the problems and disputes encountered in the exploitation of straddling stocks led the UN Conference on Environment and Development to call for an inter-governmental conference 'with a view to promoting effective implementation of the provisions' of the Law of the Sea Convention on straddling stocks and highly migratory species (which are discussed below),[37] a call that was endorsed by the UN General Assembly.[38] Such a conference was held between 1993 and 1995, and at its conclusion produced the Agreement for the Implementation of the Provisions of the United Nations Convention on the Law of the Sea of 10 December 1982 relating to the Conservation and Management of Straddling Fish Stocks and Highly Migratory Fish Stocks (hereafter the Straddling Stocks Agreement).

---

[33] Act No. 23.968 of 14 August 1991, art. 5. 20 *LOSB* 20 (1992).

[34] Decree No. 430 of 28 September 1991, partially reproduced in F. Francolanci and T. Scovazzi (eds), *Lines in the Sea* (Dordecht, Nijhoff), 1994, p. 148. See also Melzer, *op. cit.* in 'Further reading' (under 'Straddling stocks'), pp. 268–71.

[35] Law Decree No. 25977, art. 7, quoted in Melzer, *op. cit.* p. 272.

[36] Law No. 19.079, art. 154, quoted in United Nations, *op. cit.* in footnote 3, pp. 188–9.

[37] Agenda 21, chapter 17, para. 17.50, *op. cit.* in footnote 26.

[38] Resolution 47/192 (1992), 23 *LOSB* 14 (1992).

The Agreement runs to fifty articles and two annexes, so only the barest outline of its provisions can be given here. The Agreement begins by setting out the principles which should govern the conservation and management of straddling and highly migratory stocks both by the coastal State within its EEZ/EFZ and by the coastal State and other States on the high seas. These principles, which are the most detailed of their kind yet found in an international legal text, include *inter alia*: ensuring the long-term sustainability and optimum utilisation of the stocks concerned; applying the precautionary approach, which is spelt out in detail in article 6 and annex II, and means essentially being 'more cautious when information is uncertain, unreliable or inadequate' (art. 6(2)); minimising pollution, waste, discards (i.e., fish thrown back into the sea (usually dead) after being caught, because they are too small or the wrong species), catch by lost or abandoned gear, and catch of non-target species and impacts on associated or dependent species; protecting biodiversity; preventing or eliminating over-fishing and excess fishing capacity; collecting data concerning fishing activities; promoting scientific research; and implementing and enforcing measures through effective monitoring, control and surveillance. Measures taken in the EEZ/EFZ and those adopted for the high seas must be compatible in order to ensure conservation and management of stocks in their entirety, and various factors are listed (including the needs of developing coastal States) in order to determine such compatibility. Failure to agree on this matter entitles any State to invoke the elaborate settlement of disputes provisions of the Law of the Sea Convention (see chapter nineteen), which apply *mutatis mutandis* to disputes arising out of the Agreement.

Part III of the Agreement sets out the mechanisms for giving effect to the obligation to co-operate in the conservation and management of straddling and highly migratory stocks on the high seas employing the principles outlined above. Where an organisation or arrangement already exists (such as NAFO and the regional tuna commissions, discussed below), it is to be used. States fishing on the high seas for the stock concerned and relevant coastal States which are not members of such organisations or arrangements shall become members or apply the measures adopted by such organisations or arrangements. If they do not do so, they shall not fish for the stocks concerned. Where no organisation or arrangement exists, States shall establish one; and guidelines as to its scope and as to the functions of both new and existing organisations are spelt out. Article 17 reiterates that non-members of regional organisations or arrangements shall not fish for the stocks concerned, and calls on members to take measures consistent with the Agreement and international law to deter non-members from engaging in activities which would undermine the effectiveness of the measures they have agreed.

As regards compliance with and enforcement of conservation and management measures adopted by regional fisheries organisations or arrangements, the Straddling Stocks Agreement imposes duties of implementation and enforcement on flag States similar to, but in places rather more detailed than, those of the FAO Compliance Agreement, discussed earlier. Other States are to co-operate with flag States, for example by providing evidence of alleged breaches. Members of regional fisheries organisations or arrangements are to establish schemes whereby one member can board and inspect vessels of any State Party to the Straddling Stocks Agreement (even if it is not a member of the regional fisheries organisation or arrangement). If within two years of the adoption of the Agreement (i.e., by August 1997), such schemes have not been adopted, then the Agreement itself authorises one party to board and inspect the vessels of another. If there are clear grounds for believing that a vessel has engaged in any activity contrary to conservation and management measures, the inspecting State shall secure evidence and promptly inform the flag State. The latter shall either without delay investigate and, if the evidence so warrants, take enforcement action, or authorise the inspecting State to investigate: in the latter case the flag State shall either take enforcement action or authorise the inspecting State to do so. If, following a boarding and inspection, there are clear grounds for believing that the vessel has committed a serious violation, and if the flag State takes no action, the inspectors may remain on board and secure evidence and, if appropriate, bring the vessel to the nearest port. The above provisions also apply where a coastal State has clear grounds for believing that a vessel in its EEZ/EFZ has committed an offence on the high seas during the same trip. The Agreement also provides that where a vessel on the high seas is reasonably believed to have engaged in unauthorised fishing in an EEZ/EFZ, the flag State shall investigate the matter at the request of the coastal State and may authorise the latter to board and inspect the vessel. Finally, the Agreement, like the FAO Compliance Agreement, provides for port State control, but goes further by specifying that a port State may inspect vessels voluntarily in its ports and may prohibit landings of catches taken in a manner that undermines the effectiveness of conservation and management measures. In general port States have not only a right but a duty to take action to promote the effectiveness of such measures.

Parties to the Straddling Stocks Agreement are to take measures consistent with international law to deter the vessels of non-parties from undermining the effective implementation of the Agreement. Like the FAO Compliance Agreement, the 1995 Agreement is dependent for its success on wide ratification by actual and potential high-seas fishing States, as well as by relevant coastal States. If the Agreement is widely ratified (and only eighteen States had ratified by August 1998, whereas thirty ratifications are required for entry into force of the Agreement), it should improve enforcement, reduce the free rider problem and make it difficult for States to opt out of measures adopted by regional organisations (since flag States must ensure that their vessels do not undermine the effectiveness of regional conservation and management measures). Whether the Agreement will lead to improved management of straddling stocks (and highly migratory species) and satisfy the interests of coastal States will depend on whether regional organisations and coastal States can each adopt measures that are compatible, something that may well prove difficult as far as the allocation of the catch is concerned.

Rules for particular species

The rules of the Law of the Sea Convention so far expounded are considerably modified in the case of highly migratory, anadromous and catadromous species, marine mammals and sedentary species. Each of these will be considered in turn.

Highly migratory species

Highly migratory species are those species listed in Annex I of the Law of the Sea Convention and include tuna (the most commercially important), marlins, swordfish and oceanic sharks. Most such species migrate considerable distances during their life cycle, not only through the EEZs of two or more States but also on the high seas beyond. Article 64 of the Convention provides that the coastal State's normal rights and duties of fishery management in its EEZ are supplemented by an obligation to co-operate with other States fishing for highly migratory species in the region either 'directly or through appropriate international organisations with a view to ensuring conservation and promoting the objective of optimum utilisation of such species throughout the region', both within the EEZ and on the high seas. In regions where no organisation exists, the coastal State(s) and other interested States are to co-operate to establish such organisations. It will also be recalled that the 1995 Straddling Stocks Agreement applies equally to highly migratory species. Thus the combined effect of article 64 and the 1995 Agreement is that coastal States and other States fishing in the EEZ or on the high seas are to co-operate over the conservation and the management of highly migratory species through regional organisations or arrangements which either exist or which they must establish.

There are currently only three or four such regional organisations or arrangements in existence, all of which are concerned with fishing for tuna. The oldest is the Inter-American Tropical Tuna Commission, which was established by the Convention of the same name signed in 1949 to regulate tuna fishing in the Eastern Pacific. To this end the Commission's functions are to carry out scientific research and recommend conservation measures. The latter function was exercised to some degree up to 1979, by which time coastal States had extended their fisheries jurisdiction to 200 miles, but since then the Commission has effectively been unable to adopt any measures. Efforts to adapt the Convention and the Commission to a world of 200-mile zones have so far been unsuccessful, although in 1983 an interim supplementary agreement, the Eastern Pacific Ocean Tuna Fishing Agreement, was signed. However, the Agreement has not come into force. Were it to do so, it would manage the exploitation of tuna (including tuna within 200-mile zones) by means of a licensing system. In 1989 five coastal States signed an agreement establishing a rival Eastern Pacific Tuna Fishing Organisation, but this has not come into force either. It has been suggested that neither of these two agreements follows the balanced approach of the Law of the Sea Convention: the 1983 agreement minimises the role of the coastal State in its EEZ, while the 1989 agreement goes too far in the opposite direction.[39]

Elsewhere in the Pacific no international organisation at present exists. In the South Pacific the members of the Forum Fisheries Agency have co-ordinated their position in respect of distant-water vessels fishing for tuna in their EEZ/EFZs in the ways described earlier in this chapter (see p. 293). Worthy of particular note in this connection is the Treaty on Fisheries concluded in 1987 between sixteen Pacific island States and the USA. Before 1992 the USA maintained, contrary to the Law of the Sea Convention, that the coastal State had no jurisdiction over tuna (although the USA accepted that the coastal State had jurisdiction over highly migratory species other than tuna), and its fishermen fished for tuna without permission in the 200-mile zones of many of the small Pacific island States, for which tuna is a major resource. This led to seizure of US vessels and the imposition of economic embargoes by the USA in retaliation. (This position of the USA had caused similar problems in the Eastern Pacific, which partly explains the unsatisfactory situation described above.) The 1987 Treaty resolved the dispute by providing that US vessels may fish in the EEZ/EFZs of the Pacific island States concerned under a single licensing system (which also applies to fishing on the high seas for species other than albacore) and subject to the provision of technical and economic assistance by the USA. In addition, the USA is to use processing facilities, buy equipment and employ personnel from the island States concerned. US vessels must comply with all relevant national legislation of these States as well as various conservation and management measures contained in the Treaty itself, report regularly on their activities and permit observers on board. Apart from enforcement of the provisions by coastal States, the USA is also to ensure that its vessels comply by taking the necessary enforcement action both on the high seas and within EEZ/EFZs: enforcement in the latter area represents a considerable novelty, especially as any fines imposed by the USA are to be handed over to the coastal State concerned. In 1993 the Treaty, which was due to expire, was renewed for a further ten years.

Unlike the multilateral arrangements for the USA, the activities of other distant-water States fishing for tuna, such as Japan and South Korea, continue to be regulated by bilateral agreements with individual Pacific island States. Such agreements involve a degree of influence over high-seas fishing, for example through requiring the provision of catch data: in any case high seas account for only about twenty per cent of the area covered by the Forum Fisheries Agency and most is enclaved by EEZ/EFZs. In addition, in 1992 the parties to the Nauru Agreement (referred to earlier) concluded the Palau Arrangement for the Management of the Western Pacific Island Purse Seine Fishery, which introduces a licensing system for purse-seine fishing for tuna both within EEZs and on

[39] United Nations, *op. cit.* in footnote 3, p. 187.

the high seas under which the number of licences is limited, the aim being to conserve stocks and to increase licence fees.[40]

The Pacific island States originally resisted the idea of international bodies for tuna management in their region. However, since 1994 a series of meetings has been held with the aim of establishing by 2000 a 'mechanism for the conservation and management of highly migratory fish stocks' of the Western and Central Pacific 'in accordance with' the Law of the Sea Convention and the Straddling Stocks Agreement.[41] Such a mechansim might well assume responsibility for scientific research relating to tuna, which at present is co-ordinated by the South Pacific Commission, a body which otherwise has no management role in relation to tuna.

In the Indian Ocean the only international body concerned with tuna before 1991 was the Tuna Management Committee of the FAO's Indian Ocean Commission, but this body had no regulatory powers. In 1991 a number of coastal States signed an Agreement establishing a Western Indian Ocean Tuna Organisation, but this body is not one of the kind contemplated by the Law of the Sea Convention as its membership is restricted to coastal States and its aim, like that of the Forum Fisheries Agency, is primarily to promote a unified front amongst coastal States towards distant-water fishing States. However, more recently an organisation of the kind envisaged by article 64 has been set up. This is the Indian Ocean Tuna Commission, established by an agreement concluded under the auspices of FAO in 1993.[42] The objectives of the Commission, membership of which is open to both coastal States and States whose vessels fish for tuna in the Indian Ocean, are to ensure the conservation and the optimum utilisation of tuna in the Indian Ocean and to encourage sustainable development of the fishery. To this end it is to encourage and co-ordinate scientific research, adopt conservation and management measures, and keep under review economic and social aspects of the fisheries bearing particularly in mind the interests of developing coastal States. It would seem that the Commission can adopt conservation and management measures for both the high seas and zones of national jurisdiction. At the same time article XVI of the Agreement states that the Agreement does not prejudice the exercise of the coastal State's sovereign rights over fisheries in its EEZ, which implies that a coastal State may also adopt conservation and management measures for tuna within its EEZ.

Migrating between the Pacific, Indian and the South Atlantic Oceans by way of southern Australia, the southern bluefin tuna is the subject of the first agreement signed since the adoption of the Law of the Sea Convention to give effect to the principles of article 64. The Convention for the Conservation of Southern Bluefin Tuna was signed in 1993 by Australia, Japan and New Zealand, the main States fishing for this species. To achieve its objective of ensuring

---

[40] Bergin, *op. cit.* in footnote 8, pp. 294–6.
[41] Majuro Declaration, 35 *LOSB* 125 (1997).
[42] Agreement for the Establishment of the Indian Ocean Tuna Commission.

the conservation and optimum utilisation of southern bluefin tuna, the populations of which have become severely depleted in recent years, the Convention establishes a commission which is to decide (by unanimity) on a total allowable catch (TAC) and its allocation among the parties and/or other conservation measures (which apply to both high seas and national waters), develop systems to monitor fishing activities and, through a Scientific Committee, co-ordinate scientific research. The parties are to take appropriate action to deter activities by non-parties which could undermine the Convention and are to prevent their vessels from re-registering in non-parties for the purpose of circumventing the Convention.

Finally, in the Atlantic fishing for tuna, both on the high seas and in zones of national jurisdiction, is governed by the International Convention for the Conservation of Atlantic Tuna of 1966. The Convention establishes a Commission, the tasks of which are to co-ordinate scientific research and make recommendations designed to maintain populations of tuna at levels which will permit the maximum sustainable catch. To this latter end the Commission has adopted *inter alia* minimum permissible weight limits at which tuna may be caught and retained, overall catch limits for various species, gear regulations and schemes for international and port inspection. The Commission is not yet, however, fully an example of an article 64-type organisation as several Atlantic coastal States are not (yet) members.

From the above survey it can be seen that the only effective organisations of the kind contemplated by article 64 and for regulating tuna fishing on the high seas are the Commission for the Conservation of Southern Bluefin Tuna, the Indian Ocean Tuna Commission and possibly the International Commission for the Conservation of Atlantic Tuna. It will be recalled that article 64 also provides that co-operation between fishing and coastal States may take place directly, rather than through an international organisation. This is arguably the case in the South Pacific, at least as far as the USA and the Pacific island States are concerned. There are thus a considerable number of tuna fisheries which are not adequately regulated in the manner envisaged by article 64. It is to be hoped that entry into force of the Straddling Stocks Agreement will improve the situation.

Anadromous species

Anadromous species are species such as salmon, shad and sturgeon which spawn in fresh water but spend most of their life in the sea. Article 66 of the Law of the Sea Convention governs such species. It provides that the State in whose rivers such fish spawn (the State of origin) is primarily responsible for their management and shall take appropriate regulatory measures to ensure their conservation. This State can establish total allowable catches and admit foreign States to its EEZ to fish for any surplus there may be, but it is not obliged to do so. Where TACs are adopted, this must be done after consultation with other interested States, referred to below. Fishing for anadromous species beyond 200-mile limits is forbidden except where this would result in 'economic dislocation' for a State other than the State of origin. In such a situation, the State of origin is to co-operate with the other States concerned in order to minimise economic dislocation, and it is to seek to agree with them on the terms and conditions for fishing. The State of origin may adopt conservation measures for such high-seas fishing.[43] Such measures are to be enforced 'by agreement between the State of origin and the other States concerned' (art. 66(3)(d)). Where anadromous species migrate through the EEZs of States other than the State of origin (as frequently happens in practice), the State of origin and the other coastal State(s) are to co-operate with regard to conservation and management. The above provisions are the result of proposals put forward by two of the main States of origin, Canada and the USA. They argued that since the State of origin may be required to expend money to ensure the continued propagation of salmon, e.g., by reducing pollution in rivers or by providing salmon ladders, it should be entitled to the whole or at least the greater part of the fruits of its expenditure.

Article 66(5) of the Law of the Sea Convention calls on the State of origin and other interested States to implement the Convention's provisions on anadromous species, where appropriate, through regional organisations. Such organisations have been established for salmon, the principal commercially significant anadromous species, in the North Atlantic and the North Pacific, the two main salmon fishing regions. In the North Atlantic the Convention for the Conservation of Salmon in the North Atlantic Ocean was signed in 1982. This Convention prohibits fishing for salmon on the high seas, and even within 200-mile zones prohibits fishing in most areas beyond twelve miles. It establishes a North Atlantic Salmon Conservation Organisation (NASCO) through which co-operation over the conservation and management of North Atlantic salmon is to take place. NASCO has a complex structure, designed to provide a careful balance between the interests of the States of origin and other States which fish for salmon in their EEZs, and comprises a council, three regional commissions and a secretariat. The main functions of NASCO are to adopt regulations to limit fishing within EEZs by States other than the State of origin (and in practice a number of such regulations have been adopted), and to provide for consultation on matters of mutual interest relating to salmon. In recent years NASCO's efforts to manage North Atlantic salmon have been undermined by flag of convenience fishing vessels registered in States not members of NASCO fishing for salmon on the high seas. In 1990 the Council of NASCO adopted a resolution calling on its members to request the flag States concerned to prevent such fishing.[44] For flag States which are parties to the Law of the Sea Convention such fishing has become illegal since the entry into force of the Convention as such States have

[43] Article 66(2) does not say so in so many words, but it has been interpreted as having this meaning: see Burke (1994), *op. cit.* in 'Further reading' under the heading 'General works', pp. 166–9.
[44] Resolution of the Council of NASCO at its Seventh Annual Meeting, held at Helsinki from 12 to 15 June 1990, 18 *LOSB* 68 (1991).

not suffered economic dislocation because they have not traditionally fished for salmon on the high seas in the north Atlantic.

In the North Pacific the most important regional agreement is the Convention for the Conservation of Anadromous Stocks in the North Pacific Ocean, adopted in 1992, the parties to which are Canada, Japan, Russia and the USA, the major States of origin of North Pacific salmon. The Convention prohibits directed fishing for salmon on the high seas (traditionally Japan has been the only State engaging in such fishing in the North Pacific), although such fishing had been restricted under earlier agreements which the 1992 Convention effectively replaces; requires the incidental catching of salmon to be minimised to the greatest extent practicable; and stipulates that any salmon incidentally caught shall be returned to the sea. These provisions are to be enforced by flag States. In addition, authorised officials of one party may board and arrest a vessel of any other party believed to be breaching the Convention, although only the flag State may prosecute the vessel and impose penalties. The Convention also establishes the North Pacific Anadromous Fish Commission, which may *inter alia* recommend conservation measures for salmon and ecologically related species, promote co-operation over and recommend scientific research, review the operation of the Convention, and recommend amendments to the Convention. The parties are to take action, consistent with international law, to prevent non-parties from fishing inconsistently with the Convention: in practice this would seem to refer particularly to South Korea and Taiwan, which in recent years have taken considerable quantities of salmon as incidental catches. In addition, the parties are to prevent their vessels from re-registering under another flag in order to evade the Convention's provisions.

In contrast to the 1992 Convention which is only concerned with salmon fishing on the high seas, the Canada–USA Treaty concerning Pacific Salmon of 1985 deals with the issue of the interception of salmon originating in one party by vessels fishing in the 200-mile zone of the other party in the North-East Pacific. The Treaty establishes the Pacific Salmon Commission, with a complex sub-structure of panels and committees reflecting the complexity of the fishery, which involves salmon of various species originating from hundreds of different rivers along the North-East Pacific, each with its own migratory pattern. The broad function of the Commission is to recommend conservation measures and the principles of allocation which will fulfil the Treaty's objective of providing for 'each Party to receive benefits equivalent to the production of salmon originating in its waters'. In practice the operation of the Treaty has given rise to disputes between the two parties.[45]

Catadromous species

Catadromous species are species, such as eels, which spawn at sea but spend most of their lives in fresh water. In relation to such species the general rules

[45] See C. R. Horner, 'Habitat preservation and restoration under the Pacific salmon treaty', 29 *ODIL* 43–72 (1998), especially at 46–50.

governing fishing in the EEZ apply, but are supplemented by an obligation on coastal States through whose EEZs catadromous species migrate to co-operate over management (including harvesting) of these species with the State in whose waters the species spend the greater part of their life cycle: the latter State has overall management responsibility for these species (art. 67). Fishing for catadromous species on the high seas is prohibited. In practice the management of catadromous species appears to have raised few problems and there appear to be no examples of the kinds of co-operative arrangements referred to in article 67.

Marine mammals

In the case of marine mammals (whales, seals, sirenians), the Law of the Sea Convention provides that within its EEZ a coastal State is entitled to limit or prohibit the exploitation of such species rather than establishing an allowable catch and promoting the objective of optimum utilisation (art. 65). In accordance with this provision, some States, such as Australia, the United Kingdom and the USA, have prohibited whaling in their 200-mile zones.[46] International organisations may also limit or prohibit the exploitation of marine mammals, both within and beyond the EEZ (arts 65 and 120). States are to co-operate in the conservation of marine mammals, and in the case of cetaceans are to work through the appropriate international organisations, principally the International Whaling Commission (IWC), for their conservation, management and study.

The IWC has had a rather chequered history. Set up in 1948 to regulate whaling in all waters and to publish and stimulate scientific research, it failed during the first twenty-five years of its existence to prevent the over-fishing and near-extinction of many whale species, largely because quotas were set at too high levels, were set in standard units (blue whale units) rather than for individual species, and were not allocated among interested States. In 1974 a New Management Procedure was adopted which led to rather better management: in particular, catching of all but the five most populous species was prohibited. Since 1980 many small non-whaling States have joined the IWC, and as a result of this development and pressure from environmental groups, the IWC in 1982 adopted a moratorium on all commercial whaling from 1986. This measure was objected to, and therefore under the IWC Convention not binding on, Japan, Norway and the USSR, the three main whaling States, although each of these States subsequently announced that it would cease commercial whaling after 1988.[47] However, Japan and Norway, as well as some other States such as

---

[46] See Australia's Whale Protection Act, 1990; the United Kingdom's Whaling Industry (Regulation) Act, 1934 (as amended in 1976); and the USA's Marine Mammals Protection Act, 1972 (as amended) and Whaling Conservation Act, 1949 (as amended), 16 U.S.C. §916 *et seq.*

[47] In fact Japan, under pressure from the USA, withdrew its objection to the moratorium in 1988.

Iceland, have sought to get round the moratorium by engaging in relatively large-scale whaling under the pretext of scientific research, catches for which are exempt from the moratorium (as is aboriginal subsistence whaling, an area in which there is also some evidence of abuse). A further circumvention of the moratorium occurs through the use of vessels registered in flag of convenience States which are not parties to the IWC. The moratorium was reviewed by the IWC in 1990, and has been continued since then. The IWC is currently working on a Revised Management Scheme which would regulate commercial whaling if the current moratorium were to be lifted. Even if it were, commercial whaling would not be possible in the Southern Ocean, containing about eighty per cent of the world's remaining whales, which the IWC declared a whale sanctuary in 1994 (although Japan has objected to this decision), or in the Indian Ocean, which has been a whale sanctuary since 1970.

In 1993 Norway became the first country officially to resume commercial whaling following the introduction of the moratorium in 1986. Its action has been much criticised. In particular, the IWC does not consider that Norwegian whaling, which is directed solely at the minke whale in the North-East Atlantic, is scientifically justified, and in 1996 it called on Norway to cease whaling. No doubt at least partly as a result of such criticisms, Norway, together with Iceland (which left the IWC in 1992 following criticism of its scientific whaling), the Faroes and Greenland, signed an Agreement on Co-operation on Research, Conservation and Management of Marine Mammals in the North Atlantic in 1992. The Agreement establishes a North Atlantic Marine Mammal Commission (NAMMCO) which is to provide a forum for the study, analysis and exchange of information on matters relating to marine mammals and to propose measures for their conservation and rational management. The parties to the Agreement, it will be noted, all engage in whaling. So far NAMMCO has concentrated on scientific research rather than management, although a Joint Control Scheme for the Hunting of Marine Mammals was adopted in 1996.

In recent years small cetaceans (dolphins, porpoises) have become the subject of increasing attention. The IWC does not regulate such mammals, and there is considerable dispute as to whether it is legally competent to do so. Instead several regional agreements have been concluded for their conservation. In the case of the North Sea and Baltic, where populations of small cetaceans have declined significantly, probably as a result of pollution and modern types of fishing gear in which they are inadvertently caught, an Agreement on the Conservation of Small Cetaceans was concluded in 1992 under the auspices of the 1979 Bonn Convention on the Conservation of Migratory Species of Wild Animals. The Agreement requires its parties to reduce pollution harmful to small cetaceans, modify fishing gear, reduce activities which severely affect their food resources, carry out population surveys and research into the causes of their decline, and prohibit their intentional taking. To oversee and co-ordinate these actions the Agreement establishes a Secretariat, an Advisory Committee and regular Meetings of the Parties. A similar agreement for the Mediterranean and the Black Sea

– the Agreement on the Conservation of Cetaceans of the Black Sea, Mediterranean Sea and Contiguous Atlantic Area – was concluded in 1996, also under the Bonn Convention. In this connection it may also be noted that in 1993 France, Italy and Monaco signed a declaration establishing a sanctuary for marine mammals (large and small) in the western Mediterranean, including high seas, and prohibiting the use of driftnets there.[48] The inclusion of high seas within the sanctuary is justified on the basis that the area is within what would be the EEZs of the three States, were they to claim one (which they do not), and on the basis of the maxim, he who can do more can do less. Apart from the treaties mentioned above specifically concerned with small cetaceans, conservation of such species is also provided for in the 1979 Bern Convention on the Conservation of European Wildlife and Natural Habitats, which prohibits their capture and killing, and in many of the protocols on specially protected areas attached to UNEP's Regional Seas Marine Pollution Conventions, which are discussed in the next chapter (see pp. 392–3). It may also be noted that trade in most species of cetaceans (large and small) is prohibited under the 1973 Convention on International Trade in Endangered Species of Wild Fauna and Flora. Such a prohibition removes some of the incentives to killing cetaceans.

Dolphins have been the subject of specific measures. Dolphins tend to shoal with tuna, especially in tropical waters, and when tuna are fished with purse-seine nets, many dolphins are also caught and die. To try to reduce this dolphin mortality, members (and some non-members) of the Inter-American Tropical Tuna Commission in 1992 concluded an Agreement for the Reduction of Dolphin Mortality in the Eastern Pacific Ocean, which sets progressively reducing limits to the number of dolphins which may be caught each year until 1999, when the number should be less than 0.01 per cent of the 1992 population level (in comparison, the most conservative estimate of the recruitment rate for dolphins is two per cent). The Agreement also establishes a review panel to review and report on compliance with the limits established and a scientific advisory board to advise on how current purse-seine technology might be modified to make it less likely to cause dolphin mortality and on alternative ways of catching tuna. The United States has taken unilateral action to try to reduce dolphin mortality in tuna fishing by enacting legislation in 1990 which bans imports of fish caught by technology which results in the incidental killing or serious injury of marine mammals in excess of certain standards. Application of this legislation to imports of tuna from Mexico was held by a GATT dispute panel in 1991 to be contrary to GATT.[49] The decision in part was based on the fact that the measures applied to resources

---

[48] Declaration on a Sanctuary for Marine Mammals in the Mediterranean, 1993. The Declaration is summarised and discussed by T. Scovazzi in 8 *IJMCL* 510 (1993).

[49] 30 *ILM* 1594 (1991). A similar case brought against the USA by the EC and the Netherlands resulted in a similar finding by a GATT panel in 1994: see 33 *ILM* 839 (1994). Cf. also the finding by a GATT panel in 1998 that a US ban on imports of shrimps caught by methods which resulted in the incidental killing of sea turtles was also contrary to GATT: 37 *ILM* 832 (1998).

beyond US jurisdiction, and therefore has raised questions about the compatibility of GATT (WTO) obligations with the Law of the Sea Convention.[50]

Cetaceans are not the only marine mammals which are the subject of international agreement. Agreements have also been concluded for the conservation of seals. The most important current such agreement[51] is the Convention for the Conservation of Antarctic Seals of 1972. Adopted before the possible development of renewed commercial sealing in the Antarctic (such sealing having died out at the beginning of the twentieth century), and designed to have conservation measures in place before any such development, the Convention prohibits the killing of three species of seal and sets limits on the numbers of the three other species which may be caught, as well as closed seasons and areas. In fact commercial sealing has not begun again in the Antarctic. The main areas where commercial sealing currently takes place are the Canadian Arctic (where sealing is regulated by Canada unilaterally) and the Arctic waters of Russia and Norway (where regulation is by the Norway-Russia Fisheries Commission). Over the past twenty years the number of seals killed has fallen dramatically, not so much as a result of conservation measures as because of consumer boycotts of fur products and import bans on seal products by the European Union, the USA and other States. On the other hand, the unchecked growth of seal populations is not necessarily desirable as seals eat considerable quantities of fish.

Finally, there is the 1990 Agreement on the Conservation of Seals in the Wadden Sea (that part of the North Sea which is adjacent to Denmark, Germany and the Netherlands) which is concerned, not with conserving seals which are being commercially exploited, but with preserving them from the same kinds of threats as those to small cetaceans in the North Sea, discussed earlier.

Sedentary species

The final type of species for which the Law of the Sea Convention makes special provision are sedentary species. As was seen earlier (p. 285), sedentary species are considered to be part of the natural resources of a coastal State's continental shelf. Article 68 of the Law of the Sea Convention provides that Part V (on the EEZ) does not apply to sedentary species. Thus within its EEZ a coastal State is under no obligation to take any management or conservation measures in respect of such species, nor to permit foreign fishermen access to any surplus that there may be.

[50] See further United Nations, *op. cit.* in footnote 3, p. 150.
[51] Formerly the most important sealing agreement was the 1957 Interim Convention on North Pacific Fur Seals, which provided for the regulation of harvesting and the co-ordination of scientific research through the North Pacific Fur Seal Commission, but the Convention lapsed in 1985 because of opposition in the USA to the taking of marine mammals. One of the unique features of the Convention was that while only two parties (the USA and the USSR) were permitted to harvest fur seals, the other two parties (Canada and Japan) received some of the benefits of this harvest in the shape of seal skins.

Conclusions

The result of the changes in international fisheries law that have occurred since the mid- to late 1970s due to UNCLOS III, State practice and the Law of the Sea Convention is that fishing has moved from an era of international regulation (albeit relatively limited) to an era where it is regulated primarily by coastal States, although a significant element of international regulation, larger than was probably appreciated at the end of UNCLOS, remains. It was hoped that this new pattern of regulation would lead to a more effective management and equitable allocation of fishery resources than under the old regime. As regards equitable allocation, the new regime has certainly effected some transfer of benefit, in the form of increased catches, income from licence fees and access to technology, from developed to developing States, although the major transfer has been from traditional distant-water fishing States (nearly all developed States) to a relatively limited number of coastal States, many of which are also developed (and see further chapter nine, p. 177).

However, the new regime has unfortunately not led, so far at least, to improved management of fisheries, either within 200-mile zones or on the high seas. In 1995 the FAO estimated that about seventy per cent of the world's commercially important fish stocks were over-exploited or close to it.[52] In certain regions the picture is particularly bleak. Thus, for example, on the Atlantic coast of Canada the Newfoundland cod fishery collapsed in the early 1990s. The government imposed a moratorium on cod fishing in 1993, which was relaxed only in 1997 when the fishery was re-opened for very limited catches. In north-west European waters the International Council for the Exploration of the Sea reports that the spawning stock biomass of most commercial species, found largely within the 200-mile zone, are at or close to the lowest levels ever recorded. In the Black Sea, where pollution is also a major factor, catches collapsed in the mid-1980s from 1 million to 100,000 tonnes. Various explanations can be given for the lack of success of management, such as the failure of fishery managers, both national and international, to prescribe sufficiently strict conservation and management measures because of political pressures, and non-compliance by fishermen with such measures as are adopted, such non-compliance being facilitated by a lack of rigour in enforcement. The root cause, however, which lies behind these explanations, is the over-capacity of many of the world's fishing fleets, i.e., there are far more vessels than are economically justified or necessary to catch the fish available. In the EC, for example, which has one of the largest fishing fleets in the world, over-capacity is estimated to be of the order of forty per cent. Such over-capacity puts pressure on fishery managers to increase TACs above the levels recommended by scientists and adopt less stringent conservation measures of other kinds, and leads fishermen to disregard conservation measures because of the competition to catch any available fish.

---

[52] FAO, *The State of Fisheries and Aquaculture* (Rome, FAO), 1995, p. 8.

Such over-capacity also means that the world's fishing fleets are fishing well below any economically rational level. The FAO estimates that world fleets currently make a combined annual loss of $54 billion, much of which is made up by government subsidies.[53] Thus, not only has fisheries management since the later 1970s been a failure in biological terms, it also has been a failure in economic terms.

Addressing the problem of over-capacity, either at the national or international level, is extraordinarily difficult, however, because it means putting fishermen out of work. Thus, for example, the EC has spent a decade trying to reduce over-capacity, by means such as giving fishermen grants to decommission vessels, with no appreciable success so far: the fact that the EC also gives fishermen grants to build and modernise vessels hardly helps, of course. It is possible that the issue of subsidies might be addressed in the World Trade Organisation, but otherwise eliminating excess capacity would seem to come down to political will, or the lack of it, at the national level.

Unless the problem of over-capacity is seriously addressed, it seems unlikely that fisheries management will improve, either within 200 miles or on the high seas. Attempts to improve fisheries management, such as the exhortation and advice given to coastal States in such soft-law instruments as the Strategy for Fisheries Management and Development adopted by the FAO's 1984 World Fisheries Conference, UNCED's Agenda 21[54] and the FAO's Code of Conduct for Responsible Fisheries[55] and in treaties for the high seas such as the FAO Compliance Agreement and the Straddling Stocks Agreement, seem therefore unlikely to be very successful. In the case of the high seas, its basic legal nature as being open to fishing by all not only acts as a disincentive to tackle the problem of over-capacity but also continues to represent a stumbling block to better management, since treaties such as those mentioned will only be fully effective if ratified by all States fishing on the high seas.

To improve fisheries management requires not only the reduction or elimination of over-capacity but also better scientific knowledge of fish stocks and the marine ecosystem generally, as well as better conduits for the transmission of scientific advice, less tainted by political considerations, to fishery managers. Another issue which needs urgent attention is the problem of discards (unwanted fish thrown back into the sea, usually dead), which are thought to amount to the equivalent of nearly one-third of the total landed catch.

Two recent developments should also be mentioned. The first is what might be described as an attempt to 'green' international fisheries law by importing

---

[53] FAO, *World Review of Highly Migratory Species and Straddling Stocks* (Rome, FAO), 1994, p. 1.

[54] See chapter 17, Programme Area D.

[55] In addition, more practical forms of help are given to developing States through the FAO's EEZ Programme and other kinds of co-operation: for details see Kwiatkowska, *op. cit.* in footnote 2, pp. 53–7 and United Nations, *op. cit.* in footnote 3, pp. 16–18.

into it certain concepts developed in international environmental law, notably the precautionary principle/approach, sustainable development and the maintenance of biodiversity.[56] These concepts are referred to in the various soft-law instruments discussed in this chapter, as well as some of the most recent treaties such as the Straddling Stocks Agreement and the Agreement for the Establishment of the Indian Ocean Tuna Commission. It is also of interest to note that the Ministerial Declaration adopted at the Fourth North Sea Conference[57] in 1995 states that a further integration of fisheries and environmental policies should be elaborated in order to protect the North Sea environment and ensure the sustainability of fish stocks, and it recommends that the precautionary principle be applied to fisheries management.[58] Whether these developments will move beyond what seems largely to be a matter of rhetoric at this stage to make a real impact on international fisheries law, and what that impact will be, remain to be seen.

The other development is an attempt by some environmental organisations to by-pass the traditional political and legal processes and effect changes in fisheries management by dealing directly with the fishing industry. Thus, in 1996 the World Wide Fund for Nature (WWF) and Unilever (a major buyer of frozen fish) set up a Marine Stewardship Council which will establish a broad set of principles for sustainable fishing and set standards for individual fisheries. Only fisheries meeting these standards will be eligible for certification. Seafood companies will be encouraged to produce fish products only from fisheries so certified: such products will be labelled so that consumers can choose.[59] Again it remains to be seen what the impact of this development will be. Ultimately the management of marine fisheries may become less important as an increasing part of the rising consumer demand for fish is met from aquaculture and ocean ranching.

Further reading

The regime prior to the mid-1970s

F. T. Christy and A. Scott, *The Common Wealth in Ocean Fisheries* (Baltimore, Md., Johns Hopkins Press), 1965.

---

[56] For definitions of these concepts see the next chapter, p. 336. For discussion of their application to fisheries, see Hey (1996), *op. cit.* in 'Further reading' under 'General works', especially pp. 484–90 and G. J. Hewison, 'The precautionary approach to fisheries management: an environmental perspective', 11 *IJMCL* 301–22 (1996).

[57] The role and status of the North Sea Conferences are explained in the next chapter: see p. 335.

[58] See paras 13–16 of the Declaration. See also the Statement of Conclusions from the Intermediate Ministerial Meeting on the Integration of Fisheries and Environmental Issues, 1997: at http://odin.dep.no/nsc/soc.html.

[59] *WWF Arctic Bulletin*, 1996, No. 2, p. 16 and 1997, No. 2, p. 18.

D. J. Driscoll and N. McKellar, 'The changing regime of North Sea fisheries' in C. M. Mason (ed.), *The Effective Management of Resources* (London, Pinter), 1979, pp. 126–67.

J. A. Gulland, *The Management of Marine Fisheries* (Bristol, Scientechnica), 1974.

D. M. Johnston, *The International Law of Fisheries* (New Haven, Conn., Yale University Press), 1965.

H. G. Knight, *Managing the Sea's Living Resources* (Lexington, Ky., Heath), 1977.

A. W. Koers, *International Regulation of Marine Fisheries* (London, Fishing News (Books) Ltd), 1973.

The new regime

General works

P. W. Birnie and A. E. Boyle, *International Law and the Environment* (Oxford, Clarendon), 1992, chapters eleven and thirteen.

W. T. Burke, *The New International Law of Fisheries* (Oxford, Clarendon), 1994.

J. E. Carroz, 'Institutional aspects of fishery management under the new regime of the oceans', 21 *San Diego Law Review* 513–40 (1984).

R. R. Churchill, *EEC Fisheries Law* (Dordrecht, Nijhoff), 1987.

C. A. Fleischer, 'The new regime of maritime fisheries', 209 *Recueil des Cours* 95–222 (1988).

R. L. Friedheim, 'Fishing negotiations at the Third United Nations Conference on the Law of the Sea', 22 *ODIL* 209–57 (1991).

E. Hey, *The Regime for the Exploitation of Transboundary Marine Fisheries Resources* (Dordrecht, Nijhoff), 1989.

——, 'Global fisheries regulations in the first half of the 1990s', 11 *IJMCL* 459–90 (1996).

—— (ed.), *Developments in International Fisheries Law* (The Hague, Kluwer) (in press).

D. M. Johnston (ed.), *The Environmental Law of the Sea* (Gland, IUCN), 1981, especially chapter two.

P. H. Sand (ed.), *The Effectiveness of International Environmental Agreements* (Cambridge, Grotius), 1992, chapter V.

J.-P. Troadec, *Introduction to Fisheries Management*, FAO Fisheries Technical Paper No. 224, Rome, 1983.

J. A. de Yturriaga, *The International Regime of Fisheries* (The Hague, Nijhoff), 1997.

The EEZ regime

D. Attard, *The Exclusive Economic Zone in International Law* (Oxford, Oxford University Press), 1987, chapters five and six.

A. Bergin, 'Political and legal control over marine living resources – recent developments in South Pacific distant water fishing', 9 *IJMCL* 289–309 (1994).

J. E. Carroz, 'Les problèmes de la pêche à la Conférence sur le droit de la mer et dans la pratique des Etats', 84 *RGDIP* 705–51 (1980). Revised version in D. Bardonnet and M. Virally (eds), *Le nouveau droit international de la mer* (Paris, Pedone), 1983, pp. 177–229.

—— and M. J. Savini, 'The new international law of fisheries emerging from bilateral agreements', 3 *Marine Policy* 79–98 (1979).

M. Dahmani, *The Fisheries Regime of the Exclusive Economic Zone* (Dordrecht, Nijhoff), 1987.

FAO, *Report of the Expert Consultation on the Conditions for Access to the Fish Resources of the Exclusive Economic Zones*, FAO Fisheries Report No. 293, Rome, 1983.

S. Garcia, J. A. Gulland and E. L. Miles, 'The new law of the sea and access to surplus fish resources', 10 *Marine Policy* 192–200 (1986).

B. Kwiatkowska, *The 200 Mile Exclusive Economic Zone in the New Law of the Sea* (Dordrecht, Nijhoff), 1989, chapter two.

D. Mangatelle, *Coastal State Requirements for Foreign Fishing*, FAO Legislative Study No. 57, Rome, 1996.

E. Miles, *Management of World Fisheries: Implications of Extended Coastal State Jurisdiction* (Seattle, Wash., University of Washington Press), 1989.

G. Moore, 'Enforcement without force: new techniques in compliance control for foreign fishing operations based on regional co-operation', 24 *ODIL* 197–204 (1993).

——, 'National legislation for the management of fisheries under extended coastal State jurisdiction', 11 *JMLC* 153–82 (1980).

OECD, *Experiences in the Management of National Fishing Zones* (Paris, OECD), 1984.

R. W. Smith, *Exclusive Economic Zone Claims: An Analysis and Primary Documents* (Dordecht, Nijhoff), 1986 [*Smith*].

United Nations, *Conservation and Utilisation of the Living Resources of the Exclusive Economic Zone: Legislative History of Articles 61 and 62 of the United Nations Convention on the Law of Sea* (New York, United Nations), 1995.

Shared stocks

R. R. Churchill, 'Fisheries issues in maritime boundary delimitation', 17 *Marine Policy* 44–57 (1993).

J. A. Gulland, *Some Problems of the Management of Shared Sotcks*, FAO Fisheries Technical Paper No. 206, Rome, 1980.

M. Hayashi, 'The management of transboundary fish stocks under the LOS Convention', 8 *IJMCL* 245–61 (1993).

G. Munro, 'The management of shared fishery resources under extended jurisdiction' in G. Ulfstein, P. Andersen and R. Churchill (eds), *The Regulation of Fisheries: Legal, Economic and Social Aspects* (Strasbourg, Council of Europe), 1987, pp. 27–45.

High seas

W. T. Burke, M. Freeberg and E. L. Miles, 'United Nations resolutions on driftnet fishing: an unsustainable precedent for high seas and coastal fisheries management', 25 *ODIL* 127–86 (1994).

W. R. Edeson, 'The Food and Agriculture Organisation of the UN Code of Conduct for Responsible Fisheries: an introduction', 11 *IJMCL* 233–8 (1996).

FAO, *The Regulation of Driftnet Fishing on the High Seas: Legal Issues*, FAO Legislative Study No. 47, Rome, 1991.

C. C. Joyner, *Antarctica and the Law of the Sea* (Dordrecht, Nijhoff), 1992, chapter seven.

K.-H. Kock, 'Fishing and conservation in southern waters', 30 (172) *Polar Record* 3–22 (1994).

B. Kwiatkowska, 'The high seas fisheries regime: at a point of no return?', 8 *IJMCL* 327–58 (1993).

S. H. Marashi, *Summary Information on the Role of International Fishery and other Bodies with regard to the Conservation and Management of Living Resources of the High Seas*, FAO Fisheries Circular No. 908, Rome, 1996.

B. Miller, 'Combating driftnet fishing in the Pacific' in J. Crawford and D. R. Rothwell (eds), *The Law of the Sea in the Asian-Pacific Region* (Dordrecht, Nijhoff), 1995, pp. 155–70.

G. Moore, 'The Food and Agriculture Organisation of the United Nations Compliance Agreement', 10 *IJMCL* 412–6 (1995).

United Nations, *The Law of the Sea: The Regime of High Seas Fisheries – Status and Prospects* (New York, United Nations), 1992.

Straddling stocks

D. H. Anderson, 'The Straddling Stocks Agreement of 1995 – an initial assessment', 45 *ICLQ* 463–75 (1996).

D. A. Balton, 'Strengthening the law of the sea: the new agreement on straddling fish stocks and highly migratory species', 27 *ODIL* 125–51 (1996).

P. G. G. Davies and C. Redgwell, 'The international legal regulation of straddling fish stocks', 67 *BYIL* 199–274 (1996).

W.V. Dunlap, 'The Donut Hole Agreement', 10 *IJMCL* 114–35 (1995).

D. Freestone, 'Canada and the EU reach agreement to settle the *Estai* dispute', 10 *IJMCL* 397–411 (1995).

E. Melzer, 'Global overview of straddling and highly migratory fish stocks: the non-sustainable nature of high seas fisheries', 25 *ODIL* 255–344 (1994).

A. Tahindro, 'Conservation and management of transboundary fish stocks: comments in light of the adoption of the 1995 Agreement for the Conservation and Management of Straddling Fish Stocks and Highly Migratory Fish Stocks', 28 *ODIL* 1–58 (1997).

Highly migratory species

A. Bergin and M. Harvard, 'Southern bluefin tuna fishery: recent developments in international management', 18 *Marine Policy* 263–73 (1994).

FAO, *Compendium of Basic Texts concerning International Management and Development of Tuna Fisheries*, FAO Fisheries Circular No. 842, Rome, 1992.

G. Munro, 'Extended jurisdiction and the management of Pacific highly migratory species', 21 *ODIL* 289–307 (1990).

R. Shomura and H. Jayewardene, *A Review and Analysis of International Tuna Management Bodies of the World* (Rome, FAO), 1992.

Anadromous species

J. L. Bubier, 'International management of Atlantic salmon', 19 *ODIL* 35–57 (1988).

Y. L. deReynier, 'Evolving principles of international fisheries law and the North Pacific Anadromous Fish Commission', 29 *ODIL* 147–78 (1998).

F. Orrego Vicuña, 'International co-operation in salmon fisheries and a comparative law perspective on the salmon and ocean ranching industry', 22 *ODIL* 133–51 (1991).

M. Twitchell, 'Implementing the U.S.–Canada Pacific Salmon Treaty: the struggle to move from "fish wars" to cooperative fishery management', 20 *ODIL* 409–27 (1989).

Fishing

Marine mammals

S. Andresen, 'Science and politics in the international management of whales', 13 *Marine Policy* 99–118 (1989).

P. W. Birnie, *International Regulation of Whaling* (New York, Oceana), 1985.

——, 'International legal issues in the management and protection of the whale: a review of four decades of experience', 29 *Natural Resources Journal* 903–34 (1989).

D. D. Caron, 'The International Whaling Commission and the North Atlantic Marine Mammals Commission: the institutional risks of coercion in consensual structures', 89 *AJIL* 154–74 (1994).

R. Churchill, 'Sustaining small cetaceans: a preliminary evaluation of the Ascobans and Accobams Agreements' in A. E. Boyle and D. Freestone (eds), *International Law and the Sustainable Development* (Oxford, Oxford University Press), 1999, pp. 225–52.

J. Joseph, 'The tuna-dolphin controversy in the Eastern Pacific Ocean: biological, economic and political impacts', 23 *ODIL* 1–30 (1994).

G. Rose and S. Crane, 'The evolution of international whaling' in P. Sands (ed.), *Greening International Law* (London, Earthscan), 1993, pp. 159–81.

15

The prevention of
marine pollution and protection
of the marine environment

Introduction

Before 1960 there was little concern with pollution of the sea. This situation
changed, however, as a result of events such as accidents to the oil tankers
Torrey Canyon off Land's End in 1967, *Amoco Cadiz* off Brittany in 1978, *Exxon
Valdez* in Alaska in 1989 and *Sea Empress* off south-west Wales in 1996, all of
which ran aground spilling thousands of tonnes of crude oil into the sea; the
blow-outs to oil wells in the Ekofisk field in the North Sea in 1977 and Ixtoc I
off Mexico in 1979, which again resulted in vast quantities of oil being spilled
into the sea; and the discovery of DDT, a pesticide formerly used in agriculture,
and other dangerous chemicals originating from the land, in shellfish, fish and even
penguins in the Antarctic. These and many more instances have over the past
three decades or so alerted policy-makers, legislators and the public generally to
the growing problem of marine pollution.

In this chapter we examine the response of international law to this problem. Before considering the detailed rules of international law relating to marine
pollution, we shall say something about the different sources of this pollution,
both accidental and deliberate, the principal kinds of marine pollutants and their
effects, and the general framework of international law in this area. At the outset,
however, it is desirable to try to state more precisely what is meant by marine
pollution. This term is defined in article 1 of the Law of the Sea Convention,
based on a definition produced by UNESCO's Inter-governmental Oceanographic
Commission and the UN's Group of Experts on the Scientific Aspects of Marine
Pollution (GESAMP), as:

> The introduction by man, directly or indirectly, of substances or energy into the
> marine environment, including estuaries, which results or is likely to result in such
> deleterious effects as harm to living resources and marine life, hazards to human
> health, hindrance to marine activities, including fishing and other legitimate uses
> of the sea, impairment of quality for use of sea water and reduction of amenities.

The same or a very similar definition is found in a number of other conventions concerned with marine pollution. As this definition suggests, it is not the aim of international law to prevent all substances being added to the sea – many substances are harmless or are rapidly rendered so by the sea – but only those which have or are likely to have deleterious effects. For this reason, the definition has sometimes been criticised for not taking sufficient account of the need to prevent changes in the marine environment as such, and apart from any immediately identifiable possible deleterious effects.

Sources of marine pollution

Shipping

There are four main sources of marine pollution: shipping, dumping, sea-bed activities and land activities. As far as shipping is concerned, some pollution results from the operation of ships. Ships which are driven by oil-burning diesel engines (the vast majority) may discharge some oil with their bilge water; and the fumes discharged through their funnels into the atmosphere will eventually return to the sea. Some ships other than oil tankers also use their fuel tanks for ballast water and subsequently may discharge this oily ballast water into the sea. The few nuclear-powered ships (mainly submarines) may also cause some pollution. All ships, however propelled, will pollute the sea if they throw garbage overboard or discharge their sewage directly into the sea. By far the greatest amount of pollution from ships, however, comes from their cargoes. Oil, the commodity which is transported most extensively by sea, used often to be deliberately discharged at sea, notably when seawater which had been pumped into an empty oil tanker to clean out the tanks or serve as ballast was later pumped out again. This practice has greatly declined as most tankers now use the 'load on top' system (see below). Some oil, as well as other noxious cargoes like chemicals, liquid gas and radioactive matter, enters the sea as a result of accidents, such as collisions, strandings and explosions, as happened in the cases of the *Torrey Canyon, Amoco Cadiz, Exxon Valdez* and *Sea Empress*. The growing number of ships, which we noted in chapter thirteen, has increased the risk of such accidents, and the trend to larger ships makes the result of any accident more serious.

Dumping

In the 1950s and 1960s dumping at sea became an increasingly popular way of disposing of waste resulting from land-based activities. This was partly because of its relative cheapness and ease, and partly as a reaction to the tightening up of pollution controls on land. The main kinds of waste dumped include radioactive matter, military materials (including obsolete weapons and explosives), dredged materials (which account for about eighty to ninety per cent of all dumping, most of which are 'clean' and result from dredging to keep ports, rivers and other waterways open), sewage sludge (which may contain metals, oils and organic chemicals) and industrial waste (which contains a variety of different pollutants, many of them highly toxic). Although waste is dumped from ships, international conventions treat dumping as a source of pollution separate from shipping. This is partly because dumping, unlike other pollution from ships, is always deliberate and usually the *raison d'être* of a particular voyage, and partly because dumping is an extension of pollution from land (although it has to be considered separately from land-based sources because the areas where dumping takes place are obviously juridically different from land territory).

Sea-bed activities

As far as installations for exploring and exploiting sea-bed oil and gas are concerned, some deliberate pollution results from such structures, for example the disposal into the sea of domestic refuse, industrial debris and relatively small amounts of oily and chemical waste from drilling. Accidental pollution may result from blow-outs (as in the case of the Ekofisk and Ixtoc wells mentioned above); from collisions between ships and installations; or from the breaking of pipelines, either through natural wear and tear or through being fouled by a trawl. Some pollution may result from the mining of manganese nodules in the international-sea-bed area, but until commercial production begins it is difficult to assess what the impact of this will be.[1]

Land-based and atmospheric pollution

The last source, but far and away the most important, is the polluting matter entering the sea from land. This includes sewage and industrial wastes discharged into rivers or directly into the sea; chemicals used as fertilisers and pesticides in agriculture running off the land into rivers; warm water from power stations (some of them nuclear) built on coasts and estuaries; and discharges into the atmosphere of vehicle exhaust, fumes from chimneys (domestic and factory) and sprayed agricultural chemicals, all of which may eventually be precipitated into the sea.

In a report published in 1990,[2] GESAMP estimated that twelve per cent of marine pollution originated from shipping, ten per cent from dumping, one per cent from sea-bed activities, forty-four per cent from run-off and land-based discharges, and thirty-three per cent from the atmosphere (the vast majority from land-based

[1] The International Sea Bed Authority is in the course of assembling baseline data in order to monitor the environmental impact of sea-bed mining, and is trying to predict what that impact will be.

[2] GESAMP, *The State of the Marine Environment*, UNEP Regional Seas Reports and Studies No. 115, Nairobi, 1990, p. 88. In 1993 GESAMP was renamed the Group of Experts on the Scientific Aspects of Marine Environmental Protection, but its acronym is unchanged.

sources). The impact of these last two sources is very different, however. Whereas atmospheric input to the sea is normally dilute and diffuse, land-based inputs are often concentrated in particular coastal areas.

The primary approach of administrators and legislators has generally been to tackle the problems of marine pollution according to the source of such pollution, rather than dealing with the problems according to the nature of particular pollutants. The differing jurisdictional natures of land and sea make such an approach readily understandable. At the same time, however, whatever the particular source of marine pollution, attention has concentrated on tackling the more noxious and the more visible – which is not always the same – pollutants. It is therefore necessary to say a few words about some of the more serious of the many marine pollutants.

Marine pollutants

Although oil is the marine pollutant which has received most attention from legislators and attracted most public concern (perhaps because it is the most frequently obvious and visible pollutant), it is not the most noxious of marine pollutants, partly because it is eventually broken down by marine bacteria. Before it is so broken down, however, oil can cause great damage, fouling coastlines and killing sea birds, fish and other marine life. Even if they are not killed by the oil, fish can suffer damage in other ways – for example, skin cancer or disequilibrium – and shellfish are rendered inedible. Oil spills can to some extent be dealt with by keeping the oil together by means of booms and skimming it off the surface of the sea, or by dispersing it with chemicals. The former method can never be more than partially successful and can be used only when the sea is comparatively calm, while in the latter case the chemicals employed are sometimes as toxic as the oil they disperse.

Unlike oil, chlorinated hydrocarbons (such as DDT and polychlorinated biphenyls (PCBs)), heavy metals (such as lead, mercury and cadmium) and radioactive wastes are not biodegradable, nor is there any possibility of removing them from the sea once they have entered it. These substances vary in their effect, but in general they are absorbed by marine organisms, often becoming concentrated as they move up the food chain, and affecting the growth, reproduction and mortality of marine life. In some cases it is unsafe for humans to eat fish containing these substances: for example, in the 1950s in Minamata Bay in Japan forty-three people died and many more suffered blindness, muscular weakness and brain damage after eating mercury-contaminated fish.

Nutrients, such as nitrates and phosphates, contained mainly in agricultural run-off and sewage, when in small amounts are broken down by the sea and rendered innocuous, but large amounts lead to over-fertilisation, followed by de-composition and de-oxygenation of the water. This effect is particularly marked in enclosed seas such as the Baltic. When water is de-oxygenated the eggs of fish will not hatch, fish larvae are unable to develop and adult fish move to more

331

richly oxygenated waters. Sewage can also cause tides of toxic phytoplankton (which may kill or damage marine life), and contaminate seawater used for swimming and other recreational uses with micro-organisms dangerous to man.

Finally, the disposal of plastics from land and ships results in the littering of beaches and may seriously damage marine wildlife, especially marine mammals, birds and reptiles, which may ingest fragments of plastic or become trapped in plastic packaging and fishing gear.

Pollutants differ in their concentration and effects from region to region, but in general it is coastal waters which are the most polluted, while the open ocean is relatively clean.

The framework of international law relating to marine pollution

Custom

Customary international law contains few rules relevant to the question of marine pollution. In the *Corfu Channel* case (1949) the International Court of Justice said that each State was under an obligation 'not to allow knowingly its territory to be used for acts contrary to the rights of other States';[3] and in the *Trail Smelter* arbitration (1938–41), a case involving damage to property in the USA caused by noxious fumes emitted by a smelter in Canada, the arbitral tribunal held that 'no State has the right to use or permit the use of its territory in such a manner as to cause injury by fumes in or to the territory of another' State.[4] Article 2 of the High Seas Convention, which is stated to be declaratory of customary international law, provides that States must exercise the freedoms of the high seas 'with reasonable regard to the interests of other States in their exercise of the freedom of the high seas'. It could be argued that, taking the principles enunciated in Article 2 and in the *Corfu Channel* case together and extending the principle in the *Trail Smelter* case by analogy, there is a general rule of customary international law that States must not permit their nationals to discharge into the sea matter that could cause harm to the nationals of other States.[5] However, this rule appears to be too vague to be very effective, and certainly is incapable of developing, given the nature of customary international law, into the detailed emission standards or liability regimes that are required.

Customary international law also defines the extent of States' legislative and enforcement jurisdiction, a question which, as we shall see, is particularly important as far as marine pollution is concerned. However, the customary rules on jurisdiction have been considered by many States to be both inadequate and incapable of sufficiently speedy or extensive development to sustain effective action against pollution.

---

[3] [1949] *ICJ Rep.* 3, at 22.
[4] III *RIAA* 1905, at 1965.
[5] For the view that such a customary rule exists and a discussion of the relevant law and literature, see Smith, *op. cit.* in 'Further reading' under 'General', chapters 5 and 6.

Treaties

Given these deficiencies of customary international law, it is not surprising to find that the international law relating to marine pollution is contained almost wholly in treaties, of which there is now a considerable number. The first of these treaties was adopted in 1954 – although a draft treaty dealing with oil pollution from ships was drawn up in 1926 but was never opened for signature. Little attention was paid to pollution at UNCLOS I, apart from the general obligations imposed on States to prevent marine pollution by oil and radioactive waste, in articles 24 and 25 of the High Seas Convention; but since 1969, in response to growing international concern over pollution of the marine environment, a steady stream of treaties has been concluded.

Marine pollution treaties can be divided into four categories: general multilateral treaties, regional treaties, bilateral treaties and the Law of the Sea Convention. Of the general multilateral treaties, there are some half a dozen concerned with pollution from ships (details of which are given in the next section) and one concerned with dumping. There are no general multilateral treaties dealing with marine pollution from land-based sources or sea-bed activities, although some soft-law instruments exist. The treaties concerned with pollution from ships were all adopted under the auspices of the International Maritime Organisation (IMO), and the IMO exercises certain supervisory functions in the relation to them.

At the regional level there are a number of treaties dealing with all the sources of marine pollution within a single framework treaty, accompanied by protocols containing more detailed obligations for specific sources of pollution. Such treaties have been adopted for the Baltic,[6] Mediterranean,[7] Arabian/Persian Gulf and Gulf of Oman,[8] West Africa,[9] South-East Pacific,[10] Red Sea and Gulf of

---

[6] Convention on the Protection of the Marine Environment of the Baltic Sea Area, 1974, due to be replaced by the 1992 Convention of the same name when it enters into force (hereafter referred to as the 1974 and 1992 Baltic Conventions). Unlike the other treaties referred to below, the Baltic Conventions themselves contain detailed obligations and therefore do not have supplementary protocols.

[7] Convention for the Protection of the Mediterranean Sea against Pollution 1976 (hereafter referred to as the Mediterranean Convention), amended in 1995, together with its protocols on dumping (1976), co-operation in emergencies (1976), land-based sources (1980), specially protected areas (1982 and 1995), sea-bed activities (1994) and transboundary movement of hazardous waste (1996).

[8] Kuwait Regional Convention for Co-operation on the Protection of the Marine Environment from Pollution 1978 (hereafter referred to as the Kuwait Convention), together with its protocols on co-operation in emergencies (1978), sea-bed activities (1989) and land-based sources (1990). There is also a draft protocol on transboundary movement of hazardous waste.

[9] Convention for Co-operation in the Protection and Development of the Marine and Coastal Environment of the West and Central African Region, 1981 (hereafter referred to as the West African Convention), together with its protocol on co-operation in emergencies (1981). There is also a draft protocol on land-based sources.

[10] Convention for the Protection of the Marine Environment and Coastal Area of the South-East Pacific, 1981 (hereafter referred to as the South-East Pacific Convention), together

Aden,[11] Caribbean,[12] East Africa,[13] South Pacific[14] and Black Sea.[15] Many of these areas, particularly semi-enclosed seas such as the Baltic and Black Seas, are suffering particularly badly from the effects of marine pollution. With the exception of the Baltic Convention, the initiative for these agreements has largely come from, and much of the preparatory work has been done by, the United Nations Environment Programme (UNEP), as part of its Regional Seas Programme, and to a rather more limited extent the IMO. All the agreements are in force and have been widely ratified by the States of the relevant region, although not all their protocols are yet in force or widely ratified. Each of the agreements is accompanied by an Action Plan. Such Plans have also been adopted for the East Asian and South Asian Seas and the North-West Pacific Region, although there are not (as yet) any legal instruments accompanying them. In the North-East Atlantic and North Sea there is no equivalent single framework convention, but a number of *ad hoc* agreements have been adopted, dealing with co-operation in oil pollution emergencies,[16] dumping,[17] land-based sources[18] and liability for pollution resulting from sea-bed activities.[19] In addition the North Sea States

---

with its agreement and supplementary protocol on co-operation in emergencies (1981 and 1983) and protocols on land-based sources (1983), radioactive pollution (1989) and protected areas (1989). There is also a draft protocol on environmental impact assessment.

[11] Regional Convention for the Conservation of the Red Sea and Gulf of Aden Environment 1982 (hereafter referred to as the Red Sea Convention), together with its protocol on co-operation in emergencies (1982).

[12] Convention for the Protection and Development of the Marine Environment of the Wider Caribbean Region, 1983 (hereafter referred to as the Caribbean Convention), together with its protocols on co-operation in emergencies (1983) and specially protected areas (1990). There is also a draft protocol on land-based sources.

[13] Convention for the Protection, Management and Development of the Marine and Coastal Environment of the Eastern African Region 1985 (hereafter referred to as the East African Convention), together with its protocols on protected areas (1985) and co-operation in emergencies (1985).

[14] Convention for the Protection of the Natural Resources and Environment of the South Pacific Region, 1986 (hereafter referred to as the South Pacific Convention), together with its protocols on co-operation in emergencies (1986) and dumping (1986).

[15] Convention on the Protection of the Black Sea against Pollution, 1992 (hereafter referred to as the Black Sea Convention), together with its protocols on land-based sources (1992), co-operation in emergencies (1992) and dumping (1992).

[16] Agreement for Co-operation in Dealing with Pollution of the North Sea by Oil, 1969, replaced by the Agreement for Co-operation in Dealing with Pollution of the North Sea by Oil and Other Harmful Substances 1983.

[17] Convention for the Prevention of Marine Pollution by Dumping from Ships and Aircraft 1972, together with its protocol on incineration (1983). This Convention was replaced by the Convention for the Protection of the Marine Environment of the North-East Atlantic, 1992, upon its entry into force in 1998.

[18] Convention for the Prevention of Marine Pollution from Land-Based Sources, 1974, together with its protocol on atmospheric pollution (1986). This Convention has also been replaced by the 1992 Convention referred to in the previous note.

[19] International Convention on Civil Liability for Oil Pollution Damage resulting from Exploration for, or Exploitation of, Submarine Mineral Resources, 1977.

meet in conferences from time to time to discuss the problems of pollution in the North Sea. So far such conferences have been held in 1984, 1987, 1990 and 1995, each of which has adopted a declaration. These declarations, which are soft-law instruments, contain a mixture of elements – undertakings to ratify and effectively implement existing treaties; proposals to press for certain action to be taken under existing treaties and organisations (including the EC, which adopts a considerable number of measures dealing with marine pollution); and under-takings (often in imprecise and ambiguous language) to take action outside existing agreements.[20]

Action has also been taken to deal with marine pollution in the polar re-gions, which are particularly sensitive to pollution. In the Antarctic the parties to the Antarctic Treaty adopted a Protocol on Environmental Protection in 1991, Annex IV of which deals with the prevention of marine pollution from ships. Co-operation between the eight Arctic States developed later than in the Antarctic because of the Cold War and is less institutionalised. In 1991 the Arctic States adopted the Arctic Environmental Protection Strategy,[21] the objectives of which include the identification, reduction and eventual elimination of pollution. The Strategy lists existing international agreements applicable to the Arctic and notes that there are gaps in environmental protection arising therefrom. No additional legal instruments have yet been drawn up to plug these gaps. Four programmes have been established under the Strategy dealing with Arctic monitoring and assessment, conservation of Arctic flora and fauna, protection of the Arctic marine environment, and emergency prevention, preparedness and response. In 1996 an Arctic Council was set up,[22] which *inter alia* is to oversee and co-ordinate these programmes.

Some of the regional conventions mentioned above have now reached a second generation. Thus, the 1974 Baltic Convention will be replaced by a second Baltic Convention adopted in 1992 when the latter enters into force; the Mediterranean Convention and some of its protocols were revised and amended in 1995 and 1996; and the North Sea and North-East Atlantic Conventions on dumping and land-based pollution were replaced by a single new convention, the 1992 Paris Convention for the Protection of the Marine Environment of the North-East Atlantic, when it entered into force in 1998. One of the notable fea-tures of the second generation agreements is that they include, for the first time

---

[20] The texts of the 1984, 1987 and 1990 declarations are reproduced in Freestone and IJlstra (1991), *op. cit.* in 'Further reading' under 'Regional pollution agreements', pp. 3–89. The text of the 1995 declaration can be found on the internet at http://odin.dep.no/nsc/ esbjerg.html#MINISTERIAL. For a discussion of the legal nature of the declarations, see Freestone and Ijlstra (1990), *op. cit.* in 'Further reading' under 'Regional pollution agree-ments', chapters 1 and 2, and M. Pallemaerts, 'The North Sea Ministerial Declarations from Bremen to The Hague: does the process generate any substance?' 7 *IJECL* 1–26 (1992).

[21] 30 *ILM* 1624 (1991). See also D. R. Rothwell, 'International law and protection of the Arctic environment', 44 *ICLQ* 280–312 (1995).

[22] Declaration on the Establishment of the Arctic Council, 35 *ILM* 1382 (1996).

in marine pollution treaties, references to several concepts recently developed in international environmental law, such as the precautionary principle, sustainable development and biodiversity. The precautionary principle has been referred to in a number of treaties and other instruments outside the field of marine pollution as providing guidance as to when action should be taken to deal with actual or potential pollution. While definitions of the precautionary principle vary from instrument to instrument and writer to writer,[23] the definition in the Baltic Convention is reasonably representative. Article 3(2) of the Convention defines the principle as being

> to take preventive measures when there is reason to assume that substances or energy introduced, directly or indirectly, into the marine environment may create hazards to human health, harm living resources and marine ecosystems, damage amenities or interfere with other legitimate uses of the sea even when there is no conclusive evidence of a causal relationship between inputs and their alleged effects.

The Baltic Convention (art. 3(2)), the amended Mediterranean Convention (art. 4(3)(a)) and the Paris Convention (art. 2(2)(a)) all provide that their parties shall apply this principle. The principle is also espoused in the North Sea declarations and Agenda 21 adopted by the 1992 UN Conference on Environment and Development (UNCED) (see chapter 17.21 to 22). Sustainable development is a concept particularly advanced by the World Commission on Environment and Development and is defined by it as 'development that meets the needs of the present without compromising the ability of future generations to meet their own needs'.[24] The UNEP Governing Council has endorsed this definition and added that it requires 'the maintainance, rational use and enhancement of the natural resource base that underpins ecological resilience and economic growth'.[25] Biological diversity (biodiversity) is regarded as having three elements: diversity of species, genetic diversity within species and diversity of ecosystems (see art. 2 of the 1992 Framework Convention on Biological Diversity).[26] The principle of sustainable development is obviously primarily concerned with natural resources,

---

[23] See, amongst the growing literature on this topic, A. Nollkaemper, 'The precautionary principle in international environmental law. What's new under the sun?', 22 *Marine Pollution Bulletin* 107–10 (1991); D. Freestone, 'The precautionary principle' in R. R. Churchill and D. Freestone (eds), *International Law and Global Climate Change* (London, Graham & Trotman), 1991, pp. 21–39; and E. Hey, 'The precautionary concept in international policy and law: institutionalising caution', 4 *Georgetown International Environmental Law Review* 303–18 (1992).

[24] World Commission on Environment and Development, *Our Common Future* (Oxford, Oxford University Press), 1987, p. 43.

[25] Decision 15/2 of 1989, Annex II in UN General Assembly, Official Records, 44th session, supplement No. 25 (A/44/25), p. 115. The concept of sustainable development has been further developed at and since UNCED. See further Birnie and Boyle, *op. cit.* in 'Further reading' under 'General', pp. 3–6, 122–4. What is involved in sustainable development has generated a huge literature.

[26] See also M. Bowman and C. Redgwell (eds), *International Law and the Conservation of Biological Diversity* (London, Kluwer), 1996, especially chapters 1–3 and 5.

but both it and the maintainance of biological diversity require a marine environment free of significant pollution for their effective realisation. The two concepts are endorsed in article 15 of the 1992 Baltic Convention and articles 4 and 10 of the amended Mediterranean Convention, and the objective of 'sustainable management' recognised in the preamble to the Paris Convention. The concepts of sustainable development and biodiversity are also reflected and given effect in the protocols on specially protected areas attached to some of the regional conventions referred to above, which are discussed in the penultimate section of this chapter. The second-generation agreements also espouse rather longer established principles of international environmental law which are now included in marine pollution conventions for the first time. These include the polluter pays principle (under which the costs of preventing or remediating pollution are imposed on the polluter, and not on the victims of such pollution or society generally), and the principle of the use of best available techniques/technology, best environmental practice and, where appropriate, clean technology (Baltic Convention, art. 3(3)(4); Mediterranean Convention, arts 4(3)(4) and 13; Paris Convention, art. 2(2)(3)). How all these concepts and principles will be applied in practice remains to be seen.[27]

At the sub-regional level, the four Nordic States (Denmark, Finland, Norway and Sweden) have concluded two agreements dealing with marine pollution,[28] while France, Italy and Monaco in 1976 signed an Agreement relating to the Protection of the Waters of the Mediterranean Coast, and Denmark, Germany and the Netherlands signed a Joint Declaration on the Protection of the Wadden Sea in 1982.

In a number of cases States have also found it desirable to conclude bilateral agreements to deal with more specific or local questions of marine pollution. Thus, for example, Italy and the former Yugoslavia signed an Agreement on Co-operation for the Protection of the Waters of the Adriatic Sea and Coastal Zones from Pollution in 1974; Denmark and Sweden, an Agreement concerning Protection of the Sound from Pollution (1974); Canada and the USA, an Agreement relating to the Establishment of Joint Pollution Contingency Plans for Spills of Oil and other Noxious Substances (1974); Canada and Denmark, an Agreement for Co-operation relating to the Marine Environment (1983); and the Netherlands and Venezuela, an Agreement establishing a Bilateral Oil Spill Contingency Plan to Protect the Coastal and Marine Environment (1995).

In view of this extensive treaty action, much of which pre-dated UNCLOS III, it was not necessary for the conference to consider detailed standards relating to marine pollution, nor would the conference have been well suited to the

---

[27] For a critical evaluation of the inclusion of all these principles in the Paris Convention, and suggestions that they may not all be workable as they stand, see Hey, IJlstra and Nollkaemper, *op. cit.* in 'Further reading' under 'Regional pollution agreements', pp. 7–18.
[28] Agreement concerning Co-operation in Measures to deal with Pollution of the Sea by Oil, 1971 and Convention on the Protection of the Environment, 1974.

elaboration of such technically complex matters. Instead, having for the first time laid down a general duty to protect and preserve the marine environment from pollution from all sources (LOSC, arts 192 *et seq.*), the conference concentrated on defining the jurisdictional rights and obligations, both legislative and enforcement, of flag, coastal and port States. Provisions on these matters are now found in articles 207 to 234 and 236 of the Law of the Sea Convention. The remainder of the articles in Part XII (Protection and Preservation of the Marine Environment) deal with principles (arts 192–6), global and regional co-operation (arts 197–201), technical assistance (arts 202–3), monitoring and environmental assessment (arts 204–6) and responsibility and liability (art. 235).

The achievement in negotiating all the treaties mentioned above and bringing most of them into force should not be underestimated, for the conclusion of marine pollution treaties raises many economic, technical and political difficulties. The adoption of stricter anti-pollution standards means increased costs for industry and shipowners. A State is therefore very likely to be reluctant to accept stricter anti-pollution standards unless other States do the same, lest its shipping and other industries lose their competitive edge. More broadly, developing States are reluctant to accept strict anti-pollution standards which they consider may hinder their economic development, when in their view – and rightly – it is the developed States which are responsible for most marine pollution. As far as technical difficulties are concerned, there is little point in setting emission standards with which present-day technology cannot ensure compliance: on the other hand, emission standards ought to be set at the level of the most technologically advanced industry. Furthermore, the prohibition or limitation of one particular type of marine pollution should not lead to that pollution being diverted elsewhere so as to cause as great or greater harm to the environment, a problem recognised by the Law of the Sea Convention (see art. 195).

It is encouraging to see that in some areas environmental problems have led to States which can agree on little else agreeing on regional conventions to prevent marine pollution. Thus both Israel and its Arab neighbours, as well as Greece and Turkey, are parties to the Mediterranean Convention; and both Iran and the Arab States of the Gulf are parties to the Kuwait Convention. Nevertheless, there is no room for complacency. In the case of most marine pollutants there is a considerable lapse of time between the action being taken to control pollution and that action having any significant effect.

Having looked at the general framework of international law relating to marine pollution, we must now consider its provisions in more detail, looking in turn at each of the different sources of pollution.

Pollution from ships

Pollution from shipping raises a number of issues: standards to reduce or eliminate pollution; the prescription and enforcement of such standards; measures to avoid accidental pollution; action taken by coastal States in respect of pollution casualties; co-operation in dealing with emergencies; and liability for pollution damage. We shall consider each of these matters in turn.

Standards to reduce or eliminate intentional (operational) pollution

The 1954 Oil Pollution Convention

The first pollutant for which international control standards were set was oil. When an oil tanker has discharged its cargo of oil, a certain amount of the oil remains clinging to the tanks. This oil has to be disposed of before a new cargo can be taken on board.[29] One way of doing this is for tankers to wash out their empty tanks at sea. In addition, empty tankers also use seawater as ballast, and this water, containing residues of oil, has of course to be pumped out before a new cargo can be taken on board. An alternative to discharging tank washings at sea is the 'load on top' system, developed in the 1960s. In this the oily water is pumped into a special slop tank: here the oil, being lighter than water, floats to the surface and separates from the water. The almost oil-free water is then returned to the sea, and the oil residues are retained on board. The next cargo can, in most cases, then be loaded on top of the residues. Other ships also use seawater as ballast in their empty fuel tanks, and this too is eventually pumped out. Ships which use heavy oils as fuel accumulate oily sludges which eventually have to be disposed of. In each of these different ways oil may enter the sea. It was to deal with these forms of marine pollution that the International Convention for the Prevention of Pollution of the Sea by Oil was drawn up in 1954. The Convention was of limited effectiveness and is now largely of historical interest, as the International Convention for the Prevention of Pollution from Ships (hereafter referred to as the MARPOL Convention) provides that as between its parties it supersedes the 1954 Convention. Although just under twenty parties to the 1954 Convention have not (yet) become parties to the MARPOL Convention, and therefore remain bound by the earlier convention, their fleets collectively account for only a tiny proportion of the total world merchant shipping fleet.

The MARPOL Convention

The MARPOL Convention was adopted under the auspices of the IMO in 1973 and is intended to deal with all forms of intentional pollution of the sea from ships, other than dumping. Detailed pollution standards are set out in six annexes. These are concerned with oil (Annex I), noxious liquid substances in bulk (Annex II), harmful substances carried by sea in packaged forms (Annex III), sewage (Annex IV), garbage (Annex V) and air pollution (Annex VI, added in 1997).

---

[29] There are a number of reasons why this has to be done. If the oil remains, the risk of an explosion increases, drainage of the tanks may be impeded, the cargo capacity of the tank is decreased and the oily residue may be incompatible with the next cargo to be loaded.

The acceptance of Annexes I and II is obligatory for all contracting parties, but acceptance of the remaining annexes is optional. By 1978 the Convention was still a long way from receiving the necessary number of ratifications to enter into force, mainly because of the considerable economic cost and technical difficulties of complying with its provisions. In an effort to speed up ratification, a Protocol to the Convention was adopted at the IMO's Conference on Tanker Safety and Pollution Prevention, held in February 1978. The effect of the Protocol was to provide that a State could become a party to the MARPOL Convention initially by accepting only Annex I. Annex II would not become binding until three years after the entry into force of the Protocol or such longer period as might be decided by the parties to the Protocol. In this modified form the Convention and Annex I came into force in October 1983 and Annex II in April 1987. Annex III came into force in July 1992 and Annex V in December 1988. Annexes IV and VI are not yet in force. All the annexes have been amended since 1978, some several times, by means of the tacit amendment procedure (see p. 272 above). In addition, the IMO has adopted a number of resolutions giving guidance on how the Convention, its annexes and protocols are to be interpreted and applied.

The regulations dealing with oil pollution contained in Annex I are complex and detailed, and only a bare outline of them can be given here. Tankers over 150 tons must operate the load-on-top system under which limited discharges of oily water may be made while the tanker is en route, except in certain special areas, such as the Mediterranean, Baltic and Black Seas, where no discharges at all are permitted. In addition, most tankers must be fitted with with segregated ballast tanks[30] and equipment for crude oil washing.[31] Ships other than tankers must be fitted with oily water separating or filtering equipment and tanks adequate for retaining on board the sludge from heavy fuel oils, and ships above 4,000 GRT must be fitted with segregated ballast tanks. Finally, parties must provide reception facilities in their ports where ships can discharge their oily residues.

The provisions of the remaining annexes to the MARPOL Convention are extremely complex, and can be only briefly summarised here. Under Annex II the discharge of residues containing noxious liquid substances must be made to a reception facility, unless they are adequately diluted, in which case they may be discharged into the sea in accordance with detailed regulations. The annex also contains provisions for minimising pollution in the event of an accident. This last is the chief concern of Annex III, which seeks to prevent or minimise pollution from harmful substances carried in packaged forms by laying down regulations concerning packaging, marking, labelling, documentation, stowage and quantity limitations. Annex IV prohibits the discharge of sewage within four miles of land unless a ship has in operation an approved treatment plant. Between four and twelve miles from land, sewage must be comminuted and disinfected

---

[30] i.e., tanks used for ballast water must be kept separate from tanks carrying oil.
[31] A method of cleaning oil cargo tanks by using crude oil instead of water. This process leaves virtually no oily waste.

before discharge. Finally, Annex V specifies minimum distances from land for the disposal of all the principal kinds of garbage, and in some areas (such as the North Sea and Antarctic) prohibits their disposal completely: it also prohibits the disposal of all plastics. For the substances covered by Annexes II, IV and V contracting States are obliged to provide adequate reception facilities in their ports for wastes retained on board. Annex VI deals with the prevention of air pollution from ships, and limits sulphur and nitrogen oxide emissions from ship exhausts, prohibits shipboard incineration of certain substances and regulates the onboard use of ozone-depleting substances such as halons and CFCs. In addition, the IMO is in the course of drafting a seventh annex (provisionally scheduled for adoption in 2000) which would deal with the problem of environmental damage caused by the introduction of unwanted aquatic organisms in ballast water and sediment discharges.

In general it appears that the MARPOL Convention, once it eventually came into force, has made some contribution towards reducing deliberate pollution from ships. The amount of oil entering the marine environment from maritime transport (of which accidental spills account for about twenty per cent) declined from 2.13 million tonnes in 1973 to 0.57 million tonnes in 1989,[32] a decrease of nearly seventy-five per cent. Although there was evidence of defective implementation and enforcement of the 1954 and MARPOL Conventions during this period,[33] Annex I of the MARPOL Convention, which as of mid-1998 was binding on nearly ninety-four per cent of the total world fleet by tonnage, and the 1954 Convention must presumably take some of the credit for this decrease.[34] Experience with the other annexes of MARPOL is more mixed. In the case of Annex II, only seven alleged breaches of its provisions were reported during the first five years following its entry into force:[35] it is unclear whether this low number was due to a high standard of compliance or a failure to report breaches. Annexes III and V apply to a somewhat lower proportion of the world fleet than Annexes I and II, being applicable to about seventy-nine and eighty-three per cent, respectively. There have also been problems with the enforcement of Annex V. In 1992 the USA reported that the number of violations of this Annex rose from sixteen in 1989 to 118 in 1991. Of these the USA had reported 111 to the flag State, as required by MARPOL. A response was received in only thirty-five cases, and in only two of these was any action taken (a small fine in each case). The failure to reply to the USA in seventy-six of the cases was a clear breach

[32] *IMO News*, 1993, No. 3, pp. 1–2, quoting a GESAMP study, *Impact of Oil and Related Chemicals and Wastes on the Marine Environment.*

[33] R. Mitchell, 'Intentional oil pollution of the oceans' in P. M. Haas, R. O. Keohane and M. A. Levy (eds), *Institutions for the Earth: Sources of Effective International Environmental Protection* (Cambridge, Mass., MIT Press), 1993, p. 183 at 217–19.

[34] This is the view of both GESAMP, *op. cit.* in footnote 2, pp. 21, 43 and 92, and the US National Academy of Sciences in a report of 1990 summarised in *IMO News*, 1990, No. 4, p. 16.

[35] *IMO News*, 1992, No. 2, p. 9.

of MARPOL.[36] A problem common to all the annexes is the lack of adequate reception facilities in the ports of many parties. Such facilities are essential for the proper implementation of the Convention, but here there is a kind of *Catch 22* situation – ports are reluctant to provide reception facilities unless they can charge ships for their use in order to cover the cost of providing facilities, but if ships are faced with paying charges, they are likely to go to a port with no or lower charges or discharge residues illegally at sea. A further general problem is the failure to make annual reports to the IMO on the enforcement of the Convention as is required by the Convention. An IMO study of 1992 showed that thirty of the then seventy-nine parties had never submitted any report at all, and only six had fully complied by sending a report every year.[37]

Other treaties

The MARPOL Convention is the main multilateral instrument regulating pollution from ships, but there are some other, less important, instruments which should be briefly mentioned. Both the International Convention for the Safety of Life at Sea, 1974 (SOLAS Convention) (Chapter VII), and the IMO's International Maritime Dangerous Goods (IMDG) Code, adopted in 1966, contain provisions relating to the packing, marketing, labelling, documentation and stowage of dangerous goods, which have the objective *inter alia* of reducing the risk of pollution resulting from the carriage of such goods by ships. The IMDG Code is closely related to Annex III of the MARPOL Convention as the latter defines harmful substances as those which are identified as marine pollutants in the Code (over 600 substances). A code adopted by the IMO in 1993 deals with the carriage of radioactive material by ship, supplementing provisions in the SOLAS Convention, the IMDG Code and regulations of the International Atomic Energy Agency.[38] The Basel Convention on the Control of Transboundary Movements of Hazardous Wastes and their Disposal 1989, although not primarily concerned with marine pollution, is also of some relevance. Thus, article 4(2)(d) requires parties to ensure that the transboundary movement (which includes carriage by sea) of hazardous and other wastes is 'conducted in a manner which will protect human health and the environment against the adverse effects which may result from such movement,' while article 4(7)(b) requires that such wastes be packaged, labelled and transported in conformity with relevant 'generally accepted and recognised rules and standards'. The Bamako Convention on the Ban of the Import into Africa and the Control of Transboundary Movement and Management of Hazardous Wastes within Africa, 1991 has similar provisions (see arts 4(3)(m)(ii) and (t)).

---

[36] *IMO News*, 1993, No. 3, pp. V–VI. It is not clear from this report whether the violations occurred only in US waters or whether they occurred elsewhere.
[37] *IMO News*, 1995, No. 3, p. XVII.
[38] IMO Assembly Resolution A. 748 (18), as amended by Resolution A. 853 (20). It is likely that the code, known as the INF Code, will eventually be incorporated in the SOLAS Convention and thus become legally binding.

Civilian nuclear-powered ships have operated in the past, but it is a number of years since any have done so. Should such ships begin operating again, Chapter VIII of the SOLAS Convention, which lays down regulations governing non-military nuclear-powered ships, and the Code of Safety for Nuclear Merchant Ships, which the IMO adopted in 1981,[39] would help to reduce the risk of accidental or deliberate pollution arising out of the operation of such ships. In the past this question has also been dealt with by a number of bilateral agreements, e.g., the USA–UK Agreement relating to the Use of United Kingdom Ports and Territorial Waters by the N.S. *Savannah*, 1964.

The various regional conventions deal with pollution from ships in a very general way, simply referring their parties to the general multilateral provisions discussed above. Given the global nature of shipping, this approach makes good sense. Thus article 6 of the 1976 Mediterranean Convention (as amended) provides that its parties

> shall take all measures in conformity with international law to prevent, abate, combat and to the fullest possible extent eliminate pollution of the Mediterranean Sea Area caused by discharges from ships and to ensure the effective implementation in that Area of the rules which are generally recognised at the international level relating to the control of this type of pollution.

The other regional conventions are nearly all in similar vein. One exception is the Baltic Convention, Annex IV of which originally contained detailed regulations dealing with pollution from oil, noxious liquid substances in bulk, harmful substances in packaged forms, sewage and garbage. These regulations were similar to the equivalent regulations of the MARPOL Convention. However, as the annexes of the MARPOL Convention have come into force, the regulations of the Baltic Convention have been replaced by a cross-reference to the relevant MARPOL annex. This approach is followed in the 1992 Baltic Convention (see art. 8 and Annex IV). The other exception is the Protocol on Environmental Protection to the Antarctic Treaty, Annex IV of which prohibits almost all forms of pollution from ships in the Treaty area, i.e., the waters south of 60° South. In addition, the regional agreements have begun to deal with hazardous waste. Thus, article 10 of the amended Mediterranean Convention provides that its parties are to prevent pollution caused by transboundary movement and the disposal of hazardous waste, and a separate protocol on the subject was adopted in 1996. This requires its parties *inter alia* to reduce to a minimum the transboundary movement of hazardous waste (including therefore the transport of waste by sea): where such movement does take place it must be consistent with international safety standards (arts 5(3) and 6(5)). Comparable provisions are contained in the 1995 Waigani Convention to Ban Importation into Forum Island Countries and to Control the Transboundary Movement and Management of Hazardous Wastes within the South Pacific Region. A protocol on the transboundary movement of hazardous waste is also being drafted for the Kuwait Convention.

---

[39] IMO Assembly Resolution A. 491 (XII).

Having considered the standards which have been elaborated for reducing and preventing operational pollution from ships, we must now turn to a discussion of how such standards are implemented and enforced – a question which, as we have seen, has given rise to some problems with the 1954 and MARPOL Conventions.

The prescription and enforcement of pollution standards

In discussing this question it is essential to keep constantly in mind certain distinctions. First, it is necessary to distinguish between a State's competence to *prescribe* legislation for individuals or ships (legislative jurisdiction), and its competence to *enforce* legislation thus prescribed (enforcement jurisdiction). It is convenient here to sub-divide enforcement jurisdiction into the competence to *arrest* (arrest jurisdiction) and the competence of *courts* to deal with alleged breaches of the law (judicial jurisdiction). Secondly, the legislative or enforcement jurisdiction that a State has in respect of a particular vessel varies depending on whether it is a flag, coastal or port State. A *flag State* is the State whose nationality a particular vessel has. A *coastal State* is the State in one of whose maritime zones a particular vessel lies. A *port State* is the State in one of whose ports a particular vessel lies. Finally, it is necessary to distinguish between the pre-UNCLOS III rules (both customary and conventional) on the one hand, and the provisions of the Law of the Sea Convention on the other. When looking at both the pre-UNCLOS and the Law of the Sea Convention rules the general framework of the discussion will be to consider States' legislative jurisdiction first, followed by enforcement jurisdiction. Within each type of jurisdiction, the competence of flag, coastal and port States will be examined successively.

Rules adopted prior to UNCLOS III
As far as legislative jurisdiction is concerned, under customary international law a *flag State* may prescribe anti-pollution rules applicable to its vessels wherever in the world they might be. The MARPOL Convention (arts 3 and 4) obliges flag States so to apply the Convention's pollution standards. Under the Territorial Sea Convention and under customary international law a *coastal State* may prescribe any legislation relating to pollution that it wishes for foreign vessels in its territorial sea, provided that such legislation does not have the effect of hampering innocent passage (see chapter four). Parties to the MARPOL Convention are obliged to prescribe the Convention's provisions for all vessels in their territorial seas[40] (art. 4(2)). Finally, as regards *port States,* under customary

---

[40] In fact the MARPOL Convention does not use the term 'territorial sea' but 'jurisdiction'. 'Jurisdiction' clearly includes the territorial sea, and may now include the EEZ (see the discussion of the position under the Law of the Sea Convention at p. 351 below). Cf. Article 9(3) of the MARPOL Convention, which states that the term 'jurisdiction' 'shall be construed in the light of international law in force at the time of application or interpretation' of the Convention.

international law a State may adopt anti-pollution legislation for foreign vessels in its ports and even make the observance of such legislation or of particular international conventions a condition of entry to its ports, although usually, under bilateral treaties of friendship, commerce and navigation, it will have to ensure that such legislation and conditions are not discriminatory.

As far as enforcement jurisdiction is concerned, under customary international law a *flag State* may exercise judicial jurisdiction in respect of violations committed anywhere by its vessels. The flag State may arrest its vessels when they are on the high seas or in its territorial sea or ports: where the vessel is in the territorial sea or port of another State, the flag State may not arrest it, but may nevertheless institute criminal proceedings against it before its own courts provided the shipowner or master is within, or the vessel returns to, the flag State. Under the MARPOL Convention (arts 4(1) and 6(4)) a flag State is obliged to institute criminal proceedings against any of its vessels suspected of having violated the Convention. Article 19 of the Territorial Sea Convention, and customary international law, permit a *coastal State* to enforce violations of its pollution legislation committed in its territorial sea by foreign ships by arresting suspected vessels and instituting legal proceedings against them. Under the MARPOL Convention a coastal State Party to the Convention, which is obliged, as we have already seen, to prescribe the Convention's provisions for foreign ships in its territorial sea, is under the further obligation either to take legal proceedings itself against a ship which has violated the Convention's provisions in its territorial sea or to forward to the authorities of the flag State such information and evidence as it has that a violation has occurred: where they have sufficient evidence, the flag State authorities must bring legal proceedings against the vessel concerned as soon as possible (arts 4(2), 6(3) and (4)). A *port State* may exercise enforcement jurisdiction (in both its forms) against a foreign vessel that has violated the port State's anti-pollution legislation either in one of its ports or in its territorial sea. It may not take any action in respect of violations committed before the ship enters its territorial sea: however, the MARPOL Convention gives port States some role in such law enforcement. Under the Convention the port authorities may inspect a foreign vessel, and where the condition of the vessel warrants it, they may detain the vessel until it can proceed to sea without presenting an unreasonable threat of harm to the marine environment.[41] Furthermore, where the inspection indicates a violation of the MARPOL Convention, the authorities of the flag State are to be informed and must take legal proceedings if there is sufficient evidence (arts 5(2), 6, 7). Flag States must inform the IMO of the enforcement action they take against their vessels, whether acting on their own initiative or as the result of information provided by other States (arts 4(3), 6(4), 11). In addition, since article 5(4) of the Convention provides that its parties

---

[41] It should be noted that the MARPOL Convention is one of the conventions for compliance with which ships are to be inspected under the various Memorandums of Understanding on Port State Control, discussed in chapter thirteen.

must apply its requirements so as to ensure that no more favourable treatment is given to the ships of non-parties, the latter may effectively be required to observe the Convention if calling at the port of a Convention party.

The framework for the prescription and enforcement of pollution standards which had been developed prior to UNCLOS was less than satisfactory for a number of reasons. First, many flag States – especially flags of convenience – were lax in enforcing the provisions of conventions to which they were parties. This failure was compounded by the fact that these States were the only States which could take enforcement action against a vessel polluting the waters beyond the territorial sea, which is where most pollution from vessels occurs. Secondly, under both customary law and the Territorial Sea Convention there were no clear limits on the type of pollution regulations a coastal State might prescribe for its territorial sea. This could have led to widely differing and conflicting regulations which, particularly if they related to design and construction standards, might have made it impossible for a vessel to comply with all the laws to which it might become subject during the course of its voyage.

The Law of the Sea Convention
These dissatisfactions with the traditional legal framework led to two main strands of change at UNCLOS. On the one hand, the more environmentally con-scious and many non-maritime States sought to extend the enforcement powers of coastal and port States in order to compensate for the shortcomings of flag State enforcement. On the other hand, the maritime States tried to limit the legislative discretion of coastal States in order that there should be a degree of uniform-ity in coastal States' regulations. The maritime States also sought safeguards to accompany the proposed increase in the enforcement powers of coastal and port States so as to prevent undue delay to – and hence increased operating costs for – their vessels. Both groups were relatively successful in seeing their concerns met in the Law of the Sea Convention, which reflects a carefully balanced com-promise between them.

As far as the prescription of pollution standards is concerned, the Law of the Sea Convention makes no change in the traditional competence of *flag States* to prescribe their legislation for their vessels wherever they may be. It does, however, go further than the previous law, by placing an obligation on flag States to adopt pollution regulations for their vessels which 'at least have the same effect as that of generally accepted international rules and standards estab-lished through the competent international organization or general diplomatic conference' (LOSC, art. 211(2)). There is no definition of 'generally accepted international rules', although article 211(7) provides that they include *inter alia* those relating to notification of accidents likely to cause marine pollution (these rules are discussed below). Presumably 'generally accepted international rules' include the first two annexes to the MARPOL Convention, which are now widely ratified. But do they also include the provisions of the other annexes, which are not so widely ratified? 'The competent international organization' means the

IMO.[42] Do the 'standards' established by the IMO include only those found in conventions or do they include those contained in non-binding IMO Assembly resolutions? Whatever the precise scope of 'generally accepted international rules' – and it is regrettable that no guidance as to what they comprise is given – the effect of article 211(2) may be in some cases to oblige flag States to prescribe for their vessels the provisions of conventions to which they are not parties.[43] While the intention behind article 211(2) is laudable, it may discourage ratification of the marine pollution conventions because it may be felt that ratification is no longer necessary given the existence of article 211(2). Furthermore, the lack of clarity as to the meaning of 'generally accepted international rules' may give rise to disputes as to whether the obligation of article 211(2) has been complied with.

The legislative competence of *coastal States* has been reduced by the Law of the Sea Convention in respect of the kind of pollution regulations which may be adopted, but increased in respect of the geographical area to which such regulations may be applied. In the territorial sea the coastal State may prescribe pollution regulations for foreign vessels in innocent passage, provided such regulations do not 'apply to the design, construction, manning or equipment of foreign ships unless they are giving effect to generally accepted international rules or standards' (LOSC, art. 21(2)). Furthermore, such regulations must be duly publicised, must be non-discriminatory and must not hamper the innocent passage of foreign vessels (LOSC, arts 21(3), 24, 211(4)). Where the territorial sea consists of straits subject to the regime of transit passage, the coastal State's legislative competence is even more restricted. Here pollution regulations may be adopted only if they give 'effect to applicable international regulations regarding the discharge of oil, oily wastes and other noxious substances in the strait' (LOSC, art. 42(1)). Such regulations must be nondiscriminatory, must not hamper transit passage and must be duly publicised by the strait State (LOSC, art. 42(2), (3)). While the Law of the Sea Convention has restricted the scope of coastal States' legislative competence in their territorial sea, it has increased the geographical scope of their legislative competence by giving them certain powers to legislate for marine pollution from foreign vessels in their EEZ. Under article 211(5) a coastal

---

[42] Report of the UN Secretary General, 'Impact of the entry into force of the 1982 United Nations Convention on the Law of the Sea on related, existing and proposed instruments and programmes', UN Doc. A/52/491, 20 October 1997, section J, paras 8 and 9.

[43] As has been seen, art. 5(4) of the MARPOL Convention may also have this effect. Some of the provisions of these instruments may also represent customary international law, in which case the Law of the Sea Convention merely confirms obligations which exist already. For a much fuller discussion of this whole topic, see W. Van Reenan, 'Rules of reference in the new Convention on the Law of the Sea, in particular in connection with the pollution of the sea by oil from tankers', XII *NYIL* 3–44 (1981). See also G. C. Kasoulides, *Port State Control and Jurisdiction* (Dordrecht, Nijhoff), 1993, pp. 35–41 and literature cited there; the work cited in footnote 42, paras 43–6; and International Law Association, *Report of the Sixty-Seventh Conference* (London, International Law Association), 1996, pp. 158–78.

State may adopt pollution legislation for its EEZ which conforms and gives effect to 'generally accepted international rules and standards established through the competent international organization or general diplomatic conference'. Where these rules are considered inadequate to provide sufficient ecological protection for certain areas of the EEZ, the coastal State may adopt regulations implementing international rules and standards or navigational practices which the IMO has made applicable to special areas, or it may adopt additional regulations of its own, provided that these do not impose design, construction, manning or equipment standards on foreign vessels other than generally accepted international rules and standards. In each case, certain procedural requirements are laid down. These include consultation with the IMO and obtaining its approval, and giving at least fifteen months' notice of the entry into force of the coastal State's regulations (LOSC, art. 211(6)). Finally, article 234 provides that for ice-covered areas, lying 'within the limits' of the EEZ (which would seem to include the territorial sea as well as the EEZ), the coastal State may adopt non-discriminatory pollution regulations. In this case there is no requirement that design, construction, etc. standards must conform to generally accepted international rules (although the coastal State's regulations must have 'due regard to navigation'), nor are there any particular procedures to be observed.

The Law of the Sea Convention makes no changes to the legislative competence of *port States* (except to the extent necessary to accommodate their enlarged enforcement jurisdiction: see below, p. 350), but article 211(3) does provide that States which make observance of particular standards a condition for the entry of foreign vessels to their ports must give due publicity to such conditions and notify the IMO of them.

Turning now to enforcement jurisdiction, article 217 of the Law of the Sea Convention provides that *flag States* not only *may* enforce (in the sense of judicial jurisdiction) violations of pollution laws applying to their ships wherever committed, but *must* do so. In particular, flag States must lay down penalties adequate in severity to discourage violations; prohibit their vessels from proceeding to sea unless they comply with the requirements of international rules and standards; ensure that their vessels carry the certificates required by such rules; periodically inspect their vessels; and investigate alleged violations of the rules by their vessels. Where allegations are made by another State, that State and the IMO must be informed by the flag State of the action taken by it in response to the allegation. One largely theoretical question which the Law of the Sea Convention does not deal with directly is whether a flag State can arrest one of its vessels in the EEZ of another State. The answer would seem to be that it can. Article 92 of the Convention gives the flag State exclusive jurisdiction over its vessels on the high seas. By virtue of article 58(2), article 92 applies in the EEZ to the extent that it is not incompatible with the coastal State's rights. Since, as we shall shortly see, the coastal State has no general right to arrest foreign vessels in its EEZ for breach of anti-pollution regulations, it would seem that there is no coastal State right with which article 92 is incompatible, that therefore article 92 does apply, and thus that a flag State can arrest one of its vessels in the EEZ of another State.

Enforcement by *coastal States* is governed largely by article 220. Where a foreign vessel is suspected of having violated during its passage through the territorial sea the coastal State's anti-pollution legislation or applicable international rules relating to pollution from ships, the coastal State may, without prejudice to its general enforcement competence in the territorial sea as set out in section 3 of Part II of the Law of the Sea Convention (on which see chapter four above), undertake physical inspection of the vessel and, where the evidence so warrants, institute legal proceedings (LOSC, art. 220(2)). The coastal State has a power of arrest under section 3 of Part II. Where the pollution from the foreign vessel is 'wilful and serious', then the passage of that vessel is no longer innocent (see chapter four), and so the coastal State has unrestricted enforcement jurisdiction. However, where the alleged violation of the coastal State's legislation is committed by a vessel during the exercise of its right of transit passage through a strait, the coastal State may arrest the vessel only if the violation causes or threatens 'major damage to the marine environment of the straits' (LOSC, art. 233). Where an alleged violation takes place in the EEZ, the coastal State may require an offending vessel that is within its territorial sea or EEZ to give information regarding its identity and port of registry, its last and next port of call and other information required to establish whether a violation has occurred. Where the alleged violation in the EEZ has resulted 'in a substantial discharge causing or threatening significant pollution of the marine environment', the coastal State may undertake physical inspection of the vessel in the EEZ or territorial sea if the vessel has refused to give the necessary information or has given manifestly incorrect information. But only where the alleged violation has resulted 'in a discharge causing major damage or threat of major damage to the coastline or related interests of the coastal State, or to any resources of its territorial sea or exclusive economic zone' may the coastal State arrest the vessel (LOSC, art. 220(3)–(8)). Whether the distinction between a 'substantial discharge' and a 'discharge causing major damage' will be clear-cut in practice seems doubtful. It is likely that coastal States will tend to assume that any significant discharge will fall into the latter category, thus endowing themselves with the greater enforcement competence. The coastal State may exercise its enforcement powers in its territorial sea or EEZ in respect of violations not only of its own pollution rules, but also of 'applicable international rules and standards'. The effect may be that some coastal States take action to enforce the provisions of conventions to which they, and possibly also the flag State of the offending vessel, are not parties, unless 'applicable' is taken to refer to rules which are contained in a convention to which the coastal State is a party or are part of customary international law. Finally, where a coastal State has prescribed anti-pollution regulations for ice-covered areas in its territorial sea or EEZ, or both, it may enforce such regulations: no limitations or qualifications are attached to this enforcement competence (art. 234).

349

The most radical innovations made to the enforcement of marine pollution standards by the Law of the Sea Convention concern the powers given to *port States*. Article 220(1) follows customary international law – though supplementing it as a result of the introduction of the EEZ – by providing that a State may arrest in one of its ports and prosecute a vessel which is alleged to have violated that State's pollution laws or applicable international rules in its territorial sea or EEZ. However, article 218 is truly innovatory because it provides that a port State may also take legal proceedings against a vessel in one of its ports that is alleged to have discharged polluting matter *outside* that State's territorial sea or EEZ 'in violation of applicable international rules and standards established through the competent international organization or general diplomatic conference'. The port State must not take legal proceedings where the discharge occurred in the internal waters, territorial sea or EEZ of another State unless that State or the flag State so requests. Additionally, under article 219, where a port State has ascertained that a vessel in one of its ports is 'in violation of applicable international rules and standards relating to seaworthiness of vessels and thereby threatens damage to the marine environment', it shall take administrative measures to prevent the vessel from sailing until the causes of the violation have been removed, unless the vessel is going to the nearest repair yard.

Where either a port State or a coastal State arrests and proceeds against a foreign vessel for alleged violation of pollution regulations in the situations referred to above, its actions are subject to a number of safeguards set out in articles 223 to 232. These provide *inter alia* that arrests may be made only by government officials and State-owned ships and aircraft, and must be made in such a way as not to endanger navigation or the marine environment; foreign vessels may not be detained longer than necessary; legal proceedings must normally be suspended when the flag State takes proceedings in respect of the same incident; the penalties imposed for a violation must normally be limited to monetary ones; and flag States must be promptly notified of proceedings taken against their vessels. Curiously, and possibly as a result of an oversight in drafting, not all of these safeguards apply to enforcement action taken by a coastal State in ice-covered areas. The requirement that the port or coastal State must normally suspend legal proceedings if the flag State institutes proceedings, while having the desirable effect of acting as a safeguard against double jeopardy, might at first sight seem to undermine the Law of the Sea Convention's attempts to remedy the deficiencies of flag State jurisdiction by strengthening coastal and port State enforcement jurisdiction. It must be noted, however, that there is no obligation to suspend proceedings where the pollution offence was committed in the territorial sea or caused 'major damage to the coastal State', or where the flag State has not instituted proceedings within six months of the coastal or port State taking action, or where the flag State has repeatedly disregarded its duty to enforce effectively international rules in respect of violations committed by its vessels. Furthermore, article 228 appears to suggest that if the flag State begins legal proceedings but does not bring them to a conclusion, the port or coastal State may lift the suspension on its own proceedings and continue with the case.

The Law of the Sea Convention's provisions governing the prescription and enforcement of pollution standards do not apply to warships or other State-owned ships used only on government non-commercial service (LOSC, art. 236). This reflects the general international legal rules relating to sovereign immunity, and similar provisions are found in the MARPOL Convention (art. 3(3)). Like the latter provision, however, article 236 of the Law of the Sea Convention provides that 'each State shall ensure, by the adoption of appropriate measures not impairing operations or operational capabilities of such vessels or aircraft owned or operated by it, that such vessels or aircraft act in a manner consistent, so far as is reasonable and practicable, with this Convention'.

The provisions of the Law of the Sea Convention should lead to much more effective enforcement of international pollution standards. Where a flag State is lax in taking enforcement action, port and coastal States can now step in. In practice, given the difficulties of arresting a vessel in passage which is unwilling to stop and be arrested, port State jurisdiction will probably be more frequently exercised and more effective than the jurisdiction of coastal States (although there may be some doubt as to how far port States will wish to bother prosecuting vessels which have committed offences far from that State's waters or territory). The shift in recent international pollution conventions – particularly in the MARPOL Convention – away from discharge standards to construction standards which have to be certificated will facilitate the exercise of port State jurisdiction, in as much as the difficulties of proving violations of discharge standards will be avoided. At the same time the existence of port State jurisdiction may persuade flag States which have hitherto been lax in enforcing standards to take a more effective line in future – if only for reasons of national pride. It will also be recalled from chapter thirteen that the IMO is currently engaged in efforts to improve flag State enforcement of its Conventions.

So far, however, the Law of the Sea Convention appears to have had a limited impact on State practice, especially as concerns the jurisdiction of coastal and port States. As regards coastal States' jurisdiction in the EEZ, most States claiming an EEZ do no more than repeat the basic provision in article 56(1)(b) of the Convention, namely that they have jurisdiction with regard to the protection and preservation of the marine environment, although five States (Bangladesh,[44] Cape Verde,[45] Côte d'Ivoire,[46] Haiti[47] and Sri Lanka[48]) claim to be able to take

---

[44] Territorial Waters and Maritime Zones Act, 1974, s. 8. *Smith, op. cit.* in 'Further reading' under 'Pollution from ships', p. 69.
[45] Law No. 60/IV/92 delimiting the Maritime Areas of the Republic of Cape Verde, art. 16. 26 *LOSB* 24 (1994).
[46] Law No. 77–926, art. 6. *Smith, op. cit.*, p. 241.
[47] Decree No. 38 of 1977, art. 7. *Smith, op. cit.*, p. 202.
[48] Maritime Zones Law No. 27 of 1976, s. 7. *Smith, op. cit.*, p. 427.

any measures deemed necessary to prevent pollution of their EEZ. As far as we have been able to discover, only about a dozen States have so far enacted legislation which is modelled on all or part of the detailed provisions on coastal State jurisdiction contained in articles 211 and 220 of the Convention. Not all such legislation is in conformity with the Convention, however. Thus, for example, the legislation of the former Soviet Union[49] does not refer to its regulations as having to be in conformity with generally accepted rules, nor does it provide for the involvement of the competent international organisation in designating special areas. In addition, the Soviet legislation, like that of Bulgaria[50] and Romania,[51] does not provide for the suspension of criminal proceedings against foreign vessels alleged to have polluted its EEZ where the flag State has begun proceedings. Malaysia prohibits the discharge of any oil, oily mixture or pollutant in its EEZ from a vessel, which is obviously stricter than the international standards contained in MARPOL, and any vessel suspected of committing such an offence may be stopped, boarded and searched: such a vessel may be detained where Malaysia's coastline or the environment or related interests in its EEZ are damaged or threatened with damage.[52] The Swedish EEZ legislation is also not on all fours with the Convention.[53] On the other hand, the legislation of Antigua and Barbuda,[54] St Kitts,[55] St Lucia[56] and Ukraine,[57] while not reflecting all of the provisions of the Convention concerning coastal State jurisdiction, is in conformity with the Convention. In addition, several States have enabling provisions in their EEZ legislation providing for the enactment of regulations to control pollution: it may be that some such regulations have been enacted of which we are unaware. Very few States appear to have enacted legislation implementing the Convention's provisions on port State enforcement jurisdiction: the only examples of which we are aware are Belize[58] and the United Kingdom.[59] In the light of

---

[49] Decree on the Economic Zone of the USSR, 1984, arts 12–15. *Smith, op. cit.*, p. 417. For commentary, see E. Franckx, 'The new USSR legislation on pollution prevention in the exclusive economic zone', 1 *IJECL* 155 (1986) at 164–7.

[50] Act of 8 July 1987 governing the Ocean Space of the People's Republic of Bulgaria. 13 *LOSB* 8 (1989).

[51] Decree concerning the Establishment of the Exclusive Economic Zone, No. 142 of 25 April 1986, art. 11. 8 *LOSB* 17 (1986).

[52] Exclusive Economic Zone Act 1984, ss. 10(1), 15(1) and 24(1). United Nations, *The Law of the Sea: National Legislation on the Exclusive Economic Zone* (New York, United Nations), 1993, p. 186.

[53] For discussion, see S. Mahmoudi, 'Sweden's Economic Zone Act', 8 *IJMCL* 524 (1993) at 526–8.

[54] Maritime Areas Act, 1982. United Nations, *op. cit.* in n. 52, p. 12.

[55] Maritime Areas Act, 1984, s. 24. *Ibid.*, p. 303.

[56] Maritime Areas Act, 1984, s. 24. *Smith*, p. 383.

[57] Law of Ukraine on the Exclusive (Marine) Economic Zone of 16 May 1995, arts 17 and 20. 30 *LOSB* 49 (1996).

[58] Maritime Areas Act 1992, s. 24(4). 21 *LOSB* 3 (1992).

[59] Merchant Shipping (Prevention of Oil Pollution) Regs, 1996, regs. 34–9. S.I. 1996 No. 2154.

this limited and somewhat divergent practice, it must be doubtful whether those provisions of the Law of the Sea Convention relating to coastal and port State jurisdiction in respect of ships which go beyond the traditional law have become part of customary international law. Finally, in this connection, brief mention should be made of the US Oil Pollution Act of 1990.[60] The Act, passed in the wake of the *Exxon Valdez* disaster, *inter alia* requires foreign tankers calling at US ports to have double hulls. While the IMO has subsequently introduced a requirement of double hulls (as explained below), the US regulations remain stricter in some respects than the international IMO provisions. While the US measure is in accordance with the jurisdiction of port States under both customary law and the Law of the Sea Convention, it may be questioned how far it is in accordance with the spirit of the Convention, which is to discourage unilateral design and construction standards for ships.

Measures to avoid accidental pollution

A certain amount of pollution coming from ships is the result of accidents, such as hull failure, collisions and strandings, which lead to oil and other noxious cargoes entering the sea. There are provisions in the MARPOL Convention, such as the limitation on the size of tanks in an oil tanker and the requirement for double hulls or equivalent protection (introduced by amendments adopted in 1992), which are designed to reduce the scale of marine pollution when an accident occurs. Rules of international law have also been adopted to try to reduce the risk of an accident occurring in the first place. These rules are concerned with such matters as improving the seaworthiness of ships and the qualifications of crews, and regulating marine traffic in crowded waters. We examined these rules in some detail in chapter thirteen. As a result of all these measures the number of accidental oil spills has declined significantly in recent years.

Action by coastal States in respect of pollution casualties

The Intervention Convention
If an accident does occur, the question arises as to what measures a State can take to prevent or reduce pollution from a stricken vessel in the vicinity of its coasts. If the vessel is in the territorial sea, the coastal State can take any measures it considers appropriate (subject to the principle of proportionality). This is because the vessel, being no longer 'in passage', will have ceased to enjoy a right of innocent passage, and will thus be subject to the unfettered sovereignty of the coastal State. If the vessel is beyond the territorial sea, however, the position is different. The question of what powers the coastal State has in this situation

---

[60] 46 US Code §3703a.

353

was posed in 1967 in the case of the Liberian-registered *Torrey Canyon*, which, although on the high seas, was bombed by the United Kingdom authorities in the hope of reducing pollution from the vessel by setting its cargo of oil on fire. Doubts about the legality of its action led the UK government to refer the question to the IMO. The result was the adoption in 1969 of the International Convention relating to Intervention on the High Seas in Cases of Oil Pollution Casualties (hereafter referred to as the Intervention Convention). Under article I of the Intervention Convention, States Parties

> may take such measures on the high seas as may be necessary to prevent, mitigate or eliminate grave and imminent danger to their coastline or related interests from pollution or threat of pollution of the sea by oil, following upon a maritime casualty or acts related to such a casualty, which may reasonably be expected to result in major harmful consequences.

'Maritime casualty' is defined as a collision, stranding or other incident of navigation or occurrence resulting in actual or threatened material damage to a ship or its cargo (art. II). The measures taken under article I, which are not available for use against warships or other State-owned ships used for non-commercial purposes, must be proportionate to the actual or threatened damage (arts I and V). Excessive measures causing damage require the payment of compensation to the flag State (art. VI). Before taking measures under article I the State concerned must, except in cases of extreme urgency, consult the flag State and other States affected by the casualty and notify anyone likely to be affected by the proposed measures. In any case, after the measures have been taken, such States and persons, as well as the IMO, must be notified (art. III).

The Intervention Convention applies only to measures of intervention against casualties causing or threatening pollution by oil. In 1973 a Protocol to the Convention was adopted, extending coastal States' powers of intervention to casualties causing or threatening pollution by substances other than oil.

Both the Intervention Convention and its Protocol apply only to measures taken 'on the high seas'. Taken literally, this would mean that a coastal State could not rely on the powers given by the Convention and its Protocol to take action in its EEZ. Since no other convention gives powers of intervention in the EEZ, and unless such powers derive from customary international law (a question we shall consider in a moment), this would mean that a coastal State would have greater powers of intervention on the high seas than in its EEZ, which is plainly absurd. Since the EEZ concept did not exist at the time the Intervention Convention and its Protocol were drafted, it would seem not unreasonable to consider that the phrase 'high seas' should be read to mean 'beyond the territorial sea'. This position is reflected in the legislation of a number of States.[61]

---

[61] For details, and a discussion of the issues raised in the following two paragraphs, see B. Kwiatkowska, 'Creeping jursidiction beyond 200 miles in the light of the 1982 Law of the Sea Convention and State practice', 22 *ODIL* 153–87 (1991) at 173.

The Law of the Sea Convention

The Law of the Sea Convention approaches the question of intervention against maritime casualties obliquely. It does not expressly accord coastal States a right to take action in respect of casualties, but in article 221 provides that the Convention does not 'prejudice the right of States, pursuant to international law, both customary and conventional', to intervene broadly in the manner described above 'beyond the territorial sea'. The right to take such action is clearly presumed to exist.

Custom

Whether a coastal State possesses powers of intervention on the high seas under customary international law, as article 221 assumes, was, initially at least, doubtful, for otherwise it would not have seemed necessary to have concluded the Intervention Convention. The better view now is that the United Kingdom's action against the *Torrey Canyon* in 1967, coupled with its ready acceptance by other States, constituted an emerging rule of customary international law which the Intervention Convention and the Law of the Sea Convention have clarified and crystallised.

Co-operation in taking action to deal with pollution emergencies

Global conventions

Where large-scale pollution occurs, usually because of an accident to a ship, it will often be desirable that States co-operate, for example by the State which first becomes aware of the pollution warning other States which are likely to be affected, or by States assisting each other with equipment and know-how for dealing directly with a pollution emergency. Provision for such co-operation at the global level was first made to a limited extent in the MARPOL Convention. Under article 8 and Protocol 1 a ship involved in a pollution incident must report the details to the authorities of a State party (though exactly which State or States is not made clear), which in turn must relay the report to the flag State and any other State likely to be affected. In similar vein, article 198 of the Law of the Sea Convention provides that 'when a State becomes aware of cases in which the marine environment is in imminent danger of being damaged or has been damaged by pollution, it shall immediately notify other States it deems likely to be affected by such damage, as well as the competent international organizations'. Article 199 goes on to provide that affected States shall co-operate 'in eliminating the effects of pollution and preventing or minimising the damage'. To this end, States are to develop joint contingency plans for responding to pollution incidents.

More substance is given to the rather general provisions of the MARPOL and Law of the Sea Conventions by the International Convention on Oil Pollution Preparedness, Response and Co-Operation, 1990. The Convention requires parties to establish a national system (for which minimum criteria are specified) for responding promptly and effectively to oil pollution incidents (art. 6). The parties agree to exchange information relating to the research and development of such response systems and to provide technical assistance to those parties which request it (arts 7 and 8). Each party must also ensure that its ships and port authorities have an oil pollution emergency plan (art. 3). Where any oil discharged at sea is observed, the master of a ship or pilot of an aircraft must report the fact without delay to the nearest coastal State (art. 4). The latter is then to assess the situation and inform other States whose interests may be affected and the IMO (art. 5). Where the severity of the incident so justifies, any party affected by it may request assistance from any other party (art. 7): an annex to the Convention stipulates how the costs of such assistance are to be borne. The IMO is given a general role in promoting the objectives of the Convention (art. 17). Finally, the Convention exhorts its parties to conclude bilateral or regional agreements for oil pollution preparedness and response (art. 11). One example of the value of the Convention was shown even before its entry into force. During the Gulf War, in January 1991, Iraq deliberately released a huge quantity of oil into the Gulf from oil terminals in Kuwait, which threatened the Gulf with ecological disaster. The IMO, with the backing of a number of governments, responded as though the Convention were in force. It initiated clean-up operations in many threatened areas and established a centre at the IMO to co-ordinate these measures: this proved so successful it has been operating ever since.[62] At present the Convention applies only to pollution caused by oil, but the IMO is currently drafting a protocol (provisionally scheduled for adoption in 2000) to extend the Convention to hazardous and noxious substances.

Mention should also be made of the International Convention on Salvage, 1989. In the past delays were often caused when dealing with ships that had suffered accidents and threatened major pollution because of haggling over the terms of salvage: this was the case with the *Amoco Cadiz*, for example. Such delays sometimes meant that pollution resulting from accidents were worse than would otherwise have been the case. One reason for such delays has been the traditional rule of salvage of 'no cure, no pay', i.e., unless the ship is saved completely, the salvor is not entitled to be paid for his efforts. Thus, a salvor who prevented major pollution from occurring by, for example, towing a damaged tanker away from an environmentally sensitive area but who did not manage to save the ship, got nothing. There was, therefore, no incentive for a salvor to take action which could prove beneficial to the environment unless he could be sure of saving the ship. The entry into force in 1996 of the 1989 Salvage Convention will, it is hoped, remedy this situation, as it allows for the salvor to be paid if he prevents or minimises damage to the environment, even if he does not save the ship.

Finally, at the global level, it may be noted that article 13 of the Basel Convention on the Transboundary Movements of Hazardous Wastes provides that its parties, whenever they are aware of an accident occurring during the transboundary

---

[62] *IMO News*, 1991, No. 1, p. 1 and 1995, No. 2, p. 31.

movement of hazardous waste which is likely to present risks to human health and the environment in other States, shall immediately inform such States.

Regional conventions

As has been seen, some of the global agreements call for co-operation in dealing with pollution emergencies to be further developed at the regional and bilateral levels. This has already been done to a considerable extent through many of the regional pollution conventions and some bilateral agreements. The Mediterranean Convention provides, in article 9, that its parties are to co-operate in taking the necessary measures for dealing with pollution emergencies. Any party aware of an emergency must immediately notify UNEP, the Regional Oil Combating Centre for the Mediterranean (established at Malta), and other parties likely to be affected. During the first ten years of its existence the Centre was notified of over 100 alerts and accident reports.[63] The general obligation to co-operate referred to in article 9 is given more concrete detail in the Protocol concerning Co-operation in Combating Pollution of the Mediterranean Sea by Oil and other Harmful Substances in Cases of Emergency (1976). Under this Protocol the parties must maintain, individually or jointly, contingency plans (art. 3) and monitor for emergencies (art. 4). Under article 10 of the Protocol any party requiring assistance in combating a pollution emergency may call for assistance from other parties. Such assistance may include expert advice and the supply of anti-pollution equipment. The other UNEP regional conventions and the Baltic Conventions are broadly similar to the Mediterranean Convention and its Protocol, although only the Red Sea and Kuwait Conventions establish a regional emergency centre.[64]

More modest than these regional conventions is the Agreement for Co-operation in dealing with Pollution of the North Sea by Oil and Other Harmful Substances, 1983 (which replaces a somewhat similar agreement of 1969, but limited to oil pollution). Under this agreement, which applies not only to the North Sea but also to the English Channel, the ships and aircraft of the parties are requested to report to their flag State the presence of oil or other harmful substances they observe likely to constitute a serious threat to the coast or related interests of one or more parties and all casualties causing or likely to cause marine pollution. The flag State in turn must notify other States which may be affected (art. 5). For the purposes of the agreement, the North Sea is divided into zones of responsibility. A State party in whose zone the presence of oil or other harmful substance presenting a grave and imminent danger to the coast or related interest of one or more parties occurs, must make an assessment of the situation and keep the substances under observation (art. 6). A party requiring help to deal with the pollution may request assistance from other parties,

---

[63] *IMO News*, 1986, No. 3, p. 14.
[64] The Kuwait Convention Centre, the Marine Emergency Mutual Aid Centre based in Bahrain, has been quite active: for details see United Nations, *The Law of the Sea: Practice of States at the Time of Entry into Force of the United Nations Convention on the Law of the Sea* (New York, United Nations), 1994, p. 99.

and the Agreement makes provision for reimbursement by one party to another for such assistance (arts 7, 9 and 10). The agreement is serviced by the same secretariat as services the Paris Commission (formerly the Paris and Oslo Commissions) (see below, p. 383). Similar to the North Sea Agreement, but limited to co-operation in pollution emergencies involving oil only, is the Agreement between Denmark, Finland, Norway and Sweden concerning Co-operation in taking Measures against Pollution of the Sea by Oil, 1971. However, this Nordic Agreement goes further in that its parties undertake to provide themselves with equipment for dealing with any significant oil slicks at sea, and to collaborate with each other so as to achieve the greatest possible efficacy in the use of this equipment (art. 4). On the other hand, unlike the North Sea Agreement, the Nordic Agreement does not create zones of responsibility. In 1990 the EC, France, Morocco, Portugal and Spain signed the Accord of Co-operation for the Protection of the Coasts and Waters of the Northeast Atlantic against Pollution due to Hydrocarbons or Other Harmful Substances, which is similar to the North Sea Agreement. Finally at the regional level, Annex IV of the Protocol on Environmental Protection to the Antarctic Treaty provides that its parties shall develop contingency plans for marine pollution response in the Antarctic and establish procedures for co-operative response to pollution emergencies (art. 12).

Bilateral treaties
Co-operation in combating pollution has also been the subject of some bilateral agreements. For example, the USA has concluded agreements with Canada[65] and Mexico[66] which establish joint contingency plans for dealing with serious pollution threats in waters of mutual interest, and Canada has concluded a similar agreement with Denmark.[67]

Liability for pollution damage

While the primary aim of the international law relating to marine pollution should be to prevent such pollution, a subsidiary aim should be to facilitate the bringing of compensation claims by those who have suffered damage where pollution has occurred. Indeed, the existence of liability schemes favouring the victims of pollution damage may well encourage shipowners to take more care in observing the standards which are designed to prevent pollution. A person who has suffered damage from pollution – even if he can identify the vessel which has caused the pollution and can show a causal link between this pollution and the damage he has suffered (and this will often not be easy) – may face

[65] Agreement relating to the Establishment of Joint Pollution Contingency Plans for Spills of Oil and other Noxious Substances, 1974.
[66] Agreement of Co-operation regarding Pollution of the Marine Environment by Discharges of Hydrocarbons and other Hazardous Substances, 1980.
[67] Agreement for Co-operation relating to the Marine Environment, 1983.

further difficulties in bringing an action for compensation against the shipowner. First, he may find it difficult to prove fault on the part of the shipowner: most legal systems require proof of fault in most kinds of claims for compensation for damage caused by one person to another. Secondly, he may find it difficult to bring an action before the courts of his own State when the shipowner is a foreign national, because the courts may be reluctant to assume jurisdiction; and even if he succeeds, it may be difficult to enforce the judgment. Thirdly, the compensation awarded to the victim of pollution damage may exceed the financial resources of the shipowner.

The Civil Liability and Fund Conventions

The International Convention on Civil Liability for Oil Pollution Damage of 1969 (hereafter referred to as the Civil Liability Convention) and the International Convention on the Establishment of an International Fund for Compensation for Oil Pollution Damage of 1971 (hereafter referred to as the Fund Convention) attempt to overcome the difficulties which may be faced by the victims of oil pollution. The Civil Liability Convention provides that where oil escapes or is discharged from a ship and causes damage on the territory, including the territorial sea, of a contracting State, the shipowner, subject to three exceptions, is strictly liable for such damage and the cost of any preventive measures taken. The three exceptions are where the damage (1) results from war or acts of God; (2) is wholly caused by an act or omission done by a third party with intent to cause damage; (3) is wholly caused by the negligence or other wrongful act of any government or other authority responsible for the maintenance of lights or other navigational aids. In these three cases the shipowner is not liable at all (arts II and III). Where the shipowner is liable, however, his liability is limited. Originally the Civil Liability Convention expressed the limits of liability in terms of Poincaré francs, but under a 1976 Protocol the limits of liability are now expressed in terms of Special Drawing Rights (SDRs; in October 1998 one SDR was worth about £0.83 or $1.42). Under article V, as amended by the Protocol, the limits of liability are 133 SDRs for each ton of the ship's tonnage, subject to an overall limit of fourteen million SDRs. However, the shipowner's liability is unlimited if the pollution is 'the result of the actual fault or privity' of the shipowner (art. V(2)).

The above provisions are supplemented by the Fund Convention. First, the Convention provides that where the shipowner is not liable at all under the Civil Liability Convention by reason of one of the exceptions referred to above (other than war) or, in cases where the shipowner is liable but is financially incapable of meeting his obligations in full or if the pollution damage exceeds the limits of his liability, compensation will be paid to the victim from the International Oil Pollution Compensation Fund (which is established by the Convention), up to a limit of 60 million SDRs. Secondly, the Fund Convention provides that the Fund is to relieve shipowners of some of the financial burden placed on them by the Civil Liability Convention by paying that part of the shipowner's liability which is in excess of 100 SDRs per ton or 8.333 million SDRs, whichever is the less.

However, the Fund will not relieve the shipowner in this way if the pollution results from the 'wilful misconduct' of the owner or from his failure to observe the provisions of certain conventions concerned with the safety of shipping or oil pollution, where such failure is the cause of the damage (art. 5). The idea behind the Fund Convention, realised by raising the Fund's income by a levy on oil imports, is that the owners of the cargo which causes the pollution (oil companies), and not merely the shipowner, should bear a share of the liability. During the first eighteen years of its existence the Fund paid out about £120 million in respect of seventy-two incidents.[68]

The owner of a ship registered in a State party to the Civil Liability Convention and carrying more than 2,000 tons of oil as cargo must maintain insurance or other financial security sufficient to cover his maximum liability for pollution damage under the Convention (art. VII(1)). The ship is to be issued with a certificate by the authorities of the flag State to this effect (art. VII(2)). Such a certificate must be carried on board the ship, and the ship shall not be permitted 'to trade' unless it has been issued with a certificate (art. VII(4), (10)). Parties to the Convention must ensure that every ship carrying more than 2,000 tons of oil as cargo and using its ports is insured as required by article VII(1), whether the flag State of the ship is a party to the Convention or not (art. VII(11)).

As far as procedure is concerned, the Civil Liability Convention provides that the victim of oil pollution damage may bring an action for compensation only in the courts of the contracting State in whose territory the damage occurred (art. IX(1)). An action must be brought within three years of the date on which the damage occurred (art. VIII). Where an action is brought, the shipowner shall constitute a fund for the total sum representing the limit of his liability with the court or other competent authority of the State in which the claim is brought (art. V(3)). The fund is to be distributed by the court among the claimants in proportion to the amounts of their established claims (arts. V(4), IX(3)). The judgment of the court in which the action is brought is to be recognised and enforceable in all States parties to the Civil Liability Convention (art. X). Similar procedural provisions apply where a claim for compensation is brought against the International Oil Pollution Compensation Fund (arts 6–8 of the Fund Convention) .

In 1984 two Protocols to amend the Civil Liability and Fund Conventions were adopted, but neither Protocol ever came into force because the USA refused to ratify them and other States were unwilling to do so without US participation.[69] Instead, two further protocols, with similar substantive provisions to the 1984 protocols, were adopted in 1992 and, as a result of easier entry into force requirements, came into force in 1996. They require their parties to denounce the Civil Liability and Fund Conventions in their original form. For such parties the

[68] *IMO News*, 1996, No. 2, p. 86.
[69] As to the reasons why, see N. Gaskell, 'Compensation for oil pollution: 1992 Protocols to the Civil Liability Convention and the Fund Convention', 8 *IJMCL* 286–90 (1993) at 286–8.

protocols effectively create two new conventions: the 1992 Civil Liability and Fund Conventions.

The main change made by the 1992 Protocol to the Civil Liability Convention is to increase the maximum limits of liability under the Convention to three million SDRs for ships under 5,000 tons: for larger ships liability increases by 420 SDRs per ton above 5,000 tons to a maximum of 59.7 million SDRs. The Protocol also extends the geographical scope of the Convention to cover damage caused in the EEZ and the cost of preventive measures wherever taken; provides that such cost is recoverable even where there is no oil spill, provided that there was a grave and imminent threat of pollution damage; and clarifies the kinds of environmental damage that are covered by the Convention. The Protocol to the Fund Convention raises the maximum limit of liability under that Convention to 135 million SDRs (including the amount paid by the shipowner), to be increased to 200 million SDRs when certain conditions are fulfilled. In addition the Fund will no longer be required to indemnify the shipowner for part of his liability. Both Protocols provide that in future the limits of liability can be increased by means of the tacit amendment procedure.

Industry liability schemes
The world's leading tanker and oil companies established two private schemes, the Tanker Owners' Voluntary Agreement concerning Liability for Oil Pollution (TOVALOP – in force since October 1969) and the Contract regarding an Interim Supplement to Tanker Liability for Oil Pollution (CRISTAL – in force since April 1971), which broadly mirrored the provisions of the Civil Liability and Fund Conventions. These schemes were particularly important before the Conventions came into force (in June 1975 and October 1978 respectively), and were of great benefit to the victims of oil pollution damage in those coastal States not parties to the Civil Liability Convention, especially since TOVALOP covered over ninety-five per cent of the world's oil tankers. A further benefit was that CRISTAL could operate quite happily in conjunction with the Civil Liability Convention in cases where the Fund Convention was not applicable, thus providing additional compensation and relieving the shipowner of part of his liability. This was particularly useful, since only about two-thirds of the States parties to the Civil Liability Convention were parties to the Fund Convention. However, in 1995 the boards which administered TOVALOP and CRISTAL decided that the two schemes should end in February 1997 because of the increasing number of States becoming parties to the Civil Liability and Fund Conventions and because the continued existence of the schemes might discourage further ratifications.[70]

Liability for hazardous and noxious substances
After more than fifteen years' discussion within the IMO, an International Convention on Liability and Compensation for Damage in Connection with the

[70] *IMO News*, 1996, No. 2, p. 8.

Carriage of Hazardous and Noxious Substances (HNS) by Sea was finally concluded in May 1996. The Convention adopts a system of liability similar to that of the Civil Liability and Fund Conventions. Thus, the shipowner is strictly liable for: damage caused by HNS (which are widely defined but exclude radioactive matter) where such damage is in the form of loss of life or personal injury; loss of or damage to property outside the ship; loss or damage by contamination of the environment within 200 miles of land; the costs of preventive measures; and further loss or damage caused by such measures. As a *quid pro quo* for strict liability, the liability of the shipowner, who must be adequately insured, is limited. Limits are on a sliding scale depending on the size of the ship, and range from 10 million SDRs for ships under 2,000 GRT to a maximum of 100 million SDRs for ships over 100,000 GRT. A second tier of compensation, to cover situations where the shipowner is not liable (e.g., if the accident resulted from an act of war) or where the claim exceeds the shipowner's liability, is provided by the HNS Fund. The latter, which is to be financed by levies on importation of HNS cargoes, is liable up to a limit of 250 million SDRs (including compensation paid by the shipowner).

Like the Civil Liability and Fund Conventions, the HNS Convention may be regarded as an application of the 'polluter pays' principle, although as with the earlier conventions it is a qualified application, since the polluter does not necessarily pay for all harm done to the marine environment.

Liability for radioactive matter

Special liability regimes have also been elaborated for pollution damage caused by radioactive matter. Such pollution may result either from an accident to a ship carrying radioactive matter, or from the operation of or an accident to a nuclear-powered ship. In the case of the former, the Paris Convention on Third Party Liability in the Field of Nuclear Energy of 1960 and the Vienna Convention on Civil Liability for Nuclear Damage of 1963 each provides that the operator of a nuclear installation is the person exclusively liable for damage caused by a nuclear incident occurring in the course of the maritime carriage of nuclear material. In each case the operator's liability is strict but limited. The Convention relating to Civil Liability in the Field of Maritime Carriage of Nuclear Material of 1971 reaffirms the exclusive liability of the operator of the nuclear installation, and makes it clear that the shipowner is never liable for damage caused by the carriage of nuclear material unless he committed or omitted to do an act with intent to cause damage.

As far as pollution damage resulting from nuclear-powered ships is concerned, the Brussels Convention on the Liability of Operators of Nuclear Ships of 1962 provides that the operator of a nuclear ship is to be strictly liable for damage caused by a nuclear accident up to a maximum of 1,500 million Poincaré francs. However, this Convention has not yet come into force, and is unlikely to do so. In the absence of the application of the Convention, the position is as follows. At present all nuclear-powered ships are naval vessels, and therefore if faced with an action before the court of a foreign State would be able to raise the defence of sovereign immunity. When the handful of civilian nuclear-powered ships were in operation, their liability was generally governed by bilateral agreements. Thus the United States entered into agreements[71] with those States whose territorial waters or ports were visited by N.S. *Savannah* whereby the USA assumed strict liability for all damage arising out of a nuclear incident involving the *Savannah* up to a limit of $500 million. The Federal Republic of Germany entered into similar agreements[72] in respect of N.S. *Otto Hahn*: there the maximum limit of liability was DM 400 million.

Liability for other substances

The IMO is currently discussing whether it should elaborate a convention on liability and compensation for damage caused by oil from the bunkers of ships other than tankers (which are covered by the Civil Liability and Fund Conventions). At the present time a shipowner may be able to limit his liability for such damage, and for damage caused by any other substances not covered by the special liability regimes discussed above, under the 1957 or 1976 conventions on the limitation of shipowners' liability, which were discussed briefly in chapter thirteen (see p. 276). At the same conference which adopted the HNS Convention, the limits of liability under the 1976 Convention were increased significantly, and future increases made subject to the tacit amendment procedure.

Dumping

The London Convention

The growth of the practice of dumping wastes at sea and the main kinds of waste dumped were explained earlier (see p. 329). International action to control such dumping began in the early 1970s (although before that the High Seas Convention had required States to take measures to prevent marine pollution from the dumping of radioactive waste: HSC, art. 25(1)). This action has resulted in one convention that is worldwide in scope and a number of regional agreements. The global convention is the Convention on the Prevention of Marine Pollution by Dumping of Wastes and Other Matter, 1972 (hereafter referred to as the London Convention). In recent years the London Convention has undergone considerable evolution and change. In order to understand this development an account of the London Convention in its original form will be given first.

---

[71] E.g., UK–USA Agreement relating to the Use of United Kingdom Ports and Territorial Waters by the N.S. *Savannah*, 1964. For a list of other agreements of this type, see *ND VI*, pp. 770–2.
[72] E.g., Federal Republic of Germany–Liberia Treaty on the Use of Liberian Waters and Ports by N.S. *Otto Hahn*, 1970. For a list of other agreements of this type see *ND VI*, p. 772.

The London Convention defines dumping as the deliberate disposal of waste from ships and aircraft, but excluding the disposal of waste incidental to the normal operation of ships and aircraft (art. III(1)). Wastes are divided into three categories. The first category consists of the substances listed in Annex I (the 'black list'). These include organohalogen compounds, mercury, cadmium, oil, plastics and high-level radioactive wastes defined by the International Atomic Energy Agency (IAEA) as unsuitable for dumping. The dumping of substances on the black list is prohibited (art. IV(1)). The second category of wastes comprises the somewhat less noxious substances listed in Annex II (the 'grey list'). These include arsenic, lead, copper, zinc, organosilicon compounds, cyanides, fluorides, pesticides, scrap metal and radioactive matter not included in Annex I. The dumping of such substances is permitted only if a prior special permit (issued by the national authorities of a contracting party) has been obtained (art. IV(1)). In issuing a permit for the dumping of radioactive waste the parties must take full account of the recommendations of the IAEA. The third category comprises all wastes not on the black or grey lists: such wastes may nevertheless be dumped only if a prior general permit has been obtained (art. IV(1)). Annex III sets out a number of factors which are to be taken into account by the national authorities of contracting parties when issuing special and general permits. These factors include the characteristics and composition of the matter, the characteristics of the proposed dumping site, the method of deposit, the possible effects of the dumping and the practical availability of alternative land-based methods of disposal. In 1978 the parties to the London Convention adopted amendments to the annexes dealing with the incineration of wastes at sea, a method of waste disposal which began in the early 1970s. A special permit is required for the incineration of wastes listed in Annexes I and II, and such incineration must comply with the regulations set out in the revised annexes. In emergencies the above restrictions on dumping may be waived. Such situations are limited to cases where there is a danger to human life or the safety of a ship or aircraft is threatened, and if 'dumping appears to be the only way of averting the threat and if there is every probability that the damage consequent upon such dumping will be less than otherwise would occur' (art. V). Special procedures are to be followed where black list wastes are concerned.

Each party to the London Convention must take legislative action to impose the above system of regulating dumping upon (a) vessels and aircraft registered in its territory or flying its flag; (b) vessels and aircraft loading in its territory or territorial sea matter which is to be dumped; and (c) vessels and aircraft 'under its jurisdiction'[73] believed to be engaged in dumping (art. VII). The London Convention is rather imprecise about enforcement, but it would seem that this is governed by the general rules of customary law, i.e., a coastal State can take

---

[73] A term which is probably deliberately vague but which originally included the territorial sea, and under article 210 of the Law of the Sea Convention (see below) now also includes the EEZ and continental shelf.

enforcement action against any ship illegally dumping waste in its territorial sea and now, it would seem, the EEZ[74] and against any ship about to leave one of its ports for the purposes of dumping without having the necessary permit: but on the high seas enforcement will lie solely with flag States. It should be noted that under article XIII of the London Convention the parties agree to meet after UNCLOS III 'with a view to defining the nature and extent of the right and responsibility of a coastal State to apply the Convention in a zone adjacent to its coast' and that under article VII(3) the parties agree to 'co-operate in the development of procedures for the effective application of [the] Convention particularly on the high seas'. No meeting under article XIII has yet been held, nor has action been taken under article VII(3).

Parties to the London Convention must keep a record of all dumping they permit and monitor the condition of the sea for the purposes of dumping (art. VI(1)). Under article X they 'undertake to develop procedures for the assessment of liability' for damage caused by dumping: no such 'procedures' have yet been developed and in 1991 it was agreed that they should not be for the time being. Under article IX the parties are to promote support for those parties requiring assistance in the training of scientific and technical personnel, the supply of research and monitoring equipment and facilities, and in waste disposal and treatment.

Parties to the London Convention must meet not less than once every two years. These meetings may *inter alia* consider amendments to the Convention and its annexes, consider national reports on the implementation of the London Convention, and develop further guidelines for dumping in emergency situations (art. XIV). In practice the parties usually meet every year, and have *inter alia* adopted a number of guidelines on the operation of the Convention. Secretariat duties in respect of these meetings and other aspects of the London Convention are performed by the IMO.

For its first fifteen years or so the London Convention functioned in the way described above but, largely since about 1990, there have been a number of moves to restrict or phase out many kinds of dumping. This represents a departure from the traditional approach to controlling dumping, which was based on the sea's assimilative capacity, towards a precautionary approach, as well as a holistic approach towards waste management, for which the London Convention parties called in a resolution adopted in 1991.[75] The first kind of dumping to be tightened up was that concerning radioactive waste. In 1983 the London Convention parties adopted a resolution calling for a moratorium on the dumping of all radioactive material at sea (not just the high-level waste on the black list in

---

[74] At their 1988 meeting the parties concluded that a State party could enforce the Convention in respect of dumping in its EEZ and onto its continental shelf. See *Report of the Eleventh Consultative Meeting*, Doc. LDC 11/14, para. 5.4, reproduced in 4 *International Organisations and the Law of the Sea. Documentary Yearbook* 328 (1988).
[75] *IMO News*, 1992, No. 1, p. 5.

Annex I).[76] Two years later this call was renewed.[77] Following further research, amendments were adopted to the London Convention in 1993 which made the moratorium legally binding: the moratorium is to be reviewed at twenty-five year intervals. Secondly, in 1988 a resolution was adopted calling for the phasing-out of incineration at sea of noxious liquid wastes by the end of 1994 because of doubts about this method of disposing of what are normally highly toxic wastes.[78] Again this was followed by amendments to the London Convention in 1993 prohibiting the incineration of industrial waste and sewage sludge at sea. In practice incineration ended in 1991. Thirdly, in 1990 a resolution was adopted calling for an end to the dumping of industrial waste by the end of 1995.[79] This was again made legally binding by amendments to the London Convention adopted in 1993, which, like the other amendments adopted in that year, came into force in 1994. Another issue which has been discussed is whether the disposal of wastes (especially radioactive wastes) into and under the sea bed constitutes 'dumping' and is thus regulated by the London Convention. In 1990 the parties adopted a resolution in which they decided that such disposal accessed from the sea was 'dumping', but that accessed from land (by tunnel) was not.[80]

The result of the three sets of 1993 amendments is that the main substances which it is still permissible to dump (subject to the permit procedures of Annexes II and III) are dredged materials, sewage sludge, fish processing wastes, vessels and continental shelf oil and gas installations (a proposal to introduce a moratorium on the dumping of such installations was rejected at the 1995 meeting of the parties). In 1996 the parties to the London Convention adopted a protocol which reflects this situation. Re-affirming the precautionary approach, the Protocol (which for parties to it will supersede the London Convention upon its entry into force) bans the dumping of all substances except the five just listed (and one or two others such as inert, inorganic geological material and organic material of natural origin), prohibits incineration completely, and bans the export of waste to non-parties for dumping or incineration. The Protocol allows States that were not parties to the original London Convention to phase in compliance with its provisions over five years, and provides for technical assistance to be given to enable them to do so. The institutional provisions are similar to those of the original London Convention, but in addition there are provisions on settlement of disputes (amendments to the original London Convention on this matter, adopted in 1978, never came into force) and the parties are required to establish procedures and mechanisms necessary to assess and promote compliance.

---

[76] Resolution LDC. 14(7), *The London Dumping Convention, op. cit.* in 'Further reading', p. 207.
[77] Resolution LDC. 21(9), *ibid.*, p. 208.
[78] Resolution LDC. 35(11), *ibid.*, p. 235.
[79] Resolution LDC. 43(13). Reproduced in 6 *International Organisations and the Law of the Sea. Documentary Yearbook* 334 (1990).
[80] Resolution LDC. 41(13); *ibid.*, p. 332.

One consequence of the restrictions imposed on dumping by recent developments under the London Convention is the need for improved waste management on land (including recycling and the production of less waste), especially in non-OECD States, where waste management is often rudimentary.

Regional treaties

A number of treaties to deal with dumping have been adopted at the regional level. In practice such treaties are largely of significance only if their provisions are stricter than those of the London Convention, their parties include actual or potential dumping States not parties to the London Convention and/or they contain institutional arrangements which may lead to greater compliance with their provisions. The first regional treaty to be concluded was the Convention for the Prevention of Marine Pollution by Dumping from Ships and Aircraft, 1972 (hereafter referred to as the Oslo Convention). This Convention, which applies to the North-East Atlantic and North Sea, was drafted at the same time as the London Convention and therefore took a similar approach to that Convention, except that there are small variations in the black and grey lists and the institutional arrangements are different. Like the London Convention, the Oslo Convention has been considerably tightened up in recent years. Thus, the Commission established by the Oslo Convention, largely prompted by the North Sea Conferences, has adopted decisions under which the dumping of industrial waste was phased out by the end of 1995 (except for inert materials of natural origin and those industrial wastes for which it can be shown that there are no practical alternatives on land and that they cause no harm in the marine environment).[81] The dumping of sewage sludge is to be phased out by the end of 1998;[82] marine incineration (which had been regulated by a protocol of 1983) was phased out by the end of 1991;[83] and a moratorium on the dumping of oil and gas installations has been imposed.[84] The first and third of these decisions broadly parallel the London Convention amendments, although their substantive content tends to be stricter. Whether the decisions are legally binding, like the London Convention amendments, is a moot point. While the Oslo Convention does not explicitly give the Commission the competence to adopt legally binding decisions of this nature (except for incineration, where such a power is expressly given by Rule 2(3) of Annex IV), each decision begins 'the Contracting Parties to the Oslo Convention agree', which may indicate an intention to conclude an agreement in simplified form.

In 1992 the parties to the Oslo Convention signed the Convention for the Protection of the Marine Environment of the North-East Atlantic (hereafter referred

---

[81] Decision 89/1 of 14 June 1989, reproduced in Freestone and IJlstra (1991), *op. cit.* in footnote 20, p. 119. See also the associated Prior Justification Procedure, p. 121.
[82] Decision 90/1 of 23 June 1990, *ibid.*, p. 125.
[83] Decision 90/2 of 23 June 1990, *ibid.*, p. 126.
[84] Decision 95/1 of 4 August 1995.

to as the Paris Convention), which, on its entry into force in 1998, replaced the Oslo Convention (although decisions of the Oslo Commission compatible with the Paris Convention are preserved). Annex II of the Paris Convention deals with dumping. It prohibits marine incineration completely (art. 2). The only substances the dumping of which is permitted, subject to a permit system, are dredged materials, inert materials of natural origin, sewage sludge (until 1998), fish processing waste and vessels and aircraft (until 2004) (art. 3). The Convention thus prohibits the dumping of radioactive waste, but because two parties (France and the United Kingdom) wish the option of the possibility of such dumping in the future to be kept open, provision is made for periodic review of the position (art. 3(3)). In view of the 1993 amendments to the London Convention, by which both France and the United Kingdom are bound, the chances of this option becoming available must be regarded as remote. The dumping of offshore installations is governed by Annex III, article 4 of which provides that such dumping may be permitted on a case-by-case basis according to various criteria set out in that article. Thus, the provisions of the Paris Convention are similar to, but in some respects stricter than, the 1996 Protocol to the London Convention.

Chronologically the next regional agreement to deal with dumping was the 1974 Baltic Convention. From its outset the Baltic Convention took a stricter approach to dumping than the London and Oslo Conventions, reflecting the particular vulnerability of the Baltic to pollution damage. Thus, article 9 prohibits all dumping, except of dredged spoils, and even this is prohibited if the spoils contain significant quantities of certain listed noxious substances. Where such dumping is permitted, a prior special permit must be obtained. This approach is continued in the 1992 Baltic Convention (art. 11 and annex V). The new Convention also prohibits incineration (art. 10), a matter not dealt with by the 1974 Convention because it was not perceived as a problem when that Convention was drawn up, and makes it clear that 'dumping' includes disposal 'into' the sea bed (art. 2(4)). Like the other conventions, however, the two Baltic Conventions permit dumping if it appears to be the only way of averting a threat to the safety of life or of a vessel.

Only three of UNEP's Regional Seas agreements, those concerning the Mediterranean, South Pacific and Black Sea, have detailed provisions dealing with dumping, in the shape of separate protocols. The 1976 Mediterranean Protocol, as originally drafted, was similar to the original versions of the London and Oslo Conventions. In 1995 amendments were adopted to the Protocol which bring it fairly closely into line with (although it is somewhat stricter than) the 1996 Protocol to the London Convention and the 1992 Paris Convention. Thus, incineration is prohibited, and the only substances which may be dumped, subject to obtaining a prior special permit, are dredged material, fish waste, vessels (until 2000), sea-bed installations (to a limited extent) and inert uncontaminated geological materials. The 1986 South Pacific Protocol and the 1992 Black Sea Protocol are similar to the London and Oslo Conventions in their original forms, except that both the Black Sea Protocol and the South Pacific Convention (rather than the Protocol) ban the dumping of all forms of radioactive waste (the latter including disposal into and under the sea bed) and in their jurisdictional provisions reflect the Law of the Sea Convention (see below). The other six UNEP conventions simply contain a general provision calling on their parties to take all appropriate measures to prevent and reduce pollution caused by dumping and ensure effective compliance with the internationally agreed rules on the subject, although additionally in the case of the South-East Pacific Convention its 1989 Protocol on radioactive pollution prohibits the dumping (including disposal into and under the sea bed) of radioactive wastes and substances. Given that the areas to which these conventions apply are not ones where dumping has taken place to any significant degree, if at all, the absence of more detailed provisions is neither surprising nor a cause for concern.

Finally, there are a number of regional treaties which, while not primarily concerned with marine pollution, deal with dumping. First, three of the regional denuclearisation treaties, the 1985 South Pacific Nuclear Free Zone Treaty (art. 7), the 1995 African Nuclear-Weapon-Free Zone Treaty (art. 7) and the 1995 Treaty on the Southeast Asia Nuclear-Weapon-Free Zone (art. 3(3)), prohibit the dumping of any radioactive material or waste. Secondly, article 4(2) of the Bamako Convention on Transboundary Waste (referred to earlier) prohibits the dumping or incineration at sea of hazardous waste.

The Law of the Sea Convention

As with pollution from shipping, the aim of the Law of the Sea Convention in relation to dumping is not to elaborate standards to govern this form of pollution, but rather to lay down a jurisdictional framework within which such standards, developed in other fora, may be prescribed and enforced. In relation to prescription, the Convention provides that in general States must have laws to prevent, reduce and control dumping, which must be no less effective than global rules and standards and which must ensure that dumping is not carried out without their permission. More specifically, article 210(5) provides that dumping within the territorial sea and EEZ and onto the continental shelf shall not be carried out 'without the express prior approval of the coastal State, which has the right to permit, regulate and control such dumping after due consideration of the matter with other States which by reason of their geographical situation may be adversely affected thereby'. The requirement of 'due consideration' goes beyond the provisions of the London and most regional conventions relating to prior consultation, although it may do no more than reflect the requirements of customary law.[85] In relation to enforcement, article 216 provides that national laws and 'applicable international rules and standards' (the meaning of which raises the same uncertainties as the corresponding phrase in the Convention's provisions

---

[85] Birnie and Boyle, *op. cit.* in 'Further reading' under 'General', pp. 327–9.

concerning pollution from shipping, discussed earlier) are to be enforced by flag States, by coastal States in relation to dumping in their territorial seas and EEZs and onto their continental shelves, and by States in whose territories waste is loaded. The extension of coastal State jurisdiction, both prescriptive and enforcement, by the Convention to the EEZ and continental shelf is reflected in the 1996 Protocol to the London Convention and in some of the more recent regional agreements (see art. 3(2) of the 1986 South Pacific Protocol, art. 8 of the 1992 Black Sea Protocol and art. 10(1) of Annex III of the 1992 Paris Convention), as well as in the legislation of an increasing number of States.

The amount of industrial waste dumped at sea declined from a peak of seventeen million tonnes in 1982 to six million in 1987, while the amount of sewage sludge declined from a peak of seventeen million tonnes in 1980 to fourteen million in 1985.[86] For this the London and other regional dumping conventions must take some of the credit. It may be expected that as the London Convention amendments and Oslo Commission's decisions take effect and the Mediterranean Protocol's amendments come into force, the quantities of wastes dumped (other than dredged materials) will continue to decline significantly. This process may also be helped by the development of compliance mechanisms which is due under the 1996 Protocol to the London Convention, as well as under the 1992 Paris Convention (art. 23) and the amended Mediterranean Convention (art. 27). From a political point of view, the increased restrictions on dumping may be regarded as a victory for general community interests over the interests of twenty or so industrialised States.[87] As Birnie and Boyle put it, dumping 'allows a small number of industrialised States acting for their own benefit to impose pollution risks on many others, perhaps extending into future generations'.[88] At the same time some of the restrictions decided on by politicians have been queried by scientists. GESAMP, for example, has argued that for some States the dumping of sewage sludge and marine incineration remain the best environmental option for getting rid of certain kinds of waste.[89]

Pollution from sea-bed activities within national jurisdiction

The main form of pollution from sea-bed activities within national jurisdiction, and the only one considered here, is that arising from operations in the territorial

[86] *IMO News*, 1992, No. 4, pp. 15–16.
[87] An IMO survey in 1992 showed that twenty-two States still engaged in dumping, *ibid.*, p. 12.
[88] *Op. cit.* in footnote 85, p. 321.
[89] *Op. cit.* in footnote 2, pp. 14–15. See also J. Campbell, 'Legal, jurisdictional and policy issues – 1972 London Convention' in B. Ormerod (ed.), *Ocean Storage of CO2. Workshop 3* (Cheltenham, IEA), 1996, p. 127 at 128, who argues that the amendments to the London Convention are the product of an *a priori* decision to move to a more restrictive policy rather than being based on the evidence of the adverse effects of dumping.

sea and on the continental shelf for the exploration and exploitation of oil and gas. Pollution from such operations can be either deliberate or accidental. Deliberate (or operational) pollution may arise from the oil contained in drilling muds and cuttings, production water and displacement water (i.e., water displaced from containers used for storing oil); chemicals used in drilling; oil from drainage systems on platforms; and the disposal of sewage, garbage and other wastes from installations. Accidental pollution can result from a blow-out (i.e., the escape of oil or gas resulting from the loss of control over the flow from a well); rupture of a pipeline; a collision between a ship and an installation; an accident while a tanker is being loaded from an installation; or destruction of a suspended well-head or sub-sea completion system. In general both deliberate and accidental pollution is localised and relatively short-term in its effects on the marine environment.[90] We will consider deliberate pollution first, before turning to accidental pollution.

Deliberate (operational) pollution

Both the Geneva and Law of the Sea Conventions address general exhortations to States to take measures to avoid deliberate (and accidental) sea-bed pollution. Thus article 24 of the High Seas Convention provides that every State shall draw up regulations to prevent pollution from pipelines or from exploration or exploitation of the sea bed, while article 5(7) of the Continental Shelf Convention provides that States are obliged to take in the safety zones around continental shelf installations 'all appropriate means for the protection of the living resources of the sea from harmful agents'. Articles 208 and 214 of the Law of the Sea Convention require coastal States to prescribe and enforce laws to prevent pollution from sea-bed activities subject to their jurisdiction. Such laws must be 'no less effective than international rules, standards and recommended practices and procedures' (art. 208(3)). Article 208(5) of the Convention goes on to call on States to 'establish global and regional rules, standards and recommended practices and procedures to prevent, reduce and control pollution' from sea-bed activities under their jurisdiction.

No comprehensive global treaty to regulate operational pollution from offshore installations has yet been developed. One soft-law instrument, however, does exist. In 1981 a UNEP group of legal experts produced a set of Conclusions concerning the Environment related to Offshore Mining and Drilling within the Limits of National Jurisdiction.[91] The Conclusions were endorsed as guidelines for State practice by the UNEP Governing Council[92] and UN General Assembly[93]

---

[90] *IMO News*, 1993, No. 3, pp. 1–2, quoting a 1993 GESAMP report.
[91] Reproduced in Sand (1988), *op. cit.* in 'Further reading' under 'Regional Pollution agreements', pp. 226–35.
[92] Governing Council Decision 10/14 (VI) of 31 May 1982.
[93] Res. 37/217.

in 1982. The Guidelines are at a high level of generality. They recommend that States should require the authorisation of all sea-bed activities. Such authorisation should be preceded by an environmental impact assessment and should be refused if there are clear indications that the operations are likely to cause unavoidable significant adverse effects on the environment. Where an authorisation is granted, it should contain conditions to ensure that 'spillage, leakage, or wastes resulting from the operations do not endanger public health, fauna and flora and coastal regions' (para. 7). The operations of installations should be subject to regular monitoring to ensure compliance with such conditions. More specific measures to deal with certain forms of operational pollution are contained, in legally binding form, in the MARPOL Convention and the London (dumping) Convention, discussed earlier. The MARPOL Convention applies to pollution from continental shelf installations, other than the 'release of harmful substances directly arising from the exploration, exploitation and associated offshore processing of sea-bed mineral resources' (art. 2). Annex I regulates the amount of oil which can be discharged from platform drainage, while Annexes IV and V regulate the discharge of sewage and garbage. The London, Oslo (and now Paris) and Mediterranean Conventions regulate the dumping of debris from continental shelf installations, but they do not cover the disposal of wastes incidental to or derived from the normal operation of installations. The London Convention also contains the same exception as article 2 of the MARPOL Convention.

More extensive provisions to regulate pollution from sea-bed activities have been developed in regional agreements, and indeed both article 208(4) of the Law of the Sea Convention and the UNEP Guidelines call on States to harmonise their policies at the regional level. In the North Sea and North-East Atlantic the Commission established by the 1974 Convention for the Prevention of Marine Pollution from Land-Based Sources (discussed in more detail below), largely prompted by the work of the North Sea Conferences, has adopted a number of measures. These include decisions aimed at minimising discharges of oil from exploration activities and on the use of oil-based drilling muds,[94] and recommended limits on the amount of oil contained in discharges of production water and on the use and discharge of chemicals.[95] As with the Oslo Convention, discussed earlier, the 1974 Convention was replaced in 1998 by the 1992 Paris Convention. Annex III of the latter deals with 'the prevention and elimination of pollution from offshore sources'. Cast in fairly general terms, Annex III requires its parties to authorise and regulate 'the use on, or discharge or emission from, offshore sources of substances which may reach and affect the maritime area', implementing in particular the relevant applicable decisions and recommendations adopted by the Commission set up by the Convention (as well as compatible measures adopted under the 1974 Convention, which are maintained in force)

[94] Decisions 86/1 and 88/1, reproduced in Freestone and IJlstra, *op. cit.* in footnote 20, pp. 372 and 373. Decision 88/1 has been superseded by Decision 92/2.
[95] Recommendation 92/6 (replacing earlier recommendations) and Decision 96/3, on the internet at http://www.ospar.org.

(art. 4(1)). The parties are also required to use best available techniques and best environmental practice (art. 2(1)).

The 1974 Baltic Convention provided simply that 'each contracting party shall take all appropriate measures in order to prevent pollution from sea-bed activities' (art. 10). However, the Commission established by that Convention adopted a number of recommendations containing more detailed provisions on this matter, and these now form the basis of the provisions of the 1992 Convention on this subject, contained in Annex VI. After providing that before any sea-bed activity is permitted an environmental impact assessment must be carried out (thus reflecting the UNEP guidelines) and stipulating a general requirement that the parties must use best available technology and best environmental practice to prevent pollution, Annex VI contains detailed provisions on operational pollution. These minimise the use of oil-based drilling muds, require discharge of water-based mud and cuttings to be authorised, prohibit the discharge of chemicals other than in exceptional circumstances, and set a maximum oil content for production water.

All the UNEP Regional Seas conventions have a general provision similar to article 10 of the 1974 Baltic Convention quoted above. Only two of the conventions, the Kuwait Convention and the Mediterranean Convention, have gone further and developed specialised protocols on pollution from sea-bed activities. The Kuwait Protocol, adopted in 1989, is similar to the 1992 Baltic Convention, except that it spells out explicitly the MARPOL Convention's provisions on oily drainage water, garbage and sewage, whereas the Baltic Convention simply incorporates them by reference. This is important as few parties to the Kuwait Protocol are parties to MARPOL.

The Mediterranean Protocol was concluded in 1994. It is similar to the 1992 Baltic Convention and the Kuwait Protocol in requiring the prior authorisation of all sea-bed activities, the carrying out of environmental impact assessments and the use of best available technology (arts 4–8), but contains somewhat different provisions for regulating discharges of noxious substances. As far as oil and oily mixtures and drilling fluids are concerned, the parties to the Mediterranean Protocol are to elaborate standards for these matters, which must be within the maximum permissible discharge limits contained in article 10 and Annex V of the Protocol. Detailed provisions, similar to those of the MARPOL Convention, are laid down for sewage and garbage in articles 11 and 12 of the Protocol. The use of chemicals is to be governed by a chemical use plan drawn up by the operator. A State party may regulate, limit or prohibit the use of chemicals in accordance with guidelines to be adopted by the parties (art. 9(1)(2)). The Kuwait Protocol contains a similar provision (art. XI). Finally in the Mediterranean Protocol, there is a licensing system for the disposal of harmful or noxious substances similar to that of the London and regional dumping conventions. Thus, the disposal of substances listed in Annex I is prohibited; the disposal of substances listed in Annex II requires a prior special permit; and the disposal of 'all other harmful or noxious substances which might cause pollution' requires a prior general permit (art. 9(4)–(6)). The chemical use plan is presumably also subject to this licensing system. The latter system is less strict than the amended Mediterranean Protocol (discussed above), which governs dumping from installations other than that incidental to or derived from the normal operation of installations.

Finally, Offshore Oil and Gas Guidelines were adopted for the Arctic by Arctic Environmental Ministers in June 1997. The Guidelines define a set of recommended practices for those responsible for regulating offshore oil and gas activities. Such practices include environmental impact assessment, environmental monitoring, waste management and decommissioning.[96]

The result of the international legislative action described above is that in the Baltic, Mediterranean, Persian/Arabian Gulf and, to a lesser a extent, the North Sea there exists, on paper at least, a range of measures which should minimise operational pollution from sea-bed activities. Whether they will do so in practice depends on how well the provisions of the various treaties are implemented and observed, once they have come into force. Effective regional standards are necessary because national practice can diverge in the absence of such standards. An example of this can be seen by comparing the practice of the two major oil-producing States of the North Sea, Norway and the United Kingdom. In the period 1981–6 inclusive, before the adoption of any standards by the Paris Commission, installations on the United Kingdom's continental shelf, where offshore activity was roughly two to three times greater than on the Norwegian shelf, discharged seven times as much oil from operational sources as did installations on the Norwegian shelf.[97]

Prevention of accidental pollution

One of the more obvious ways to reduce the chances of accidental pollution is for States to prescribe and rigorously enforce strict construction and operating standards for installations and pipelines used in the exploration and exploitation of sea-bed resources, as the Law of the Sea Convention (art. 194(3)(c)) and the UNEP Guidelines (section F) emphasise. No such standards have yet been developed at the global level apart from the IMO's non-binding Code for the Construction and Equipment of Mobile Offshore Drilling Units,[98] which obviously applies to only a limited range of installations. At the regional level the Mediterranean Protocol provides that a party shall not authorise sea-bed activities unless satisfied that 'the installation has been constructed according

---

[96] *WWF Arctic Bulletin* 1997, No. 2, p. 9 and No. 3, p. 6.

[97] R. R. Churchill and J. Gibson, *The Implementation of the North Sea Declarations by the United Kingdom. An Assessment.* Third North Sea Conference, Greenpeace Paper 17 (1990), pp. 118–20.

[98] IMO Assembly Resolution A. 414 (XI) of 1979. Units constructed after 1991 are recommended to follow the revised version of the Code contained in IMO Assembly Resolution A. 649 (16) of 1989.

to international standards and practice and that the operator has the technical competence and the financial capacity to carry out the activities' (art. 4(1)), and this is reinforced by article 15 and Annex VI, which *inter alia* require the operator of an installation to have adequate equipment, maintained in good working order, for preventing accidental pollution. The parties to the Mediterranean Protocol are also jointly to develop guidelines on these matters (art. 23(1)(c)). With the exception of this last provision, the Kuwait Protocol contains similar obligations (arts VI and VII). Neither of the Baltic Conventions contains any provisions on preventing accidental pollution, apart from a general obligation to use best available technology.

In north-west Europe coastal States met several times during the 1970s and 1980s in an informal Diplomatic Conference on Safety and Pollution Safeguards in the Development of North West European Offshore Mineral Resources. This conference studied the safety of installations and personnel and pollution safeguards, but eventually abandoned attempts to produce a treaty or a code of conduct on these matters. It may also be noted that under various bilateral agreements Norway and the United Kingdom co-operate over safety standards for certain North Sea installations and pipelines.[99] Elsewhere, under the Canada–Denmark Agreement of 1983 the parties undertake to take measures to ensure that offshore installations are 'designed, constructed, placed, equipped, marked, operated and maintained in such a manner that the risk of pollution of the marine environment is minimised' (art. V).

As regards the question of avoiding accidental pollution resulting from collisions between ships and installations, there are some general rules of international law which are relevant. In chapters eight and nine it was pointed out that sea-bed installations must not be placed where interference may be caused to the use of recognised sea lanes essential to international navigation, and must be properly marked and lit. In addition, the IMO has recommended that fairways or routeing systems for shipping should be established through offshore exploration areas where the proliferation of oil installations or traffic patterns warrant it.[100] Such fairways have been established in the Gulf of Mexico (done in fact before the IMO recommendation) and elsewhere. Compliance by ships with fairways may be enforced by the coastal State in its territorial sea, but beyond that limit enforcement lies solely with the flag State (cf. chapter thirteen, p. 268). The IMO has also recommended that ships not involved with the offshore oil industry should avoid certain areas, such as the Gulf of Campeche, because of the degree of offshore oil and gas activity in such areas.[101]

---

[99] See, for example, the Agreement relating to the Transmission of Petroleum by Pipeline from the Ekofisk Fields and Neighbouring Areas to the United Kingdom, 1973, art. 8; and the Agreement relating to the Exploitation of the Frigg Field Reservoir and the Transmission of Gas therefrom to the United Kingdom, 1976 arts 7, 8, 17 and 18.

[100] IMO Assembly Resolution A. 671 (16) of 1989, revoking and replacing Resolution A. 379 (X) of 1977.

[101] IMO Assembly Resolution A. 527 (XIII) of 1983.

Where large-scale accidental pollution has occurred, for example as the result of a blow-out, the various conventions dealing with co-operation in pollution emergencies, referred to earlier when discussing pollution from shipping, apply. These include the 1990 Oil Pollution Preparedness Convention, which specifically requires operators of offshore installations to have oil pollution emergency plans (art. 3(2)) and to notify the coastal State of the discharge or presence of oil. Similar obligations, in rather more detail, are contained in the 1992 Baltic Convention (Annex VI, regs 6 and 7), the Kuwait Protocol (art. VIII) and the Mediterranean Protocol (arts 16–18 and annex VII), and recommended in the UNEP Guidelines (section G). In addition the Association of Southeast Asian Nations (ASEAN) has adopted an Oil Spill Regional Action Plan, with a contingency plan for offshore installations.[102] Furthermore, the offshore oil industry in many areas has its own schemes for dealing with accidents: for example, since 1978 North Sea operators have been grouped into ten (originally six) 'Sector Clubs', within each of which plans have been developed for operators to assist each other with fire-fighting vessels and other equipment in the event of an emergency.[103]

Liability

As with pollution from shipping, it is desirable that the victims of pollution from sea-bed operations should be able to obtain effective compensation for the damage they have suffered, and this is called for by the UNEP Guidelines (section H). Although article 235 of the Law of the Sea Convention, all the UNEP Regional Seas agreements and the Baltic Conventions contain a general provision committing their parties to develop special liability regimes for all forms of marine pollution, only two attempts have so far been made to lay down a special liability regime for sea-bed pollution. The first, in north-west Europe, is the Convention on Civil Liability for Oil Pollution Damage resulting from Exploration for and Exploitation of Sea-bed Mineral Resources, which was signed in 1977. The Convention has not entered into force and is unlikely ever to do so, having not yet received a single ratification of the four necessary for its entry into force. The Convention was modelled on the 1969 Civil Liability Convention (discussed above) and thus was based, with some exceptions, on the principle of strict, but limited, liability. The operator of a continental shelf installation causing pollution damage was automatically liable for that damage and for the cost of any remedial measures taken unless he could prove that the damage resulted from war or an act of God or from an abandoned well more than five years after it was abandoned, or from an intentional or negligent act done by the person suffering pollution damage (art. 3). As a *quid pro quo* for this strict liability,

---

[102] United Nations, *op. cit.* in footnote 64, p. 77.
[103] J. Side, 'North-west Europe – clean seas and emergency services', 19 *Marine Pollution Bulletin* 153–5 (1988).

the operator's liability was limited to forty million SDRs (art. 6), although it was open to a State party, if it so wished, to provide that the liability of the operators of installations on its continental shelf should be higher or even unlimited in respect of pollution damage caused in that State (art. 15). In any case, an operator's liability was unlimited if the pollution damage 'occurred as a result of an act or omission by the operator himself, done deliberately with actual knowledge that pollution damage would result' (art. 6(4)). The rest of the 1977 Convention dealt, in a manner broadly similar to the 1969 Convention, with compulsory insurance (which had to provide cover of not less than thirty-five million SDRs) (art. 8); the procedure for bringing claims (the limitation period was shorter than in the 1969 Convention, but there was a wider choice of forum) (arts 10 and 11); and the recognition of judgments (art. 12). The main reason for the failure of any State to ratify the Convention appears to be dissatisfaction with the Convention's provisions on limits of liability, and the existence of a generally superior industry scheme (discussed below).

The second attempt to develop a special liability regime for sea-bed pollution is the 1994 Mediterranean Protocol. Article 27 of the Protocol calls on its parties to co-operate in developing such a regime 'as soon as possible'. Until they have done so, each party shall ensure that every operator on its continental shelf is liable for pollution damage for which he shall pay 'prompt and adequate compensation', and shall carry adequate insurance cover for this purpose.

Although the 1977 Convention has not entered into force, the advantages which it would bring for both operators and the victims of pollution damage have been provided for in north-west European waters by an industry scheme – the Offshore Pollution Liability Agreement (OPOL)[104] – which has been in existence since 1975. OPOL, whose parties are oil companies operating in north-west European waters, broadly parallels the Convention, rather as the industry schemes of TOVALOP and CRISTAL paralleled the 1969 Civil Liability and 1971 Fund Conventions in respect of pollution from shipping. Unlike the 1977 Convention, the limits of liability in OPOL are expressed in US dollars and not SDRs. The upper limit of liability is US $100 million (raised from the initial limit of $25 million).

Pollution from mining in the international sea bed area

Article 145 of the Law of the Sea Convention provides that the International Sea Bed Authority is to adopt rules to prevent pollution from deep-sea mining, particular attention being paid to the consequences of 'such activities as drilling, dredging, excavation, disposal of waste, construction and operation or maintenance of installations, pipelines and other devices related to such activities'.

---

[104] The text of OPOL in its 1986 version is reproduced in Freestone and IJlstra, *op. cit.* in footnote 20, p. 319. OPOL was further amended in 1992.

Assuming such rules fall within the category of 'rules, regulations and proced-ures [relating to] prospecting, exploration and exploitation in the Area' (and article 17 of Annex III and paragraph 5(k) of Section 1 of the Annex to the 1994 Agreement relating to the Implementation of Part XI of LOSC strongly suggest this is the case), pollution rules are to be framed by the Legal and Technical Commission and formally adopted by the Council and Assembly (LOSC, arts 160(2)(f), 162(2)(o), 165(2)(e). In carrying out these functions the various bodies concerned are to take into account the work of PrepCom on this question (1994 Agreement, section 1, para. 16). Provisions on environmental protection are con-tained in the Draft Regulations on Prospecting and Exploration for Polymetallic Nodules in the International Seabed Area, produced by the Legal and Technical Commission in March 1998 and currently being considerd by the Council. In addition to pollution regulations adopted by the Authority, article 209 requires States to adopt national legislation which is no less effective than the Authority's regulations.

As far as the enforcement of pollution regulations in the Area is concerned, article 215 states that enforcement is to be governed by the provisions of Part XI. In fact this part contains no provisions specifically dealing with enforce-ment. Article 139 of the Law of the Sea Convention suggests that in respect of activities by companies, whether private or State-owned, enforcement will be by the State whose nationality the company bears; and in respect of activities by the Enterprise enforcement will be by the Enterprise and the Authority. It should be noted, however, that even in respect of non-Enterprise operations the Authority appears to have residual enforcement powers. Under article 153 the Authority is to 'exercise such control over activities in the Area as is necessary for the purpose of securing compliance with' its regulations, and every applicant for sea-bed mining undertakes to accept such control (LOSC, Annex III, art. 4(6)(b)). Furthermore, under article 162(2) the Council may 'issue emergency orders, which may include orders for the suspension or adjustment of operations, to prevent serious harm to the marine environment arising out of activities in the Area' (sub-paragraph w) and 'establish appropriate mechanisms for directing and super-vising a staff of inspectors who shall inspect activities in the Area to determine' whether the Authority's regulations are being complied with (sub-paragraph z). In addition, the Legal and Technical Commission, at the request of the Council, is to supervise activities in the Area (LOSC, art. 165(2)(c)).

The Basic Conditions of Prospecting, Exploration and Exploitation, set out in Annex III, will also help to secure compliance with the Authority's pollution regulations. Prospecting is to be conducted only after the Authority has received a satisfactory written undertaking that the proposed prospector will comply with the Authority's pollution regulations and will accept verification by the Author-ity of compliance (LOSC, Annex III, art. 2(1)(b)). Exploration and exploitation are to take place only in accordance with a contract between the operator and the Authority, and one of the conditions of such contracts is that the Authority's pollution regulations are strictly observed (LOSC, Annex III, arts 3, 4). Failure to do so will lead to the contract being suspended or terminated, and monetary penalties being imposed on the contractor (LOSC, Annex III, art. 18). Furthermore, the Council is not to allow exploration and exploitation in areas 'where substantial evidence indicates the risk of serious harm to the marine environment' (LOSC, art. 162(2)(x)). Under paragraph 7 of section 1 of the 1994 Agreement, an application for approval of a plan of work must be accompanied by an assessment of the potential environmental impacts of the proposed activities.

For any sea-bed mining which might take place outside the framework of the Convention (an increasingly unlikely possibility: see chapter twelve) – little international law is at present applicable: at most the MARPOL and London Conventions would to some extent apply.

Land-based sources of marine pollution

Although pollution from land is the most significant source of marine pollution, only a limited amount of international legislative action has so far been taken to tackle this form of pollution. This is not perhaps surprising. Land-based pollution is the most 'national' source of marine pollution. It emanates from an area that is under the sovereignty of a State and in which other States enjoy no rights (unlike the position in relation to other forms of marine pollution). There is only one State (the territorial State) that can legislate for such pollution and enforce that legislation (unlike shipping or dumping). Furthermore, different national traditions of legislation and policy make it difficult for countries to agree on a uniform approach. For example, there have been differences between the United Kingdom and its EC partners over the question of whether EC directives should be based on uniform emission standards or water quality standards. Proponents of the former view argue that such standards make the cost of taking anti-pollution measures the same for all industries, while proponents of the latter view (such as the United Kingdom) argue that the capacity of some water areas to break down pollutants more quickly should be recognised. National differences are, of course, even more marked between rich and poor States. Added to these difficulties is the fact that there are so many different pollutants produced by a wide variety of activities and that there are various ways for them to enter the sea from land. Furthermore, much of this pollution is difficult to monitor, and its control and reduction is often costly.

Articles 207 and 213 of the Law of the Sea Convention provide that States shall prescribe and enforce laws and regulations to prevent, reduce and control pollution from land-based sources, including rivers, estuaries, pipelines and outfall structures, especially of persistent toxic or noxious substances, taking into account and implementing internationally agreed rules, standards and recommended practices and procedures. In relation to the latter, article 207(4) calls on States to 'endeavour to establish global and regional rules, standards and recommended practices and procedures to prevent, reduce and control pollution of the marine environment from land-based sources, taking into account characteristic regional features, the economic capacity of developing States and their need for development'. As will be seen below, a number of regional treaties have been concluded to deal with land-based sources of marine pollution, but no global treaty on the matter has yet been drawn up. However, a number of soft law instruments of global application have been adopted.

The first of these is the set of 'Guidelines for the Protection of the Marine Environment against Pollution from Land-Based Sources', drawn up by UNEP in 1985.[105] The main objective of the Guidelines is to assist States in developing national legislation and international agreements on land-based pollution. The Guidelines are intended to be a checklist of basic provisions rather than a model agreement. Agenda 21, adopted at the 1992 UN Conference on Environment and Development, suggested that the Guidelines should be revised, and invited UNEP to convene an intergovernmental meeting on land-based marine pollution. Agenda 21 also called for the development and strengthening of regional agreements and suggested a number of matters for priority action in tackling pollution (chapter 17.25 to 28). UNEP accepted Agenda 21's invitation and held a number of meetings which revealed a division of opinion over whether to consider adopting a legally binding instrument or to continue the non-binding approach. The latter prevailed, and the meetings culminated in the adoption in November 1995 of the Washington Declaration and Global Programme of Action on Protection of the Marine Environment from Land-Based Activities.[106] This is a fresh soft-law instrument, rather than a revision of the original Guidelines, which were considered to be out of date and impracticable to update. In the Declaration States 'declare their commitment to protect and preserve the marine environment from the impacts of land-based activities' in the ways set out in the Programme of Action. The latter is a lengthy and complex document, and only the barest outline of its provisions can be given here. It begins by recalling the relevant provisions of the Law of the Sea Convention and various principles endorsed by UNCED such as the precautionary approach, the polluter pays principle and sustainable development, and states that its aim is to assist States in taking action individually or jointly to reduce land-based pollution. Chapters II to IV then set out objectives and actions to be taken at the national, regional and international level. The last of these puts considerable emphasis on promoting access to technology and knowledge and on making funding available to developing countries through such mechanisms as the World Bank's Global Environment Facility. Chapter V sets out recommended approaches to different categories of pollutant and lists those that require priority action. These are sewage (in relation to which UNEP is requested to propose a plan to address the global nature of the problem of inadequate management and treatment of waste water), persistent organic

---

[105] The text of the Guidelines is reproduced in 14 *Environmental Policy and Law* 77–83 (1985) and in Sand, *op. cit.* in footnote 91, pp. 235–54.
[106] The Declaration and Programme of Action are reproduced in 26 *Environmental Policy and Law* 37–51 (1996). The Declaration only is reproduced in 31 *LOSB* 76 (1996).

pollutants (for the reduction or elimination of which a global, legally binding instrument should be developed[107]), radioactive substances, heavy metals, oil, nutrients and litter. Unlike the original UNEP Guidelines, the Programme of Action contains various provisions for its implementation and further development. These include securing formal endorsement of those parts of the Programme of Action that are relevant to other organisations (including the UN Commission on Sustainable Development) and incorporating the relevant provisions into their work programmes; establishing a clearing-house mechanism to provide decision-makers in all States with direct access to relevant sources of information, practical experience and scientific and technical expertise; and providing for periodic inter-governmental review of the Programme of Action.

Although it is expected that the Programme of Action will result in the adoption of at least one global and legally binding instrument, at present the only treaties regulating land-based pollution of the sea are regional. There are an increasing number of such agreements. In fact, given the wide variations between regions in the extent and nature of marine pollution from land-based sources, a regional approach to this form of pollution makes much sense.

The Paris Convention

The first regional convention to tackle land-based marine pollution in detail was the Convention for the Prevention of Marine Pollution from Land-based Sources, 1974 (hereafter referred to as the Paris Convention), which applies to the North-East Atlantic and North Sea and covers all pollution emanating from land (arts 2, 3). The Convention regulates land-based pollution by dividing pollutants into four categories. The first category (the 'black list') consists of the most noxious pollutants, and includes organohalogen compounds, mercury, cadmium, persistent synthetic materials and oil (Part I of Annex A). Parties to the Paris Convention have undertaken to 'eliminate' pollution by such substances, 'if necessary by stages', although no timetable for doing so is set (art. 4(1)). The second category (the 'grey list') consists of rather less noxious pollutants, including organic compounds of phosphorous, silicon and tin, phosphorous, non-persistent oils, arsenic and heavy metals (Part II of Annex A). Pollution by these substances must be strictly limited, and each contracting party has had to introduce a system of permits to regulate the discharge of such pollutants (art. 4). Radioactive substances come into a special category because, as we have seen earlier, they are already the subject of research and recommendations by various international organisations. In respect of these substances contracting parties have undertaken to 'adopt measures to forestall and, as appropriate, eliminate pollution' (art. 5). The final category consists of all other pollutants. No special measures are required of contracting parties in the case of such other pollutants, but they have to try to reduce pollution by such substances, taking into account relevant circumstances

---

[107] In fact negotiations for such an instrument began in 1996.

such as the nature and quantity of the pollutants in question, the state of the waters which may be affected, and so on (art. 6). Where pollution (other than from substances on the 'black list') from the territory of one State is likely to prejudice the interests of another State, the States concerned are to consult together with the object of negotiating a co-operation agreement (art. 9). No such agreements appear yet to have been concluded.

Implementation and enforcement of the Paris Convention's provisions are carried out by the national authorities of the parties (art. 12), but the Convention has also established a Commission, the functions of which include overall supervision of the implementation of the Convention; reviewing the state of the seas in the Convention area; assessing the effectiveness of control measures and, where appropriate, recommending additional measures; reviewing and distributing information from contracting parties on the state of the seas in the Convention area and measures taken to reduce pollution; and recommending amendments to the different lists of pollutants (art. 16). Recommendations of the Commission, which must be adopted by a majority of not less than three-quarters of the parties, are binding on all the parties unless objected to (art. 18).

Since it came into being, the Commission has devoted much time to studying the sources of the more noxious pollutants – an essential preliminary before taking any regulatory measures. In relation to the latter there was in the early years of the Commission an intense debate over whether to use uniform emission standards (UES) or water quality objectives (WQO). As a result, for the first substances for which it adopted discharge standards – mercury, hydrocarbons, cadmium and organohalogen compounds – the Commission set both UESs and WQOs. The 1987 and 1990 North Sea Declarations called for the two approaches to be combined,[108] and in any case the debate between the two approaches has been overtaken by the new strategy adopted by the Paris Commission in the late 1980s, which was largely prompted by the North Sea Conferences. In 1989 the Commission adopted a Recommendation on the Principle of Precautionary Action[109] under which polluting emissions of substances that are persistent, toxic and liable to bioaccumulate are to be reduced at source by the use of best available technology. The latter is defined in general terms in another Recommendation adopted on the same day,[110] and has subsequently been defined in specific terms for particular industrial sectors (e.g., secondary iron and steel plants,[111] pharmaceutical industry[112]). This change represents a shift in philosophy from a substance-by-substance approach, which is difficult where many discharges are indirect, to a more holistic one. At the same time the Commission has been able to adopt many more regulatory measures than in the 1980s (e.g.,

---

[108] For a further discussion on this issue, see Churchill and Gibson, *op. cit.* in footnote 97, pp. 56–62.
[109] Recommendation 89/1, in Freestone and IJlstra, *op. cit.* in footnote 20, p. 152.
[110] Recommendation 89/2 on the Use of Best Available Technology, *ibid.*, p. 153.
[111] Recommendation 90/1, *ibid.*, p. 156.
[112] Recommendation 92/5.

concerning PCBs, organohalogens, heavy metals, oil and nutrients). This has been accompanied by improved monitoring of States' implementation of the Convention and the Commission's measures. The Quality Status Reports produced for the North Sea Conferences suggest that there have been improvements in some respects in the marine environment of the North Sea, for which the Paris Commission may claim some of the credit, but deteriorations in other respects.

The Paris Convention, together with the Oslo Convention, was replaced by a single new convention, the 1992 Convention for the Protection of the Marine Environment of the North-East Atlantic (also known as the Paris Convention), upon its entry into force in 1998. The new Convention abandons the black/grey list approach of the original Paris Convention. Thus, article 3 and Annex I require the parties to take 'all possible steps to prevent and eliminate' land-based pollution. To this end programmes and measures are to be drawn up by the new commission established by the Convention, according to priorities indicated in Appendix 2 (although, as with the original Convention, no timetable is laid down) which are to require the use of best available techniques for point sources and best environmental practice for point and diffuse sources. Best available techniques and best environmental practice are defined in general terms in Appendix I. Each party must ensure that point source discharges are subject to authorisation or regulation, which implement any relevant Commission decisions. Any relevant decisions and recommendations of the original Paris Commission not incompatible with the new Convention remain in force. In fact between 1994 and 1998 the Commission had followed the approach of the 1992 Convention by adopting a number of recommendations on best available techniques and best environmental practice (rather than simply best available technology as before) for particular sectors.[113]

It is appropriate briefly to outline here some of the general provisions of the 1992 Paris Convention. The parties are to review the quality of the marine environment and the effectiveness of measures taken under the Convention at regular intervals (art. 6), and are to carry out research to further the aims of the Convention (art. 8). The functions of the new Paris Commission are similar to those of the previous Oslo and Paris Commissions, but the Convention clarifies the legal status of decisions and recommendations adopted by the Commission (arts 10 and 13). The parties are to report at regular intervals on implementation of the Convention (art. 22). On the basis of such reports the Commission is to assess parties' compliance with the Convention and measures adopted thereunder: 'when appropriate' the Commission is to 'decide upon and call for steps to bring about full compliance' (art. 23). This last provision represents a novel and potentially important step compared with current practice. The contribution

---

[113] E.g., Recommendations 94/5 (on the textile processing industry) and 96/1 (on aluminium electrolysis plants). The text of Paris Commission Decisions and Recommendations adopted since 1993 can be found on the Internet at http://www.ospar.org.

the 1992 Convention may make to reducing marine pollution in the North-East Atlantic will largely depend on how the Commission functions in practice. In this respect the EC has a crucial role. The overwhelming majority of members of the Commission comprise the EC and its member States. It remains to be seen whether disputes over the division of competence between the EC and its member States will arise, as happened in the early years of the original Paris Commission (the EC was not a member of the Oslo Commission), and frustrate the work of the Commission, especially as the 1992 Convention covers subjects which fall outside the remit of the Paris Commission. Another possibility is that the EC and its member States will drive through or block decisions against the wishes of non-EC members. The EC itself has adopted a number of measures which are concerned with reducing land-based marine pollution, but lack of space prevents any discussion of their details.[114]

The Baltic Conventions

The first Baltic Convention was drawn up at much the same time as the Paris Convention and adopts a not dissimilar approach. Article 6(1) lays down a general obligation on States parties to 'take all appropriate measures to control and minimise land-based pollution'. Certain noxious pollutants listed in Annex II, such as heavy metals, hydrocarbon compounds, radioactive materials, oil and acids, may be discharged only if a permit has been issued by a State party. The parties are to co-operate in the development of common criteria for the issue of such permits. Under article 5 the parties undertake to 'counteract the introduction' into the marine environment of DDT and its derivatives and PCBs from any source. They shall control and minimise pollution from other pollutants by aiming to attain the goals and applying the criteria enumerated in Annex III: these are concerned with the treatment of sewage, industrial wastes and the discharge of cooling water. The Commission set up by the Convention is to define these goals and criteria more precisely. This the Commission has so far done by adopting more than fifty recommendations: these deal *inter alia* with pollutants used in agriculture, the treatment of sewage, waste water from industrial plants (including pulp and paper mills and iron and steel plants), oil, mercury, cadmium, DDT and PCBs.[115] Commission recommendations are not legally binding, but parties report on their implementation, as well as on implementation of the Convention generally. Like the Paris Commission, the Baltic Commission has in recent years moved away from controlling emissions of individual

---

[114] As to which see N. Haigh, *Manual of Environmental Policy: the EC and Britain* (Harlow, Longman), 1992. The EC shares competence with its member States in relation to marine pollution. See the declaration it made on confirming its signature of the Law of the Sea Convention.

[115] For a list of, and links to the texts of, Commission recommendations, see http://www.helcom.fi.reclist.html.

substances to identifying best available technology for particular industrial sectors. In 1990 Baltic Governments adopted a Declaration (rather in the way the North Sea States have done), calling for a restoration of the Baltic marine environment, setting up a Joint Comprehensive Action Programme to reduce emissions, and establishing a Task Force whose members include *inter alia* international financial institutions such as the European Investment Bank and the World Bank. The Task Force is to identify and analyse investment projects for pollution control. It is anticipated that about 18 billion ECU will be spent over a twenty-year period to deal with the most severely polluted areas ('hot spots'), most of which are in former Communist States and virtually all of which concern land-based sources. It is considered that this is more cost-effective than a more general approach to reducing pollution. Nevertheless, it is expected to be many years before the effects of all the above measures are known.

In the meantime the legal framework will change when the 1992 Baltic Convention enters into force. This Convention represents a somewhat different and rather stricter approach than the 1974 Convention which it replaces. Thus, article 6(1) provides that the parties are to prevent and eliminate pollution by using *inter alia* best environmental practice for all sources and best available technology for point sources. Criteria for identifying such practice and technology are set out in Annex II. Under article 6(2) the parties are to implement and develop specific programmes, guidelines and emission standards. Harmful substances from point sources may only be discharged if a prior special permit has been obtained (art. 6(3)). Under article 5 and Annex I parties are to 'prohibit, totally or partially' the use of certain substances from any source, including DDT, PCBs and PCTs, and 'endeavour to minimise and, wherever possible, to ban' the use of various listed pesticides. Clearly the effect of the above provisions is to give States considerable latitude in what action they take, especially as no timetables are laid down. How far land-based pollution is reduced in practice will largely depend on what recommendations are adopted by the Commission (which remain non-binding), how far they are complied with (the new Convention tightens up reporting obligations, but, unlike the 1992 Paris Convention, does not contain any provisions on assessing compliance), and the nature of the 'hot spots' financing programme referred to above.

UNEP Regional Seas agreements

Each of the nine UNEP Regional Seas agreements contains a general provision committing its parties to take all appropriate measures to prevent, reduce and control pollution from land-based sources. Only four of the agreements – those for the Mediterranean, South-East Pacific, Arabian/Persian Gulf and Black Sea – have so far gone on to develop detailed provisions in separate protocols. The Caribbean and West African Conventions are in the course of elaborating such protocols.

The Mediterranean Protocol

The 1980 Protocol to the Mediterranean Convention is in many ways similar to the 1974 Paris Convention. The Protocol covers all pollution emanating from land except that discharged into the atmosphere, which is to be the subject of a subsequent annex to the Protocol (art. 4): such an annex was adopted in 1991. The parties to the Protocol are to 'eliminate' pollution by the substances listed in Annex I (which is similar to the Paris Convention's 'black list') (art. 5) and 'strictly limit' pollution by the substances listed in Annex II (which is much more extensive than the Paris Convention's 'grey list') by means of permits (art. 6). More guidance is given than in the Paris Convention as to when such permits may be issued: see Annex III. In order to fulfil these obligations, the parties are to agree on timetables and measures such as common emission standards, and also adopt common guidelines and criteria relating to pipelines used for coastal outfalls; effluents requiring separate treatment; the quality of seawater; and the control and progressive replacement of products and processes causing significant marine pollution (art. 7).

The parties must inform each other through UNEP of the measures they have taken, the results achieved and difficulties encountered in applying the Protocol (art. 13). Meetings shall be held every two years for the purposes *inter alia* of keeping implementation of the Protocol under review; amending the annexes to the Protocol; and adopting the timetables, measures, guidelines and criteria referred to above (art. 14). In implementation of the Protocol the parties have adopted measures concerning the quality of bathing water and shellfish water, the quality of shellfish for human consumption, mercury in marine products, cadmium, organohalogen compounds, solid litter, pathogenic micro-organisms and pesticides. In 1993 an evaluation of the Protocol carried out by UNEP found that the majority of parties had not effectively implemented or complied with these measures.[116]

In 1996 the Protocol was the subject of major amendments, which are designed *inter alia* to take into account the objectives laid down in the Washington Global Programme of Action, referred to earlier. Like the 1992 Paris and Baltic Conventions, the amendments abandon the distinction between black and grey lists and move away from a substance-by-substance approach to one based on sectors of activity. The emphasis is placed on adopting timetables for the phasing-out of substances that are toxic, persistent and liable to bioaccumulate, taking account of best available techniques for point sources and best environmental practice for point and diffuse sources, including where appropriate clean production technologies. The amendments also tighten up reporting procedures.

The other UNEP protocols

The South-East Pacific and Black Sea Protocols are, on paper, similar in many respects to the Mediterranean Protocol in its original form, including the absence

---

[116] Report of the UN Secretary General on the Law of the Sea, UN Doc. A/49/631 (1994), para. 100.

of any precise amounts or time limits by which reductions in emissions of black and grey list substances are to be effected. The fourth UNEP protocol, the Kuwait Protocol, is very different from the others. Under article IV the parties undertake to implement action programmes based on 'source control' as outlined in Annex I. This involves controlling and progressively replacing products, installations and industrial or other processes causing significant pollution to the marine environment, including changing raw materials, changing manufacturing processes and recycling. Secondly, recognising the difficulties faced by industries in treating effluent but endeavouring not to inhibit industrial development, the parties undertake to implement industrial location planning programmes and joint and/or combined effluent treatment (art. V and Annex I). Thirdly, the parties undertake to develop guidelines, standards and criteria for the quality of seawater used for specific purposes and regulations for waste treatment and discharges, and to require polluters to obtain a permit (art. 6 and Annex III). With its emphasis on tackling land-based marine pollution at the source of the polluting process, the Protocol is in many ways a very advanced document. However, the parties are given almost complete discretion as to the degree and time of any action taken, and the effectiveness of the Protocol therefore depends entirely on what implementing action, if any, is in practice taken by the parties either individually or jointly.[117]

Rivers

Most pollutants entering rivers will eventually finish up in the sea. It therefore follows that treaties adopted specifically to curb pollution of rivers will also help to reduce marine pollution. Such treaties will be most significant in regions where there is no agreement dealing in detail with land-based marine pollution or where there is such a regional agreement but not all riparian States of the river concerned are parties to that regional agreement. It must also be remembered that treaties dealing with river pollution will be governed primarily by the interests and concerns of the riparian States, which may not always take sufficient account of the need to protect the marine environment.

There are a considerable number of treaties dealing with the pollution of rivers. At the global level the United Nations in 1997 adopted a Convention on the Law of the Non-Navigational Uses of International Watercourses, based on draft articles drawn up by the International Law Commission in 1994. The Convention *inter alia* requires States to prevent, reduce and control pollution of an international watercourse that may cause significant harm to other riparian States or their environment, and to take all measures with respect to an international watercourse that are necessary to protect and preserve the marine environment.

---

[117] For brief surveys of action taken under this and the other protocols referred to above, see the section on 'Oceans' in the annual surveys of the *Yearbook of International Environmental Law*.

At the regional level the UN Economic Commission for Europe (UNECE) in 1992 adopted a Convention on the Protection and Use of Transboundary Watercourses and International Lakes. The Convention requires its parties to prevent, control and reduce pollution of waters that has or is likely to have an 'adverse effect on the environment . . . within an area under the jurisdiction of another Party' (arts 1 and 2). In taking such action parties are to be guided by the precautionary principle, the polluter pays principle and the needs of future generations. Specifically they are *inter alia* to control emissions at source using low- or non-waste technology, license and limit discharges from point sources by requiring use of best available technology for hazardous substances, require the use of best environmental practices for inputs of nutrients and hazardous substances from diffuse sources and, where appropriate, define water quality objectives. Unlike the UN Convention, the UNECE Convention does not refer to pollution of the marine environment as such, although the area to which the obligation to control pollution relates, areas 'under the jurisdiction of another party', is wide enough to include the territorial sea and probably also the EEZ of a coastal State party. In addition, bodies established by riparian States are to co-operate with 'bodies established by coastal States for the protection of the marine environment directly affected by' pollution from riparian States (art. 9(4)). Like the UN Convention, the UNECE Convention is essentially of a framework nature, and requires its parties to enter into bilateral or regional pollution agreements where they do not exist and to adapt existing agreements if necessary to eliminate contradictions with the basic principles of the Convention. On the basis of this provision, agreements have been concluded for the Danube,[118] Meuse[119] and Scheldt.[120]

One of the most significant river pollution regimes, which pre-dates the UNECE Convention by some years, is that for the Rhine, which is the source of a significant proportion of the pollution of the North Sea. This regime includes two agreements concluded in 1976. The first of these, the Convention concerning Protection of the Rhine against Pollution by Chlorides, together with a Protocol of 1991, is aimed at reducing the discharge of chlorides into the Rhine. The aim of the second agreement, the Convention on the Protection of the Rhine against Chemical Pollution, is to eliminate the discharge of the most noxious chemical pollutants, and control the discharge of less noxious chemicals by means of a system of permits. The International Commission for the Protection of the Rhine, established in 1950, has a role in monitoring and implementation under both agreements. A further agreement of 1996[121] prohibits the discharge of waste from boats on the Rhine. In 1987 the riparian States adopted an Action Programme

---

[118] Convention on Co-Operation for the Protection and Sustainable Use of the Danube, 1994. Much of the pollution of the Black Sea is caused by upper riparian States of the Danube, in particular Austria and Germany.
[119] Convention for the Protection of the Meuse, 1994.
[120] Convention for the Protection of the Scheldt, 1994.
[121] Convention on the Collection, Deposit and Disposal of Waste generated during Navigation on the Rhine and Inland Waterways.

for the Rhine, one of the objectives of which is to improve the water quality of the North Sea.[122]

Liability

Unlike the case with shipping or sea-bed activities, there are no specific multilateral agreements to facilitate the bringing of claims for compensation by a national of one State who has suffered damage from pollution emanating from another State. The one, and geographically limited, exception is the Nordic Convention on the Protection of the Environment, article 3 of which provides that a national of one Nordic State may bring an action before the court of another Nordic State to prevent a particular pollution from continuing or to claim compensation for damage suffered. If an individual is unwilling or unable to proceed, his role in instituting proceedings may be taken over by the Supervisory Authority which each State party has established for this purpose. The lack of other agreements is not surprising. With land-based pollution it is often difficult to identify the source of the pollution, and to establish a causal link between that source and the damage suffered. It is likely, therefore, that only in exceptional cases will an action for compensation have any chance of success, and the Nordic Convention itself has been of limited practical application. On the other hand, it might be desirable to introduce provisions similar to the Nordic Convention in other regions in order to facilitate the bringing of actions by litigants before foreign courts. This is something which is encouraged by article 235(3) of the Law of the Sea Convention and on which the parties to the Mediterranean Convention are currently elaborating a protocol. In addition, it should be noted that article 235(2) of the Law of the Sea Convention provides that

> States shall ensure that recourse is available in accordance with their legal systems for prompt and adequate compensation or other relief in respect of damage caused by pollution of the marine environment by natural or juridical persons under their jurisdiction.

This provision, of course, is not limited to cases of damage caused by land-based pollution.

Atmospheric pollution

As was mentioned near the beginning of this chapter, a good deal of pollution enters the sea, especially open-ocean basins, via the atmosphere. Although

---

[122] For further discussion of the prevention of pollution of rivers, including rivers outside Europe, see Birnie and Boyle, *op. cit.* in 'Further reading' under 'General', chapter 6; Sand (1992), *op. cit.* in 'Further reading' under 'General', chap. VI; and P. Sands, *Principles of International Environmental Law*, Vol. I (Manchester, Manchester University Press), 1991, chapter 9.

pollution from the atmosphere is essentially a form of land-based pollution, the Law of the Sea Convention treats it as a separate source of marine pollution. Articles 212 and 222 provide that States shall prescribe and enforce legislation to prevent marine pollution from the atmosphere, applicable to the air space under their sovereignty and to their vessels and aircraft. Article 212(3) calls on States to establish global and regional rules to prevent atmospheric pollution. A number of such rules have been adopted. They may be divided into two broad categories: rules to control and reduce atmospheric emissions specifically in the context of preventing marine pollution, and controls on atmospheric emissions adopted generally or primarily to deal with pollution of land territory, which incidentally may help to reduce marine pollution.

The former include controls on incineration of wastes at sea adopted by the London and some of the regional dumping conventions and Annex VI to MARPOL on atmospheric emissions from ships, all of which were discussed in detail earlier. In addition, some of the regional conventions on land-based pollution have provisions specifically concerned with pollution via the atmosphere. Thus, a protocol to the 1974 Paris Convention, adopted in 1986, extends the scope of that Convention to atmospheric pollution, and a number of the measures adopted by the Paris Commission since then concern atmospheric emissions. The 1992 Convention, which has replaced the 1974 Convention, includes emissions into the air from sources on land in its definition of land-based sources of marine pollution (art. 1(e)), and the provisions of the Convention relating to such sources, described earlier, accordingly apply to atmospheric emissions. In this connection it may also be noted that the Third North Sea Conference (1990) called for a fifty per cent reduction in atmospheric emissions of certain listed substances by 1999. Unlike the 1974 Paris Convention, the 1974 Baltic Convention from the outset specifically included atmospheric emissions from sources on land within its definition of land-based marine pollution (art. 2(2)). The subsequent provisions of the Convention on such pollution (art. 6) include an obligation on its parties to endeavour to use best practical means in order to minimise airborne pollution of the Baltic by the noxious substances listed in Annex II. The 1992 Baltic Convention also includes atmospheric emissions within its definition of land-based sources. Its provisions concerning pollution from such sources, which were outlined earlier and which are rather different from those of the 1974 Convention, accordingly apply to atmospheric emissions without there being any provisions relating specifically to such emissions. Like the 1974 Paris Convention, the Protocol to the Mediterranean Convention on land-based sources of marine pollution did not originally apply to atmospheric emissions, but this omission was made good by an annex of 1991. The 1996 amendments to the Protocol amend this annex by providing that in case of atmospheric emissions the general obligations to eliminate pollution, especially of toxic, persistent and bioaccumulative substances, 'shall apply progressively to appropriate substances and sources listed in Annex I to [the] Protocol as will be agreed by the Parties' (Annex III, paragraph 3).

Of the other UNEP Regional Seas agreements having protocols on land-based sources of marine pollution, the Kuwait, South-East Pacific and Black Sea protocols all include atmospheric emissions within their scope. Their provisions (outlined above) accordingly apply to atmospheric emissions without there being any specific provision concerning such emissions, although the Black Sea Convention (not Protocol) does provide, in article XII, that its parties shall adopt legislation and take measures to prevent, reduce and control marine pollution from or through the atmosphere; but no further details are given as to how or by when this should be done. Four of the remaining UNEP Regional Seas agreements (the Caribbean, East African, South Pacific and West African Conventions) contain a similar provision, while the Red Sea Convention includes atmospheric emissions within the scope of its general obligation to reduce pollution from land-based sources. What this brief survey suggests is that, except possibly in the case of the Paris and Baltic Conventions, the various regional marine pollution conventions have so far done little in practice to curb pollution from atmospheric emissions. More has been done under the general agreements on atmospheric pollution, to which we now turn.

Of such agreements perhaps the most important is the UN Economic Commission for Europe's Convention on Long-Range Transboundary Air Pollution of 1979. Under this Convention, which was particularly inspired by the problems of 'acid rain', contracting parties are obliged gradually to reduce and prevent air pollution. The Convention itself contains no precise details as to how or when this shall be done. Instead a series of protocols has been elaborated setting specific emission targets. The first protocol, adopted in 1985, provided that State parties to it were to reduce sulphur dioxide emissions by thirty per cent of 1980 levels by 1993, a target that was in fact met by all but one of the twenty-one parties. This protocol has been followed by a further protocol, adopted in 1994, which requires substantially greater reductions in sulphur dioxide emissions, the figure varying from State to State, the overall figure being 50.8 per cent, to be achieved in three steps by 2010. A protocol of 1988 required its parties to stabilise emissions of nitrogen oxides (like sulphur dioxide, a source of acid rain) at 1980 levels by 1994, while a protocol of 1991 required its parties to reduce emissions of volatile organic compounds by thirty per cent of 1988 levels by 1999 or, for parties with relatively low emissions, to stabilise emissions by the same date. Further protocols to deal with other kinds of pollutants are currently under elaboration. Secondly, mention may be made of the Vienna Convention for the Protection of the Ozone Layer (1985) and its Montreal Protocol on Substances that deplete the Ozone Layer (1987). One of the consequences of depletion of the ozone layer is an increase in ultra-violet radiation which damages the phytoplankton near the ocean surface, thus reducing the sea's biological productivity. In the Antarctic there are already signs that this increase has damaged the eggs and larvae of fish and krill.[123] The Montreal Protocol sets a series of target

---

[123] *The Guardian*, 20 March 1997.

dates by which the production and consumption of various ozone-depleting substances, such as CFCs, halons and methyl bromide, are to be reduced and phased out completely. A third agreement is the 1963 Nuclear Test Ban Treaty (discussed in chapter seventeen), one of the consequences of which is the end of pollution of the sea by radioactive fallout from nuclear weapons testing in the atmosphere. Fourthly, the International Civil Aviation Organization has adopted various measures to reduce polluting emissions from aircraft. Finally, in the broader context of protecting the marine environment, the Framework Convention on Climate Change, adopted in 1992, is of some relevance. One of the widely predicted consequences of the unchecked growth in emissions of carbon dioxide and other greenhouse gases is an increase in average global temperatures, with the consequent melting of ice in polar regions and a significant rise in sea levels. The Convention requires its parties, especially developed States, gradually to stabilise and reduce emissions of carbon dioxide. Timetables and target figures for so doing are laid down in the Kyoto Protocol, adopted in December 1997. All the above measures, although not specifically concerned with marine pollution, are nevertheless contributing to its reduction, and more generally to protection of the marine environment.

Protection of special areas

In recent years the emphasis has shifted from concern with protecting the marine environment simply by trying to reduce and prevent pollution to a realisation of the need to take more positive measures to conserve marine life and habitats. This trend is illustrated to some extent in the Law of the Sea Convention itself, article 194(5) of which provides that measures taken under Part XII (on the protection and preservation of the marine environment) 'shall include those necessary to protect and preserve rare or fragile ecosystems as well as the habitat of depleted, threatened or endangered species and other forms of marine life', and is perhaps best exemplified in the protocols on specially protected areas attached to some of the UNEP Regional Seas Conventions.

The first of these UNEP protocols to be concluded was the Protocol on Mediterranean Specially Protected Areas, adopted in 1982. The Protocol applies to the territorial sea, and also to such 'wetlands or coastal areas' designated by each party (art. 2). Article 3 requires the parties to establish 'to the extent possible' protected areas in order to safeguard in particular 'sites of biological and ecological value; the genetic diversity, as well as satisfactory population levels, of species, and their breeding grounds and habitats; representative types of ecosystems, as well as ecological processes'. The parties are to 'endeavour to undertake the action necessary in order to protect' such areas (art. 3) and 'progressively take the measures required' in such areas (art. 7), which may include introducing a planning and management system for an area, prohibiting pollution, regulating the use of the area for navigation, fishing and sea-bed exploitation, prohibiting the destruction of plant and animal life, and taking any other measure aimed at safeguarding ecological and biological processes. In adopting all such measures the parties are to take into account the traditional activities of their local populations, but this must not be done in such a way as to endanger the maintenance of ecosystems protected under the Protocol or substantially reduce animal and plant populations. The parties are also to try to create a network of protected areas in the Mediterranean.

In 1995 a new Protocol concerning Specially Protected Areas and Biological Diversity in the Mediterranean was adopted, which, upon its entry into force, will replace the 1982 Protocol for parties to it. The new Protocol is similar to the 1982 Protocol as regards the establishment of specially protected areas, although more guidance is given on management plans, but it provides in addition for the establishment of Specially Protected Areas of Mediterranean Importance (SPAMIs). SPAMIs are to be created by a decision of the parties to the Protocol and are to include sites which are important for conserving biodiversity in the Mediterranean, contain ecosystems specific to the Mediterranean or habitats of endangered species, or are of special interest at the scientific, aesthetic, cultural or educational levels. SPAMIs may be created both within areas of national jurisdiction and on the high seas. In the latter case the protection and management measures applying in the SPAMI are those prescribed by the States proposing the SPAMI: other parties must comply with such measures but enforcement must be in accordance with international law. The other major change made by the new Protocol is an obligation on its parties to take action, both individually and co-operatively, to conserve fauna and flora. In particular they are to regulate and prohibit activities having adverse effects on endangered or threatened species or their habitats.

The protocols to the East African, South-East Pacific and Caribbean Conventions, adopted in 1985, 1989 and 1990 respectively, contain provisions on the establishment of protected areas very similar to those of the first Mediterranean Protocol. Unlike that Protocol, the East African and Caribbean Protocols go on to require their parties to conserve endangered or threatened species of fauna and flora listed in appendices to the Protocols and protect their habitats: this obligation also applies outside protected areas. Although none of the other five UNEP Conventions has a protocol on specially protected areas, both the West African Convention (in article 11) and the South Pacific Convention (article 14) contain a provision which reflects the essence of the Protocol system.

As regards regions outside the UNEP Regional Seas Programme, the 1992 Baltic Convention, unlike its 1974 predecessor, contains provisions on conservation. Article 15 provides that the parties, individually and jointly, are to take 'all appropriate measures' to conserve natural habitats and biodiversity, protect ecological processes, and ensure the sustainable use of natural resources. To this end the parties are to 'aim at adopting subsequent instruments containing appropriate guidelines and criteria'. In the North Sea the more recent North Sea Ministerial Declarations have introduced a concern for conservation. Thus, the

Third Declaration (1990) calls for an improvement in the protection of marine wildlife and the adoption of a common and co-ordinated approach to developing species and habitat protection.[124] This call is repeated, emphasised and developed in the Fourth Declaration (1995),[125] in response to which the parties to the 1992 Paris Convention have adopted an annex to that Convention dealing with the protection of species and habitats.

In connection with the regional conventions discussed above, mention may also be made of the Convention on Biological Diversity, adopted at the Rio Earth Summit in 1992. The Convention, which is very much of a framework nature, requires its parties *inter alia* to develop national strategies for the conservation and sustainable use of biological diversity, both on land and at sea, which should include, as appropriate, the establishment of protected areas, the protection of ecosystems and habitats, and the protection of threatened species. The Convention establishes a Conference of the Parties which is to meet periodically to try to put some flesh on the bare bones of the Convention. At its second meeting, held in 1995, the Conference decided that one of its priority areas should be marine biodiversity, and in the following year adopted the Jakarta Mandate on Marine and Coastal Biological Diversity, under which a strategy to preserve marine biodiversity is being elaborated, the elements of which are likely to include an emphasis on integrated marine and coastal area management and the precautionary approach.[126]

Finally in discussing protected areas, mention may be made of the work done by the IMO, although rather different from the approach of the regional conventions discussed above. In 1991 the IMO Assembly adopted a resolution containing a set of Guidelines for the Designation of Special Areas and the Identification of Particularly Sensitive Sea Areas.[127] Special areas are those which are the subject of stricter measures under the MARPOL Convention and were discussed earlier. Particularly Sensitive Sea Areas (PSSAs) are areas which need special protection through action by the IMO because of their significance for recognised ecological, socio-economic or scientific reasons and which may be vulnerable to damage by maritime activities. The kind of measures which might be taken for such areas include designation as a special area under MARPOL, the adoption of routeing measures including designation as an area to be avoided, compulsory pilotage, the adoption of a vessel traffic management system, special construction requirements and speed restrictions (on all of which see chapter thirteen). Measures for PSSAs lying beyond the territorial sea would need to be international in character, i.e., based on an existing treaty. The first PSSA to be designated by the IMO is the Great Barrier Reef Marine Park. This area, which straddles

---

[124] Para. 39 and Annex 5 of the Declaration, which is reproduced in Freestone and IJlstra, *op. cit.* in footnote 20, p. 3.

[125] Paras 1–9 of the Declaration, *loc. cit.* in footnote 20.

[126] See further M. M. Goote, 'The Jakarta Mandate on Marine and Coastal Biological Diversity', 12 *IJMCL* 377–89 (1997).

[127] Resolution A. 720 (17).

Australia's internal waters, territorial sea and EEZ, 'should' be avoided by all ships over 500 GRT and ships 'should act' in accordance with Australia's system of pilotage. A second PSSA, the Sabana-Camaguey archipelago off Cuba, was designated in 1997. The fact that no further PSSAs have been designated has raised some doubts over the utility of PSSAs. Areas requiring special protection are also dealt with in the Law of the Sea Convention. Article 211(6) provides that in its EEZ a coastal State may, where existing international rules are inadequate and after consulting the IMO, establish an area for which the coastal State may prescribe laws for the prevention of pollution from vessels 'implementing such international rules and standards or navigational practices as are made applicable, through the [IMO], for special areas'. Additional national measures may be adopted, provided that they do not lay down design, construction, manning or equipment standards for foreign vessels and provided that they have been approved by the IMO. The enforcement of such laws is governed by the general rules of the Convention relating to enforcement by a coastal State in its EEZ (see p. 349 above).

Other matters

Many of the more recent treaties, as well as some soft-law instruments such as Agenda 21, contain provisions other than those discussed above, which are important, if not quite so central, for the prevention of marine pollution and protection of the marine environment. For reasons of space only the barest summary of such provisions can be given. They include the requirement to carry out an environmental impact assessment before any development which could have a significant adverse impact on the marine environment (see, e.g., LOSC, art. 206; 1992 Baltic Convention, art. 7; amended Mediterranean Convention, art. 4(3)(c); Agenda 21, chapter 17.22); an obligation not to transfer pollution from one medium to another (see, e.g., LOSC, art. 195; 1992 Baltic Convention, art. 3(6); 1992 Paris Convention, art. 2(4)); a prohibition on introducing alien species into the marine environment (e.g., LOSC, art. 196; the UNEP Regional Seas protocols on protected areas); a call for integrated coastal zone management (e.g., amended Mediterranean Convention, art. 4(3)(e); Agenda 21, chapter 17A); and greater access for the public to environmental information and participation in regional commission meetings (e.g., 1992 Baltic Convention, art. 17; 1992 Paris Convention, arts 9 and 11; amended Mediterranean Convention, arts 15 and 20).

Conclusions

As this chapter shows, a vast amount of international law dealing with marine pollution has been adopted in recent years. With the exception of UNEP's

Regional Seas Programme, where some work still remains to be done, especially in the form of developing further protocols, particularly on land-based pollution, the time has now come for a period of consolidation as far as treaty-making is concerned. The international community should concentrate on four main tasks. First, it should seek to bring into force those conventions that are not yet in force and to increase the number of ratifications of all conventions. Secondly, it should ensure that the various regional commissions and meetings of the parties function effectively, and that where they have not yet done so they adopt the various measures required for the protection of the marine environment of the region concerned. This is especially necessary in the case of pollution from land-based sources. Thirdly, there is a need significantly to improve implementation of, and compliance with, existing international rules. This requires, amongst other things, increased technical and economic assistance to developing countries through such mechanisms as the IMO's Technical Co-Operation Programme and the World Bank's Global Environmental Facility, and the development of sophisticated non-compliance mechanisms for which the most recent regional marine pollution treaties call and models for which can be found in agreements in other areas, such as the Montreal Protocol on Substances that Deplete the Ozone Layer. Finally, there needs to be increased monitoring of the effects of existing rules on marine pollution, with the aim of seeing what deficiencies there are in the rules and whether further international legislative action is desirable. This assumes, of course, that there is agreement on what the aims of such action should be, which there may not be. Some may argue that the aim should be to prevent all pollution, others that the sea's assimilative capacity should not be exceeded, and yet others for some other goal.

Further reading

General

P. W. Birnie and A. E. Boyle, *International Law and the Environment* (Oxford, Clarendon), 1992, chapters 6–8.

R. B. Clark, *Marine Pollution* (Oxford, Clarendon), 4th edn, 1997.

E. Du Pontavice and P. Cordier, *La Mer et le Droit* (Paris, Presses Universitaires de France), 1984, chapter 3.

K. Hakapää, *Marine Pollution in International Law* (Helsinki, Suomalainen Tiedeakatemia), 1981.

D. M. Johnston (ed.), *The Environmental Law of the Sea* (Gland, IUCN), 1981.

H. Ringbom (ed.), *Competing Norms in the Law of Marine Environmental Protection* (The Hague, Kluwer), 1997.

P. H. Sand, *The Effectiveness of International Agreements* (Cambridge, Grotius), 1992, chapters IV and X.

B. D. Smith, *State Responsibility and the Marine Environment* (Oxford, Clarendon), 1988.

G. J. Timagenis, *International Control of Marine Pollution* (New York, Oceana), 1980.

United Nations, *The Law of the Sea: Protection and Preservation of the Marine Environment. Repertory of International Agreements relating to Sections 5 and 6 of Part XII of the United Nations Convention on the Law of the Sea* (New York, United Nations), 1990.

Pollution from ships

D. W. Abecassis and R. L. Jarashow, *Oil Pollution from Ships* (London, Stevens), 2nd edn, 1985.

W. Chao, *Pollution from the Carriage of Oil by Sea: Liability and Compensation* (The Hague, Kluwer), 1996.

T. L. McDorman, 'Port State enforcement: a comment on article 218 of the 1982 Law of the Sea Convention', 28 *JMLC* 305–22 (1997).

R. M. M'Gonigle and M. W. Zacher, *Pollution, Politics and International Law. Tankers at Sea* (Berkeley, Cal., University of California Press), 1979.

R. B. Mitchell, *Intentional Oil Pollution at Sea: Environmental Policy and Treaty Compliance* (Cambridge, Mass., MIT Press), 1994.

G. Plant, 'Legal environmental restraints upon navigation post-*Braer*', 10 *OGLTR* 245–68 (1992).

S. Z. Pritchard, *Oil Pollution Control* (London, Croom Helm), 1987.

C. Redgwell, 'The greening of salvage law', 14 *Marine Policy* 142–50 (1990).

Safer Ships, Cleaner Seas. Report of Lord Donaldson's Inquiry into the Prevention of Pollution from Merchant Shipping, London, 1994, Cm. 2560. For the British Government's response, see Cm. 2766 (1995).

R. W. Smith, *Exclusive Economic Zone Claims: An Analysis and Documents* (Dordecht, Nijhoff), 1986 [*Smith*].

P. C. Szasz, 'The Convention on the Liability of Operators of Nuclear Ships', 2 *JMLC* 541–69 (1971).

D. Wilkinson, 'Moving the boundaries of compensable environmental damage caused by marine oil spills: the effect of two new international protocols', 5 *Journal of Environmental Law* 71–90 (1993).

Dumping

P. Birnie, 'Are twentieth-century marine conservation conventions adaptable to twenty-first century goals and principles?', 12 *IJMCL* 488 at 514–31 (1997).

IMO, *The London Dumping Convention: The First Decade and Beyond* (London, IMO), 1991.

E. J. Molenaar, 'The 1996 Protocol to the 1972 London Convention', 12 *IJMCL* 396–403 (1997).

C. Nihoul, 'Dumping at sea', 16 *Ocean and Shoreline Management* 313–26 (1991).

R. Parmenter, 'Radioactive waste dumping at sea' in P. Sands (ed.), *Greening International Law* (London, Earthscan), 1993, pp. 140–58.

J. B. Skjaerseth, 'Towards the end of dumping in the North Sea: an example of effective international problem solving?', 16 *Marine Policy* 130–40 (1992).

United Nations, *The Law of the Sea: Pollution by Dumping* (New York, United Nations), 1985.

Pollution from sea-bed activities

S. Berge, J. M. Markussen and G. Vigerust, *Environmental Consequences of Deep Sea-bed Mining: Problem Areas and Regulations* (Lysaker, Fridtjof Nansen Institute), 1991.

B. A. Dubais, 'The 1976 London Convention on Civil Liability for Oil Pollution Damage from Offshore Operations', 9 *JMLC* 61–78 (1977).

S. M. Evans, 'Control of marine pollution generated by offshore oil and gas exploration and exploitation', 10 *Marine Policy* 258–70 (1986).

M. Gavouneli, *Pollution from Offshore Installations* (London, Kluwer), 1995.

T. IJlstra, 'Pollution from offshore installations: the Kuwait Protocol', 21 *Marine Pollution Bulletin* 8–10 (1990).

A. L. C. de Mestral, 'The prevention of pollution of the marine environment arising from offshore mining and drilling', 20 *Harvard International Law Journal* 469–518 (1979).

T. Scovazzi, 'The fifth protocol to the Barcelona Convention on the Protection of the Mediterranean', 10 *IJMCL* 542–5 (1995).

Pollution from land-based sources

S. Kuwabara, *The Legal Regime of the Protection of the Mediterranean against Pollution from Land-Based Sources* (Dublin, Tycooly), 1984.

B. Kwiatkowska, 'Marine pollution from land-based sources: current problems and prospects', 14 *ODIL* 315–35 (1984).

J. G. Lammers, *Pollution of International Watercourses* (The Hague, Nijhoff), 1984.

A. Nollkaemper, *The Legal Regime for Transboundary Water Pollution: Between Discretion and Consent* (Dordrecht, Nijhoff), 1993.

M. Qing-Nan, *Land-Based Marine Pollution* (London, Graham & Trotman), 1987.

Special Issue of *Marine Policy*, vol. 16 (1992), pp. 3–72.

Protection of special areas

D. Freestone, 'Protected areas and wildlife in the wider Caribbean', 5 *IJECL* 362–8 (1990).

——, 'The conservation of marine ecosystems under international law' in M. Bowman and C. Redgwell (eds), *International Law and the Conservation of Biological Diversity* (London, Kluwer), 1996, pp. 91–107.

K. Gjerde and D. Freestone (eds), 'Particularly Sensitive Sea Areas – an important environmental concept at a turning point', 9 *IJMCL* 431–578 (1994).

Regional pollution agreements

W. Anderson, *The Law of Caribbean Marine Pollution* (The Hague, Kluwer), 1997.

P. Ehlers, 'The Helsinki Convention 1992: improving the Baltic Sea environment', 8 *IJMCL* 191–214 (1993).

M. Fitzmaurice, *International Legal Problems of the Environmental Protection of the Baltic* (Dordrecht, Nijhoff), 1992.

D. Freestone and T. IJlstra (eds), *The North Sea: Perspectives on Regional Environmental Co-operation* (London, Graham & Trotman), 1990.

——, *The North Sea: Basic Legal Documents on Regional Environmental Co-operation* (Dordrecht, Graham & Trotman), 1991.

P. M. Haas, 'Protecting the Baltic and North Seas' in P. M. Haas, R. O. Keohane and M. A. Levy (eds), *Institutions for the Earth: Sources of Effective Environmental Protection* (Cambridge, Mass., MIT Press), 1993, pp. 133–82.

——, *Saving the Mediterranean. The Politics of International Environmental Co-operation* (New York, Columbia University Press), 1990.

E. Hey, T. IJlstra and A. Nollkaemper, 'The 1992 Paris Convention for the Protection of the Marine Environment of the North-East Atlantic: a critical analysis', 8 *IJMCL* 1–49 (1993).

The Oslo and Paris Commissions, *The First Decade* (London, Oslo and Paris Commissions), 1984.

S. Saetevik, *Environmental Co-operation between the North Sea States: Success or Failure?* (London, Belhaven), 1988.

P. H. Sand, *Marine Environment Law in the United Nations Enviroment Programme* (London, Tycooly), 1988.

T. Scovazzi, 'The recent developments in the "Barcelona system" for the protection of the Mediterranean against pollution', 11 *IJMCL* 95–100 (1996).

Special Issues on 'Toxics reduction programmes in the North Sea and Baltic Sea: a comparative perspective', 13 *IJMCL* 299–471 (1998).

16

Marine scientific research and the transfer of technology

Introduction

Marine scientific research serves a wide variety of purposes. Adequate and effective scientific research is a basic precondition for the rational exploitation of the sea's resources. For example, the harvesting of a particular stock of fish at levels which do not lead to overfishing can be achieved only if there is constant monitoring of the size of and recruitment to the stock. Exploitation of offshore oil is possible only where the necessary geological research has been carried out to locate oilfields. The study of waves, currents, the sea bed and weather helps to make navigation safer. Furthermore, the preservation of the marine environment is also dependent on scientific research – first, to discover what substances cause what kinds of harm to the sea and its living organisms, and, secondly, to find ways in which pollution can be abated or eliminated. Marine research may also be more or less directly linked to military uses of the sea: for example, by trying to improve the ability to detect submarines. Finally, marine scientific research may also help to tell us more about the earth generally. Thus, it is study of the sea floor which has largely prompted the theory that the earth's outer layer consists of a number of large, moving plates, while studies of the oceans' circulation are an important part of research into global climate change.

This chapter begins by examining the scope of the competence to conduct marine scientific research. It then goes on to deal with the legal status of installations used in conducting research and with international co-operation in marine research. Finally, the chapter considers a question separate from, but related to, marine scientific research: the transfer of marine technology.

Scope of the competence to conduct marine scientific research

Until the middle of the twentieth century legal controls on the conduct of marine scientific research were not perceived to be necessary, and indeed the law of the sea literature up to this time contains virtually no mention of scientific research. This may be explained partly by the generally prevailing attitude that scientific research should be free of governmental controls, and partly by the modest scale and limited practical application of marine scientific research. It is the great increase in marine research since the Second World War, together with a better appreciation of its practical application to resource and military purposes, that has led the international community to introduce controls on marine scientific research, first in the Geneva Conventions and latterly, and more extensively, in the Law of the Sea Convention.

The 1958 rules

High seas

Under the Geneva regime marine research was generally regarded as a freedom of the high seas, even though not mentioned in the list of freedoms in article 2 of the High Seas Convention. However, this list was expressly stated not to be exhaustive, and in its commentary on the draft article which eventually became article 2, the International Law Commission specifically referred to marine research as an example of a freedom not mentioned in the article. Furthermore, scientific research has been conducted on the high seas by the vessels of many different States for the past century or more without giving rise to any recorded protest.

Territorial sea and internal waters

The restrictions on marine research laid down in the Geneva Conventions related to research in the territorial sea and on the continental shelf. As regards the former, the territorial sea was subject to the sovereignty of the coastal State, and the only right which other States enjoyed there was the right of innocent passage (see chapter four). It therefore followed that research in the territorial sea was permissible only where the coastal State had given its consent and subject to any conditions which it had laid down. The one possible exception would have been if, during the course of exercising its right of innocent passage through the territorial sea, a vessel had engaged in activities incidental to its passage through the territorial sea which might also have been regarded as 'research'. The taking of hydrographic soundings, for example, might have been regarded both as a prudent safety measure incidental to passage and as research into the hydrography of the sea bed. However, this question was controversial, and it may be that 'research' would always take the vessel outside the concept of 'passage'. Even if a vessel could have engaged in research while exercising the right of innocent passage, the coastal State would have been able to prescribe conditions regulating such research (see TSC, art. 17). Although the Geneva Conventions said nothing about internal waters, it is clear from the legal status of such waters in customary international law (see chapter three) that research could be undertaken there only with the consent of the coastal State.

Continental shelf

Research on the continental shelf was dealt with by article 5 of the Continental Shelf Convention. Article 5(1) began by stating that the 'exploration of the continental shelf and the exploitation of its natural resources must not . . . result in any interference with fundamental oceanographic or other scientific research carried out with the intention of open publication'. This broad principle was, however, considerably qualified by article 5(8), which read:

> The consent of the coastal State shall be obtained in respect of any research concerning the continental shelf and undertaken there. Nevertheless, the coastal State shall not normally withhold its consent if the request is submitted by a qualified institution with a view to purely scientific research into the physical or biological characteristics of the continental shelf, subject to the proviso that the coastal State shall have the right, if it so desires, to participate or to be represented in the research, and that in any event the results shall be published.

The result was that both pure and applied research on the continental shelf required the consent of the coastal State, but in the case of the former consent should not 'normally' be withheld if the various conditions as to participation, publication, etc. were complied with. While the broad intent of article 5(8) was reasonably obvious, the details of its drafting gave rise to many difficulties. For instance, two interpretations were possible of the phrase 'research concerning the continental shelf and undertaken there'. One was that it meant that consent was required only where the research both concerned the continental shelf and was physically undertaken on the shelf, i.e., on the sea bed: the other was that consent was required both for research concerning the continental shelf – whether conducted on the sea bed or in the superjacent waters – and for research conducted on the sea bed, whether it concerned the continental shelf or not. As to which interpretation was correct, the *travaux préparatoires* of the Continental Shelf Convention gave little guidance, while the practice of parties to the Convention,[1] though not conclusive, appeared to support the second interpretation. Whichever interpretation was right, it is clear that consent was not required for research in the superjacent waters which did not concern the continental shelf: such research came under the high-seas freedom of research and was not subject to coastal State interference, as article 5(1) made clear.

The second sentence of article 5(8) also raised a number of difficulties. The distinction it made between pure and applied research was not necesssarily easy to apply in practice. What might have begun and been intended as 'pure' research might, once the research had actually been undertaken and its results analysed, have turned out to have significant practical implications. Furthermore, the article gave no guidance as to what might have been 'normal' situations in which consent to pure research should have been given. There were further problems. What was a 'qualified' institution? At what stages in a project should

---

[1] Discussed in Soons, *op. cit.* in 'Further reading' under 'Competence to conduct marine scientific research', pp. 66–82.

coastal State participation have begun and ended? The imprecision of the Continental Shelf Convention's definition of the outer limit of the continental shelf (see chapter eight) also added to the uncertainties surrounding marine research on the continental shelf.

Exclusive fishing zone

A further restriction on scientific research arose in customary international law after the adoption of the Geneva Conventions with the development of the concept of the exclusive fishing zone (see chapter fourteen). The majority of States which claimed an exclusive fishing zone also claimed the competence to regulate fisheries research within that zone where such research involved the taking of fish. The lack of protests against such claims suggests that that limitation on marine research became part of customary international law. On the other hand, no States prior to UNCLOS III appear to have claimed the competence to regulate fisheries research in their exclusive fishing zones where such research did not involve the taking of fish, although there was in the past a certain amount of discussion amongst writers as to whether such a claim would have been permissible.

The controls on research introduced by the exclusive fishing zone and article 5(8) of the Continental Shelf Convention (which is often thought also to have represented customary international law) appear in practice to have led to a definite restriction of marine scientific research. A study of requests made between 1972 and 1978 by US vessels to undertake research in areas under other States' jurisdiction shows that seven per cent of such requests were rejected by the coastal State concerned – in nearly half these cases no reason was given – and a further twenty-one per cent of the requests were subject to inordinate (and therefore costly) delays.[2]

The Law of the Sea Convention

UNCLOS III was faced with much stronger demands for controls over marine scientific research than the Geneva Conference had been. These demands came chiefly from the developing countries and were inspired by two principal factors. First, the developing countries felt that they would be unable to benefit fully from the right to exploit the resources off their coasts which the introduction of the 200-mile EEZ would give them unless they had control over the research in those waters that might have application to resource exploitation. The second factor was the suspicion among at least some developing countries that research vessels, particularly those of the major military powers, were often used for espionage: these suspicions had been fuelled by incidents like that in 1968 involving the *Pueblo,* where a US ship posing as a research vessel was found by

[2] W. S. Wooster, 'Research in troubled waters. US research vessel clearance experience 1972–1978', 9 *ODIL* 219–39 (1981).

North Korea, allegedly inside its twelve-mile territorial sea, engaged in spying. The demands for greater controls over marine scientific research were resisted first and foremost by the scientific community. They had found the existing controls, which had begun to be applied from the mid-1960s onwards with the entry into force of the Continental Shelf Convention and the development of the exclusive fishing zone, burdensome, and feared that further controls would lead to proposed research projects being refused or being made subject to undesirable conditions or long bureaucratic delays. They argued that scientific research benefited all mankind, and that the unity of the ocean demanded that its study be restricted by the fewest man-made boundaries. These concerns of the scientists were taken up at UNCLOS by the developed States, which are responsible for the overwhelming proportion of marine research at present being conducted. Nevertheless, the demands of the developing countries for greater controls over marine scientific research have largely been met by the Law of the Sea Convention, although these controls are to some extent more precisely, and therefore more narrowly, formulated than those of the Geneva Conventions. The major areas subject to controls are the EEZ and continental shelf, but the Law of the Sea Convention also makes changes to the position adopted by the Geneva Conventions for other maritime zones.

High seas

As far as the high seas are concerned, marine research is now specifically mentioned as a freedom of the high seas (LOSC, art. 87), and all States may conduct research there (art. 257). However, it must be borne in mind that, in contrast to the Geneva regime, under the Law of the Sea Convention the sea bed and subsoil of the high seas beyond the continental shelf are now the international sea bed area. All States have the right to engage in research in the Area (LOSC, art. 256), provided that it is carried out 'exclusively for peaceful purposes and for the benefit of mankind as a whole' (art. 143(1)). A further condition is that set out in article 143(3), which requires States to 'promote international co-operation in marine scientific research in the Area by . . . effectively disseminating the results of research and analysis when available, through the [International Sea Bed] Authority or other international channels when appropriate'. Where 'research' moves on to the stage of 'prospecting' or 'exploring' it is no longer unrestricted, but becomes subject to the provisions of Annex III (see chapter twelve). The Convention contains no precise guidance as to how 'research', 'prospecting' or 'exploring' are to be distinguished.

Territorial sea

The basic principle that research in the territorial sea may be conducted only with the consent of, and subject to the conditions laid down by, the coastal State is affirmed by the Law of the Sea Convention (art. 245). Although not specifically stated in the Convention, the same principle applies to research in archipelagic waters: this follows from the legal status of such waters (see chapter six). Unlike the Geneva Convention, the Law of the Sea Convention makes it clear that research may not be undertaken while a ship is exercising a right of innocent passage: any research or survey activities render the passage non-innocent (LOSC, art. 19). Nevertheless, the problem of distinguishing between prohibited 'research' and permissible acts incidental to passage, which we noted above, is not resolved by the Convention. It is left to pragmatism and the good sense of the States concerned. A vessel engaged in transit passage through straits or archipelagic sea lanes passage through archipelagic waters may not carry out any research or survey activity without the prior authorisation of the strait or archipelagic State (LOSC, arts 40, 54).

EEZ and continental shelf

The most important provisions of the Law of the Sea Convention dealing with controls over marine scientific research are those relating to research in the EEZ and on the continental shelf, contained in articles 246 to 255. These provisions adopt the same basic approach as article 5(8) of the Continental Shelf Convention. Thus all research in the EEZ and on the continental shelf requires the consent of the coastal State (LOSC, art. 246(2)).[3] Like the Continental Shelf Convention, the Law of the Sea Convention seeks in essence to distinguish between pure and applied research, although nowhere does the Convention in fact use these precise terms. Unlike the Continental Shelf Convention, however, an attempt is made to define each of the two categories of research. Applied research is that which is of 'direct significance for the exploration and exploitation of natural resources'. Such research clearly impinges directly upon the interests of the coastal State in exercising its sovereign rights over its natural resources. The same is true of research which is particularly intrusive upon the coastal State's maritime zones. For that reason two other categories of research are assimilated to the archetypical 'applied research': first, research which involves drilling into the continental shelf, the use of explosives or the introduction of harmful substances into the marine environment; and second, research which involves the construction, operation and use of artificial islands, installations and structures (LOSC, art. 246(5)). For convenience we treat all these classes of research under the heading of 'applied research'. What will be labelled here as pure research is research which is carried out 'exclusively for peaceful

---

[3] The Convention contains no definition of 'marine scientific research'. In the view of many writers such research is to be distinguished from hydrographic surveying activities. Since the Convention is silent on the question of such activities in the EEZ (unlike the position in the territorial sea, as we have seen), and since such activities can be regarded as embracing the safety of navigation, they should be regarded as an internationally lawful use of the sea related to the freedom of navigation and therefore permissible for all States in the EEZ by virtue of art. 58 of the Convention. See Soons, *op. cit.*, p. 157, and J. A. Roach and R. W. Smith, *United States Responses to Excessive Maritime Claims* (The Hague, Nijhoff), 2nd edn, 1996, pp. 425–7, 446–8. More controversially, the USA takes the view that military surveys are permissible under the same principle: Roach and Smith, pp. 448–9, and see chapter nineteen.

purposes and in order to increase scientific knowledge of the marine environment for the benefit of all mankind' (LOSC, art. 246(3)).

In the case of pure research, consent must 'in normal circumstances' be given. In view of the difficulties that have been faced by marine scientists in the past, it is important to note that coastal States 'shall establish rules and procedures ensuring that such consent will not be delayed or denied unreasonably' (LOSC, art. 246(3)). In the case of applied research, the coastal State has a complete discretion whether to give its consent or not. It also has the same discretion when the researcher has provided inaccurate advance information as to the nature and objectives of the project or if the researcher has outstanding obligations to the coastal State from a prior research project (LOSC, art. 246(5)). It is important to note that any dispute over whether a coastal State has improperly withheld consent is not subject to any form of compulsory third-party settlement except compulsory conciliation under Annex V of the Convention (for details see chapter nineteen): but even there the coastal State's discretion to withhold consent for applied research or in the other circumstances listed in article 246(5) may not be called into question (LOSC, art. 297(2)). In certain circumstances – where the proposed research project is to be carried out by an international organisation of which the coastal State is a member or where the coastal State does not respond within four months of being furnished with the necessary advance information by the researching State – consent is implied (LOSC, arts 247, 252).

Those wishing to undertake research in a foreign State's EEZ or on its continental shelf are subject to a number of obligations. First, they must provide the coastal State with specified information about the proposed project at least six months in advance (LOSC, art. 248). Secondly, they must allow the coastal State to participate or be represented in the project (LOSC, art. 249(1)(a)). Thirdly, they must provide coastal States with the results of the research and ensure that such results are made internationally available as well as assisting the coastal State, if requested, in assessing and interpreting the results and data of the research (LOSC, arts 249(1)(b) to (e)). Failure to comply with these obligations entitles the coastal State to suspend the research or require its cessation (LOSC, art. 253). In the case of pure research, it would seem from the wording of articles 246(1) and 249(2) that the coastal State is not entitled to lay down any conditions other than those just mentioned. In the case of applied research, on the other hand, article 249(2) provides that the list of conditions laid down in article 249(1) is without prejudice to the conditions which the coastal State may prescribe for applied research in its EEZ. Finally, whether research be pure or applied, it must be so conducted that it does not unjustifiably interfere with the legitimate activities of the coastal State (LOSC, art. 246(8)).

Compared with the Continental Shelf Convention, the distinction drawn in the Law of the Sea Convention between pure and applied research is much clearer, and should give rise to fewer difficulties as to the types of research projects for which consent should normally be given. The obligation on the coastal State not to delay unreasonably in giving consent and the provisions on implied consent are also an improvement on the Continental Shelf Convention, as are the provisions specifying the conditions to which pure research may be subject and the amount of notice required. On the other hand, what is meant by 'normal circumstances' is little clearer than the corresponding phrase in the Continental Shelf Convention, except that article 246(4) stipulates that 'normal circumstances' can exist in spite of the absence of diplomatic relations between the coastal State and the researching State. The implication is that circumstances are 'normal' except where there is hostility or serious tension between the coastal State and the researching State.[4]

A further problem concerns research carried out in the water column above the continental shelf where the latter extends beyond 200 miles. It is not clear whether coastal State consent is required where the research is directed at the sea bed (cf. the similar problem raised by the Continental Shelf Convention, discussed above). Article 246(2) simply speaks of coastal State consent for research '*on* the continental shelf' (emphasis added), which may suggest that consent is only required for research physically taking place on the sea floor. This suggestion is supported by article 257 which provides that all States have the right to conduct 'research *in* the water column beyond the limits' of the EEZ (emphasis added). Whatever be the correct interpretation of article 246(2), whether it is that consent is required for research taking place in the water column directed at the sea bed, or whether consent is required only for research physically taking place on the sea bed, the potential restrictions on research are lessened by article 246(6). The latter provides that a coastal State may not withhold its consent for the carrying out of research of direct significance for the exploration and exploitation of natural resources 'on' its continental shelf beyond the 200-mile limit outside those areas it has designated as areas in which exploitation or detailed exploratory operations are to take place. Within such areas the problem of the meaning of the phrase 'on' the continental shelf will, of course, be more acute.

It will be recalled from chapter nine that some 100 or so States have so far claimed an EEZ. These claims vary widely in how they deal with marine scientific research. A few States claim no jurisdiction over research. This is notably the case with the USA: however, it has said that it will recognise the claims of other States which are 'exercised reasonably in a manner consistent with international law'.[5] Secondly, many States (in fact the majority) claim simply 'jurisdiction' or 'exclusive jurisdiction' over research, or 'exclusive jurisdiction to authorise, regulate and control scientific research', with no further elaboration. Thirdly, the legislation of some States (such as Côte d'Ivoire,[6]

---

[4] See further B. H. Oxman, 'The Third United Nations Conference on the Law of the Sea: the Eighth Session (1979)', 74 *AJIL* 1 (1980) at 26.

[5] Statement by the President of the USA, 10 March 1983. 22 *ILM* 464 (1983).

[6] Law No. 77–926. art. 6. United Nations, *The Law of the Sea: National Legislation, Regulations and Supporting Documents on Marine Scientific Research in Areas under National Jurisdiction* (New York, United Nations), 1989 (hereafter UN (1989)), p. 81; *Smith, op. cit.* in 'Further reading', p. 241.

Honduras,[7] Indonesia,[8] Morocco[9] and Tanzania[10]) requires the consent of the coastal State to be given for research in the EEZ, but contains no further details. Somewhat more detailed is the legislation of Bulgaria,[11] Gabon,[12] Ghana,[13] Iceland,[14] Maldives,[15] Mexico,[16] Portugal,[17] Romania,[18] Senegal[19] and Venezuela,[20] which broadly reflects the basic outline of the Convention regime. The only States which so far have adopted legislation which deals fully with all (or nearly all) the matters in the Convention are Malaysia,[21] Poland,[22] Russia,[23] Spain[24] and

[7] Decree No. 921 of 13 June 1980 on the Utilisation of Marine Natural Resources, art. 1(C). UN (1989), p. 133; *Smith, op. cit.*, p. 205.

[8] Act No. 5 of 18 October 1983 on the Indonesian Exclusive Economic Zone, art. 7. UN (1989), p. 138; *Smith, op cit.*, p. 227. The accompanying 'elucidation of the Act' provides for implied consent along the line of the LOSC regime.

[9] Act No. 1–81, art. 5. UN (1989), p. 177; *Smith, op. cit.*, p. 303.

[10] Territorial Sea and Exclusive Economic Zone Act, 1989, ss. 9 and 10. 13 *LOSB* 38 (1989).

[11] Decree No. 2210 of 1 September 1987 on Law on the Maritime Spaces of the People's Republic of Bulgaria, arts 55–7. UN (1989), p. 51.

[12] Law No. 9/84 establishing an Exclusive Economic Zone of 200 Nautical Miles, and Note on Rules governing Marine Scientific Research Activites. UN (1989), p. 107.

[13] Maritime Zones (Delimitation) Law 1986, and Information required for Permission to allow Foreign Research Ships to carry out Research in the Ghanaian Exclusive Economic Zone. UN (1989), p. 119.

[14] Law No. 41 of 1 June 1979, arts 9 and 10. UN (1989), p. 134; *Smith, op. cit.*, p. 209.

[15] Regulations for Marine Scientific Research in the Maritime Zones of the Republic of Maldives, 1988. UN (1989), p. 161. It is, however, questionable whether all of the conditions applied to foreign researchers are compatible with the Law of the Sea Convention. Like the legislation of Gabon, Ghana, Mexico, Portugal and Senegal, the Maldives regulations do not distinguish between pure and applied research.

[16] Mexican Federal Act relating to the Sea of 8 January 1986, art. 22, and Requirements applicable to Marine Scientific Research Projects carried out by Foreign Nationals in the Territorial Sea, on the Continental Shelf and in the Exclusive Exconomic Zone of Mexico, 1976. UN (1989), p. 172.

[17] Decree Law No. 52/85 of 1 March 1985. UN (1989), p. 217.

[18] Decree No. 142 of 25 April 1986, art. 10. UN (1989), p. 221.

[19] Note on Conditions governing Maritime Scientific Research in Senegal, 1988. UN (1989), p. 229.

[20] Act establishing an Exclusive Economic Zone along the Coasts of the Mainland and Islands of 26 July 1978, art. 9 and Directive No. MD-EMC-D1-004–79 of 1 February 1980. UN (1989), p. 284.

[21] Exclusive Economic Zone Act 1984, ss. 16–20. UN (1989), p. 158.

[22] Act concerning the Maritime Areas of the Polish Republic and the Marine Administration, 21 March 1991, arts 28–32. 21 *LOSB* 66 (1992).

[23] The first of this legislation is in fact that of the former Soviet Union: see Decree on the Economic Zone of 28 February 1984, arts 8–11, and Decree of 19 December 1985. UN (1989), p. 258; 1 *IJECL* 386 (1986). See also the accompanying article by E. Franckx, 'Marine scientific research and the new USSR legislation on the economic zone', in *ibid.*, pp. 367–83. The Soviet legislation has now been supplemented by the Federal Law on the Continental Shelf of the Russian Federation, 1995, arts 23–30, 32 *LOSB* 59 (1996).

[24] Royal Decree No. 799/1981 of 27 February 1981 concerning Regulations Applicable to Marine Scientific Research Activities in Areas under Spanish Jurisdiction. UN (1989), p. 235.

Ukraine,[25] whose legislation follows very closely the Convention's provisions for the most part. On the other hand, the legislation of two States diverges significantly from the Law of the Sea Convention. Trinidad and Tobago stipulates that the results of research done on its continental shelf are its property and may be published only with its express consent, that research data and specimens are its property, and that its consent is required for the participation of researchers who are not its nationals or nationals of the flag State of the research vessel.[26] Secondly, Brazil's legislation provides that authorisation for research (whether pure or applied, it seems) will only be given if the research 'contributes to Brazil's scientific and technological development' and derives from contracts with Brazilian institutions, except where no such institution has shown an interest in entering into such contracts: in addition, the information required from, and conditions which may be imposed on, foreign researchers are considerably more onerous than is permitted under the Convention.[27] Finally, it may be of interest to note that since the adoption of the Convention Italy has issued regulations for research on its continental shelf (Italy does not claim an EEZ) which are broadly in accordance with the Convention, except that there is no provision for implied consent.[28] In addition, a number of other States, probably influenced more by the Continental Shelf Convention than the Law of the Sea Convention, require consent for research activities relating to their continental shelves.

With the entry into force of, and increasing participation in, the Law of the Sea Convention, the question of what represents customary international law concerning marine research is of decreasing importance. Nevertheless, the above practice, nearly all of which pre-dates the entry into force of the Convention, supports the conclusion that the principle of coastal State consent for research in the EEZ and on the continental shelf is now part of customary international law. However, many of the details of the Convention regime, such as the period of notice and implied consent, are not now, and are probably incapable of becoming, part of customary international law because of the paucity of State practice and because they do not seem to have the fundamentally norm-creating character necessary for an emergent rule of customary law. In addition, the question of opposability (see chapter one) will be crucial in determining the validity of individual claims.

In addition to these EEZ claims, most of the twenty or so States which still claim or in the past have claimed a 200-mile exclusive fishing zone claim the

[25] Law of Ukraine on the Exclusive (Marine) Economic Zone of 16 May 1995, arts 13–15. 30 *LOSB* 49 (1996).
[26] Guidelines for the Conduct of Marine Scientific Research in Areas under the Jurisdiction of the Republic of Trinidad and Tobago. UN (1989), p. 254.
[27] Decree No. 96,000 of 2 May 1988, arts 2, 5, 15 and 16. UN (1989), p. 42. This Decree, which applies to the continental shelf and 'waters under Brazilian jurisdiction', was adopted before Brazil reduced its territorial sea from 200 to 12 miles and established a 200-mile EEZ. It is not clear if the legislation applies to the EEZ.
[28] Note of 9 July 1984 by the Ministry of Foreign Affairs on Regulation of Scientific Research by Foreign Vessels in Areas under Italian Jurisdiction. UN (1989), p. 140.

jurisdiction to control fisheries research in the zone where it involves the taking of fish. Although the validity of such claims may again turn on the issue of opposability in individual cases, it is likely that in general such claims now represent a rule of customary international law, first, because there have been no protests to such claims (as far as we are aware), and secondly, because similar claims made in respect of twelve-mile exclusive fishing zones were – as we have seen – generally accepted.

There does not seem to be much information publicly available about the practical operation of the consent regime now established by most coastal States. One of the few public studies made shows that in the case of the USA between 1983 and 1995 the State Department processed over 1,600 requests for US vessels to conduct marine scientific research in the territorial seas and EEZs of 140 States. Of these requests, only 43 were denied and a further 148 were cancelled, mainly because of non-compliance by the researchers with the Convention's requirements. The main problems faced by the USA include delays in responding to its requests, last-minute denial of permission, requiring data to be held in confidence, and slow or incomplete staffing and co-ordination among interested coastal State bureaucracies.[29]

This experience lends support to the conclusion which can be drawn from the survey of State practice above, namely that many States do not yet have, or at least until very recently did not have, the necessary detailed legislation or administrative procedures in place to operate properly the consent regime provided for in the Convention, with the consequent problems that this poses for both foreign scientists and the authorities of coastal States. With the entry into force of, and increasing participation in, the Law of the Sea Convention, this problem may be expected gradually to lessen. It may also lessen as a result of the fact that in 1991, on the basis of the advice of a group of technical experts, the UN published a guide (see the reference in 'Further reading') recommending how the consent regime of the Convention should be implemented, including suggested forms for making requests to conduct research and for coastal States' response to such requests. In addition, at the regional level the Baltic Marine Environment Protection Commission has recommended the Baltic States to simplify and speed up procedures for dealing with applications for research, while the EC Commission has made proposals for similar action to be taken by EC Member States.[30]

---

[29] Roach and Smith, *op. cit.* in footnote 3, pp. 438–41. For an earlier study of US experience, in the period 1979–85, see J. A. Knauss and M. H. Katsouros, 'Recent experience of the United States in conducting marine scientific research in coastal State exclusive economic zones', in T. A. Clingan (ed.). *The Law of the Sea: What Lies Ahead?* (Honolulu, Hawaii, Law of the Sea Institute), 1988, pp. 297–309. For the difficulties experienced by German research vessels, see Plasmann and Röben, *op. cit.* in 'Further reading' under 'Competence to conduct marine scientific research', pp. 376–85.

[30] U. Jenisch, 'Jurisdictional aspects of marine scientific research in the Baltic Sea', 10 *IJMCL* 106 (1995), at 111–12. See also A. H. A. Soons, 'The regulation of marine scientific research by the European Community and its Member States', 23 *ODIL* 259 (1992) at 273–5.

Furthermore, the International Council for the Exploration of the Sea (ICES) (further discussed at pp. 416 below) in 1984 adopted a resolution in which it noted that 'research has occasionally been impeded by bureaucratic procedures' and called on its Member States to 'simplify relevant procedures to the extent possible, for example by keeping the time required for advance notification to a minimum, and by considering the use of a standard clearance information form'.[31]

General principles governing marine research

Wherever marine research be conducted – whether on the high seas or in one of the coastal State's jurisdictional zones – it must conform to certain broad principles laid down by the Law of the Sea Convention. Under article 240, marine scientific research must be conducted 'exclusively for peaceful purposes'; with appropriate scientific methods and means compatible with the Convention; so as not unjustifiably to interfere with other legitimate uses of the sea; and in compliance with all relevant regulations adopted in conformity with the Convention. A further general principle is that contained in article 241, which provides that 'marine scientific research activities shall not constitute the legal basis for any claim to any part of the marine environment or its resources'. Only the first of these principles is likely to raise problems. It may suggest that research primarily intended to have military application is prohibited. However, article 240 should be read in the context of the Convention as a whole. Article 88 of the Convention, it will be recalled, reserves high seas for 'peaceful purposes', and the provisions governing other maritime zones have what are in effect similar prescriptions. Accordingly, article 240(a) is probably best understood as a restatement in the context of marine scientific research of a principle which would in any event be applicable by virtue of other provisions of the Convention. It follows that article 240(a) should be interpreted in the same sense as the 'peaceful purposes' requirement in article 88. As we note below (see chapter seventeen), that provision is generally understood, in line with the terms of article 301 of the Convention ('Peaceful uses of the sea'), to forbid no more than the use of the seas for aggressive action in violation of international law.

An assessment of the LOSC regime

The Law of the Sea Convention, by adopting a twelve-mile territorial sea and the concept of archipelagic waters where research is entirely subject to coastal State consent, and by imposing coastal State controls on research in the EEZ and on the continental shelf, has, in comparison with the Geneva Conventions and previous customary international law, considerably increased the areas of sea where marine scientific research is restricted and controlled. These areas, moreover, are those which are of the greatest interest to marine scientists and where

[31] Text of the Resolution given in a letter of 15 July 1987 to the authors from the General Secretary of ICES. A standard form has in fact been adopted: see Soons, *op. cit.* in footnote 30, p. 273.

consequently most marine scientific research takes place. On the other hand, the coastal State's controls in the EEZ and on the continental shelf are somewhat more clearly formulated than those of the Continental Shelf Convention, but there may still be scope for a coastal State unreasonably to deny or delay foreign research. Whether coastal State controls will operate so as not to restrict marine scientific research unreasonably still, it seems, remains to be seen. Certainly such controls add to the work of marine scientists in terms of complying with notification procedures, providing access for coastal State scientists to projects and often instructing them as to the details and methodology of the project. These factors will almost certainly increase the cost of marine scientific research. Coastal State controls may also prove to be an inhibiting factor in carrying out the research necessary for co-operative marine management, notably as regards fish stocks which migrate between EEZs and/or between EEZs and the high seas and the protection of the marine environment from pollution.

The scientific research provisions of the Law of the Sea Convention may to some extent soon become obsolete. A significant and increasing proportion of marine scientific research is carried out by remote sensing from satellites. This is a form of research for which the Convention makes no provision, and it is not clear whether it is legally possible, or feasible in practice, for a coastal State to require consent for such research in relation to its maritime zones.

The legal status of research installations

While much marine scientific research is carried out on ships, such research also often involves the emplacement of fixed structures, buoys and other floating objects in the sea, and more recently the use of unmanned submersibles. The legal status of such objects, often referred to as ocean data acquisition systems (ODAS), began to be studied by the Intergovernmental Oceanographic Commission (IOC) of UNESCO in collaboration with the IMO in the 1960s. In 1969 they published a report on 'Legal Problems associated with Ocean Data Acquisition Systems (ODAS)'.[32] A preliminary draft convention was produced in the following year[33] and discussed at a diplomatic conference held in 1972. The conference decided to defer finalisation and adoption of the draft until after the conclusion of UNCLOS III, although it was agreed to publish three of the annexes to the draft Convention (on notification; marking and signals; and construction arrangements and other safety provisions) as voluntary guidelines for national measures. In the event many of the matters relating to the legal status of ODAS dealt with by the draft convention are now covered by the Law of the Sea Convention.

[32] IOC Technical Series No. 5 (1969).
[33] Doc. SC/IOC EG-1 (IV)/12, 17 September 1970, Annex III.

The central provision of the Law of the Sea Convention is article 258. It reads:

> The deployment and use of any type of scientific research installations or equipment in any area of the marine environment shall be subject to the same conditions as are prescribed in this Convention for the conduct of marine scientific research in any such area.

The effect of this provision would seem to be as follows. In the territorial sea and archipelagic waters the deployment and use of research installations and equipment will require the consent of the coastal State. It follows from the legal nature of these waters that such installations and equipment will be subject to the jurisdiction of the coastal State. In the EEZ and on the continental shelf the consent of the coastal State will again be required. Since the definition of applied research in the EEZ and on the continental shelf includes research which involves the construction and operation of 'artificial islands, installations and structures', the deployment and use of research installations and equipment which take the form of 'artificial islands', 'installations' or 'structures' will be subject to the discretionary powers a coastal State enjoys in respect of applied research, regardless of the kind of research which is to be carried out from such research installations and equipment. It further follows from articles 60 and 80 that a coastal State will have jurisdiction over such research installations and equipment. No guidance is given in the Convention as to the characteristics, in terms of size, permanence and so on, that an object must possess in order to qualify as an 'installation' or 'structure'.[34]

Where the research installations and equipment do not take the form of 'artificial islands', 'installations' or 'structures'– and floating buoys and other floating objects probably come into this category – but such objects are used for applied research, the coastal State has a discretion to refuse their deployment. Under article 249(2) the coastal State may impose such conditions on the deployment of these types of ODAS as it sees fit, and this provision may well be broad enough to give the coastal State jurisdiction over such objects. On the other hand, where floating research objects are used for pure research, the coastal State should not normally withhold its consent to the deployment and use of such objects. There would appear to be no provision giving the coastal State jurisdiction over such objects once consent has been given, at least provided that nothing is done that entitles the coastal State to exercise its rights under article 253 to suspend or order the cessation of research. On the other hand, the emplacing State, while it would presumably have legislative jurisdiction over the object on a quasi-territorial basis analogous to flag State legislative jurisdiction

---

[34] See further T. Treves, 'Military installations, structures and devices on the seabed', 74 *AJIL* 808–57 (1980); R. Zedalis, 'Military installations, structures and devices on the seabed: a response', *ibid.*, vol. 75, pp. 926–33 (1981); and T. Treves, 'Reply', *ibid.*, pp. 933–5.

over ships, would have no enforcement jurisdiction in the coastal State's EEZ or on its continental shelf because there is no provision of the Law of the Sea Convention which gives it such jurisdiction in these areas. Since it appears that no State would have enforcement jurisdiction over the object (and such jurisdiction does not appear to be an entirely theoretical matter: it would, for example, be required in order to take action against anyone unauthorisedly interfering with the object), to decide who should have jurisdiction it is necessary to have recourse to article 59 (the formula for resolving conflicts regarding the attribution of rights and jurisdiction in the EEZ – see chapter nine).

On the high seas the researching State is free to deploy any research installation or equipment, whether to be used for research of the water column and superjacent air space or for research of the sea bed and subsoil (i.e., the international sea bed area). Such installations and equipment will be subject to the jurisdiction of the researching State.[35]

Further provisions relating to the deployment of research installations and equipment are set out in articles 259 to 262. Such objects do not have the status of islands, nor do they affect the delimitation of maritime zones (LOSC, art. 259). It is possible, however, to establish safety zones of up to 500 metres in radius around such objects, and flag States must ensure that their ships respect such zones (LOSC, art. 260). Deployment of research installations and equipment must not 'constitute an obstacle to established international shipping routes' (LOSC, art. 261), and such objects must bear identification marks indicating the State of registry or the international organisation to which they belong and have adequate internationally agreed warning signals to ensure safety at sea and safety of air navigation (LOSC, art. 262).

Following the conclusion of UNCLOS III, the IOC and IMO each decided to take up their work again on the draft convention on ODAS, although no timetable for this has been set and progress on the matter has so far been fairly slow. Although some provisions of the original draft convention, such as those covering the deployment of ODAS and certain jurisdictional matters, are probably now redundant in the light of the Law of the Sea Convention's provisions (unless it be thought desirable to repeat the latter in an ODAS Convention in order to cover the eventuality of some of the major researching States not becoming parties to the Law of the Sea Convention), there are a number of matters in the draft which are not dealt with by the Law of the Sea Convention. These include the recovery and return of ODAS found in maritime zones under the jurisdiction of a foreign State, liability for unauthorised interference with ODAS, the registration of ODAS, and safety rules covering ODAS. The last two of these could usefully lead to a development of the provisions of article 262 of the Law of the Sea Convention.

---

[35] It should also be noted that under the pre-UNCLOS law the rules governing the deployment and use of ODAS in the territorial sea and on the high seas were the same as those of the Law of the Sea Convention.

International co-operation in marine scientific research

Much marine research is carried out on a purely national basis, but international co-operation does take place, and indeed is encouraged by the Law of the Sea Convention (see in particular arts 143 and 242). Such co-operation may be on an *ad hoc* basis for specific projects; however, much international co-operation is institutionalised, in both non-governmental and inter-governmental international organisations. The former, which include the International Council of Scientific Unions and its subsidiary, the Scientific Committee on Oceanic Research, fall outside the ambit of this book. Within this ambit, however, are the considerable number of inter-governmental organisations concerned with marine scientific research.

At the global level, there are several UN bodies. Of the specialised agencies, the Food and Agriculture Organisation (FAO) undertakes a good deal of fisheries research; much of the work of the World Meteorological Organisation (WMO) is concerned with weather observation at sea; and in 1960 UNESCO established an Intergovernmental Oceanographic Commission (IOC) to 'promote scientific investigation and related ocean services, with a view to learning more about the nature and resources of the ocean through the concerted action of its members'.[36] According to article 2 of its Statutes, the IOC's functions include promoting and co-ordinating the development and transfer of marine science and technology, making recommendations to strengthen education and training programmes in marine science and technology, promoting scientific investigation of the oceans, and promoting and co-ordinating observation and monitoring of the marine environment. The IOC has organised and co-ordinated a number of co-operative investigations, particularly in the Indian Ocean, eastern central Atlantic, Mediterranean and Pacific. It has also studied the legal problems connected with ODAS and freedom of research, and established various ocean services such as the International Oceanographic Data Exchange programme. Apart from the UN's specialised agencies and the United Nations Environment Programme (UNEP), which supports the scientific work of other organisations, there are also bodies co-ordinating the activities of the various parts of the UN system concerned with marine scientific research: two such are the Group of Experts on the Scientific Aspects of Marine Environmental Protection (GESAMP) and the Intersecretariat Committee on Scientific Programmes relating to Oceanography.[37] Outside the UN system but still on the global level is the International Hydrographic Organisation, established in 1970 as the successor to the International Hydrographic Bureau. Its functions are to co-ordinate the activities of national

---

[36] Art. 1(2) of the Statutes of the IOC.
[37] For further information on the work of the UN relating to marine research, see L. M. Alexander, 'Organizational responses to new ocean science and technology developments', 9 *ODIL* 241 (1981) at 249–56, and the UN Secretary General, *Annotated Directory of Intergovernmental Organizations concerned with Ocean Affairs*, UN Doc. A/Conf. 62/L. 14 (1976), pp. 11–105.

hydrographic offices, to bring about the greatest possible uniformity in nautical charts and documents; to adopt reliable and efficient methods of carrying out and exploiting hydrographic surveys and developing hydrographical sciences and the techniques employed in descriptive oceanography.

Much research co-operation takes place at the regional level. The oldest and perhaps foremost regional organisation is the International Council for the Exploration of the Sea (ICES), founded as long ago as 1902. It promotes and co-ordinates research relating to fisheries, and more recently pollution, in the North Atlantic, North Sea and Baltic, and gives scientific advice to fisheries and pollution organisations and commissions. In 1990 a convention was signed establishing the North Pacific Science Organisation, closely modelled on ICES, the functions of which are to promote and co-ordinate research in the North Pacific relating to fisheries and marine pollution. Originally performing a function similar to that of ICES for the Mediterranean was the International Commission for the Scientific Exploration of the Mediterranean, founded in 1919, but much of its work has now been taken over by the General Fisheries Council for the Mediterranean. A number of other regional fisheries organisations either conduct their own research (e.g., the International Pacific Halibut Commission, the Inter-American Tropical Tuna Commission) or more commonly co-ordinate the research of their member States (e.g., the Northwest Atlantic Fisheries Organisation, the International Committee for the Conservation of Atlantic Tunas). More generally, the Organisation for Indian Ocean Marine Affairs Co-Operation (IOMAC), established by an agreement of 1990, *inter alia* promotes co-operation in marine science and technology among Indian Ocean States, while the South Pacific Applied Geoscience Commission (SOPAC), also established by an agreement of 1990, has as its tasks the provision of information on the physical environment of coastal and nearshore areas to assist member States with resource and environmental management, the search for sea-bed minerals and the co-ordination of geological and geophysical research. Finally, States may also co-operate in marine research at the bilateral level. Thus, for example, in 1971 Portugal and Spain concluded an Agreement concerning Oceanographic Co-operation whereby they undertake to co-operate in the oceanographical research essential to making an inventory of the marine resources in the areas of interest to them.

Greater use of international co-operation in research projects, involving developing countries and the coastal States of the region where the project is being carried out, may help to mitigate the drawbacks of the controls given by the Law of the Sea Convention to a coastal State in its EEZ and on its continental shelf, because in such cases coastal State consent is likely to be obtained more quickly.

The transfer of marine technology

Related to the question of marine scientific research is that of the transfer of marine technology. In general terms, of course, transfer of technology has a compass going far beyond the law of the sea. Developing countries have long felt that one of the more important reasons for their economic backwardness is that they lack much of the technology which developed countries enjoy, and that without a substantial transfer of technology their economies will not adequately develop. In the 1970s they called for a New International Economic Order, one of the central features of which was to be the transfer of technology.[38] Negotiations began on an International Code of Conduct for the Transfer of Technology. However, by the late 1980s and early 1990s, with the collapse of Communism and the apparent triumph of capitalism as the prevailing global economic philosophy, calls for a New International Economic Order had largely ceased and the negotiations on the proposed Code of Conduct were effectively abandoned. Nevertheless, UNCLOS, having taken place mainly during the 1970s, was not unaffected by developing States' demands for the transfer of technology, and the Law of the Sea Convention deals with this matter in four places.

The first, and most concrete, is in the provisions on the international sea bed regime. Section 5 of the Annex to the Agreement relating to the Implementation of Part X1 (which replaces the rather more onerous provisions of article 5 of Annex III) requires anyone who applies to engage in mining in the international sea bed area in certain circumstances to help facilitate the acquisition of sea-bed mining technology by the Enterprise and/or developing countries. These provisions are discussed further in chapter twelve (p. 249). In addition, articles 144 and 274 require the International Sea Bed Authority to train nationals of developing countries, to make technical documentation on sea-bed mining available to developing countries, and to assist such countries in the acquisition of sea-bed mining technology. In carrying out these functions the Authority must act subject to 'all legitimate interests including, *inter alia*, the rights and duties of holders, suppliers and recipients of technology'.

The second place where the Law of the Sea Convention deals with the transfer of technology is in article 62, which provides that the conditions which a State may impose on the vessels of other States wishing to fish in its EEZ include the requirement to train personnel and transfer fisheries technology. In practice such conditions are found in many bilateral agreements: see, for example, the EC's Fisheries Agreements with Senegal (1979) and Guinea-Bissau (1980).[39] Thirdly, article 202 provides that States shall, directly or through international organisations, promote programmes of scientific, educational, technical and other assistance to developing States for the protection and preservation of the marine environment and the prevention of marine pollution. Such assistance may include the training of scientific and technical personnel, the supply of equipment and facilities, the enhancement of developing States' capacity to manufacture

---

[38] See especially UN General Assembly Resolutions 3201 (S VI) and 3202 (S VI) of 1974.
[39] For further examples see J. E. Carroz and M. J. Savini, 'The new international law of fisheries emerging from bilateral agreements', 3 *Marine Policy* 79 (1979) at 88–91.

such equipment, and the development of research, monitoring and educational programmes.

Finally, Part XIV of the Convention deals with the transfer of technology in general. This part essentially takes the form of a number of *pacta de contrahendo*: the lack of concrete legal obligations is largely explained by the novelty of the subject and the opposition of developed States to precise commitments.[40] Article 266 calls on States, directly or through international organisations, to co-operate in promoting the development and transfer of marine science and technology on fair and reasonable terms and conditions. To facilitate the transfer of marine technology, States are to promote the establishment of generally accepted guidelines, criteria and standards (LOSC, art. 271). The means envisaged for the development and transfer of marine technology include the establishment of programmes of technical co-operation, holding conferences and symposia on scientific and technological subjects, exchanges of scientists and technologists, undertaking joint ventures and the establishment of national and regional marine scientific and technological research centres (LOSC, arts 269 and 275–7).

Clearly the effectiveness of these provisions will depend on what action is taken to implement them, now that the Convention has entered into force, not least the action taken by international organisations, for which the Convention envisages a significant role. In this respect it is noteworthy that some international organisations have been engaged for many years in the transfer of marine technology: for example, the FAO has done considerable work in facilitating the transfer of fisheries technology to many developing States, while the IMO provides technical assistance to developing States in the fields of shipping safety and pollution, as well as assisting in the training of maritime personnel; and UNESCO, mainly through the IOC, has assisted in the transfer of technology through its research, information exchange and training programmes. In addition, a number of regional, mainly UN-sponsored, centres of technology transfer have been set up in Asia, Africa, Latin America and the Middle East, although none of them is specially for marine technology.

Apart from transfer of technology through international organisations, a certain amount of technology is already being transferred through bilateral agreements for scientific and technological co-operation and, probably more extensively, by transnational corporations through investment in foreign subsidiaries, joint ventures, technical assistance agreements and licensing arrangements. The activities of transnational corporations are viewed as particularly controversial by developing countries since the transfer of proprietary technology is the virtual preserve of transnational corporations because of their control of patents, methods of manufacture, channels of distribution and industrial processes.[41] Little improvement in this position is likely to result from the provisions of the Law of the Sea

---

[40] M. H. Nordquist (ed.), *United Nations Convention on the Law of the Sea. A Commentary* (Dordrecht, Nijhoff), Vol. 1V, 1991, p. 669.
[41] See Boczek, *op. cit.* in 'Further reading' under 'Transfer of technology', pp. 11–12.

Convention, which in Boczek's view 'do not lay down clear legal obligations but only establish certain standards of conduct which to a large extent reflect the already existing practice . . . and are not likely to have any immediate discernible legal effect upon the transfer of marine technology'.[42]

Further reading

Competence to conduct marine scientific research

L. Caflisch and J. Piccard, 'The legal regime of marine scientific research and the Third United Nations Conference on the Law of the Sea', 38 *ZAORV* 848–901 (1978).

R. J. Dupuy and D. Vignes (eds), *Traité du Nouveau Droit de la Mer* (Brussels, Bruylant), 1985, chapter 18 (or chapter 20 of the English edition, 1991).

O. Freymond, *Le Statut de la Recherche Scientifique Marine en Droit International* (Geneva, Georg), 1978.

B. Kwiatkowska, *The 200-mile Exclusive Economic Zone in the New Law of the Sea* (Dordrecht, Nijhoff), 1989, chapter 4.

W. Plasmann and V. Röben, 'Marine scientific research: State practice versus law of the sea' in R. Wolfrum (ed.), *Law of the Sea at the Crossroads* (Berlin, Dunker & Humblot), 1991, pp. 373–92.

W. S. Scholz, 'Oceanic research – international law and national legislation', 4 *Marine Policy* 91–127 (1980).

R. W. Smith, *Exclusive Economic Zone Claims: An Analysis and Primary Documents* (Dordecht, Nijhoff), 1986 [*Smith*].

A. H. A. Soons, *Marine Scientific Research and the Law of the Sea* (Deventer, Kluwer), 1982.

T. Treves, 'Principe du consentement et nouveau régime juridique de la recherche scientifique marine' in D. Bardonnet and M. Virally (eds), *Le Nouveau Droit International de la Mer* (Paris, Pedone), 1983, pp. 269–85.

W. S. Wooster (ed.), *Freedom of Oceanic Research* (New York, Crane Russak), 1973.

United Nations, *The Law of the Sea: National Legislation, Regulations and Supplementary Documents on Marine Scientific Research in Areas under National Jurisdiction* (New York, United Nations), 1989 [UN 1989].

——, *The Law of the Sea: Marine Scientific Research. A Guide to the Implementation of the Relevant Provisions of the United Nations Convention on the Law of the Sea* (New York, United Nations), 1991.

——, *The Law of the Sea: Marine Scientific Research. Legislative History of Article 246 of the UN Convention on the Law of the Sea* (New York, United Nations), 1994.

Legal status of research installations

N. Papadakis, *The International Legal Regime of Artificial Islands* (Leiden, Sijthoff), 1977, chapters 6–9.

R. J. R. Rao, 'The international legal regime of ODAS and other offshore research installations', 22 *IJIL* 375–95 (1982).

---

[42] *Ibid.*, pp. 33–4.

International co-operation

K. A. Bekiashev and V. V. Serebriakov, *International Marine Organisations* (The Hague, Nijhoff), 1981.

H. Charnock, 'Marine science. Organising the study of the oceans', 8 *Marine Policy* 120–36 (1984).

E. Miles, 'IOC data and information exchange: implications of the Law of the Sea Convention', 7 *Marine Policy* 75–89 (1983).

W. Sullivan, 'Constituting the IOC as a more autonomous or independent body', 4 *Marine Policy* 290–308 (1980).

Transfer of technology

B. A. Boczek, *The Transfer of Marine Technology to Developing Nations in International Law*, Law of the Sea Institute Occasional Paper No. 32, Honolulu, Hawaii, 1982.

Y. Li, *Transfer of Technology for Deep Sea Mining: The 1982 Law of the Sea Convention and Beyond* (Dordrecht, Nijhoff), 1994.

P. Roffe, 'Technology issues in the international agenda: a review of two decades of multilateral deliberations in the United Nations and GATT' in R. Wolfrum (ed.), *Law of the Sea at the Crossroads* (Berlin, Dunker & Humblot), 1991, pp. 285–317.

17

Military uses of the sea

Introduction

The 1958 and 1982 Conventions on the Law of the Sea were intended to regulate the uses of the seas in time of peace. The United Nations conferences on the Law of the Sea consciously avoided negotiation of the rules applicable to military operations on the seas. Consequently, the extent to which rights and duties under the conventions are modified or suspended in time of war is a controversial matter, compounded by the uncertainty of the Law of Treaties on this point. This does not, however, mean that all activities at sea by military vessels and aircraft are equally controversial. Routine law enforcement, of fishery and customs laws for example, is plainly regulated by those Conventions whether the enforcement is carried out by 'civilian' or military units, and certain other matters are regulated by other specific treaties. Here, the law is reasonably clear.

In recent years there has been a good deal of practice concerning the use of force at sea. While the naval aspects of the Vietnam war were pursued in a remarkably cautious manner, generally minimising the impact upon non-combatant activities and avoiding action on the high seas, subsequent armed conflicts have seen very substantial interference with third States' rights at sea. This is particularly true of the Falklands/Malvinas conflict of 1982 and the Iran/Iraq war of 1980–8. This chapter seeks to outline the limits of the controversy and to describe the main instruments and the emerging principles governing military uses of the seas.

The law of the sea and laws of war

There is a well-defined body of Laws of War at Sea, deriving in part from conventions, notably those drafted by the Hague Peace Conference of 1907, and in part from customary law.[1] These laws recognised and regulated such traditional

---

[1] See H. Lauterpacht (ed.), *Oppenheim II, op. cit.* in 'Further reading' at the end of this chapter; C. J. Colombos, *International Law of the Sea*, 6th edn (London, Longman), 1967, Part II; L. Doswald-Beck, 'The *San Remo Manual on International Law Applicable to Armed Conflicts at Sea*', 89 *AJIL* 192–208 (1995).

belligerent rights as the right to visit and search neutral merchant ships on the high seas in order to intercept contraband goods destined for the enemy and the right to maintain a close and effective blockade of enemy ports. They also defined the rights and duties of neutrals to prevent the use of their territorial waters as bases of naval operations by belligerents (although innocent passage by belligerents was not regarded as a violation of neutrality). Those laws presupposed the existence of a legal state of war, as distinct from the normal state of peace. But since the outlawing of war by the Kellogg–Briand Pact (the Pact of Paris) in 1928, and the wider prohibition in article 2(4) of the United Nations Charter of the threat or use of force against the territorial integrity or political independence of a State, it is not clear if international law can now recognise a state of war so as to trigger the application of the Laws of War in the traditional way. This question is of little practical importance in relation to the laws governing the hostilities between the combatants, because the key instruments (such as the Geneva Conventions of 1949) expressly apply 'to all cases of declared war or of any other armed conflict.' The question is of great practical importance in relation to the law of neutrality, which governs relations between the combatants and non-combatants.[2]

There are two broad approaches to this issue. One view, probably the most widely held, is that force may now be lawfully used only with the authorisation of the United Nations Security Council (or the General Assembly, acting under the 'Uniting for Peace' resolution) or alternatively in exercise of the inherent right of self-defence preserved by article 51 of the United Nations Charter. On this view, all actions formerly referred to the Laws of War and the law of neutrality must now seek their justification under one of these two headings.

The other view is that, regardless of the legality of the use of force in international relations, when force is used on a large scale it is regulated by the Laws of War and the law of neutrality.

Evidence can be found to support both views. For instance, during the Iran/Iraq war of 1980–8, the United States used the language of the traditional law of war and neutrality to describe the rights of belligerents and of neutrals in the conflict. It referred, for example, to rights of belligerents and neutrals, rights of ships in convoy, and so on. Such statements appear to evidence a belief in the continued applicability of at least some of the Laws of War. The United Kingdom, on the other hand, carefully avoided that language, referring instead to the rights that States involved in armed conflicts possess under article 51 of the UN Charter. The difference in the views is significant. For example, under the traditional laws of war and neutrality belligerents would have a right systematically to stop and search all neutral vessels and to seize contraband, whereas under article 51 combatants would have only the right to stop and search particular

---

[2] See C. J. Greenwood, 'The concept of war in modern international law', 36 ICLQ 283–306 (1987); R. W. Tucker, *The Law of War and Neutrality at Sea* (Washington D.C., Naval War College), 1955.

ships suspected on reasonable grounds of taking arms to the other side for use in the conflict. [3]

The best view seems to be that at least the principles, if not the detailed rules *eo nomine*, of the Laws of War and the law of neutrality apply to international armed conflicts. The precise ground for their application may be unclear: some would claim that the principles apply because of the survival of the Laws of War and the law of neutrality; others would say that the principles illuminate the manner in which the right to use force in self-defence or with UN authorisation must be exercised.

There have been many recent episodes in which military force has been used at sea. Uses of force authorised by the UN are uncommon. During the Cold War, the existence of the permanent members' (PR China, France, Russia, UK, USA) power of veto in the Security Council was a substantial obstacle to UN authorisation. The episode in 1966 when the United Kingdom was authorised by Security Council Resolution 221 to blockade the (then Portuguese) port of Beira, through which oil was being taken to support the Smith regime in Rhodesia, was a rare example of a UN authorisation to use force at sea, and force was indeed used in pursuance of it. Two Greek ships attempting to run the blockade, the *Joanna V* and the *Manuela*, were boarded, and later shots were fired across the bows of the French tanker *Artois*, in order to enforce the oil import ban.

The massive military operation launched by land, sea and air in the Gulf in 1991 in response to the invasion of Kuwait by Iraq was covered by Security Council Resolution 678, which authorised the 'Coalition' forces to use 'all necessary means' to secure the implementation of Security Council resolutions that had, *inter alia*, demanded the withdrawal of Iraqi forces from Kuwait. Yet there was a persistent (and probably deliberate) ambiguity concerning the nature of Operation Desert Storm, as it was known. It was not clear whether the adoption of the Security Council resolution meant that the resolution thereafter constituted the sole basis on which the Coalition might lawfully use force, or whether the resolution merely 'approved' the exercise of a right of collective self-defence by Kuwait and its allies, which right survived and might extend beyond the limits of the resolution.[4] The latter point would have been of crucial importance had the Coalition sought to pursue objectives not clearly covered by the resolution.

---

[3] For the US statements see US State Department, *Special Report No. 166. US Policy in the Persian Gulf* (Washington D.C., US Government), 1987; cf. de Guttry and Ronzitti, *op. cit.* in 'Further reading', p. 188. See also the Swedish declaration that the LOSC does not affect the rights and duties of neutral States provided for in 1907 Hague Convention XIII (25 *LOSB* 36 (1994)), and the reference by the International Court in the *Nicaragua* case to the application of 1907 Hague Convention VIII (on automatic submarine contact mines) in time of war ([1986] *ICJ Rep.* 12 at 112). On the other hand, it might be argued that the specific authorisations given by the UN Security Council in the 1990s to intercept vessels in the Gulf and off the coast of the Former Yugoslavia suggest that the traditional laws no longer apply.
[4] See, e.g., M. Weller, 'The UN and the *jus ad bellum*' in P. Rowe (ed.), *The Gulf War 1990–91 in International and English Law* (London, Routledge), 1993, pp. 29–54.

UN-authorised actions have occurred more frequently since the end of the Cold War,[5] but are still not common. Self-defence, permitting States threatened by an immediate armed attack upon themselves or their ships or aircraft to use force proportionate to the threat in order to avert the threat, is in practice the more important basis for the use of armed force at sea. Indeed, the United Kingdom conducted the whole of the 1982 naval conflict over the Falkland Islands/Islas Malvinas on the basis of its rights of self-defence. After dispatching a naval task force to repossess the islands after their occupation by Argentina, the United Kingdom established for the protection of the task force a 200-mile 'maritime exclusion zone' (MEZ), measured from a single point in the middle of the islands rather than from baselines, which Argentinian warships and naval auxiliaries were forbidden to enter. This zone was soon replaced by a 200-mile 'total exclusion zone' (TEZ), which was stated to apply

> not only to Argentine warships and Argentine naval auxiliaries but also to any other ship, whether naval or merchant vessel, which is operating in support of the illegal occupation of the Falkland Islands by Argentine forces.
> The Exclusion Zone will also apply to any aircraft, whether military or civil which is operating in support of the illegal occupation. Any ship and any aircraft whether military or civil which is found within this Zone without due authority from the Ministry of Defence in London will be regarded as operating in support of the illegal occupation and will therefore be regarded as hostile and will be liable to be attacked by British Forces.

The establishment of the TEZ avoided the necessity for determining whether any ship or aircraft in the area in fact presented an immediate threat to the task force, in circumstances where the time taken to make such a determination could have given a decisive advantage to the other ship or aircraft. All unauthorised ships and aircraft in the zone were deemed to be threatening and so liable to attack in self-defence. It should be noted that, contrary to what was at the time a widely held misconception, the TEZ was stated to be

> without prejudice to the right of the United Kingdom to take whatever additional measures may be needed in exercise of its right of self-defence, under Article 51 of the United Nations Charter.

Thus, when the Argentinian cruiser *General Belgrano* presented, in the view of the United Kingdom, a threat to the task force, it was sunk notwithstanding that it was some way outside the zone. The TEZ was replaced, after the cessation of hostilities, by a 150-mile 'Falkland Islands Protection Zone', which Argentinian ships and aircraft were asked not to enter without permission of the British Government.[6]

[5] See Security Council resolutions 665 (on the Gulf), 787 (on the Adriatic) and 875 (on Haiti) for provisions on interception at sea.
[6] For the texts of the official statements on the zones see the UK *Parliamentary Debates* (Hansard), House of Commons, 6th Series, Vol. 21, col. 1045, 7 April 1982 (MEZ in effect from 12 April 1982); *ibid.*, Vol. 22, col. 296, 28 April 1982 (TEZ in effect from 30

The 1958 and 1982 Law of the Sea Conventions make no provision for any such zones, but the Falklands zones were generally respected.[7] Similar zones were established, and generally respected, in the Gulf, during the Iran–Iraq conflict. The Gulf conflict also saw a variant of the exclusion zones established by the combatants. The United States announced the existence of moving protective 'bubbles' around its warships. A Notice to Mariners in 1986 stated that 'Surface and subsurface ships and craft that close U.S. naval forces within five nautical miles without making prior contact and/or whose intentions are unclear to such forces may be held at risk by U.S. defense measures. (*sic*)'[8] The difficulty with such moving zones is that if the course of the warship is notified in advance the risk that it might be attacked is increased, but if its course is not notified in advance ships and aircraft may have no way of knowing when they come within the protective bubble. It seems unlikely that moving zones will be accepted or tolerated by the international community as readily as fixed exclusion zones have been.

The 1980–8 Gulf war gave rise to many other questions concerning the use of force at sea. One of the most difficult issues concerned the use of force to protect non-national ships. In the closing months of the war, when attacks on neutral shipping intensified, shipowners began to re-flag their vessels under the US or UK flags in order to attract the protection of US and British warships stationed in the Gulf. The practice, which could have had serious political and military implications had the conflict and the re-flagging continued on a large scale, gave rise to difficult questions concerning the need for a 'genuine link' between the ship and the flag, and also concerning the right or duty of warships to protect third-State merchant ships from attack by the combatants. These questions remain unresolved. They were largely avoided in practice, but only because the Iran/Iraq war ended soon after the problem arose.[9]

The Cuban 'quarantine' of 1962 illustrates a further point. When powerful States feel strongly enough, legal rules are unlikely to be effective constraints upon their actions. The United States did not obtain Security Council consent before mounting the Cuban quarantine in order to prevent the importation of missile parts from the Soviet Union to the island. The Organisation of American

---

April 1982); *ibid.*, Vol. 28, col. 235, 22 July 1982 (Falkland Islands Protection Zone – FIPZ – in effect from 22 July 1982). The texts are reproduced in *UKMIL 1982*, pp. 539 (MEZ), 542 (TEZ), 556–7 (FIPZ). See further R. P. Barston and P. W. Birnie, *op. cit.* in 'Further reading'.

[7] See, on this and on other episodes, G. K. Walker, 'State practice following World War II, 1945–1990' in R. J. Grunawalt (ed.), *Targeting Enemy Merchant Shipping* (Newport, Rhode Island, US Naval War College), 1993, pp. 121–221.

[8] Text from A. de Guttry and N. Ronzitti (eds), *op. cit.* in 'Further reading', p. 139. A similar Notice to Airmen is reprinted *ibid.*, p. 140. The opacity of the language may be a source of difficulty.

[9] See J. S. Davidson, 'United States protection of reflagged Kuwaiti vessels in the Gulf war', 4 *IJECL* 173–91 (1989); A. V. Lowe, 'Self-defence at sea' in W. E. Butler (ed.), *The Non-Use of Force in International Law* (Dordrecht, 1989), pp. 185–202.

States approved the exercise, but this approval patently could not establish its legality (see art. 53 of the United Nations Charter); nor was the threat to the United States sufficiently proximate to justify the use of force in self-defence.

Military uses of the sea in peacetime

Military activities in the seas relate to a variety of functions of naval vessels. First, there is the duty of routine law enforcement in national waters, usually in relation to fisheries, customs and immigration laws. Secondly, in preparation for their other roles, navies commonly engage in manoeuvres and weapons testing on the 'high seas', as they were under the 1958 rules. Third, the larger maritime States, following Lord Grey's dictum that 'Diplomacy without force is like an orchestra without instruments', use their navies for the projection of national power and influence. This third function covers several types of action. It may involve no more than flying the flag in some part of the world to remind allies and enemies alike that the naval State has a military presence in the area. This is readily observable at times of particular tension in the Middle East, for instance, when both American and Russian fleets are to be found deployed in the Mediterranean or Indian Ocean. It may involve a more immediate display of force as, for example, when the Royal Navy asserted its right of passage through the Corfu Channel after Albanian shore batteries had fired on other passing British warships, or when the US Destroyer Division 31 sailed through the Lombok and Malacca straits to assert its right of passage after the Indonesian archipelagic waters claim of 1957. There may even be direct action against a hostile vessel such as occurred when the United States ship *Pueblo* was seized in 1968 by North Korean vessels for spying, allegedly within Korean territorial waters.

Another example arose when, during the 'cod wars' of 1958–76, the Royal Navy sought to defend British trawlers from attempts by Icelandic naval vessels to enforce fishing regulations against them, the British view being that the laws constituted unwarrantable extensions, first to twelve, and then to fifty and 200 miles, of jurisdiction on to the high seas, and were inadmissible under international law. And navies may also be used to provide logistic support for land-based actions, as they were during the American landing in Lebanon in 1958 and, more recently, during the 1991 Operation Desert Storm in the Gulf.

Some of the problems to which these give rise, such as the questions of rights of passage for warships, the establishment of contiguous zones for security purposes, and the legality of high-seas weapons tests, have been discussed in previous chapters. The important point is not that these legal questions are insoluble, but that the uncertainty which persists makes it possible for coastal or flag States intent for political reasons on, say, denying passage to foreign warships to do so under the colour of the enforcement of legal rights. That is equally true of the remaining issues, not treated elsewhere, which arise from naval operations.

Of the many issues that could be chosen to illustrate the impact of the law of the sea on military activities, two will suffice. The first stems from the establishment of the EEZ. In the declarations which they made on signature or ratification of the 1982 Convention several States, including Brazil, Cape Verde, India, Malaysia, Pakistan and Uruguay, announced that they do not consider the Convention to authorise the carrying out of military exercises or manoeuvres, or the deployment of military installations, in the EEZ without the permission of the coastal State.[10] Some States have adopted this position in their legislation.[11] Since this position, if widely adopted, would close off enormous areas of the seas for such routine military activities, it is not surprising that the position has not been accepted by naval powers: Germany, Italy and the Netherlands, for instance, have expressly rejected it.[12] The problem lies in the fact that although the freedoms of navigation and overflight and other internationally lawful uses of the seas related to them are preserved in the EEZ (LOSC, arts 58, 87), it is not clear whether such activities as exercises involving weapons testing are included within those freedoms. Nor is it clear how the question is to be resolved: on one view, exercises and so on are included within the permitted freedoms; on another, they are unattributed rights falling for decision under article 59 of the Convention (see chapter nine).[13]

The second problem concerns the deployment of monitoring devices such as the United States' Sonar Surveillance Systems which lie on the continental shelf off the coasts of the United States, in the North Sea, and in the Mediterranean. These devices might be regarded as 'structures', and therefore within the provisions of article 60 of the Convention, which gives the coastal State the exclusive right to authorise the construction and operation in the EEZ of installations and structures which may interfere with the exercise of its rights in that zone. Similar provisions would apply to their deployment on the continental shelf beneath the high seas (LOSC, art. 80). On the other hand it might be argued that a right to lay them in the EEZ or on the continental shelf arises by the application, or extension by analogy, of the freedom to lay submarine cables and pipelines (LOSC, arts 58, 79, 87) subject only to the duties not to interfere with coastal

---

[10] See the lists of declarations and protests in the UN paper, *The Law of the Sea. Declarations and statements with respect to the United Nations Convention on the Law of the Sea* (New York, United Nations), 1997, p. 84, and at http://www.un.org/Depts/los/los_decl.htm.

[11] E.g., Brazil (23 *LOSB* 17 (1993), art. 9) and Iran (24 *LOSB* 10 (1993), art. 16).

[12] See the 1997 UN paper, *op. cit.* in footnote 10, pp. 29, 31, 35. See also B. A. Boczek, 'Peace-time military activities in the exclusive economic zone of third countries', 19 *ODIL* 455–68 (1988); S. Mahmoudi, 'Foreign military activities in the Swedish economic zone,' 11 *IJMCL* 365–86 (1996); S. Rose, 'Naval activity in the exclusive economic zone – troubled waters ahead', 21 *ODIL* 71–103 (1990).

[13] See further A. V. Lowe, 'Some legal problems arising from the use of the seas for military purposes', 10 *Marine Policy* 171–84 (1986); B. Kwiatkowska, 'Military uses in the EEZ: a reply', *ibid.*, Vol. 11, pp. 249–50 (1987) and A. V. Lowe, 'Rejoinder', *ibid.*, pp. 250–2.

State rights in the zone and to deploy them with due regard to the interests of other users of the seas. However, some jurists regard their deployment as different in nature from the immersion of cables and pipelines, and outside that freedom.[14] The only thing that can be said with confidence is that it is most unlikely that the major naval powers will cease from the use of the seas for military exercises and the deployment of such systems, no matter what the Convention might say.

Special treaties concerning military uses

Apart from treaties dealing with rules of naval warfare,[15] which we cannot consider here for reasons of space, there are three main categories of international agreement concerning military uses of the seas.

First, there are treaties regulating the kind and quantity of naval power that the parties are allowed to possess. For example, the 1922 Washington Treaty for the Limitation of Naval Armament, the first of a series of such treaties made during the inter-war years, limited the number, size and armament of the navies of the signatories – Great Britain, the United States, France, Italy and Japan. The treaty lapsed at the end of 1936. Post-war naval policy has generally been to increase, rather than limit, naval forces. The most notable exception is the Strategic Arms Limitation Agreement (SALT) of 1972 between the United States and the then Soviet Union which *inter alia* limits the number and armament of submarines carrying nuclear missiles. A successor to SALT, agreed in 1979, was not ratified by the American Senate. Such treaties as these are, though often simple in appearance, extraordinarily complex political agreements, often involving accommodations on other issues, such as territorial claims and economic relations.

A second set of treaties limits the right to test and deploy certain weapons. The Nuclear Test Ban Treaty of 1963 was the first significant agreement, prohibiting nuclear weapon test explosions in the atmosphere or under water, including territorial waters and high seas. Most States – with the exception of China and France – are parties to this treaty. It was supplemented in 1971 by the Treaty on the Prohibition of the Emplacement of Nuclear Weapons and other Weapons of Mass Destruction on the Sea Bed, which prohibits the emplacement of such weapons (which could include biological and chemical weapons of mass destruction) and of installations specially designed to store, test or use them, on the sea bed beyond twelve miles from the shore. Each party has the right to verify through observation the compliance of other parties.

[14] See T. Treves, 'Military installations, structures and devices on the seabed', 74 *AJIL* 808–57 (1980); R. Zedalis, 'Military installations, structures and devices on the seabed: a response, *ibid.*, Vol. 75, pp. 926–33 (1981), and T. Treves 'Reply', *ibid.*, pp. 933–5.
[15] See, e.g., the works by Ronzitti, *The Law of Naval Warfare*, Doswald-Beck (ed.), and Fischer and von Heinegg, in 'Further reading'.

Four regional treaties have similar aims, but apply only to areas under the jurisdiction of the parties and only to nuclear weapons. The Treaty of Tlatelolco, 1967, the parties to which are Latin-American States, prohibits the testing, deployment and use of nuclear weapons both on the sea bed and in the superjacent waters. At present, it is limited to the waters over which the parties have sovereignty, which is generally understood to mean the (twelve-mile) zone of sovereignty recognised in international law; but the treaty is capable of extension to a very much wider area of the Pacific and Atlantic at such time as all nuclear powers and all Latin-American States adhere to it.[16]

Further west, the Treaty of Raratonga, which was concluded in 1985 by States members of the South Pacific Forum, applies in an area south of the equator, including Australia and extending to the meridian of 115° west. Parties are bound to prevent the stationing and testing of nuclear devices within their territory, including internal, archipelagic and territorial waters, and remain free to decide whether to allow visits of foreign ships and aircraft carrying nuclear weapons to visit their ports or to transit their waters in any manner not included in rights of innocent passage or transit or archipelagic sealanes passage, which rights are to be respected. New Zealand, in particular, has taken steps to secure a ban on such visits to its ports. While some nuclear powers are parties to Protocols of both treaties, which bind those powers to the main provisions of the treaties, it is not likely that this will inhibit deployment of nuclear missile submarines beyond territorial sea limits in the regions covered: indeed, the United Kingdom takes the view that the transportation of nuclear missiles through the Treaty area does not violate the Treaty of Tlatelolco.

More recently, in 1995 the Organization of African Unity adopted the Pelindaba Text on the African Nuclear-Weapon-Free Zone which, *inter alia*, prohibits the stationing of nuclear explosive devices within the territory, including internal and archipelagic waters and territorial seas, of States parties. The ten States of South-East Asia made a similar agreement, the Treaty on the South-East Asia Nuclear-Weapon-Free Zone, in 1995. The latter Treaty implies that its provisions do not impede the exercise of rights of innocent and transit passage and archipelagic sealanes passage, at least if prior notice of the passage is given.[17] Nonetheless, the treaties allow considerable latitude in their application, and it remains to be seen how they will be applied in practice.

The final category of agreements concerns the conduct of naval operations. Clearly there is some overlap with the other categories. The treaties of Tlatelolco and Raratonga could affect submarine operations, and the 1930 London Naval Treaty – one of the inter-war arms limitation agreements – contained in its 1936 Protocol important rules concerning submarine warfare, which were reaffirmed

---

[16] The treaty was reinforced by an IAEA–USA agreement for the application of IAEA safeguards to US nuclear activities within the area of application of the Tlatelolco treaty: see 28 *ILM* 1345 (1989).

[17] See article 7.

in the 1937 Nyon Agreement under which the Mediterranean powers organised patrols for the suppression of piratical submarine attacks during the Spanish Civil War. The 1930 treaty expired at the beginning of 1937, while the other treaties terminated with outbreak of the Second World War. Some other agreements are solely concerned with the operational matters. The second Hague Convention of 1907, limiting the use of pacific blockade, is one example. And more recently the United States and the Soviet Union, seeking to reduce the chances of nuclear war breaking out by accident, concluded the Agreement on the Prevention of Incidents on and over the High Seas, 1972. This agreement and its 1973 Protocol include rules of conduct for naval surveillance and other operations on the high seas, and provide for the exchange of information concerning actual and potential incidents. They apply also to EEZs, and thus support the view that military manoeuvres are permissible in those waters. Similar agreements were concluded between the Soviet Union and other western States.[18]

Demilitarisation of the seas

Finally, mention must be made of efforts within the United Nations to demilitarise some sea areas. The General Assembly adopted a series of resolutions endorsing the idea of the establishment of nuclear-free zones in Africa, the Middle East, South Asia, the South Pacific and Latin America; such zones are based upon the voluntary assumption by the States concerned of obligations not to deploy nuclear missiles within these zones (see GA Res. 3472B (XXX)). These UN proposals have been given concrete application in the various regional treaties on nuclear-weapons-free zones, noted above. More ambitious is the solemn designation of the Indian Ocean by the General Assembly as a zone of peace (see GA Res. 2832 (XXVI)). It has so far proved impossible to implement this resolution, not least because of the vagueness of the concept. Some States regard it as involving total demilitarisation of the area; others, including the major powers, see the deployment of conventional and nuclear weapons as essential to the maintenance of peace, rather than a threat to it. At present it seems unlikely that the resolution will find concrete expression.[19]

Finally, it may be noted that neither article 301 of the Law of the Sea Convention, headed 'Peaceful uses of the seas' which obliges all States to refrain

[18] Canada,1989, 18 *LOSB* 25 (1991); France, 1989, 16 *LOSB* 23 (1990); Germany, 1988, 14 *LOSB* 15 (1989); Italy, 1989, 16 *LOSB* 35 (1990); Netherlands, 1990; United Kingdom, 1986, 10 *LOSB* 97 (1987). These are known as 'Incsea' agreements. See also the USSR–USA Agreement on the Prevention of Dangerous Military Activities, 1989, which supplements the provisions of the original USSR–USA Incsea agreement; and cf. T. J. Nagle, 'The Dangerous Military Activities Agreement: minimum order and superpower relations on the world oceans', 31 *VJIL* 125–44 (1990).

[19] See S. P. Subedi, *Land and Maritime Zones of Peace in International Law* (Oxford, Clarendon Press), 1996, pp.15–16 and *passim*.

from the threat or use of force in any manner inconsistent with the principles of international law embodied in the United Nations Charter when using the seas, nor article 88 of the Convention which reserves the high seas for 'peaceful purposes', nor article 141, which reserves the International Sea Bed Area exclusively for peaceful purposes, is generally understood to forbid anything other than aggressive actions at sea.[20] Certainly the major naval powers do not regard any of these articles as imposing restraints upon routine naval operations.

Further reading

R. P. Barston and P. W. Birnie, 'The Falkland Islands/Islas Malvinas conflict. A question of zones' 7 *Marine Policy* 14–34 (1983).

J. Cable, *Gunboat Diplomacy*, 3rd edn (London, Macmillan), 1991.

H. L. Cryer, 'Legal aspects of the *Joanna V* and *Manuela* incidents, April 1966', 2 *Australian Yearbook of International Law* 85–98 (1966).

L. Doswald-Beck, *San Remo Manual on International Law applicable to Armed Conflicts at Sea* (Cambridge, Cambridge University Press), 1995.

W. J. Fenrick, 'Legal limits on the use of force by Canadian warships engaged in law enforcement', 18 *Canadian Yearbook of International Law* 113–45 (1980).

——, 'Legal aspects of targeting in the law of naval warfare', 29 *Canadian Yearbook of International Law* 238–81 (1991).

H. Fischer and W. H. von Heinegg, *The Law of Naval Warfare: A Select Bibliography* (Bochum, Universitätsverlag Brockmeyer), 1989.

A. de Guttry and N. Ronzitti (eds), *The Iran–Iraq War (1980–1988) and the Law of Naval Warfare* (Cambridge, Grotius), 1993.

T. Halkiopoulos, 'Interférence des règles du nouveau droit de la mer et celles du droit de la guerre' in R.-J. Dupuy and D. Vignes (eds), *Traité du Nouveau Droit de la Mer* (Paris, Economica), 1985, pp. 1095–104.

W. H. von Heinegg, 'Visit, search, diversion, and capture in naval warfare', Part I, the traditional law, 29 *Canadian Yearbook of International Law* 283–328 (1991); Part II, developments since 1945, 30 *Canadian Yearbook of International Law* 89–136 (1992).

——, 'The law of armed conflict at sea' in D. Fleck (ed.), *The Handbook of Humanitarian Law in Armed Conflicts* (Oxford, Oxford University Press), 1995, pp. 405–83.

H. Lauterpacht (ed.), *Oppenheim's International Law*, Vol. II, *Disputes, War and Neutrality*, 7th edn (London, Longman), 1952 [*Oppenheim II*].

F. C. Leiner 'Maritime security zones: prohibited yet perpetuated', 24 *VJIL* 785–807 (1984).

H. S. Levie, *Mine Warfare at Sea* (Dordrecht, Nijhoff), 1991.

A. V. Lowe, 'Self defence at sea' in W. E. Butler (ed.), *The Non-Use of Force in International Law* (Dordrecht, Nijhoff), 1989, pp. 184–202.

L. Lucchini, 'Les opérations militaires en mer en temps de paix', 88 *RGDIP* 9–45 (1984).

J. H. McNeil, 'Neutral rights and maritime sanctions: the effects of two Gulf wars', 31 *VJIL* 631–43 (1991).

---

[20] See B. A. Boczek, 'Peaceful purposes provisions of the United Nations Convention on the Law of the Sea', 20 *ODIL* 359–89 (1989).

P. Merciai, 'La démilitarisation des fonds marins', 88 *RGDIP* 114–203 (1985).

R. W. G. de Muralt, 'The military aspects of the UN Law of the Sea Convention', 32 *Netherlands International Law Review* 78–99 (1985).

D. P. O'Connell, *The Influence of Law on Sea Power* (Manchester, Manchester University Press), 1975.

——, 'International law and contemporary naval operations', 44 *BYIL* 19–85 (1970).

B. H. Oxman, 'The regime of warships under the United Nations Convention on the Law of the Sea', 24 *VJIL* 809–63 (1984).

G. P. Politakis, 'From action stations to action: US naval deployment, "non-belligerency", and "defensive reprisals" in the final year of the Iran–Iraq war', 25 *ODIL* 31–60 (1994).

M. Pugh, *Maritime Security and Peacekeeping: a framework for United Nations operations* (Manchester, Manchester University Press), 1994.

H. B. Robertson, Jr (ed.), *The Law of Naval Operations* (Newport, Rhode Island, Naval War College), 1991.

N. Ronzitti, 'Demilitarization and neutralization in the Mediterranean', 6 *Italian Yearbook of International Law* 33–54 (1985).

——, (ed.), *The Law of Naval Warfare* (Dordrecht, Nijhoff), 1988.

F. V. Russo, 'Neutrality at sea in transition: State practice in the Gulf war as emerging international customary law', 19 *ODIL* 381–99 (1988).

B. Vukas, 'L'utilisation pacifique de la mer, dénucléarisation et désarmement' in R.-J. Dupuy and D. Vignes (eds), *Traité du Nouveau Droit de la Mer* (Paris, Economica), 1985, pp.1047–94.

See also the invaluable series of *International Law Studies* published by the US Naval War College, Newport, Rhode Island, and now including over sixty volumes.

18

Landlocked and geographically disadvantaged States

Introduction

Of the world's approximately 190 States, forty-two have no sea coast. Of these forty-two States, fifteen are in Africa,[1] thirteen in Europe,[2] twelve in Asia[3] and two in Latin America.[4] Not only do these landlocked States suffer from the lack of direct access to the sea and its resources, but many of them are also deficient in natural land resources and thus are amongst the world's poorest States. In addition to landlocked States, there are quite a number of States which are said to be geographically disadvantaged as far as the sea is concerned – for example, because their coastline is very short in proportion to the size of their land territory, e.g., Iraq and the Democratic Republic of the Congo (formerly Zaire); or because the presence of neighbouring States prevents the generation of maritime zones (especially a continental shelf and EEZ) commensurate with the length of their coastline or the size of their territory, e.g., Germany, Singapore and Togo; or because their EEZ is poor in natural resources, e.g., Jamaica, Nauru and Tanzania. Obviously the degree of disadvantage varies enormously from one State to another. Later in this chapter we shall consider a more precise definition of geographically disadvantaged States.

As far as the law of the sea is concerned, landlocked and geographically disadvantaged States raise three main questions: (1) the right of landlocked States' ships to navigate on the sea; (2) the access of landlocked and geographically disadvantaged States to marine resources; and (3) the access of landlocked States to the sea. Nearly all the international law dealing with these questions has been developed since the end of the First World War in 1918. This development has

[1] Botswana, Burkina Faso, Burundi, Central African Republic, Chad, Ethiopia, Lesotho, Malawi, Mali, Niger, Rwanda, Swaziland, Uganda, Zambia and Zimbabwe.
[2] Andorra, Austria, Belarus, Czech Republic, Holy See, Hungary, Liechenstein, Luxembourg, Macedonia, Moldova, San Marino, Slovakia and Switzerland. The status of the Holy See as a State is somewhat controversial.
[3] Afghanistan, Armenia, Azerbaijan, Bhutan, Kazakhstan, Kyrgyzstan, Laos, Mongolia, Nepal, Tajikistan, Turkmenistan and Uzbekistan.
[4] Bolivia and Paraguay.

taken place in a number of forums, principally the League of Nations (particularly its two Conferences on Communications and Transit, held in 1921 and 1923); UNCTAD; and UNCLOS I and III. At UNCLOS I the question of landlocked States was discussed by the Fifth Committee, which had before it a memorandum submitted by the Preliminary Conference of Landlocked States, held in February 1958[5] (the question of landlocked States not having been considered by the ILC). At UNCLOS III no separate committee to deal with questions relating to land-locked and geographically disadvantaged States was established: instead such questions were discussed in each of the conference's three main committees. In order to try to improve their negotiating position at the conference, the land-locked and some geographically disadvantaged States formed themselves into a group comprising fifty-five States (about a third of the total conference member-ship). Although the States which were members of this group were very diverse politically, economically and geographically (and included both developed and developing States, and States from both East and West), they agreed on trying to obtain at UNCLOS III confirmation of the existing navigational rights of land-locked States; transit rights through States lying between landlocked States and the sea; access to the resources of neighbouring coastal States' EEZs; and proper recognition of their interests in the international sea bed regime. As we shall see, these demands met with mixed success.

The navigational rights of landlocked States

Before 1914 there was doubt as to whether under customary international law ships of a landlocked State had the right to sail on the sea and fly the flag of that State. Those who denied such a right, principally France, Great Britain and Prussia, argued that, since landlocked States had neither maritime ports nor warships, they could not verify the nationality of merchant vessels nor exercise effective control over them. However, under the Treaty of Versailles, 1919 (art. 273) and the other peace treaties concluded at the end of the First World War the parties agreed to recognise the flag flown by the vessels of a landlocked party which were registered at a specified place in its territory, which was to serve as the port of registry of such vessels. The right thus accorded to some landlocked States was put on a more general footing in the Declaration recognising the Right to a Flag of States having no Sea Coast, adopted at the 1921 League of Nations Conference on Communications and Transit.[6] Since then the view that landlocked States have the same navigational rights as coastal States has become firmly established. Thus both the Geneva Conventions and the Law of the Sea Convention provide specifically that the ships of all States, whether coastal or landlocked, have the right of innocent passage in the territorial sea and freedom

---

[5] UNCLOS I, *Official Records*, Vol. VII, pp. 67–79.
[6] 7 *LNTS* 14.

of navigation in the waters beyond (TSC, art. 14(1); HSC, arts 2(1), 4; LOSC, arts 17, 38(1), 52(1), 53(2), 58(1), 87, 90). These rights now also appear to be the same under customary international law. At present only thirteen landlocked States (Austria, Azerbaijan, Czech Republic, Ethiopia, Hungary, Kazakhstan, Laos, Luxembourg, Malawi, Paraguay, Slovakia, Switzerland and Turkmenistan) possess merchant fleets[7] and so exercise these rights in practice.

Access to ports

The right to navigate through the territorial sea and EEZ and on the high seas is of limited benefit to landlocked States unless they also have the right to use the ports of a coastal State (particularly an adjoining coastal State), and a right of access to the sea across the territory of States lying between landlocked States and the sea. The latter question will be considered in the final section of this chapter. As regards the use of ports, we saw in chapter three that under customary international law there is no general right of access to ports (except for ships in distress). Rights of access are, however, granted under bilateral treaties of friendship, commerce and navigation and, for the forty States parties to it (which include six landlocked States), under the 1923 Convention and Statute on the International Regime of Maritime Ports. The Law of the Sea Convention provides that 'ships flying the flag of landlocked States shall enjoy treatment equal to that accorded to other foreign ships in maritime ports' (LOSC, art. 131). The scope of this provision is not entirely clear. Does treatment include – as it does specifically under the 1923 Convention – access to ports? Or does article 131 simply deal with the treatment to be accorded to a vessel of a landlocked State which already enjoys a right of access under some other provision? If the latter is the case (as some commentators have suggested[8]), the article would seem to be of little practical application, for the obligation it contains already results from the 1923 Convention and from most, if not all, bilateral treaties giving access. In either case the treatment to be enjoyed is that 'accorded to other foreign ships'. This need not be most-favoured-nation treatment: indeed, there seems nothing in the Law of the Sea Convention to prevent the port State offering least-favoured-nation treatment.

The access of landlocked and geographically disadvantaged States to marine resources

The question of the access of landlocked and geographically disadvantaged States to marine resources has three main aspects: the access of such States to

---

[7] Lloyds Register of Shipping, *World Fleet Statistics 1995* (1996), pp. 11–13.
[8] See, e.g., M. H. Nordquist (ed.), *United Nations Convention on the Law of the Sea 1982. A Commentary* (The Hague, Nijhoff), Vol. III, 1995, p. 453.

the resources of the high seas; the role of such States in the international sea-bed regime; and the access of such States to the resources of the EEZ. Landlocked and geographically disadvantaged States have never sought access to the re- sources of the territorial sea of other States, presumably because this zone is part of a coastal State's territory, and thus other States have never been accorded any general right of access to its resources.

Access to high-seas resources

As far as access to high-seas resources is concerned, article 2 of the High Seas Convention and article 87 of the Law of the Sea Convention each provide that the freedoms of the high seas may be exercised by all States, whether coastal or landlocked. This means that landlocked (and geographically disadvantaged) States have access to and may exploit the living resources of the high seas (and at least formerly sea-bed nodules, if such exploitation could be regarded as a freedom of the high seas – see chapter twelve). It also means that landlocked and geo- graphically disadvantaged States can engage in non-resource uses of the high seas, such as scientific research, overflight and the laying of submarine cables and pipelines, as well as navigation.

International sea-bed regime

As far as the second aspect of access to marine resources is concerned, land- locked and geographically disadvantaged States have sought to ensure that they play a full part in the international sea-bed regime and do not suffer because of their geographical situation. The Law of the Sea Convention contains a number of provisions specifically aimed at promoting the interests of landlocked States and, to a lesser extent, geographically disadvantaged States. Thus, article 148 formulates as one of the guiding principles of the international sea-bed regime that:

> The effective participation of developing States in activities in the Area shall be promoted as specifically provided for in this Part [i.e., Part XI], having due regard to their special interests and needs, and in particular to the special need of the landlocked and geographically disadvantaged among them to overcome obstacles arising from their disadvantaged location, including remoteness from the Area and difficulty of access to and from it.

In the same vein, article 152 provides that the International Sea Bed Authority is not to act discriminatively in exercising its powers, but may nevertheless give 'special consideration for developing States, including particular consideration for the landlocked and geographically disadvantaged among them', as provided for in Part XI of the Convention. Article 160(2)(k) requires the Assembly of the Authority to consider problems of a general nature in connection with activities in the Area arising in particular for developing States, as well as those problems for States in connection with activities in the Area that are due to their geographical location, particularly for landlocked and geographically disadvantaged States.

It should be noted that all these provisions apply only to *developing* landlocked and geographically disadvantaged States.

The Law of the Sea Convention also provides for the special representation of landlocked and geographically disadvantaged States on the thirty-six-member Council, the only organ of the Authority which has limited State membership. Six members of the Council are to be elected from among developing States representing special interests. Such interests include, *inter alia,* being landlocked and geographically disadvantaged (1994 Agreement, section 3, para. 15(d) of Annex). Furthermore, in electing members of the Council, the Assembly must ensure that landlocked and geographically disadvantaged States (the latter are not defined – except in relation to rights in the EEZ: see p. 438 – and neither group this time is limited to developing States), 'are represented to a degree which is reasonably proportionate to their representation in the Assembly' (LOSC, art. 161(2)(a)). In the first elections to the Council, held in March 1996, four landlocked States – Austria, Paraguay, Ukraine and Zambia – were elected to the Council, as well as a number of States which are generally regarded as geographically disadvantaged.

However, the Law of the Sea Convention contains no special provisions for landlocked and geographically disadvantaged States as far as the effect of sea-bed mining on land-based producers or the distribution of the Authority's revenues are concerned. As to the former, it is developing States generally for which the Convention makes special provision (see LOSC, arts 150(h), 151(10)). In the case of the latter, it is again developing States generally which are to receive preferential treatment (see LOSC, arts 140, 160(2)(f)), although it should be noted that when distributing the revenues it receives from a coastal State's exploitation of the resources of its continental shelf beyond the 200-mile limit the Authority is to take into account 'the interests and needs of developing States, particularly the least developed and the land-locked among them' (LOSC, art. 82(4)).

Taken together, the above provisions offer landlocked and geographically disadvantaged States less guarantee of active participation in and benefit from the international sea-bed regime than they sought.

Access to EEZ resources

The extension of coastal State jurisdiction resulting from the Law of the Sea Convention's provisions on the EEZ and continental shelf means a considerable diminution in the area of the high seas and international sea bed, and therefore in the marine resources available to landlocked and geographically disadvantaged

States. By way of compensation these States proposed at UNCLOS III that they should be given access to both the living and non-living resources of the EEZ and continental shelf of neighbouring States. As far as non-living resources were concerned, the aspirations of landlocked and geographically disadvantaged States were firmly rejected by coastal States because their proposals would have deprived coastal States of their vested continental shelf rights. On the other hand, landlocked and geographically disadvantaged States have been given limited access to the living resources of neighbouring EEZs.

In chapter fourteen we saw that under the Law of the Sea Convention a coastal State is to establish the total allowable catch for the fish stocks in its EEZ and that that part of the total allowable catch which the coastal State's vessels are not capable of harvesting (the surplus) is to be made available to other States. Articles 69(1) and 70(1) provide that landlocked States and geographically disadvantaged States have

> the right to participate, on an equitable basis, in the exploitation of an appropriate part of the surplus of the living resources of the exclusive economic zones of coastal States of the same subregion or region, taking into account the relevant economic and geographical circumstances of all the States concerned (LOSC, arts 69(1),70(1))

and in conformity with articles 61 and 62. The terms and modalities of such participation are to be established by the States concerned through bilateral, sub-regional or regional agreements, taking into account various specified factors (LOSC, arts 69(2), 70(3)). Where the harvesting capacity of a coastal State reaches the point which would enable it to harvest the whole of the total allowable catch in its EEZ, the coastal State and other States concerned 'shall cooperate in the establishment of equitable arrangements on a bilateral, sub-regional or regional basis to allow for participation' by developing landlocked States and developing geographically disadvantaged States of the same sub-region or region in the exploitation of the living resources of the EEZs of coastal States of the sub-region or region, 'as may be appropriate in the circumstances and on terms satisfactory to all parties', and taking into account various specified factors (LOSC, arts 69(3), 70(4)).

For the purpose of Part V of the Law of the Sea Convention, concerning the EEZ, 'geographically disadvantaged States' comprise coastal States (1) whose geographical situation makes them dependent upon the exploitation of the living resources of the EEZs of other States in the sub-region or region for adequate supplies of fish for the nutritional needs of their population or parts thereof, or (2) which can claim no EEZ of their own (LOSC, art. 70(2)). The right to equitable participation in the surplus, given by articles 69(1) and 70(1), applies in the case of developed landlocked States and developed geographically disadvantaged States only to the EEZs of other developed States; and here regard also has to be had to the extent to which the coastal State, in giving access to other States to the living resources of its EEZ, has taken into account the need to minimise detrimental effects on fishing communities and economic dislocation in States whose nationals have habitually fished in its zone (LOSC, arts 69(4), 70(5)).

The rights given to landlocked and geographically disadvantaged States by articles 69 and 70 may not be directly or indirectly transferred to third States or their nationals unless all the States concerned agree (LOSC, art. 72). It is always open to coastal States to grant to landlocked and geographically disadvantaged States rights greater than those laid down in the above provisions (LOSC, arts 69(5), 70(6)). On the other hand, a coastal State 'whose economy is overwhelmingly dependent on the exploitation of the living resources of its exclusive economic zone' is under no obligation to allow access by other States to these resources (LOSC, art. 71).

The rights given to landlocked and geographically disadvantaged States by the above provisions are fairly tenuous, and largely depend on how much a coastal State is prepared to concede in negotiating an agreement. The language of the provisions is also vague and ill-defined. Perhaps the most serious failing in this regard is the lack of any definition of 'region' or 'sub-region', and the failure to explain the distinction between these two terms. The difficulties arising from this can be illustrated by the case of landlocked Chad. To which 'region' does it belong for the purposes of article 69? It borders four coastal States–Libya, Sudan, Cameroon and Nigeria. Is the 'region' to which it belongs therefore the Mediterranean, the Red Sea or the Gulf of Guinea? Or does it belong to all three?

Although, as we saw in chapter fourteen, many coastal States have already claimed 200-mile EEZs or fishing zones, there appear as yet to be no agreements providing for the access of landlocked States to such zones.[9] This is scarcely surprising, since no landlocked State yet possesses a marine fishing industry and very few landlocked States have an inland fishing industry. It may be wondered, in the light of the cost and formidable difficulties for landlocked States of starting a marine fishing industry, whether giving such States some access to the living resources of neighbouring States' EEZs is really the most effective way of providing an equitable share of marine fish resources for landlocked States. It would have been a more economic and effective division of labour to provide that, rather than landlocked States attempting to establish their own fishing

---

[9] Although there are no agreements providing for the access of landlocked States, two States provide for such access in their national legislation. See Morocco, Decree No. 1–81–179 of 8 April 1981, art. 13 and Togo, Ordinance No. 24 of 16 August 1977, art. 4. *Smith, op. cit.* in 'Further reading' at the end of this chapter, pp. 303 and 439. Note also art.16 of the 1991 Convention on Fisheries Co-operation among African States bordering the Atlantic Ocean, which provides that 'parties affirm their solidarity with land-locked African States and with Geographically Disadvantaged States of the Region and shall establish active co-operation with them'. In addition, the 1992 Agreement between Bolivia and Peru concerning the Establishment of a Binational Technical Commission for a Complimentarity Programme between Peruvian and Bolivian Fishing Enterprises includes the possibility for Bolivia to enter into joint ventures with Peruvian companies to engage in fishing activities.

industries, the more developed coastal States should be obliged to give land-locked States part of their catch or a cash equivalent. As regards geographically disadvantaged States, it is difficult to say whether any have been given access to neighbouring States' 200-mile economic or fishing zones in pursuance of article 70, both because of the difficulty of deciding which States are geographically disadvantaged within the meaning of article 70 and because access might be accorded for reasons other than that a State is geographically disadvantaged.

Related to the question of the access of landlocked and geographically dis-advantaged States to the EEZs of neighbouring coastal States is the subject of marine scientific research. Part XIII of the Law of the Sea Convention, which deals with research, contains one provision specifically concerning landlocked and geographically disadvantaged States. Under article 254 third States and international organisations undertaking a pure research project in the EEZ of a coastal State must notify neighbouring landlocked and geographically disadvant-aged States of that project: the latter States must also be given an opportunity to participate in the project 'whenever feasible', and in any case must be given an assessment of the results of the project. In so far as the rights of fisheries exploitation given to landlocked and geographically disadvantaged States are of practical benefit, the right given in article 254 may be a useful supplement, although somewhat limited. This is because the right is confined to projects con-cerning pure research and does not apply where the project is directly concerned with fishery resources. The right is also limited because there are no obligations on the coastal State when conducting research in its EEZ corresponding to those on third States and international organisations under article 254.

The access of landlocked States to the sea

The navigational rights of landlocked States (particularly their exercise for the pur-poses of engaging in seaborne trade) and the rights of access of landlocked States to marine resources would be of little practical benefit unless landlocked States also enjoy a right for their nationals and goods to cross the territory of States lying between them and the sea (which will be referred to as a right of transit). Whether and to what extent there is such a right of transit in international law is therefore an important question which we must now consider.

Customary law

It is controversial whether there is a general right of transit in customary interna-tional law. In the *Right of Passage* case (1960) the International Court of Justice found that Portugal enjoyed a right of transit across Indian territory between the various enclaves it at that time possessed in India. The Court found this right derived from a local custom and therefore it did not consider it necessary to decide whether a right of transit existed as a general rule of customary international law.

The evidence for such a general rule is scant (the most recent State practice apparently being characterised by frequent denials of transit rights), and the considerable treaty practice on the subject which we shall consider in a moment suggests the absence of such a rule or at least casts considerable doubt on its existence, since if such a rule of customary international law was clearly to be found, treaty rules would not be necessary.[10] Of course, local customary rules may always exist, as in the *Right of Passage* case.

Quite separately the question has been asked whether under customary international law there exists a right of transit in relation to one specific mode of transit – navigation on international rivers. Opinion is divided, but the view of the majority of writers appears to be that under customary international law there is no right for vessels of one State – at least of a non-riparian State – to navigate a river passing through another State.[11] Again, as we shall see, this is a right that is sometimes conferred by treaty.

Treaty law

Although a general right of transit probably does not exist under customary international law, such a right has been granted in a number of treaties. The Convention and Statute on Freedom of Transit of 1921 obligates the parties 'to facilitate free transit' of goods and persons across their territory by rail or waterway on routes in use convenient for international transit without distinction as to nationality. Only dues to defray expenses and reasonable tariffs may be charged. The Convention is general in scope and is not limited to, nor does it deal specifically with, landlocked States or access to the sea. A further disadvantage of the Convention is the relatively low number of contracting parties – forty-eight as at the end of September 1998, of which twelve are landlocked. Article V of the General Agreement on Tariffs and Trade (1947), now also incorporated in the 1994 GATT, provides for a general 'freedom of transit' along lines similar to those of the 1921 Convention. For this freedom to be exercised by a party to GATT, its nationals or their goods must not only pass through the territory of a party to GATT, but both the State of origin and the State of destination must also be parties to GATT. In spite of the high number of parties to GATT – 126,

---

[10] Some writers have, however, claimed that a right of transit exists in customary law, e.g., Lauterpacht, *op. cit.* in 'Further reading' and J. E. S. Fawcett, 'Trade and finance in international law', 123 *Recueil des Cours* 215 (1968), at 266–7. Against this view see, e.g., Caflisch (see the references in 'Further reading', 1977 and 1978, at pp. 361–4 and 77–9, respectively) and Vasciannie, *op. cit.* in 'Further reading', chapter 8.

[11] See, e.g., Baxter, *op. cit.* in 'Further reading', pp. 149–59, R. Jennings and A. Watts, *Oppenheim's International Law* (London, Longman) 9th edn, 1992, p. 582, and Vitanyi, *op. cit.* in 'Further reading', chapter 4. See also the *Faber* case (1903) where the German Commissioner of the Germany–Venezuela Mixed Claims Commission thought there was a general right of navigation on rivers (X RIAA 438, at 444–5); the Venezuelan Commissioner (pp. 448–9) and the Umpire (pp. 464–7), however, disagreed. In any case, the question was essentially *obiter*.

of which twenty-three are landlocked – this triple requirement (which also applies in the case of the 1921 Convention) is a considerable limitation on the freedom granted by article V.

The High Seas Convention, unlike the two earlier treaties, dealt with transit specifically in relation to the access of landlocked States to the sea. Article 3 provided:

> 1 In order to enjoy the freedom of the seas on equal terms with coastal States, States having no sea-coast should have free access to the sea. To this end States situated between the sea and a State having no sea-coast shall by common agreement with the latter, and in conformity with existing international conventions, accord:
>
> (a) To the State having no sea-coast, on a basis of reciprocity, free transit through their territory; and
>
> (b) To ships flying the flag of that State treatment equal to that accorded to their own ships, or to the ships of any other States, as regards access to sea ports and the use of such ports.
>
> 2 States situated between the sea and a State having no sea-coast shall settle, by mutual agreement with the latter, and taking into account the rights of the coastal State or State of transit and the special conditions of the State having no sea-coast, all matters relating to freedom of transit and equal treatment in ports, in case such States are not already parties to existing international conventions.

This article in fact conferred no direct rights on landlocked States. Rights of access and transit were to be agreed between landlocked and coastal States in separate treaties. It was thus a *pactum de contrahendo*, requiring parties to the High Seas Convention to enter into negotiations for such treaties in good faith. Although according to its preamble the High Seas Convention was generally declaratory of customary international law, this would not seem to have been the case as far as article 3 was concerned, because, as has already been suggested, no right of transit exists under customary international law. Furthermore, unlike the rest of the Convention, article 3 was not the result of the ILC's largely codifying work, but was added at the 1958 Geneva Conference in response to the recommendations of the Preliminary Conference of Landlocked States.

Since the adoption of the High Seas Convention in 1958 a number of bilateral treaties have been signed,[12] as well as an important multilateral treaty – the Convention on Transit Trade of Landlocked Countries of 1965. Article 2 of this Convention grants freedom of transit across a State lying between a landlocked State and the sea (the transit State) for goods travelling by road, rail or river between the landlocked State and the sea. No customs duties may be levied on goods in transit, and only dues to defray expenses and reasonable charges may be levied (arts 3, 4). Transit must not be hindered by administrative or customs

---

[12] For examples, see Delupis, *op. cit.* in 'Further reading', pp. 105–8, and UN Doc. A/AC 138/37.

practices (art. 5). Exceptions to all these provisions may be made on grounds of public health and security, or in case of emergency and war (arts 11–13). The great drawback with this Convention is the low number of ratifications. Only thirty-six States are parties (as of September 1998), of which twenty are landlocked. However, of these twenty, only nine (Belarus, Burkina Faso, Chad, Czech Republic, Hungary, Mali, Mongolia, Niger and Slovakia) adjoin transit States which are also parties to the 1965 Convention, and so can obtain any practical benefit from its provisions.

In addition to the above treaties which deal with transit by a number of different modes of transport, there are also treaties dealing with transit by only one mode of transport. The Convention and Statute on the International Regime of Railways of 1923, which has twenty-six parties (five of which are land-locked), contains a number of provisions designed to facilitate the international traffic of goods and persons by railway. The Convention and Statute concerning the Regime of Navigable Waterways of International Concern of 1921 gives its twenty-eight parties (six of which are landlocked) a right of navigation on international rivers. In addition, there is a number of treaties dealing with individual rivers. The most important of these, so far as landlocked States are concerned, are the treaties relating to the Rhine,[13] Danube[14] and Niger,[15] which give freedom of navigation on these rivers to all States, including those riparian States that are landlocked, viz. Switzerland; Austria, Slovakia and Hungary; and Burkina Faso, Chad, Mali and Niger respectively. As far as transit by air is concerned, a number of multilateral treaties dealing with civil aviation – the Convention on International Civil Aviation (1944), article 5, the International Air Services Transit Agreement (1944) and the International Air Transport Agreement (1944) – give aircraft varying rights of transit, but in practice bilateral agreements are at least, if not more, important. Finally, the facilitation of road transit is provided for by the widely ratified multilateral Convention on Road Traffic of 1968 (replacing the 1949 Convention on Road Traffic) and a host of bilateral agreements.

The Law of the Sea Convention

Although quite numerous, the existing multilateral treaties dealing with transit are each in one way or another not wholly satisfactory for landlocked States. At UNCLOS III these States therefore pressed for the Law of the Sea Convention to contain a guaranteed right of transit. At first sight their demands appear to have been satisfied. Article 125(1) provides that:

[13] Convention for Rhine Navigation, 1868, as amended.
[14] Convention regarding the Regime of Navigation on the Danube, 1948.
[15] Act regarding Navigation and Economic Co-operation between the States of the Niger Basin, 1963, and Agreement concerning the Niger River Commission and the Navigation and Transport on the River Niger, 1964. The 1964 Agreement has been superseded by the Convention creating the Niger Basin Authority, 1980.

Land-locked States shall have the right of access to and from the sea for the purpose of exercising the rights provided for in this Convention including those relating to the freedom of the high seas and the common heritage of mankind. To this end land-locked States shall enjoy freedom of transit through the territory of transit States by all means of transport.[16]

However, what appears to be an absolute right of transit becomes considerably qualified when one reads paragraphs 2 and 3 of article 125. They provide:

2 The terms and modalities for exercising freedom of transit shall be agreed between the land-locked States and transit States concerned through bilateral, sub-regional or regional agreements.

3 Transit States, in the exercise of their full sovereignty over their territory, shall have the right to take all measures necessary to ensure that the rights and facilities provided for in this Part [i.e., Part X] for land-locked States shall in no way infringe their legitimate interests.

The exercise of the right of transit will therefore in practice very much depend on the terms and modalities agreed between transit States and landlocked States and on the measures taken by transit States under article 125(3). It is clear that a transit State must in good faith seek to conclude a transit agreement (what happens where the States concerned cannot reach agreement is not entirely clear),[17] and that the terms and modalities of such an agreement, as well as unilateral measures taken by a transit State, cannot be such that they effectively negate the right of transit in principle. Furthermore, such terms and modalities and unilateral measures must comply with the provisions of articles 127 and 130, which deal with customs duties and other charges and measures to avoid delays in a way similar to that of the 1965 Convention on Transit Trade of Landlocked Countries.

In the case of some landlocked States, particularly those of Africa, the right of transit may not be exercisable in practice because of the lack of navigable rivers, railways or adequate roads. Article 129 of the Law of the Sea Convention recognises this problem and provides that in these situations the States concerned 'may co-operate' in taking remedial measures. While the details of how such measures are to be taken can of course only be agreed on by the States concerned at a bilateral or regional level, the Convention might nevertheless have contained a stronger exhortation to co-operate in this matter. In practice co-operation on such issues of infrastructure in Africa has taken place through regional organisations such as the Economic Community of West African States and the Southern African Development Community.

---

[16] But 'means of transport' is defined in article 124 as excluding pipelines and air transport, unless the States concerned agree to the contrary.

[17] Where one party has not shown good faith, there is presumably breach of an international obligation (and cf. art. 300 of the Law of the Sea Convention): in any case the Convention's provisions on settlement of disputes could be invoked by the dissatisfied party.

Nearly all the multilateral treaties on transit, particularly the High Seas Convention and the Law of the Sea Convention, contemplate the conclusion of bilateral treaties to regulate transit rights in detail. There are in fact quite a number of these treaties, particularly in relation to the landlocked States of Europe, Latin America and, to some extent, Asia (for examples, see the works of Delupis, Glassner, Govindaraj and the UN Secretariat listed in 'Further reading' at the end of this chapter). In Africa there is an important regional transit agreement, the Northern Corridor Transit Agreement,[18] which gives a right of transit to Burundi, Rwanda and Uganda to the Kenyan port of Mombasa. This agreement is one of the most comprehensive and detailed transit agreements yet concluded. In spite of the existence of bilateral and regional transit treaties, multilateral treaties such as the 1965 Convention and the Law of the Sea Convention which confer a general right of transit remain of great importance. In negotiating with a transit State a landlocked State is in a weak bargaining position because it usually has little to offer the transit State in return for the favour it is seeking. It therefore strengthens the position of a landlocked State in negotiating a new bilateral treaty or renewing an existing treaty if it can point to a general right of transit laid down in a multilateral convention.

The special problems experienced by landlocked and geographically disadvantaged States in relation to the law of the sea appear now to have received general recognition. On the other hand, the rights that have been accorded to these States do not deal with those problems in a manner wholly to their satisfaction. Furthermore, the rights themselves, particularly those relating to access to the living resources of neighbouring EEZs and to transit, are subject to so many qualifications and limitations and are expressed in such imprecise language that it is doubtful how much practical benefit they will give (as a matter of law) to landlocked and geographically disadvantaged States. This may explain why so few landlocked States, currently just over a quarter, have so far ratified the Law of the Sea Convention.

Further reading

L. M. Alexander, 'The "disadvantaged" States and the Law of the Sea', 5 *Marine Policy* 185–93 (1981).

—— and R. D. Hodgson, 'The role of geographically disadvantaged States in the law of the sea', 13 *San Diego Law Review* 558–82 (1976).

R. R. Baxter, *The Law of International Waterways* (Cambridge, Mass., Harvard University Press), 1964.

L. C. Caflisch, 'Land-locked and geographically disadvantaged States and the new law of the sea' in *The Law of the Sea*, Thesaurus Acroasium, Vol. VII, Thessaloniki, 1977, pp. 341–404.

[18] The agreement was signed on 19 February 1985 and came into force on 15 November 1986. We have been unable to locate the text of the agreement. A summary of its provisions is given in 11 *Commonwealth Law Bulletin* 1001–2 (1985) and 13 *ibid.* 641–3 (1987).

——, 'Land-locked States and their access to and from the sea', 49 *BYIL* 71–100 (1978).

——, 'What is a geographically disadvantaged State?', 18 *ODIL* 641–63 (1987).

——, 'The Fishing Rights of Land-Locked and Geographically Disadvantaged States in the Exclusive Economic Zone' in B. Conforti (ed.), *La Zona Economica Esclusiva* (Milan, Giuffre), 1983, pp. 29–48.

I. Delupis, 'Landlocked States and the law of the sea', 19 *Scandinavian Studies in Law* 101–20 (1975).

R.-J. Dupuy and D. Vignes (eds), *Traité du Nouveau Droit de la Mer* (Brussels, Bruylant), 1985, chapter 9 and pp. 905–30 (*passim*) (chapter 9 and pp. 1074–1100 (*passim*) of the English edition, 1991).

J. H. E. Fried, 'The 1965 Convention on Transit Trade of Landlocked States', 6 *IJIL* 9–30 (1966).

M. I. Glassner, *Access to the Sea for Developing Land-locked States* (The Hague, Nijhoff), 1970.

——, *Bibliography on Landlocked States* (The Hague, Nijhoff), 4th edn, 1995.

V. C. Govindaraj, 'Land-locked States and their right of access to the sea', 14 *IJIL* 190–216 (1974).

E. Lauterpacht, 'Freedom of transit in international law', 44 *Transactions of the Grotius Society* 313–56 (1958–59).

R. Makil, 'Transit rights of land-locked countries', 4 *Journal of World Trade Law* 35–51 (1970).

Memorandum submitted by the Preliminary Conference of Landlocked States, UNCLOS I, *Official Records*, Vol. VII, pp. 67–79.

A. M. Punal, 'The rights of landlocked and geographically disadvantaged States in exclusive economic zones,' 23 *Journal of Maritime Law and Commerce* 429–59 (1992).

A. M. Sinjela, *Land-locked States and the UNCLOS Regime* (New York, Oceana), 1983.

R. W. Smith, *Exclusive Economic Zone Claims: An Analysis and Primary Documents* (Dordrecht, Nijhoff), 1986 [*Smith*].

J. Symonides, 'Geographically disadvantaged States in the 1982 Convention on the Law of the Sea', 208 *Recueil des Cours* 283–406 (1988).

United Nations, *The Law of the Sea: Rights of Access of Land-Locked States to and from the Sea, and Freedom of Transit – Legislative History of Part X, Articles 124–132, of the United Nations Convention on the Law of the Sea* (New York, United Nations), 1987.

UN Secretariat, 'The question of free access to the sea of land-locked countries', UNCLOS I, *Official Records*, Vol. I, pp. 306–35.

UN Secretary General, 'Study of the question of free access to the sea of landlocked countries and of the special problems of landlocked countries relating to the exploration and exploitation of the resources of the seabed and the ocean floor beyond the limits of national jurisdiction', UN Doc. A/AC 138/37 (1971).

S. C. Vasciannie, *Land-Locked and Geographically Disadvantaged States in the International Law of the Sea* (Oxford, Clarendon Press), 1990.

B. Vitanyi, *The International Regime of River Navigation* (Alphen aan den Rijn, Sijthoff), 1979.

I. J. Wani, 'An evaluation of the Convention on the Law of the Sea from the perspective of landlocked States', 22 *VJIL* 627–65 (1982).

19

Settlement of disputes

Settlement of disputes under general international law

The law of the sea presents many opportunities for disputes. Adjacent or opposite States may disagree over the boundaries separating their respective maritime zones; one State may claim the right to conduct naval manoeuvres in the EEZ of another State which denies that such a right exists; a fisherman may challenge the right of a foreign State to arrest him for fishing fifty miles from its coasts. These three examples (and many more may be found in previous chapters) illustrate different kinds of dispute which may arise. For the purposes of settlement, the important distinction is between the first two examples, which represent inter-State or international disputes, and the third, which represents disputes between a State and an individual. However, as we shall see, disputes of the latter kind may become translated into international disputes proper.

Municipal courts

When an individual has, to use our example, been arrested under foreign laws which in his view violate international law, he may attempt to raise the issue with the arresting officer or, if that is unsuccessful, with the municipal court before which he is brought for trial. The response of the court to arguments based upon international law will be determined largely by the standing of international law in the legal system concerned. For example, under English and Scottish law domestic statutes invariably prevail, in accordance with the doctrine of parliamentary sovereignty, over international customary law and treaties. Accordingly, when it was argued in the case of *Mortensen* v. *Peters* (1906) that the conviction of the Danish captain of a Norwegian ship for fishing in the Moray Firth was contrary to international law because it involved a claim to jurisdiction over a foreign ship more than three miles from shore, the conviction was nevertheless upheld. The Scottish Court of Justiciary held that even if the statute under which Mortensen was convicted was contrary to international law, the court was bound to give effect to the intention of Parliament and enforce it. The remedy for the consequent breach of international law is then diplomatic (see below). In this case the British government subsequently pardoned the fishermen and repaid their fines.

Other States have different rules.[1] In States with civil law systems (based upon comprehensive legislative codes descended from Roman law rather the mixture of judicial decisions and statute which characterises the English and other common law systems) treaties are commonly given precedence over domestic legislation – at least over prior, if not over later, legislation. Some States, such as Germany, also give customary international law this status. In such States it is therefore possible in at least some cases (depending upon the precise rules of the legal system in question) for international law to be invoked to prevent the application of the local law. Thus, in the French case of the *Sally* and the *Newton* (1806), the jurisdiction of the French courts to prosecute assaults committed on board American ships in French ports was held to be ousted by a rule of international law reserving matters of 'internal discipline' to the flag State (see chapter three). Each legal system has its own rules for determining the relationship between municipal and international law, but most adopt a position somewhere between the 'nationalism' of English law and the 'internationalism' of German law. Thus in the USA, for example, the self-executing provisions of treaties have direct effect and overrule prior (but not later) statutes, but statutes prevail over customary law.

Whatever the doctrine espoused by their States, it is the usual practice of courts to construe statutes, wherever possible, so as not to conflict with the international obligations of their State. So, for instance, the English Court of Appeal in *Post Office* v. *Estuary Radio Ltd* (1968) decided that any ambiguity in the Order defining British territorial waters should be resolved so as to accord with the provisions of the Territorial Sea Convention 'in so far as that is a plausible meaning of the express words of the Order.'[2]

Diplomatic protection

It may be that municipal courts insist upon enforcing the legislation which is alleged to conflict with international law. If so, if the dispute is to be pursued, it must be taken up on behalf of the aggrieved individual and continued as a dispute between States. A State could take up such a case by espousing the complaint of the individual that international law has been breached. In such cases, the State is said to exercise the right of diplomatic protection. That right extends to the State's nationals (including companies incorporated in the State) and to ships and aircraft flying the State's flag. In the absence of some link of nationality of this kind, diplomatic protection may not be exercised. Furthermore, diplomatic protection is a right, and not a duty: the individual has no right to insist upon his State exercising diplomatic protection on his behalf; nor, indeed, to

---

[1] See M. Fitzmaurice and C. Flinterman (eds), *L. Erades. Interaction between International and Municipal Law* (The Hague, Asser), 1993.
[2] [1968] 2 QB 740 at 757.

prevent his State from doing so. In taking up an individual case a State is, in law, asserting its own rights, which have been challenged when they were exercised by the State through one of its nationals: it is not asserting the rights of the individual concerned as such. The State is said to have suffered an 'indirect wrong' in such circumstances. When the dispute is taken up by the individual's national State in this way, the dispute becomes one between two States: the one exercising diplomatic protection and the one whose actions are challenged. For example, the United Kingdom took up the cases of British trawler owners denied access to or arrested in 'Icelandic' fishing grounds during the successive 'cod wars' of 1958–76 against Iceland.

Settlement of inter-State disputes

Some disputes arise out of a direct violation of one State's rights by another. Those disputes involve 'direct wrongs', and are on the international plane from the outset. Examples are disputes over maritime boundaries, and cases involving the armed forces, which are considered to embody the sovereignty of the State. The *Corfu Channel* dispute between the United Kingdom and Albania, discussed in chapter four, is an instance of the latter. International disputes of this kind never go before municipal tribunals, it being a rule of international law that no State should be required to submit to the courts of another.

States are under an obligation to settle disputes by peaceful means, whether the dispute concerns a direct or an indirect wrong (see article 33 of the UN Charter, and the 1982 Manila Declaration on Peaceful Settlement of Disputes between States, UN GA Res. 37/10, (1982)). Unless they are bound by treaty to have recourse to any specific procedure, States are free to use any means of their own choosing for the settlement of disputes. The most common means for settling international disputes are negotiation, enquiry, mediation, conciliation, arbitration or judicial settlement. It is true that the sequence of dispute settlement procedures in this list, which is taken from article 33 of the UN Charter, reflects an increasing level of involvement by third parties. But the list does not represent a progression, with States exhausting the possibilities of one procedure before trying another. The list is more in the nature of a toolbox, from which States can choose the dispute settlement procedure most suited to the dispute in question, and States may use different means at different stages of the dispute. There is, for example, no reason why States should not decide to seek a ruling from the International Court as a prelude to detailed negotiations for a settlement of the dispute. Indeed, this was the role given to the Court in the *North Sea Continental Shelf* cases.

Negotiations

Once a dispute arises on the international plane, it is normal first to seek a settlement by negotiation. Indeed, in cases where a State is exercising its right of diplomatic protection, negotiations may have been started before the individual has been convicted, or even arrested. This is typically the case where the source of the dispute is a piece of legislation. It is not unusual for diplomatic representations, which may lead to negotiations, to be made while the legislation is still at its Bill stage, before final adoption by the legislature. During the disputes over the American liquor laws in the 1920s diplomatic negotiations proceeded in respect of the general issue, rather than specific cases, and produced in 1924 a series of bilateral treaties embodying the agreed settlement.

Whether or not they lead immediately to the resolution of the dispute, negotiations perform a vital role. They serve to identify the precise issue at the heart of the dispute, separating it from the common ground between the parties and from peripheral issues. They may also identify other procedures that may be pursued in order to settle the dispute.

Fact-finding and conciliation commissions

If negotiations do not resolve the dispute, it may be necessary or desirable to involve a third party. This may involve no more than the provision of good offices, where the third party acts as an essentially passive channel of communication between the disputants, or mediation, in which case the third party plays a more active role, attempting to find a basis for agreement between them. In some cases the third party may play a more conclusive role, settling disputed questions of fact or law or both. For example, in the dispute following the seizure of the *Red Crusader* (1962) much turned upon the question whether the fishing vessel was within or without the Faroese fishing zone, and the United Kingdom (as flag State) and Denmark agreed to set up a commission of enquiry to settle the matter.

Occasionally, a conciliation commission may be established to investigate the dispute and propose the terms of a settlement. This occurred in relation to the continental shelf around Jan Mayen island, disputed between Norway and Iceland, who agreed to the establishment of a conciliation commission and accepted its recommendations. Several treaties on the law of the sea, such as the 1969 Oil Pollution Intervention Convention and the 1993 Indian Ocean Tuna Agreement, provide for the 'compulsory' conciliation of disputes between their parties.

Arbitration

Where questions of law are concerned, the parties may decide to refer the dispute for a 'judicial' settlement. There is no judicial tribunal with compulsory jurisdiction in international law, and the parties to the dispute must agree to submit a case to a tribunal. Third-party settlement may take different forms. The basic choice is between recourse to the International Court of Justice in The Hague, to which we refer below, and recourse to arbitration, of which several varieties may be distinguished.

450

The parties may agree to set up an *ad hoc* arbitral tribunal whose composition and terms of reference they jointly determine. This course was adopted in the *Anglo-French Continental Shelf* arbitration of 1977. The Permanent Court of Arbitration ('PCA') – which is really no more than a panel of arbitrators – may be used in this connection, each State nominating from the panel two arbitrators who together choose a fifth as umpire. Tribunals established under the PCA system gave awards in the *Muscat Dhows* (1905) and *North Atlantic Coast Fisheries* (1910) cases, among others. Alternatively, there may be a standing tribunal with jurisdiction over disputes arising between the States in question, such as the US-Panamanian General Claims Commission, which decided the case of the *David* (1933). Such standing tribunals, which had something of a vogue in the inter-war period, are not now common. It is, however, relatively common for treaties to provide for disputes to be settled by arbitral tribunals established according to procedures laid down in the treaty. The 1992 Convention for the Protection of the Marine Environment of the North-East Atlantic is one of many treaties which provides for the establishment of arbitral tribunals to settle disputes between States parties concerning the interpretation or application of the treaty. Article 32 of the 1992 Convention obliges parties to submit to arbitration: any State may require another to arbitrate a dispute arising under the Convention. By contrast, many other treaties simply encourage recourse to arbitration. For instance, article 22 of the 1976 Barcelona Convention for the Protection of the Mediterranean Sea Against Pollution provides that if parties cannot settle disputes arising under the Convention by means of their own choosing the dispute shall *upon common agreement* be submitted to arbitration. Here, unilateral references of disputes to arbitral tribunals are not possible.

In the case of all international tribunals, whether arbitral tribunals or the International Court of Justice or other special tribunals, cases arising from indirect wrongs can be brought before them only when local remedies – that is to say, the system of appeals in municipal courts, and any other appeals which the municipal legal system might offer – have been exhausted. As we have noted, a dispute which arises from a direct wrong, between two States rather than an individual and a State, does not have to be submitted to a municipal court, and so there will in such cases be no question of exhausting local remedies.

The International Court of Justice

States have often preferred to take disputes to the International Court of Justice (or, before 1945, its predecessor, the Permanent Court of International Justice), rather than to arbitration. The International Court is a very highly respected body, whose judges are lawyers of the highest reputation, representing all of the world's major legal systems, and often having very extensive experience of international litigation. The Court's procedures are well known, and its rulings carry very great weight.

The International Court has some disadvantages, as compared with arbitration. The Court's workload has now increased to the point where delay in dealing with cases has become a significant problem. The parties cannot themselves dictate the procedure to be followed in the case, and they are not wholly free to determine the composition of the bench. The judges are elected for nine-year terms by the UN General Assembly and Security Council in accordance with the Court's Statute. However, each party to a dispute has a right to appoint a judge of its choosing if there is no judge of its nationality on the bench. Furthermore, the parties may agree to put a dispute before a chamber of the Court. If they do, the parties may choose those judges who will constitute the chamber. This was done, for example, in the *Gulf of Maine* case. The Court itself allocates judges each year to two special chambers: a Chamber of Summary Procedure to handle cases in an accelerated manner, and a Chamber for Environmental Matters.

The International Court has some significant advantages over arbitration. It is a standing tribunal, with excellent premises, funded (the Court would say under-funded) by the UN rather than by the parties. The parties do not have to arrange for accommodation, translation and so on, or for the drafting of rules of procedure. Moreover, about sixty States[3] have opted under article 36(2) of the Statute to accept the Court's jurisdiction in advance of any specific dispute arising. The case concerning the *Land and Maritime Boundary between Cameroon and Nigeria* is a recent (1994) example of a case put before the Court on the basis of article 36(2) declarations ('Optional Clause' declarations) made by the two States concerned.

Acceptance of the Court's jurisdiction cannot be withdrawn once proceedings have been instituted against that State. Thus, the *Nuclear Tests* cases were brought against France in 1974, despite the fact that it refused to co-operate. Such a refusal would ordinarily have prevented arbitration of the issue, because arbitration depends upon the willingness of both parties to agree to and participate in the arbitral process.[4] While the refusal of France to appear before the International Court detracted from the proceedings, there is no doubt that recourse to the Court put considerable pressure upon France to comply with the applicable rules of international law.

Article 36(2) is not the only route by which a dispute may be brought before the International Court. The disputing States may decide by special agreement to submit the dispute to the Court, as did the three States involved in the *North Sea Continental Shelf* cases. In addition, many bilateral and multilateral treaties provide that any dispute arising out of the interpretation or application of the treaty is to

---

[3] For lists of the States see the *Yearbooks* of the Court or the ICJ internet site, http://www.icj-cij.org, or the *United Nations Treaty Series* database, at http://www.un.org/Depts/Treaty/bible.htm. Among the permanent members of the Security Council, only the United Kingdom currently has such a declaration in force.

[4] Though States may agree in advance that once an arbitral tribunal is validly seised of a dispute the refusal of one party to co-operate shall not prevent the tribunal from proceeding to render an award.

be referred to the Court. An example of a treaty containing such a compromissory clause, as these provisions are known, is the Iceland–United Kingdom Agreement of 1961, and it was on this treaty that the Court's jurisdiction was founded in the *Fisheries Jurisdiction* case (1974). Even where there are no declarations under article 36(2) of the Statute and no special agreement or treaty containing an applicable compromissory clause, a State may be prepared to accept the Court's jurisdiction. If a State chooses to defend itself in the Court when another State institutes a case against it, the Court may assert jurisdiction on the basis of the doctrine of *forum prorogatum*. This kind of jurisdiction is highly exceptional, one of the very few cases which the Court has decided on this basis being the *Corfu Channel* case (1949). It will be noted that all the ways in which a case may come before the Court (and, indeed, all forms of third-party dispute settlement in international law) are based upon the consent of both the States concerned.

The International Court was intended to have a prominent role in the settlement of disputes arising from the 1958 Geneva Conventions on the Law of the Sea. An optional protocol provided that all disputes arising from the interpretation or application of the Conventions should be referred to the International Court, unless the parties agreed within a reasonable time upon some other means of peaceful settlement. Just over thirty States accepted this obligation in relation to the 1958 Conventions to which they were parties. Its unpopularity, like that of declarations under article 36(2) of the Court's Statute, derives mainly from an unwillingness on the part of States to accept an open-ended obligation to submit future disputes, whose nature is almost impossible to predict, to any particular settlement procedure. In fact, no case has been referred to the Court under the optional protocol.

The International Court has frequently been criticised as ineffectual because it is powerless to compel States to appear before it. That criticism is misdirected. It is the governments of States which have refused to give the Court the power to demand that they appear before it. Despite the general reluctance of States to bind themselves to use particular dispute settlement procedures, UNCLOS III adopted an elaborate system for the settlement of maritime disputes. It did so in order to provide some assurance that the delicate balance of rights and duties established in the 1982 Law of the Sea Convention would be respected in practice, by facilitating action against States violating the Convention. This system applies to disputes involving States parties: disputes with non-party States are subject to the principles and procedures outlined above. We turn now to a description of the main features of the LOSC system.

Settlement of disputes under the Law of the Sea Convention

Consensual settlement

The scheme in the 1982 Convention has two parts. Section 2 of Part XV of the Convention sets out the range of tribunals to be used under the 'compulsory' settlement procedures that are commonly thought of as the essence of the Convention's dispute settlement procedures. However, it is important to recognise that those compulsory procedures are of secondary importance. Section 1 (General Provisions) of Part XV of the Convention sets out the fundamental principles concerning dispute settlement.

First, article 279 stipulates that States are obliged to settle their disputes by peaceful means, and refers to the provisions of article 33 of the UN Charter. Article 280 provides that States have the right to settle any dispute between them by peaceful means of their own choosing. The same principle applies to disputes between States and non-State entities, such as the International Sea Bed Authority and the Enterprise and the deep-sea-bed mining companies.

When a dispute arises the parties must 'proceed expeditiously to an exchange of views regarding its settlement by negotiation or other peaceful means' (article 283). Those means might have been established in advance by agreement between them: for example, fisheries disputes between EC States would have to be submitted, under the EC Treaty, to the Court of Justice of the European Communities. If they have not been established in advance, the parties are free to have recourse to any procedure they choose, judicial or non-judicial, although the Convention singles out the possibility of recourse to voluntary and non-binding conciliation for explicit mention. Certain provisions, such as article 264 concerning marine scientific research, appear to limit this freedom and to oblige the parties to use the 'compulsory' settlement procedures in section 2 of Part XV to resolve the dispute, but their practical effect is unclear. It might be said that if there arises a difference between the parties, which they agree to pursue in a particular fashion, no 'dispute' arises.

If the parties to a dispute fail to reach a settlement through agreed procedures, one of them may invite the other to submit to the conciliation procedure laid out in the Convention (LOSC, article 284 and Annex V). If this invitation is accepted, each party chooses two conciliators of which one may be one of its nationals, from a list to which each State party to the Convention is entitled to nominate four people. The four conciliators chosen select a fifth, who acts as chairman of the conciliation panel. The panel has one year within which to hear the parties and report, making any recommendations that it sees fit. If the report is accepted and implemented, all is well. If it is not, or if the invitation to conciliate is rejected, the conciliation procedure is deemed to be terminated.

The scope of 'compulsory' settlement obligations

Only where settlement is not possible by means freely chosen by the parties to the dispute do the elaborate compulsory dispute settlement provisions of the 1982 Convention come into play. Section 2 of Part XV of the LOSC sets out the 'compulsory procedures entailing binding decisions' to which, according to articles 286 and 287, parties must have recourse if the means chosen by them fail to settle the dispute. That obligation is subject to a number of exceptions. The exceptions are designed to take out of the compulsory settlement process certain categories of dispute that touch upon vital interests of the State, such as the State's boundaries, security, and some aspects of its control over its offshore resources. Without these exclusions there was a risk that some States would have been deterred from accepting the Convention. Certain exclusions are prescribed by the Convention itself.

The first is general. Article 297(1) provides that no dispute concerning the exercise by a coastal State of its sovereign rights or jurisdiction within its EEZ is subject to the 'compulsory procedures entailing binding decisions' set out in Section 2 of Part XV of the LOSC unless it is alleged (a) that the State has violated the freedoms set out in the Convention of navigation, overflight, and pipe- and cable-laying, and other internationally lawful uses of the seas, or (b) that a State exercising any such freedom has violated the Convention or coastal laws adopted in conformity with the Convention, or (c) that the coastal State has, in breach of the LOSC, exercised its jurisdiction in a manner inconsistent with certain internationally adopted rules and standards on marine pollution.

Secondly, under LOSC article 297(2) States are not obliged to submit to the compulsory procedures disputes arising from the refusal to give permission to conduct marine scientific research in their EEZs or continental shelves. If such a dispute is not submitted to those procedures, it must be submitted to the 'compulsory conciliation' procedure under section 2 of Annex V of the Convention. This procedure is the same as the ordinary conciliation procedure described above, except that States cannot choose not to participate. The conciliation commission would proceed with its work (exactly how is not clear) without the co-operation of a defaulting State. The conciliation commission may not question a State's exercise of its discretion to refuse consent but could, presumably, find that the refusal was based upon patently impermissible grounds.

Similar provisions in article 297(3) apply to certain EEZ fisheries disputes. States are not obliged to accept article 287 procedures in relation to disputes concerning their sovereign rights over EEZ fisheries, including disputes arising from failures to determine total allowable catches and coastal harvesting capacities, the allocation of surpluses to other States, and the terms of conservation measures. However, where it is alleged that the coastal State has manifestly failed to ensure that the maintenance of EEZ fish stocks is not seriously endangered, or that it has arbitrarily refused to determine total allowable catches or harvesting capacity or to allocate a surplus to other States, the 'compulsory conciliation procedure' is to operate (LOSC, article 297(3)).

The Convention also gives States parties the right to impose further limitations, thereby opting out of the compulsory dispute settlement procedures in respect of any or all of three defined categories of dispute. These optional exceptions, set out in article 298(1) of the Convention, cover (a) disputes concerning delimitation and claims to historic waters, (b) disputes concerning military activities and law enforcement activities, and (c) disputes in respect of which the Security Council is exercising its functions. Two of these categories – disputes concerning military activities and disputes in respect of which the UN Security Council is exercising its functions – are rooted in the need for deference to States' sovereign rights and to international settlement procedures. If disputes in these categories are excluded from the 'compulsory' procedures, the disputing States are subject only to the general obligation to reach a settlement by peaceful means. The other category, delimitation disputes, is excepted from the general regime because of lack of agreement on the criteria for historic title to areas of the seas, and on delimitation criteria and procedures more generally at UNCLOS III. If a State declares that it will not accept compulsory settlement of disputes over the boundaries of its territorial sea, EEZ or continental shelf, and such a dispute arises which is not settled by negotiation within a reasonable time, either State party may insist that the matter be referred to 'compulsory conciliation'. Furthermore, the disputing States are obliged to negotiate an agreement on the basis of the conciliation commission's report. If they do not do so, they must agree upon some other procedure for settling the dispute.

Surprisingly, few States have, as yet, invoked the optional exceptions under article 298.[5] Some, such as France and Russia, have excepted all three categories of dispute. Others have excepted only some: Iceland and Italy, for instance, have excepted only questions of continental shelf delimitation; and Cape Verde has excepted only disputes concerning military operations and law enforcement. Where a State exercises this right to exclude certain categories of dispute from the compulsory settlement procedures, the exclusion operates reciprocally, so that the State cannot itself institute compulsory settlement procedures in respect of such disputes against other States parties. States are, of course, always free to agree upon reference of the dispute to any procedure they choose, even if they have excluded it from the compulsory dispute settlement provisions.

Subject to the foregoing qualifications, all disputes concerning the application or interpretation of the 1982 Convention (and of the 1995 Straddling Stocks Agreement) must be submitted to the 'compulsory' Part XV procedures.

Forums for 'compulsory' dispute settlement

The disputing parties are given considerable freedom in choosing the precise 'compulsory procedure' that must be pursued in order to seek a settlement of the dispue. There are four main choices: the International Tribunal for the Law of the Sea; the International Court of Justice; an 'Annex VII' arbitral tribunal; and an 'Annex VIII' special arbitral tribunal.

---

[5] The UN paper, *The Law of the Sea. Declarations and statements with respect to the United Nations Convention on the Law of the Sea* (New York, United Nations), 1997, pp. 102–4, updated by the list at www.un.org/Depts/los/los_decl.htm, lists around a dozen States parties, and a number of signatories, as having indicated that they wish to exclude article 298 disputes. The parties are Argentina, Cape Verde, Chile, France, Iceland, Italy, Norway, Portugal, Russia, Tunisia and Uruguay; in addition, Cuba, Guinea-Bissau and the Philippines made declarations whose exact meaning is not clear.

The International Court of Justice was discussed above, and no further comment on it is necessary.

The International Tribunal for the Law of the Sea (ITLOS) was established under Annex VI of the LOSC. It has twenty-one members having 'recognized competence in the field of the law of the sea', elected by the Parties to the Convention so as to ensure the representation of the world's principal legal systems. Not all members will necessarily be present in every adjudication: the tribunal's quorum in plenary session is eleven, and it is empowered to operate through special chambers of three or five members (LOSC, Annex VI, art. 15). It has set up a chamber of summary procedure and two seven-person chambers, for fisheries and environmental disputes. The ITLOS may also work through its eleven-person Sea Bed Disputes Chamber, which may itself operate through three-person *ad hoc* chambers (LOSC, Annex VI, section 4). The Tribunal selects its own president.[6]

Arbitral tribunals under Annex VII of the Law of the Sea Convention may be established for disputes between States, and also for disputes involving international organisations, such as the European Community. Tribunals are to be composed of five members, one chosen by each of the parties and the other three members chosen jointly by the parties, from a panel to which each State party to the Convention may nominate four people. If the disputants cannot agree upon the three jointly chosen arbitrators, these are to be appointed by the President of the Law of the Sea Tribunal. Arbitrators must have some experience in maritime affairs, but not necessarily in the Law of the Sea: it is, therefore, possible to select arbitrators whose expertise lies in a technical field, such as fisheries management or environmental matters.

Special arbitral tribunals under Annex VIII of the LOSC may be established to deal with four categories of specialised disputes: (1) fisheries; (2) environmental protection; (3) marine scientific research; and (4) navigation (including pollution and dumping from ships). Special arbitral tribunals are limited, like Annex VII tribunals, to disputes to which States and international organisations are parties. States parties to the Convention may nominate two experts in the relevant field (who may be technical, rather than legal, experts) to each of four lists, each list dealing with one of these categories and maintained respectively by the FAO, UNEP, IOC and IMO. Each party to the dispute may choose two arbitrators (of whom only one may be a national) for each case, preferably from the appropriate list. The President of the arbitral tribunal, who is to be a national of a third State, is chosen by agreement between the parties, failing which the Secretary General of the United Nations is to make the appointment unless the parties agree upon some other appointing authority. Special arbitral tribunals may also be used as fact-finding commissions to inquire into and establish the facts in relation to disputes within the four specialised categories. This must be

---

[6] The Tribunal heard its first case in 1997: see Lowe, *op. cit.* in 'Further reading' at the end of this chapter.

done by agreement between the parties. In such cases, the findings of fact are conclusive between the parties, who are then free to choose some other process, such as negotiation or arbitration, for the settlement of the dispute.

These bodies – the ICJ, ITLOS, and Annex VII and Annex VIII arbitral tribunals – all apply the rules of the Convention and other rules of international law, although the disputants may agree to request a decision *ex aequo et bono* – that is, one based on general principles of fairness and equity (LOSC, article 293). Any of these bodies may, if it thinks it necessary, appoint two or more non-voting scientific experts to sit with it while it is hearing a case (LOSC, article 289). All decisions are taken by majority vote, all are reasoned, and all are final and binding on the parties.

States parties to the Convention may indicate which of the four means for the settlement of disputes concerning the interpretation or application of the Convention they have chosen, at any time on or after signature of the Convention. Any State party to the Convention that has not selected one of the available forums under article 287 is deemed to have accepted 'Annex VII' arbitration. Any dispute that is not settled by means chosen by the parties or by the voluntary conciliation procedure under section 1 of this Part of the Convention must be submitted to one of these forums at the request of any party to the dispute. If the parties have chosen the same forum under article 287, it goes to that body; if not, the dispute is to be referred to an 'Annex VII' arbitral tribunal unless the parties otherwise agree.

Practice in the choice of article 287 forums is varied. Perhaps surprisingly, given the sensitivity of States to international dispute settlement obligations, most States have as yet made no choice, although they are free to do so at any time in the future. Among those who have chosen, the Law of the Sea Tribunal (chosen by Argentina, Belgium, Germany, Greece, Oman, Tanzania, and Uruguay, among others) and the International Court (chosen by States including Belgium, Finland, Germany, Oman and Spain, among others, but explicitly rejected by Algeria, Cuba and Guinea-Bissau) are the most popular. States need not choose the same forum for every purpose. For example, some eastern European States have chosen 'Annex VII' arbitration as the 'basic' means for dispute settlement, but have chosen Annex VIII special arbitration for disputes concerning fisheries, environmental protection, scientific research and navigation, and the Law of the Sea Tribunal for disputes concerning the prompt release of detained vessels and their crews (see LOSC, art. 292).

It should be noted that special provision is made for the settlement of disputes arising from the exploration and exploitation of the international sea bed area and its resources (LOSC, Part XI, section 6). These provisions are complicated, not least because not only States, but also the International Sea Bed Authority and its organs, the Enterprise, and individual contractors (which may be State-owned industries or commercial operators), may all be parties to disputes, which may concern not only the Convention but also rules laid down by the Authority and the terms of contracts and licences. Article 188 stipulates that inter-State disputes concerning the exploitation of the international sea bed area are to be submitted to the special Sea-Bed Disputes Chamber of the International Tribunal on the Law of the Sea, and not to any other form of settlement. Disputes concerning contracts would be submitted to commercial arbitration under UNCITRAL rules; but any question of the interpretation of Part XI of the Convention and its associated Annexes to which a commercial dispute gives rise must be submitted to the Sea-Bed Disputes Chamber of ITLOS. That may prove a cumbersome procedure in the context of essentially commercial disputes, because all States parties to the Convention have a right to intervene in such proceedings before the Chamber (LOSC, Annex VI, articles 32 and 40). (See further, chapter twelve.)

Provisional measures

It may be that one of the parties is proposing to take action which would prejudice the rights of the other even if the dispute were ultimately to be settled in the other's favour. For example, if one State is proposing to insist on a right of innocent passage for a cargo that the other regards as so inherently dangerous as to prejudice the safety of its coastal communities, there is little point in deciding in favour of the coastal State if the passage has taken place and an accident resulted. In such cases, or if it is necessary to prevent serious harm to the environment, the 'article 287' forum hearing the case may prescribe appropriate provisional measures. This power is modelled on that under article 41 of the Statute of the International Court of Justice (which Greece tried, unsuccessfully, to invoke in the *Aegean Sea Continental Shelf (Interim Measures)* case (1976) in order to prevent Turkish vessels conducting seismic surveys on the disputed shelf). Unlike the position in the ICJ Statute, however, the LOSC clearly provides that provisional measures are binding. If the case is to be heard by an arbitral tribunal that has not been constituted at the time, provisional measures may be indicated by the Law of the Sea Tribunal (LOSC, art. 290).

General principles applicable in dispute settlement

Almost every dispute has characteristics that mark it out from others, but there are nevertheless some general points of importance which may be made in conclusion.

Locus standi

Not every State will have the right to institute proceedings in respect of any violation of the Law of the Sea Convention that might arise. Generally, a State must show that it has some particular legal right, such as the right of innocent passage, or the freedom of navigation on the high seas, which has been infringed. An international tribunal would not accept a complaint by a State that some other State's rights have been infringed: the State would not have *locus standi* to present such a case. Sensible as this rule is in cases where at least one State is in fact directly affected, it hampers the enforcement of the law when a 'community interest' is at stake. For example, it is usually difficult to show that any particular State's legal rights are infringed by pollution of the high seas and so, although the world at large may suffer from such pollution, it may be that no individual State has *locus standi* to bring proceedings in respect of it. The question of defending community interests was raised, but not resolved, in the *Nuclear Tests* cases (1974) where Australia and New Zealand based their claims in part upon the right of the international community to be preserved from radioactive fall-out, apart from any direct infringement of their own rights. But this area of international law is still developing, and the institution of community proceedings – the *actio popularis*, as it is known – may yet be recognised. In some cases a similar result has been achieved by giving an international organisation the power to initiate action to protect community interests: see, for example, the role of the supervisory authorities under the 1974 Nordic Convention on the Protection of the Environment, which can bring actions in the courts of any State party.

Deciding the case

Disputes arising under the Law of the Sea Convention or any other international treaty will usually be decided by the interpretation of the treaty in question. The rules for interpretation are conveniently summarised in the 1969 Vienna Convention on the Law of Treaties. The basic rule is that the treaty must be interpreted in good faith in accordance with the ordinary meaning to be given to its terms in their context and in the light of the treaty's object and purpose: 'context' here includes not only the treaty and its preamble and annexes, but also any other instruments, such as protocols, made in connection with the treaty. Any subsequent agreement between the parties concerning interpretation must be taken into account, as must any subsequent practice of parties in the application of the treaty which establishes their (perhaps tacit) agreement concerning its interpretation. Comparison of authentic texts in different languages may also clarify the meaning: the Law of the Sea Convention has six authentic texts, in Arabic, Chinese, English, French, Russian and Spanish (LOSC, art. 320), although it was in fact negotiated primarily in English. Egypt, in its declaration made on ratification of the Convention,[7] pointed out the discrepancies between the various versions of the Convention and stated that it would 'adopt the interpretation which is best corroborated by the various official texts of the Convention'. If the meaning remains ambiguous or obscure, recourse may be had to the preparatory works *(travaux préparatoires)* and circumstances of the conclusion of the treaty, as supplementary means of interpretation. However, UNCLOS III

---

[7] 25 *LOSB* 12 (1994).

does not have a comprehensive official record of its *travaux préparatoires*, and some of the critical parts of the final text of the 1982 Convention were the product of unrecorded negotiations. This reduces the importance that can properly be given to the conference records as an aid to interpretation.

Disputes over matters not regulated by treaty would be determined by the application of customary international law, as established by the general practice of States. Customary law may be supplemented by general principles of law recognised by civilised nations (such as the rule that no one may profit from his own wrong).

Where neither treaty nor customary law contains rules determining the dispute, it is necessary to fall back upon certain presumptions. The most significant are those concerning maritime jurisdiction: in the absence of 'other rules', coastal States are presumed to have complete jurisdiction over ships of all flags in their territorial seas, and ships on the high seas are subject only to the jurisdiction of their flag State. Unfortunately, in the case of the EEZ, where many disputes are likely to arise, there is no presumption either way, disputes being resolved on the basis of the elusive criteria of article 59 of the Law of the Sea Convention (see chapter nine).

Other general rules of international law, such as that requiring the use of minimum force when effecting an arrest, whether it be after hot pursuit, as in the case of the *I'm Alone* (1935) or in any other circumstances, will also be applied.

Finally, we must emphasise a point made at the beginning of this book. The law of the sea is no more than a part of international law. An understanding of the principles of international law concerning nationality, international claims, State responsibility and so on is essential for a proper understanding of the law of the sea.

Further reading

A. O. Adede, *The System for Settlement of Disputes under the United Nations Convention on the Law of the Sea* (Dordrecht, Nijhoff), 1987.

A. E. Boyle, 'Dispute settlement and the Law of the Sea Convention: problems of fragmentation and jurisdiction', 46 *ICLQ* 37–54 (1997).

J. A. Charney, 'The implications of expanding international dispute settlement systems: the 1982 Convention on the Law of the Sea', 90 *AJIL* 69–75 (1996).

David Davies Memorial Institute of International Studies, *International Disputes: The Legal Aspects* (London, Europa), 1972.

M. P. Gaertner, 'The dispute settlement provisions of the Convention on the Law of the Sea', 19 *San Diego Law Review* 577–97 (1982).

International Journal of Marine and Coastal Law, Special Issue. The International Tribunal for the Law of the Sea: establishment and prompt release procedures, Vol. 11, No. 2, (pp. 137–232) (1996).

A. V. Lowe, 'The *M/V Saiga*: the first case in the International Tribunal for the Law of the Sea', 48 *ICLQ* 187–200 (1999).

J. G. Merrills, *International Dispute Settlement*, 3rd edn, (Cambridge, Grotius), 1998.

M. H. Nordquist, S. Rosenne and L. B. Sohn (eds), *United Nations Convention on the Law of the Sea*, Vol. V (Dordrecht, Nijhoff), 1989.

S. Oda, 'The International Court of Justice viewed from the Bench', 244 *Recueil des Cours* 9, at 127–55 (1993.vii).

K. Oellers-Frahm, 'Arbitration – a promising alternative to dispute settlement under the Law of the Sea Convention', 55 ZAOR 457–78 (1995).

R. Ranjeva, 'Le règlement des différends' in R. J. Dupuy and D. Vignes (eds), *Traité du Nouveau Droit de la Mer* (Paris, Economica), 1985, pp. 1105–67.

W. Riphagen, 'Dispute settlement in the 1982 United Nations Convention on the Law of the Sea' in C. L. Rozakis and C. A. Stephanou (eds), *The New Law of the Sea* (Amsterdam, North Holland), 1983, pp. 281–301.

T. Treves, 'The Law of the Sea Tribunal: its status and scope of jurisdiction after November 16, 1994', 55 *ZAORV* 421–51 (1995) (and see T. Eitel, 'A comment', *ibid.*, 452–6).

Appendix 1

Claims to maritime zones

This table sets out the current claims made by States to a territorial sea, exclusive fishing or exclusive economic zone, continental shelf and other maritime zones. Unless otherwise stated, the breadths of zones are given in nautical miles and are measured from the baseline. Dates in brackets refer to the year when the claim was first made. Where the claim is embodied in legislation, the date is the year in which the legislation was enacted: this is not always the same as the year in which the legislation entered into force. Where an entry in the EEZ, EFZ or other zones columns is blank, it means that no claim has been made to such a zone: in the case of the continental shelf column it means that no claim to a precise area of continental shelf has been made. 'CZ for LOSC purposes' means a contiguous zone for the purposes set out in the Law of the Sea Convention, viz. the control to prevent and punish infringement of customs, fiscal, immigration or sanitary regulations. States are arranged in alphabetical order and a summary of claims is given at the end. The information has been taken from *Limits in the Seas* No 36, seventh revision (1995) and issues of the *Law of the Sea Bulletin*, with some additions and updating by the authors. As far as possible the information is correct as at 1 January 1998.

State	Territorial sea	EEZ or EFZ	Continental shelf	Other maritime zones
Albania	12 (1990)			
Algeria	12 (1963)	EFZ of 32–52 (1994)		
Angola	20 (1975)	200 EFZ (1975)		
Antigua and Barbuda	12 (1982)	200 EEZ (1982)	200 or outer edge of continental margin (1986)	24 CZ for LOSC purposes (1982)
Argentina	12 (1991)	200 EEZ (1991)	200 or outer edge of continental margin (1991)	24 CZ for LOSC purposes (1991)
Australia	12 (1990)	200 EEZ (1994)	200 or outer edge of continental margin (1994)	24 CZ for LOSC purposes (1994)
Bahamas	12 (1993)	200 EEZ (1993)	CSC definition (1970)	
Bahrain	12 (1993)			24 CZ (purposes not specified) (1993)
Bangladesh	12 (1971)	200 EEZ (1974)	Outer limit of continental margin (1974)	18 CZ for LOSC purposes plus security (1974)

State	Territorial sea	EEZ or EFZ	Continental shelf	Other maritime zones
Barbados	12 (1977)	200 EEZ (1978)		
Belgium	12 (1987)	EFZ up to median line with neighbouring States (1978)	Up to median line with opposite and adjacent States (1969)	
Belize	12 (1992)	200 EEZ (1992)		
Benin	200 (1976)			
Bosnia and Herzegovina	Not known			
Brazil	12 (1993)	200 EEZ (1993)	200 or outer edge of continental margin (1993)	24 CZ for LOSC purposes (1993)
Brunei Darussalam	12 (1982)	200 EEZ (1993)		
Bulgaria	12 (1951)	200 EEZ (1987)	'Natural prolongation of its land territory . . . to the limits established by the continental shelves of opposite and adjacent States' (1987)	24 CZ for LOSC purposes (1987)
Cambodia	12 (1969)	200 EEZ (1978)	200 (1982)	24 CZ for LOSC purposes plus security (1982)
Cameroon	50 (1974)			
Canada	12 (1970)	200 EEZ (1996)	200 or outer edge of continental margin (1981)	100 anti-pollution zone in Arctic waters (1970). 24 CZ for LOSC purposes (1996)
Cape Verde	12 (1977)	200 EEZ (1977)	200 (1992)	24 CZ for LOSC purposes (1992)
Chile	12 (1986)	200 EEZ (1986)	350 around Easter and Sala y Gomez Islands (1985); otherwise not defined	24 CZ for LOSC purposes (1986)
China	12 (1958)	200 EEZ (1996)		24 CZ for LOSC purposes plus security (1992)
Colombia	12 (1970)	200 EEZ (1978)		
Comoros	12 (1976)	200 EEZ (1976)		
Congo	200 (1977)			
Congo, Democratic Republic of	12 (1974)	EEZ up to boundaries with neighbouring States (1992)		
Costa Rica	12 (1972)	200 EEZ (1975)	CSC definition (1967)	
Côte d'Ivoire	12 (1977)	200 EEZ (1977)	200 metres (1967)	

State	Territorial sea	EEZ or EFZ	Continental shelf	Other maritime zones
Croatia	12 (1991)	EEZ to limit established in accordance with international law (1994)	Up to limits with neighbouring States (1991)	
Cuba	12 (1977)	200 EEZ (1977)	200 metres (1954)	
Cyprus	12 (1964)		To depth of exploitation (1974)	
Denmark	3 (1966)	200 EEZ (1996)	CSC definition (1963)	4 customs zone (1928). 12 anti-liquor smuggling zone (1926). 24 zone for jurisdiction over archaeological and cultural remains (1984)
Djibouti	12 (1979)	200 EEZ (1979)		24 CZ for fiscal, health and immigration matters (1979)
Dominica	12 (1981)	200 EEZ (1981)		24 CZ for LOSC purposes (1981)
Dominican Republic	6 (1967)	200 EEZ (1977)	200 or outer edge of continental margin (1977)	24 CZ for LOSC purposes (1977)
Ecuador	200 (1966)		100 miles beyond 2,500-metre isobath (1985)	
Egypt	12 (1958)	200 EEZ (1983)	CSC definition (1958)	24 CZ for security, navigation, fiscal and sanitary matters (1983)
El Salvador	200 (1950)			
Equatorial Guinea	12 (1970)	200 EEZ (1984)		
Eritrea	12 (1991)			
Estonia	12 (1993)	EEZ up to limit established in agreement with neighbouring States (1993)		
Fiji	12 (1976)	200 EEZ (1977)	CSC definition (1970)	
Finland	12, except for Gulf of Finland where outer limit is 3 miles from median line (1995)	EFZ to equidistance line with neighbouring States (1981)	Defined as in arts 1 and 6 of CSC (1965)	
France	12 (1971)	200 EEZ (1976) (not in Mediterranean)		24 customs zone (1987). 24 CZ for cultural and archaeological remains (1989)
Gabon	12	200 EEZ (1984)		24 CZ for LOSC purposes (1984)

State	Territorial sea	EEZ or EFZ	Continental shelf	Other maritime zones
Gambia	12 (1969)	200 EFZ (1977)		18 CZ to prevent and punish infringement of any law (1969)
Georgia	Not known			
Germany	12 (1994) (less in some parts of Baltic)	EEZ up to specified limits (in most cases continental shelf boundaries with neighbouring States) (1994)	CSC definition (1964)	
Ghana	12 (1986)	200 EEZ (1986)	200 (1986)	24 CZ for LOSC purposes (1986)
Greece	6 (1936)		CSC definition (1969)	10 security zone (1913)
Grenada	12 (1975)	200 EEZ (1978)		
Guatemala	12 (1939)	200 EEZ (1976)	200 or outer edge of continental margin (1994)	
Guinea	12 (1980)	200 EEZ (1980)		
Guinea Bissau	12 (1978)	200 EEZ (1978)		
Guyana	12 (1977)	200 EEZ (1977)	200 or outer edge of continental margin (1977)	
Haiti	12 (1972)	200 EEZ (1977)	To depth of exploitation (1977)	24 CZ for customs, fiscal and security matters (1977)
Honduras	12 (1965)	200 EEZ (1980)	200 or outer edge of continental margin (1982)	24 CZ for unspecified purposes (1982)
Iceland	12 (1979)	200 EEZ (1979)	200 or outer edge of continental margin (1979)	
India	12 (1967)	200 EEZ (1976)	200 or outer edge of continental margin (1976)	24 CZ for LOSC purposes plus security (1976)
Indonesia	12 (1957)	200 EEZ (1980)	To depth of exploitation (1969)	
Iran	12 (1959)	EEZ up to equidistance line with neighbouring States or such other line as may be agreed (1993)	As EEZ	24 CZ for security, customs, maritime, fiscal, immigration, sanitary and environmental purposes (1993)
Iraq	12 (1958)			
Ireland	12 (1988)	200 EFZ (1976)		Jurisdiction over wrecks and archaeological objects on its continental shelf (1987)
Israel	12 (1990)		To depth of exploitation (1953)	

Appendix 1

State	Territorial sea	EEZ or EFZ	Continental shelf	Other maritime zones
Italy	12 (1974)		CSC definition (1967)	
Jamaica	12 (1971)	200 EEZ (1991)	200 or outer edge of continental margin (1996)	24 CZ for LOSC purposes (1996)
Japan	12 – 3 in some straits (1977)	200 EEZ (1996)	200 or beyond to be established in accordance with art. 76 LOSC (1996)	24 CZ for LOSC purposes (1996)
Jordan	3 (1943)			
Kenya	12 (1969)	200 EEZ (1979)		
Kiribati	12 (1983)	200 EEZ (1983)		
Korea, North	12 (1955)	200 EEZ (1977)		50 security zone (1977)
Korea, South	12 – 3 in Korea Strait (1977)	200 EEZ (1996)		24 CZ for LOSC purposes (1995)
Kuwait	12 (1967)		Up to boundaries with neighbouring States (1949)	
Latvia	12 (1990)	200 EEZ (1993)		
Lebanon	12 (1983)			
Liberia	200 (1976)		CSC definition (1969)	
Libya	12 (1959)			
Lithuania	12 (1992)			
Madagascar	12 (1985)	200 EEZ (1985)	200 or to limit determined with adjacent States, or 100 miles beyond 2,500-metre isobath (1985)	24 CZ for LOSC purposes (1985)
Malaysia	12 (1969)	200 EEZ (1980)	CSC definition (1966)	
Maldives	12 (1975)	Polygonal EEZ, from 37 to 310 (1976)		
Malta	12 (1978)	25 EFZ (1978)	CSC definition (1966)	24 CZ for LOSC purposes (1978)
Marshall Islands	12 (1984)	200 EEZ (1984)		24 CZ for LOSC purposes (1984)
Mauritania	12 (1988)	200 EEZ (1978)	200 or outer edge of continental margin (1978)	24 CZ for LOSC purposes (1988)
Mauritius	12 (1970)	200 EEZ (1977)	200 or outer edge of continental margin (1977)	
Mexico	12 (1969)	200 EEZ (1976)	200 or outer edge of continental margin (1986)	24 CZ for LOSC purposes (1986)
Micronesia	12 (1988)	200 EEZ (1988)		
Monaco	12 (1973)			

State	Territorial sea	EEZ or EFZ	Continental shelf	Other maritime zones
Morocco	12 (1973)	200 EEZ (1981)	CSC definition (1958)	24 CZ for LOSC purposes (1981)
Mozambique	12 (1976)	200 EEZ (1976)		
Myanmar	12 (1968)	200 EEZ (1977)	200 or outer edge of continental margin (1977)	24 CZ for LOSC purposes plus security (1977)
Namibia	12 (1990)	200 EEZ (1990)	200 or outer edge of continental margin (1990)	24 CZ within which it exercises 'any powers which it may consider necessary to prevent the contravention of any fiscal law or any law relating to customs, immigration or health' (1991)
Nauru	12 (1971)	200 EFZ (1978)		
Netherlands	12 (1985)	200 EFZ (1977)		
New Zealand	12 (1977)	200 EEZ (1977)	200 or outer edge of continental margin (1977)	24 CZ for LOSC purposes (1996)
Nicaragua	200 (1979)		200 metres (1948)	
Nigeria	30 (1971)	200 EEZ (1978)	CSC definition (1969)	
Norway	4 (1812)	200 EEZ (1976)	200 or outer edge of continental margin (1985)	10 customs zone (1921)
Oman	12 (1972)	200 EEZ (1981)	CSC definition (1972)	24 CZ for LOSC purposes (1989). 50 pollution control zone (1974)
Pakistan	12 (1966)	200 EEZ (1976)	200 or outer edge of continental margin (1976)	24 CZ for LOSC purposes plus security (1976)
Palau	3 (1978)	200 EFZ (1978)		
Panama	200 (1967)			
Papua New Guinea	12 (1977)	200 EFZ (1977)	CSC definition (1977)	
Peru	No territorial sea claim as such but maritime dominion of 200 in which it exercises sovereignty and jurisdiction 'without prejudice to the freedoms of international communication, in accordance with the laws and treaties ratified by the State' (1993)	200 EFZ (1947)	200 (1947)	

State	Territorial sea	EEZ or EFZ	Continental shelf	Other maritime zones
Philippines	No precise claim	200 EEZ (1978)	To where depth admits of exploitation (1968)	
Poland	12 (1978)	EEZ up to boundaries defined by international treaties (1991)		
Portugal	12 (1977)	200 EEZ (1977)	CSC definition (1969)	
Qatar	12 (1992)	EEZ corresponds to limits of continental shelf (1974)		24 CZ for 'all rights and purposes provided for in International Law' (1992)
Romania	12 (1951)	200 EEZ (1986)	CSC definition (1961)	24 CZ for LOSC purposes (1990)
Russia	12 (1909)	200 EEZ (1984)	200 or outer edge of continental margin (1995)	
Saint Kitts and Nevis	12 (1984)	200 EEZ (1984)	200 or outer edge of continental margin (1984)	24 CZ for LOSC purposes (1984)
Saint Lucia	12 (1984)	200 EEZ (1984)	200 or outer edge of continental margin (1984)	24 CZ for LOSC purposes (1984)
Saint Vincent	12 (1983)	200 EEZ (1983)	200 (1983)	24 CZ for LOSC purposes (1983)
Samoa	12 (1971)	200 EEZ (1977)		
São Tomé e Príncipe	12 (1978)	200 EEZ (1978)		
Saudi Arabia	12 (1958)	EFZ of unspecified area (1974)		18 CZ for security, navigation, fiscal and health matters (1958)
Senegal	12 (1985)	200 EEZ (1985)	200 or outer edge of continental margin (1976)	24 CZ for LOSC purposes (1985)
Seychelles	12 (1977)	200 EEZ (1977)	200 or outer edge of continental margin (1977)	
Sierra Leone	200 (1971)			
Singapore	3 (1878)			
Slovenia	Not known			
Solomon Islands	12 (1978)	200 EEZ (1978)		
Somalia	200 (1972)			
South Africa	12 (1977)	200 EEZ (1994)	200 or outer edge of continental margin (series of straight lines joining listed co-ordinates) (1994)	24 CZ for LOSC purposes (1994); 24 maritime cultural zone (1994)

State	Territorial sea	EEZ or EFZ	Continental shelf	Other maritime zones
Spain	12 (1977)	200 EEZ (1978); 'fishing protection zone' in the Mediterranean up to the median line with neighbouring States (1997)	To depth of exploitation (1969)	24 CZ for unspecified purposes (1992)
Sri Lanka	12 (1971)	200 EEZ (1976)	200 or outer edge of continental margin (1976)	24 CZ for LOSC purposes plus security (1976), 200 pollution prevention zone (1976)
Sudan	12 (1960)		CSC definition (1970)	18 CZ for LOSC purposes plus security (1970)
Suriname	12 (1978)	200 EEZ (1978)		
Sweden	12 (1979)	EEZ up to existing continental shelf boundaries or equidistance line with neighbouring States (1992)	CSC definition (1966)	
Syria	35 (1981)		CSC definition (1963)	41 CZ for LOSC purposes plus security (1963)
Tanzania	12 (1989)	200 EEZ (1989)		
Thailand	12 (1966)	200 EEZ (1981)		24 CZ (1995)
Togo	30 (1977)	200 EEZ (1977)		
Tonga	12 (1978)	200 EEZ (1978)		
Trinidad and Tobago	12 (1969)	200 EEZ (1986)	200 or outer edge of continental margin (1986)	24 CZ (1986)
Tunisia	12 (1973)			24 CZ (1986)
Turkey	6 – 12 in Black and Mediterranean Seas (1964)	200 EEZ in Black Sea (1986)		
Tuvalu	12 (1983)	200 EEZ (1983)		24 CZ for LOSC purposes (1983)
Ukraine	12 (1991)	200 EEZ (1995)		
United Arab Emirates	12 (1993)	200 EEZ (1993)	200 or outer edge of continental margin (1993)	24 CZ for LOSC purposes (1993)
United Kingdom	12 (1987)	200 EFZ (1976)		
United States of America	12 (1988)	200 EEZ (1983)		
Uruguay	200 (1969)		CSC definition (1963)	
Vanuatu	12 (1978)	200 EEZ (1978)	200 or outer edge of continental margin (1981)	24 CZ for LOSC purposes (1981)

State	Territorial sea	EEZ or EFZ	Continental shelf	Other maritime zones
Venezuela	12 (1956)	200 EEZ (1978)	CSC definition (1956)	15 zone for purposes of 'maritime supervision and policing, national security and the safeguarding of the national interests' (1956)
Vietnam	12 (1964)	200 EEZ (1977)	200 or outer edge of continental margin (1977)	24 CZ for LOSC purposes plus security (1977)
Yemen	12 (1967)	200 EEZ (1977)	200 or outer edge of continental margin (1977)	24 CZ for security, customs, sanitary and fiscal matters (1977)

This table does not include the Federal Republic of Yugoslavia (Serbia and Montenegro).

Summary of claims

1. *Territorial sea*

Three miles: four
Four miles: one
Six miles: two (excluding Turkey)
Twelve miles: 121 (including Turkey)
Twenty miles: one
Thirty miles: two
Thirty-five miles: one
Fifty miles: one
200 miles: ten
No precise claim / not known: five

2. *EFZ or EEZ*

Twenty-five-mile EFZ: one
32–52 mile EFZ: one
200-mile EFZ: nine
EFZ up to boundaries with neighbouring States: two
EFZ of unspecified area: one
200 mile EEZ: ninety-three
EEZ up to boundaries with neighbouring States: six
Other EEZ: three

3. *Continental shelf*

CSC definition: twenty-three
200 metres: three
200 miles:* forty-four
200 miles or edge of continental margin: thirty-three
Up to boundary with neighbouring States: five
To depth of exploitation: six
Edge of continental margin: one
350 miles: one
100 miles beyond 2,500-metre isobath: two (including Madagascar)
No precise claim: thirty (not including Chile)

* This includes claims to a 200-mile continental shelf as such, and claims to a 200-mile EEZ or territorial sea where no precise claim is made to a continental shelf.

4. *Other zones*

Fifteen-mile contiguous zone: one

Eighteen-mile contiguous zone plus
security: four (including Gambia)

Twenty-four-mile contiguous zone for
LOSC purposes: thirty-three
(including Djibouti)

Twenty-four-mile contiguous zone for
LOSC purposes plus security: eleven
(including Egypt, Haiti and Iran)

Twenty-four-mile contiguous zone for
unspecified/unknown purposes: seven

Forty-one-mile contiguous zone for
LOSC purposes plus security: one

Four-mile customs zone: one

Ten-mile customs zone: one

Twelve-mile anti-liquor smuggling
zone: one

Twenty-four-mile customs zone: one

Ten-mile security zone: one

Fifty-mile security zone: one

Fifty-mile pollution control zone: one

200-mile pollution control zone: one

Twenty-four-mile zone for wrecks/cultural
remains: three (including South Africa)

Continental shelf: jurisdiction over wrecks
and archaeological remains: one

100-mile anti-pollution zone in Arctic
waters: one

Appendix 2

Ratifications of the UN Convention on the Law of the Sea, its Implementation Agreements and the Geneva Conventions

Table A shows which States have signed and ratified the UN Convention on the Law of the Sea (LOSC), the Agreement relating to the Implementation of Part X1 of the Convention (the 1994 Implementation Agreement) and the Agreement for the Implementation of the Provisions of the Convention relating to the Conservation and Management of Straddling Fish Stocks and Highly Migratory Fish Stocks (the 1995 Implementation Agreement). Table B shows which States have ratified the four Geneva Conventions – the Convention on the Territorial Sea and the Contiguous Zone (TSC), the Convention on the High Seas (HSC), the Convention on Fishing and Conservation of the Living Resources of the High Seas (FC) and the Convention on the Continental Shelf (CSC). In each table the date refers to that on which the State concerned deposited its instrument of ratification, accession, etc. An 'x' in Table A indicates signature of the Convention and its Implementation Agreements. In Table B States in round brackets are those which have signed the Law of the Sea Convention, while States in square brackets are those that have ratified the Convention. As between the latter the Convention prevails over the Geneva Conventions. The position is shown as at 9 July 1998.

Table A

	LOSC	1994 Implementation Agreement	1995 Implementation Agreement
Afghanistan	x		
Albania			
Algeria	11. 6.1996	11. 6.1996	
Andorra			
Angola	5.12.1990		
Antigua and Barbuda	2. 2.1989		
Argentina	1.12.1995	1.12.1995	x

473

Table A (*Cont'd*)

	LOSC	1994 Implementation Agreement	1995 Implementation Agreement
Armenia			
Australia	5.10.1994	5.10.1994	x
Austria	14. 7.1995	14. 7.1995	x
Azerbaijan			
Bahamas	29. 7.1983	28. 7.1995	16. 1.1997
Bahrain	30. 5.1985		
Bangladesh	x		x
Barbados	12.10.1993	28. 7.1995	
Belarus	x		
Belgium	x	x	x
Belize	13. 8.1983	21.10.1994	x
Benin	16.10.1997	16.10.1997	
Bhutan	x		
Bolivia	28. 4.1995	28. 4.1995	
Bosnia and Herzegovina	12. 1.1994		
Botswana	2. 5.1990		
Brazil	22.12.1988	x	x
Brunei Darussalam	5.11.1996	5.11.1996	
Bulgaria	15. 5.1996	15. 5.1996	
Burkina Faso	x	x	x
Burundi	x		
Cambodia	x		
Cameroon	19.11.1985	x	
Canada	x	x	x
Cape Verde	10. 8.1987	x	
Central African Republic	x		
Chad	x		
Chile	25. 8.1997	25. 8.1997	
China	7. 6.1996	7. 6.1996	x
Colombia	x		
Comoros	21. 6.1994		
Congo	x		
Cook Islands	15. 2.1995	15. 2.1995	
Costa Rica	21. 9.1992		
Côte d'Ivoire	26. 3.1984	28. 7.1995	x
Croatia	5. 4.1995	5. 4.1995	
Cuba	15. 8.1984		
Cyprus	12.12.1988	27. 7.1995	

Appendix 2

Table A (*Cont'd*)

	LOSC	1994 Implementation Agreement	1995 Implementation Agreement
Czech Republic	21. 6.1996	21. 6.1996	
Democratic People's Republic of Korea	x		
Democratic Republic of the Congo	17. 2.1989		
Denmark	x	x	x
Djibouti	8.10.1991		
Dominica	24.10.1991		
Dominican Republic	x		
Ecuador			
Egypt	26. 8.1983	x	x
El Salvador	x		
Equatorial Guinea	21. 7.1997	21. 7.1997	
Eritrea			
Estonia			
Ethiopia	x		
European Community	1. 4.1998	1. 4.1998	x
Fiji	10.12.1982	28. 7.1995	12.12.1996
Finland	21. 6.1996	21. 6.1996	x
France	11. 4.1996	11. 4.1996	x
Gabon	11. 3.1998	11. 3.1998	x
Gambia	22. 5.1984		
Georgia	21. 3.1996	21. 3.1996	
Germany	14.10.1994	14.10.1994	x
Ghana	7. 6.1983		
Greece	21. 7.1995	21. 7.1995	x
Grenada	25. 4.1991	28. 7.1995	
Guatemala	11. 2.1997	11. 2.1997	
Guinea	6. 9.1985	28. 7.1995	
Guinea Bissau	25. 8.1986		x
Guyana	16.11.1993		
Haiti	31. 7.1996	31. 7.1996	
Holy See			
Honduras	5.10.1993		
Hungary	x		
Iceland	21. 6.1985	28. 7.1995	14. 2.1997
India	29. 6.1995	29. 6.1995	
Indonesia	3. 2.1986	x	x

Table A (*Cont'd*)

	LOSC	1994 Implementation Agreement	1995 Implementation Agreement
Iran (Islamic Republic of)	x		17. 4.1998
Iraq	30. 7.1985		
Ireland	21. 6.1996	21. 6.1996	x
Israel			x
Italy	13. 1.1995	13. 1.1995	x
Jamaica	21. 3.1983	28. 7.1995	x
Japan	20. 6.1996	20. 6.1996	x
Jordan	27.11.1995	27.11.1995	
Kazakhstan			
Kenya	2. 3.1989	29. 7.1994	
Kiribati			
Kuwait	2. 5.1986		
Kyrgyzstan			
Lao People's Democratic Republic	5. 6.1998	5. 6.1998	
Latvia			
Lebanon	5. 1.1995	5. 1.1995	
Lesotho	x		
Liberia	x		
Libyan Arab Jamahiriya	x		
Liechtenstein	x		
Lithuania			
Luxembourg	x	x	x
Madagascar	x		
Malawi	x		
Malaysia	14.10.1996	14.10.1996	
Maldives	x	x	x
Mali	16. 7.1985		
Malta	20. 5.1993	26. 6.1996	
Marshall Islands	9. 8.1991		x
Mauritania	17. 7.1996	17. 7.1996	x
Mauritius	4.11.1994	4.11.1994	25. 3.1997
Mexico	18. 3.1983		
Micronesia (Federated States of)	29. 4.1991	6. 9.1995	23. 5.1997
Monaco	20. 3.1996	20. 3.1996	
Mongolia	13. 8.1996	13. 8.1996	
Morocco	x	x	

Table A (*Cont'd*)

	LOSC	1994 Implementation Agreement	1995 Implementation Agreement
Mozambique	13. 3.1997	13. 3.1997	
Myanmar	21. 5.1996	21. 5.1996	
Namibia	18. 4.1983	28. 7.1995	8. 4.1998
Nauru	23. 1.1996	23. 1.1996	10. 1.1997
Nepal	x		
Netherlands	28. 6.1996	28. 6.1996	x
New Zealand	19. 7.1996	19. 7.1996	x
Nicaragua	x		
Niger	x		
Nigeria	14. 8.1986	28. 7.1995	
Niue	x		x
Norway	24. 6.1996	24. 6.1996	30.12.1996
Oman	17. 8.1989	26. 2.1997	
Pakistan	26. 2.1997	26. 2.1997	x
Palau	30. 9.1996	30. 9.1996	
Panama	1. 7.1996	1. 7.1996	
Papua New Guinea	14. 1.1997	14. 1.1997	x
Paraguay	26. 9.1986	10. 7.1995	
Peru			
Philippines	8. 5.1984	23. 7.1997	x
Poland	x	x	
Portugal	3.11.1997	3.11.1997	x
Qatar	x		
Republic of Korea	29. 1.1996	29. 1.1996	x
Republic of Moldova			
Romania	17.12.1996	17.12.1996	
Russian Federation	12. 3.1997	12. 3.1997	4. 8.1997
Rwanda	x		
Saint Kitts and Nevis	7. 1.1993		
Saint Lucia	27. 3.1985		9. 8.1996
Saint Vincent and the Grenadines	1.10.1993		
Samoa	14. 8.1995	14. 8.1995	25.10.1996
San Marino			
São Tomé and Principe	3.11.1987		
Saudi Arabia	24. 4.1996	24. 4.1996	
Senegal	25.10.1984	25. 7.1995	30. 1.1997
Seychelles	16. 9.1991	15.12.1994	20. 3.1998
Sierra Leone	12.12.1994	12.12.1994	

Table A (*Cont'd*)

	LOSC	1994 Implementation Agreement	1995 Implementation Agreement
Singapore	17.11.1994	17.11.1994	
Slovakia	8. 5.1996	8. 5.1996	
Slovenia	16. 6.1995	16. 6.1995	
Solomon Islands	23. 6.1997	23. 6.1997	13. 2.1997
Somalia	24. 7.1989		
South Africa	23.12.1997	23. 12.1997	
Spain	15. 1.1997	15. 1.1997	x
Sri Lanka	19. 7.1994	28. 7.1995	24.10.1996
Sudan	23. 1.1985		
Suriname	9. 7.1998	9. 7.1998	
Swaziland	x	x	
Sweden	25. 6.1996	25. 6.1996	x
Switzerland	x	x	
Syrian Arab Republic			
Tajikistan			
Thailand	x		
The former Yugoslav Republic of Macedonia	19. 8.1994	19. 8.1994	
Togo	16. 4.1985	28. 7.1995	
Tonga	2. 8.1995	2. 8.1995	31. 7.1996
Trinidad and Tobago	25. 4.1986	28. 7.1995	
Tunisia	24. 4.1985	x	
Turkey			
Turkmenistan			
Tuvalu	x		
Uganda	9.11.1990	28. 7.1995	x
Ukraine	x	x	x
United Arab Emirates	x		
United Kingdom	25. 7.1997	25. 7.1997	x
United Republic of Tanzania	30. 9.1985	25. 6.1998	
United States of America		x	21. 8.1996
Uruguay	10.12.1992	x	x
Uzbekistan			
Vanuatu	x	x	x
Venezuela			
Viet Nam	25. 7.1994		
Yemen	21. 7.1987		

Yugoslavia	5. 5.1986	28. 7.1995	
Zambia	7. 3.1983	28. 7.1995	
Zimbabwe	24. 2.1993	28. 7.1995	
Total number of ratifications	127	91	18

Table B

	TSC	HSC	FC	CSC
(Afghanistan)		28. 4.1959		
Albania		7.12.1964		7.12.1964
[Australia]	14. 5.1963	14. 5.1963	14. 5.1963	14. 5.1963
[Austria]		10. 1.1974		
(Belarus)	27. 2.1961	27. 2.1961		27. 2.1961
(Belgium)	6. 1.1972	6. 1.1972	6. 1.1972	
[Bosnia and Herzegovina]	1. 9.1993	1. 9.1993	12. 1.1994	12. 1.1994
[Bulgaria]	31. 8.1962	31. 8.1962		31. 8.1962
Burkina Faso		4.10.1965	4.10.1965	
(Cambodia)	18. 3.1960	18. 3.1960	18. 3.1960	18. 3.1960
(Canada)				6. 2.1970
(Central African Republic)		15.10.1962		
(Colombia)			3. 1.1963	8. 1.1962
[Costa Rica]		16. 2.1972		16. 2.1972
[Croatia]	3. 8.1992	3. 8.1992		3. 8.1992
[Cyprus]		23. 5.1988		11. 4.1974
[Czech Republic]	22. 2.1993	22. 2.1993		22. 2.1993
(Denmark)	26. 9.1968	26. 9.1968	26. 9.1968	12. 6.1963
(Dominican Republic)	11. 8.1964	11. 8.1964	11. 8.1964	11. 8.1964
[Fiji]	25. 3.1971	25. 3.1971	25. 3.1971	25. 3.1971
[Finland]	16. 2.1965	16. 2.1965	16. 2.1965	16. 2.1965
[France]			18. 9.1970	14. 6.1965
[Germany]		26. 7.1973		
[Greece]				6.11.1972
[Guatemala]		27.11.1961		27.11.1961
[Haiti]	29. 3.1960	29. 3.1960	29. 3.1960	29. 3.1960
(Hungary)	6.12.1961	6.12.1961		
[Indonesia]		10. 8.1961		
Israel	6. 9.1961	6. 9.1961		6. 9.1961
[Italy]	17.12.1964	17.12.1964		
[Jamaica]	8.10.1965	8.10.1965	16. 4.1964	8.10.1965
[Japan]	10. 6.1968	10. 6.1968		
[Kenya]	20. 6.1969	20. 6.1969	20. 6.1969	20. 6.1969
Latvia	17.11.1992	17.11.1992		2.12.1992

Table B (*Cont'd*)

	TSC	HSC	FC	CSC
(Lesotho)	23.10.1973	23.10.1973	23.10.1973	23.10.1973
Lithuania	31. 1.1992			
(Madagascar)	31. 7.1962	31. 7.1962	31. 7.1962	31. 7.1962
(Malawi)	3.11.1965	3.11.1965	3.11.1965	3.11.1965
[Malaysia]	21.12.1960	21.12.1960	21.12.1960	21.12.1960
[Malta]	19. 5.1966			19. 5.1966
[Mauritius]	5.10.1970	5.10.1970	5.10.1970	5.10.1970
[Mexico]	2. 8.1966	2. 8.1966	2. 8.1966	2. 8.1966
[Mongolia]		15.10.1976		
(Nepal)		28.12.1962		
[Netherlands]	18. 2.1966	18. 2.1966	18. 2.1966	18. 2.1966
[New Zealand]				18. 1.1965
[Nigeria]	26. 6.1961	26. 6.1961	26. 6.1961	28. 4.1971
[Norway]				9. 9.1971
(Poland)		29. 6.1962		29. 6.1962
[Portugal]	8. 1.1963	8. 1.1963	8. 1.1963	8. 1.1963
[Romania]	12.12.1961	12.12.1961		12.12.1961
[Russian Federation]	22.11.1960	22.11.1960		22.11.1960
[Senegal[1]]	25. 4.1961	25. 4.1961	25. 4.1961	25. 4.1961
[Sierra Leone]	13. 3.1962	13. 3.1962	13. 3.1962	25.11.1966
[Slovakia]	28. 5.1993	28. 5.1993		28. 5.1993
[Slovenia]	6. 7.1992	6. 7.1992		
[Solomon Islands]	3. 9.1981	3. 9.1981	3. 9.1981	3. 9.1981
[South Africa]	9. 4.1963	9. 4.1963	9. 4.1963	9. 4.1963
[Spain]	25. 2.1971	25. 2.1971	25. 2.1971	25. 2.1971
(Swaziland)	16.10.1970	16.10.1970		16.10.1970
[Sweden]				1. 6.1966
(Switzerland)	18. 5.1966	18. 5.1966	18. 5.1966	18. 5.1966
(Thailand)	2. 7.1968	2. 7.1968	2. 7.1968	2. 7.1968
[Tonga]	29. 6.1971	29. 6.1971	29. 6.1971	29. 6.1971
[Trinidad and Tobago]	11. 4.1966	11. 4.1966	11. 4.1966	11. 7.1968
[Uganda]	14. 9.1964	14. 9.1964	14. 9.1964	14. 9.1964
(Ukraine)	12. 1.1961	12. 1.1961		12. 1.1961
[United Kingdom]	14. 3.1960	14. 3.1960	14. 3.1960	11. 5.1964
United States of America	12. 4.1961	12. 4.1961	12. 4.1961	12. 4.1961
Venezuela	15. 8.1961	15. 8.1961	10. 7.1963	15. 8.1961
[Yugoslavia]	28. 1.1966	28. 1.1966	28. 1.1966	28. 1.1966
Total number of ratifications	51	62	37	57

[1] Senegal purported to denounce the TSC and FC in 1971, and the CSC in 1976.

Index